SECURITY ANALYSIS
Principles and Technique

"Many shall be restored that now are fallen and many
Shall fall that now are in honor."

HORACE—*Ars Poetica.*

SECURITY ANALYSIS
Principles and Technique

BENJAMIN GRAHAM, *Visiting Professor of Finance,*
Graduate School of Business Administration,
University of California at Los Angeles

DAVID L. DODD, *Professor of Finance, Emeritus,*
Graduate School of Business, Columbia University

SIDNEY COTTLE, *Senior Financial Economist,*
Stanford Research Institute

with the collaboration of CHARLES TATHAM, *Manager*
Public Utilities Department, Bache & Co.

FOURTH EDITION

McGRAW-HILL BOOK COMPANY

New York   *Toronto*
San Francisco   *London*

SECURITY ANALYSIS

07-023957-6

2425262728   HDHD 898765432

PREFACE*

The three previous editions of *Security Analysis* were published in 1934, 1940, and 1951. Like this volume, they dealt with three main topics: (1) the orderly, comprehensive, and critical analysis of a company's income account and balance sheet; (2) the formulation of appropriate criteria for the selection of well-protected bonds and preferred stocks, and (3) approaches to the selection of common stocks for investment purposes. It does not seem to us that the first two divisions present any new difficulties of great magnitude, or require significant changes in our handling of them. But we cannot say the same about common-stock investment.

All our previous editions were written and published under market conditions quite different from those of 1960–1961. On the former occasions it was possible to combine conservative investment principles with a generally favorable attitude toward the current purchase of common stocks. In the original (1934) publication our cautious viewpoint was almost compulsory, in the light of the 1929–1932 debacle. In fact it took a certain amount of courage for us to assert that there was such a thing as sound investment in common stocks. When we revised the book in 1940 we had the benefit of the market decline of 1937–1938 to justify our conservative standards, and they were similarly acceptable in 1951 after the bear market of 1946–1949.

This perhaps fortuitous concordance enabled us to maintain virtually unchanged through the three editions certain criteria of a "reasonable price" at which a given common stock or group of stocks might be bought for investment. These criteria took into account the wide fluctuations of former stock markets; they leaned heavily on average earnings for a number of past years; they established upper limits for a permissible price in relation to such earnings. Favorable possibilities of future growth were to be looked for and taken advantage of when feasible; but the investor—as distinguished from the speculator—was to

---

* We ask the reader to bear in mind that our manuscript was virtually completed and this preface drafted toward the end of 1961, when prevailing sentiment was in strong disagreement with our conservative position.

keep the premium paid for such prospects within a modest maximum. We did not claim that these conservative criteria of "value" or "justified price" proceeded from mathematical laws or other a priori principles. They were definitely empirical in their origin. True, they sounded plausible enough when viewed in the light of experience, but it was their conformity with the long-term behavior of the stock market that gave them most of their authority. We might say with some confidence that our principles and measures of common-stock investment worked out quite well in practice during the two decades following 1934.

Beginning sometime in 1955, our value standards and the actual market level parted company, and the gap has tended to widen through the ensuing years. Thus we are not able to proceed in 1960–1961 with the same comforting assurance as formerly that our standards are in accordance with both long-term and recent-term experience. In this respect we face a three-pronged dilemma, which we share with all serious-minded security analysts. If we persist in clinging to our old, highly conservative standards of common-stock appraisal, we risk not only the certain charge of old-fogyism, but a real possibility of failing to recognize important changes in the underlying structure of common-stock values. If, at the other extreme, we embrace the general optimism and adopt the long-term expectations of high and virtually uninterrupted earnings growth which are used to justify the market quotations of 1960–1961, we would surely be repeating the practices, and probably repeating the errors, of former bull markets. Finally, if we adopt some middle ground and raise our standards of value to some "compromise position," we shall satisfy neither the prevalent views of the investment community nor the critically minded who insist that standards be justified by hewing close to past experience or by employing persuasive theoretical reasoning.

We deal with this problem in the only way that seems practical to us —by formulating our value standards anew in accordance with our best judgment, and by presenting these results to the reader for what they are. He may accept, reject, or modify them as he decides.

At this point we should add a word of caution. We believe that there are sound reasons for anticipating that the stock market will value corporate earnings and dividends more liberally in the future than it did before 1950. We also believe there are sound reasons for giving more weight than we have in the past to measuring current investment value in terms of the expectations of the future. But we fully recognize that both views lend themselves to dangerous abuses. The latter has particularly been a cause of excessively high stock prices in past bull markets. However, the danger lies not so much in the emphasis on future earnings as on a lack of standards used in relating earnings growth to current values. Without standards no rational method of value measurement is possible.

In connection with the reformulation of our value standards, two points are to be made. First, the post-World War II world has been characterized as "brave" and "new." Brave it is, indeed, but we are not positive that it is equally new. While we recognize marked contrasts with the decade of the thirties, we can be skeptical about a complete break with the past. The government has assumed large responsibilities in preventing or remedying mass unemployment. This Federal involvement is a new factor, and we consider it important in its potential effect on the business cycle and on stock values. But other considerations, such as inflation and the population "explosion," are by no means as new as many think. To assist the student in reaching his own conclusions as to the relation between the future and the longer past (an essential task) the "historical record" has been expanded and set forth in much more detail. In this connection, the economic factors which concern the investor most immediately are reviewed over the period since 1900 as far as available data make the investigation possible. In addition, numerous references are provided to basic studies bearing on specific aspects of the record. We encourage the student to delve into these references. He may find not only his perspective sharpened but also some of today's sacred bulls gored.

Second, the reformulation of our views on common-stock investing has resulted in broadening the portions of the book which deal with trends and with growth stocks. The importance of these two subjects needs no reemphasis. Here, again, in the hope of assisting the student toward his own decision, we have cited more than formerly the writings of others on these subjects. To keep the book's length within bounds we have condensed our former chapters on stockholder-management relations, and we have relegated some material to the Appendix.

Our title page notes the advent of a new principal author, Sidney Cottle, who has taken a major part of the work of revision from the shoulders of its original authors. We are happy to retain the collaboration of Charles Tatham, who is responsible for the chapters on public utility analysis and has rendered other aid. We acknowledge with deep thanks the physical help and kind indulgence accorded by Stanford Research Institute, which has granted Dr. Cottle leave from his Institute duties. Others, who helped with former editions, are remembered with gratitude.

The Preface to the 1951 edition closed with the following paragraph:

Our final word is addressed to the student-reader who may be planning to make security analysis his calling, and to whom we have ventured to dedicate this third edition. Security analysis is on the verge of attaining some measure of formal recognition as a professional discipline. It will demand better training and more rigorous thinking from its members than it has done in the past. We think it offers rewards fully commensurate with its demands and responsibilities. The "average" analyst will probably fare about the same as the average member of any other profession. But for the outstanding man—who combines native ability, a flair for the subject, and a courageous, independent spirit —the sky is the limit.

Since 1951 our profession has made great strides in numbers, capabilities, and influence. We wish it even greater success in the years ahead.

Benjamin Graham
David L. Dodd
Sidney Cottle
Charles Tatham

CONTENTS

PART ONE

SURVEY AND APPROACH

CHAPTER ONE

INTRODUCTION. THE ARRAY OF

SECURITIES. ECONOMIC BACKGROUND

The objectives of security analysis are twofold. First, it seeks to present the important facts regarding a publicly held corporate stock or bond issue in a manner most informing and useful to an actual or potential owner. Second, it seeks to reach dependable conclusions, based upon the facts and applicable standards, as to the safety and attractiveness of a given security at the current market price or at some assumed price.

To do these jobs creditably the analyst needs a wide equipment. He must understand security forms, corporate accounting, the basic elements that make for the success or failure of various kinds of businesses, the general workings not only of our total economy but also of its major segments, and finally the characteristic fluctuations of our security markets. He must be able to dig for facts, to evaluate them critically, and to apply his conclusions with good judgment and a fair amount of imagination. He must be able to resist human nature itself sufficiently to mistrust his own feelings when they are part of mass psychology. He must have courage commensurate with his competence.

In these preliminary chapters we shall try to cover, briefly, a number of important matters that determine or affect the general work of the analyst. There is first his field of work—the vast array of securities that lie before him for possible analysis. Then there is the broad economic background of security values or, in more precise terms, the behavior of the economy. We shall view this mainly in terms of the historical developments since the turn of the century. We turn next to the scope and

1

limitations of security analysis itself, viewed as a systematic activity with practical objectives. This brings us to two basic considerations that must enter constantly and prominently into the analyst's final judgment and decisions—(1) the behavior characteristics of the security markets and (2) the various investment policies that are suitable for different classes of security owners. This section will include also some groundwork material of definition and classification that will lead into the body of our work.

A. THE FIELD OF SECURITY ANALYSIS

Ignoring unusual and ambiguous cases, we may divide securities into two main groups: (1) civil obligations and (2) bonds and stock of corporations. Civil obligations are those of nations, states, municipalities, and the like. They may be subjected to a specialized and frequently elaborate form of analysis. The securities of this type extant in 1960 are summarized in Table 1-1.

Table 1-1. Civil Obligations Outstanding in 1960

(000,000,000 omitted)

Type	Amount at par
United States government interest-bearing debt	$283.2
Long-term debt of individual states	18.1
Long-term debt of local governments and agencies	47.7*
Dollar bonds of foreign nations and subdivisions	5.2*
International Bank for Reconstruction and Development	2.1

* 1959 data.

SOURCES: U.S. Department of Commerce, Bureau of the Census, *Statistical Abstract of the United States*, 1961, p. 389; U.S. Department of Commerce, Bureau of the Census, *Summary of Governmental Finances in 1959*, August 1960, p. 20; National Industrial Conference Board, *The Economic Almanac*, 1960, p. 509; U.S. Department of Commerce, Bureau of the Census, *Compendium of State Government Finances in 1960*, 1961, p. 9; International Bank for Reconstruction and Development, *Fifteenth Annual Report, 1959–1960*, 1960, p. 37.

Corporate Securities. In 1959 there were 990,000 active corporations in the United States. Each of them has shares and possibly bonds outstanding; and any of these could theoretically be referred to a security analyst for study. However, the great majority of companies are purely private affairs—"close corporations"—and they do not come within the purview of practical analysis. We may limit the latter to companies that have securities with a quoted market. There are about 3,000 such enterprises whose bonds or stocks are traded on security exchanges. In addition there is a vast and somewhat indefinite "unlisted market," which by liberal count could be said to include some 25,000 corporations. For most of these, however, the market is so inactive as to be virtually nonexistent.

Perhaps a more practical census of securities as subject to analysis may be made from such investment services and manuals as Moody's and Standard & Poor's. These are the companies for which statistical data are regularly made public. Figures for 1960 indicate the totals shown in Table 1-2.

Primary Common Stocks. We shall have occasion at various points in this book to distinguish between "primary" (or "first-line" or "standard") and "secondary" common stocks. As in most distinctions of quality or degree, it is impossible to set a clear-cut dividing line here. Primary common stocks are those of large and prominent companies, generally with a good record of earnings and of continued dividends. They are included, somewhat as a matter of course, in widely diversified portfolios of financial institutions. There may be some three hundred issues of this type about which there would be little dispute and perhaps a similar

Table 1-2

1. Companies described in Moody's Manuals:
   Public utilities... 821
   Transportation (railroads, busses, airlines, etc.)...................... 1,041
   Industrials... 4,383
   Banks and finance... 8,641
2. Securities quoted in Standard & Poor's Monthly "Guides":
   Bonds... 2,566*
   Stocks.. 4,182*
3. Securities quoted in "over-the-counter" daily sheets of National Quotation Bureau on an average business day:
   Bonds... 1,900
   Stocks.. 6,900

   * As of August 1961.

number that may enter and leave the select circle from year to year or which would be recognized as "standard" by some authorities and not by others.

Secondary Common Stocks. Many more common stocks are marginal, in the sense that they are regarded as very close to the primary grade and are expected to reach that privileged status in due course. Others are thought by their particular adherents to be "just as good" as the typical standard stock. (This is often an error in judgment, made under conditions of speculative enthusiasm and fated to prove highly expensive.) However, we suggest that some 80 percent of the listed stock issues and perhaps 90 percent or more of the unlisted ones clearly belong in the "secondary" category. This fact influences their market-price behavior in significant ways, which the analyst must not fail to take into account.

B. ECONOMIC BACKGROUND OF SECURITY VALUES

The soundness of a security purchase is determined by future developments and not by past history or statistics. But the future cannot be analyzed; we can seek only to anticipate it intelligently and to prepare for it prudently. Here the past comes in—through the back door, as it were—because long experience tells us that investment anticipations, like other business anticipations, cannot be sound or dependable unless they relate themselves to past performance. In measuring past performance we should give consideration to both trends and averages.

In spite of the tremendous and frequently tragic events of 1914–1962 and the major transformations in the economic, social, and political scene, it is our underlying thesis that they do not justify a revolutionary change in the *basic* principles of sound investment. This does not mean— as we shall subsequently discuss—that the apparently increased postwar stability in the economy and the improved growth may not warrant some modification in both standards of value and the approach employed.

Historical Evidence as a Base. We have always held that an understanding of change and the factors of change should appropriately influence investment decisions. But it is change which is caused by the more basic, enduring factors and not by abnormal, fleeting forces that should bring substantial modifications in investment principles. Although there are some marked differences between the decade of the thirties and the decade of the fifties, it is our view that the past decade may represent much more a modification of the *long-run* past than a departure from it. (In fact, it may be that the 1930's represented more of a departure than did the 1950's.) Therefore we propose to the reader that he evolve his investment principles from a careful appraisal of the facts and the lessons of the last sixty years. This proposal may come as a shock—certainly as an unrealistic doctrine—to those who hold that the world has broken away from its mooring to the past.

To assist the student in his examination of the past, a summary review of the country's economic development since the early 1900's is presented in the following section of this chapter—"Economic Considerations." From it the security analyst may gain additional perspective and improved insight into some of the post-World War II changes and may find clues helpful to an appraisal of the implications of these changes for the future.

C. ECONOMIC CONSIDERATIONS

The five economic problems which concern the investor most immediately are: (1) the general price level, (2) business profits, (3) dividends, (4) interest rates, and (5) security-price movements. Let us consider the historical record of each of these in turn.

1. The General Price Level. The movements of consumer and wholesale prices over the span from 1900 through 1960 are set forth in Chart 1-1. There are some significant differences in the two price series. For example, in World War I wholesale prices rose much higher than did consumer prices; subsequently, in the early 1930's, they fell substantially more. At the same time, an examination of the two series leads to several common conclusions.

First, although inflation has received marked attention in the invest-

Chart 1-1. Consumer and Wholesale Price Indexes, 1900–1960
(1947–1949 = 100)

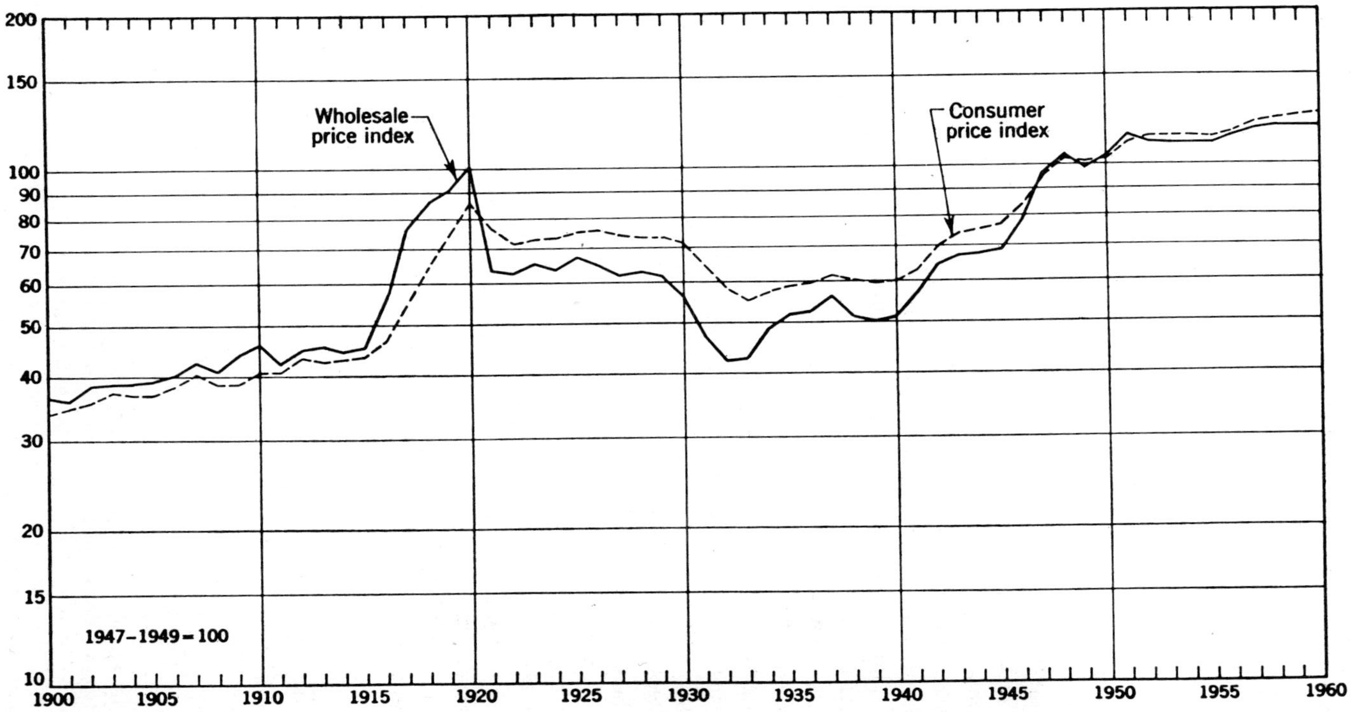

ment literature of the last few years, it is certainly not a new phenomenon. Over the six-decade span since 1900, wholesale prices increased at an annual rate compounded of 1.7 percent and consumer prices at a rate of 1.9 percent.

Second, the economic impact of the two world wars has shown itself very clearly in the level of general prices. World War I produced a sharp inflation, followed by a severe deflation (1921–1922) and then by recovery and stabilization at a level well above the prewar benchmark. Another and severer price decline took place in the Great Depression of the early 1930's, followed again by partial recovery and moderate stability. The World War II period was characterized by a reasonably effective control over prices. In fact, it was not until Congress removed price controls in 1946 that significant price inflation occurred. However, in contrast to the post-World War I situation, it has not been followed thus far by any pronounced deflation.

Third, there is an outstanding similarity in the broad pattern of prices in the 14-year post-World War II span from 1947 through 1960 and the 16-year pre-World War I period from 1900 through 1915.[1] In fact, as shown by the tabulation below, the annual average increase in consumer prices was identical in both periods and was nearly so for wholesale prices. If Chart 1-1 is again referred to, the comparability of the 1900–1915 and 1947–1960 price movements in each series will be noted in the narrowness of the price fluctuations as well as in the degree of inflation. The comparative annual average rates of increase are:

Prices	1900–1915	1947–1960
Consumer prices[2]	2.0%	2.0%
Wholesale prices	1.6	1.5

Long-term Trend Inflationary. These historic movements of the general price level have injected a recurrent element of uncertainty and confusion into the thinking of investors. In our opinion, they carry the lesson that the long-term trend is toward inflation. It is questionable, moreover, whether in the future this upward price movement will be interrupted by periods of deflation as severe as some of those prior to World War II.

[1] A set of charts, entitled the *Growth Reckoner*, prepared in 1959 by the Committee for Economic Development, indicates that much of the price rise of the postwar period is roughly comparable to the rise from 1910 to 1915.

[2] The absolute percentage changes in consumer prices from the first year in each decade through the last year are as follows:

1900–1909	+13.9%	1930–1939	−16.8%
1910–1919	+82.3	1940–1949	+69.9
1920–1929	−14.5	1950–1959	+21.2

For this reason, it is quite probable that inflation is a more important consideration than deflation. Nevertheless, investment policy must accommodate itself, as far as it can, to both possibilities.

Common stocks are by no means an ideal protection or "hedge" against inflation, but they do more for the investor on this point than either bonds or cash. Hence we conclude that the history of prices since 1900 carries a strong argument for the inclusion of a substantial proportion of common stocks in the ordinary investment portfolio. This conclusion, however, must be tempered in its application. As the already-cited record brings out, inflation is not new. It is therefore most doubtful whether the movements of general prices over the last few years—in themselves— justify a completely new evaluation of common stocks.[3] For this reason, inflation should not be allowed to influence unduly investor thinking.

Chart 1-2, which compares the changes in the "real income"—i.e., dollar income divided by the price level—derived from high-grade bonds and that derived from leading common stocks from 1913 through 1960, supports our contention in regard to the propriety of investing a significant proportion of a portfolio in common stocks except under abnormally high market conditions.

2. Business Conditions and Business Profits. Across time the aggregate earnings of business have moved irregularly but undeniably upward. This fact may be readily seen from Chart 1-3. Although the data are not entirely consistent throughout, they clearly show the increase in business earnings over the last 52 years and provide a basis for comparing the growth with that of the economy—as measured in terms of Gross National Product (the market value of the nation's output of final goods and services).

The relationship of business earnings and GNP is a factor which merits careful consideration by the analyst. There are some weaknesses in the statistics across the 52-year span, but it is doubtful that they are sufficient to destroy perspective. Examination of the data shows that for the entire period from 1909 through 1960, corporate earnings averaged 5.3 percent of GNP. The 52-year span may be divided roughly into two halves, around a 5-year gap: the period from, say, 1909 through 1929 which preceded the Great Depression and the period from 1935 through 1960 which followed it. The periods are not identical in numerous respects, and certainly there have been pronounced structural changes in the economy in the post-World War II years. Nevertheless, the two spans have a fair measure of comparability. Both include a world war, inflation, prosperity, relative stability, and recessions. For the 21 years from 1909 through 1929, corporate earnings averaged 6.1 percent of GNP; in the 1935–1960 period, they averaged 5.5 percent. In the 1947–1960 span,

---

[3] We concur in the view that "the factor of inflation, insofar as it applies to stocks at all, applies through its effects upon the stock's dividend-paying ability, and not through its effect upon the evaluation of the dividend-paying ability." A. Bernhard, *The Evaluation of Common Stocks*, Simon and Schuster, Inc., New York, 1959, p. 38.

Chart 1-2. Stocks vs. Bonds for Maintaining Real Income

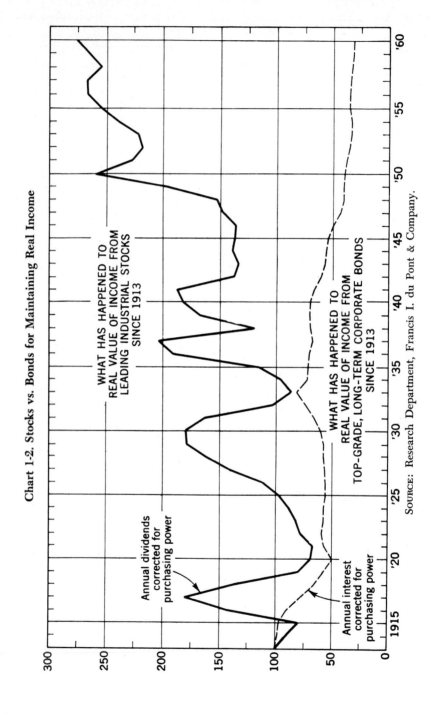

SOURCE: Research Department, Francis I. du Pont & Company.

Chart 1-3. Gross National Product and Corporate Net Income before and after Taxes, 1909–1960.

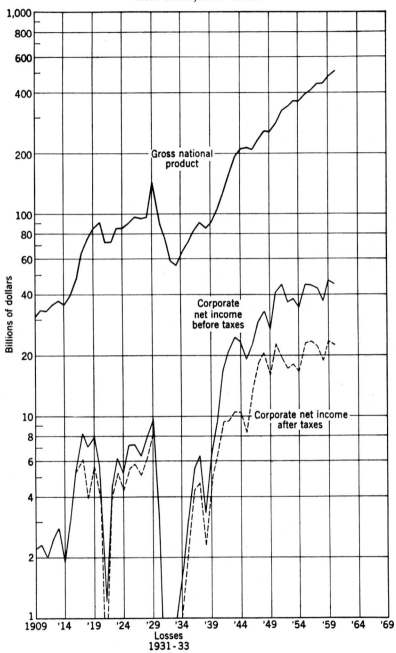

the average was 5.5 percent. In the last six years, 1955–1960, the average dropped to 5.0 percent, which is well below the 1909–1929 average and moderately below the 1935–1960 level. Perhaps one of the questions which invites examination is whether the corporate earnings share of the GNP has definitely become somewhat smaller.

If the analyst does some probing behind this relationship, he will discover a most interesting fact: In contrast to the pronounced decline in net corporate earnings as a percent of GNP, earnings before taxes and before depreciation—but after adjustment for inventory profits and losses —have had a remarkably consistent relationship to GNP across time.[4] The analyst may profitably give some thought to this fact. Because, if he can reach an over-all opinion as to the probable course of taxes and as to depreciation and the probability of inventory profits and losses (fundamentally the amount of inflation that may be anticipated), he may then be in a position to judge with reasonable reliability the average relationship of net corporate earnings to GNP over a period of time.

While the dollar amount earned is important in appraising business performance and essential in arriving at a per-share valuation figure, it is not the best measure of profitability. Dollar earnings should also be considered in relation to the volume of sales from which they are derived and to either (or both) the amount of capital or the amount of assets necessary to their production. For this reason we have also included data showing the rate of return earned on total capital by a group of major corporations. To our knowledge, a consistently compiled series is not available for the last 50 years; however, the following data set forth the return on total capital for a quarter of a century.[5]

Adjusted Return Earned on Total Capital

1935	6.9%	1948	15.0%	1935–1939	8.0%
1936	9.7	1949	12.2	1940–1944	9.5
1937	10.3	1950	15.0	1945–1949	11.4
1938	5.5	1951	12.6	1950–1954	12.2
1939	7.8	1952	11.0	1955–1959	10.9
1940	9.3	1953	11.1		
1941	10.7	1954	11.1		
1942	9.4	1955	12.9		
1943	9.1	1956	12.0		
1944	9.0	1957	10.9		
1945	7.5	1958	8.8		
1946	9.5	1959	9.7		
1947	13.0	1960	8.9		

[4] For example, in 1929 the pretax and predepreciation (and inventory-adjusted) earnings figure for all nonfinancial corporations was 12.0 percent of GNP; in 1936–1937 it was 9.8 percent; 12.5 percent in 1947–1960; and 12.6 percent in 1955–1960.

[5] Data 1935–1955 from S. Cottle and T. Whitman, *Corporate Earning Power and Market Valuation,* Duke University Press, Durham, N.C., 1959. Data for 1956 by

The figures for the post-World War II period are somewhat controversial. This is particularly true from the standpoint of the impact of inflation on corporate earnings and on the adequacy of depreciation.[6] These are shortcomings not of the return-on-capital type of analysis (or any other rate-of-return approach) but of the basic data from which they are computed. We do not live in a perfect world, and the analyst cannot expect to find "perfect" data. This should not deter him from examining carefully available pertinent material and gleaning from it as much as possible. Approached from this point of view, an analysis of the foregoing return-on-total-capital data points up two facts worthy of note: (1) the change in the structure of corporate profits and (2) the improved stability of the earnings rates in the 1947–1960 period.

Profit Structure. The earnings rate on total capital is the product of the "earnings margin" (earnings available for total capital divided by sales) and capital turnover (net sales divided by total capital). Consequently, changes in the return earned on total capital can result only from changes in either one or both of these two ratios. Chart 1-4 provides a graphic comparison of the rate of return on total capital, profit margin, and capital turnover for the 1935–1959 span.

The difference between the prewar (1935–1939) and postwar (1947–1959) levels for both the profit margin and capital turnover is striking. It is clear that American industry is operating on a much narrower profit margin after taxes than in the five-year span immediately prior to World War II. It is also clear that capital turnover has increased substantially. On balance, the increase in the turnover rate has somewhat outweighed the decline in the profit margin, with a resultant moderate gain in the return on capital. This fact emphasizes that the analyst needs to give thought to capital turnover, as well as to the return on sales, in examining the profitability of a company.

Amplitude of the Cyclical Swings of Business. It is exceedingly doubtful that *any* economy can remain continuously at "full throttle." Certainly, some ebb and flow in industrial activity and corporate earnings must be anticipated. Thus it is not the probability of future swings which is the primary concern but, rather, the probable amplitude of those swings. The extent of the downturns is particularly pertinent. In this regard, a review of the experience of the last three decades may be helpful.

---

one of the authors and subsequently by Stanford Research Institute. The return represents (*a*) net income after taxes plus interest on long-term debt *minus* an adjustment equivalent to the amount of Federal income taxes that would have been due had interest charges not been deductible for tax purposes, divided by (*b*) net worth plus long-term debt.

[6] See "Corporate Profits and Rates of Return in the Fifties Adjusted for Comparison with Those of the Twenties," *Capital Goods Review,* Machinery and Allied Products Institute, No. 38, May 1959.

Chart 1-4. Composite Industry Performance
Earnings Rate on Total Capital
Earnings Available Total Capital to Sales
Sales to Total Capital,
1935–1959

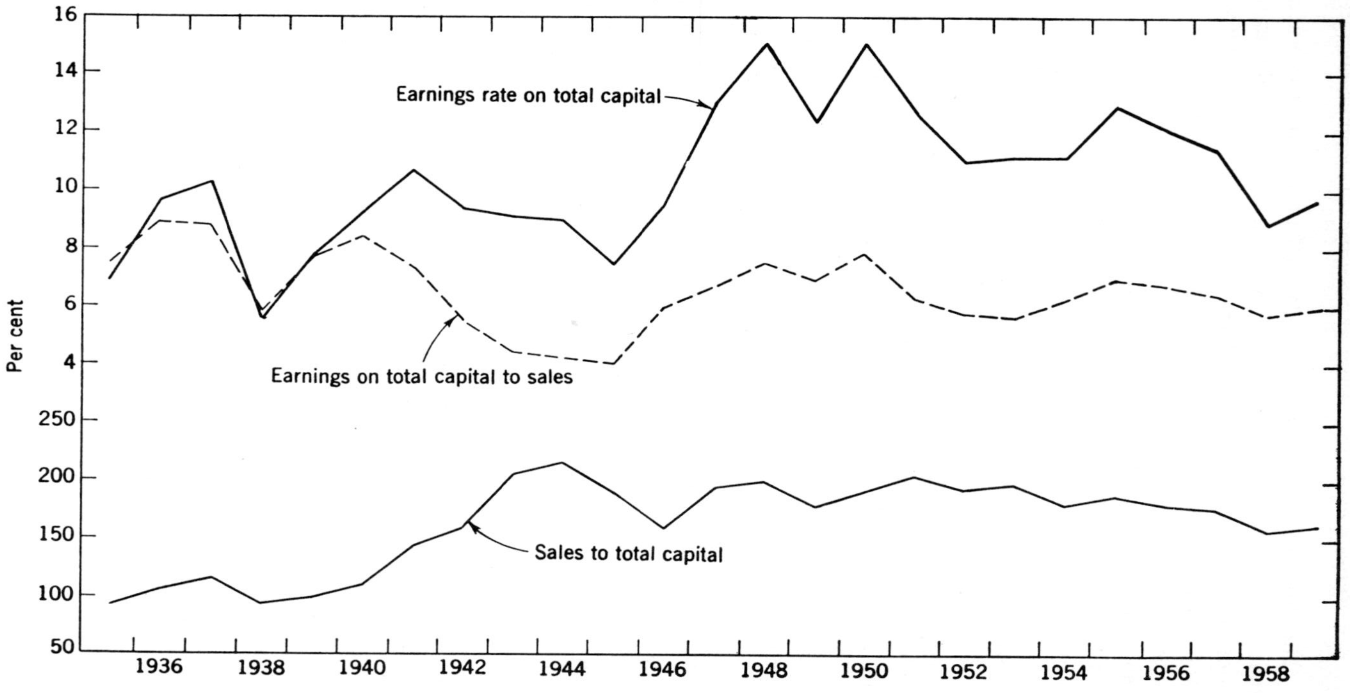

Earnings rate on total capital

Earnings on total capital to sales

Sales to total capital

Per cent

16 14 12 10 8 6 4   250 200 150 100 50

1936 1938 1940 1942 1944 1946 1948 1950 1952 1954 1956 1958

12

The business depression of 1929–1933 was drastically out of proportion not only to the preceding business expansion but to all the earlier depressions for which satisfactory data are available. The decline in 1937–1938, while much less severe than its predecessor, was nevertheless substantial. In fact, we failed to regain our economic stride—and to solve the problem of abnormally high unemployment—until the United States entered World War II. The expansion of our industrial output and of the level of general business in the ensuing war and postwar years was— like the Great Depression—a phenomenon of unexampled character. Thus, in the three decades from 1929 to 1959 there have been downward and upward movements of business, apparently unconnected, which have dwarfed all the recorded cyclical swings of the past.

To date there have been four post-World War II recessions. The first occurred in 1948–1949, the second in 1953–1954, the third in 1957– 1958, the last in 1960–1961. The extent and the duration of all four periods of contraction were substantially less than in the depressions of 1920–1921, 1929–1933, and 1937–1938; hence they have been given the milder designation of "recessions."[7]

The probable amplitude of future business downturns may be approached from two standpoints. On the one side, barring the results of a destructive war, few today would hold that a depression of the amplitude of the early 1930's will recur. Furthermore, although the number would be greater, only a minority would contend that a decline more severe than that of 1937–1938 will again be encountered. On the other side, a majority might conceivably conclude that future recessions could exceed in severity those of the post-World War II period.

The relevant legislation, governmental policies, and business practices of the last two or three decades have, for the most part, tended toward stability.[8] It appears, therefore, that—from a cyclical point of view— the economic climate within which business operates has improved ma-

---

[7] Geoffrey Moore measured the severity of eight out of the last nine business-cycle contractions in terms of ten indicators of aggregate economic activity. These contractions, beginning with the mildest, are ranked in the tabulation below, and the percentage change in a single indicator—the Federal Reserve Board Index of Industrial Production—is shown in parentheses. (It will be seen that a ranking based on the percentage decline in the Index of Industrial Production would not in every instance be the same as that resulting from the use of numerous measures.)

1926–1927	(− 7%)	1957–1958	(− 13%)
1953–1954	(− 10%)	1920–1921	(− 30%)
1948–1949	(− 9%)	1937–1938	(− 32%)
1923–1924	(− 18%)	1929–1933	(− 52%)

Geoffrey H. Moore, "Measuring the 1957–58 Recession," *Analysts Journal*, February 1959, p. 18.

[8] For a penetrating review of postwar economic changes, see Arthur E. Burns, "Progress Towards Economic Stability," *The American Economic Review*, March 1960.

terially.[9] If so, the investment attractiveness of common stocks *as a class* has risen. It would be logical, then, for this improved attractiveness to be expressed in a higher multiplier of earnings and a lower dividend yield than would otherwise be appropriate.

From the foregoing we should not assume that the success of all undertakings is thereby assured or that some well-established companies or even industries may not have less attractive earnings experiences in the future than they have had in the past. To emphasize this fact, we should like to return to the record and point out the strikingly divergent postwar and prewar earnings patterns of different corporate groups.

Industry Divergence. Surprising as it may seem, a number of important American industries were less profitable in the post-World War II prosperity than in the prewar span from 1935 to 1939. Table 1-3 compares the composite earnings rates on total capital in the two five-year spans—1955–1959 and 1935–1939—for the major corporations in each of 32 principal industrial groupings.

Note that, although the weighted composite earnings rate was nearly 38 percent higher in 1955–1959 than in 1935–1939, one-half of the industries had lower returns on total capital in the latter period than in the former. Various explanations can be offered in the individual cases. Nevertheless, the fact remains that all industries do not participate equally in prosperity. In our dynamic industrial economy, the relative profitability and growth of industries—as well as companies—are subject to marked and continual change.

There are other divergences in the patterns of different corporate groups to be pointed out. In the past 45 years the railroad group has declined from preeminence to a tertiary and a relatively unprofitable position, while the same period has seen an almost uninterrupted growth and stability in the operating public utility companies, other than tractions.

In the field of "industrials"—comprising mainly manufacturing, mining, and trade—the already-noted experience has been so variegated as to counsel strongly against generalizations. Some authorities have seen in this record a standard pattern—repeated successively by each industrial group—of expansion, slowing down, decline, and complete decay or extinction. Our view of the same material is decidedly different. We believe the most striking characteristic of our large American businesses (e.g., those big enough to warrant their listing on the New York Stock Exchange) is their repeated pendulum swings from better to poorer results and back.

A remarkably small percentage of our large enterprises have actually "gone out of business" through voluntary liquidation or a sheriff's auc-

---

[9] Moreover, the amount of available economic data has been expanded substantially. And at the same time, the ability to analyze and interpret its cyclical implications has also improved.

tion. Those that have ended their corporate existence have usually effected this via a merger or sale as a going concern, a method which has meant continuance of function if not of name.[10] As will be seen later, this somewhat controversial point may be of the greatest importance in the determination of a sophisticated investment policy.

Table 1-3. Comparative Changes in Earnings Rates on Total Capital by Industries, 1955–1959 and 1935–1939

Industries	Change, 1935–1939 to 1955–1959	1955–1959	1935–1939
Steel	+216.1%	9.8%	3.1%
Paper and allied products	+106.0	10.3	5.0
Copper	+ 90.6	10.1	5.3
Building materials	+ 70.3	12.6	7.4
Oil	+ 69.8	10.7	6.3
Rubber	+ 68.4	9.6	5.7
Corn products	+ 67.9	13.6	8.1
Department stores	+ 45.3	7.7	5.3
Dairy products	+ 34.7	10.1	7.5
Textile fabrics	+ 32.6	5.7	4.3
Grocery chain stores	+ 31.8	11.2	8.5
General industry machinery	+ 17.7	11.3	9.6
Electrical supplies and equipment	+ 16.0	11.6	10.0
Aircraft	+ 6.5	14.7	13.8
Grain-mill products	0	7.8	7.8
Nonferrous metals	0	13.1	13.1
Chemicals	− 5.6	10.3	10.9
Auto parts and accessories	− 10.0	12.5	13.9
Toilet preparations and soap	− 10.4	12.1	13.5
Mail-order houses	− 13.0	10.7	12.3
Containers	− 17.1	9.2	11.1
Proprietary drugs	− 18.6	25.3	31.1
Agricultural machinery	− 20.7	6.5	8.2
Meat packing	− 22.0	3.2	4.1
Automobiles	− 24.4	15.5	20.5
Ethical drugs	− 27.4	17.5	24.1
Cigarettes	− 28.1	10.5	14.6
Packaged foods	− 28.7	12.9	18.1
Limited-price variety stores	− 36.5	8.0	12.6
Apparel and accessories chains	− 38.1	14.3	23.1
Radio and television	− 51.1	6.9	14.1
Distilling	− 57.2	6.2	14.5
Composite	+ 37.5	11.0	8.0

SOURCE: Stanford Research Institute.

[10] A study of the 100 corporations which—in terms of assets—were the largest in the United States in 1929 reveals that in the subsequent three decades (including the Great Depression) only eight went into receivership and of these only one involved a 100 percent loss for the common stockholders. Moreover, at the end of 1958, 50 were among the 100 largest industrial corporations, and five were among the 50 largest merchandising firms listed by *Fortune* magazine.

Table 1-4. Percent of Earnings Paid Out in Cash Dividends. All Corporations, Dow-Jones Industrial Average, and Standard & Poor's Composite Stocks, 1926–1960

Year	All corporations*			Dow-Jones Industrial Average			Standard & Poor's 500 Stock Composite Index		
	Earnings (in billions)	Dividends (in billions)	Payout rate	Earnings per share	Dividends per share	Payout rate	Earnings per share	Dividends per share	Payout rate
1926	n.a.	n.a.	.....	$14.97	$7.42	50%	$1.24	$0.69	56%
1927	n.a.	n.a.	.....	12.39	8.29	67	1.11	0.77	69
1928	n.a.	n.a.	.....	16.64	9.76	59	1.38	0.85	62
1929	$8.3	$5.8	70%	19.94	12.75	64	1.61	0.97	60
1930	2.5	5.5	220	11.02	11.13	101	0.97	0.98	101
1931	−1.3	4.1	.....	4.09	8.40	205	0.61	0.82	134
1932	−3.4	2.6	.....	0.51 (d)	4.62	.....	0.49	0.50	102
1933	−0.4	2.1	.....	2.11	3.40	161	0.44	0.44	100
1934	1.0	2.6	260	3.91	3.66	93	0.49	0.45	92
1935	2.2	2.9	132	6.34	4.55	72	0.77	0.47	61
1936	4.3	4.5	105	10.07	7.05	70	1.03	0.72	70
1937	4.7	4.7	100	11.49	8.78	76	1.19	0.80	67
1938	2.3	3.2	139	6.01	4.98	83	0.63	0.51	81
1939	5.0	3.8	76	9.11	6.11	67	0.87	0.62	71
1940	6.5	4.0	62	10.92	7.06	65	1.06	0.67	63
1941	9.4	4.5	48	11.64	7.59	65	1.18	0.71	60
1942	9.5	4.3	45	9.22	6.40	69	1.00	0.59	59
1943	10.5	4.5	43	9.74	6.30	65	0.93	0.61	66
1944	10.4	4.7	45	10.07	6.57	65	0.94	0.64	68

Year									
1945	8.3	4.7	57	10.56	6.69	63	0.98	0.66	68
1946	13.4	5.8	43	13.63	7.50	55	1.03	0.71	69
1947	18.2	6.5	36	18.86	9.21	49	1.63	0.84	52
1948	20.3	7.2	35	23.07	11.50	50	2.28	0.93	41
1949	15.8	7.5	47	23.54	12.79	54	2.32	1.14	49
1950	22.8	9.2	40	30.70	16.13	52	2.83	1.47	52
1951	19.7	9.0	46	26.59	16.34	62	2.42	1.41	58
1952	17.2	9.0	52	24.76	15.48	62	2.40	1.41	59
1953	18.1	9.2	51	27.23	16.11	59	2.52	1.45	58
1954	16.8	9.8	58	28.40	17.47	62	2.76	1.54	56
1955	23.0	11.2	49	35.78	21.58	60	3.62	1.64	45
1956	23.5	12.1	51	33.34	22.99	69	3.40	1.74	51
1957	22.3	12.6	56	36.08	21.61	60	3.38	1.79	53
1958	19.1	12.4	65	27.95	20.00	72	2.89	1.75	61
1959	23.8	13.4	56	34.31	20.74	61	3.41	1.83	54
1960	22.8	14.0	61	32.21	21.36	66	3.31	1.95	59
Weighted averages:									
1926–1929			n.a.			60			62
1935–1939			103			73			70
1941–1945			47			66			63
1947–1951			40			54			50
1955–1959			55			64			52
1955–1960			56			64			54

* U.S. Department of Commerce, *Survey of Current Business.*

3. Dividends. Tax considerations, capital-expenditure programs, financing plans, and numerous other factors play a role in shaping dividend policies. Basically, as a result of the widespread desire of managements to maintain payments to stockholders, dividend payments are more stable than earnings. Except for the wider cyclical fluctuations of profits, the over-all pattern of corporate dividends has followed that of earnings with reasonable closeness.

Table 1-4 shows the total of all corporate earnings and dividends and the payout rate for each of the last 32 years. It also shows the per-share earnings, dividends, and payout rate for the Dow-Jones Industrial Average and Standard & Poor's Composite over the 35-year period from 1926 through 1960.

Prior to the 1929–1933 depression, roughly 60 percent of the earnings of industrial enterprises were paid out in cash dividends. In the years just prior to World War II there was some tendency toward a modest rise in the percentage of earnings disbursed. Note from Table 1-4 that the payout rate for the Dow-Jones Industrial Average rose from nearly 60 percent in 1926–1929 to over 73 percent in 1935–1939, and for Standard & Poor's Composite stock the payout rose from 62 to 70 percent. (The increase in the proportion of corporate earnings distributed to stockholders in the form of cash dividends was undoubtedly affected by the surtax on undistributed profits in 1936–1937 and may also have been aided by Section 102 of the Internal Revenue Code imposing a penalty tax on improper accumulation of surplus. The latter was replaced by Section 531 of the 1954 Code.)

From 1941 until the early 1950's the tremendous needs for corporate capital resulting from a combination of business expansion and inflation' reduced the payout rate substantially. For all corporations, it dropped to 47 percent in the five-year span 1941–1945 and to 40 percent in the like period from 1947 through 1951. For the Dow-Jones shares, the percent paid out declined to 66 percent and 54 percent, respectively, in the same two five-year spans. For the Standard & Poor's series the decline was to 63 and 50 percent. In each of the subsequent years the payout rate has been well above the 1947–1951 average for both the "all corporations" and the Dow-Jones groups. For the Standard & Poor's stocks, the payout dropped below the 1947–1951 average in 1955, and the 1955–1960 average of 54 percent was only moderately above the 1947–1951 average of 50 percent. In all instances, the payout has remained below the 1935–1939 level.

The higher payout rate in recent years was to be expected. In our 1951 edition we noted that the extremely low proportion of earnings distributed as cash dividends "would seem a temporary phenomenon." At the same time, in view of the relatively high capital-expenditures level anticipated for corporations for the rather indefinite future, a voluntary return to a payout level as high as 1935–1939 would appear doubtful.

The use of annual stock dividends to represent currently reinvested profits may become increasingly prevalent, and this may make for lower cash payout rates for growing companies. In general, good growth and low rates of cash disbursements may logically be expected to go together.

Once again, the wide diversity of industry experience is to be pointed out. It may be seen from Table 1-5 that 27 out of 32 major industrial

Table 1-5. Percent of Earnings Paid Out in Cash Dividends by 32 Major Industrial Groups, 1955–1959 and 1935–1939

Industrial group	Payout rate, percent	
	1955–1959	1935–1939
Electrical supplies and equipment........	69.7	84.3
Apparel and accessories chains...........	68.4	77.5
Limited-price variety stores.............	65.9	71.0
Copper.................................	67.6	63.9
Automobiles...........................	65.5	74.6
Chemicals.............................	62.8	70.3
Corn products.........................	61.2	114.9
General industrial machinery...........	61.2	78.3
Nonferrous metals.....................	60.8	66.5
Proprietary drugs.....................	58.9	74.1
Department stores.....................	58.7	72.1
Glass and metal containers.............	57.9	77.8
Meat packing..........................	57.5	74.2
Cigarettes.............................	57.5	101.8
Ethical drugs.........................	57.2	87.9
Dairy products........................	55.4	83.3
Building materials.....................	55.3	82.5
Paper and allied products..............	55.2	48.5
Distilling.............................	54.2	36.7
Toilet preparations and soap............	54.0	67.3
Mail-order houses.....................	53.0	66.0
Packaged foods........................	52.6	89.5
Steel..................................	52.6	55.3
Grain-mill products....................	52.3	66.6
Automobile parts and accessories........	50.7	56.9
Agricultural machinery.................	50.5	39.5
Textile fabrics........................	49.5	71.3
Aircraft...............................	48.0	54.0
Oil....................................	47.8	54.4
Radio and television...................	43.8	65.0
Grocery chain stores...................	41.9	75.8
Rubber................................	39.6	35.3

groups had lower average payout rates in 1955–1959 than in 1935–1939. Note that in the latter five-year span the percent of earnings paid out ranged from a low of about 40 percent for a group of rubber companies to a high of 70 percent for the electrical supplies and equipment group. In the prewar period, the range, which was from 35 percent to 115 percent, was distorted by the maintenance of dividends when losses were encountered or earnings were almost nonexistent.

4. Interest Rates. The record of sixty years of interest rates on high-grade bonds is an interesting one (Chart 1-5). World War I ushered in

Chart 1-5. Comparative Bond and Stock Yields
Standard & Poor's A1⁺ Bonds and Industrial Stocks, 1900–1960

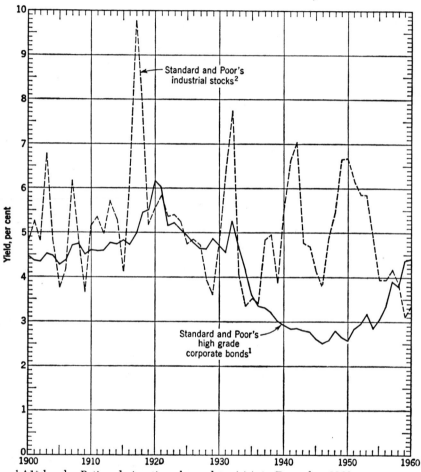

¹ A1⁺ bonds: Rating designation changed to AAA in December 1960.
² 1900–1925: Alfred Cowles and Associates, *Common Stock Indexes, 1871–1937,* Principia Press, Inc., Bloomington, Ind., 1939.

a substantial rise in the interest rate, which was considered the normal concomitant of large-scale government financing. However, after several irregular movements associated with the business cycle—including a sharp rise in 1920 to a high to date for this century—the bond rate declined throughout most of the 1930's. This decline took place despite the fact that the Treasury was going heavily into debt through New

Deal deficit financing. Then came World War II with its incredible expansion of the Federal debt from $40 billion to $240 billion. Nevertheless, instead of rising, the bond interest rate fell further during this period. These unorthodox events resulted from artificial controls resorted to by the Federal government. A new period for interest rates began in 1951,

Table 1-6. Comparative Yields on Government and Corporate Bonds, and Preferred Stocks, 1940–1960

Year	Taxable long-term U.S. Treasury bonds	U.S. savings bonds	Municipal tax-free bonds	High-grade corporate bonds	High-grade preferred stocks
1940		2.90%	2.50%	2.92%	4.14%
1941		2.90	2.10	2.84	4.08
1942	2.27%	2.90	2.36	2.85	4.31
1943	2.29	2.90	2.06	2.80	4.06
1944	2.38	2.90	1.86	2.78	3.99
1945	2.34	2.90	1.67	2.61	3.70
1946	2.19	2.90	1.64	2.51	3.53
1947	2.24	2.90	2.01	2.58	3.79
1948	2.43	2.90	2.40	2.80	4.15
1949	2.28	2.90	2.21	2.65	3.97
1950	2.32	2.90	1.98	2.59	3.85
1951	2.60	2.90	2.00	2.84	4.11
1952	2.68	3.00	2.19	2.95	4.13
1953	2.90	3.00	2.72	3.18	4.27
1954	2.52	3.00	2.37	2.87	4.02
1955	2.80	3.00	2.53	3.04	4.01
1956	3.06	3.00	2.93	3.38	4.25
1957	3.47	3.25	3.60	3.91	4.63
1958	3.23	3.25	3.56	3.80	4.45
1959	4.10	3.75	3.95	4.38	4.69
1960	3.99	3.75	3.73	4.41	4.75

SOURCE: Standard & Poor's *Statistics*.

when the so-called "Treasury–Federal Reserve accord" brought an end to an inflexible policy of pegging the prices and yields on Treasury obligations. Since then the yield on all types of bonds (except United States Savings issues) has tended to rise or fall according to the state of business conditions and the accompanying monetary policy of "tight" or "easy" money.

Table 1-6 above shows the comparative 1940–1960 yields of taxable long-term United States government bonds, United States Savings Bonds, Series E and H, tax-free municipal bonds, and the highest-grade corporate bonds. The dividend yields of high-grade preferred stocks is also presented, since these are competitive with bonds. The data show clearly the superior attractiveness, until 1956, of United States Savings Bonds as against other taxable bonds. This relationship greatly simplified the problem of bond selection for the individual investor not in a high tax bracket. In recent years, however, the Savings Bonds have lost their yield advantage.

Stock Yields and Bond Yields. Examination of Chart 1-5 shows that the annual dividend yield on industrial stocks has been less than the yield for highest quality bonds in only 15 out of the last 61 years. Note, however, that on two occasions the annual stock yields remained below annual bond yields for a continuous 3-year period. This was true from 1919 through 1921 and from 1933 through 1935. Both spans included years in which dividends were extremely low. The longest uninterrupted period in which stock yields exceeded bond yields was the 23 years from 1936 through 1958. Over the span from 1926 through 1960, for which stock-yield data have been compiled by Standard & Poor's, stock yields averaged 137 percent of bond yields. Annual stock yields in 1959 were lower than in any year in the last 60. In 1959 stock yields were 71 percent of bond yields—in other words, just about half of their ratio for the preceding 33 years. (In 1960 the yield rose slightly but was still less than 77 percent of the high-grade bond yield.) The student will note that *in the past* a drop in stock yields below bond yields, caused by rising stock prices, has proved a sure indication that the market had entered a dangerously high level.

5. Security Prices. The price history of high-grade bonds (and high-grade preferred stocks) is necessarily the reverse of the course of interest rates, which was set forth in Chart 1-5.

If the price movement of common stocks over the last nine decades—1871–1961—is examined, 12 major stock-price cycles can be discerned in the period 1871–1949. Since 1949, the price declines have been so limited that we have designated these fluctuations "stock-price swings" rather than "cycles" (Table 1-7).

A review of Table 1-7 and a visual examination of any long-term price chart for a composite group of stocks—such as Standard & Poor's Composite or the Dow-Jones Industrial Average—emphasize two major facts. First, stock prices are subject to pronounced fluctuations. Second, the famous new-era bull market which began in 1921, reached a dizzy peak in 1929, and terminated its collapse in June 1932, represented a cycle which in both duration and magnitude exceeded by far every other major price movement in the 1871–1949 span. It is our considered opinion that this prodigious bull market constituted nothing but a mass speculative orgy—like the South Sea and Mississippi Bubbles of two centuries earlier—without any special foundation in economic or political developments. (In this case, however, the speculation produced portentous economic and political results.)

Everyone recognizes that the post-World War II period has been characterized by a tremendous upsurge in common-stock prices, the extent and duration of which is not yet a matter of completed history. The most generally accepted view is that the bull market began in 1949. Standard & Poor's Composite Index dropped to a low of less than 14 in June 1949. The high to the end of 1961 (and the high up to the time of this writing) is 72.6. Accordingly, measured from the 1949 low, this represents a rise of 434 percent, which has extended—with some interruptions (Table 1-7)—over a period of 12½ years. Accordingly, taking June 1949

Table 1-7. Major Stock-price Cycles, 1871–1949, and Stock-price Swings, 1949–1961

Trough		Peak		Percent	
Date	Low price	Date	High price	Rise from low	Decline to next low
Jan. 1871	4.44	April 1872	5.13	17	47
June 1877	2.73	June 1881	6.58	141	36
June 1885	4.24	May 1887	5.90	39	35
Aug. 1896	3.81	Sept. 1902	8.85	132	29
Oct. 1903	6.26	Sept. 1906	10.03	60	38
Nov. 1907	6.25	Dec. 1909	10.30	65	34
Dec. 1914	6.80	July 1919	9.51	40	32
Aug. 1921	6.45	Sept. 1929	31.92*	395	86
June 1932	4.40	Mar. 1937	18.68	322	54
Mar. 1938	8.50	Jan. 1939	13.23	56	55
Apr. 1942	7.47	May 1946	19.25	158	30
June 1949	13.55	Jan. 1953	26.66	97	15
Sept. 1953	22.71	July 1956	49.74	119	19
Dec. 1957	40.33	Aug. 1959	60.71	50	14
Oct. 1960	52.30	Dec. 1961†	72.64	39	

* This figure and subsequent data based on daily closing prices; previous figures based on monthly average.

† High to May 1962.

Source: Standard & Poor's Long-term Composite Price Index, 1871–1961.

as the starting point, the present bull market exceeds both the extent and duration of the 1921–1929 market. To what extent the sequels will resemble each other is a matter not of history but of prediction, and our views thereon are reserved for a later chapter. At this point we are assuming that history has some relevance to the investor's policies. Even if he feels that the 1921–1932 cycle is to be excluded from consideration, as a unique phenomenon, he must still be impressed by the magnitude of the declines from lesser market peaks since 1900. We should therefore consider it most doubtful that common stocks can be purchased without regard to the level of the market and without an eye on historic fluctuations in prices.

CHAPTER TWO

THE SCOPE AND LIMITATIONS

OF SECURITY ANALYSIS

"Analysis" connotes the careful study of available facts with the attempt to draw conclusions therefrom based on established principles and sound logic. It is part of the scientific method. But in applying analysis to the field of securities we encounter the serious obstacle that investment is by nature not an exact science. The same is true, however, of law and medicine, for here also both individual skill (art) and chance are important factors in determining success or failure. Nevertheless, in these professions analysis is not only useful but indispensable, so that the same should probably be true in the field of investment and possibly in that of speculation.

The importance and prestige of security analysis have tended to increase over the years, paralleling roughly the steady improvement in corporation reports and other statistical data which supply its raw material. An exception may be seen in the new-era markets of 1927–1933. Both the advance and the decline in stock prices were so extreme during this period that the conclusions suggested by informed and conservative security analysis were found to have little practical utility. This was the more true because the business depression of the early 1930's was so unexpectedly severe as to vitiate many conclusions regarding safety and value that had been reasonable in the light of past experience. On the other hand, the market and business cycles since 1933—like those before 1927—have provided a suitable proving ground for security analysis. In periods of extended prosperity, there is always the hazard of undue optimism, particularly in terms of the glamour stocks of the moment. This has been evidenced in the stock market since the late 1950's. Nevertheless, we believe that in broad terms security analysis has met these challenges satisfactorily.

It should be added that since the enactment, mainly in 1933–1935, of the various laws administered by the Securities and Exchange Commission, there has been a significant improvement in the quality and quantity of the published corporate data, which in turn has added to the scope

24

and dependability of security analysis. Furthermore, the increased attention given by major corporations to their annual reports since 1946 has improved their informational value.

THREE FUNCTIONS OF SECURITY ANALYSIS

The functions of analysis may be described under three headings: descriptive, selective, and critical.

1. Descriptive Function. Descriptive analysis limits itself to marshaling the important facts relating to an issue and presenting them in a coherent, readily intelligible manner. But there are gradations of accomplishment and of related skill in this descriptive function. The least imaginative type is found in the familiar and indispensable statistical presentations of the various security manuals and similar descriptive services.[1] Here the material is accepted essentially in the form supplied by the company; the figures are set down for a number of successive years; then certain standard calculations are added—e.g., earnings per share, number of times fixed charges were earned.

A more penetrating descriptive analysis can often go much farther than this in presenting the published figures. In many cases the analyst needs to make various kinds of adjustment of the material in order to bring out the true operating results in the period covered and particularly in order to place the data of a number of companies on a fairly comparable plane. He must consider such matters as contingency reserves, special allowances for depreciation, "LIFO" versus "FIFO" inventory accounting, nonrecurring gains and losses, nonconsolidated subsidiaries, and many other possible items.

On a still higher level of analysis would rank the evaluation of favorable and unfavorable factors in the position of the issue. This might include consideration of the changes within the company over a long period of years, a detailed comparison with others in the same field, and projections of earning power on various assumptions as to future conditions.

2. The Selective Function. The senior analyst must be ready to pass judgment on the merits of securities. He is expected to advise others on their purchase, sale, retention, or exchange. Many laymen believe that if a security analyst is worth his salt, he will be able to give good advice of this sort about any stock or bond issue at any time. This is far from true. Certain times and security situations are propitious for a sound analytical judgment; others the analyst may be poorly qualified to handle; for many others his study and his conclusions may be better than nothing but still of questionable value to the investor. Furthermore, we should acknowledge that there are some serious differences of opinion among practicing security analysts as to the basic approach to the selective

---

[1] These include Moody's and Standard & Poor's.

function. Let us develop this question by a progression from its less to its more controversial aspects.

a. Analysis of Senior Securities. The analysis of high-grade bonds follows well-established principles. The object is to make as sure as possible that interest payments will be met in the future without difficulty or doubt. The accepted method is to require an ample margin of safety in the past, which is counted on to protect against possible adverse developments that lie ahead. The techniques and standards used in this work are by no means uniform, but the differences in practical conclusions between one competent analyst and another are not likely to be striking. These conclusions may include determination of a suitable price and yield for the issue, to bring it in line with the current interest level for its class. Investment-grade preferred stocks are dealt with generally in the same manner as bonds.

On the other hand, the analysis of second-grade or speculative bonds and preferred stocks is an almost nonexistent technique. Although the field is a fairly large one, little serious effort has been made to cultivate it intensively. The reason is, probably, that this group presents difficulties in analysis out of proportion to the popular interest therein. Thus the market for such issues is generally left to find its own level without benefit of studious inquiry. These levels are often highly irrational, and at their extreme points they will usually offer interesting and rewarding opportunities for value analysis. (As will be seen, a common-stock approach may be quite useful in this field.)

b. Common-stock Analysis. The analysis of common stocks is, of course, the most fascinating part of our subject. Its objective generally is to help the investor or speculator to "do well" in common stocks, by selecting those that will pay a good return or increase in price or both. A proper analysis will take into account all the important points in the company's past record and present position, and it will apply informed judgment to the projection of future results. We believe there are three schools of thought, or philosophies, in approaching this task.

Three Approaches. The first and oldest approach places primary emphasis on anticipated market performance. This we term the "anticipation" approach. The second and third approaches rest on valuation—one on *absolute* values, the other on *relative* values.[2]

The anticipation approach is typified by the numerous published lists which suggest stocks which will "outperform" the market over some specified time span, such as the next twelve months. In this approach it is assumed that the present market price is, by and large, an appropriate reflection of the present situation of a stock, including the general opinion of its future. But the price, say, a year from now will probably be quite

[2] For a further discussion of relative values, see R. A. Bing, "The Appraisal of Stocks," *Analysts Journal,* May 1958, pp. 41–46.

different from today's, though it will be appropriate for the conditions of a year hence. The function of the security analyst, then is to anticipate the new situation, to select the stocks that will benefit most therefrom, and to reject those that will fare badly. He does this by a detailed study of the business position and prospects of the various companies. The presumption is that his work and skill will enable him to make a more nearly accurate projection of future results than is already implicit in the present market price. This approach, clearly, does not involve seeking an answer to the question: What is the stock worth?

The second concept stands in marked contrast. It attempts to value a stock independently of its current market price. If the value found is substantially above or below the current price, the analyst concludes that the issue should be bought or disposed of. This independent value has a variety of names, the most familiar of which is "intrinsic value."[3] It may also be called "indicated value," "central value," "normal value," "investment value," "reasonable value," "fair value" (in some legal proceedings), and "appraised value."

In earlier years there was a great deal of skepticism in Wall Street as to whether intrinsic value had any valid existence at all apart from the market price. The common saying was: "A security is always worth what you can sell it for, no more and no less." This view is no longer prevalent in such a dogmatic form. The possible existence of an intrinsic value differing from price is now generally conceded, although vestiges of doubt remain as to the extent to which the concept has practical usefulness in security operations.

The third approach, although a member of the valuation family, is concerned with *relative* rather than *intrinsic* value. Instead of accepting the complete independence of intrinsic value from the current level of stock prices, in estimating relative value the analyst more or less accepts the prevailing market level and seeks to determine the value of a stock in terms of it. That is, he derives the capitalization rate for an individual issue in terms of the rate at which the earnings or dividends for a cross section of the market—such as the Dow-Jones Industrial Average—are being capitalized or from the capitalization rate for a specific industry or other group which typifies the market for the individual share he is seeking to evaluate. His efforts, therefore, are devoted fundamentally to appraising the *relative* attractiveness of individual issues in terms of the then existing level of stock prices and not to determining the fundamental worth of a stock. This approach is valid when employed in connection with capital committed to permanent full investment in common stocks, a commitment which now appears to be accepted for many in-

[3] We do not know when the term "intrinsic value" was first applied to investments, but it is referred to in a pamphlet published in 1848, *Stocks and Stock-jobbing in Wall Street*, by William Armstrong, p. 12.

vestment funds. (Of course, the relative attractiveness of a list of stocks could also be determined by arraying them in terms of the relationship of their intrinsic values to their current market prices.)

Intrinsic Value. Let us consider in a little more detail what the analyst ordinarily means by intrinsic value and then what problems and obstacles arise in connection therewith.

A general definition of intrinsic value would be "that value which is justified by the facts, e.g., assets, earnings, dividends, definite prospects, including the factor of management." The primary objective in using the adjective "intrinsic" is to emphasize the distinction between *value* and *current market price,* but not to invest this "value" with an aura of permanence. In truth, the computed intrinsic value is likely to change at least from year to year, as the various factors governing that value are modified. But in most cases intrinsic value changes less rapidly and drastically than market price, and the investor usually has an opportunity to profit from any wide discrepancy between the current price and the intrinsic value as determined at the same time.

The most important single factor determining a stock's value is now held to be the *indicated average future earning power,* i.e., the estimated average earnings for a future span of years. Intrinsic value would then be found by first forecasting this earning power and then multiplying that prediction by an appropriate "capitalization factor." To illustrate this process we have selected one of our largest corporations—General Motors.

Early in 1948 we presented a valuation of General Motors common stock.[4] It assumed that the average future per-share earnings at $4.50 to $5.50. (Adjusted for subsequent splits to the end of 1959 (6 for 1), this would equal $0.75 to $0.92.) It also assumed a fair multiplier for these earnings to be between 14 and 16.[5] Combining the earnings and the multiplier, the indicated range of value of General Motors common was between 63 and 88 (adjusted, 10½ to 15).

At first glance this range of value may appear too broad and thus too indefinite to be of practical use. But that is not true at all. If the investor could rely on the analyst's conclusions here, he could have bought General Motors with confidence during 1948–1949, for its price in those years averaged only 60 (adjusted 10), and it held consistently below the mean figure (76 or 12½ adjusted) of intrinsic value. The normal range of price fluctuations of General Motors over a stock-market cycle is considerably wider than is covered by this intrinsic-value "band."

Ten years later General Motors was entrenched in a much higher area

---

[4] See the address by Benjamin Graham before the National Federation of Financial Analysts on Mar. 4, 1948, entitled "Two Ways of Making (and Losing) Money in Securities," printed in a supplement in the *Analysts Journal* covering this meeting.

[5] This would be equivalent to a so-called "capitalization rate" of between about 7 and 6¼ percent.

of value than in 1948. An elaborate valuation study—made by Nicholas Molodovsky, an editor of the *Financial Analysts Journal,* in the May 1959 issue—boiled down to the following simple computation:

	1958	1970
"Level-of-earnings trend".........	$3.30	$4.30
Appropriate multiplier............	13.7	13.5
Theoretical value.................	45	58
Current price....................	35	

Molodovsky concluded that General Motors had a reasonable expectancy of long-term capital gain of more than 50 percent, and that with a current yield of 5½ percent, it represented an attractive purchase. (The following year the stock rose to above 58.)

If the valuation of a given issue is sound, it can provide a guide to an advantageous buying-and-selling policy. But what do we mean, in this context, by the phrase, "if the valuation is sound"? It could conceivably mean a price that the investor should feel justified in paying and in having paid, without regard to what the market does thereafter. He could be entirely satisfied by the future earnings, dividends, and balance-sheet position, even though the market quotation declined and then continued disappointingly low. But the investor does not actually have to make this choice between the world of value and the world of market prices. Experience affirms that in a sufficient number of cases the price and the soundly ascertained value do tend to converge as time goes on.[6] The valuation approach is thus not at all an unrealistic one, in the sense that it deals with concepts that play no part in the actual behavior of the market price. Its limitations and weaknesses stem rather from the lack of precision and of full dependability that are always associated with calculations of the economic future.

Estimates of Earning Power and Multipliers. Any estimate of earning power extending over future years may easily fall wide of the mark, since the major business factors of volume, price, and cost are all largely unpredictable. Assuming that profits develop as anticipated, there remains a similar doubt as to whether the multiplier, or capitalization rate,

[6] This statement, by its terms, does not apply to inherently speculative issues since these do not admit of a "soundly ascertained value." We consider "growth stocks" at high price-earnings ratios basically in this category. Later we suggest some rules for determining the maximum "investment value" of such issues, but we do not imply that the market price may be relied on to converge with such conservative valuations. In other words, a genuine growth stock will typically appear to be selling too high by our valuation standards, and the true investor may do well to avoid it for this reason. But both the price and the ultimate value may often develop independently of, and contrary to, any given valuation.

will prove correctly chosen. A valuation may be very skillfully done in the light of all the pertinent data and the soundest judgment of future probabilities; yet the market price may delay adjusting itself to the indicated value for so long a period that new conditions may supervene and bring with them a new value. Thus, even though the price ultimately converges with that new value, the old valuation may have proved undependable.

These handicaps that are attached to the value approach should be clearly recognized by the analyst, and they should make him modest and circumspect in its use. In particular he must use good judgment in distinguishing between securities and situations that are better suited and those that are worse suited to value analysis. Its working assumption is that the past record affords at least a rough guide to the future. The more questionable this assumption, the less valuable is the analysis. Hence this technique is more useful when applied to senior securities (which are protected against change) than to common stocks; more useful when applied to a business of inherently stable character than to one subject to wide variations; and, finally, more useful when carried on under fairly normal general conditions than in times of great uncertainty and radical change.

Fields for Value Analysis. We have selected a series of six quite diverse examples to illustrate the scope of value analysis. Many others will appear in later sections of this book.

Example 1: *Selection among Security Classes.* In the 1951 edition at this point we showed that the individual investor should buy United States Savings Bonds in preference to any other type of taxable bond. This conclusion followed clearly from the relative yields obtaining at that time, together with the important option that United States Savings bondowners had to demand repayment on specified terms at short notice. This option did indeed prove valuable in subsequent years when bond yields advanced sharply and bond prices had substantial declines. In 1962 the advantage of United States Bonds over other taxable issues had largely disappeared because of the change in comparative yields.

However, in 1962 a general conclusion of opposite import may be drawn with regard to investment in high-grade preferred stocks. Because of the tax situation and the resultant yield relations, most such issues are unsuitable for investment by an individual. Their dividends are fully taxable to him but tax-exempt as to 85 percent thereof when received by a corporate owner. In 1961–1962 the yields on investment-grade preferreds became almost identical with those obtainable on good corporate bonds. In 1949, contrastingly, preferred stocks yielded 50 percent more than bonds of similar quality ratings. Nearly all such preferred stocks are now unintelligent purchases by individual investors and should be held only by corporations which enjoy the special tax advantage therefrom.

Example 2: *Railroad Income Bonds at High Prices.* This group of securities has at certain times sold at prices which offered no chance of appreciable profit but carried the risk of substantial market decline. As an illustration, we shall use the Chicago & Northwestern Railway Income 4½s, which in 1946 sold as high as 98¼. A competent security analyst would have suggested their sale at that price. The reasoning did not relate to any specific projections of the earnings of the Northwestern, but rather to the inherent nature and the characteristic market behavior of income bonds as a class. They are subject to wide fluctuations in price, responding emphatically to changes in business conditions or sentiment. Their upper limit could not be much above 100, because of their limited coupon and their call price of 101⅛. On the other hand, past experience showed that their low quotation could easily prove to be 50 percent below the current market. The case for selling was thus reasonably conclusive. The range for the 1947–1961 span was from a high of 83½ to a low of 42½.

Example 3: *Clearly Undervalued Common Stocks.* Between 1947 and 1957 it was possible to find numerous common stocks selling substantially under their minimum value as shares of an ordinary private business. This was particularly evident to the security analyst in the case of issues showing satisfactory earnings but obtainable below the net current assets alone available for the common stock. The following describes an opportunity of this sort existing at the end of 1957:

It is the Hoover Company (vacuum cleaners). In addition to its domestic business it controls three foreign subsidiaries, of which the most important is the 53 percent owned Hoover, Ltd., of England. The American company has a substantial equity interest in the undistributed earnings of the English affiliate. Since this equity is not reported directly in either the income account or the balance sheet, the parent company's earnings and asset value are both understated.

The Hoover American shares appeared undervalued at the end of 1957 because they were selling at only 4.3 times their full 1957 earnings and less than 7 times their 10-year average earnings. The undervaluation was emphasized by the company's strong position and long record of successful operation and by the fact that the English shares were being accorded a more liberal valuation in the London market. Table 2-1 provides the basic information on the American company.

Example 4: *A Clearly Overvalued Common Stock.* It is much more difficult and risky for an analyst to declare that a common stock is definitely overvalued than to recommend those selling at bargain prices. (The "overvalued" issue is likely to be quite popular at the time and capable of advancing much farther in the market.) In some cases the particular circumstances will demonstrate overvaluation without any reasonable doubt. Such an instance was presented by Studebaker-Packard common at or near its high level of 29 in 1959. The analyst could find

Table 2-1. The Hoover Company

Capitalization: common A and B (shares)	1 708,000
Price (December 1957)	14
Market value of common	$23,900,000
Preferred stock	1,540,000
Total capitalization at market	25,440,000

1957 results:

Sales	$53,139,000.
Net after taxes	3,944,000.
Net for common	3,871,000.
Earned per share, as reported	2.27
Add equity in English company's 1957 earnings	1,710,000.
Per share	1.00
Earned per American share (adjusted)	3.27
Dividend 1957	1.10
Average earnings for common 1948–1957 as reported	1.61
Estimated average earnings, including British equity	2.25

Balance-sheet position, December 1957:

Net current assets, less preferred	$19,434,000.
Fixed and miscellaneous assets, net	7,032,000.
Investment in foreign companies, at cost	1,908,000.
Total	$28,374,000.

Common equity per books per share	$16.66
Add equity in surplus and reserves of English subsidiary	7.09
Adjusted equity per share	$23.75

four different and impressive reasons for terming the stock overpriced, as follows:

1. The stock was selling 56 percent above the price at which it could have been obtained concurrently by buying the convertible preferred stock, which became exchangeable for the common stock in about a year; intrinsically the preferred was worth more rather than less than its exchangeable value into common.

2. The reported earnings of $4.36 per share for the common did not allow for the potential doubling of the common issue through conversion of the preferred. This adjustment—essential for proper analysis—would have cut the 1959 earnings nearly in half.

3. The true earnings were again being doubled by reason of carry-forward tax credits from large losses in previous years. Not only was this benefit temporary, but its very existence indicated the unimpressive nature of the company's past record. (After the adjustments required under this and the preceding paragraph, the "earning power" implied in the 1959 figures would be reduced to only $1 per share instead of the reported $4.36.)

4. The company had long been at a competitive disadvantage as compared with the larger auto makers. Its turn-around from huge deficits to earnings in 1959 was chiefly due to the sudden popularity of compact-sized cars, which Studebaker was able to offer before the "Big Three" decided to produce them. This was obviously a short-lived advantage, and the company's prosperity in future years was far from assured.

Sequel: The company did little better than break even in 1960 and 1961. The price of the common collapsed to 6½ in 1960.

Example 5: *Price-Value Relationships Changing in Time.* It is our thesis that almost any issue can conceivably be attractive at one selling price and unattractive at another. Because of the wide fluctuations in market conditions, these opposite situations frequently obtain for the same issue at different times.

For an illustration we use Foremost Dairies Company in 1949 and 1955. In 1949 the stock, based on the mean price for the year, was selling at approximately 5 times earnings. Principally because Foremost was not as well known as a number of other corporations in the same field and because of a low payout rate, the multiplier in 1949 was about 80 percent of the average for eight other reasonably comparable companies. Taking the debt and preferred issues at par and the common at the 1949 mean price, the market was valuing the company at about $12 million compared with a net tangible asset value of approximately $10 million. In sharp contrast, in 1955 Foremost's common stock was selling at a price-earnings ratio of 19.6, or more than 155 percent of the average for the eight reasonably comparable companies. Taking the debt and other prior claims at par and the common at the mean price for the year, the market valuation was about $210 million compared with net tangible assets of less than $107 million. Although the company had become well known and although the payout rate was now relatively high, the return being earned on total capital was not significantly changed. The 1947–1949 average return was a little over 10 percent, and the 1950–1954 average was about 11.5 percent. Although it is quite possible that the analyst may not have considered Foremost's shares an outstanding bargain in 1949 (though such a judgment would have proved sound), it is doubtful that careful comparative examination would not have indicated overvaluation in 1955. Subsequently the price dropped 50 percent below the 1955 peak.

Example 6: *Arbitrage Operations.* While this field is relatively specialized, it is particularly well suited to the processes of security analysis. These opportunities are available in varying quantities and classes, depending on the times. During the late 1930's and afterwards, a wide scope for such operations was found in the breaking-up of public utility holding companies, pursuant to the drastic legislation of 1935. In the 1940's and early 1950's, profits at the annual rate of 20 percent or better could be made by arbitraging the securities of railroads going through reorganization. The operation consisted in buying existing bonds and selling against them the "when-issued" securities to be exchanged for them under the reorganization plan. The indicated proceeds were always substantially more than the cost. The major risk involved was that of a failure of the plan to be carried out; the minor risk was that consummation would be delayed so long as to make the operation relatively unattractive. An experienced security analyst could have appraised these risks intelligently and could have determined that most of the arbitrage operations were well worth entering upon.

In recent years numerous arbitrage opportunities have been presented by corporate mergers and take-overs. These, too, have required analytical skill and judgment in weighing the risks against the indicated profit.

Securities Not Suited to Valuation Analysis. Two general types of issues do not lend themselves satisfactorily to the intrinsic-value approach. The first are those that are essentially speculative in character, meaning thereby that their apparent value is almost entirely dependent upon the vicissitudes of the future. An extreme example would be the stock of a company controlling a promising but still undeveloped invention—such as Polaroid Corporation in 1940. In the same category belong shares of high-cost or marginal producers, which may have no earning power or else very high earnings according to the price-cost situation of the moment. The same unstable situation may be created by a speculative capitalization structure, in which the senior securities are disproportionately large and the common stock becomes exceedingly sensitive to changes affecting earnings or value.[7]

The other type of speculative commitment is often found in the common stock of a strong enterprise that is considered to have unusually favorable prospects of continued growth. The difficulty for the analyst here is to place a sound arithmetical valuation on an optimistic outlook. Since common stocks of this kind are favorites among both admitted speculators and self-styled investors, they present an unusually difficult area for the advisory function of security analysis. It is our view that most growth stocks reach price levels that make them speculative rather than investment issues—a view which apparently is not shared by those who buy them.

3. The Critical Function of Security Analysis. This third function is apart from the appraisal and selection of individual securities. It is concerned more with the role of the security analyst as a financial statesman —with the contribution which he can make to finance and to the financial community. His broad experience in the analysis and appraisal of securities should provide him with insight into the financial practices and policies of corporations. Moreover, because—either directly or indirectly —he is guiding the investment of funds, the analyst is concerned with these practices and policies as they affect the investor. For example, the security analyst is interested in seeing that securities, especially bonds and preferred stocks, be issued with adequate protective provisions, and —more important still—that proper methods of enforcement of these convenants be part of accepted financial practice.

[7] For a discussion of typical leveraged situations, see Missouri Pacific class B common stock and other issues, as set forth in Chap. 48.

It is a matter of great moment to the analyst that the facts be fairly presented, and this means that he must be highly critical of accounting methods. Finally, he must concern himself with all corporate policies affecting the security holder, for the value of the issue which he analyzes may be largely dependent upon the acts of the management. In the category of corporate policies are included questions of capitalization setup, of dividend and expansion policies, of managerial capacity and compensation, and even of continuing or liquidating an unprofitable business.

On these matters of varied import the senior analyst should be competent to express critical judgments, looking to the avoidance of mistakes, to the correction of abuses, and to the better protection of those owning bonds or stocks.

Security Analysis as a Discipline. Our field of work developed for many years as a hit-or-miss affair, requiring no special equipment by the practitioner except a "feeling for figures," and following no standard rules or procedures. It has always suffered from a serious handicap in that the viewpoint of analysts in most of the brokerage houses and elsewhere has been unduly influenced by short-term stock-market considerations. The founding of the *Analysts Journal* (now the *Financial Analysts Journal*) by the New York Society of Security Analysts, in 1945, was an important step toward raising the standards and improving the techniques of the profession. The *Journal* has made many contributions toward better methods and better thinking.[8]

Certification for Analysts. For a number of years attention was given intermittently to a proposal that security analysts be given a professional standing by setting up a rating or certification generally similar to that of certified public accountants. It has been something of an anomaly that customers' brokers (the former "customers' men") in Wall Street are required to pass specific tests of knowledge and fitness, whereas no corresponding requirements are made of a man who is to become a security analyst. Now, as the consequence of the continuing, earnest work of a number of leading analysts, the establishment of the Institute of Chartered Financial Analysts has become a fact. The Institute has set for itself a challenging and most important but not an easy task. We hope it will receive wide support, and we wish it complete success.

[8] It is published bimonthly by the National Federation of Financial Analysts Societies.

CHAPTER THREE

THE BEHAVIOR OF THE SECURITY MARKETS

The security analyst operates in the area of marketable securities, and he is deeply concerned with their price behavior. The price to be paid or received for a security is an integral part of any complete analysis. Almost any security may be a sound purchase at some real or prospective price and an indicated sale at another price. When an analyst recommends an issue for long-time holding, he should be implying to the purchaser that its long-term price behavior, in relation to its purchase price, is likely to be reasonably satisfactory. We do not believe that short-run price movements—the day-to-day or month-to-month variations—are a valid or profitable concern of the security analyst. But the broader fluctuations of the market, which are tied in with the accepted concept of business cycles, should not be left out of his reckoning.

A competent analyst should have sufficient familiarity with the important behavior patterns of the securities markets so that he can form intelligent conclusions about the *probable* price-movement characteristics of various types of security issues. In the accepted view, security analysis hinges largely upon a general anticipation of the future earnings position of the company under study. We would add as an essential part of each analysis a similar general anticipation, based on adequate observation, of the broad pattern of price fluctuations that is likely for the security. The second formulation, like the first, may exert a considerable influence upon the analyst's practical recommendations.

Our survey in this chapter will divide securities into classes appropriate for a study of price fluctuations. This will parallel, in part, our later classification for purposes of intensive analysis.

A. HIGH-GRADE BONDS

High-grade bonds are, by definition, exempt from present or future doubt as to prompt payment of interest or principal. Putting aside for the moment considerations arising from call provisions, we may say that their price should be controlled mainly by the going rate of interest for their maturity bracket. If the basic interest rate declines, the price of a high-grade bond should rise so as to bring down its own yield accordingly; and conversely, the price should fall when interest rates advance.

Example: This principle is illustrated in Table 3-1.

In this area, therefore, the main point of anticipation is the future course of interest rates. As it happens, this point does not lend itself well to analytical technique. The reason is that today's interest rates already reflect, in some part at least, whatever changes in relevant economic factors can now be reasonably projected. Hence an expectation that future rates will be higher or lower than the present usually will be a matter more of economic than of security analysis.

Thus in the field of high-grade bonds the analyst does not ordinarily concern himself with price anticipations. He knows from experience that while price fluctuations do occur they are only rarely so wide as to affect the finances or confidence of those holding this type of security. The

Table 3-1. High-grade Bonds

Year	Yield on Standard & Poor's A1[+] corporate bonds, percent	Price of Atchison, Topeka & Santa Fe General 4s/1995
1937	High 3.42	Low 106¾
1946	Low 2.44	High 141
1953	High 3.39	Low 106
1954	Low 2.81	High 124¾
1959	High 4.59	Low 89

financial institutions that make up the largest body of owners are permitted by law to ignore market variations in these issues when presenting their annual statements of condition.[1]

There are some market-price indications in this group, however, that the analyst might well take into account. For issues of long maturity, a small change in the general interest rate may produce a change in principal value equal to several years' income.

As Table 3-1 indicates, the moderate change in interest rates between 1953 and 1954 brought a rise of about 18 percent in the principal value of Atchison General 4s. Note also that in 1959 this issue was selling at 89 which was 37 percent below the 1946 peak of 141. There is more than a suggestion in this example that the purchase of high-grade long-term bonds at historically high premiums is not good business.

Call Provision an Adverse Arrangement. The analyst should appreciate also that the "call provision" introduced in most bond issues after World War I operated to deprive investors of most of the price advantage that should have accrued to them by reason of the drastic fall in interest rates that took place after 1933. These provisions are discussed in detail in Chapter 23.

[1] Instead, they can show these at "amortized cost"—i.e., at cost increased or decreased to reflect the gradual approach of repayment at par on the maturity date.

B. HIGH-GRADE PREFERRED STOCKS

These issues, by definition, are subject to no doubts—present or future —as to regular payment of the stipulated dividend. If such doubt should arise, the market price may be seriously affected even though the dividend is actually uninterrupted. An examination of the price behavior of preferred stocks rated as high-grade indicates that they are by no means insensitive to broad changes in business conditions, or to even moderate changes in the going interest rate.

Example: From April 1946 to October 1948 the dividend yield on high-grade preferred stocks, as measured by Standard & Poor's Index, rose from 3.42 to 4.28 percent, and between November 1954 and December 1959 it rose from 3.91 to 4.90 percent. In the first period the price of National Biscuit 7 percent Preferred (a highest-grade issue) declined from 205 to 162½, and in the second span the price dropped from 183½ to 142. The shrinkages in principal value were 20 and 23 percent, respectively, and in each instance were approximately equivalent to six years' dividends. If the all-time high of 205 is compared with the December 1959 price, the loss is in excess of 30 percent and is equivalent to exactly nine years' dividends. The security analyst may well hesitate here—even more than in the case of first-grade corporate bonds—to recommend preferred issues at price levels considerably above the average levels of the past.

C. SECOND-GRADE SENIOR SECURITIES

We may define these securities, provisionally, as bonds and preferred stocks classified by Moody's and Standard & Poor's below the first three ratings. Taking all such issues together, we find them subject to unexpectedly large price variations. In the following table we give examples illustrative of various subclasses in this large group.

Second-grade senior securities	High price, 1955	Low price, 1956–1959
Chicago, Milwaukee, St. Paul & Pacific Income 4½s, Series B/2044	79¼	49½
Servomechanisms Convertible Debenture 5s/1966	108½	70
Bigelow-Sanford 4½% Cumulative Preferred	85⅞	56
United States Smelting, Refining, and Mining 7% Cumulative Preferred, par $50	70½	44

The range of price fluctuations for a second-grade bond issue over a longer period of years (1925–1959) is illustrated by the accompanying selected figures for Northern Pacific general mortgage 3s, due 2047.

Year	High price	Low price
1925		59¼
1927	73¾	
1931		46¾
1936	85¼	
1940		31½
1946	94¾	
1949		56⅛
1951	76	
1953		64
1955	81	
1956		63¼
1957	70	
1959		55

In this group, more characteristically perhaps than in any other, is to be noted the tendency of the securities market to swing between opposite extremes. In bull markets these second-grade issues will often sell close to their maximum possible prices. For, unlike common stocks, their principal value is in fact limited by their stipulated interest or dividend rate or by call provisions. On the other hand, the market record shows repeatedly that this class of issue suffers a severe price decline when the general market turns downward. The conclusion is obvious. Security analysts should not allow themselves to be deceived by currently prosperous conditions and by current optimism about the future to the extent that they recommend such issues as attractively yielding investments—without regard to the risks of serious loss implicit in their pattern of price fluctuation.

D. COMMON STOCKS

The major purpose at this point in examining the price behavior of common stocks is to consider whether price is an important factor in the purchase of investment-quality shares. The investor, in developing his approach to the acquisition of common stocks, must weigh the magnitude of the hazard that the price paid will prove too dear in terms of subsequent levels of the market. Thus our primary concern here is with cyclical declines. The extent of such declines in major stock-price cycles between 1871 and 1949 was shown in Table 1-7. These fluctuations offered a recurrent warning of the dangers of paying bull-market prices for common stocks which appear to be out of line in terms of value.

In the post-World War II period the price-level factor has appeared much less important in the purchase of common stocks. It is well known that numerous issues have enjoyed pronounced price rises over most of the postwar span—certainly over the last decade. For these shares, the downswings represented little more than pauses in the upward movement. Furthermore, the same is generally true of the familiar stock averages.

As a result of the experience of the 1950's, the once-accepted tenet that investment-grade common stocks could be soundly purchased at all times without regard to their price has again been adopted by many investors. This doctrine holds that, even if the price paid proved comparatively high, it would be of only temporary discomfort, and the long-range investor could expect eventually that the underlying secular increase in price would fully vindicate his commitment. Is this point of view now justified?

In our opinion, the conclusion of Edgar Lawrence Smith in the early 1920's that there should be a long-term rise in the value of a well-diversified list of quality stocks was—and continues to be—sound.[2] However, we are *not* of the opinion that the historic long-run growth in value warrants purchasing investment-grade (or any other) stocks at *any* price. A bull market of record duration can lead to an all-pervasive optimism and unless restraint is exercised can also lead to a market psychology somewhat analogous to that of the late 1920's. Furthermore, if the fluctuations in the Dow-Jones Industrial Average over the eight-year period from the 1921 low to the 1929 high are examined, it will be found that the greatest decline between the high price in one year and the low price in the succeeding year (18.6 percent) was about the same as the maximum decline over the decade of the 1950's (17.5 percent). Thus, if history has meaning, the mere fact that there was no significant reversal in the market during the 1950's does not in itself establish that a substantial cyclical decline cannot occur in the future. In addition, an examination of individual share experience establishes that in the postwar period some prominent issues have become substantially overpriced and have been subjected to significant readjustment.

The following brief tabulation will illustrate this point by three examples representing different classes of common stocks.

Issue	Class of stock	High	Low
Amerada Petroleum.......	Investment*	147 in 1957	55 in 1960
Thiokol Chemical.........	Growth	72 in 1959	29 in 1960
Studebaker-Packard.......	Speculative	29 in 1959	6½ in 1960

* A favorite issue of the mutual funds in 1957.

When we pass from the first-line common stocks to the less prominent and less strongly entrenched issues, we find these price fluctuations be-

[2] Edgar Lawrence Smith, *Common Stocks as Long Term Investments*, The MacMillan Company, New York, 1924. See also Winthrop B. Walker, *A Re-examination of Common Stocks as Long Term Investments*, thesis for the Graduate School of Banking at Rutgers University, The Anthoenser Press, Portland, Maine, 1954.

come progressively wider and of more significance in the analyst's judgment. Some typical examples of the range of price variations for primary and secondary common stocks are given in Table 3-2.

It might appear from these figures that the most useful and profitable work of the security analyst would consist in detecting the overvaluations created in bull markets and the undervaluations created in bear markets. The student should note, however, that during a large part of the cycle the market is in neutral ground and does not lend itself to the broad critical evaluations just referred to. The practical question is whether the security analyst should be opposed in principle to common-stock

Table 3-2

Year	American Can* (P)	American Cyanamid* (P)	TransWorld Airlines‡ (S)	Bullard* (S)
1937 high...............	30¼	9¼†	20⅛	20⅜
1942 low................	14⅛	7⅛†	6⅞	7⅜
1946 high...............	26⅝	15⅞	64	21⅜
1948–1949 low...........	19	8¼	8⅝	5½
1952–1953 high...........	36	31⅜	23¾	28⅝
1953 low................	31⅝	20⅞	12¾	17½
1955–1956 high...........	49⅛	39¾	35½	47⅞
1957–1958 low...........	37¼	33⅛	9¼	9⅜
1958–1959 high...........	52⅜	65¼	24⅝	24⅞

P = primary stock. S = secondary stock.
* Adjusted for stock splits and dividends.
† Class B shares.
‡ Adjusted for 10 percent stock dividend.

investment in these intermediate periods, on the ground that it would be shrewder to wait for a definitely depressed market level. We doubt that such a viewpoint would prove advantageous. Let us, however, postpone our discussion of this matter until the chapter on investment policy (Chapter 5).

Central Value. Prior to the long bull market of the 1950's, there appeared to be a tendency for the typical leading issue to fluctuate around a median level, which corresponded fairly well with business valuations made independently of price and in accordance with rational techniques of appraisal. This is perhaps only another way of saying that "intrinsic value" and price tended to converge at midpoints or "normal" levels of the market, thus correcting discrepancies established at the extremes of bull and bear movements. Thus the actual averaging of high and low prices over past years could often give some clue to a future "normal level." But, since there has not been a true bear market since 1949, this old rule has not been applicable over the last decade—neither will it be applicable in the future unless the stock market resumes its pre-1950 characteristics.

In the smaller and less prominent companies, which constitute the major portion of the "secondary issues," there was a pronounced tendency for such median market prices to fall below the apparent value of the business as such. The upsurge of the 1950's has carried the prices of most of the secondary issues above this depreciated-value area. Nonetheless, many unpopular issues have remained in or relapsed to subvalue levels— for the most part awaiting some take-over by another company or similar spectacular development, to equalize price with the minimum valuation of the business. The reasons for the relatively poor price behavior of these issues as a class are various. One is the special risk or instability factor in a smaller enterprise, exemplified by its greater vulnerability to severe business depression or even recession. A second reason is the tendency of public interest to be concentrated in the larger and better-known companies, in which trading activity is naturally heavier because of the larger number of shares, and heavier still because of the very concentration of interest. The multiplication of the number of quoted common stocks into the thousands makes it impossible for investors generally to maintain any degree of familiarity with the typical issue of smaller size. The "investment funds" normally show a pronounced partiality to the leading issues and a tendency to hold a secondary stock only when its prospects are regarded as unusually favorable.

The security analyst, wishing to proceed realistically, should recognize as "normal" some degree of deficiency between the average price and the indicated value of a randomly chosen secondary stock. This means that when such issues sell at what seems—in relative terms—a fair price, they are in fact overpriced from the standpoint of experience. It also means that, by the nature of the security markets, offerings of common stocks that introduce a company for the first time to the public are likely to have an unsatisfactory price sequel for a number of years in the future.

The Relationship between Intrinsic Value and Market Price. The general question of the relation of intrinsic value to the market quotation may be made clearer by the accompanying chart, which traces the various steps culminating in the market price. It will be evident from the chart that the influence of what we call analytical factors over the market price is both partial and indirect—partial, because it frequently competes with purely speculative factors which influence the price in the opposite direction; and indirect, because it acts through the intermediary of people's sentiments and decisions. In other words, the market is not a weighing machine, on which the value of each issue is recorded by an exact and impersonal mechanism, in accordance with its specific qualities. Rather should we say that the market is a voting machine, whereon countless individuals register choices which are the product partly of reason and partly of emotion.

Relationship of Intrinsic Value Factors to Market Price

I. General market factors
II. Individual factors

A. Speculative
  1. Market factors
    a. Technical
    b. Manipulative
    c. Psychological
  2. Future-value factors
    a. Management and reputation
    b. Competitive conditions & prospects
    c. Possible and probable changes in volume, price, and costs
B. Investment
  3. Intrinsic-value factors
    a. Earnings
    b. Dividends
    c. Assets
    d. Capital structure
    e. Terms of the issue
    f. Others

Attitude of public toward the issue

Bids and offers } Market price

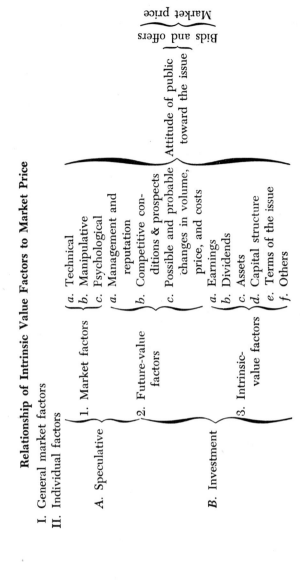

43

SECURITY ANALYSIS AND MARKET ANALYSIS

Security analysts identified with Wall Street brokerage houses are frequently stock-market analysts as well. Perhaps the historical reason is that the majority of their "clients" have been speculatively inclined, and when they asked the analyst to recommend a "good investment" they really meant a common stock that was likely to advance in price. Moreover, the widely held view that it is the chief function of the security analyst to anticipate changing conditions has made the stock market itself a primary factor of analysis. There are now some carefully reasoned arguments that common-stock investment cannot be carried on successfully unless aided by reasonably close anticipations of the important movements of the stock market.

For our part, we do not believe that market analysis and security analysis can be profitably combined by the ordinary practitioner. But since this subject is complicated and controversial we shall postpone its further consideration until our last chapter.

Undervalued Situations When the Market Appears High. We shall conclude with a practical observation that is based on experience rather than theory. When the general market is high there are always a number of individual issues that appear definitely undervalued by objective standards and consequently even more attractive in contrast to the inflated level of other stocks. The analyst may be tempted to recommend these as unusual opportunities. But that is a time that calls for especial caution. Not only may the "neglected security" continue neglected for the remainder of the bull market, but when the downturn comes it is likely to decline in price along with the general market and to fully as great an extent. In a word, beware of "bargains" when most stocks seem very high.

SUMMARY

The security analyst should be concerned with those fluctuations in security prices which tend to create opportunities to buy at less than indicated value and to sell at more than such value. He should not devote his attention to short-term market movements, as such, nor to precise timing of changes in the market's direction, for either major or minor swings. The recurrent but highly irregular stock-market cycles are of prime interest to the analyst, because their low ranges and high ranges almost always mark areas of undervaluation and overvaluation for both standard and secondary common stocks in general, and for second-grade senior issues as well. In intermediate areas of the general market, or during its minor downturns, there are significant price fluctuations in many secondary stock issues. These will produce many undervaluations in such securities, of interest to the analyst, during the long periods when standard stocks remain in an intermediate range.

THE FACTOR OF MARKETABILITY

A standard requirement for security investments is that they should be readily marketable. Marketability in the case of a listed issue may be measured by the amount of the issue dealt in over a period, such as a month or a year. In the case of unlisted issues the test may be the close-ness of the market—i.e., ordinary spread between the bid price and the asked price—and also the number of bids and offers appearing on the daily quotation sheets.[3] Some of the financial services have stressed the importance of marketability by giving "salability ratings" for each security they analyze. Other things being equal, it is obviously better to own a readily marketable security than one with a poor market. But a problem of security analysis enters when value must be sacrificed to marketability. The specific question is whether the investor should avoid an otherwise attractive issue because it is relatively inactive. Viewing investment practice as a whole, we are convinced that the factor of marketability has been overemphasized, with rather unfavorable consequences for the investor.

The speculator or market trader has a real need for high marketability because he may want to buy or sell in a few minutes' time. The typical investor has no similar requirement. He is rarely compelled by financial exigencies to sell his holdings; even when that happens, he usually has a fair amount of time in which to complete his liquidation. The need for immediate sale, when it seems to be present, is almost always due to his voluntary decision to turn out of his holdings. A decision of that kind, made and executed in haste, is more likely to prove wrong than right. In a typical case of bear-market hysteria or pessimism the investor would be better off if he were not able to sell out so readily; in fact, he is often better off if he does not even know what changes are taking place in the market price of his securities.

The time for the investor to sell is when his securities are high—which usually means when a bull market is well under way. At such a time the marketability of nearly all issues improves greatly. In the case of the typical secondary stock it is almost a law of the market place that mar-ketability improves as the price advances. Thus the investor will have no particular difficulty about selling out to realize a substantial profit. If he has to sacrifice a fraction of a point to make the sale (or to acquire his holdings in the first place), that is a small price to pay for an advan-tageous investment. The extra dividend yield in a year's time will almost always take care of any such penalty.

The spread between the selling price to the public and the redemption price of investment fund shares runs in general between 6 and 8 percent. This is the amount that an investor would lose if he bought and then

---

[3] These are compiled by the National Daily Quotation Service and distributed to the "over-the-counter" or unlisted-trading houses.

resold immediately, or if he resold later when the underlying value was unchanged. Substantial as this figure is, it has not interfered with the marketing of investment fund shares on an increasing scale to the public. By contrast, most secondary issues which the experienced investor is likely to reject as "not readily marketable" will have a smaller spread in the actual trading market than the investment company shares.[4]

The problem of acquiring or disposing of large blocks of an issue with poor marketability may be a real one for large-scale investors such as the financial institutions. Most individual investors, if they practice full-scale diversification, will rarely own more than a few hundred shares of any one issue. Both purchases or sales of such size can ordinarily be made at or about the quoted market in the case of nearly all listed issues and also of most of the unlisted issues with daily published quotations. Our practical experience has taught us that if investment operations are conducted without haste—as they should be—it is usually possible both to buy and to sell quite substantial amounts of any issue which is interesting to the security analyst without unduly affecting its quoted market price.

Marketability Secondary. We conclude therefore that it is better to sacrifice quick marketability to attractive value rather than vice versa. For every point lost in the spread between bids and offers, the buyers of a true bargain issue may expect to gain perhaps ten points in increased dividend returns plus ultimate improvement in selling price.

Much of the emphasis on marketability emanates from the stock-brokerage business. This is readily understandable. Brokers are in business to earn commissions. It is easier to get orders and to execute them in active than in inactive stocks. Market traders, who—in former days at least—supplied the bulk of brokerage commissions, concentrate their interest on the active issues. This bread-and-butter situation has an important and not too favorable effect upon the profession of security analysis as it is practiced by members of brokerage-house staffs. They are likely to overemphasize the popular and active issues in their work, and to slur over the values presented by less marketable secondary issues.

This attitude tends to create a vicious cycle, since it makes active issues more active and inactive ones more inactive. Stock brokers and their security analysts might be better advised to cultivate an interest among their investment-minded clients in securities which have intrinsic value rather than immediate salability to recommend them. This is a type of business which can be built up gradually but steadily; it produces satisfied customers; and it may offer a welcome source of commissions during periods when general market trading is at a low ebb.

[4] The National Association of Security Dealers has a semiformal limit of a 5 per-cent spread between the price paid by its members for a security and that charged on immediate resale to a customer.

CHAPTER FOUR

INVESTMENT AND SPECULATION

When the analyst passes from the stage of description to the higher stage of security selection his frame of reference widens. He now considers not only securities but security holders as well. His recommendation that an issue be purchased must be in accord with the objectives of the proposed security holder.

The first and most basic step in the formulation of a program for the acquisition—and management—of a security portfolio is to distinguish clearly between investment and speculation. As will be seen from the following, it is our view that security analysis is primarily useful to the investor and that it can perform only a limited service at best on the speculator's behalf.

General Connotations of the Term "Investment." "Investment" or "investing," like "value" in the famous dictum of Justice Brandeis, is "a word of many meanings." Of these, three will concern us here. The first meaning, or set of meanings, relates to putting or having money in a business. A man "invests" $1,000 in opening a grocery store; the composite "return on investment" for the major companies in the steel industry (including long-term debt and net worth) averaged 8.9 percent during 1956–1960.[1] The sense here is purely descriptive; it makes no distinctions and pronounces no judgments. Note, however, that it accepts rather than rejects the element of risk; the ordinary business investment is said to be made "at the risk of the business."

The second set of uses applies the term in a similar manner to the field of finance. In this sense all securities are "investments." We have investment dealers or brokers, investment companies[2] or trusts, investment lists. Here, again, no real distinction is made between investment and other types of financial operations such as speculation. Investment is a

---

[1] From data compiled by the Division of Economics Research, Stanford Research Institute.

[2] Note that in October 1939 the SEC listed under the title of "Investment Company" the offering of stock of "The Adventure Company, Ltd.," a new enterprise promoted by "The Discovery Company, Ltd." The fact that 1-cent par-value stock was offered at $10 per share, although not really significant, has a certain appropriateness.

47

convenient omnibus word, with perhaps an admixture of euphemism—
a desire to lend a certain respectability to financial dealings of miscellaneous character.

Alongside these two indiscriminate uses of the term "investment" has always been a third and more limited connotation—that of investment as opposed to speculation. The usefulness of such a distinction is generally taken for granted. It is commonly thought that investment, in this special sense, is good for everybody and at all times. Speculation, on the other hand, may be good or bad, depending on the conditions and the person who speculates. It should be essential, therefore, for anyone engaging in financial operations to know whether he is investing or speculating and, if the latter, to make sure that his speculation is justifiable.

The difference between investment and speculation, when the two are thus opposed, is understood in a general way by nearly everyone; but when we try to formulate it precisely, we run into perplexing difficulties. In fact, something can be said for the cynic's definition that an investment is a successful speculation and a speculation is an unsuccessful investment. It might be taken for granted that United States government securities are an investment medium, while the common stock, say, of Superior Oil Company in 1957—which had paid no dividends since 1955 and had shown a large decline in earnings—must certainly have been a speculation. Yet operations of a definitely speculative nature may be carried on in United States government bonds (e.g., by specialists who buy large blocks in anticipation of a quick rise); and on the other hand, Superior Oil was rated in 1957 as having "investment merit" (Fitch). Incidentally, it sold that year as high as $2,000 per share!

It is certainly desirable that some exact and acceptable definition of the two terms be arrived at, if only so that we may know as clearly as possible what we are talking about. A more forceful reason, perhaps, might be that the failure properly to distinguish between investment and speculation was in large measure responsible for the market excesses of 1928–1929 and the calamities that ensued—as well as, we think, for much continuing confusion in the ideas and policies of would-be investors. Also, it may well have been a factor in some of the overvaluations which occurred in the late 1950's.

A Proposed Definition of Investment. Investment should be identified with safety, but the safety must be more than a mere expectation. The concept can be really useful only if it is based on something more tangible than the psychology of the purchaser. Safety must be assured or at least strongly indicated by the application of definite and well-established standards.

Had this attitude been taken by the purchaser of common stocks in 1928–1929, the term "investment" would not have been the tragic misnomer that it was. But in proudly applying the designation "blue chips" to the high-priced issues chiefly favored, the public unconsciously revealed the gambling motive at the heart of its supposed investment selections. These differed from earlier common-stock investments in the one vital respect that the buyer did not determine, by the application of firmly established standards of value, that they were worth the price paid. The market made up new standards as it went along, by accepting the current price, however high, as the sole measure of value. Any idea of safety based on this uncritical approach was clearly illusory and replete with danger. Carried to its logical extreme, it meant that no price could possibly be too high for a good stock, and that such an issue was exactly as "safe" after it had advanced to 200 as it had been at 25.

We conclude, therefore, that expected safety must be based on study and standards. At the same time, investment does not necessarily require the existence of current income for the purchaser. The investor may at times legitimately base his purchase on a return which is accumulating to his credit and which will be realized by him after a longer or shorter wait. With these observations in mind, we suggest the following definition of investment as one in harmony with both the popular understanding of the term and the requirements of reasonable precision:

An investment operation is one which, upon thorough analysis, promises safety of principal and a satisfactory return. Operations not meeting these requirements are speculative.

Certain implications of this definition are worthy of further discussion. We speak of an "investment operation" rather than an issue or a purchase, for several reasons. It is unsound to think always of investment character as inhering in an issue per se. The price is frequently an essential element, so that a stock (and even a bond) may have investment merit at one price level but not at another. Furthermore, an investment might be justified in a group of issues, which would not be sufficiently safe if made in any one of them singly. In other words, diversification might be necessary to reduce the risk involved in the separate issues to the minimum consonant with the requirements of investment. (This would be true, in general, of purchases of common stocks for investment.)

In our view it is also proper to consider as investment operations certain types of arbitrage and hedging commitments which involve the sale of one security against the purchase of another. In these rather specialized operations the element of safety is provided by the combination of purchase and sale. This extension of the ordinary concept of investment appears to the writers to be entirely logical.

The phrases, "thorough analysis," "promises safety," and "satisfactory return" are all chargeable with indefiniteness, but the important point is that their meaning is clear enough to prevent serious misunderstanding. By "thorough analysis" we mean, of course, the study of the facts in the light of established standards of safety and value. An "analysis," made in 1959 that recommended investment in Thiokol Chemical common—or many similar issues—at a price forty times its current and a hundred times its average earnings, merely because of its excellent prospects, would be clearly ruled out, as devoid of all quality of thoroughness.

The "safety" sought in investment is not absolute or complete; the word means, rather, protection against loss under reasonably likely conditions or variations. A safe bond, for example, is one which would suffer default only under exceptional and highly improbable circumstances. Similarly, a safe stock is one which holds every prospect of being worth the price paid except under quite unlikely contingencies. Where study and experience indicate that an appreciable chance of loss must be recognized and allowed for, we have a speculative situation.[3]

"Satisfactory return" is a wider expression than "adequate income," since it allows for capital appreciation or profit as well as current interest or dividend yield. "Satisfactory" is a subjective term; it covers any rate or amount of return, however low, which the investor is willing to accept, provided he acts with reasonable intelligence.

It may be helpful to elaborate our definition from a somewhat different angle, which will stress the fact that investment must always consider the price as well as the quality of the security. Strictly speaking, there can be no such thing as an "investment issue" in the absolute sense, i.e., implying that it remains an investment regardless of price. In the case of high-grade bonds and preferred stocks, this point may not be important, for their prices are rarely so inflated as to introduce serious risk of loss of principal.[4] But in the common-stock field this risk may frequently be created by an undue advance in price—so much so, indeed, that in our opinion the great majority of common stocks of strong companies must be considered speculative a good part of the time after a bull market is well under way, simply because their price is too high to warrant safety of principal in any intelligible sense of the phrase. We must warn the reader that prevailing Wall Street opinion does not agree with us on this point; and he must make up his own mind which of us is wrong.

Nevertheless, we shall embody our principle in the following additional criterion of investment: *An investment operation is one that can be justified on* **both** *qualitative and quantitative grounds.*

Analysis and Speculation. It may be thought that sound analysis should produce successful results in any type of situation, including the confessedly speculative, i.e., those subject to substantial uncertainty and risk. If the selection of speculative issues is based on expert study of the companies' position, should not this approach give the purchaser a considerable advantage? Admitting future events to be uncertain, could we

[3] For the relationship between "safety" and "market-price" fluctuations, see Chap. 16 of *The Intelligent Investor*, 2d rev. ed., by Benjamin Graham, Harper & Brothers, New York, 1959.

[4] Yet the example of Atchison, Topeka and Santa Fe General 4s/1995 selling at 141 in 1946 (given in Chap. 3) might be said to illustrate a "serious risk" in a high-grade bond. It subsequently declined to 89.

not count on the favorable and unfavorable developments to cancel out each other, more or less, so that the initial advantage afforded by sound analysis will carry through into an eventual average profit? This is a plausible argument but a deceptive one; and its overready acceptance has done much to lead analysts astray. It is worthwhile, therefore, to detail several valid arguments against placing chief reliance upon analysis in speculative situations.

In the first place, what may be called the mechanics of speculation (in the sense of active trading) involves serious handicaps to the speculator, which may outweigh the benefits conferred by analytical study. These disadvantages include the payment of commissions and interest charges, the so-called "turn of the market" (meaning the spread between the bid and asked price), and, most important of all, an inherent tendency for the average loss to exceed the average profit, unless a certain technique of trading is followed which is opposed to the analytical approach.

The second objection is that the underlying analytical factors in speculative situations are subject to swift and sudden revision. The danger, already referred to, that the intrinsic value may change before the market price reflects that value is therefore much more serious in speculative than in investment situations. A third difficulty arises from circumstances surrounding the unknown factors, which are necessarily left out of security analysis. Theoretically these unknown factors should have an equal chance of being favorable or unfavorable, and thus they should neutralize each other in the long run. For example, it is often easy to determine by comparative analysis that one company is selling much lower than another in the same field, in relation to earnings, although both apparently have similar prospects. But it may well be that the low price for the apparently attractive issue is due to certain important unfavorable factors which, though not disclosed, are known to those identified with the company—and vice versa for the issue seemingly selling above its relative value. In a speculative situation those "on the inside" often have an advantage of this kind which nullifies the premise that good and bad changes in the picture should offset each other, and which loads the dice against the analyst working with some of the facts concealed from him.

The Value of Analysis Diminishes as the Element of Chance Increases. The final objection is based on more abstract ground, but, nevertheless, its practical importance is very great. Even if we grant that analysis can give the speculator a mathematical advantage, it does not assure him a profit. His ventures remain hazardous; in any individual case a loss may be taken; and after the operation is concluded, it is difficult to determine whether the analyst's contribution has been a benefit or a detriment. Hence the latter's position in the speculative field is at best uncertain and somewhat lacking in professional dignity. It is as though the analyst and

Dame Fortune were playing a duet on the speculative piano, with the fickle goddess calling all the tunes.

By another and less imaginative simile, we might more convincingly show why analysis is inherently better suited to investment than to speculative situations. In Monte Carlo the odds are weighted 19 to 18 in favor of the proprietor of the roulette wheel, so that on the average he wins $1 out of each $37 wagered by the public. This may suggest the odds against the untrained investor or speculator. Let us assume that, through some equivalent of analysis, a roulette player is able to reverse the odds for a limited number of wagers, so that they are now 19 to 18 in his favor. If he distributes his wagers evenly over all the numbers, then whichever one turns up he is certain to win a moderate amount. This operation may be likened to an investment program based upon sound analysis and carried on under propitious general conditions.

But if the player wagers all his money on a single number, the small odds in his favor are of slight importance compared with the crucial question whether chance will elect the number he has chosen. His "analysis" will enable him to win a little more if he is lucky; it will be of no value when luck is against him. This, in exaggerated form perhaps, describes the position of the analyst dealing with essentially speculative operations. Exactly the same mathematical advantage which practically assures good results in the investment field may prove entirely ineffective where luck is the overshadowing influence.

It would seem prudent, therefore, to consider analysis as an adjunct or auxiliary rather than as a guide in speculation. It is only when chance plays a subordinate role that the analyst can properly speak in an authoritative voice and accept responsibility for the results of his judgments.

OTHER ASPECTS OF INVESTMENT AND SPECULATION

Relation of the Future to Investment and Speculation. It may be said, with some approximation to the truth, that investment is grounded on the past whereas speculation looks primarily to the future. But this statement is far from complete. Both investment and speculation must meet the test of the future; they are subject to its vicissitudes and are judged by its verdict. But what we have said about the analyst and the future applies equally well to the concept of investment. For investment, the future is essentially something to be guarded against rather than to be profited from. If the future brings improvement, so much the better; but investment as such cannot be founded in any important degree upon the expectation of improvement. Speculation, on the other hand, may always properly—and often soundly—derive its basis and its justification from prospective developments that differ from past performance.[5]

[5] Common-stock investment may reasonably count upon a normal or cautiously estimated growth rate in the future to justify the price paid or to supply the required

Types of "Investment." Assuming that the student has acquired a fairly clear concept of investment in the distinctive sense that we have just developed, we have still to deal with the confusing effect of the prevalent use of the term in the broader meanings referred to at the beginning of this chapter. It might be useful if some descriptive adjective were regularly employed, when care is needed, to designate the particular meaning intended. Let us tentatively suggest the following:

1. Business investment: Referring to money put or held in a private business.
2. Financial investment or investment generally: Referring to securities generally.
3. Sheltered investment: Referring to securities regarded as subject to small risk by reason of their prior claim on earnings or because they rest upon an adequate taxing power. (These would be in the area of bonds, preferred stocks, and guaranteed common stocks.)
4. Analyst's investment: Referring to operations that, upon thorough study, promise safety of principal and an adequate return.

Evidently these different types of investments are not mutually exclusive. A good bond, for example, would fall under all four headings. Unless we specify otherwise, we shall employ the word "investment" and its relatives in the sense of "analyst's investment," as development in this chapter.

Types of Speculation. The distinction between speculation and gambling assumes significance when the activities of Wall Street are subjected to critical scrutiny. It is more or less the official position of the New York Stock Exchange that "gambling" represents the creation of risks not previously existing—e.g., race-track betting—whereas "speculation" applies to the taking of risks that are implicit in a situation and so must be taken by someone. A formal distinction between "intelligent speculation" and "unintelligent speculation" is no doubt open to strong theoretical objections, but we do think that it has practical utility. Thus we suggest the following:

1. Intelligent speculation: the taking of a risk that appears justified after careful weighing of the pros and cons
2. Unintelligent speculation: risk taking without adequate study of the situation

In the field of small, privately-owned business most well-considered enterprises would belong in the class of intelligent speculations as well as

---

margin of safety. In so doing it continues, on a conservative basis, the pattern of long-term growth demonstrated in the past. This point is discussed further at the end of the chapter.

representing "business investments" in the popular sense. If the risk of loss is slight—an exceptional occurrence—a particular business venture may qualify as an analyst's investment in our special sense. On the other hand, many ill-conceived businesses must be called unintelligent speculations.

In the field of finance common-stock *investment* would typically be made in a diversified group of leading issues at prices within the range of their intrinsic values, or in a group of secondary issues at less than their appraised values—i.e., on a "bargain basis." Many successful common-stock purchases may be made on terms other than the above—at prices which we would regard as too high for true investment, or without adequate diversification. According to our view, these commitments are speculative in spite of subsequent success. Occasionally, some quite unintelligent speculations may have succeeded splendidly; but few, if any, unintelligent speculators have successful *careers*.

We believe, moreover, that a sound analyst's investment can be made under most conditions by buying a diversified list of standard common stocks, or of carefully selected secondary stocks that appear to be definitely undervalued. Here the element of diversification is counted upon to offset the recognized risk existing in the individual securities.

It is possible to argue, however, that issues with a high degree of speculative risk individually may be made part of an investment operation, provided (1) the chances of gain definitely outweigh those of loss and (2) there is ample diversification. Examples of this sort would include low-priced common stocks meeting certain quantitative conditions, and even very low-priced "option warrants," although these latter are nothing but long-term "calls" upon, or rights to buy, certain shares at prices much above their current levels. This is a marginal area in which distinctions between investment and speculation become blurred. Actually, not enough careful study has been given to group operations of this sort to warrant a final opinion about them.

An Additional Criterion of Investment Operations: The Margin-of-safety Concept. Our approach to security analysis will show a basic characteristic of true investment, which we believe may be taken also as its touchstone or distinguishing feature. This is the presence of a measurable margin of safety. In the case of bond or preferred-stock investment this margin is usually determined by the excess of earning power over interest or dividend requirements, or of the value of the enterprise above the senior claims against it. In the case of a common stock it should be represented (1) by the excess of calculated intrinsic value over the price paid, or (2) by the excess of expected dividends for a period of years above a normal interest return, or (3) by a corresponding calculation related to expected earnings.

This concept of the margin of safety as the underlying element in every investment operation will serve to unify the approach to investment, through all forms of securities, from the highest-grade bond down to those common stocks of secondary quality which may be considered to present investment opportunities because their price is well below indicated minimum value.

The Companion Concept of Diversification. In order to take proper advantage of the margin-of-safety principle in investment operations it is almost always essential that the investor practice adequate diversification. A margin of safety does not guarantee an investment against loss; it merely assures that the probabilities are against loss and, in the case of common stocks, that the probabilities favor an ultimate profit. The individual probabilities may be turned into a reasonable approximation of certainty by the well-known practice of "spreading the risk." This is the cornerstone of the insurance business, and it should be a cornerstone of sound investment.

The importance of diversification varies, however, with the class of investment. Obligations of the United States need no outside diversification to buttress their safety. In fact, the purchase of other securities will diminish the safety of the portfolio, at least slightly, and if such purchases are made, it should be for other reasons than spreading the risk. A single corporate bond issue of the highest grade is undoubtedly a sound investment by itself; but here prudence recommends diversification, since it brings added assurance at no cost. But whenever the investment quality arises out of the disparity between price and indicated value—as in attractive common stocks and in "bargain" senior issues—diversification becomes an integral part of the reasoning and the practice. In this field the analogy between investment and insurance becomes very close.

There is a well-known argument *against* diversification based on Andrew Carnegie's maxim: "Put all your eggs in one basket and watch the basket." We believe this counsel has an application to security investment but only within its strictest interpretation. An investor may concentrate heavily on the shares of one corporation provided that he has a *personal connection* with it—as an executive or a member of a controlling group. Many large fortunes have been built up over the years by such concentration. But where the close personal connection with the company is lacking, that policy rarely works out well. When the choice is in fact a very good one, there is a tendency to sell out at a comparatively early stage of the long-term advance. Any other kind of choice will, of course, appear to be a mistaken one during periods of declining prices.

Growth Stocks in Relation to Investment and Speculation. In this edition we are haunted, as it were, by the spectre of "growth stocks"—by the question how best to deal with them in the context of our basic principles. As we revise this chapter we are confronted with a widespread conviction that "a good growth stock" or a "well-selected growth stock" is the best investment. Obviously, "good" or "well-selected" may not be defined here with benefit of hindsight; the words must refer to processes of selection actually carried out by competent security analysts. Let us summarize our views on this matter in a series of brief propositions:

1. By definition, a "growth stock" has increased its per-share earnings at materially above the average rate of other issues and is expected to continue to do so for many years in the future.

2. In our view, security analysts as a whole cannot estimate the future earnings pattern of one or more such growth stocks with sufficient accuracy to provide a firm basis for valuation in the majority of cases.

3. The inherent uncertainty about the rate and duration of future growth makes the intrinsic value of such issues at least partially speculative—in spite of the strength and quality of the business.

4. Our concept of "investment value" requires that the uncertainty as to future growth be reflected in relatively modest projections and capitalization rates. The investment value, so arrived at, must necessarily fall most of the time below the market prices of such issues, which are based either on no calculations or on what we should call "speculative calculations."

5. Growth stocks have been purchasable in the past at prices which would meet our criteria of investment value, and perhaps this will occur again. But, under the conditions obtaining at the beginning of the 1960's, we must say that virtually all the recognized growth stocks were selling on a speculative basis. Therefore, they could not constitute investments as we have defined the term.

6. A number of these issues will prove profitable, and a number unprofitable. We do not know what the aggregate or representative result will be. However, we are inclined to the view that growth-stock purchases *as a whole* did not yield outstanding results during the 1950–1959 decade—a period one would think of as especially favorable to this class of security.[6]

7. The price history of General Electric, one of our premier growth companies, contains an interesting illustration of the tendency of this type of common stock to take on speculative aspects in the market—a tendency which dates from the great bull market of the 1920's and has continued ever since. Observe from the appended table that the percentage decline in the mild business recession of 1960–1961 was greater than that shown in the full-scale depression of 1920–1921.

Changing Aspects of the Investment Quality of Common Stocks. During the past half-century the investment and speculative characteristics of common stocks as a whole have undergone a series of changes, some of which are as subtle as they are important. Before World War I the typical common stock was basically speculative, for reasons related chiefly to the company itself. The capitalization structure was often top-heavy, the working capital inadequate, the management deficient in various respects, the published information sketchy and unreliable. The junior issue's dividend history was nonexistent or erratic, its earnings subject to

[6] For some evidence in this connection, see footnote 22, p. 431.

wide fluctuations, and its market action to crass manipulation. Virtually all these defects have been greatly ameliorated and even abolished, as far as today's representative common stocks are concerned. Along with this improvement has come an upgrading in the public standing of common stocks generally—so much so that virtually all the many hundred different issues seen in the portfolios of investment funds are considered to be "investment" rather than "speculative" issues.

Nonetheless, we suggest that in relatively recent years at least two developments have exerted their influence in the opposite direction. The first of these is the rapid stepping up of technological change. This has

Table 4-1. General Electric Company

(Share prices adjusted to capitalization of 1930–1953)*

Year	Low price	High price	Rise	Decline
1918	32			
1919		44	35%	
1921	27½			35%
1929		101	266	
1932	8			91
1937		65	633	
1938	27¼			59
1946		52	91	
1946	33			35
1960		300	809	
1961	182			39

* The shares were split 4 for 1 in 1930 and 3 for 1 in 1954.

created opportunities for spectacular growth of profits for many companies, but it has also threatened the position of many others which have fallen behind in the technological race. To some degree these contrary occurrences can be projected well in advance by an unusually competent analyst who does some unusually penetrating research of his own. But, broadly speaking, we think that modern technology has injected an important new factor in the affairs of many companies, which is not amenable to dependable prediction and which for that reason must be recognized as fundamentally speculative.

The second and more important development relates to the shift of investment emphasis from values established by the past record to values to be achieved *solely* by future growth. This would be an entirely logical proceeding if security analysts and investors could be sure that their predictions of future earnings changes are reasonably reliable. An accurate forecast of the long-term future is infinitely more valuable than the most elaborate dissection of the past. But we are skeptical of the ability of all but the most gifted analysts to chart with precision the growth rate of a given company for many years ahead. A large part of the market's valuation of our most popular common stocks is closely tied in with prophecies as to their future rate of growth; were the earnings actually to increase much more slowly than anticipated or not at all, the value justified by the past rate of earnings alone would be only a minor fraction of the price the "investor" pays.

Our view is that in many of these cases the valuation process itself has given a speculative character to the purchase of these shares, which is quite independent of their undoubted "investment quality" in terms of the business itself. Such speculation is not necessarily unsound and unwise; it may prove highly successful because of the speculator's abilities or good fortune. But whatever the outcome, we think good semantics and prudent conduct require that purchases of common stocks at prices that rely heavily on future developments to justify the commitment, be recognized as at least partially speculative in their nature.[7]

[7] For a more detailed presentation of this viewpoint, see the address of Benjamin Graham, "The New Speculation in Common Stocks," reprinted in the *Analysts Journal,* June 1958.

CHAPTER FIVE

INVESTMENT POLICY

By investment policy we mean the allocation of the available funds among the various types of securities, including variations in such proportions under changing conditions and decisions to hold cash for future commitments. In this chapter we shall set forth briefly the established investment policies presently followed by well-defined classes of investors, consider the general problem of investment timing, and add some suggestions of our own that may be helpful in the broad field of investment policy.

Security owners are conveniently divided into two main groups—institutions and individuals. In terms of average size of holdings and purchases the financial institutions bulk largest in the investment picture.[1] Their investment policies are well standardized and are readily explicable in the light of their respective functions and obligations. The patterns followed by individuals tend to be much less clear-cut and consistent.

INSTITUTIONAL POLICIES

The so-called "institutional buyers" of securities fall into a number of subgroups, which may be classified in accordance with the degree of governmental control exercised over their selection of investments. Our listing is as follows:

Subgroup 1. *Investment choice subject to comprehensive controls*
      a. Life insurance companies
      b. Mutual savings banks

[1] It has been estimated that financial intermediaries hold 25 percent or more of the common stocks outstanding and about 90 percent of the corporate bonds. See R. F. Murray, "Institutional Influences on the Stock Market," *Analysts Journal*, May 1958, pp. 15–16. Also, by the same author, "Changing Share-ownership and Effect on the Market," *Commercial and Financial Chronicle*, Apr. 7, 1960, p. 9. For figures at the end of 1959, see table on p. 215 of *Journal of Finance*, May 1961.

　　　　　　　c. "Restricted" trust funds[2]
　　　　　　　d. Commercial banks (including trust companies)
Subgroup 2. *Investment choice subject to partial controls*
　　　　　　　a. Fire and casualty insurance companies
Subgroup 3. *Investment choice not controlled*
　　　　　　　a. "Unrestricted" trust funds, including "commingled trusts";
　　　　　　　　　pension funds
　　　　　　　b. (Most) philanthropic and educational institutions
　　　　　　　c. Regulated investment companies ("investment funds,"
　　　　　　　　　"mutual funds," "investment trusts")

Discussion of Subgroup 1. The most comprehensive regulation of investment policy is found in the laws of most states governing the operations of life insurance companies and savings banks. These must limit their purchases to bonds meeting specific tests of safety (plus, in some cases, a similar but narrower choice among preferred stocks) and to well-secured first mortgages on real estate. The proportion which can be invested in common stocks is restricted to a low figure. At the end of 1959, the common-stock holdings of life insurance companies aggregated at market value $2,954 million, or 2.6 percent of total assets.

The investments of trust funds are subject to regulations of a similar type, unless freed from such restrictions by the maker of the instrument.[3] The laws in this respect and the interpretation of them by the courts, however, have undergone some liberalization in recent years. Although the movement to liberalize the investment statutes began in the mid-1930's and there was some buying of common stocks by trust funds late in that decade, it was not until the post-World War II inflationary pressures began to be felt that trust funds made a significant move toward investing in common stocks.[4] Prior to 1940, there were nine states which had adopted the "prudent-man rule" and ten "legal-list" states which permitted equities in any form.[5] By 1961, 40 states had adopted the "prudent-

---

　　[2] These are listed as "institutional" because most trust funds are administered by trust departments of banks.

　　[3] The importance of trust funds is indicated by the fact that personal trust funds alone, which are administered by banks, have been estimated at $80 billion, or an amount nearly as large as the total assets of all life insurance companies. This estimate is exclusive of corporate trusts, employees' trusts, community trusts, institutional trusts, common trust funds, and funds in connection with other fiduciary relationships. R. W. Goldsmith and Eli Shapiro, "An Estimate of Bank-administered Personal Trust Funds," *Journal of Finance,* March 1959, p. 11.

　　[4] For a discussion from the investment manager's point of view, see Morton Smith, "Changing Concepts of Trust Investment Policy," *Trust Bulletin,* September 1957, pp. 11–17, 53–56.

　　[5] M. A. Shattuck, "The Development of the Prudent Man Rule for Fiduciary Investment in the United States in the Twentieth Century," 12 *Ohio State Law Journal,* Autumn 1951, pp. 491ff. See also, American Law Institute, *Restatement of the Law of Trusts,* 2d ed., 1959, Vol. I; and A. W. Scott, *The Law of Trusts,* 2d ed., Little,

man rule" and a number of the other states allowed some common-stock holdings.[6] Perhaps the biggest move toward common stocks came when the New York State Legislature in 1950 adopted a statute which permits up to 35 percent of restricted funds to be invested in common stocks.

The strict statutory provisions pertaining to life insurance companies, savings banks, and trust funds have represented a long-standing endeavor to protect policyholders, depositors, and trust beneficiaries—traditionally widows and orphans—against loss through overrisky investments. Good bonds and good real estate mortgages can be counted on to pay interest and principal punctually and to maintain stable dollar values in spite of economic vicissitudes. They do not, however, provide any protection against the erosion of real values in periods of inflation, and for that reason the statutory prohibitions against common stocks have been progressively relaxed.

Common Stocks as a Partial Protection against Inflation. In the last generation the idea of safety has been extended in the minds of many investors to include protection against loss of purchasing power of income or principal because of price inflation. Two world wars have produced spectacular rises in the general price level, a substantial part of which appears to be of permanent nature. The prevalent tendency toward unbalanced government budgets even in peacetime has accentuated fears as to the future purchasing power of the dollar. Securities bearing fixed rates of interest or dividends supply no protection against inflation; but there is a likelihood of obtaining at least partial protection against this adverse development by the ownership of common stocks. These considerations have had a definite influence in recent years upon the creators of trust funds, whether by will or otherwise. It is becoming more and more common in these instruments to set aside even the now more liberal statutory restrictions on investment media, so as to permit the trustees in their judgment to purchase all kinds of securities, including common stocks.

Investment Policy of Commercial Banks. Commercial banks have somewhat more latitude of choice in their portfolios than managers of restricted trust funds, but they are in effect closely regulated by a combination of specific restrictions and the conservative supervision of state and national bank examiners. Faced with the problem of minimizing the danger of loss of principal, banks confine themselves to securities

---

Brown & Company, Boston, 1956, Vol. III, pp. 1689ff. In essence, this "prudent-man rule" requires the trustee to exercise the judgment and care, under the circumstances prevailing, which men of ordinary prudence would employ in the management of their own affairs—not in regard to speculation, but in the permanent disposition of their funds, considering both income and safety of capital.

[6] Arthur Wiesenberger, *Investment Companies*, 1961, New York, p. 86.

with the least financial risk. For this reason and because of the tremendous expansion of the national debt since 1932, there has been a heavy increase in the percent of bank investments in the form of United States government securities. The tabulation below shows what percent of the total investments of all commercial banks over the last three decades has been in United States government securities.[7]

June 1929	36.1%
June 1935	64.6
June 1940	69.7
June 1945	92.6
June 1950	85.4
June 1955	79.0
June 1959	74.7

A more detailed breakdown of the total investments of all insured commercial banks on June 10, 1959, is as follows:

Types of securities	Amount (in millions)	Per cent
United States government obligations:		
Direct:		
Maturing or redeemable in 5 years or less	$47,599.5	58.2
Maturing in 5–10 years	8,245.8	10.1
Maturing in 10–20 years	3,945.3	4.8
Maturing in 20 years or more	509.1	0.6
Nonmarketable	1,154.6	1.4
Guaranteed	9.6	.....
Total	$61,463.9	75.2
Municipal securities (obligations of states and political subdivisions)	$16,798.7	20.5
Other bonds, notes, and debentures	3,084.9	3.8
Corporate stocks	519.7	0.6
Total securities	$81,858.2	100.0

SOURCE: Federal Deposit Insurance Corporation, *Report No. 51, Assets, Liabilities and Capital Accounts, Commercial and Mutual Savings Banks*, June 10, 1959.

Although United States government obligations remain by far the major investment media, the tax-exempt status plus the higher effective yield of municipal bonds have made them more attractive in recent years. Note that corporate bonds (included in "other bonds, notes, and debentures") constitute a very small percent of total investments. This may be adequately explained by the limited yield differential between high-grade corporate issues and government obligations.

[7] Board of Governors of the Federal Reserve System, *Banking and Monetary Statistics,* Washington, 1959, p. 19.

Federal regulations permit all bonds of "investment quality" to be valued on an amortized cost basis without reference to the current market price. Bank regulatory authorities generally consider investment-quality bonds to be those in the top four ratings. These ratings are made by two major statistical organizations, Moody's and Standard & Poor's, and they have been accorded official recognition. The ratings designate the "intrinsic risks" which exist in a security, i.e., the degree of security of principal and the likelihood of prompt payment of interest over a term of years.[8] Moody's Investors Service has 9 ratings running from the highest, Aaa, down to the lowest, C. Standard & Poor's has 11 ratings previously running from A1+ down to D, and now from AAA down to D.

Subgroup 2. Fire and Casualty Insurance Companies. The state laws governing these concerns require, in general, that they invest certain minimum portions of their funds in high-grade bonds. The fact that the allocation of the (generally larger) balance is in the discretion of the management results in significant differences between companies. This is shown by the fact that the common-stock component of 50 of the largest companies at the end of 1958 ranged from a low of less than 2 percent to a high in excess of 84 percent of the market value of total investments. The aggregate figures for these 50 companies, whose total admitted assets amounted to $13 billion (65 percent of the assets of all of the fire and casualty companies contained in *Moody's Bank & Finance Manual*, 1959) show the following distribution of holdings among the three groupings: government securities (United States government, agency, state, and municipal bonds) 49 percent; other bonds and preferred stocks, 8 percent; and common stocks, 43 percent.[9]

Subgroup 3. Investment Policies Not Controlled by Law. Those administering "unrestricted" trust funds and the endowment resources of philanthropic and educational establishments endeavor conscientiously to combine the conflicting objectives of safety and a satisfactory income yield. In our earlier discussion we made note of the marked move in recent years toward the increased role of common stocks in trust-fund portfolios. This trend has been equally, if not more, pronounced in this subgroup. In the 1950 edition we reproduced some data from a study showing the breakdown by type of securities of the combined portfolios of 43 common trust funds. In the following tabulation, these data are compared with similar information for 183 "discretionary" common trust funds as of the end of 1958. In addition to the substantial increase in common stocks, the heavy decline in government bonds (including state

---

[8] The quoted phrase is from a lecture by E. V. Vogelius of Moody's Investors Service, reprinted in the *Commercial and Financial Chronicle*, Aug. 24, 1950, p. 712. This lecture contains interesting views not only about bond ratings themselves but also about the factors that determine the quality of the bond issue.

[9] In a few instances includes preferred stocks.

and municipal issues) and preferred stocks and the contrasting increase in corporate bonds are to be noted.

Types of securities	About the end of 1949	About the end of 1958*
United States government bonds, state and municipal bonds.	37.1%	9.3%
Other bonds..	11.4	24.0
Preferred stocks...	15.0	8.1
Common stocks..	34.2	57.0
Other securities and cash...	2.3	1.6
Total..	100.0	100.0

* *Trusts and Estates,* April 1959, p. 342.

A survey of a representative group of college and university portfolios shows that as of mid-1958 common stocks amounted to 57 percent of total investments.[10] It is coincidental, but nevertheless striking, that this figure is identical with that for discretionary common trust funds. Available sketchy information implies that the common stock portion of charitable-foundation portfolios may be somewhat lower, perhaps nearer to 45 percent, which is close to the 43 percent for fire and casualty insurance companies.

We think the proportionate distribution of stocks and bonds just presented may be taken as indicative of the "middle-ground" investment policy, as it was established at the start of the 1960's. That is, a division of the portfolio roughly equally between variable-value (principally common stocks) and fixed-value (principally investment-quality bonds) securities. The breakdown of the fixed-value portion among United States government and agency bonds, tax-exempt state and municipal issues, corporate bonds, and high-grade preferred stocks, will rest primarily on relative yields, tax considerations, and maturity requirements (if any). This middle-ground investment policy is presumably suited to the needs of institutions and individuals desiring to be realistically conservative in an economy characterized by both long-term inflationary tendencies and (apparently) by less cyclical instability than before World War II. However, the concurrent growth of the common-stock component in portfolios and of the level of stock prices in the 1950's raises the somewhat disquieting question whether this "middle-ground" policy may not have been in good part a bull-market phenomenon, and thus subject to possible substantial revision.

[10] *College and University Investment Policies,* Wood, Struthers & Company, New York, June 1958. A subsequent study by Boston Fund of 65 major college and university endowments reveals that at June 1959 approximately 56 percent of the market value was in common stocks.

INVESTMENT POLICY FOR INDIVIDUALS

It is accepted doctrine that the investment needs and the appropriate policies of individuals will vary with their particular circumstances. In the past this resulted in a kind of parallelism between classes of individual security buyers and classes of institutions. Since widows and orphans need safety above all else, all of their capital, like the funds of life insurance companies, was generally placed in the most conservative securities. However, in more recent years the experience and threat of inflation, the need for higher income, and possibly the brilliant performance of the stock market, have combined to introduce a fair-sized component of better-grade common stocks even into portfolios of the widow-and-orphan category.

At the other extreme from this group, a wealthy businessman may feel he can afford to risk substantial sums in new, uncertain, but promising enterprises, or to speculate in the ups and downs of the stock market. His policy would correspond to that of the more avowedly speculative investment funds.

No doubt the typical investor with fairly large resources occupies a middle position in the spectrum of safety vs. opportunity. He is likely to be attracted by the intermediate or compromise policy of the discretionary common-trust funds. If he has engaged in the services of an investment-counsel firm, he will probably find that they will recommend this middle-ground pattern as the most satisfactory in its over-all results.

Investment Companies or Funds. These institutions invest their own capital in securities, and by so doing they provide investment management for the money of those who have bought their shares. The typical company owns mainly common stocks, generally diversified among many different industries.[11] The investment philosophy represented by the predominant sector of these companies may be summarized thus: All individual investors should have at least a portion of their funds committed to common stocks. But this area of investment requires a high degree of experience and skill to avoid serious pitfalls. It is logical, therefore, for individuals—and even trustees and smaller institutions—to do their common-stock investing indirectly by buying investment-fund shares, and thus command expert management for this portion of their total portfolio.

It is not to be supposed, however, that all or even the majority of individual investors have classified themselves in the above fashion and have

---

[11] There are also some that buy only bonds, others that specialize in a particular industry, and others that spread their holdings broadly among bonds, preferred stocks, and common stocks. According to a release issued by the National Association of Investment Companies, the net assets of 24 closed-end and 155 open-end funds aggregated nearly $17.5 billion at the end of 1959. Of this total, less than $1 billion was in cash and bonds.

adopted and adhere to a corresponding investment policy. The average security buyer makes up his policy as his funds become available. He is likely to be speculation-minded in rising markets and a penitent conservative after a drastic fall. His choice of securities is largely influenced by the arts of salesmanship to which he is exposed.

A significant transition in the thinking of the individual investor has taken place within the last decade. A survey made for the Federal Reserve Board in 1948, which attracted wide attention, showed that over 90 percent of the persons canvassed were opposed to investment in common stocks, either because they thought them too risky or because they were unfamiliar with them. Since that date, and particularly since the early 1950's, the American people have become stockholders at an amazing rate. Between 1956 and 1959 the increase was at an annual average rate of about 1.3 million. As a result, in excess of 15 million Americans, or about one adult out of seven, hold shares in corporate enterprises.[12]

Two Classes of Security Buyers. It would be most useful, we think, to classify security buyers into two groups—defensive investors and aggressive or enterprising investors. Defensive investors are those who should place their chief emphasis upon freedom from effort, annoyance, and the necessity for making frequent investment decisions. The great majority of individual security holders belong in the defensive category. Their specific training and experience with bonds and stocks are not adequate to warrant their making independent decisions about the selection of securities or exercising a sufficient degree of control over the recommendations of their advisers—unless such advice be confined to simple and clearly sound areas of investment.

The Defensive Investor. We believe the defensive investor should divide his funds into two parts. The first part should be placed in United States government bonds or in the tax-free issues of state and municipal bodies. The second part should be placed in a diversified list of leading common stocks, purchased at a reasonable price level. The relative proportions of the two parts will depend largely on the subjective feeling of the investor—but it should normally fall between a 75 to 25 percent and a 25 to 75 percent division.

The defensive investor may properly do his common-stock purchasing through the medium of investment-fund shares.[13] This policy would appear especially sensible for the small investor, but it would not be illogical for the investor with substantial means as well.

[12] New York Stock Exchange, *Share Ownership in America: 1962*, New York. On June 3, 1959, "public individuals" accounted for 53.5 percent of the New York Stock Exchange volume. *A Portrait of the Stock Market*, New York Stock Exchange, October 1959, p. 1.

[13] These are officially known as "investment companies." The "open-end" issues—redeemable on demand—are often referred to as "mutual funds." The popular title for all these companies is "investment trusts," which originated with their early legal form as actual trusts.

The chief requirement for all defensive investors is that they exercise firmness in the application of the simple principles of sound procedure outlined above. The main hazards they face are of three kinds, viz., being tempted into (1) stock-market speculation, (2) buying second-rate issues, (3) buying good common stocks at excessive prices. It is the duty of conscientious security analysts to assist defensive investors to escape these pitfalls by clinging tenaciously to the unexciting but safe path of standard, conservative investment.

The Enterprising Investor. The distinguishing feature of individuals in this class is their willingness and ability to devote time and care to the selection of sound and attractive investments. Their chief objective should be by training, intelligence, and guidance to take advantage of the numerous opportunities in normal markets to buy securities for considerably less than they are worth or to choose companies with better than average prospects when such securities are obtainable at reasonable market levels. The enterprising investor may take a calculated risk at times—if he is convinced that his chances of profit sufficiently outweigh the hazard of loss. But through careful selection coupled with adequate diversification he should succeed in reducing his over-all risk factor to a minimum.

The enterprising investor need not be a full-fledged security analyst in his own right. He may depend on others for detailed analyses and for ideas and advice as well. But the decisions will be his own, and in the last reckoning he must rely upon his own understanding and judgment. The first rule of intelligent action by the enterprising investor must be that he will never embark upon a security operation which he does not fully comprehend and which he cannot justify by reference to the results of his own study and experience. The endeavor to make money in securities is a business undertaking, and it must be conducted in accordance with business principles.

Relation of United States Government Bonds to Investment Policy. In the 1951 edition we strongly recommended United States Savings Bonds for the defensive investor. The logic behind this recommendation may be readily seen from Table 1-6. The Series E issue, with its attractive yield, offered—particularly to the small investor—a form of security which was so far superior to other first-grade bond investments that there was no point in his buying anything else in the field. The Series E and H bonds are safer than the best corporate issues, completely protected against any interim loss in market value, and until 1955 provided a higher yield. (Exception: In 1953, by a very narrow margin, highest-grade corporate bonds offered a higher yield.)

At the onset of the 1960's, long-term United States government bonds yielded about $\frac{1}{2}$ of 1 percent more than the E and H Savings Bonds. The latter, however, had certain advantages in the right of the holder to cash in the bonds *at his option,* as well as in various matters of convenience attaching to them. Thus the defensive investor may have considered buying either or both of these two classes of United States bonds. Also, in 1960 the yield on long-term government bonds was not appreciably less than that on the highest-grade corporate bonds. Under these conditions—which have actually existed for about twenty years— there has been no good reason for the *individual* investor to buy the best corporate bonds in preference to governments, nor would there be unless at least one-half percent additional yield may be obtained.

In our opinion, the purchase of second-grade corporate bonds to obtain yields less than one-third above that presently available on long-term governments would be questionable. The risks of permanent or temporary loss in this category would, we believe, far outweigh the yield differential. The only logical alternative to United States government bonds, in the fixed-income field, is found in tax-free issues, which hold an especial advantage for investors in high-income brackets. This consideration is treated in the next section.

Senior Corporate Securities Inappropriate for Individuals. If our analysis is correct, we are led to the conclusion that the individual should invest the fixed-value portion of his fund in United States government issues or in well-rated tax-exempt bonds, and concentrate his time and talents on the appraisal and selection of common stocks. On this logic, high-grade corporate securities are presently appropriate investments *only* for *non*individual buyers—particularly the large financial institutions such as insurance companies, savings banks, and possibly pension funds.

Tax Considerations in Investment Policy. In the last generation the tax burden upon the investor class has become increasingly heavy. As a consequence, the taxation aspects of investment alternatives have been claiming more and more attention. This is part of the personal factor, since tax effects vary with the individual. Let us discuss the three major considerations that enter here.

1. *Tax-free vs. Taxable Bonds.* Bonds of states, municipalities, and various public authorities are free of Federal income tax and generally of state income tax in the state where issued. High-grade tax-exempt issues could be bought in early 1960 to yield 3.87 percent against 4.47 percent from first-grade corporate bonds. If a married couple had an income of $10,000, above exemptions, their top tax bracket would be 26 percent. The same figure would apply to a single man with income of $5,000, above exemptions. Thus, for incomes at these levels, the net return after taxes on the corporate bonds would be 3.31 percent. Consequently, there would be a decided advantage in buying prime tax-free rather than prime corporate issues. The same observation would hold in general if we compared second-grade, higher yielding corporate issues with correspondingly higher yielding tax-exempt issues.

For example, tax-free bonds of the Chicago Transit Authority could be bought in May 1960 to yield 4.55 percent to maturity. For a wealthy investor in the 60 percent tax bracket, this yield would be equivalent to a return of 11.38 percent on a taxable bond or preferred stock.

Since the 1960 rate of corporation income tax is 52 percent (or 54 percent on consolidated returns)[14] it follows that tax-free bonds will yield a higher net return to corporations than would taxable bonds of equivalent grade.

The security analyst, acting as investment adviser, must be alert to the fact that a large proportion of security buyers may find important income advantages in purchasing tax-free bonds.

2. *The Tax Position of Preferred Stocks.* Preferred stocks generally have a quite different tax position for the individual and for the corporation buyer. Their dividends are fully taxable to individual owners, but a corporate owner pays tax on only 15 percent thereof.[15]

There is thus a very substantial tax reason for the purchase of preferred stocks rather than bonds by corporations, but no similar reason in the case of individual investors generally. The logical result is that preferred stocks should be bought only by corporations, just as it is logical that tax-free bonds should be bought only by investors in high enough income brackets to benefit substantially from this feature. (There may be exceptional conditions which make preferred-stock buying a more logical policy taxwise for individuals—for example, in Pennsylvania because of local tax conditions, or in the case of certain convertible stock issues. The reader is warned here that we have certain objections in principle to preferred-stock investment, to be developed later, which are independent of tax considerations.)

3. *Capital Gains vs. Income.* "Long-term capital gains" are the profits realized from the sale of securities (and other "capital assets") owned for more than six months. Under existing law (1960) they are taxed at only half the rate applicable to regular income (not tax-free), and furthermore their maximum tax rate is 25 percent. For most investors, therefore, there would be a substantial tax advantage in realizing profits in the form of long-term capital gains rather than as ordinary income.

The choice between the two types of investment reward is rarely presented in a form as clear-cut as that between a tax-free and a taxable security. It is possible at times to slant the general investment policy in one direction rather than the other, for opportunities frequently arise to select securities that are more interesting from the standpoint of a reasonably dependable long-term price appreciation than for income.

---

[14] Revenue Act of 1951.

[15] Preferred stocks of rate-regulated electric, gas, water, and telephone utility companies, issued prior to Oct. 1, 1942, or for the purpose of refunding such issues or bonds issued prior thereto, are an exceptional case. Approximately 73 percent of their dividends are taxable to corporate owners since this proportion is allowed as a credit for tax purposes to the issuing company.

The security analyst, again viewed here as an investor adviser, must bear this factor in mind.

Timing Considerations in Investment Policy. The old rule for the ordinary investor was that he should buy sound securities when he had funds available. If he waited for lower prices he would be losing interest on his money; he might "miss his market," even if prices declined; in any case, he was turning himself into a stock trader or speculator. Much of this view retains its validity. However, the time when the investor should clearly not buy common stocks is during the upper ranges of a bull market. For most issues this is tantamount to saying that he should not buy them at prices higher than can be justified by conservative analysis —which is something of a truism. But, as we pointed out previously, this warning applies also to the purchase of apparent "bargain issues" when the general price level seems dangerously high.

There are two other major questions of investment timing. The first is whether the investor should try to anticipate the movements of the market—endeavoring to buy just before an advance begins or in its early stages, and to sell at corresponding times prior to or at the onset of a full-scale decline. We state dogmatically at this point that it is impossible for all investors to follow timing of this sort, and that there is no reason for any typical investor to believe that he can get more dependable guidance here than the countless speculators who are chasing the same will-o'-the-wisp. Furthermore, the major consideration for the investor is not when he buys or sells but at what prices.

This is an aspect of the "timing" philosophy that has been almost completely overlooked. The speculator will always be concerned about timing because he wants to make his profit in a hurry. But waiting for a profit is no drawback to an investor, as compared with having his money uninvested for a similar period. He will have no advantage in remaining uninvested until a propitious "buying signal" is given, unless he thereby succeeds in buying at a sufficiently lower price to offset his loss of dividends. This means that timing, as such, does not benefit the investor unless it coincides with pricing. Specifically, if his aim is to buy and sell repeatedly, then his timing policy must enable him to repurchase his shares at a cost substantially under his previous selling price. We do not believe that the popular approaches to stock-market timing for the average investor—e.g., the famous Dow theory—will accomplish this for the investor. This question is considered in our final chapter on stock-market analysis.

A more serious question of timing policy, in our opinion, is presented by what were, at least formerly, the pronounced cyclical movements of the stock market. Should the investor endeavor to confine his buying to the lower reaches of the recurrent bear markets and correspondingly plan to sell out in the upper ranges of the recurrent bull markets? In such a policy, timing and pricing would clearly coincide—he would be buying at the right time because he would be buying at the right price, and vice versa.

No one can tell in advance how such an investment philosophy will work out in the years to come. Presumably its theoretical justification must be sought in the market's past history. If this is studied with some care, the indications it yields will not be found too encouraging.

If the relatively minor, as well as the major, stock-price "swings" over the 1885–1921 period are examined, it will be seen that—although they are certainly not identical—they are roughly comparable. (Appendix Note A sets forth the dates, duration, and amplitudes of the 11 swings over the 1885–1921 span. Table 1-7 provides data for the "major stock-price cycles" from 1871 to 1946 and for the "swings" since that date.) The average duration for the 11 fluctuations was 40 months (the median was 37 months) and the range was from a minimum of 30 months to a maximum of 50 months. Moreover, with only moderate exceptions, the amplitudes of the cycles were also fairly comparable. Thus these market swings were sufficiently regular to support the idea that about every three to four years the investor could buy his stocks at reasonably well-defined cheap levels and sell them out at reasonably well-defined dear levels. But since 1921 the stock-price cycles have been much less homogeneous in their successive forms. For example, the duration and amplitude of the 1921–1933 cycle exceeded by far those of any other price cycle in the span from 1871 to 1921. Furthermore, most analysts characterize the 12-year span from late 1949 through 1961 as one bull market. As a result it is exceedingly difficult to "regularize" the stock-market cycles of the last 35 years. In the period from 1949 through 1956, Standard & Poor's Composite Price Index was at a higher level at the end of each year than at the beginning in every instance except one—1953. Moreover, within any single year, the decline from the high price in that year to the subsequent low price in the same year was insignificant, except in 1953, when it amounted to approximately 15 percent. In fact, for the eleven-year span from 1948 through 1959 the maximum decline in the Index was less than 22 percent. In our opinion, the earlier cyclical movements may no longer be considered as a basis for any simple form of investment timing.

Formula-timing Plans. Certain compromise methods have been devised—primarily in the early post-World War II years—which seek to take some advantage of the stock market's cycles without running (for the most part) the risks of a complete miscalculation. These are known as "formula plans" or "formula-timing plans." The essence of such plans is that the investor automatically sells stocks after a given price rise and buys after a given price decline. The recurrent and relatively moderate stock-price fluctuations of the first quarter of the century and from the mid-1930's through World War II generally lent themselves very well to formula-plan action. In the light of this historic record and of the com-

paratively moderate and frequent market oscillations encountered by
investors shortly after the war, these plans gained considerable acceptance in the late 1940's and early 1950's. In fact, they almost became a
fad. They enjoyed special popularity with the finance committees of col-
leges, philanthropic institutions, and the like, where the trustees are
justifiably anxious to mitigate the responsibilities of common-stock investment with the aid of reasonable-appearing impersonal devices. (Formula timing appears to have originated in 1938 with the administrators
of the Yale University and Vassar College endowments.)

Statistics are not available, but, basing our judgment on some familiarity with the subject, we may say that formula plans have fallen considerably from grace in recent years. There are probably three principal
explanations for the decline in popularity. First, an extended market
movement—either upward or downward—puts any type of timing program to a severe test. This was especially true of the 1953–1956 bull-
market spurt in which stock prices rose almost without interruption and
more than doubled. (Standard & Poor's Composite Stock Index rose by
120 percent and the Dow-Jones Industrial Average by 105 percent.)
Under such circumstances, a buy-and-hold program will outdo any other
timing arrangement. Second, some plans were ill-conceived and inadequately tested before their adoption. Careful testing against the historic
record would have raised serious doubts at the outset in some instances.[16]
Subsequent experience has shown this to be the case. (Contrary to prevalent opinion, the adoption of a formula plan—if properly considered—
involves the exercise of substantial judgment.) Third, the unsatisfactory
performance of some plans plus the fact that the word "formula" occasionally has undesirable connotations (among other things, some feel it
sounds too "pat") have caused a number of investors either to shift away
from formula plans or, at least, to disclaim their use. However, in a surprising number of instances the examination of the management of conservative institutional funds will disclose the imprint of formula timing—
or something closely resembling it.

Fundamentally, there are two types of formula-timing plans: constant-
ratio and variable-ratio. The first involves the establishment of simple
schedules under which—with a given price change in the market or the
value of the fund—stocks are sold (or bought) and bonds are bought
(or sold) to adjust the fund to a predetermined and fixed stock/bond
ratio. The original Yale Plan followed this course. The variable-ratio plan
requires the selection of a central or base price *for* the stock market.
Having done this—presumably on an annual basis—the investor sells and
buys on a prescribed schedule or scale with the objective of holding a
smaller proportion in common stocks at high prices and a larger proportion at low prices. One approach is to sell only above a selected median
for the market and to buy only at or below it. Another approach is to

[16] See Cottle and Whitman, *Investment Timing: The Formula Plan Approach,*
McGraw-Hill Book Company, Inc., New York, 1953, for some illustrative tests.

establish a market range and then gradually reduce stocks as the market rises in the range and increase stocks as the market declines. There are an unlimited number of variations in detail on these alternative types of plans.[17]

Although significant differences in risk and, therefore, in possible performance can be introduced into formula plans, it is our view that no one plan has a priori or guaranteed advantage over all others.

Our thinking is favorable to the principle of formula timing, primarily because it brings compulsion upon the investor to sell when the crowd is buying and to buy when the crowd lacks confidence. It is especially suited for investment portfolios which have a substantial common-stock component of the cross-section type, and presumably concentrated in the leading, well-known issues.[18] Investors who devote their efforts to the selection of undervalued securities will ordinarily measure their buying and selling opportunities by the relation between price and objective value for such issues. But a formula plan—requiring the development of a median for the market—would have a collateral interest of some importance for them, if it should indicate dangerously high levels for the *general* market. That would be the time for caution in all purchases. One additional point is to be emphasized. The adoption of a formula plan inherently involves (or should, if properly done) some definite decisions on the investor's part in regard to basic investment objectives. This is all to the good. Too frequently the individual investor and occasionally even institutions may concentrate on the selection of specific issues and sweep under the rug decisions in regard to fundamental and long-run portfolio objectives.

Dollar Averaging. Dollar averaging (or "dollar-cost averaging") consists of investing at regular intervals a fixed dollar amount in a selected stock or group of stocks. In this way the investor buys more shares at low prices than at high prices and thus is assured of a lower average cost per share than the average of the market price. This cost advantage is the inevitable result of the mathematical fact that: since the number of shares bought with a constant amount of money increases as the price declines, the average cost per share must be less than a simple average

---

[17] For a further discussion of formula plans, see Lucile Tomlinson, *Practical Formulas for Successful Investing*, Wilfred Funk, Inc., New York, 1955; Edgar S. Genstein, *Stock Market Profit without Forecasting*, Investment Research Press, South Orange, N.J. 1954; H. G. Carpenter, *This Is Investment Management*, Scarborough Press, Scarborough, N.Y. 1956. Articles will also be found in the *Journal of Finance, Financial Analysts Journal, Commercial and Financial Chronicle,* and other similar publications.

[18] This is typically true of the endowment funds of educational and charitable enterprises. The formula-timing idea is particularly applicable in such cases for an added reason of importance. The responsibility for a basic and long-run (although not irrevocable) decision in regard to investment-timing policy is assumed by the entire board, thus relieving the finance committee of the need for making frequent and controversial buy-or-sell decisions.

of market prices. This fact is readily illustrated in Table 5-1. Note from the table that dollar averaging would have provided, under the assumed market fluctuations, a per-share cost of $73.73, whereas the average of the quarterly prices was $77.27. Thus, through investing a constant dollar amount rather than buying a constant number of shares each quarter, the decrease in the cost per share would have been $3.54, or nearly 5 percent.

The increasing amount of favorable attention accorded this comparatively simple idea rests on the opinion that over a period of time it will provide a satisfactory average price for common-stock holdings. The soundness of the opinion may be evaluated by (1) an examination of the

Table 5-1. Comparison of Average Per-share Cost under Dollar Averaging and Average Market Price

Market price of stock	Quarterly investment	Shares purchased	Cumulative average cost per share	Cumulative average market price
100	$1,000	10.0	$100.00	$100.00
90	1,000	11.1	94.78	95.00
80	1,000	12.5	89.28	90.00
70	1,000	14.3	83.50	85.00
60	1,000	16.7	77.40	80.00
50	1,000	20.0	70.92	75.00
60	1,000	16.7	69.10	72.86
70	1,000	14.3	69.20	72.50
80	1,000	12.5	70.26	73.33
90	1,000	11.1	71.84	75.00
100	1,000	10.0	73.73	77.27

results that would have been obtained from employing dollar averaging over periods of the past and (2) an appraisal of the underlying assumption on which it rests.

We have made numerous historical tests of performance. In addition to confirming the favorable findings of others, the tests brought out two additional facts of importance. First, variations in the frequency of purchase can produce substantial differences in cost in the early phases of an acquisition program, but over a sufficient period of time these differences become inconsequential. Furthermore, it would be impossible to predict at the outset which time interval for successive purchases would do best in the early stages. For example, in a *steadily rising market* a program which makes a full year's commitment at the beginning of each year would—as long as the bull market lasted—outperform a program which purchases shares at regular intervals *throughout* the year (say, monthly) and thus at progressively higher prices. In a *steadily declining* market the reverse is true; the program which makes a full commitment at the beginning of the year buys at the highest cost for the year. Over an entire cycle, with a fairly comparable up- and down-swing, these opposite effects tend to cancel out and thus the differences in per-share costs become nominal.

The second notable fact developed by our studies is the minor influence of the level of stock prices at the starting point on long-run per-share cost. Certainly the results will vary widely in the early stages between funds initiated at significantly different market levels, but the variance will diminish and eventually become insignificant as the programs continue. The result is inevitable, because the longer each program is followed the less influential becomes either a single purchase or the purchases over a short span of time. We have concluded that, insofar as the long-run effects are concerned, if adherence over at least ten years is assured, a dollar-averaging program may be initiated at any market level or in any phase of the cycle. This conclusion is a coldly statistical one and puts aside psychological considerations. The investor must appraise his own emotional characteristics and his intestinal and financial fortitude (or, if it be an institution, those of the finance committee).

We would add an important word of caution. Dollar averaging rests on the fundamental assumption that the resulting average per-share cost will prove reasonable in terms of subsequent average market levels. The validity of this assumption depends on two essentials: (1) that the acquisition period will be sufficiently long to span *at least* a full stock-price cycle of reasonable amplitude and (2) that the future secular trend of stock prices will not be downward. If the first condition is met by the investor, the second will most likely be met by the market.

An examination of the basic characteristics of common stocks *as a class* leads us to the view that neither the evidence of the past nor the economic knowledge of the present point to a *secular* decline in stock prices.[19] Thus, in our opinion, it can be assumed with considerable confidence that this prerequisite of successful dollar averaging will be met.

With the investor rests the responsibility for the conclusion as to the other prerequisite—continuing the program through a full cycle. It is quite possible that the average individual will not have available for the investment a sufficient sum to acquire a carefully diversified list of stocks[20] at regular intervals over a period of years (say, not less than five

[19] The same will certainly not be true of specific individual issues.

[20] The importance of diversification is effectively demonstrated by R. W. Bidwell in an article entitled, "Magic Formula? Dollar Averaging Sometimes Can Lead to Losses," *Barrons*, Feb. 3, 1958, p. 9. He points out that a quarterly investment in General Motors from 1939 through 1957 would have provided 300.6 percent appreciation, in Woolworth a loss of 11.2 percent, and in Tri-Continental Corporation a gain of 531.8 percent. His conclusion in this regard is that "Dollar averaging, like any sound investment program, requires adequate diversification if it is to succeed with a minimum of risk."

Investment trust shares can, of course, be substituted. In fact, some funds offer specific arrangements which fit with the dollar-averaging concept.

and preferably something like ten or more); therefore dollar averaging may prove more practical for the institutional than for the individual investor.

Certain institutions, such as all types of insurance companies, are more likely to find feasible an approximation to the concept of dollar averaging. They have substantial funds available for additional common-stock investment each year, and they can arrange to make their purchases at quarterly or some other regular interval.

However, for most investors, we think, the real implication of dollar averaging is that it prevents them from putting more money in stocks at higher prices than they did at lower prices—which is a common failing—and that it never lets a lower price level scare them away from buying.

CHAPTER SIX

NATURE AND SOURCES OF THE

ANALYST'S INFORMATION

Most of the corporate data used by the security analyst will have come originally from two parallel sources. The first is information sent by the company to the stockholders or the press; the second is material filed with a regulatory body—most often the SEC. Nearly all this information is reproduced or condensed by the financial services as it becomes available. For many analytical purposes it is sufficient to take the material at second hand, from the various manuals, supplements, or the current information service of Moody's and Standard & Poor's. But for a full-scale analysis the practitioners will generally find it advisable to consult the original sources to make sure that nothing of importance is overlooked.

The amount of material available varies to an extraordinary degree when the entire body of quoted securities is surveyed. At one extreme we have unlisted issues which are subject to no regulatory controls, and for which the published data can range from a complete story down to literally nothing at all.[1] At the other extreme we have the Class I railroads, which include all lines of any importance. These file quarterly with the ICC a large eight-page form that presents statistics in the greatest profusion about nearly every phase of their physical operations and finances. In addition they supply weekly figures of cars loaded on their lines and received from connections.

Reports to Commissions Other Than the SEC. Quite a few classes of companies are in industries subject to regulation by public agencies and are required to file financial statements with them which are open to

[1] It is a fact that in the case of some unlisted securities the company does not make public any financial statements. For example, the United States National Bank of San Diego is quoted on the over-the-counter market but does not publish an income statement.

public inspection. Most of these reports are considerably more elaborate than the average published statement. These categories may be listed as follows:

Railroads. We have already mentioned the quarterly statements that are filed with the ICC. Even more complete annual reports are also required by the Commission. Much of the data so furnished is reproduced in the annual "Statistics of Railways in the United States" (the "blue book") published by the ICC.

Public Utilities. In virtually every state, public utility companies are subject to comprehensive regulation by state public service commissions.[2] These regulatory bodies generally have jurisdiction over rates, issuance of securities, property acquisitions, standards of service, accounting methods, etc. Comprehensive and detailed annual reports are required to be filed by the companies, and these reports are open to inspection by the public at the commissions' offices. Usually these reports contain substantially more detailed financial and operating statistics than are set forth in the annual reports to stockholders. Monthly operating statements are in some cases also filed and are likewise available for public inspection.

In addition to submitting information to state commissions, all interstate electric and natural-gas companies file similarly detailed annual reports with the Federal Power Commission. These reports can be inspected at the Commission's headquarters in Washington, and, in certain cases, at its regional offices.

While virtually all the material included in these commission reports is of interest and importance, it is usually presented in such a manner that the analyst needs to do considerable further work to bring out its true significance. Certain of the statistical services assemble these data together with the appropriate ratios and unit figures for various periods of years.

Banks. Detailed call reports are filed regularly (three or four times annually) with state banking departments or a Federal agency (Federal Reserve Bank or Comptroller of the Currency). Although these reports are not available for public inspection, the summary balance sheet—"face" of the call report—is published in the official newspaper for the county in which the bank's head office is located.

Insurance Companies. Detailed annual statements of uniform character (the so-called "convention reports") are filed with the insurance department of each state in which the concern does business. In addition, an audit is made every three years by the state of domicile (with the participation of other state departments). These audits are also open to inspection.

---

[2] In the states Iowa, Minnesota, and South Dakota, the commissions do not at the date of this writing have jurisdiction over electric and gas utilities, and in certain others the jurisdiction of the commission is limited.

Pipe Lines, Express Companies, Interstate Trucking Companies, Freight Forwarders. Reports in considerable detail are made by these concerns to the ICC.

Companies Subject to SEC Regulations. Most of the securities that come before the analyst for study will be listed on a registered securities exchange, or will have been subject to a public offering since 1933, or both. In such cases there will be material of three sorts available for the analyst, viz:

1. *The Basic Registration Statement (or Prospectus).* This statement provides a detailed description of the company's business and properties and will often serve as a starting point for detailed analysis. In the case of old-line concerns, much of the data contained in the registration statement can be carried back for earlier years by references to the security manuals.

2. *Annual Data.* It is here that the dualism between voluntary and required data is most manifest. Each concern with listed securities must file annually with the SEC a form (10-K for most companies) which contains a balance sheet and income account in prescribed detail and which also adds material that may be needed to bring the registration statement up to date. Similar requirements are imposed with respect to unlisted securities registered for sale under the Securities Act of 1933 if the amount involved exceeds $2 million.

These reports are not circulated among the stockholders or even released to the press, but they are available for inspection at the offices of the Commission, or at the security exchanges. In addition thereto, each company publishes its own annual statement for distribution among stockholders and the general public. These reports vary greatly in amount of detail as between concerns. They may contain substantially more or substantially less data than are contained in the 10-K form filed with the SEC.

Although there is a pronounced tendency toward making company annual reports more complete and informative, in some cases it is still necessary to go to the commission forms for such a basic item as the volume of business or sales. We might mention also that the figure of rents (and royalties) paid in each year, which must be given in the 10-K form, for years was never published elsewhere. Recently, however, there has been a tendency to show in a footnote the annual rental or leases expiring beyond one year.

3. *Interim Figures.* Since 1936 the SEC has required nearly every listed enterprise to file with it semiannual sales figures. (The chief exception appears to be the sugar producers.) Consequently this is the interim information that is now most uniformly available for companies generally. The majority of concerns also supply their quarterly net income figures, generally in the form of press releases which are given adequate publicity.

There are a number of variations from this model pattern of quarterly sales and earnings figures. A few companies—notably Caterpillar Tractor

—now publish both figures monthly. Nearly all the mail-order houses and chain stores supply sales data monthly, but not profits.[3]

It is still customary for all the meat packers and most of the sugar producers to announce their profits not more frequently than semi-annually. American Crystal Sugar, which reports profits quarterly, is an exception. On the other hand, it is the fashion for most companies to issue quarterly reports. Allied Chemical Corporation, for a long time one of the few that published figures only once a year, issued its first semiannual statement in 1950 and subsequently began reporting quarterly.

It was originally the accepted view that companies with a pronounced seasonal bias in their results should not publish interim figures, on the ground that these could be misleading. As we have seen, this prejudice has been almost entirely overcome in the matter of publishing quarterly sales. It is now assumed that the investing public will make due allowance for seasonal variations in interpreting the figures. The same sophistication could no doubt be counted upon in the use of interim profit figures. One method of overcoming the objection to seasonally unstable interim figures is by publication of successive twelve-month totals at quarterly intervals. This is a sound idea, but at this time it is practiced by only a few industrial concerns—e.g., General Refractories and American Zinc, Lead, and Smelting—although it is the general practice among the utilities.

Nature of the Information Supplied. The forms prescribed by the SEC assure the analyst of a respectable minimum of financial information about each company that files an annual report with the Commission. The uniform divisions of the income account and the balance sheet, and the other material required on the 10-K reports, are summarized in Appendix Note 7, page 672 of the 1951 edition.

Additional Material in Comprehensive Reports. Many companies go beyond the SEC requirement in their statements to stockholders. The United States Steel Corporation holds an honorable position as perhaps the first large industrial enterprise to tell its whole financial story to its owners. Since 1901 its annual reports have been a model of comprehensiveness. In addition to the data required on the SEC forms, U.S. Steel has supplied figures on the following items:

1. Production and sales in units; rate of capacity operated
2. Division of sales as between
    a. Domestic and foreign
    b. Intercompany and outsiders
3. Details of operating expenses
    a. Wages, wage rates, and number of employees
    b. State and local taxes paid
    c. Selling and general expense
    d. Maintenance expenditures, amount and details

[3] In fact, Woolworth, Kresge, and Kress announce their sales once a month and their earnings only twice a year.

4. Details of capital expenditures during the year
5. Details of inventories
6. Details of properties owned
7. Number of stockholders

In recent years the annual report has been considered by many companies as a major vehicle for enlisting the goodwill of stockholders toward management. Great efforts have been made to turn out reports that are attractive in appearance and satisfying in their content. The *Financial World* has made annual awards for the best financial reports, and these contests have aroused considerable emulation among companies.[4]

In many reports the management seeks to give stockholders a comprehensive idea of the company's business, properties, personnel, progress, and problems. Illustrations, once frowned upon as unconservative, are now standard features. Some reports are made especially useful by the inclusion of annual figures going back five to fifty years.[5]

Some Important Information Still Not Generally Available. The improvement in corporate reporting in the last generation has been so far-reaching that it may seem hypercritical to stress some deficiencies that remain to be supplied in the generality of annual statements.[6] The areas in which further information is particularly needed include: breakdown of sales by products or product lines and by consuming industries, research and development costs, long-term lease arrangements, wages and salaries ("employee statistics"),[7] foreign operations, capital expenditures, inventory valuation, and depreciation.

The desirability of as much uniformity as possible within industries in the reporting of financial information has been stressed by the Committee on Corporate Information of the National Federation of Financial Analysts and by an executive of the New York Stock Exchange.[8] The

[4] See Appendix Note 8, p. 674 of the 1951 edition, for further reference to these awards.

[5] However, after a review of about 5,000 annual reports in the *Financial World's* Nineteenth Survey of Annual Reports, it was stated that "a large number of publicly held corporations . . . fail to give comparative figures" (i.e. for two years). "The Annual Report and the Stockholder," *Financial World*, June 17, 1959, pp. 39–40.

[6] For a discussion of annual reports, see such articles as, C. T. Horngren, "Disclosure: 1957," *Accounting Review*, October 1957, pp. 598–604; and "Disclosure: What Next?," *Accounting Review*, July 1959, pp. 381–388; "The Annual Report and the Stockholder," *Financial World*, June 17, 1959. See especially the comprehensive review of the subject in A. R. Cerf, *Corporate Reporting and Investment Decisions*, University of California Printing Department, 1961. He concludes that "a significant need for improvement is evident in the reporting of many firms."

[7] "How Accountants Can Help Improve Corporate Annual Reports," *Controller*, May 1959, pp. 255–256. Data pertaining to assets per employee and average hours worked per employee, as well as compensation, can be most helpful. A review of 150 major corporations listed on the New York Stock Exchange indicates that approximately one-half are not currently reporting wages and salaries.

[8] E. Linwood Savage, Jr., "Conclusions Regarding Annual Reports," *Analysts Journal*, February 1954, pp. 51–53; Phillip L. West, "The Reporting of Earnings to Stockholders," *Journal of Accountancy*, February 1959, pp. 27–32.

Committee suggested that, through intra-industry cooperation, managements "should see to it that financial figures are comparable or that the
necessary supplementary information is supplied so that the analyst can
make them comparable."

In addition, there have been suggestions that companies supply information pertaining to fixed and variable costs in order that analysts
might more accurately estimate profits at various levels of activity.[9]
Clearly such information would be helpful to the skilled analyst, particularly if he is primarily concerned with projecting earnings on a year-by-
year basis. Prevailing on corporate management to provide the data may
prove to be a long-range undertaking but this should not deter the effort.

Additional Financial and Physical Data Are Important. The dollar
figures supplied in the balance sheet and income account should be supplemented by certain additional information of a quantitative sort. The
analyst would like to have the following material if he can get it:

1. Orders booked and unfilled orders
2. Productive capacity where relevant
3. Production in units where relevant
4. Division of products by principal classes or departments, in dollar
amounts or in percentage of total
5. Data on concentration of business with a few customers, if it exists, and
any significant dependence on exports
6. Description of property owned, including types of buildings and combined floor area

Most of this information is contained in registration statements relating
to security offerings or in proxy material bearing on mergers and the
like. It is not so frequently supplied in the annual reports themselves, so
that some of the original material tends to become out of date. Security
analysts are making something of an organized effort to obtain this material from companies which have so far withheld it.

Unlisted Companies. The original pressure both for detailed reports
to stockholders and for the publication of interim figures came largely
from the New York Stock Exchange, which paved the way for the SEC's
even more extensive regulations in this area. The unlisted companies
with unregistered securities, being exempt from such authoritative influences, have tended to limit both the amount of information revealed
and its frequency. In fact, the great majority of unlisted companies do
not vouchsafe interim figures of either sales or profits.

Certain exceptions, notably in the banking group, have been developing in recent years. Within the last decade the most important com-

---

[9] A discussion of the value of fixed and variable costs data is set forth in Sidney
M. Robbins, "The Need for More Complete Cost Data in Annual Reports," *Analysts
Journal,* February 1957, pp. 9–11. For an interesting approach from the corporate
point of view, see Marshall K. Evans, "Profit Planning," *Harvard Business Review,*
July-August 1959, pp. 45–54.

mercial banks whose shares are widely held have been publishing details concerning their earnings and expenses in their annual and interim reports to shareholders. In 1942 the Committee on Bank Management and Research of the New York State Bankers Association issued and recommended general use by banks of a "Condensed Operation Earnings Report for Shareholders and Others," showing details of operating earnings, operating expenses, and a reconcilement of surplus and undivided profits. This recommendation has been widely followed.

In different fashion the semiannual results of most insurance companies have become available through the activities of specialists in the shares, who obtain them from the companies and present them in published compilations.[10]

Supplementary Information. The security analyst uses a vast amount of economic statistics which relate either to business as a whole or to a particular industry. Most of this material may be found in the weekly and monthly publications of the Department of Commerce. The monthly *Survey of Current Business* is indispensable.

Trade Journals. Many important summary figures are published at frequent intervals in the various trade journals. In these publications will be found also a continuous and detailed picture of the current and prospective state of the industry. Thus it is usually possible for the analyst to acquire without undue difficulty a background of fairly complete knowledge of the history and problems of the industry with which he is dealing. In some cases he obtains unofficial data relating to individual concerns. In the various trade papers he can find out the weekly output (estimated) of each motor-car maker, or the current rate of production of the major steel and copper companies, or an estimate of the season's crop for each sugar producer.[11]

Official Documents. In times past, when many corporations were highly secretive about their affairs, the wide-awake analyst was often able to unearth little-known information in various kinds of official documents. (Examples were reports of the Federal Trade Commission, the United States Coal Commission, and others.) Nowadays, the corresponding opportunities are likely to be found in the elaborate hearings and lengthy opinions of the SEC and the ICC, which sometimes contain important factual material not elsewhere to be found.

Requests for Direct Information from the Company. Published information may often be supplemented to an important extent by private in-

---

[10] The SEC has asked Congress for power to require the unlisted companies with more than $3 million of assets and more than 300 stockholders to file with it the same kind of reports as do the listed companies, but this legislation has not been passed. However, any unlisted company which has filed a Registration Statement with the SEC in connection with a stock offering which has an aggregate value of $2 million—computed at the offering price—for all shares of that class is also required to file with the Commission annual data similar to those filed by listed firms.

[11] Much of this type of data is republished in the *Wall Street Journal*.

quiry of or by interview with the management.[12] There is no reason why stockholders should not ask for information on specific points, and in many cases part at least of the data asked for will be furnished. It must never be forgotten that a stockholder is an owner of the business and an employer of its officers. He is entitled not only to ask legitimate questions but also to have them answered, unless there is some persuasive reason to the contrary.

Until recently, at least, insufficient attention has been paid to this all-important point. The courts have generally held that a bona fide stockholder has the same right to full information as a partner in a private business. This right may not be exercised to the detriment of the corporation, but the burden of proof rests upon the management to show an improper motive behind the request or the possibility of injury to the business as a result of disclosure of the information.

Compelling a company to supply information involves expensive legal proceedings, and hence few shareholders are in a position to assert their rights to the limit. Experience shows, however, that vigorous demands for legitimate information are frequently acceded to even by the most recalcitrant managements. This is particularly true when the information asked for is no more than that which is regularly published by other companies in the same field. Few questions of this sort asked at annual meetings go unanswered.

In recent years there has been an increasing tendency for managements to give frank and adequate answers to pertinent queries. This includes the explanation of obscure or unusual items in the financial statements. Excellent working arrangements have been established between security analysts and corporation executives, largely through the activities of the New York Society of Security Analysts and similar groups in other cities. The luncheon meetings of these organizations are addressed by scores of company heads each year, who often give behind-the-scenes pictures of their concerns' operations, problems, and prospects.

[12] In May 1962 the Corporation Relations Committee of The New York Society of Security Analysts published an excellent guide to appropriate behavior by both security analysts and company officials in connection with such interviews.

CHAPTER SEVEN

QUANTITATIVE AND QUALITATIVE FACTORS IN SECURITY ANALYSIS. THE MARGIN-OF-SAFETY CONCEPT

After the analyst has learned what information he can get and where to find it, he faces the harder question: what use to make of it.

Analyzing a security involves an analysis of the business. Such a study could be carried to an unlimited degree of detail; hence practical judgment must be exercised to determine how far the process should go. The circumstances will naturally have a bearing on the decision. A buyer of a $1,000 bond would not deem it worth his while to make as thorough an analysis of an issue as would a large insurance company considering the purchase of a $500,000 block. The latter's study would still be less detailed than that made by the originating bankers. Or, from another angle, a less intensive analysis should be needed in selecting a high-grade bond yielding 4¼ percent than in trying to find a well-secured issue yielding 6 percent or an unquestioned bargain in the field of common stocks.

The Technique and Extent of Analysis Should Be Limited by the Character and Purposes of the Commitment. The equipment of the analyst must include a sense of proportion in the use of his technique. In choosing and dealing with the materials of analysis he must consider not only inherent importance and dependability but also the question of accessibility and convenience. He must not be misled by the availability of a mass of data—e.g., in the reports of the railroads to the Interstate Commerce Commission—into making elaborate studies of nonessentials. On the other hand, he must frequently resign himself to the lack of significant information because it can be secured only by expenditure of more effort than he can spare or the problem will justify. This would be true frequently of some of the elements involved in a complete "business analysis"—as, for example, the extent to which an enterprise is dependent upon patent protection or geographical advantages or favorable labor conditions which may not endure.

The Value of Data Varies with the Type of Enterprise. Most important of all, the analyst must recognize that the value of a particular kind of

85

data varies greatly with the type of enterprise which is being studied. The five-year record of gross or net earnings of a utility or a large chain-store enterprise may afford, if not a conclusive basis, at least a reasonably sound one for measuring the safety of the senior issues and the attractive-ness of the common shares. But the earnings statements for the same period of a small manufacturing enterprise, in a competitive field, may have so slight a bearing on the future earnings as to be virtually value-less. The same, of course, applies to any other type of speculative enter-prise. (Nevertheless, in the early 1960's the shares of innumerable small manufacturing concerns were offered to the public on the strength mainly of a satisfactory five-year record.)

Quantitative vs. Qualitative Elements in Analysis. It is convenient at times to classify the elements entering into an analysis under two head-ings: the quantitative and the qualitative. The former might be called the company's statistical exhibit. Included in it would be all the useful items in the income account and balance sheet, together with such additional specific data as may be provided with respect to production, unit prices, costs, capacity, unfilled orders, etc. The various items may be subclassified under the headings: (1) capitalization, (2) earnings and dividends, (3) assets and liabilities, and (4) operating statistics.

The qualitative factors, on the other hand, deal with such matters as the nature of the business; the relative position of the individual company in the industry (this factor verges on the quantitative because of the significant amount of data that can be developed and analyzed); its physical, geographical, and operating characteristics; the character of the management; and, finally, the longer-term outlook for the unit, for the industry, and for business in general. Questions of this sort are not dealt with ordinarily in the company's reports. For their answers the analyst must look to miscellaneous sources of information of greatly varying dependability—including a large admixture of mere opinion.

Broadly speaking, the important quantitative factors lend themselves to much more precise consideration in appraising a specific company than do the qualitative factors. The former are fewer in number, more easily obtainable, and better suited to the forming of definitive conclu-sions. Furthermore, the financial results in themselves epitomize such qualitative elements as the ability of a reasonably long-entrenched man-agement. This point of view does not minimize the importance of qualita-tive factors in appraising the performance of a company, but it does indicate that a detailed study of them—to be justified—should provide sufficient additional insight to assist significantly in appraising the com-pany.

QUALITATIVE FACTORS

The qualitative factors upon which most stress is laid are the nature of the business and the character of the management. These elements are exceedingly important but they are also exceedingly difficult to deal with. The problem in the first is the scope of the undertaking and in the second is the lack of objective measures.

Nature and Prospects of the Business. Industry Analysis. Let us consider, first, the nature of the business, in which concept is included the general idea of its future prospects. If the analyst (or investor) is so situated that he can undertake industry analysis in depth, he will find that a substantial amount of valuable data can be compiled. However, for several reasons, we have put this subject among the qualitative factors. First, we doubt that many are in a position to undertake penetrating industry studies; second, the notions of investors as to what is a "good business" and what is not are often based on surmise and bias as well as on a knowledge of the specific facts and conditions in the industry; and, third, substantial judgment is involved in predicting the influence of broad industry conditions on the future performance of a specific company.

The specific role that industry studies should play in investing is a much debated subject. At one extreme is the view that industry selection is all-important and company selection almost inconsequential.[1] At the other is the view that not only is company selection by far the dominant consideration but that industry data are of doubtful significance because of such factors as the growing multi-industry character of our major corporations.[2] It is probably safe, however, to conclude that it is still an established canon of investment in common stocks that one should first select the most promising industry or industries and then pick out the best companies in those industries.

It is our opinion that the existence of an attractive industry outlook is not a *sine qua non* for the purchase of a specific common stock. Well-known examples exist of companies which, over a period of years, have moved counter to the experience of their industry.[3] For this reason, there

---

[1] "Beside the selection of the industry, other considerations of investment are unimportant." E. S. Mead and Julius Grodinsky, *The Ebb and Flow of Investment Values,* Appleton-Century-Crofts, Inc., 1939, p. 4.

[2] In the period since World War II, ever-widening product diversification has been changing an increasing number of corporate enterprises into multi-industry undertakings. Consequently, the classification of complex corporate entities by industries is becoming more difficult. Nevertheless, we find that with few exceptions the transition of major corporations is an evolving process and that a change in their dominant characteristics occurs gradually. Moreover, within most of the industries of primary consequence there remains across time a "hard core" of companies which, from an investment standpoint, are significantly comparable. Therefore, if industry data are used as broad—rather than exact—indicators of the earnings and financial patterns of the principal segments of our industrial structure, they constitute helpful analytical tools.

[3] Denver and Rio Grande Western Railroad is one of the relatively few listed companies whose common shares advanced *more than tenfold* in price between 1949 and 1961. During this period the earnings of the railroad industry as a whole declined.

is also the danger of overemphasizing the general outlook for an industry in selecting individual issues. Not all the companies in an industry with a particularly bright outlook may enjoy its good fortunes, nor may all of the firms in an industry with a dark prognostication suffer a decline.

Whatever the differences of opinion as to the place of industry studies in common-stock investing, it is clear that the performance of a company cannot be completely or permanently isolated from the economic climate of the industry (or industries) within which the major portion of its activities occur. Consequently, industry information has an essential role to play in the evaluation of individual companies.

If industry data are important, does it follow that industry *studies* are of equal importance? At this early stage of our book we must express some reservations as to the basic utility of that great mass of industry studies which represent primarily a "warm-over" of readily available and usually familiar data. Insofar as these studies relate to the past, the elements dealt with have already influenced the results of the companies in the industry and the average market price of their shares. There is a danger in emphasizing the favorable or unfavorable position of the industry *in addition* to the high or low earnings produced by this position, for that means counting cause and effect as two factors in the valuation instead of one, as they really are. Insofar as they relate to the future, the studies generally assume that past characteristics and trends will continue. We find these forward projections of the past to be misleading at least as often as they are useful.

To make a significant contribution to common-stock investing, industry analysis must be undertaken in sufficient depth to generate new information and to reveal more fully than before the anatomy of the industry. Moreover, comparative analysis is at the heart of industry studies just as much as of company studies. Therefore an industry's performance should be examined also in terms of the experiences of other industries.[4] Industry studies of this type, through providing clearer insight into the forces operative in an industry and through bringing into better focus the relative performance of the industry, should make possible a more accurate appraisal of the future.

Such studies are particularly valuable when they lead to well-founded conclusions differing from those in vogue. Typically, these conclusions would forecast the *reversal* of a condition or trend that had been so long continued as to be accepted as permanent in Wall Street. Reversals of this kind are surprisingly frequent. In particular, World War II and its aftermath produced extraordinary changes in the relative profitability of industry groups. This fact is illustrated in Table 7-1, which shows average earnings on total capital in 1935–1939 and 1954–1958 for 32 industries. Note particularly the sharp drop in relative profitability of the distill-

[4] This point is examined in some detail by Sidney Cottle in "Appraising the Chemical Industry and Components," *Commercial and Financial Chronicle*, June 25, 1959.

Table 7-1. 1935–1939 Return on Total Capital Compared with 1954–1958

Rank-ing	Industry	1935–1939 return, percent	Rank-ing	Industry	1954–1958 return, percent
1	Proprietary drugs.....	31.1	1	Proprietary drugs.....	23.2
2	Ethical drugs.........	24.1	2	Aircraft.............	19.3
3	Apparel and accessories chains.............	23.1	3	Automobiles	16.9
4	Automobiles..........	20.5	4	Ethical drugs.........	16.1
5	Packaged foods.......	18.1	5	Apparel and accessories chains.............	14.5
6	Cigarettes...........	14.6	6	Corn products........	13.7
7	Distilling............	14.5	7	Nonferrous metals....	13.7
8	Radio and television...	14.1	8	Building materials....	12.7
9	Automobile parts and accessories..........	13.9	9	Packaged foods.......	12.2
10	Aircraft.............	13.8	10	Toilet preparations and soap...............	12.2
11	Toilet preparations and soap...............	13.5	11	Electrical supplies and equipment..........	11.8
12	Nonferrous metals....	13.1	12	General industrial machinery.............	11.8
13	Limited-price variety chains.............	12.6	13	Automobile parts, etc..	11.7
14	Mail-order houses.....	12.3	14	Oil..................	11.3
15	Chemicals...........	10.9	15	Mail-order houses.....	10.8
16	Containers..........	10.8	16	Grocery chain stores...	10.8
17	Electrical supplies and equipment...........	10.0	17	Copper..............	10.7
18	General industrial machinery.............	9.6	18	Paper and allied products...............	10.4
19	Grocery chain stores...	8.5	19	Steel................	10.3
20	Agricultural machinery	8.2	20	Chemicals...........	9.3
21	Corn products........	8.1	21	Cigarettes...........	9.8
22	Grain-mill products...	7.8	22	Dairy products.......	9.8
23	Dairy products.......	7.5	23	Rubber.............	9.7
24	Building materials....	7.4	24	Containers..........	9.4
25	Oil..................	6.3	25	Grain-mill products...	8.3
26	Rubber.............	5.7	26	Limited-price variety chains.............	8.1
27	Department stores....	5.3	27	Department stores....	8.0
28	Copper..............	5.3	28	Radio and television...	6.8
29	Paper and allied products...............	5.0	29	Distilling............	6.2
30	Textile fabrics........	5.0 4.2	30	Agricultural machinery	5.9
31	Meat packing.........	4.1	31	Textile fabrics........	5.3
32	Steel................	3.1	32	Meat packing.........	3.3

SOURCES: 1935–1939 data: Cottle and Whitman, *Corporate Earning Power and Market Valuation, 1935–1955*, Duke University Press, Durham, N.C., 1959; 1954–1958 data: Stanford Research Institute.

ing, radio and television, cigarette, limited-price variety chains, and agricultural machinery industries. In contrast, there was a marked improvement in the relative profitability of the building materials, corn products, steel, paper and allied products, copper, and oil industries. The average rate of return for the first five industries declined from 12.8 percent in 1935–1939 to 7.4 percent in 1954–1958, whereas the average for the second group of six industries jumped from 5.9 to 11.5 percent.

An industry analysis—unless it involves the compilation of composite sales, assets, earnings, and other financial data for the major units in the industry—is not subject to technical problems of the types met in security analysis. We shall assume that the student has the statistical and economic training necessary for the collection and interpretation of such industrial data and descriptive material as will aid him in understanding the nature of a business with which he is to deal in his work of security analysis. We shall assume also that, although the student will not typically be undertaking industry studies of the scope and penetration envisaged in the preceding paragraphs, he will include in an intensive examination of an individual security a consideration of the industry-wide conditions which have contributed to the specific company's performance. The subject of industry analysis will be dealt with in more detail in Chapter 19 and will then be illustrated by an examination of the chemical and public utility industries.

The Factor of Management. Picking a company with a good management is considered by many to be even more important than picking a company in a promising industry. Management is a factor about which little tangible information is available.[5] Objective tests of managerial ability are few and not too scientific. In most cases the investor must rely upon a reputation which may or may not be deserved. The most convincing proof of capable management lies in a superior comparative record over a period of time. But this brings us back to the quantitative data.

There is a strong tendency in the stock market to value the management factor twice in its calculations. Stock prices reflect the large earnings which the good management has produced, *plus* a substantial increment for "good management" considered separately. This amounts to "counting the same trick twice," and it proves a frequent cause of overvaluation.

But the management factor does assume quite independent importance where a significant change therein has recently taken place or may be considered probable. In such cases future results may be very different from those of the past. Typically, but by no means always, changes in

---

[5] *Forbes Magazine* publishes annually its ratings of the management of many companies; the method was changed in 1962. The American Institute of Management distributes to its members periodical "management audits," of an elaborate sort, pertaining to selected companies.

management are for the better; they are often brought about because of results so unsatisfactory as to demand a drastic shake-up. In this area, particularly, we think the analyst may profit from personal contacts with the new directing heads. His investigations may lead him to expect future results by no means discounted in the current price.

The Trend of Future Earnings. Since the middle 1920's, increasing importance has been laid upon the trend of earnings.[6] Needless to say, a record of increasing profits is a favorable sign and should be given full weight in an appraisal. If the trend approach assists in interpreting this record, then, by all means, it should be employed. If a graphic array of the sales, earnings, or other data for a company, an industry, or the economy as a whole reveals reasonably consistent secular growth,[7] it is both appropriate and desirable to measure this growth through either a visually or a mathematically fitted trend line.

Although we commend to the student this use of trend lines, we also want, at the same time, to stress the fundamental difference between the use of a trend line to measure past performance and its use as a means of projecting future performance. To estimate future earnings by projecting the past trend and then accepting that projection as a basis for valuing the business may be sound in specific instances, but it must be used with extreme caution. It is essential that the analyst be fully aware of the implications of what he has done.

Figures and a mathematical equation are involved in computing a trend, and some people believe that for that reason a trend projection is "mathematically sound." But while a definite trend shown in the past is a fact,[8] a "future trend" is only an assumption. Factors of economic adjustment and readjustment, militating against the maintenance of abnormal prosperity or depression in the economy as a whole, are equally opposed to the indefinite continuance of either a *pronounced* upward trend or a *marked* decline for an individual company or industry. By the time the trend has become clearly identifiable, conditions may well be ripe for a change.

[6] This has been true particularly since 1949. For a discussion of the use of trend projections (growth rates) in appraising common stocks, see such articles as J. G. Buckley, "A Method of Evaluating Growth Stocks," *Financial Analysts Journal*, March-April 1960, pp. 19–21; and N. Molodovsky, "Valuation of Common Stocks," *Analysts Journal*, February 1959, pp. 23ff.

[7] If a secular trend is a straight line on arithmetic paper, the growth is in terms of a constant annual *amount*. If it is a straight line on semilogarithmic paper, the growth is in terms of a constant annual *rate* (percent). The latter presentation is almost always the more useful to the analyst.

[8] In 1951 we analyzed the Dow-Jones Industrial Average over the periods from 1897 to 1950 and from 1926 to 1950 and could find no objective standard for determining the specific trend line which should be employed. Therefore, while the data represent facts, it does not necessarily follow that a specific trend line is a "fact." A single line may not fully describe a time series. Cottle and Whitman, *Investment Timing: The Formula Plan Approach*, McGraw-Hill Book Company, Inc., 1953, Chap. 7.

A trend represents the relationship of the individual data in a time series. Thus, like any statistical measure, it is derived from the data for the period selected and is, of course, subject to any fundamental distortions which exist in the data. To illustrate: A trend fitted to an index of sales for the major corporations in the aircraft industry shows a growth rate of 26 percent per annum over the 1947–1957 period. However, an analyst should have had serious doubts about projecting this trend. For one thing, it was distorted by the fact that sales were extremely low in 1947–48. This, in itself, indicated that (unless strong supporting factors could be found) an extrapolation of the 1947–1957 rate would represent an overstatement of future growth. (It so happened that—after adjustment for acquisitions and mergers—there was practically no increase in the aggregate sales of these major corporations over the 1957–1960 span.)

Trends are certainly one of the tools which the analyst should have in his analytical kit. But they are only *one* of the tools and, therefore, should take their place along with *individual* and *average* figures of the past. The analyst must not take undue comfort from the fact that they can be computed according to mathematical formulas. Not only does their use involve a number of subjective decisions (period for which computed, type of trend, etc.), but also situations will occur where trend analysis is of questionable value.

A trend projection has an air of definiteness which may mislead the unwary; it should be used only as a rough index of what may be expected from the future. Furthermore, a trend projection—which can be indefinitely extended—should not be allowed to serve, palliate, or obscure a financial condition which, in terms of past experience and present earnings levels, appears to be unsatisfactory. This important point may be clarified by the following example.

In 1929 nearly all public utility holding-company systems showed a continued growth of earnings, but the fixed charges of many were so heavy—by reason of pyramidal capital structures—that they consumed nearly all the available earnings. Investors bought bonds of these systems freely on the theory that the small margin of safety was no drawback, since earnings were certain to continue to increase. They were thus making a clear-cut prediction as to the future, upon the correctness of which depended the justification of their investment. If their prediction was wrong—as it proved to be in 1931–1932—they were bound to suffer serious loss.

Trend Essentially a Qualitative Factor. Later in this book, in our discussion of the valuation of common stocks, we shall point out that the placing of undue emphasis on the trend is likely to result in errors of overvaluation or undervaluation. This is true because no theoretical limit may be fixed on how far ahead the trend should be projected; and therefore the process of valuation, while seemingly mathematical, is in reality psychological and quite arbitrary. For this reason we consider the trend as a *qualitative* factor in its practical implications, even though it may be stated in quantitative terms.

Qualitative Factors Resist Even Reasonably Accurate Appraisal. The projected trend is, in fact, a statement of future prospects in the form of a fairly exact prediction. In similar fashion, conclusions as to the nature of the business and the abilities of the management have their chief significance in their bearing on the company's outlook. These qualitative factors are therefore all of the same general character. They all involve the same basic difficulty for the analyst, viz., that it is impossible to judge how far they may properly reflect themselves in the price of a given security. In most cases, if they are recognized at all, they tend to be overemphasized. We see the same influence constantly at work in the general market. The recurrent excesses of its advances and declines are due at bottom to the fact that, when values are determined chiefly by the outlook, the resultant judgments are not subject to any mathematical controls and are almost inevitably carried to extremes.

The Importance of Qualitative Factors in Current Analytical Thinking. The reader will have noted that in our view security analysis should be primarily a process of *measurement*—either of safety, in the case of a typical bond, or of value, in the case of a typical common stock. This has led us to prefer the "valuation approach" to the "anticipation approach" in our earlier discussion (page 26), and it has caused us now to express misgivings as to the consequences of placing undue emphasis on non-measurable factors of quality. It is only fair to add that our attitude is by no means the accepted one among working analysts generally. The concept that the *primary* job of security analysis is to select "good and promising" companies is widely held not only by investors but among analysts themselves.

The very real and basic issue here may be expressed in extreme fashion by these two opposite dicta: (1) "Make sure of the right quality, and the price will take care of itself"; (2) "Make sure of the right price, and the quality will take care of itself."

Although these propositions may appear in conflict, they are not mutually exclusive. The quality of a security may be so good as to justify a very high price; and, conversely, the price may be so low as to offset very poor quality. Many experienced investors and investment advisers are convinced that the dangers of overpaying for stocks of strong and promising companies are much less than those of buying poor quality issues because they seem to offer a lot of assets or earnings or income return for the money.

The latter viewpoint is certainly true when applied to the operations of untrained security buyers. They are easily led astray by an *apparently* attractive price or yield to buy low-grade securities that will come to grief. We believe that in most such cases a competent security analyst would have shown that the security was in reality not attractively priced, and that the unwary investor had been deceived by a temporarily good showing or had overlooked elements of serious weakness.

Requirements of Defensive Investors. The solution of this problem was anticipated in our proposed self-classification of security buyers into defensive and aggressive investors. It is advisable for the defensive investor to require first quality in all his selections. He will get this ordinarily by buying the securities of large, well-known enterprises, which his adviser can certify to him as prosperous, well managed, and strongly entrenched. We think he will do well to require of the analyst some assurance also that the price he is to pay is not inordinately high in terms of accepted standards of value.

The enterprising investor, working with or as a security analyst, may range more freely over the area of varied quality. Within limits he may trade off, as it were, the qualitative against the quantitative factors, making sure that the composite result indicates an underlying value well in excess of price. Thus he may accept a management rated less than top grade, a past record less than brilliant, a future prospect less than alluring, provided these factors are overdiscounted in the price to be paid. Needless to say, however, if he thinks the company is headed for bankruptcy, or even for steadily declining earnings, he is most unlikely to buy any of its securities, no matter how low their price.[9]

Security Analysis and the Future. The kind of security analysis we regard as a most rewarding discipline is concerned primarily with values which are supported by the facts and not those which depend largely upon expectations. In this respect the analyst's approach is diametrically opposed to that of the speculator, meaning by that term one whose success turns upon his ability to predict or guess future developments. The analyst must of course take possible future changes into account, but his primary aim is not so much to *profit* from them as to guard against them. Broadly speaking, he views the business future as a hazard which his conclusions must encounter rather than as the source of his vindication.

Three Offsets to the Hazards of the Future. The hazards of the unknown future may be met by the security analyst in several ways. He may place his prime emphasis upon the presence of a large margin of safety for the security, which should be able to absorb whatever adverse developments are reasonably likely to occur. In such cases he will be prepared to see unsatisfactory earnings for the issue during recession periods, but he will expect (1) that the company's financial strength will carry it unharmed through such a setback and (2) that its *average* earnings will be enough to justify fully the bond or stock purchase he is recommending. In other cases the analyst may emphasize the factor of *inherent stability*. Here the nature of the industry or the company is supposedly such as to immunize it in large measure from the recurrent ad-

---

[9] After bankruptcy comes, surprisingly profitable opportunities are often presented by the senior securities selling at too depressed levels.

versity that befalls most enterprises. Stability of this kind has been possessed by nearly all the public utility groups—electricity, gas, water, telephone—by well-established chain stores, by certain makers of trademarked goods for public consumption, and by others.

Finally, the analyst may properly give considerable weight to the future prospects themselves, and he should favor companies which his own study and judgment tell him have better than average expectations. In his common-stock selections he will value such concerns more liberally than others. But he must beware of carrying such liberality to the point of enthusiasm, for at that point he loses the sober moderation that distinguishes the investment approach from the speculative one. The security analyst is on safest ground when he treats favorable expectations as an added reason for a purchase which would not be unsound if based on the past record and the present situation.

Inherent Stability a Qualitative Factor. The element of inherent stability, above referred to, has particular appeal to the security analyst, because it minimizes the risk that new conditions will upset his calculations derived from the past record. Stability, like the trend, may be expressed in quantitative terms—as, for example, by stating that over the last three decades the earnings of National Biscuit Company were never less than five times the preferred dividend requirements; or that the net income of the United States Tobacco Company between 1937 and 1959 varied only between $1.11 and $2.08 per share of common. But in our opinion stability is really a qualitative trait, because it derives in the first instance from the character of the business and not from its statistical record. A stable record suggests that the business is inherently stable, but this suggestion may be rebutted by other considerations.

Example 1. The Bon Ami Company reported remarkably stable earnings in the 18 years from 1929 through 1946. This is shown by the figures for selected years set forth in the accompanying table.

Year	Net income
1929	$1,703,000
1932	1,339,000
1935 (low year)	1,246,000
1939	1,839,000
1946 (high year)	2,611,000

At the 1946 and 1947 high prices the company sold in the market for about $25 million, even though both the net tangible assets and the annual sales were only about $5 million.

The business was dependent on a single well-known trademarked product. Toward the end of this period of steady operations, its field was subjected to an important technological change leading to replacement of old cleansing agents by new detergents. Thus in 1946 the company was more vulnerable to competitive forces than its past record had indicated.

A steady decline in earnings commenced in 1947. By the end of 1958 the company was operating at a deficit of nearly $1 million, and the market price of the company's stock had fallen to $3 million—a loss of 88 percent from the high figure of 1947.[10]

Example 2. A striking example of this type, which some of our readers will remember, was presented by the real estate bonds issued by S. W. Straus and Company in the late 1920's. Straus did an enormous business in this field, with the effective use of a slogan, such as "Fifty years in business without loss to a single investor." The customers naturally assumed that this excellent record was an assurance of future stability. But the fact was that the Straus business had *changed* radically in the 1920's, from a small concern engaged in conservative forms of real estate financing to a huge enterprise concentrating on volume of business with little regard to prudence and care. When the losses did come they were colossal.

QUANTITATIVE FACTORS

Margin of Safety as the Basic Quantitative Factor. At the end of Chapter 4 we pointed out that the presence of a margin of safety is the distinguishing characteristic of true investment. In like manner the margin of safety may be thought of as the most fundamental quantitative concept in security analysis. A given bond is approved as a safe investment because it has an adequate safety margin; this margin is expressed quantitatively by the analyst and is compared with specific quantitative criteria. Similarly, we consider that the analyst works most effectively in the field of common stocks when he is able to work out a valuation that exceeds the current market price by a goodly margin. In the selection of primary or leading common stocks for conventional investment, such a margin between value and price has not ordinarily been present. But prior to about 1957 common-stock investments did possess a quantitative margin of safety of another kind—viz., the substantial excess of the expected annual dividend over the interest rate on high-grade bonds. As this margin was realized over the years, it could be viewed as a sinking fund to amortize the cost of these diversified stock holdings down to a point where an ultimate loss becomes highly improbable. In our view the loss of the second type of margin of safety, in consequence of the market advance and increased popularity of common stocks in the late 1950's, poses the central problem facing the security analyst at the beginning of the 1960's.

---

[10] In the earlier editions of this work we used the example of Studebaker Preferred stock, the dividend on which had been earned not less than twenty-three times in each year from 1922 to 1929, but which went into receivership in 1933 (see pp. 43 and 44 of the 1940 edition). The 1959 performance of Studebaker-Packard Corporation, referred to on page 31, was of quite different character.

Since the major portion of this book will be devoted to the analysis of the quantitative factors behind security values, we shall not expand our discussion at this point.

SUMMARY

To sum up this discussion of qualitative and quantitative factors, we may express the dictum that the analyst's conclusions must always rest upon the figures and upon established tests and standards. These figures alone are not *sufficient;* they may be completely vitiated by qualitative considerations of an opposite import. A security may make a satisfactory statistical showing, but doubt as to the future or distrust of the management may properly impel its rejection. Again, the analyst is likely to attach prime importance to the qualitative element of inherent *stability,* because its presence means that conclusions based on past results are not so likely to be upset by unexpected developments. It is also true that he will be far more confident in his selection of an issue if he can buttress an adequate quantitative exhibit with unusually favorable qualitative factors.

But whenever the commitment depends to a major degree upon these qualitative factors—whenever, that is, the price is considerably higher than the figures alone would justify—then, the analytical basis of approval is lacking. In the mathematical phrase, a satisfactory statistical exhibit is a *necessary* though by no means a *sufficient* condition for a favorable decision by the analyst.

At the end of the 1950s and the beginning of the 1960s investors seemed to be basing many of their valuations and decisions on the almost unqualified acceptance of markedly rising trends of earnings projected for a number of years ahead. Some may say that these projected earnings constitute part, indeed the principal part, of the company's "statistical exhibit." We think that projections of increased earnings have "statistical validity" only when organically connected with a growth trend of the past, and that even then, they must be treated with caution and conservatism in reaching investment valuations.

CHAPTER EIGHT

CLASSIFICATION OF SECURITIES

Securities are customarily divided into the two main groups of bonds and stocks, with the latter subdivided into preferred stocks and common stocks. The first and basic division recognizes and conforms to the fundamental legal distinction between the creditor's position and the partner's position. The bondholder has a fixed and prior claim for principal and interest; the stockholder assumes the major risks and shares in the profits of ownership. It follows that a higher degree of safety should inhere in bonds as a class while greater opportunity of speculative gain—to offset the greater hazard—is to be found in the field of stocks. It is this contrast, of both legal status and investment character, as between the two kinds of issues, which has provided the point of departure for the usual textbook treatment of securities.

OBJECTIONS TO THE CONVENTIONAL GROUPING

1. Preferred Stock Grouped with Common. While this approach is hallowed by tradition, it is open to several serious objections. Of these the most obvious is that it places preferred stocks with common stocks, whereas, so far as investment practice is concerned, the former undoubtedly belong with bonds. The typical or standard preferred stock is bought for fixed income and safety of principal. Its owner considers himself not as a partner in the business but as the holder of a claim ranking ahead of the interest of the partners, i.e., the common stockholders. Preferred stockholders are partners or owners of the business only in a technical, legalistic sense; but they resemble bondholders in the purpose and expected results of their investment.

2. Bond Form Identified with Safety. A weightier though less patent objection to the radical separation of bonds from stocks is that it tends to identify the bond form with the idea of safety. Hence investors are led to believe that the very name "bond" must carry some especial assurance against loss. This attitude is basically unsound and on frequent occasions is responsible for serious mistakes and loss. The investor has been spared even greater penalties for this error by the rather accidental fact that fraudulent security promoters have rarely taken advantage of the investment prestige attaching to the bond form.[1] It is true beyond dispute that bonds as a whole enjoy a degree of safety distinctly superior to that of the average stock. But this advantage is not the result of any essential virtue of the bond *form;* it follows from the circumstance that the typical American enterprise is financed with honesty and intelligence and does not assume fixed obligations without a reasonable expectation of being able to meet them. But it is not the obligation that creates the safety, nor is it the legal remedies of the bondholder in the event of default. *Safety depends upon and is measured entirely by the ability of the debtor corporation to meet its obligations.*

The bond of a business without assets or earning power would be every whit as valueless as the stock of such an enterprise. Bonds representing all the capital placed in a new venture are no safer than common stock would be and are considerably less attractive. For the bondholder could not possibly get more out of the company by virtue of his fixed claim than he could realize if he owned the business in full, free and clear.[2] This simple principle seems too obvious to merit statement; yet because of the traditional association of the bond form with superior safety, the investor has often been persuaded that by the mere act of limiting his return he has obtained an assurance against loss.

3. Failure of Titles to Describe Issues with Accuracy. The basic classification of securities into bonds and stocks—or even into three main classes of bonds, preferred stocks, and common stocks—is open to the third objection that in many cases these titles fail to supply an accurate description of the issue. This is a consequence of the fact that a large percentage of securities do not conform to the standard patterns but instead modify or mingle the customary provisions.

Briefly stated, these standard patterns are as follows:

1. The bond pattern comprises
   a. The unqualified right to a fixed interest payment on fixed dates.
   b. The unqualified right to repayment of a fixed principal amount on a fixed date (usually subject to the right of the company to call the issue prior to maturity).
   c. No further interest in assets or profits, and no voice in the management.

---

[1] For an example of fraudulent sales of bonds, see Securities Act of 1933: Release No. 2112, dated Dec. 4, 1939, relating to the conviction of various parties in connection with the sale of American Terminals and Transit Company bonds and Green River Valley Terminal Company notes. In 1956 the Commission entered a stop order in connection with the proposed issuance by Frozen Food Storage, Inc., of $1,750,000 principal amount of convertible debentures. The *Annual report* of the SEC for the fiscal year ended June 30, 1957 (p. 42) states: "Registrant was virtually without assets and was looking entirely to the proceeds of this financing for its capital requirements." The *Annual Report* for fiscal 1959 (pp. 172–173) reports the conviction of several persons in connection with the sale of certificate bonds of Selected Investments Trust Fund.

[2] See Appendix Note 1, p. 725, for data on Court-Livingston Corporation, illustrating this point. For other examples, see pp. 590–593 of the 1940 edition of this book.

2. The preferred-stock pattern comprises
   a. A stated rate of dividend, usually cumulative,[3] in priority to any payment on the common. (Hence full preferred dividends are mandatory if the common receives any dividend; but if nothing is paid on the common, the preferred dividend is subject to the discretion of the directors.)
   b. The right to a stated principal amount in the event of dissolution, in priority to any payments to the common stock.
   c. Either no voting rights, or voting power shared with the common.
3. The common-stock pattern comprises
   a. A prorata ownership of the company's assets in excess of its debts and preferred-stock issues.
   b. A prorata interest in all profits in excess of prior deductions.
   c. A prorata vote for the election of directors and for other purposes.

Bonds and preferred stocks conforming to the above standard patterns will sometimes be referred to as *straight bonds or straight preferred stocks.*

Numerous Deviations from the Standard Patterns. However, almost every conceivable departure from the standard pattern can be found in greater or less profusion in the security markets of today. Of these the most frequent and important are identified by the following designations: *income* bonds; *convertible* bonds and preferred stocks; bonds and preferred stocks with *stock-purchase warrants* attached; *participating* preferred stocks; common stocks with *preferential features; nonvoting* common stock. (The 1920s produced the device of making bond interest or preferred dividends payable either in cash or in common stock at the holder's *option.*) The *callable feature* now found in most bonds and preferred stocks is now so common as to constitute a feature of the standard patterns for such issues.[4]

Of less frequent and perhaps unique deviations from the standard patterns, the variety is almost endless.[5] We shall mention here only the glaring instance of Great Northern Railway Preferred stock, which between 1898 and 1954 was in all respects a plain common issue; and also the resort by the former Associated Gas and Electric Company to the insidious and highly objectionable device of bonds convertible into preferred stock *at the option of the company*—which were, therefore, not true bonds at all.

[3] The SEC study referred to in the preceding footnote showed that 93 percent of preferred-stock issues had cumulative dividend rights. *Ibid.,* pp. 21–22.

[4] Preferred stocks which are nominally noncallable may sometimes be retired at their "fair value" as fixed by the company, but subject to appraisal rights by dissenting holders. This is accomplished under a New Jersey statute permitting "reduction of capital" through retirement of an entire class of stock. Johnson and Johnson retired all of its 16,000 shares of $8 preferred in this way in 1950, offering the holders $215 in cash or $200 in new $4 second preferred.

[5] The reader is referred to Appendix Note 3 of the 1934 edition of this work for a comprehensive list of these deviations, with examples of each. To save space, that material has been omitted from subsequent editions.

These were wiped out in the bankruptcy of that company which ended in 1946.

More striking still is the emergence of completely distinctive types of securities so unrelated to the standard bond or stock pattern as to require an entirely different set of names. Of these, the most significant is the option warrant—a device which during the years prior to 1929 developed into a financial instrument of major importance and tremendous mischief-making powers. The option warrants issued by a single company—American and Foreign Power Company—attained in 1929 an aggregate market value of more than a *billion dollars*, a figure exceeding our national debt in 1914.[6] A number of other newfangled security forms, bearing titles such as "allotment certificates" and "dividend participations," could be mentioned.[7]

The peculiarities and complexities to be found in the present-day security list are added arguments against the traditional practice of pigeonholing and generalizing about securities in accordance with their *titles*. While this procedure has the merit of convenience and a certain rough validity, we think it should be replaced by a more flexible and accurate basis of classification. In our opinion, the criterion most useful for purposes of study would be the *normal behavior* of the issue after purchase—in other words, its risk-and-profit characteristics as the buyer or owner would reasonably view them.

NEW CLASSIFICATION SUGGESTED

With this standpoint in mind, we suggest that securities be classified, for analysis, under the following three headings:

Class	*Representative issue*
I. Securities of the fixed-income and stable-value type	A high-grade bond or preferred stock
II. Senior securities of the fluctuating-value type	
A. Well-protected issues with profit possibilities	A high-grade convertible issue
B. Inadequately protected issues	A lower-grade bond or preferred stock
III. Common-stock type	A common stock

An approximation to the above grouping could be reached by the use of more familiar terms, as follows:

[6] Warrants have again become prominent in corporate financing, some companies issuing several series of warrants. (For a discussion, see Chap. 44.)

[7] In June 1939 the SEC set a salutary precedent by refusing to authorize the issuance of "capital-income debentures" in the reorganization of the Griess-Pfleger Tanning Company, on the ground that the devising of new types of hybrid issues had gone far enough. See *SEC Corporate Reorganization Release No. 13*, dated June 16, 1939. The court failed to see the matter in the same light and approved the issuance of the new security. Fortunately, the issue was later paid off in full.

   I. Investment bonds and preferred stocks
  II. Speculative bonds and preferred stocks
     A. Convertibles, etc.
     B. Low-grade senior issues
 III. Common stocks

The somewhat novel designations that we employ are needed to make our classification more comprehensive. This necessity will be clearer, perhaps, from the following description and discussion of each group.

Leading Characteristics of the Three Types. The first class includes issues, of whatever title, which are bought in the reasonable expectation that the income therefrom will continue unchanged and that their market quotation will not deviate greatly from the purchase price.[8] The owner's dominant interest lies in the safety of his principal, and his sole purpose in making the commitment is to obtain a steady income. In the second class, prospective changes in the value of the principal assume real significance. In Type A, the investor hopes to obtain the safety of a straight investment, with an added possibility of profit by reason of a conversion right or some similar privilege. In Type B, a definite risk of loss is recognized, which is presumably offset by a corresponding chance of profit. Securities included in Group IIB will differ from the common-stock type (Group III) in two respects: (1) they enjoy an effective priority over some junior issue, which gives them a certain degree of protection; and (2) their profit possibilities, however substantial, have a fairly definite limit, in contrast with the unlimited percentage of possible gain theoretically or optimistically associated with a fortunate common-stock commitment.

Issues of the fixed-income, stable-value type include all *straight* bonds and preferred stocks of high quality selling at a normal price. Besides these, the following securities belong in this class:

1. Sound convertible issues where the conversion level is too remote to enter as a factor in the purchase (similarly for participating or warrant-bearing senior issues)

2. Guaranteed common stocks of investment grade

3. "Class A" or prior-common stocks occupying the status of a high-grade, straight preferred stock (*Example:* Montgomery Ward class A stock)

[8] The actual fluctuations in the yields and prices of long-term investment bonds since 1900 have been so wide and so frequent as to suggest that these price changes must surely be of more than minor importance. It is true, nonetheless, that the investor habitually acts *as if* they were of minor importance to him, so that, subjectively at least, our criterion and title are justified. To the objection that this is conniving at self-delusion by the investor, we may answer that on the whole he is likely to fare better by overlooking the price variations of high-grade bonds than by trying to take advantage of them and thus transforming himself into a trader. We have substituted the phrase "fixed-income and stable-value" for "fixed-value," which we formerly employed. For convenience we shall usually refer to this type as "fixed-income" issues.

On the other hand, a bond of investment grade which happens to sell at any unduly low price would belong in the second group, since the purchaser might have reason to expect and be interested in an appreciation of its market value.

Exactly at what point the question of price fluctuation becomes material rather than minor is naturally impossible to prescribe. The price level itself is not the sole determining factor. A long-term 3 percent bond selling at 60 may have belonged in the fixed-income, stable value class (e.g., Northern Pacific Railway 3s, due 2047, between 1922 and 1930), whereas a one-year maturity of any coupon rate selling at 80 would *not*— because in a comparatively short time it must either be paid off at a 20-point advance or else default and probably suffer a severe decline in market value. We must be prepared, therefore, to find marginal cases where the classification (as between Group I and Group II) will depend on the personal viewpoint of the analyst or investor. Such marginal cases will crop up everywhere in security analysis.

Any issue which displays the main characteristics of a common stock belongs in Group III, whether it is entitled "common stock," "preferred stock," or even "bond." American Telephone and Telegraph Company Convertible 4½s, when they sold at about 200 in 1929, provided an apposite example. The buyer or holder of the bond at so high a level was to all practical purposes making a commitment in the common stock, for the bond and stock would not only advance together but also decline together over an exceedingly wide price range. Still more definite illustration of this point was supplied by the Kreuger and Toll Participating Debentures at the time of their sale to the public. The offering price in 1928 was so far above the amount of their prior claim that their title had no significance at all and could only have been misleading. *These "bonds" were definitely of the common-stock type.*[9]

The opposite situation is met when issues, senior in name, sell at such low prices that the junior securities can obviously have no real equity, i.e., ownership interest, in the company. In such cases, the low-priced bond or preferred stock stands virtually in the position of a common stock and should be regarded as such for purposes of analysis. A preferred stock selling at 10 cents on the dollar, for example, should be viewed not as a preferred stock at all, but as a common stock. On the one hand it lacks the prime requisite of a senior security, viz., that it should be followed by a junior investment of substantial value. On the other hand, it carries all the profit features of a common stock, since the amount of possible gain from the current level is, for all practical purposes, unlimited.

The dividing line between Groups II and III is as indefinite as that between Groups I and II. Borderline cases can be handled without undue difficulty, however, by considering them from the standpoint of either

[9] See Appendix Note 10, p. 675, of the 1951 edition for the terms of this issue.

category or of both. For example, should a $5 preferred-stock issue selling at 30 be considered a low-priced senior issue or the equivalent of a common stock? The answer to this question will depend partly on the exhibit of the company and partly on the attitude of the prospective buyer. If real value may conceivably exist in excess of the par amount of the preferred stock, the issue may be granted some of the favored status of a senior security. On the other hand, whether or not the buyer should consider it in the same light as a common stock may also depend on whether he would be amply satisfied with a possible 250 percent appreciation or is looking for even greater speculative gain.[10]

From the foregoing discussion the real character and purpose of our classification should now be more evident. Its basis is not the title of the issue, but the practical significance of its specific terms and status to the owner. Nor is the primary emphasis placed upon what the owner is legally entitled to demand, but upon what he is likely to get or is justified in expecting, under conditions which appear to be probable at the time of purchase or analysis.

---

[10] Numerous examples of this kind may be found in any bear market, e.g., St. Louis–San Francisco Preferred paying $5 and selling as low as 31 in 1949. Compare Interstate Department Stores Preferred, which sold at an average price of 30 in 1932–1933 and then advanced to 107 in 1936–1937. A similar remark applies to some low-priced bonds.

PART TWO

ANALYSIS OF FINANCIAL STATEMENTS

CHAPTER NINE

ANALYSIS OF THE INCOME ACCOUNT:

GENERAL PROCEDURE

All security analysis involves the analysis of financial statements. True, the weight given to the financial material may vary enormously, depending upon the kind of security studied and the basic motivation of the prospective purchaser. The standing of investment-grade bonds and preferred stocks is decisively controlled by the financial record. They must meet specific tests of safety, which turn upon such criteria as the relation of past earnings to fixed charges (and preferred dividends), the dividend record, the relation of funded debt to property account, the working-capital position, the volume of business done, and others. While qualitative factors may be important in this area, they cannot be determinative of safety without support from the actual figures.

Past Record Is Pertinent to the Future. In the selection of common stocks much more emphasis is placed upon *future expectations* as the primary basis of attractiveness and value. In theory these expectations may be so different from past performance that the latter could be virtually irrelevant to the analysis. But this separation of the future from the past rarely occurs in practice. A tendency toward an underlying continuity in business affairs makes the financial record the logical point of departure for any future projection. Thus it is only the trader on market movements or the heedless speculator following tips or hunches who will ignore the statistical showing of a common stock. The investment approach to every kind of security—which is the analytical approach—requires the proper application of income-account and balance-sheet analysis.

In Chapter 2 we pointed out that the descriptive function of security analysis involves the marshaling of the important facts relating to an issue and their presentation in a coherent, readily intelligible manner. Analysis of financial statements plays a major part in this descriptive function. We propose to devote this section of our book to an exposition of such analysis up to the point where the indicated results are actually to be used in the evaluation and the choice of securities.

The Typical Pattern of an Analytical Study. Every reasonably complete analysis of a corporate issue has three major divisions. The first describes the company's business and properties (it may include also some historical data and some details about the management). The second contains financial material, viz.: (1) the capitalization, (2) the record of earnings and dividends for a considerable number of years, and (3) a recent balance sheet. The third division discusses the prospects of the enterprise and the merits of the security.

Kinds of Analytical Studies. 1. *The Prospectus.* The prospectuses which are issued in connection with new security offerings are in reality elaborate but incomplete analytical studies. They supply a wealth of information about the company and the specific issue, often in overwhelming detail. They frequently include a discussion of factors that may make for either larger or smaller profits in the future.[1] They lack, however, any comparisons of the enterprise with others in the same industry. Nor does a prospectus include any arguments, pro or con, about the merits of the offering itself, or any specific recommendation that the issue be purchased as an attractive investment or speculation. (In many common-stock offerings the outer page of the prospectus carries the statement that the shares are "being offered as a speculation." The purpose of this warning is to relieve the underwriters of possible liability for failure to indicate the presence of substantial risk.)

2. *Brokerage-house Releases.* The analytical studies or "circulars" issued by brokerage houses cover a wide range of scope and competence. Some are not really analyses at all, but thinly disguised recommendations that the issue be bought for a quick profit because the short-term prospects seem favorable. At the other extreme we find really penetrating and scholarly presentations of the salient factors bearing on the worth of the issue. Nearly all these documents include a specific conclusion, which is

---

[1] There is actually a tendency to emphasize the unfavorable or risky aspects of the business. This frankness will presumably relieve the issuers and underwriters from future liability for lack of "full disclosure." The rather discouraging statements in the typical prospectus of a relatively new or small company do not seem to prevent the sale of its securities—either because the buyers do not really read the prospectus, or because the warnings therein are taken as a matter of course.

almost invariably a direct or implied recommendation to buy.[2] The latter fact follows from the economics and the psychology of the brokerage business. An analysis without a conclusion seems pointless and unprofitable; a recommendation to sell would nearly always be of interest only to that small portion of the clientele who own the securities.

3. *Reports by Investment Services.* The larger investment services—Standard & Poor's, Moody's, and Value Line—publish condensed analytical reports about most of the listed and a number of the unlisted stock issues. These follow a uniform pattern for each service. They include a conclusion about the current attractiveness of the issue—often necessarily in guarded language.

Uses of the Income Account. The indications furnished by the income account may be analyzed and discussed from various angles. These include the *average* results for the period, the *minimum* for any year, and the *trend* over the years. In many common-stock "write-ups" considerable and perhaps excessive attention is paid to the *current* figure, which may be misleading. The more progressive analysts are now using past income accounts primarily as a guide to formulating estimates of future earnings, or "earning power," which will serve as the chief basis of their conclusions respecting the merits of a common stock.

The importance attached to the income account in security analysis makes it the more essential that the published figures be studied with discernment. A really good job of income-account analysis may be anything but a simple matter. Many complications may have to be unraveled, many quirks or special entries guarded against, many variations between companies equalized. The broad study of corporate income accounts may be classified under three headings, viz.:

1. *The accounting aspect.* Leading question: "What are the true earnings for the period studied?"

2. *The business aspect.* Leading question: "What indications does the earnings record carry as to the future earning power of the company?"

3. *The aspect of security valuation.* Leading question: "What elements in the earnings exhibit should the analyst take into account and what standards should he follow, in endeavoring to arrive at a reasonable valuation of the shares?"

In this and the ensuing chapters we shall deal with the accounting aspect of statement analysis, treating first the income statement and then the balance sheet. Discussion of the other two facets will be postponed until it can be fitted into our comprehensive attack upon the theory and technique of common-stock investment.

[2] The attitude of Merrill, Lynch, Pierce, Fenner & Smith, Inc., the largest stock-brokerage firm, is an exception to this generalization. Their analytical circulars concentrate on giving the facts and frequently list the favorable and unfavorable elements in parallel columns. Recommendations are generally avoided.

Basic Procedures in Arriving at "True Operating Earnings" (or Ordinary Earnings) for the Period Studied. The analyst must start, of course, with the assumption that the figures he is studying are not fraudulent. This means basically that the various items of assets and liabilities in the balance sheet are honestly stated as they would appear on the books without omissions, fictitious entries, or other juggling of the accounts. It means further that where discretion is used in valuing assets or estimating liabilities, such estimates are based on informed and honest judgment.

Nearly all the published annual reports have been audited by independent public accountants and bear their certification. This is now a requirement of law as applied to companies with listed securities and those which have made a public offering of an unlisted issue in an amount exceeding $2 million. (There were some 600 of the latter in 1949 and over 3,700 as of July 1960.) The auditing procedures have been tightened up considerably since 1933, partly through the efforts of the accountants themselves and partly at the insistence of the SEC. Not only have the possibilities of outright fraud been greatly reduced, but—what is of more practical importance—the analyst is now supplied with the year's results in sufficient detail and with enough explanatory comment to permit him to interpret the figures intelligently.

Prior to the SEC legislation, which began in 1933, it was by no means unusual to encounter semifraudulent distortions of corporate accounts. The misrepresentation was almost always for the purpose of making the results look better than they were, and it was generally associated with some scheme of stock-market manipulation in which the management was participating. In our 1934 and 1940 editions we gave considerable attention to misleading artifices. But if we repeated the examples here, we should ourselves be misleading, in that we might influence the reader to believe that they were related to present-day practices. It is still quite possible for the accounts to be manipulated in either gross or subtle fashion by promoters of new enterprises, or even in some established but unlisted companies not subject to the audit requirements of the SEC. But our considered opinion is that intentionally deceptive reports—which constituted a very real abuse before 1933—are now so infrequent and unimportant as to permit us to dismiss the subject here.[3]

Accountants' Results and Analysts' Results. Since the reports of nearly all companies are honestly compiled and are certified by their auditors as conforming with accepted accounting principles, why should it be

---

[3] Sometimes, of course, the accounts are falsified by a defaulting employee, but in most such cases the loss is paid by a surety company. There was an incident of this kind involving the Mergenthaler Linotype Company in 1946, and another involving fictitious assets claimed by a company taken over by H. L. Green, Inc., in 1959. The debacle of United Industrial Corporation, suspended from NYSE trading in 1961, appears to have involved fraudulent overstatement of assets and profits.

necessary for the security analyst to meddle with the figures? The reason is basically that accepted accounting principles allow considerable leeway in the statement of results. This leeway permits the company to report its earnings on a basis that may not reflect the true operating results for the year (including its interest in affiliated companies) as the analyst would present such results. Furthermore, it permits considerable variations in the basis of accounting between different companies in the area of inventory valuation and depreciation. It is an important job of the analyst to restate and interpret the figures, not so much in accordance with permissible practices of accounting as in the form most enlightening to the investor.

It should be pointed out that since 1939 something of a revolution has taken place in accounting procedures as a result of the promulgation of a number of accounting research bulletins by the Committee on Accounting Procedure of the American Institute of Certified Public Accountants. These bulletins have recommended sweeping changes in a number of vital matters.[4] Nearly all the important companies have changed their accounting to comply with these recommendations, and more will certainly do so in the future. Practically all these modifications are in the direction of making the corporate statements conform more closely to what we should call a security analyst's concept of proper reporting to stockholders.

Professional vs. Practical Implications. A distinction needs to be drawn between the importance of financial-statement analysis as a matter of necessary procedure by the professional analyst, and its importance in leading to the most successful selection of securities—particularly common stocks. If the practitioner is to use the past record as the starting point for his study, he must present the figures adequately and accurately. If he fails to make the corrections required by sound techniques, then he has done a bad professional job of analysis. From that point of view we consider a comprehensive training in income-account and balance-sheet analysis an essential part of the financial man's education.

It is not equally true that such competent marshaling of the figures can be depended on to lead to successful choices of securities. We are convinced that this is broadly the case in the analysis and choice of bonds and preferred stocks for investment, for in these the overriding question is whether the issue meets certain minimum standards of safety based on past performance. But in the common-stock field values have come to be dependent to a preponderant extent upon expectations as to the *rate of future growth* of earnings. Consequently the success of a common-stock purchase will be determined largely (1) by whether such expectations will have been fulfilled, (2) by whether *subsequent* expectations as to the future growth rate are more or less favorable than the earlier

---

[4] See Appendix Note 2, p. 726, for a list of the more important bulletins.

ones, and (3) by changes, up or down, in the market's basis of capitalizing such expectations.

These newer determinants of market value and the success of common-stock purchases are by no means closely related to the past record. In view of the increased preoccupation with the tempo of the future, much of the analyst's work in an accurate presentation of the past record may appear rather irrelevant and of little practical value when applied to the choice of common stocks. We should be unrealistic if we did not recognize that such is the current situation.

Nonetheless, we think that the analyst should continue to do this searching and critical work as before—and for several reasons. First, he must maintain his professional standards in whatever he does, even though the market may seem to pay little heed to his presentations. Second, it is still true that in a number of individual instances this critical analysis will lead to worthwhile conclusions as to the overvaluation of certain issues and, particularly, as to the undervaluation of others. Third, the standard analytical procedure still consists of applying an appropriate multiplier to the current level of earnings. To do this properly for a given company it is necessary that the current level of earnings be determined as accurately as possible. Finally, the stock markets of the future may return, at least part way, to the criteria of earlier decades, and may shift the emphasis somewhat from future projections, which will perhaps have proved too unreliable, back toward the less challengeable record of actual past performance.

FIVE STEPS IN THE ANALYSIS OF INCOME STATEMENTS

In order to arrive at the indicated earning power for the period studied, the analyst should follow a standard procedure consisting of five steps:

1. He will eliminate nonrecurrent items from a single-year analysis. But he will include most of them in a long-term analysis.
2. He will exclude deductions or credits arising from the use of contingency and other arbitrary reserves.
3. He will endeavor to place the depreciation (or amortization) allowance and the inventory valuation on a basis suitable for comparative study.
4. He will adjust the earnings for the operations of subsidiaries and affiliates to the extent they are not included but available.
5. He will adjust the income tax deduction to place it in proper relationship to the adjusted earnings before tax.

NONRECURRENT ITEMS

As is evident from the name, nonrecurrent profits or losses are those which arise for reasons outside the regular course of the business. The entries are of two main types. In one case the item relates entirely to events taking place in past years, such as the following:

1. Payments of back taxes or tax refunds, not previously provided for, and interest thereon (this may be accompanied by adjustments in depreciation reserves)

2. Results of litigation or other claims (e.g., renegotiation, damage suits, public utility rate controversies) relating to prior years

The other type of special transaction has its origin in the year covered by the report but is nonetheless of an exceptional character which sets it off from the ordinary operations. The following are examples of this category:

3. Profits or loss on the sale of fixed assets—or of investments, for a non-investment company

4. Adjustments of investments to market value, for a noninvestment company; or write-down of nonmarketable investments

5. Write-downs or recoveries of foreign assets

6. Proceeds of life insurance policies collected

7. Charge-offs in connection with bond retirements and new financing

Except for refinancing costs, which are almost invariably charged against surplus, the treatment of these nonrecurring items in annual reports varies widely. One school of accountancy favors showing them in the income statement, to make the latter "all-inclusive." Another school prefers to exclude at least some of them from income because they do not reflect current operating results. When they do appear in the income account they are generally identified as separate items, but they are not necessarily segregated from ordinary income in a clear-cut manner. Under the requirements of the SEC such segregation is required to be made in registration statements and in subsequent annual reports to the Commission (on Form 10-K).

The now standard and appropriate treatment of nonrecurrent items in annual reports and by the financial services may be illustrated by the following typical example:

Example: In 1959 American Viscose showed net income of $10,481,000, followed by a special credit of $3,000,000, representing "adjustment of provision for Federal income taxes and renegotiation for prior years." Moody's *Manual* shows the company as earning $3.01 per share before special credit and $3.98 per share after special credit.

Alternatively, a transaction clearly related to prior years may properly appear in the surplus account only, with full exclusion from the current year's income.

Example: In 1957 Zenith Radio showed regular income of $8,165,000; in addition a large settlement of $10,000,000 received in patent litigation was credited directly to earned surplus account.

Less acceptable methods of reporting nonrecurrent items will be treated below.

Twofold Status of Nonrecurrent Items in Analysis. Most of the non-recurrent items play a double and contradictory role in security analysis. They should be excluded in arriving at the results for a single year, but they should be included in the over-all results for a period of years. A substantial refund of overpaid taxes, for example, has nothing to do with the year's operating profit, and it is a misuse of language to call it part of the "earnings" of the year in which it was received. Yet under the former accounting rules of the ICC, these and similar items were required to be included in the income account of railroad companies, while various losses were chargeable only to surplus.

However, in a seven- or ten-year analysis of average earnings, a tax refund pertaining to the period belongs in the picture just as much as the profits or losses against which it accrued. In a long-range analysis of past results the best rule is to take in every *real* profit or loss item unless it is quite unrelated to the normal operations of the business. Voluntary mark-ups or mark-downs of capital items, such as plant or intangibles, should not be considered a "real" gain or loss. We should exclude also a profit or loss from a major sale of property, considering it not related to the company's operations; but smaller and repeated sales of fixed assets could be regarded, contrariwise, as incidental to a continuing business.

Rules for the Treatment of Nonrecurrent Items. It is clear that where substantial nonrecurring items exist there cannot be any completely satisfactory statement of earnings *by single years;* for neither the inclusion nor the exclusion of such items will do full justice to the situation. We doubt, in any event, that really worthwhile indications of *earning power* and intrinsic value could be obtained from a study of the current year's results alone. Fuller consideration of this point must be reserved for the discussion of the significance of the earnings record in Chapter 33.

Regardless of the basic issue just raised, the security analyst does face the problem of properly interpreting, and perhaps restating, the earnings reported for relatively short periods of time. This will require a logical and consistent approach to the various kinds of nonrecurrent items.

The student may be helped by the following three suggested rules for the treatment of nonrecurrent items in the income account:

1. Small items should be accepted as reported. For convenience we may define "small" as affecting the net result by less than 10 percent in the aggregate.

2. When a large item is excluded, a corresponding adjustment must be allowed for in the income tax deduction.

3. Most nonrecurrent items excluded from the single year's analysis must nevertheless be included in a statement of long-term or average results.

Gain or Loss from Disposal of Capital Assets. The most frequent and important nonrecurrent items arise from the sale or other disposition of capital assets—i.e., plants or equipment. The standard treatment now, as for other similar transactions, is to show them in the account, but in a separate position after (ordinary) net income.

Example: Kennecott Copper Company's 1960 report showed the following:

Net before taxes	$163.0 million
Income taxes	85.6
Net income	77.4
Special item	dr. 36.2
Balance to surplus	41.2

The special item was a loss on sale of the company's South African mining investment. It did not carry a tax credit, except as a capital-loss carry-forward against capital gains for the next five years.

The gain or loss on such disposition may be excluded from the income account, but it is important that any tax saving from the loss be *not* credited to income.[5]

Example 1: Proper tax treatment.

American Viscose in 1958 gave up its Roanoke plant at a considerable loss. It deducted $2,462,000 "cost of closing plant" from the year's income; but the loss of $7,836,000 on the disposal of the plant, less $4,422,000 tax saving therefrom, was charged to "a special depreciation reserve provided from earnings in prior years." The full tax allowance was then charged against the year's reported pretax earnings of $9,600,000.

Example 2: Improper tax treatment.

Pennsylvania Railroad, 1955: Under the old accounting rules of the ICC (changed in 1956), the railroads were required to deduct loss on property abandonments from *surplus*, but the tax saved thereby was credited to income.

In 1955 Pennsylvania Railroad reported consolidated net income of $50,208,000 after income taxes of only $1,608,000. The system saved $12,505,000 in taxes by reasons of loss on property retired, charged to surplus. Most of the remaining net income was offset by the 85 percent dividend credit and by a tax saving of $7,418,000 from amortization of emergency facilities. (These items will be treated later.)

For a proper statement of the 1955 earnings the analyst would have deducted the two tax savings, thus reducing the per-share income from the reported $3.99 per share to an adjusted $2.80 per share.

Overstatement of Ordinary Income. An obvious type of distortion arises from the failure to separate a large gain on the sale of a capital asset from the ordinary income of the year. If the company published its per-share earnings with the inclusion of such an extraordinary profit, the financial services are likely to reproduce these misleading per-share figures.

[5] For comments on the taxes applicable to gains realized on the sale of capital assets see p. 195.

Example: Unexcelled Chemical Company, 1960.

A headline in the *Wall Street Journal* reads, "Unexcelled Chemical Profit hit $2.40 per share, up from $1.44." The income account for the two years breaks down as follows:

(000 omitted)

	1960	1959
Sales.................................	$3,597	$7,003
Net before profit on sale of assets......	338 (d)	501
Profit on sale of assets...............	2,338	259
Income tax..........................	630	0
Profit as reported...................	1,370	760
Profit per share, as reported..........	$2.40	$1.44
Profit per share before special items....	*	$0.97†
Price range..........................	28¼–14⅛	20¼–11⅞

* Deficit.
† Note that no tax was paid in 1959 because of prior years' deficits.

Reporting of Per-share Earnings in Financial Press and Services.
The Unexcelled Chemical example illustrates the natural tendency for the press to report per-share earnings as given out by the company in its releases. The financial services will subject the reports to some further scrutiny and endeavor to allow in their calculations for the effect of nonrecurrent or extraordinary items. Yet these, too, tend to reproduce the often misleading per-share figure published by the company and to make their correction or amplification in the form of a footnote.[6]

Example: The Stock Guide, published monthly by Standard & Poor's, reports earnings per share, with variable treatment of special items. The 1959 earnings of Geo. A. Fuller Company, for instance, are given as $5.62 per share, with footnote addition: "Includes spec. credit of $2.54"; while those of Gamble-Skogmo appear as $1.50 in 1960, "excluding special income of $5.69."

It would be a salutary change if the financial services adopted the uniform practice of stating the per-share earnings *before* special items, and presented the effect of the special items in a footnote or other secondary position.

Losses on Foreign Operations. Such losses have frequently arisen through both political and financial (foreign-exchange) disturbances. Many companies with diversified foreign interests set up reserves, usually by charges to income, to absorb possible future losses of this kind. The income account is thus spared if and when the loss arises. We give examples of this procedure in our next chapter on reserves.

[6] However, Moody's *Industrial Manual* for 1961 gives the 1960 per-share earning of Unexcelled Chemical Company as $2.40, with no alternative figure or footnote.

If no reserve has been set up for the purpose, a loss of this kind may be charged either to income or to surplus.

Example 1: Coca-Cola charged to consolidated earned surplus in 1960 the sum of $2,033,000, representing "loss of investment in Cuban assets (net of applicable income tax effect)." About 5 percent of the year's profit was involved.

Example 2: Swift and Company charged its Cuban loss of $2,787,000, net of tax, to income as a special item. This amounted to 15 percent of the net income before the deduction.

The analyst would accept the allocations to income and to surplus shown in the above examples because there is no convincing reason to insist that one treatment rather than the other be followed.

CAPITAL GAINS AND LOSSES OF FINANCIAL OR REAL ESTATE COMPANIES

Financial companies are those whose assets are almost exclusively in the form of cash, receivables, and securities. They include banks, insurance companies, investment companies or funds, holding companies that do not report on a consolidated basis, and credit or finance companies.[7] In all but the latter group, investment in marketable securities is a major or at least a significant part of the business. Gains or losses from the investment portfolio, both realized and unrealized, will usually be of significant size in relation to what is called their ordinary or operating income. Should such changes in portfolio values be viewed as recurrent or nonrecurrent items in the analysis of income accounts of financial companies?

The question does not admit of a categorical answer. These gains and losses are certainly recurrent in the sense that they occur every year in a greater or less amount, and they are without doubt related to the regular business operations. But they are not recurrent in the sense that under "normal operating conditions" the business would be geared to make a certain "normal profit" out of security price movements. By contrast, the interest and dividend income from the securities owned is reasonably stable and predictable.

There seems to be a sharp distinction between realized and unrealized profits or losses. The former are necessarily entered on the books; they have income tax consequences; in the case of most investment funds, realized profits result in corresponding distributions to stockholders.[8] On

---

[7] The customary classification of financial companies—e.g., as comprised in Moody's *Bank & Finance Manual*—includes real estate concerns but excludes the holding-company group.

[8] Under Sects. 851–52 of the 1954 Internal Revenue Code—so-called "regulated investment companies" may reduce or avoid corporate income tax by distributing their regular income and their realized security profits in a prescribed manner.

the other hand, an increase in market value over cost may be recognized only in a footnote to the balance sheet. Whether or not a security profit or loss is "real" until it is realized through sale may be debated. But in the case of financial companies the issue is less important than it appears. The real distinction is between the *over-all long-term results*, which are of major significance, and the more or less fortuitous changes in security values during the single year.

In a single-year analysis the student should group together the realized and unrealized portfolio gain or loss. (This is done in the standard or conventional form of reporting the income account of insurance companies.) The figures for the twelve months should be presented in two parts: (1) ordinary income and (2) portfolio profit or loss. Comparatively little significance will attach to the latter component because it is governed mainly by security-market conditions in the year; but the former may serve as a guide to future projections.

In a long-term analysis the portfolio results must always play a part; for investment funds their significance is usually controlling in determining the relative accomplishment of the management. In former editions we were able to suggest that the period taken for study be one between substantially equal levels of the stock market. For such a span the portfolio profit and loss would properly enter into the analysis on a par with the other components of earning power, and they would provide a measure of the skill of the management in this important part of the operations of a financial company. Such comparisons could have been made between 1924 and 1934; between 1926 and 1940; between 1936 and 1945 (or 1949).

Beginning with 1951, the stock market advanced into new high ground for year-end figures, and comparisons on an "even-Stephen" price-level basis could no longer be made. It is still useful, however, to compare the over-all results of various funds for a five- to ten-year period. But such studies should seek to bring together companies with similar general policies and portfolio compositions. It is obvious, for instance, that an all-stock fund would be expected to show better results during a rising market than would a balanced fund, containing a substantial bond component.

We supply herewith a comparison of two investment funds for the periods 1936–1949 and 1951–1960, and another of two insurance companies for the 1951–1960 span. These may illustrate both a suitable method of procedure and the varying significance of portfolio-value changes for the two types of financial enterprises.[9]

Comment: These calculations are based on reported figures, plus cer-

---

[9] Elaborate analyses of investment-company results, on various bases, are to be found in *Wiesenberger's Investment Companies* and in *Johnson's Investment Company Charts.* The method we employ above is relatively simple, and sufficiently informing for most purposes.

Table 9-1. Performance of Two Investment Funds and a Market Index during Two Periods

A. The thirteen years 1937–1949 inclusive

	Lehman Corporation*	Massachusetts Investors Trust*	Standard & Poor's Composite Index
Asset value:			
December 1949	$ 52.82	$27.67	$16.49
December 1936	45.73	28.87	16.59
Gain in 13 years	$ 7.09	–$ 1.20	–$ 0.10
Capital-gain dividends	14.76†	1.31	
Total capital gains	$ 21.85	$ 0.11	–$ 0.10
Ordinary dividends	18.64	13.51	9.43
Over-all gain	$ 40.49	$13.62	$ 9.33
Percent of 1936 value:			
Total capital gains	47.8%	0.4%	–0.1%
Ordinary dividends	40.7	46.8	56.8
Total gain	88.5%	47.2%	56.7%
(Total distributions)	(71%)	(52%)	(57%)

B. The ten years 1950–1960 inclusive

	Lehman Corporation*	Massachusetts Investors Trust*	Standard & Poor's Composite Index
Asset value:			
December 1960	$108.24	$79.02	$58.11
December 1950	57.70	33.27	20.57
Gain in 10 years	$ 50.54	$45.75	$37.54
Capital-gain dividends	39.35	8.38	—
Total capital gains	$ 89.93	$54.13	$37.54
Ordinary dividends	22.04	22.02	16.51
Over-all gain	$111.97	$76.15	$54.05
Percent of 1950 value:			
Total capital gains	155.9%	162.7%	182.5%
Ordinary dividends	38.2	66.2	80.6
Total gain	194.1%	228.9%	263.1%

Adjustment to equalize total distributions to Standard & Poor's rate

	Lehman Corporation*	Massachusetts Investors Trust*	Standard & Poor's Composite Index
Total distributions	$ 61.39	$30.40	$16.51
Total distribution as percent of 1950 value	107%	91%	81%
Excess over S&P total	26	10	—
Estimated gain on reinvested excess	102‡	115‡	—
Added gain as percent of 1950 value	26	12	—
Adjusted total gain	220	241	263%

* All figures based on 1936 shares.

† Estimated dividends paid out of security profits.

‡ Extra investment is assumed for average of five years and yielding half the 10-year profit rate.

         Analysis of Financial Statements

tain adjustments which we deem desirable. The underwriting results include an equity in increased unearned-premium reserve, discussed later (page 130). The tax allowances assume, in part, an average ordinary rate of 50 percent in the decade. They also deduct a 25 percent tax payable on realization of untaken security profits.

The disparate results of Home and Seaboard are representative of the widely different conditions governing the fire and casualty lines on the one hand and the surety lines on the other during the decade. More than half of the over-all gain of Home Insurance must be attributed to the stockmarket rise; for Seaboard Surety the figure is slightly over 20 percent.

Table 9-2. Two Insurance Companies' Results for Ten Years, 1951–1960,
per Share of Stock Outstanding December 1960

	Home Insurance Company			Seaboard Surety Company		
	Before tax	Related tax	After tax	Before tax	Related tax	After tax
Adjusted underwriting results.................	−$ 5.90	cr. $ 2.95	−$ 2.95	$25.95	$12.98	$12.98
Interest and dividends....	34.32	6.72	27.60	12.65	2.51	10.14
Capital gains:						
Taken...............	8.32	....	....	0.29		
Unrealized............	28.28	....	....	8.43		
Total capital gains...	$36.60	9.15	27.45	$ 8.72		
Total.............	$65.02	$12.92	$52.10	$47.32	$17.67	$29.65

Profits from Real Estate Sales. Public interest in real estate companies has increased in recent years. Their shares have been sought as vehicles of capital gains, and in some cases they have been made to appear more attractive by a policy of paying tax-free "dividends."[10] The analysis and evaluation of their results are complicated by a double ambiguity, relating to (1) the significance of their depreciation charges and (2) the significance of their profits from property sales. We deal with the latter point here, and with the former in our section on "Cash Flow" (page 177).

The current "fair value" of real estate holdings is not ascertainable in

[10] Prior to 1959 shares of real estate companies had proved relatively unpopular in the market, and they tended to sell well below their realizable asset value in terms of the properties owned. This disparity led to the decision in 1958 to liquidate the largest diversified concern of this sort, General Realty and Utilities Company.

the same way as the value of a portfolio of marketable securities. Thus, while the analyst can determine quite accurately what has happened to the asset values behind an investment of an insurance company's shares over a given period, he has no similar comprehensive measure of the asset value of real estate shares. He can, and should, separate the profits on real estate sales from the recurrent earnings realized through rentals. But he is not in a position to state with confidence what the "true earnings" of such an enterprise have been over a period of years, since the relationship between "earnings" and increases in property values—realized and unrealized—must be a cloudy one. In all probability he would have to confess that real estate operations in periods of rising or fluctuating values do not lend themselves to the concept of an established or continuing earning power.

An appropriate way of presenting the results of real estate concerns may be illustrated by the following:

Table 9-3. Results of Two Real Estate Companies

(Dollar figures in thousands)

1951–1960	City Investing Co. (year ends March)		Tishman Realty & Construction Co. (year ends September)	
	Amount	Per share	Amount	Per share
Profit from real estate sales after tax:				
High..............	(1953) $3,600		(1953) $3,810	
Low..............	(1952) 434		(1960) 494	
Average..........	$1,210	$1.06	$2,560	$1.26
Average profits from rentals, etc..............	390	0.34	*200* (d)	−0.10
Total profit........	$1,600	$1.40	$2,360	$1.16
Price range, 1960.......	25–17		22–14½	

The variant statements of per-share earnings of City Investing Company in financial publications illustrate the inherent ambiguity of the capital-gains component of real estate operations.

Table 9-4. Profits per Share As Reported. City Investing Company§

Year	By Moody's		By *Financial World*‡
	*	†	
1960	$0.93	. . . . .	$0.93
1959	0.97	. . . . .	0.97
1958	0.85	$0.22	0.85
1957	0.76	0.29	0.76
1956	1.07	0.30	1.07
1955	1.33	0.28	1.34
1954	1.37	. . . . .	2.43
1953	3.82	. . . . .	6.95
1952	1.01	. . . . .	1.28
1951	. . . . .	. . . . .	1.79

* Including real estate profits.
† Excluding real estate profits.
‡ In 12-year Stock Record, 1949–1960.
§ Adjusted to 1960 shares.

Moody's *Bank & Finance Manuals* show the City Investing profits *before* real estate profits for 1955–1958 as the preferred figure, the larger ones being footnoted. In other years, only the inclusive calculation appears. In the case of Tishman, all the services seem to include its profits on real estate sales in their *only* per-share figures.

CHAPTER TEN

EFFECT OF RESERVES UPON THE
INCOME ACCOUNT

Reserves have played a prominent but not always a helpful part in corporate accounting. In recent years recourse to them has been much reduced, but it is still necessary for the security analyst to understand their use and misuse. They have been set up for a wide variety of purposes. These may be classified under three main headings, viz.: (1) to reduce assets from original book value to some more appropriate figure, (2) to reflect liabilities of a somewhat indefinite character or of uncertain payment date, arising from past events, and (3) to provide for expected or merely possible losses arising from future events.

Reserves appear both in the income account and in the balance sheet. In the former they reflect current allowances or credits; in the latter they show net sums accrued to date. The balance-sheet figures are ordinarily larger than those in the single year's income account; but in their effect on common-stock prices and common-stock values, the income-account figures are likely to be more important. Consequently, most of our treatment of reserves will be found in the present section relating to the earning statements, but there will be cross references to our balance-sheet discussion.

Newer and More Limited Use of the Term "Reserve." The use of reserves in corporate accounts is at present nearing the end of a long transition. Some years ago the American Institute of Certified Public Accountants (AICPA) initiated a campaign to limit the use of the term "reserve" to a relatively narrow area and to abandon many of its former applications in both the income account and the balance sheets.[1]

The Institute's recommendations have largely been put into effect by corporate managements and auditors. We consider this an important change for the better. In former times the widespread use of voluntary

[1] *Accounting Research Bulletin No. 34,* issued by the Institute in October 1948, recommended that the use of the word "reserve" be limited to indicating "that an undivided portion of the assets is being held or retained for general or specific purposes." This would exclude reserves to reduce the value of specific assets and also any "reserve" that can be identified as a liability to creditors.

or discretionary reserves—presumably for the purpose of stabilizing the reported earnings—has served in many cases to obscure the true earning power of corporations, not only for single years but also over long periods of time.

The case against reserves as a whole may be stated in two sentences: Most of the former reserves that were necessary and proper might better have been called something else, e.g., "deduction," "provision," "liability," or "accrual." Most reserves that may properly be called by that name are not necessary, and are likely to create more confusion than enlightenment. There may be a few types of reserve that require a separate place in the balance sheet (as the equivalent of long-term liabilities, not bearing interest); but these may best be viewed as exceptions to a salutary rule.

Recognition should go to Chrysler Corporation for taking the lead in the complete elimination of the use of reserves. At the end of 1944 the balance sheet, in typical fashion, showed four reserve items as liabilities, or quasi-liabilities, aggregating $54 million. Two years later the word "reserve" had disappeared from the report, nor did it show any items equivalent to a reserve in the customary position between Current Liabilities and Stockholder's Investment.[2] To effect this transformation, Chrysler followed three practices, which we consider should be standard in security analysis:

1. So-called "reserves" against specific assets were deducted from such assets. (They were designated as "provision for doubtful accounts" and "accumulated depreciation.")
2. Reserves representing sums expected to be paid out as an expense or as a liability were made part of the Current Liabilities and included in the item "accrued insurance, taxes, and other expenses."
3. Reserves for future contingencies were eliminated by transferring them to the stockholders' investment account, i.e., capital and surplus.[3]

A program of this kind is not as radical as it may seem. It affects reserves against assets only by changing their name and making sure they are deducted directly from the related item. It affects reserves that are true liabilities by designating them as such and by including them preferably in the Current Liability total. But it does cut cleanly in the field of Contingency Reserves—those provisions which managements were fond of setting up in good years to cushion the impact of later adversity. In our view, such reserves do not belong in the accounts proper, but only in glosses or comments that express the management's cautious view of the future.

A Partial List of Frequently Used Reserves. The above ideas, expressed in 1951, have been adopted fairly rapidly since then but far from uni-

---

[2] By contrast, the reports of many insurance companies still show most of their liabilities under the heading of various "Reserves."

[3] The chief reserve of this kind in December 1944 was $40 million for postwar plant rehabilitation. A small part of this was drawn upon in the next two years, before the transfer to surplus.

versally. Since the security analyst will probably have to deal for a long time with reserves of many species, we still deem it advisable to discuss these categories in proper sequence and in some detail. Despite the semantic objection to the term reserve, noted above, we shall apply it for convenience to all the various "provisions," "deductions," etc., that may be called items of the reserve type. These will include any provision for future payments which need not be stated either as a current liability or as a long-term debt.

1. *Valuation Reserves.* The standard reserves to reduce assets are those (*a*) against receivables (for doubtful accounts) and (*b*) against fixed assets (for depreciation and other amortization). Reserves are also used frequently (*c*) to mark down marketable securities to current price, (*d*) to reduce other investments and foreign-exchange holdings to estimated current value or less, and (*e*) to mark down inventories to some figure below both cost and market.

2. *Liability Reserves.* Reserves to reflect liabilities arising from the past include the following types: (*f*) for taxes, when noncurrent or uncertain in amount, (*g*) for renegotiation, (*h*) for pensions, (*i*) for workmen's compensation and other employee benefits, (*j*) for profit sharing or bonus, (*k*) for claims in litigation and similar liabilities.

There are other liability reserves especially important in specific industries, for example: (*l*) in insurance: for losses, unearned premiums, policy reserves; (*m*) in the credit field: against bank loans, mortgage loans, etc., and for unearned finance charges: (*n*) in publishing: for unexpired subscriptions; (*o*) in transportation: for injuries and damages; (*p*) in shipping: for recapture of subsidy; (*q*) in public utilities: for rate adjustments and refunds. (*r*) The account designated General Reserves plays a major role in the analysis of savings-and-loan-association shares.

3. *Reserves against Future Developments.* Reserves to provide for possible future losses—i.e., not actually incurred as yet—include the following: (*s*) for inventory decline, related to (*e*) above; (*t*) plant replacement and similar costs, related to (*b*); (*u*) for proposed plant changes and abandonments; (*v*) for contingencies of various descriptions.

It should be pointed out that reserves against receivables, investments and foreign exchange—(*a*) and (*d*) above—may be in good part against expectable losses rather than those actually incurred or clearly indicated.

GENERAL RULES FOR TREATMENT OF RESERVE ITEMS

Reserves will appear on the balance sheet either explicitly or by reference. They are provided by charges to (1) the income account, (2) some surplus account, or (3) the capital account. The last has been rare except in public utilities. The significance of reserves in income-account analysis varies greatly with the type and size of the item. We recommend the following three rules for treating reserves, corresponding to the rules given above for noncurrent items (page 112):

1. Small items should be accepted as they appear. (We have defined "small" as affecting the final result by less than 10 percent in the aggregate.)

2. Reserve appropriations *allowed for income tax purposes* should be considered ordinary deductions from current income, unless they relate clearly to a nonrecurrent item or have some other special characteristic.[4]

3. Reserve appropriations *not* allowed for income tax purposes should ordinarily be excluded from—i.e., added back to—the income account.

The following comments and examples may elucidate the application of these three rules to actual analysis. They are keyed to the letters utilized on page 123, but they do not exhaust the list. However, reserves relating to depreciation and to inventory accounting—items (*b*), (*e*), (*s*), and (*t*) above—are of such importance and complexity that we shall deal with them separately in the following three chapters, as also with contingency reserves (*v*).

a. Reserves for Bad Debts, Uncollectible Accounts, and Collection Expenses. These are nearly always accepted as stated. They are tax-deductible if properly computed.[5] For companies doing an installment selling or a lending business, this item is of importance and may require special scrutiny.

c. Reserves for Marketable Securities. The reserves here provided are not tax-deductible until losses are actually realized (except for security dealers). Many companies reflect price declines on securities owned by adding a parenthetical note or footnote in their statements instead of setting up a formal reserve. Examples of such reserves would be rare in 1961, except among commercial banks.

For nonfinancial companies, such reserves should be regarded as nonrecurrent, but they are rarely important enough to require adjustment of the income account. In the analysis of *financial companies* it does not seem practicable to distinguish between unrealized depreciation (or "quotational losses") on portfolio securities and losses actually taken. We have discussed on page 115 above the inherent difficulties of properly evaluating this important area in the results of banks, insurance companies, and investment funds.

d. Reserves against Other Investments. These generally apply to subsidiary or affiliated companies. In the case of holdings valued in foreign

---

[4] Examples of the latter are (*a*) reserves for accelerated amortization at the 20 percent rate; (*b*) reserves against intangible drilling costs at the 100 percent rate; (*c*) general reserves of savings and loan companies. All of these are discussed later.

[5] In 1947 and subsequent years, commercial banks were permitted to build up a reserve against loans by deductions from taxable income in accordance with a "United States Treasury formula." In their reports to stockholders, many banks showed only the tax savings as a charge against current income, and they created the balance of the required reserves by a transfer from various reserves previously set up on the books.

For example, Chase National Bank of New York in 1949 increased its bad-debt reserve by $8 million, of which $3 million was charged to income.

exchange, it is usually difficult to distinguish between a reserve for a current shrinkage and one for possible future shrinkage.

Example: Firestone Tire & Rubber Company showed $19,866,000 as "reserve for foreign investments" in its 1959 balance sheet. This had been provided by various charges to income over the years. In the 1960 fiscal year the company used $3,306,000 of this reserve to write off its investment in Cuba and $1,821,000 to reduce the value of other foreign assets. These losses were therefore not reflected in the income account for 1960.

f. Tax Reserve; g. Renegotiation Reserve. The ordinary provision for income tax should be regarded as a current liability. It is usually carried as such but is sometimes designated as a "reserve for income tax." During the periods of the excess-profits tax, 1941–1946 and 1950–1953, the amount of the tax liability was often quite uncertain, partly because of controversial aspects of the credit allowed against income (measured by prewar earnings or by invested capital) and partly because of doubt as to the amount of the current year's earnings after renegotiation.[6] The result was that allowance was frequently made for renegotiation and taxes combined, and generally in round amounts. There are many examples of both overestimates and underestimates of these two reserves and of others connected therewith.

Example 1: Republic Aviation Corporation.

Year	Earnings as first reported	Earnings as later adjusted for renegotiation settlements
1943	$3,026,000*	$2,176,000
1944	3,691,000†	2,348,000

* After contingency- and operating-reserve deductions of $2,844,000.
† After contingency-reserve deduction of $1,450,000.

Example 2: Curtiss-Wright Corporation. During 1941–1945 this company reported net income of $90.6 million after provision for taxes renegotiation and various contingencies. However, during 1946–1949 it credited surplus with a total of $52.7 million, representing reductions in such reserves, as follows: (1) for taxes, $17.5 million; (2) for war contingencies, $18.4 million; (3) for service guarantees, $16.8 million.

Example 3: Boeing (Airplane) Company, in 1956–1959, provided by

[6] Renegotiation is the process by which the profits realized on war contracts, if found excessive, can be reduced to a reasonable figure and a refund made to the government. The original renegotiation machinery was under the direction of the War Contracts Price Adjustment Board, which also handled "repricing" of contracts prior to their completion. Renegotiation expired in 1945, but it was revived in 1948 and now applies to all negotiated military contracts.

charges to surplus for results of renegotiation covering past years. In 1958, for example, it charged $2,750,000 to provide for a $6,000,000 renegotiation in 1955, less taxes. This would have reduced the 1955 profits by about 9 percent. The failure of the company to provide a reserve for renegotiation reflected its contention that no refund was due; the consequence was a rather minor overstatement of earnings for the post-Korea period.

This topic will be discussed again, from a somewhat different approach, in our chapter on the reconcilement of the tax deduction and the reported income (Chapter 15).

For most companies engaged importantly in war work the actual earnings for 1941–1946 could be calculated only retrospectively, in the light of subsequent adjustments, and by comparison of the balance sheets rather than of the income statements. This technique, which is the only one proper for every long-term study of earnings, is explained in Chapter 16 below, page 221.

h. Pension Reserves and Provisions. Liability for pensions has become an increasingly important factor in corporate accounts. The terms of settlement of the steel strike of 1948 established, for the benefit of all eligible workers, a general pattern of pensions which will supplement those to be received under social security. Prior to 1949, pension plans were already in effect in a large but minority portion of listed companies.

The financial arrangement for the typical pension scheme has two sections. One provides for "current service" and takes care of the liability accruing year by year, by reason of services performed subsequent to the adoption of the plan. The cost of this provision is obviously a current charge against income, as an additional expense for wages and salaries. The other section of the pension plan relates to liability for "past services," i.e., to rights to pension that have accrued by the terms of the plan but prior to its initiation. Such liabilities can be very large.

Example: U.S. Steel. A calculation was made by United States Steel Corporation in its proxy material for the special meeting of stockholders held in February 1950 to ratify the pension agreement with the union. This showed a total liability for past service of no less than $677 million, of which $103 million had already been provided by trusteed funds and $574 million was unfunded. Thus the new plan resulted in an additional cost or liability for past service alone of over $20 per share of stock, as against a stated equity of $64 per share at the end of 1949 and an average market price in that year of 23½. (These figures relate to the 1949 shares.)[7]

United States Treasury regulations covering the tax-deductibility of allowances for past services provide that the maximum annual charge

[7] Similarly, Endicott Johnson calculated its liability for past-service pensions at the end of 1946 at $20 million, which compared with a stated equity for the common of $52 million.

against taxable income shall be 10 percent of the calculated lump-sum liability. As a minimum, the company must provide and deduct the annual interest requirements on the lump-sum liability. In its proxy statement referred to above, U.S. Steel calculated the annual cost for past service on the minimum basis (plus $5 million for retired employees), which amounted to only $12½ million. This amounted to about 40 cents per share after tax credit. On a 10-year basis of amortization it would have been about four times as much.

Between 1950 and 1957 U.S. Steel charged earnings with almost a flat annual rate of $37,000,000 for past-service pension liability, thus amortizing it on about a 15-year basis. But in the business recession of 1958 the company not only made no provision for past services but even reversed as much as $61,000,000 of its accumulated provision and *credited* this amount to current income. In 1959 and 1960 no debit or credit was made to income for past-service account. (In the meantime the charge for "current services" had grown from $59,600,000 in 1951 to $104,600,000 in 1959.)

These variations in the past-service provision have functioned somewhat as the equivalent of an old-fashioned contingency reserve and have reduced the fluctuations in reported net income between good years and bad. A similar consequence results from the gearing of the depreciation allowance to the rate of operations. Finally, there was a fortuitous reduction of charges to earnings in the poorer years caused by the rapid running out of the 20 percent accelerated amortization of defense facilities.[8] The results of this threefold variation in charges against U.S. Steel's earnings may be observed from the following summary table covering the years 1955, 1957, 1958, and 1960:

Table 10-1. U.S. Steel Corporation

(Dollar figures in millions)

	1955	1957	1958	1960
Net for common stock before following deductions:...............................	$666.1	$708.2	$420.3	$487.4
Past-service pensions......................	36.0	38.0	cr 61.0*	......
Amortization of defense facilities..........	147.7	115.8	57.2	13.8
Other depreciation and depletion..........	137.5	160.2	147.7	194.6
Total of deductions....................	$321.2	$314.0	$143.9	$208.4
Net for common as reported..............	$344.9	$394.2	$276.4	$279.0
Earned per share.........................	$ 6.01	$ 7.33	$ 5.13	$ 5.16
Ratio of depreciation to gross plant (Moody's Manual)†...............................	6.35%	5.37%	3.74%	3.40%

* Added back to income.

† For similar reasons this ratio for Youngstown Steel dropped from 7.00 percent to 3.02 percent in 1958.

[8] These last two items are discussed in the next chapter.

There was a reduction in excess of $170,000,000 between 1957 and 1958 in the three deductions listed above. After tax allowance this came to about $1.50 per share. On the same basis as 1957 (or 1955) the 1958 earnings would have been only $3.60 a share rather than the reported $5.13. A similar calculation, comparing the 1960 with the 1955 reports, shows that the variations in the three types of deductions helped the 1960 earnings, net, by about $1 per share. From the standpoint of approved accounting methods, the variations in the pension appropriations may perhaps be criticized as essentially arbitrary and aimed at equalizing earnings.[9]

Other Methods of Dealing with Past-service Liability. A number of companies have charged the cost of past-service annuities in a lump sum to surplus. In most such cases the amount was not large enough to make any real difference in annual earnings per share if it had been amortized over, say, ten years against earnings.[10]

A different and more satisfactory treatment of the matter was shown by General Cable Corporation in 1949. In that year it paid out $2,013,000 to cover its past-service obligation in full. It charged 10 percent of this sum, or $201,000, to income and carried forward the balance of $1,812,000 as an asset under the title of Prepaid Expense and Deferred Charges, to be written off in the next nine years. Thus, despite the lump-sum payment, its reports to stockholders and its tax returns were on this point in agreement.

Effect of Liability for Past Service. The broad question for the analyst is whether payments for the account of past services under a pension plan should be considered (1) a discharge of a past obligation, (2) a nonrecurrent charge against earnings, or (3) an ordinary operating expense. We might pause for a moment to reflect on the practical significance of each of these choices.

If liability for past service is considered a fixed obligation as at the date of the plan's adoption, the result will be paradoxical. The asset or balance-sheet value of the common stock will be reduced, often by a substantial percentage as in our Endicott Johnson and U.S. Steel examples. On the other hand, there would then be either no charge against current earnings as this liability is discharged, or perhaps only an interest charge, if the obligation is computed on a discounted or present-value basis.

---

[9] "An important objective of income presentation should be the avoidance of any practice that leads to the equalization of income." *Restatement and Revision of Accounting Research Bulletins,* issued by the American Institute of Certified Public Accountants (AICPA), 1953, p. 59. The other variations in amortization charges are not open to this objection, since they result from admissible methods consistently applied.

[10] Note, however, that when Union Carbide charged off $2,919,000 for this purpose against surplus in 1945—an excess-profits-tax-year—it took the resulting tax saving of $2,423,000 as a credit to income. This would require correction by the analyst.

Hence, if the value of the company or of its common stock were to be calculated exclusively by capitalizing current or future earning power— as is done so often in Wall Street—then setting up the large pension liability at once will actually result in a higher valuation than would the alternative of charging the annual installments against income.

The effect of treating the annual payments as a nonrecurrent charge will also be contradictory. This would mean that they will be ignored in calculating the "true earnings" for a single year but will be deducted from the long-term results. But obviously, any *regular* charge that figures in the long-term analysis should also be deducted in a single year's analysis. For otherwise the result would be simply to create an unnecessary difference between the successive short-term and the long-term results. (It is only the irregular nature of large nonrecurrent items that makes it preferable to exclude them from a single-year analysis.)

Both practical and logical reasoning suggest that the annual pension payments on account of past service be included as an ordinary charge against income, provided each amount is not more than, say, one-tenth of the total liability. Such payments are allowed as annual deductions for tax purposes. They are not so much the result of happenings in the distant past as of a voluntary or union-enforced decision to pay out sums in the future. They will represent actual and regular cash disbursements over a period of years, not offset by additional assets for the company. Thus they come much closer to being an ordinary and current expense than the discharge of a past debt—such as, for example, the paying off of a serial bond issue.[11]

A Basic Anomaly in Security Analysis. The attention of the reflective student is called to the contrast between the burden of past-service costs viewed as a *principal amount* and the same burden viewed as an annual charge against earnings. The U.S. Steel figures quoted above express this contrast vividly. If fully stated in the balance sheet, the past-service liability would have reduced the stockholders' 1949 equity by about one-third. But stated as an *annual* cost, on the minimum basis used by the company, it reduced the 1949 earnings per share of common stock from $5.40 to $5, or less than 8 percent. Furthermore, such annual cost, before tax credit, amounted to less than 1 percent of the 1949 sales.

A little thought will show a close analogy between this situation and the broader question of *corporations' liability for their share of the Federal debt.* On the basis of their contribution to total tax revenues, American corporations may be said to be liable for, and carrying, at least 30 percent of the national debt, i.e., about $85 billion of principal liability in 1960. If this item were entered on each corporate balance sheet with some equitable apportionment among companies, it would cancel out a quarter of the total equity shown for common stockholders

[11] An estimate of future earnings may include some years following termination of the annual past-service charge, thus increasing the reported profits.

by companies paying income taxes in 1958. (This equity was $305 billion, the income before tax $43.7 billion, the tax liability $18.8 billion.) Yet the annual interest burden on this enormous debt amounted to some $2.2 billion, or about 5 percent of the aggregate earnings before tax of companies with net income.

1. **Reserves of Insurance Companies.** In the fire and casualty insurance business, damage claims—both those litigated and those settled peaceably—are a basic part of the operations. The results for any year and the equity shown for the stockholders will depend in large measure on the method followed in computing reserves for unsettled and unreported losses. The regulatory bodies require that specific formulas be followed in settling up the minimum reserves for personal injury claims in automobile insurance and for workmen's compensation claims. (If the company's own estimate, on a "case basis," indicates a larger liability, that figure must be used instead.) Liability under other types of claims is a matter for management to determine, subject to a triennial or quadrennial check by insurance-commission examiners. There is room for a considerable degree of either overestimation or underestimation in this field.[12]

The reserves for unearned premiums also play a major role in the accounting of insurance companies. In this area there is a conflict of accounting treatment which has given rise to much confusion among insurance-company investors and has undoubtedly served at times to depress unduly the price of their shares. There is also some needless confusion and inaccuracy in the treatment of this item by financial agencies analyzing insurance-company statements.

Unearned-premium Liability Overstated. The unearned-premium reserve represents that part of premiums received which is applicable to the unexpired portion of the policies. Under the standard accounting prescribed by the state insurance commissioners, the full amount of unearned premiums must be shown as a liability. There are, however, two different reasons for concluding that the true liability is considerably less than that required to be shown. In the first place, on the basis of many years' experience, it is known that the losses will run only between one-half and two-thirds of the premiums received, so that there is always a very considerable equity later realized from the reserve. This equity can usually be turned into cash immediately, if the company so desires, by the process of reinsurance, under which another company assumes the risk upon payment to it of about 60 or 65 percent of the unexpired premium.

Second, the chief reason the stockholders have so large an equity in the unearned-premium reserve is that the company has paid out a considerable amount of acquisition expense—mainly in the form of agents'

---

[12] This question formed the nub of a controversy over the solvency of Rhode Island Insurance Company in 1949–50, which ended by placing the company in receivership. In the life insurance field the so-called "policy reserves" involve more intricate computations. They are a matter for actuarial analysis rather than security analysis.

commissions—in order to put the business on the books. In ordinary accounting, such costs paid in advance would be entered as an asset under the title Prepaid Expense. In fact, they would be directly analogous to the unearned premiums themselves, which are a similar asset to a business which has paid them.

Varying Treatment of Unearned-premium Reserves. As we have already stated, the official reports of insurance companies include *no* prepaid expense or other credit to offset part of the liability for unearned premiums. Nor are the financial statements to stockholders presented on different accounting bases. But in the management's comments in the body of the report, in prospectuses and registration statements, and in analyses of the results by financial services, it is now the custom to adjust the official figures to reflect an equity in the unearned premiums. This has been done in a variety of ways:

1. For a great many years the services credited earnings with 40 percent of the increase in the reserve of five insurance companies and 35 percent of that of casualty companies. (Nearly all such companies now operate in both fields.)

2. After 1956 Moody's *Bank & Finance Manual* changed from the flat-credit basis to a credit equivalent to the ratio of each company's over-all expenses (excluding losses and loss expense) to premiums written.[13] The theory is that this percentage represents the approximate cost of putting additional business on the books. It still runs at about 40 percent for most agency companies but is considerably less for the direct writers. However, this addition to earnings makes no allowance for the tax already saved on the prepaid expense—a fact reflected only in the services' footnotes.

3. A more conservative method, which we have favored as consistent with sound accounting generally, is to take credit for the prepaid expense at the over-all rate, but to reduce this by 50 percent to reflect the tax benefit already received. (An exception could be made, of course, for companies operating at a loss even with the prepaid-expense credit.)

Calculations in a Recent Prospectus. The prospectus of Hanover Insurance Company, dated July 1961, makes adjustments of its official earnings substantially in accordance with our recommended method. The equity in unearned premiums is calculated at rates related to the expense and loss experience of two merged companies, and works out at about 30 percent over-all. Allowance is then made for the tax effect of this addition to profits. The figures are complicated by a simultaneous adjustment to exclude gains and losses on security sales and by a loss carry-forward during the period covered. In the year 1956 the earnings are shown as increased from $1.22 to $1.98 per share, entirely because of the unearned-premium equity.[14]

---

[13] *Best's Insurance Reports* have apparently done the same in most cases.

[14] In 1960 they were reduced from $3.83 to $2.55, chiefly through elimination of security profits.

m. Reserve for Unearned Finance Charges. The accounting for finance charges "paid" by the borrower in advance—by having them added to his debt—is essentially identical with that for insurance premiums paid on issuance of the policy. A reserve is set up for that portion of the finance charges that have not yet been earned by the passage of time. The amount is properly deductible from the receivables themselves on the asset side, along with the bad-debt reserve.

Undoubtedly the stockholders have some sort of equity in these unearned finance charges, since they should offset certain expenses incurred in putting the business on the books, as do the unearned-premium reserves. It is not customary to allow for such an equity in any official calculation of earnings or net worth. However, as illustrated below, in one way or another some finance companies are now endeavoring to relieve earnings of part of the cost of acquiring and developing business.

Example 1: In 1960 Standard Financial Company credited income with $199,000, representing a portion of the year's finance charge, for the purpose of offsetting acquisition costs. This procedure increased the per-share earnings by about 20 percent.

Example 2: See our discussion of Seaboard Finance Company's "deferred-development cost" (below, Chapter 12). This had a substantial effect on the reported earnings.

n. Reserve for Unexpired Subscriptions. The liability of newspaper and magazine publishers for unexpired subscriptions is also of the same nature as that for unearned premiums. It is usually of important size and undoubtedly includes an equity component for the shareholders.

Example: Curtis Publishing Company showed on its 1960 balance sheet an intermediate liability of $49,000,000 for "advance payment on subscriptions." This amount was about $1\frac{1}{2}$ times the common stockholders' equity.

q. Reserve for Rate Adjustments. Public utility companies have frequently been subject to regulatory proceedings looking to a reduction in their rates and charges. In some cases such reductions, if ordered, will be retroactive. In recent years proceedings of this type have been initiated against a number of natural gas pipe-line companies. Some of the companies have set up reserves against current earnings for refunds that may later be ordered; others have not.

Example 1: Peoples Gas, Light and Coke Company reserved $5.3 million in its June 1961 year, out of net income of $31.7 million, for "possible rate readjustments" that may be ordered against its subsidiary pipeline company. This reserve reduced earnings by one-sixth. A reserve of similar magnitude was set up in the previous year. (The analyst would accept these reserves as a proper reduction from earnings.)

Example 2: In contrast to the foregoing, Texas Eastern Transmission Company set up no similar reserves in 1959–1960, and charged refunds, when ordered, against surplus instead of income, or against previous year's income on a restated basis. In consequence the company reported average earnings for the two years of $2.05 per share, against an actual or corrected figure of $1.25.

Comment: The analyst should pay serious attention to charges of this magnitude, which are kept out of the current-income account and the current reported per-share earnings. These refunds, together with other divergences not presently revelant, apparently caused the disappearance for income tax purposes of both Texas Eastern's current earnings and its large accumulated book surplus in 1961, so that some of that year's dividends were stated to be tax-free to the stockholders. Ironically, these combined developments seemed to make the shares more rather than less attractive to "investors," because of the lure of "tax-free" dividends.

r. General Reserves of Savings and Loan Associations. The shares of these associations or of holding companies therefore have become popular investment or speculative media in recent years. The industry has been of growing importance in the field of mortgage loans, mainly to owners of residential property. Virtually all the funds so used have been obtained in the form of savings accounts from the general public. These pay an attractive rate of interest and are guaranteed—up to $10,000 per account—against ultimate loss by the Federal Savings and Loan Insurance Corporation, an instrumentality of the United States government.

It is in the income and balance-sheet accounting of these companies that the analysis and interpretation of *reserves* becomes of overshadowing importance. These companies are both required and permitted by Federal and state regulations to set up substantial reserves by annual tax-deductible charges against net profits. These are designated as General Reserves in the companies' reports. Their purpose is to create "a Federal insurance reserve which, once established, is available only to cover possible losses on loans."[15] They may thus be considered at the same time as a "valuation reserve" against the concerns' principal liabilities. On the mandatory side, the reserve must be added to each year until it reaches 5 percent of the aggregate insured accounts; thereafter this 5 percent must be maintained on the new totals, and a minimum of 10 percent of net earnings before interest on savings accounts must be appropriated to the reserve. On the permissive side, the tax-deductible feature applies to whatever reserves are so set aside, until surplus, undivided profits, general reserves, and capital stock equals 12 percent of the insured accounts.

The effect of these provisions has been to eliminate nearly all the taxable income of these companies through "appropriations to general reserves." Nonetheless, these general reserves are bracketed in the balance sheets with the stockholders' equity; the "book value per share" is calculated in the statements with full inclusion of the reserves; most

---

[15] Quoted from the 1960 Annual Report of TransWorld Financial Company, Note 8, p. 19.

importantly, earnings per share are calculated in the reports to stock-holders before transfers to general reserves. These reserves are also con-sidered part of the tangible equity of companies acquired by purchase.

In sum, the additions to reserves are considered to form part of the earnings and accumulated capital in the companies' statements, but for tax purposes they constitute allowances for bad debts and offsets against the loans-receivable account. What is their true nature—or, at least, how may they be treated most intelligently by the security analyst?

Let us consider various possible approaches to the problem.

Approach 1: Assume the companies' treatment of the general reserves is correct, and that to all intents and purposes they form part of the earnings and equity. We think that there are at least three serious ob-jections to this viewpoint—which is the one that appears to have governed the market's attitude toward savings-and-loan-company shares.

a. The general reserve is designated in the Internal Revenue Code as a "bad-debt reserve." Some part of the amounts set aside for this purpose is undoubtedly needed by the nature of the business, which is by no means free from actual and possible losses on mortgage loans. To the extent that the re-serve is so needed it should not be regarded as the equivalent of profits. In an important respect, therefore, the general reserves differ from ordinary earnings and stockholders' equity.

b. The general reserves cannot be used for the payment of cash dividends.[16]

c. To the extent that these reserves are not clearly needed to provide for future bad debts, they constitute a tax advantage accorded to these companies and not to other mortgage lenders. As such, they have been under strong attack by commercial banks and the United States Treasury, which complains that this prosperous industry pays virtually no income tax. The possibility of a change in the favorable tax status of these shares must be taken seriously into account.

Approach 2: Apply the general rule suggested above (page 124) that reserves against receivables permitted by the tax law be con-sidered proper deductions from income. On this basis the industry would have virtually no "real earnings," just as it has virtually no tax-able earnings. This is obviously an attitude too drastic for the analyst to take under the circumstances, since the annual appropriations to re-serves have been much larger than ordinary provisions for bad debts.

Approach 3: The analyst would make his own calculation of an ap-propriate reserve for losses and his own allowance for the special tax status of the remaining deduction permitted under present (1961) law. This might be done as follows:

a. Assume that an appropriate bad-debt allowance would be 10 percent of the net income before deducting interest paid on savings accounts. This is the

---

[16] Some companies—e.g., Great Western Financial Corporation—charge *stock divi-dends* paid to this reserve, others to the combined equity and reserve account on the balance sheet. This seems essentially a matter of bookkeeping.

provision that will have to be made in later years, under the regulations of the Federal Savings and Loan Insurance Corporation.

b. Assume that the remainder of the earnings now transferred to the general reserve occupy an intermediate position between tax-free and fully taxable profits—i.e., subject them to a theoretical deferred-tax liability at the rate of 25 percent.

The effect of such treatment of the 1960 results of two California savings and loan associations would be as follows:

Table 10-2

(000 omitted)

	Trans World Financial	Financial Federation, Inc.
As reported:		
Net before interest	$4,791	$14,500
Interest paid	3,535	9,615
Income tax	13	91
Earnings before general reserves	1,243	4,794
Transferred to general reserves	1,272	4,481
As adjusted by the analyst:		
Net before interest	$4,791	$14,500
Bad-debt reserve—10 percent	479	1,450
Interest paid	3,535	9,615
Balance for general reserve and deferred income tax	778	3,435
Deferred income tax—25 percent	194	859
Adjusted net income	584	2,576
Number of shares outstanding	1,354	1,262
Earned per share:		
As published	$0.95	$3.80
As adjusted	0.43	2.02
Price range—1961	10–47	57–164*

* Before 5-for-4 split in 1962.

The treatment of general reserves suggested above would reduce the calculated earnings of the two savings and loan companies by about one-half; in fact, the result is about equivalent to deducting the full 52 percent corporate income tax, with no separate provision for bad-debt reserve.

The subject has been treated at some length in order to provide an adequate illustration of the independent procedures sometimes demanded of the analyst in his dealing with reported earnings. The reader is free, of course, to substitute some other method of revision which he deems more suitable to the facts. But that the earnings of this group as published must be revised, we think admits of little argument.

u. Reserve for Plant Changes and Abandonments. An item of this kind is involved in some rather spectacular entries appearing in the 1959 annual report of Armour & Company. In that year the directors determined on a policy of major rearrangement of facilities and heroically made provision for losses and shrinkages involving no less than $71,000,000 before taxes and $43,800,000 after tax savings. This huge sum breaks down into three parts, as follows:

1. A provision of $12,900,000 to write down the net value of certain facilities to their Federal-tax basis. This was apparently done by increasing the depreciation reserve and carried no tax offset.

2. A loss of $28,800,000 actually taken in 1959, arising from disposition of facilities, separation payments, etc. The tax saving of $13,300,000 against this loss was deducted from ordinary income, as an income tax equivalent, and the balance of $15,500,000 formed part of the "special item," charged at the end of the income account.

3. The company set up a reserve of $15,300,000, after tax credit of $14,-900,000, for anticipated charges in connection with "replacement and relocation of facilities." About $2,200,000 of this reserve appeared on the liability side to take care of the expense component, and the remaining $13,100,000—representing expected net loss on property sales—was deducted from the fixed-asset account. In the next year about one-third of each reserve was drawn upon to absorb realized expenses and losses.

The net cost of $43,800,000 for this program appeared at the end of the 1959 income account as a "Special item." The year's results may be summarized as follows:

(000 omitted)

Net earnings before taxes	$27,151
Income-tax provision (none actually paid)	13,085
Net income after tax	14,066
Per share of common	$2.73
"Special item"	*dr.* 43,787
Net income and special item	*dr.* 29,721

It is interesting to observe that the financial services ignored the large "special item" altogether and reported Armour's 1959 earnings as $2.73 per share, unamplified. Nor did the extraordinary loss prevent the shares from rising from 12 in 1958 to 37 in 1959 and to 54 in 1961.

If the Armour developments of 1959 are compared with the opposite phenomenon of Unexcelled Chemical in the next year (page 114) we are inclined to think that together they throw some light on the strongly optimistic bias of the contemporary market. Unexcelled had an operating loss, coupled with a large profit on the sale of a subsidiary or division. In this instance, the market treated the "special item" as the equivalent of ordinary earnings. But it took the contrary course in the case of Armour by completely ignoring the heavy loss involved in its "special item." Apparently the emphasis was placed on Armour's prospects of bettering its profit margin as a result to the drastic changes, and on the skill of the Unexcelled management in buying and selling businesses at a profit. In more conservative times the exhibit of neither company for the years in question would have been greeted with enthusiasm.

CHAPTER ELEVEN

INVENTORY VALUATIONS AND INVENTORY
RESERVES. CONTINGENCY RESERVES

From the standpoint of security analysis the problems of inventory accounting and of depreciation accounting bear a generic relationship to each other. Both may have an important bearing on the reported earnings, and in both cases the amounts are determined in accordance with principles and theories rather than as the simple result of cash or credit transactions during the year under review. Let us discuss them together briefly, before concentrating in this chapter on the inventory question.

Methods of Valuing Inventories and Calculating Depreciation. The standard method of valuing merchandise inventory is to carry it "at cost or market, whichever is lower." The standard method of calculating depreciation (and other amortization) is to write down each depreciable item from cost to salvage value by regular charges against income extending over its expected life. Until recently the chief job of the security analyst in these fields has been to make sure that the standard accounting practices were followed in the corporate reports he examined. The departures he found were generally in the direction of overstatement of income, e.g., by failure to mark down inventory to market or by omitting or skimping the depreciation charge. More rarely, the income and assets were understated by an overconservative policy in valuing inventory or figuring depreciation and amortization.

Since the end of World War II the questions of inventory valuation and depreciation policy have taken a somewhat different complexion. Many corporate managements have felt that the standard accounting practice was not well suited to a protracted period of rising prices. On the one hand, profits were increased by a nonrecurrent and probably illusory gain arising from the marking up of inventory values to their ever-higher replacement levels. On the other hand, they claimed that the tax-allowed depreciation, based on cost, was becoming grossly inadequate to provide for the replacement of worn-out facilities at these same higher levels. Many companies changed their accounting practices in order to minimize the impact of inflationary forces upon the income

137

account. The issues involved here have implications beyond the area of accurate reporting to the stockholders. They have led to a vigorous demand for the right to charge higher depreciation against earnings for tax purposes; they have also figured prominently in labor disputes where the "real" profits of business and its consequent "ability to pay" have been in controversy.

It should be added that, although price-level changes had a marked effect on inventory valuations and corporate profits in the immediate postwar years and in 1950 and to a less degree in 1956, the influence on the decade has been rather small. This is shown by the following summary:

Table 11-1

	All nonfinancial corporations		
	Profits before taxes (in billions)	Inventory mark-up included (in billions)	Ratio
Average 1946–1949.........	$25.9	$2.9	11.2%
Average 1950–1954.........	34.7	1.3	3.7
Average 1955–1959.........	38.7	1.3	3.4
1960....................	38.9	0	0

However, the stock market's apparent expectation of substantial inflation in the coming years suggests that the subject is still of considerable importance.

Security Analyst's Approach to the Question. The security analyst is interested in these matters from two practical standpoints. First, he must make up his mind as to what treatment of inventory and depreciation will supply the most helpful approach to calculating the "normal" earning power and—less importantly—the actual asset values. Secondly, to the extent possible, he must develop means of placing all companies in a given industrial group on the same accounting basis, as regards inventories and depreciation, to permit a proper comparative analysis.[1]

[1] Some indication of the intensity of intellectual ferment concerning the effects of changes in the purchasing power of money upon the "accuracy" and usefulness of financial statements may be gained by a search of the issues since 1947 of the following accounting journals: the *Journal of Accountancy*, the *Accounting Review*, the *NAA Bulletin*, the *Accountant*, and the *New York Certified Public Accountant*. Literally scores of articles appeared in these journals during that period, discussing the valuation of inventories and fixed assets as well as the related problems of amortization charges and reserves. The list is far too long to cite in detail here. For example, the *NAA Bulletin*, August 1961 (section 1), has four articles dealing with "accounting during inflation." We suggest that the interested student check the *Business Periodicals* or some comparable index for articles on this subject.

INVENTORY CALCULATION

"FIFO" and "LIFO." The two most important ways of calculating inventory values are known as "first-in, first-out" (FIFO) and "last-in, first-out" (LIFO). FIFO represents the formerly standard "lower of cost or market" method. LIFO inventories must always be carried at cost, but cost is calculated on a basis different from that used in FIFO. There are some additional and less usual methods of figuring inventory values.

Difference between "FIFO" and "LIFO." The basic difference between FIFO and LIFO is generally illustrated by a company's coal pile. If the coal bought is piled on top and the coal used is taken from the bottom, we have a typical case of first-in, first-out. The old coal is used up first, and the stock remaining would naturally be valued on the basis of the most recent purchases. But if we assume that the coal used is taken off the top, we should then have the typical last-in, first-out situation. The coal on hand at the inventory date would represent some old or original purchase, and it could be valued at an unchanging price from year to year.

It is evident that during a period of sharply rising prices, the effect of FIFO is to mark up inventories to about current replacement cost. Hence computed earnings are increased by a special profit arising from the sale of older and cheaper materials at advancing quotations. Under the same circumstances the LIFO method will hold down the carrying value of a given quantity of inventory to its original low level and thus exclude year-to-year inventory profits from the reported earnings.

The first-in, first-out method was almost universal before the recent inflation, for the reason that it corresponded to the actualities of business. In continuous production or mechandising, the older goods are normally sold first, if at all possible, so that those remaining on hand may be fresh and up to date. The newer LIFO idea is thus in reality a somewhat artificial concept, which recommends itself, however, because of its stabilizing effect upon corporate results. Beyond this, it has the support of economic theory. For in calculations of national income—such as those now elaborately developed by the Department of Commerce—it is settled practice to exclude gains or losses from "inventory valuation," as unrelated to the actual production and distribution of goods. Finally, the LIFO method is a permitted method of accounting, subject to certain limitations, under the Internal Revenue Code (the tax law).

The difference between the FIFO (formerly the "standard") and the LIFO methods of computing cost of goods sold and inventory on hand can be illustrated by the following simplified and hypothetical example (Table 11-2): A company starts with 10 million pounds of copper, buys 10 million pounds each year for three years, and sells the same amount each year at a 2-cent advance above current cost price. The initial cost is 10 cents; the average and closing cost price is 15 cents the first year, 20

Table 11-2

	First year		Second year		Third year	
First-in, first-out method						
Proceeds of goods sold		$1,700,000		$2,200,000		$1,200,000
Cost of goods sold:						
Opening inventory	$1,000,000		$1,500,000		$2,000,000	
Purchases	1,500,000		2,000,000		1,000,000	
Totals	$2,500,000		$3,500,000		$3,000,000	
Less closing inventory (lower of cost or market)	1,500,000	1,000,000	2,000,000	1,500,000	1,000,000	2,000,000
Gross profit		$ 700,000		$ 700,000		–$ 800,000
Last-in, first-out method						
Proceeds of goods sold		$1,700,000		$2,200,000		$1,200,000
Cost of goods sold (same as purchases during year)		1,500,000		2,000,000		1,000,000
Gross profit		$ 200,000		$ 200,000		$ 200,000
Closing inventory		1,000,000		1,000,000		1,000,000

cents the second year, and 10 cents the third year. We assume that the company has no operating expenses.

Obviously the company ends up where it started in inventory and has made a continuous profit of 2 cents per pound. Common sense would insist that the company has made $200,000 each year. But the standard or FIFO method of accounting would show a profit of $700,000 in the first year, the same in the second year, and a loss of $800,000 in the third year. Under the tax law prior to 1939, when no carry-back or carry-forward of losses was permitted, the company would have been subject to income tax on $1,400,000. Under present law, the tax on that amount would have been subject to a refund resulting from the third year's loss of $800,000.

However, by the last-in, first-out method, the profit would work out as $200,000 each year—the sensible figure—and income tax would be payable on this amount.

The example we have taken places the LIFO method in a particularly favorable light, because it excludes two complicating factors, viz., (1) a fall in market price below the original unit value and (2) significant changes in the quantity of the inventory at various price levels.

In the first of these cases the inventory must still be carried at cost—which is now above market—not only for tax purposes but also in all reports to stockholders or for credit purposes. However, the security analyst would normally allow for the shrinkage in the value of the inventory below the carrying figure. To that extent the superior stability of LIFO against FIFO would be diminished.

When the quantities in the inventory change from year to year, under LIFO certain irregularities in the results become unavoidable. Two of these cases are discussed in Appendix Note 3, on page 727.

Most LIFO companies have followed that method since 1941 or have made retroactive adjustments to that year. There are numerous exceptions, of course.

Example: Caterpillar Tractor uses the price levels at January 1, 1947. Federated Department Stores carries the greater part of its inventory on a 1941 basis, a lesser part on a 1951 basis, and a small amount at FIFO.[2]

It should be borne in mind that under the LIFO method the earlier year's price level applies continuously only to that quantity of the inventory owned in the starting year (and subsequently held). Virtually all companies have increased the physical quantity of their stocks since 1941, to take care of their expanded business. Those increments to physical inventory are taken in for LIFO at the prices ruling in the year they were first acquired. Hence most LIFO companies which started from a 1941 base have had to mark up the average price level of the enlarged inventory by a substantial extent.

[2] The starting year of LIFO is usually not stated in the annual reports. The analyst can often trace it back through the *Moody's Industrial Manuals*.

Example: Figures of May Department Stores for selected years (LIFO began in 1940) will show this development, as follows:

(000,000 omitted)

Year	Inventory as reported on LIFO basis	"LIFO difference"	Inventory on FIFO basis
January 1947...........	$41.0	$ 8.5	$49.5
January 1957...........	56.5	16.1	72.6
January 1961...........	82.7	17.1	99.8

Although wholesale prices advanced over 50 percent from the end of 1946 to the end of 1960, the "LIFO difference" of May Department Stores remained at about 21 percent of the inventory. Its average LIFO cost has thus apparently kept pace with the price rise because of the expanding quantities.

Reserve for LIFO Adjustment. Instead of valuing inventories directly on a LIFO basis, a few companies have valued them on a FIFO basis but set up a reserve to reduce the net value to LIFO.

Example: Maytag Company established such a reserve (shown as an intermediate liability) to mark down its inventory to a 1946 price basis. At the end of 1959 the amount of the reserve (less tax credit) was nearly $1.5 million against inventory of $15.6 million. (The reserve system was discontinued at the end of that year.)

In a few cases the inventory reserve marked down the account to a LIFO basis without taking the tax offset into consideration.

Example: Stewart Warner Corporation followed this practice between 1946 and 1956, making an apparently excessive reduction of about $4.5 million, or approximately $3.30 per share, in reported earnings and equity. The year of largest effect was 1950, in which the company reduced inventory by $1.9 million for LIFO basis adjustment without taking the related tax credit of more than $1 million. The analyst should have raised the reported earnings either to a proper LIFO equivalent basis, or to a FIFO basis, depending on which approach he had elected to follow consistently. The figures are as follows:

Table 11-3. Stewart Warner Corporation, 1950

	Earnings (in thousands)	Per share*
Earnings as reported..................	$4,585	$3.58
Add tax credit not taken...............	1,076	
Earnings adjusted to full LIFO basis....	5,661	4.41
Add balance of LIFO reduction.........	840	
Earnings adjusted to FIFO basis.......	6,471	5.07

* On the 1,282,000 shares before split in 1960. (An excess profits tax was applicable in the second half of 1950.)

The Normal-stock or Basic-stock Method of Inventory Valuation. An older and more radical method of minimizing fluctuations due to inventory values has been followed by certain companies for some years past. This method is based on the theory that the company must regularly carry a certain physical stock of materials and that there is no more reason to vary the value of this "normal stock" from year to year—because of market changes—than there would be to vary the value of the manufacturing plant as the price index rises or falls and to reflect this change in the year's operations. In order to permit the base inventory to be carried at an unchanging figure, the practice is to mark it down to a very low unit-price level—so low that it should never be necessary to reduce it further to get it down to current market.

Examples: As long ago as 1913 National Lead Company applied this method to three principal constituents of its inventory, viz., lead, tin, and antimony. The specified base stocks of these metals were carried at the end of 1960 at about $4 million against current value of about $18 million. However, expansion of the company's operations has built up its total inventory to $102 million at carrying value.

A number of other companies have used or are using this method, including American Metals, American Smelting and Refining, Eagle-Picher (since 1943), Corn Products, Plymouth Cordage, and Endicott Johnson.

THE ENDICOTT JOHNSON CASE

This company's affairs may be of interest to the reader for two quite opposite reasons. In the first place it has been the chief exponent of the normal-stock method of inventory accounting. In consequence it reduced its reported earnings per share between 1945 and 1959 by about one-half, as against the prevailing FIFO inventory basis, and by so doing had marked down its 1959 equity from $74.20 to $48.50 per share. By not taking credit for the related tax saving on the inventory mark-down the company about doubled the unfavorable effect of its policy on earnings and net assets. For a good part of this period a restatement of the profits and net assets on the conventional inventory basis would have made the common stock look quite attractive at its average market price.

On the other hand, a closer study of the company's development through the years would have indicated a definite lack of progress—in fact, a retrogression—in such vital elements as growth of sales, maintenance of profit margins, maintenance of rate of earnings on capital. This would still have been true after the company's inventory accounting had been equalized with that of its chief competitors. A purchase of the shares inspired by an upward correction of its reported earnings would have brought relatively disappointing results.

The moral therefrom is that security analysis cannot *confine itself* to the type of examination and possible restatement of the figures that we have been discussing in the present section of the book. We repeat that this work is essential to competent analytical procedures, but it is far from sufficient to provide guides to successful investment.[3]

Difference between LIFO and Normal-stock Methods. The typical inventory valued by the normal-stock method consists of a substantial portion of the total carried at a very low cost price, with the balance carried at the conventional first-in, first-out or current-replacement-cost method. The typical LIFO inventory has various segments of cost, depending on how much was owned in the initial or base year and how much was added in various subsequent years. More important, when part of a normal-stock inventory is sold, bringing the amount on hand below the basic requirement, it is necessary to charge earnings with a reserve for the replacement of the deficiency. In effect this cancels out the large profit made on the sale.

Example: Archer-Daniels-Midland Company combines the LIFO and the normal-stock principles. It carries certain oil inventories at LIFO cost based on early 1942 prices. When such inventories fall below normal quantities it provides a reserve charged against income, to cover the difference between replacement cost and LIFO cost, less related tax credit. The reserve is shown as a current liability. When the inventory is replaced, the excess cost is charged to such reserve instead of a current income. During 1945–1949 considerable amounts were added to and taken out of the reserve, as is shown in Table 11-4.

Table 11-4. Earnings before and after Inventory Adjustments.
Archer-Daniels-Midland Company

(000 omitted)

Date June 30–	Inventory		Reserve for replacement of LIFO inventory less tax credit	Net income for year	
	FIFO portion	LIFO portion		Before inventory adjustment	After inventory adjustment
1945	$25,663	$3,796	$1,232	$ 4,440	$ 3,538
1946	21,494	2,353	3,720	9,092	6,604
1947	31,243	2,271	8,421	20,374	15,673
1948	40,527	3,860	5,720	9,648	12,349
1949	18,968	7,318	1,831	8,153	12,042

It will be noted that the smaller the LIFO portion of the inventory shown to be on hand, the larger the reserve provided for replacement.

[3] Endicott-Johnson discontinued its base-stock inventory policy in 1961 and transferred the reserve to surplus. The reader is referred to pp. 115–116 of the 1951 edition for a detailed analysis of the 1946–1949 figures.

This method takes out of reported earnings the profit realized on liquidation of inventory, in addition to eliminating the gain from higher prices of the balance left on hand.[4] Under LIFO no such replacement reserve is required—or permitted as a taxable deduction—though it may be provided at the management's election. On the whole, the normal-stock method probably produces more conservatively stated and more stable earnings over an extended period of time than the LIFO method.

The Retail Method of Inventory Valuation. An accepted method of valuing retailers' inventories—including those of department stores and chain stores—starts with the current retail selling price of each item, from which is deducted an appropriate "mark-on." The resulting value gives a calculated replacement cost, which corresponds to the expected realization less normal expense and profit. It is regarded as more closely reflecting the true value of the inventory to the store than either the actual recorded cost of each item or its current quotation in the wholesale market.

Retail stores that follow the LIFO method use a special technique, based on index numbers of retail prices. The inventory in each department is first valued as above, and then the "cost" is reduced in proportion to the advance in the particular price level—say, since 1941—shown by the official index numbers.

The Security Analyst and Inventory Methods. If there are two generally similar companies, one of which reports on the LIFO and the other on the FIFO basis, the second will probably have shown considerably larger earnings than the former during 1946–1959. Should the analyst accept both earnings statements as "correct"? If not, what adjustments should he make?

It is clear that the two companies cannot fairly be *compared* unless a substantially similar method of inventory valuation is applied to each. For this purpose either the LIFO or the FIFO method could properly be used, if the data are available. Since most companies are still on the conventional FIFO,[5] it would seem logical to mark up the inventories and earnings of the LIFO concerns to conform with the majority. This method has the advantage of setting up a uniform criterion for all comparisons—i.e., the current replacement cost of the inventory on hand, subject to appropriate mark-downs for nonstandard or slow-moving items. Some companies on a LIFO basis supply this replacement (or FIFO) figure for their inventory value somewhere in their annual report; others will give this information on request.

Examples: Several of the large department stores—e.g., Allied, Federated, Macy, May—give the amount of the LIFO difference.

[4] See Appendix Note 3, p. 727, for some peculiar results from the use of the LIFO method by U.S. Steel in the last quarter of 1949.

[5] *Accounting Trends and Techniques* for 1960 showed that 194 companies out of the 600 covered used the LIFO inventory-cost method.

American Radiator gives the LIFO difference and also the amount of inventory on LIFO and FIFO.

Falstaff Brewing states the percentage on LIFO but not the LIFO difference.

In certain cases it may be possible to form a reasonably accurate estimate (including proper tax allowance) by using the differentials disclosed by two companies in the same industry.[6]

However, such comparisons could easily be misleading. The difficulties confronting the analyst in this general matter were vividly shown by the divergent results of Armour & Company and Swift & Company between 1945 and 1949. Both companies stated that they were on a LIFO basis as to part of their inventory, but they did not supply data as to the dollar amounts involved in that portion and in the other. The reported earnings were as shown in Table 11-5.

Table 11-5. Earnings of Armour and Swift, 1945–1949

(000 omitted)

Year ended about October 31	Earnings reported	
	Armour	Swift
1945	$ 9,173	$13,304
1946	20,791	16,395
1947	22,950	22,335
1948	*1,965* (d)	27,889
(First half 1949)	(*6,513* (d))	(Not reported)
1949	558	25,826

Armour & Company passed its common dividend in July 1948 and its preferred dividend in April 1949. At the annual meeting in February 1950 the president explained that because its LIFO base was limited, it had been protected to the extent of only $9 million out of a total decline of $27 million in inventory values experienced in the first half of 1949.

Evidently this was a case in which careful investigation by the analyst was necessary before he could draw sound conclusions based on purported use of a LIFO basis by the meat-packing companies.

Which Basis Should the Analyst Use? A strong argument has been made by many authorities against recognizing any "profits" that are caused by price-level advances.[7] We believe that adequate reporting to

---

[6] See Appendix Note 15, p. 688, of the 1951 edition for a 1947 example.

[7] They were called "fool's profits" in a book under that title by Arundel Cotter, published in 1940. See also an article entitled "Fantasy of Figures: Responsibility of Accountants," by Alden R. Wells in the *Commercial and Financial Chronicle*, Apr. 20, 1950, p. 36. He criticizes the American Institute of Accountants for not favoring both the LIFO basis of inventory and the replacement basis of depreciation in order to avoid overstatement of profits.

stockholders should clearly segregate the portion of the year's result that is attributable to changes in the price level. This may properly be designated as an "extraordinary item"; together with the tax consequence, it should be segregated from the ordinary operating results of the year. In balance-sheet studies, on the other hand, we think the current-replacement basis is the most informing one for the analyst to use provided the information is available. It would put all companies in the same industry in a comparable position. It would avoid the use of price levels related to dates arbitrarily selected in the past. If the analyst believes the current price level is vulnerable, he can make allowances in his calculations for any expected degree of decline.

At this point let us insert the observation we made here in the 1951 edition:

There are some grounds for believing that the 1940–1949 average on the LIFO basis would give a closer approximation to the 1950–1959 average than the same period's result on a FIFO basis, since the LIFO method would supply a partial correction for an inflationary factor that should not be counted on to recur in the future—though it may.

Our caution against expecting the 1940–49 inflationary factor to recur in the future was at least partially correct since the rise in wholesale prices in the 1950's was only about one-sixth that in the 1940's. This is evident from the following Department of Labor statistics:

Year	Wholesale price index (annual average)	Increase in decade
1940	51.1	
1950	103.1	102%
1960	119.5	16%

But the generally expansive economy of the 1950's produced an unforeseen jump in corporate profits. (The average earnings of the Standard & Poor's 500-Stock Composite rose from $1.36 in 1940–1949 to $2.97 in 1950–1959.) Hence a conservative restatement of the earnings of the 1940's—although supported by the views of most financial authorities —would have brought us farther away from rather than closer to a correct projection of the next decade.

This is one of the countless examples and reasons that may be adduced for a modest, non-Olympian attitude on the part of the securities analyst when he enters on his inescapable task of projecting from the past into the future.

Inventory Reserves in Arbitrary Amounts. The use of inventory reserves is by no means coextensive with the LIFO concept. It has long been customary, in good years, for companies to provide a reserve for future inventory losses by charges against earnings.[8] These have usually been in some round amount, with no announced basis of calculation. They were thus in the nature of a contingency reserve, to which subject we shall now turn.

RESERVES FOR CONTINGENCIES

A reserve for contingencies, as its name implies, is intended to absorb future losses or liabilities of a rather indefinite character. Such a reserve may be created by a charge to earnings or to surplus; or even by the intermediate device of charging it to profit and loss account *after* the payment of dividends. These reserves, like all others, are not in themselves cash funds. They may be represented or offset on the asset side by a corresponding *contingency fund,* in cash or securities, but this is now a rare occurrence. A contingency reserve is in reality indistinguishable from an earmarked portion of the surplus account, with the purpose of the earmark being quite indefinite.

The effect of setting up contingency reserves varies with the procedure followed. Until recently the standard pattern was to deduct the reserved amount from the earnings of a prosperous year, thus reporting profits smaller than were actually realized. Then in a later year when some extraordinary loss occurred (or the particular kind of loss anticipated when the reserve was created), the shrinkage was charged against the reserve instead of against current earnings. Thus the profits of the later and less favorable year were bolstered up by the reverse process of that used in the earlier year.

Contingency reserves have been favored by many managements, but they are frowned on by most security analysts. In the old days the reserve appropriations were often undisclosed, except possibly in the balance sheet. For many years past the New York Stock Exchange and (later) the SEC have insisted that full information about such reserves be supplied to the stockholders. Managements, familiar both with the vicissitudes of business and with the tendency of the stock market to exaggerate both temporary prosperity and temporary adversity, have viewed contingency reserves as a valuable device for more nearly equalizing the earnings in good and bad times. The analysts, however, object to the arbitrary nature and amount of such reserves. They prefer to see the earnings stated as they actually are, leaving the equalizing and averaging to be done by the stockholders, with the aid of their advisers. The views adopted by the accounting profession regarding contingency reserves and implemented some years ago by strong recommendations run along parallel lines.

[8] No less than 170 companies out of 541 covered in *Accounting Techniques* reported some sort of inventory reserve in 1948. But in 1960 the number had shrunk to 45 out of 600, indicating a lesser fear of sudden shrinkage in value.

Since the last edition of this work, contingency reserves have almost disappeared as a factor of moment in corporate reports. They have lingered on in some balance sheets, but rarely appear as income-account deductions or credits.[9] Consequently, we omit our former rather detailed treatment of the subject at this point (pages 121–126 of the 1951 edition). It gave a number of examples of the use of contingency reserves to equalize reported earnings during the 1940's.

One of the chief contingencies reserved against in the past has been a future decline in inventory values. Such reserves are now sometimes set up, with accountants' consent, by entries solely within the surplus account. The over-all result will be to report *earnings* as if there were no contingency reserve to draw on, but to reflect the appearance and disappearance of the danger of price declines by transfers between free and appropriated surplus. These items would correspond to the comments or warnings by management, which we recommend generally instead of moves to state the year's earnings as something different from their actual amounts.

Certain permitted accounting practices do serve to cushion the fluctuations of earnings between good and bad years. These include the LIFO method (directly or by reserves equivalent thereto) and the variation of depreciation rates in accordance with the rate of operations. Such methods are nonarbitrary in nature and are definitely related to past and current happenings rather than to possible future events.

[9] *Accounting Trends and Techniques* for 1960 reported 48 balance sheets with, and 552 without contingency reserves; 13 of the former were listed as part of the equity. In 1950 there were 155 with and 445 without such reserves.

CHAPTER TWELVE

THE RELATION OF DEPRECIATION AND
SIMILAR CHARGES TO EARNING POWER

A critical analysis of an income account must pay particular attention to the amounts deducted for depreciation and kindred charges. These items differ from ordinary operating expenses in that they do not signify a current and corresponding outlay of cash. They represent the estimated shrinkage in the value of the fixed or capital assets, due to wearing out, to using up, or to their approaching extinction for whatever cause. The important charges of this character may be classified as follows:

1. Depreciation (and obsolescence), replacements, renewals, or retirements
2. Depletion or exhaustion
3. Amortization of leaseholds, leasehold improvements, licenses, etc.
4. Amortization of patents

All these items may properly be embraced under the title "amortization," but we shall sometimes refer to them generically as "depreciation items" or simply as "depreciation," because the latter is a more familiar term.

Leading Questions Relative to Depreciation. The accounting theory that governs depreciation charges appears simple enough. If a capital asset has limited life, provision must be made to write off the (unsalvaged) cost of that asset by charges against earnings distributed over the period of its life. But behind the appearance of simplicity lie complications of a fivefold character. First, we find that accounting rules themselves may permit a value other than cost as the basis of the amortization charge. Second, a variety of choices is permitted as to the allocation of depreciation expense over time periods in the life of the asset. Third, certain companies may not follow accepted accounting practice in stating their amortization deduction in the income account. Fourth, in many cases a company will use one permitted basis of amortization in its tax returns and another in its published statements. Fifth, there are occasions when an allowance justified from an accounting standpoint will fail to meet the situation properly from an investment stand-

150

point. Apart from these technical issues, a broader tendency has recently become manifest to regard the depreciation deduction as in some sense "unreal" and to concentrate attention on earnings before amortization, or "cash flow." These problems will engage our attention in this and the next chapter.

The Analyst's Basic Approach to Depreciation. In this rather complex area we suggest that the analyst be guided by the following basic principles:

1. He should want the amortization provision to be adequate by conservative standards.

2. He should seek, as far as possible, to apply uniform measures of depreciation, making necessary adjustments therefor in his comparative studies.

3. As generally in his work, he must maintain a sense of proportion here and concern himself only with items that might have an appreciable influence on his conclusions.

Importance of Amortization Charges in Corporate Accounts. The attention that the analyst will give to a specific question about depreciation will vary with its significance for his final results. If a company has a relatively small amount of fixed assets, its amortization charge will have only a minor influence on its profits. Hence the analyst can readily accept the company's provision, which in any case is apt to be fully adequate. This situation will be found generally in the major divisions of financial, trade, and service enterprises. In the manufacturing field the plant investment and associated depreciation is less important for light operations of the assembly type than for heavy and integrated operations. In mining, oil and gas production, and the great public utility and railroad industries, the fixed assets bulk very large, and amortization is correspondingly important.

The relationship between depreciation, etc., and other major financial elements for various industry groups in the year 1959 is summarized in Table 12-1. It will be observed that for manufacturing companies generally the amortization charge was more than 75 percent of the earnings after such deduction. In fact, profits before amortization were divided fairly evenly among depreciation, income taxes, and final net income. (In 1959 the aggregate depreciation figure for all manufacturing corporations equaled about 2.8 percent of sales and over 6 percent of the gross plant and equipment account.) The ratios for all manufacturing companies may be compared with the aggregate for the 29 industrial giants in the DJIA, which we have compiled for 1959. In addition, we present composite material for the Class I railroads.

The figures in our table demonstrate that for most industries the depreciation and amortization allowance is of major importance in relation to net income. Consequently the analyst must deal with the question of what is "normal" or adequate depreciation for companies generally or for industrial groups, and he must concern himself with detecting and evaluating individual or group departures from these norms.

Standard Methods of Computing Depreciation. There are four theoretical approaches to the writing off of property during its useful life, and each of these is found in practice. The most usual approach for many

Table 12-1. All Corporations with Net Income, 1958.° Gross Receipts, Depreciation, etc., Income Taxes, and Net Income for Various Industrial Groups

(000,000 omitted)

Corporation	Gross receipts	Depreci- ation, etc. ¶	Net before tax	Income tax	Net after tax
All corporations..............	$632,300	$19,983	$44,148	$18,814	$25,333
Major groups:					
Mining†..................	7,867	1,106	1,185	483	702
Construction..............	23,227	408	933	356	576
Manufacturing............	290,847	10,113	20,156	9,377	10,778
Transportation and public					
utilities................	47,357	4,525	6,096	2,994	3,002
Wholesale trade..........	93,922	539	2,326	939	1,387
Retail trade..............	87,356	899	2,782	1,194	1,588
Finance, insurance, real es-					
tate...................	51,560	1,294	8,669	2,724	5,945
Service..................	14,146	726	1,063	412	651
Selected subgroups:					
Oil and gas‡..............	35,451	3,197	2,097	761	1,336
Tobacco manufacturing....	4,469	28	513	265	248
Chemical manufacturing....	22,140	1,097	2,644	1,253	1,391
Electric and gas utilities....	15,459	2,133	2,477	1,255	1,222
Banking.................	10,406	227	3,228	1,207	2,021
Insurance carriers.........	27,809	134	1,662	579	1,083
Real estate...............	6,334	732	1,334	405	929
Class I railroads§.........	10,452	604	843	266	557
Dow-Jones Industrial Average§	66,843	3,722	10,302	4,546	5,756

* Years ended between July 1958 and June 1959.
† Includes oil and gas producers.
‡ Entire industry. Net income reduced here by percentage depletion not shown on income statements.
§ 1959 year.
¶ Includes depreciation, amortization, and depletion.

decades has been the "straight-line" method, which charges off each year the same percentage of book cost less estimated salvage. A more conservative method assumes that an asset loses a larger portion of its economic value in the earlier years of use than in the later years; hence the depreciation charge gradually diminishes over the asset's life. The tax law now permits this technique to be applied with respect to property acquired after 1953.[1] (The companies may choose between essentially equivalent applications—one called the "declining-balance" and the other the "sum-of-the-digits" method.)

Strangely enough, a third respectable approach to depreciation permits *smaller* deductions in the earlier years than in the later ones. This amortization charge is set aside—actually or just for purposes of computation—and will be increased by earning compound interest until the property is retired. Hence an earlier year's depreciation allowance can be larger than a later year's, because the first sum will earn interest for a longer period of time. This method has been considered appropriate for public utility companies and has been prescribed by utility commissions in a number of states.

The fourth standard method is based on the principle that wear and tear is a function not only of the passage of time but also of the use made of the facilities. Companies using this approach will vary the depreciation rate in some proportion to the rate of operations during the period.

A Typical Statement of Depreciation Policy. The depreciation policies of the more important companies are summarized in the detailed descriptions appearing in the financial manuals. They must be set forth in a registration statement and prospectus covering the sale of securities and in proxy statements relating to mergers and similar transactions.

The following statement—expressed in highly succinct terms—sets forth the depreciation policy of Crown Cork & Seal Company. It appears in its proxy statement of October 1961, relating to its proposed merger with Crown Cork International Corporation.

Depreciation was based on the estimated lives of the assets computed on the straight-line method. The lives assigned to properties for depreciation purposes are:

Buildings.........................	40 to 50 years
Machinery and equipment.............	12½ to 25 years
Office furniture and fixtures............	15 years
Autos and trucks....................	4 to 6 years
Capping and bottling machines.........	5 to 25 years

Assets and reserve are relieved on retirement of fixed assets; gain or loss (therefrom) is credited or charged to income; maintenance and repairs are charged to expense; renewals and replacements are capitalized.

The range of annual rates indicated by the above schedule would run from 25 percent on autos to 2 percent on buildings. The over-all rate for the first half of 1961 works out at 4.1 percent.

Accelerated Amortization of War Facilities. An important departure from the standard approaches to depreciation was made in the "acceler-

---

[1] A similar method was permitted prior to 1954 but only if it had been followed consistently from the outset.

ated-depreciation" provisions of the income tax laws, in order to spur the expansion of productive capacity in World War II and the Korean War. With respect to new facilities deemed useful for the war effort, the companies were awarded "certificates of necessity" which entitled them to write off the cost of all or part of such facilities in 60 equal monthly installments. (A charge-off of the balance was permitted at the end of World War II.)

Brief Survey of Corporate Practices. Prior to the SEC legislation of the 1930's, corporate practices with respect to depreciation were often quite irregular. While most companies no doubt conformed to the accepted straight-line procedures, the exceptions were numerous. There were instances in which important companies made no provision whatever for amortization in their published statements.[2] In a few cases the same result was achieved by writing down fixed assets to $1 on the balance sheet, thus making a depreciation charge unnecessary except on later additions.[3] Most public utility concerns formerly used the so-called "retirement-reserve" basis of depreciation, which was too low and overstated net income.

On the other hand, a number of concerns followed ultraconservative practices, either consistently or on special occasions. They charged certain plant expenditures to expense instead of capitalizing them;[4] they used large depreciation allowances to write off the "water,"—i.e., undisclosed intangibles in the property account; during periods of high prices they wrote down plant additions to "normal cost" by extra amortization charges to income.[5]

After World War I many companies increased their depreciation rates by a procedure which was accepted by the accounting profession. This consisted of writing up the value of fixed assets in the balance sheet to current replacement costs—say, 50 percent above actual cost—and then charging standard depreciation rates against the higher carrying value. (The extra depreciation was not deductible for income tax purposes.)

The student should note, in passing, the directly opposed financial philosophies involved in the write-ups to replacement costs in the 1920's and the write-downs to $1 in the 1930's. In the earlier period asset values were still important, and the companies were eager to write up their net worth, even if that meant reducing their reported profits by reason of

[2] This was true of the Cities Service system for many years before 1930.

[3] For examples of this curious and soon-abandoned practice—baldly intended to increase the reported earnings—see our discussion of U.S. Industrial Alcohol Company, Safety Car Heating and Lighting Company, and four other concerns on pp. 489–492 of the 1940 edition.

[4] See our discussion of National Biscuit in the years 1911–1925 and of American Can, *ibid.*, pp. 453–455.

[5] The outstanding example of these two practices in the past was U.S. Steel. See Appendix Note 4, p. 728, for a summary of its varying amortization policies since 1901.

the higher amortization required. By the 1930's the emphasis had shifted so completely from asset values to earning power that several concerns did not hesitate to reduce their book worth drastically in order to relieve earnings of the depreciation charge.

After the SEC reforms, the grosser kinds of abuses in corporate reporting pretty well disappeared. Depreciation policies were divulged by all registered companies, and they rarely failed to conform to accepted accounting rules. However, within these rules there was room for some rather wide divergencies in amortization policy, particularly in the treatment of accelerated amortization of war facilities and in certain write-downs of high-cost plant additions.

Post-SEC Practices. Between, say, 1935 and 1954 the vast majority of companies used the straight-line method of depreciation applied to the cost of their assets, as required on tax returns. But the law was amended in 1954 to permit deduction of the more liberal declining-balance or sum-of-the-digits depreciation with respect to new property additions. Most publicly held companies appear to have adopted this tax-saving procedure on their tax returns.[6] But the practice with respect to reports to stockholders has been sharply divided. Many concerns now use the higher-tax return figure in their published statements; perhaps as many retain the lower straight-line rates—with resultant higher net earnings—in their reports. Where the latter practice is followed, proper accounting requires a charge against the year's profits for future taxes to be incurred by reason of the different bases of depreciation. Most companies make such a provision for future taxes; but the analyst must now struggle with special problems in the railroad and public utility fields because of regulatory requirements and in the case of oil companies because of their peculiar philosophy on the subject of intangible drilling costs.

In Table 12-2 we summarize the depreciation allowances of the companies in the Dow-Jones Industrial Average in 1949 and 1959. This will give the reader an idea of how policies vary among large companies, and of the dollar magnitudes involved.

Depreciation took a much larger percentage of net earnings in 1959 than in 1949. This was due in part to the more liberal policies followed, but in greater degree to the much higher plant investment in 1959 and to the lower rate of net profit thereon. The over-all depreciation rate on the gross plant account advanced from 4.5 percent to 5.1 percent. Had the 1949 rates been followed in 1959 and tax paid on the increased profit, the earnings on the DJIA unit would have advanced from $34.31 to $35.78, a rise of 4.3 percent. This quick calculation may reflect reasonably well the true measure of the change in depreciation policy in recent years.

[6] However, the corporation income tax statistics for 1957 indicate that the vast majority of corporations calculated depreciation by the straight-line method on their tax returns in that year.

Are the Newer Depreciation Rates Overliberal? A rather remarkable change has occurred in the attitude of the financial community toward depreciation in the past decade. In 1947–1949 most emphasis was laid on the claimed inadequacy of the rates allowed by the tax law and used by

Table 12-2. Comparative Depreciation Allowances in 1959 and 1949 for Companies in the Dow-Jones Industrial Average°

Company	1959				1949		
	Gross plant	Depreci- ation, etc.	Depreci- ation/ plant (percent)	Method used†	Gross plant	Depreci- ation, etc.	Depreci- ation/ plant (percent)
Allied Chemical..........	$ 1,019	$ 55.0	5.4 %	SD	$ 416	$ 15.1	3.7 %
ALCOA................	1,519	73.1	4.8	SD	696	15.7	2.3
American Can...........	786	34.5	9.4	SL	304	10.9	3.6
American Tel and Tel.....	22,205	1,054.7	4.7	SL	9,433	321.0	3.4
American Tobacco.......	124	5.2	4.2	SL	71	2.8	4.0
Anaconda..............	1,206	51.5	4.3	DB	637	10.3	1.7
Bethlehem Steel.........	2,267	97.5	4.3	DB	1,186	31.0	2.7
Chrysler...............	1,149	72.1	6.3	SL	207	19.4	9.3
du Pont...............	1,977	143.1	7.5	SL	867	72.5	8.3
Eastman Kodak.........	687	41.6	6.0	SD	329	16.9	5.1
General Electric.........	1,566	119.9	7.6	SL	684	52.9	7.7
General Foods..........	221	14.0	6.3	SD	113	4.9	4.3
General Motors.........	6,186	413.7	6.7	RA	1,176	110.4	6.3
Goodyear..............	789	49.7	6.3	SD	330	19.6	5.9
International Harvester...	689	41.7	6.0	SL	426	20.3	4.7
International Nickel......	597	14.6	2.5	U	294	8.2	2.8
International Paper......	886	57.4	6.3	DB	307	14.5	4.7
Johns-Manville..........	304	16.8	5.5	SD	118	5.2	4.4
Owens-Illinois...........	354	17.7	5.0	SD	136	6.5	4.8
Procter & Gamble.......	596	22.5	3.8	SL	195	6.5	3.3
Sears Roebuck...........	565	31.5	5.5	SD	272	20.5	7.5
Standard Oil of Calif......	3,185	141.0	4.5	SL	1,382	75.7	5.5
Standard Oil of N.J......	9,863	527.7	5.3	SL	3,742	184.3	4.9
Swift..................	489	22.3	4.5	SD	289	12.7	4.4
Texaco................	4,109	278.0	6.7	SL	1,377	92.3	6.7
Union Carbide..........	1,974	121.6	6.2	SD	694	27.5	4.0
United Aircraft..........	288	28.5	9.9	SD	88	6.5	7.4
U.S. Steel..............	5,892	190.0	3.2	‡	3,068	120.0	3.9
Westinghouse...........	753	46.7	6.2	SL	312	14.0	4.3
Woolworth.............	380	23.2	6.1	SL	195	9.4	5.8
Total.................	72,575	3,687.0	5.1		29,644	1,327.5	4.5

* Based on issues in the Average in 1959.
† Method used in 1959 reports to stockholders, keyed as follows:
    SL = straight line
    SD = sum of year's digits (post 1953)
    DB = double declining balance (post 1953)
    RA = rapid amortization (before and after 1953)
     U = unstated
‡ Rate dependent in part on percentage of use of facilities.

corporations. Such rates were based on the book cost of the assets and did not reflect their higher replacement cost. At present there is a tendency to regard the more liberal rates now allowed by the tax law as in some way excessive. More generally, the fact that amortization charges are larger than formerly is taken as an indication that the true earnings are larger than reported. It is this belief that has turned the attention of

Wall Street to the earnings *before* depreciation or the "cash flow." This change in attitude is perhaps the natural concomitant of the enormous rise in the ratio of stock prices to reported earnings. When stock prices were very low in 1949, investors readily believed that the true profits were lower than reported; now that prices are very high by old standards, investors readily believe that their true earnings are higher than reported.

In our previous edition we gave considerable space to the controversy over reproduction-cost depreciation as against the original-cost basis. A calculation made by the National City Bank of New York in 1949 concluded that depreciation charges for all nonfinancial companies would have to be increased by 62 percent to provide for replacement cost instead of original cost. Had this change been made, the average profits for 1946–1948 would have been reduced by about 13 percent.[7]

Neither the replacement-cost issue nor the inventory-valuation issue has been as important in recent years as it was between 1946 and 1952. From 1953 through 1960 wholesale prices increased only 9 percent, and the "inventory-value adjustment," used by the Department of Commerce to offset the effect of price rises, has averaged only 2 percent of corporate profits before taxes. It is still true, however, that current depreciation allowances will not provide for present replacement costs of the assets involved. A number of companies have supplied various figures showing the difference between depreciation taken and that required to cover replacement cost. In the case of Bristol-Myers, Inc., the required increase in 1959 was 27.4 percent. If the same step-up of depreciation was applied to the Dow-Jones Industrial group, and tax credit taken, the net result would be to reduce the reported earnings by some 10 percent. This is about twice the percentage *increase* in earnings that would have followed from the use of the lower 1949 depreciation rates in 1959.

This discussion may well have suggested that there is no such thing as a "scientific" or uniquely correct basis for calculating depreciation and hence of establishing whether a given policy produces too high or too low an allowance. But we are inclined to the view that the rates now in use are not excessive. There are, we think, two rather basic reasons for accepting them as appropriate. The first is that there is as yet no evidence that plant accounts are being written down too quickly to too low a figure. We recognize that the record is extremely short since the more liberal write-off of assets was permitted and that the year-by-year relationship of sales and profits to net plant in the postwar period has at times been distorted by overutilization of capacity and by inflation. Nonetheless, in the last three years both sales and profits were lower in relation to net plant than in the preceding recession years of 1949 and

---

[7] An additional reduction of slightly larger amount would have been required to cancel the profits ascribable to the inflation-caused mark-up of inventory values.

1954; this would still have been true if the 1958–1960 earnings had been upgraded by applying 1949 depreciation rates. The second reason is that the speeding up of technological change has undoubtedly increased the obsolescence factor in many businesses; there is greater danger than heretofore that equipment will have to be scrapped before the end of its normal life.[8]

Let us add some over-all figures bearing on the question whether depreciation charges are larger than necessary and thus include some "concealed profits" accruing to the shareholders. Depreciation, depletion, and amortization charges for all corporations rose from $4.3 billion in 1946 to $22.8 billion in 1960. This quintupling of the allowance in 14 years does give an impression of liberality verging on excess.[9] But the data disclose that over a 15-year period the percentage rise in depreciation has kept in line, more or less, with the rise in plant and equipment expenditures. In dollar figures, such outlays aggregated $413 billion in 1946–1960, while total amortization allowances were $194 billion. The 1960 depreciation etc. was almost exactly 5 percent of the total outlays on new plant and equipment for the preceding 20 years (figures for 1941–1945 are partly estimated). This implies, somewhat indirectly, that current rates are geared to an over-all life-span of twenty years. In view of the speed-up of technological change, this period hardly appears too short.

Our conclusion for the analyst is that he should accept the tax basis of depreciation as the norm for the typical company, and that for comparative and other purposes he should adjust to this basis the earnings of most of the companies that use lower rates on their reports than on their tax returns. (The situation of the public utilities differs in this respect from that of other companies. It is discussed in Chapter 21.) Our rule would not apply, also, to certain 100 percent and 20 percent charge-offs discussed later.

Let us pass on now to various illustrations of depreciation analysis in the study of financial statements.

Three Standard Methods Illustrated. The 1960 reports of three large corporations will illustrate, respectively, the straight-line method, the (post-1953) accelerated method, and the rate-of-use method of calculating depreciation.

---

[8] In 1961 the United States Treasury began a policy of reducing the assigned lives—and thus of increasing the annual depreciation allowed—on various types of industrial machinery, giving as its reason the fact that "advancing techniques engender further advances and make even recently developed equipment economically outmoded long before it is physically worn out." (*Business Week*, Oct. 14, 1961, p. 32.)

[9] See article "Cheer for Stockholders" by R. G. Klein in *Barron's*, Dec. 18, 1961, p. 9. The writer suggests that the rise in depreciation allowance will lead to a more generous dividend policy.

American Can retained the straight-line basis in its published reports, but after 1953 it adopted the accelerated-depreciation basis for tax purposes. It deducted a reserve for deferred taxes equal to the income tax difference between the two bases.

Allied Chemical follows its tax return on its published statements. It applies straight-line rates to property acquired before 1954 and the "sum-of-the-digits" accelerated rates to post-1953 additions, which represented about 43 percent of the gross property account at the end of 1960.

U.S. Steel also uses its tax-return basis on its statements. However, its depreciation rates are reduced when the actual operating use is less than a predetermined average, but not in as great proportion as the reduction in operating use. Details are not published, but its 1937 report stated that the minimum depreciation rate is more than 50 percent of the regular rate.

(Dollar figures in millions)

	American Can	Allied Chemical	U.S. Steel
Average gross property......................	$824.0	$1,042.9	$6,097.5
Depreciation................................	$ 38.0	$ 50.3	$ 208.4
Ratio to property...........................	4.61%	4.82%	3.42%
Deferred income tax for year.................	$ 4.5	none	none
Indicated extra depreciation on tax return......	$ 9.0	....	....
Total depreciation on tax return..............	$ 47.0	....	....
Ratio to property...........................	5.70%	4.85%	3.42%

The effect of the rate-of-use method employed by U.S. Steel was indicated in our Table 10-1 on page 127. As that table shows, the ordinary depreciation taken in 1958 (operating rate 59.2 percent) was lower than that taken in 1957 (operating rate 85.5 percent), although the plant account subject thereto was considerably larger.

Effect of Variations in Useful Life Assigned. In most cases the life assigned to various types of property—and the resultant rates of depreciation applied under a particular permitted method—are reasonably uniform from company to company. Here and there an exception arises which the analyst should take into account in his study of the figures.

Example: The useful life assigned to leased computing equipment appears to vary rather significantly among various lessor companies. They also use different basic methods of depreciation. Because of the large dollar amounts involved, this double variation has an appreciable effect on reported earnings. Control Data Corporation assigns a useful life of only four years and depreciates by the declining-balance method. Hence it writes off 50 percent of cost the first year, 25 percent the second, and 12½ percent in each of the third and fourth years. IBM uses the sum-of-the-digits method applied to a five-year life. This produces a 33⅓ percent write-off the first year, 26⅔ percent the second, etc. By contrast, Sperry-Rand employs the straight-line method over a seven-to-eight-year period; hence its rate each year is between 12½ percent and 14.3 percent of cost.

A thoroughgoing comparison of reported earnings, in cases such as these, should seek to equalize the annual depreciation charges, to the extent justified by the character of the property.

The Deferred-tax Deduction. When a company takes accelerated depreciation on its tax return but charges only the lower straight-line rate on its books, it will have to make up the tax difference later. For the time will come when all of the annual depreciation still required on its books will no longer be tax deductible because the steadily declining depreciation charge allowed by the accelerated methods will fall below the fixed straight-line amount.[10] Hence approved accounting practice requires that a reserve for deferred taxes, equivalent to the tax currently saved, be deducted from the year's earnings. Companies following this procedure—e.g., American Can above—show their net earnings increased by about one-half the difference between book depreciation and tax depreciation, the other half having been absorbed by the deferred tax. For American Can this increase amounted to about 30 cents per share, or 18 percent.

If the analyst, in comparing companies, wishes to put the results of all of them on a standard (Allied Chemical type) depreciation basis, he need simply deduct an adjustment about equal to the deferred tax for the year from the earnings of companies reporting on the straight-line basis. However, in many cases the required information is unavailable. Of the thirty companies in the Dow-Jones Industrial Average, fourteen apparently used the straight-line method in 1960. Of these six set up a reserve for deferred taxes; two stated that this reserve was added to the depreciation allowance itself and thus could not be identified; and six gave no indication that they used the accelerated method on their tax returns.[11]

The railroads and other carriers have been required by the ICC to use in their accounts the straight-line method of calculating depreciation for both post-1953 additions and for defense facilities entitled to the 20 percent-per-day amortization. They were expressly prohibited, also, from setting up the deferred-tax reserve in their accounts to provide for the ultimate payment of the tax currently saved. In 1961 the ICC proposed further to prohibit all companies under its jurisdiction—chiefly railways

---

[10] Under the sum-of-the-digits method this will occur in the sixth year of assets with a 10-year life, in the thirteenth year of assets with a 20-year life, etc. The declining-balance method will produce closely similar results.

[11] See Table 12-2 above for classification of the depreciation policies of the 30 DJIA companies in 1959.

and truckers—from adjusting their official figures in their reports to stockholders so as to show a reserve for deferred tax. The latter rule has been vigorously opposed by the accounting profession, on the ground that it compels the companies to overstate their profits, and it deprives the public of significant financial information.[12]

The railways have generally followed the procedure of indicating in a footnote the amount of the year's tax saving on amortization, but this is not deducted by the financial services in reporting earnings per share.

Example: Western Pacific Railroad reported net income of $2.21 per share in 1960, but noted tax savings aggregating $964,000 from use of sum-of-the-years'-digits depreciation and 20 percent amortization of defense facilities on its tax return. The normal and proper adjustment for these items would have reduced the stated per-share earnings by 53 cents, or 24 percent.

It is clear that the profits of railroad companies generally have been substantially overstated in recent years, by order of the ICC. This accounts, at least to some degree, for what appeared to be an abnormally low ratio of price to earnings for the carrier shares.

The public utility companies have been governed in the deferred-tax matter by varying regulations of the commissions under whose authority they operate. This point is treated in Chapter 21.

A very few industrial companies fail to allow for the deferred income tax, where it is indicated.

Example: Bird & Son. The 1959 report of this rather large maker of building products, etc., shows that it failed to set up the usual reserve for deferred income tax. It states that the management is of "the opinion that as a result of future replacements and additions to the company's plants the reduction in taxes represents, in effect, a permanent tax reduction and not a deferment to future years." (Note 3 to balance sheet.) The omission of the deferred tax increased 1958 net by over 60 percent and 1959 net by about 16 percent.

The company claimed, in essence, that it expects to operate in the future on a basis that will never require it to draw on a deferred-tax reserve of this type; hence there is no point in setting it up. Its reasoning would presumably be sound (1) if the company could be sure of adding new plant at a rate which will create deferred-tax advantage equal to that which will have to be drawn on when the diminishing tax-allowed rates on old plant fall below the straight-line rate; and (2) if no adverse changes are made in the benefits allowed by the 1954 tax amendments. Since these are questions that cannot be answered with certainty, the accountants have decided that an indicated future tax liability related to

[12] See *Business Week*, Mar. 25, 1961, p. 101, for a discussion of various aspects of this controversy. (In early 1962 the ICC apparently rescinded the rule referred to above.)

current operations should be currently provided for. We consider this a conservative and proper viewpoint.

It is interesting to observe that the reason given by Bird & Son is basically that behind the failure of oil and gas companies to set up a deferred-tax reserve for amounts saved through their treatment of intangible drilling costs (below, page 165). But while the Bird auditors took exception to this procedure in their certificate, the accountants do not officially object to its use by oil and gas producers.

Varying Treatment of Amortization of Defense Facilities. A number of companies deducted in their statements the full 20 percent annually allowed on certificate-of-necessity facilities, while others applied only regular rates and set up a deferred-tax reserve for the tax difference.[13] The case of Aluminum Company of America (ALCOA) is interesting because it switched from one method to another.

Example: In the years 1951–1954 ALCOA charged the full 20 percent amortization to income, the amount being $65,000,000 in excess of normal depreciation. In 1955 it reversed this procedure retroactively, set up a deferred-tax reserve of $34,000,000 on this amount, and credited the $31,000,000 balance to surplus. By 1958 the deferred-tax reserve had increased to its maximum of $83,700,000. In 1959–1960 the reserve decreased by $5,000,000 indicating that regular depreciation charges drawing on this reserve had begun to exceed the small remaining credits at the 20 percent rate.

By changing over to the reserve basis, ALCOA increased appreciably its average reported earnings during 1955–1958—from $2.67 to $3.48 a share. However, the total increase from this source for the 1951–1958 period, aggregating some $4 per share, will have to be deducted from earnings of later years, corresponding about equally to the gradual absorption of the deferred-tax reserve.

Two Policies Compared. A comparison of the amortization policies in this area of ALCOA and U.S. Steel suggests some rather conflicting conclusions as to what is appropriate. U.S. Steel charged the full 20 percent annual rate to earnings on its emergency facilities in World War II and on its Korean War defense facilities covered by certificates of necessity in 1950–1953. (In addition, it charged off $200,000,000 of accelerated depreciation on plant additions in 1947–1949, which was not tax deductible. This was at the rate of 10 percent per annum.) From a strict accounting standpoint the ALCOA policy was probably the more suitable one, since the useful life of the subject facilities in each case was certain to extend beyond the five-year amortization period. The accounting principle is that the cost of these as of all other depreciable assets should be spread over their expected useful life "in such a way as to allocate it as

---

[13] As a special case, Caterpillar Tractor amortizes in its reports one-half of its "defense facilities" at the 20 percent rate and one-half at the straight-line rate.

equitably as possible to the periods during which services are to be obtained from the use of the facility."[14]

On the other hand, the practical effect of the drastic charge-off policy of U.S. Steel was to absorb these capital costs during a period of great economic activity and near-capacity operations in the industry. What this really amounted to was an extension of the two accepted methods by which depreciation may vary from the straight-line rule: (1) by charging more in the earlier than in the later years and (2) by charging more at higher than at lower rates of operation.

AMORTIZATION CHARGES OF MINING AND OIL COMPANIES

These important sectors of the industrial field are subject to special factors bearing on amortization. In addition to ordinary depreciation on buildings, equipment, etc., they must allow for depletion of their ore, oil, and similar reserves. In the case of mining companies there is the factor of exploration and development expense. The corresponding charges for oil and gas producers would come under the headings of unproductive leases, dry holes, and drilling costs, in which "intangible drilling costs" have a special accounting and tax status. These items are significant in their bearing on the true profits, and they are often troublesome to the analyst because of varying methods followed by different enterprises in dealing with them in their accounts.

Depletion Charges. Depletion represents the using up of exhaustible capital assets, mainly underground, by turning them into products for sale. It applies to companies producing oil and gas, metals and many other minerals, sulphur and other chemicals from deposits, clay, limestone, etc. It also applies to timber companies, although their "wasting asset" is above ground and may be renewed by reforestation. As the holdings, or reserves, of these products are exhausted, their value must be gradually written off through charges against earnings. In the companies' own accounts such charges are made by deducting that percentage of the cost of the property which the mineral, etc., extracted bears to the total content. This is the so-called "units-of-production" method, and it is applied also to measure the depreciation on wells and other equipment, the service life of which is governed by the same factors. For tax purposes, however, two important departures from the standard method of computing depletion have been permitted, viz., discovery depletion and percentage depletion. Since discovery depletion has been all but completely superseded by the percentage option, we shall not discuss it here.

Percentage depletion may be taken by exploiters of almost every form of wasting asset. Under the 1954 Internal Revenue Code, the depletion computed by taking a specified percentage of the *sales value* of the

[14] American Institute of Certified Public Accountants (AICPA), Accounting Research Bulletin No. 43, p. 76.

product cannot exceed 50 percent of the net income (before depletion) of each producing property.[15] The percentage of sales value allowed includes the following:

Oil and gas wells................ 27½%
Sulphur and uranium............ 23
Metal mines.................... 15
Coal, asbestos................. 10
Sand, gravel, clay............. 5

It is important to observe that a good part of an active company's exploration and development expense does not have to be deducted from the net income of a separate deposit or oil well subject to percentage depletion. Hence the depletion allowance may add up to a great deal more than 50 percent of the company's over-all net income. In fact many producers report substantial net incomes with no tax allowance whatever. How this comes about may be indicated by the approximate figures based on the 1959 report of Texas Pacific Coal & Oil Company (see Table 12-3).

Table 12-3. Texas Pacific Coal & Oil Company, December 31, 1959

(In thousands)

	Tax return (our estimate)	Income as reported
Sales of products.............................	$25,900*	$25,900
Expenses and taxes, less other income..............	8,800	8,800
Depreciation.................................	1,600	1,600
Amortization of intangible drilling costs............	....	2,400
Intangible drilling costs, charged to developed holdings (estimated).............................	3,100	....
Balance.......................	$12,400	$13,000
Depletion....................	6,200*	400
Balance after depletion......................	$ 6,200	$12,600
Intangible costs charged to undeveloped holdings (estimated).................................	$ 900	....
Dry holes and abandoned wells....................	2,500	2,500
Lease rentals and surrendered leases................	2,900	2,900
Net income......................	$ 100 (d)	$ 7,200

* Percentage depletion of 27½ percent of sales would equal $7,122,000; this exceeds 50 percent of our calculated net income before depletion; consequently the maximum depletion allowable under the statute is $6,200,000.

In Table 12-3 the indicated intangible drilling costs are somewhat arbitrarily divided to produce a tax-depletion allowance which leaves no final taxable income. In fact, the company showed no tax payable in 1959 against its income of $7,200,000.

[15] The taxpayer is not given an election to choose between the cost or valuation depletion and the percentage depletion, but is required to compute both ways and claim the *larger* of the two. As a practical matter the percentage depletion is usually the larger.

The actual ratio of tax paid to reported income varies to a striking degree among companies in the same depletion-subject industry.

Examples:

(Dollar figures in millions)

	Phelps Dodge	Kennecott Copper	Phillips Petroleum	Continental Oil
1960 net before tax............	$57.1*	$163.0	$169.9	$70.8
Income tax..................	21.1	85.6†	54.0	9.6
Net income.................	30.0	77.4	112.9	61.2
Tax as percent of net before tax	37%	52%	32%	14%

* After deducting $1.3 million "depletion of mines."
† Includes $53.9 million of foreign income taxes.

The percentage depletion allowed by the tax law has been under growing attack from the Treasury and elsewhere. The analyst must consider in his evaluations the possibility of changes being made adverse to the companies which have been paying no tax or very little tax on a large reported net income.

Accounting for Intangible Drilling Costs. Table 12-3 includes figures on intangible drilling costs of a typical oil and gas producing company. These represent the labor and overhead costs incurred in drilling wells, as distinguished from the cost of pipe and other tangible materials. The income tax law gives the concerns the option of either capitalizing such intangible costs, subject to regular amortization over the life of the well, or of writing off the full cost in the year incurred. The standard policy, of course, is to take the 100 percent write-off on the tax returns in order to get the important tax benefits. The active and expanding producers have in the past decade spent more money each year on new producing wells than the accruing amortization on their past investment. Hence they have always kept ahead of the tax collector in their intangible drilling accounts. For that reason, as indicated above (page 162) most of the companies have felt they could report earnings to stockholders on the basis of capitalizing the drilling costs—thus producing a higher net profit —without setting up any reserve for deferred income tax because of the higher deductions on their tax returns. The Texas Pacific Coal & Oil figures in Table 12-3 illustrate the effect of this prevalent treatment— which we shall call "Method *A*"—on the income account.

A second or intermediate "Method *B*," used by a very few companies, follows the accepted practice in other industries and deducts a charge from earnings equal to the tax saved. But instead of showing this amount as a reserve for future income tax it is added to the depreciation reserve—as is done by Johns-Manville, Woolworth, and others in different fields.

Examples: Texaco, Inc., has followed this method since 1951. In 1959 it added $50,000,000 to its depreciation reserves, representing deferred tax on about $100,000,000 of net increase in intangible drilling investment.

The third, "Method *C*," used by relatively few high-profit companies, writes off 100 percent of the intangible costs both on the tax return and on the published reports. These costs are added both to the gross property account and to the depreciation reserves, and are taken out when the property is abandoned.

Examples: Amerada Petroleum, Continental Oil,[16] Superior Oil. Shell Oil gives us an example of a change from Method *C* to Method *B*, made at the end of 1958. As a consequence it reduced its accumulated depreciation reserve and increased stockholders' equity by $206 million and raised its net income for 1958 from $118.5 million to $128.6 million.

The effect of the choice among the three methods upon the reported earnings per share may be approximated by an examination of the Texas Pacific Coal & Oil and Texaco figures for 1959, and from a corresponding estimate for Amerada, as follows:

Table 12-4. 1959 Earnings per Share of Three Oil Companies

	Amerada*	Texaco	Texas Pacific Coal & Oil
Method *A*..............	(Estimated) $4.95	(Estimated) $6.65	Reported $1.85
Method *B*..............	(Estimated) 4.38	Reported 5.85	(Estimated) 1.65
Method *C*..............	Reported 3.81	(Estimated) 5.05	(Estimated) 1.45
Average price, 1959.....	88	76	25
Multiplier of reported earnings.............	23.1	13.0	13.5
Multiplier of earnings under Method *B*.....	20.1	13.0	15.2

* In 1960 Amerada changed its accounting policy by capitalizing intangible drilling costs of productive wells drilled in Libya. This raised the 1960 earnings from $3.84 to $4.37 and those of 1959, retroactively, from $3.81 to $4.08.

It will be observed that the popular Method *A* gives earnings about 15 percent higher than by Method *B* and 30 percent higher than by Method *C*. We consider the intermediate procedure to be preferable to the others. As we see it, intangible drilling costs represent actual investment just as do labor costs anywhere else. Hence they should, be amortized as are other capital costs. The tax saved by the full charge-off on the tax return should be deducted from earnings in some suitable manner, so as to be drawn on in the future.[17]

[16] Continental Oil changed to Method *A* in 1961.

[17] Metal mining companies have a similar option for the treatment of mine-development expense, and the accounting method varies. Anaconda Company capitalizes such expense *less* the related tax savings—giving a net income and net asset result similar to that for Texaco.

Depletion of Mining Companies. Depletion is no longer an important item in the published accounts of mining companies. A number of such enterprises, such as Anaconda and Kennecott Copper, have made no deduction for depletion in either their income statement or their balance sheet. Others show a deduction based on the cost of their mining properties, but this figure is almost always comparatively small.

Example: American Smelting & Refining Company showed $1,931,000 deducted for depletion in 1960. Its final net was $23,700,000.

In former years some concerns deducted in their income accounts the full amount of the percentage or discovery-value depletion allowed by the tax law. For most purposes, including intercompany comparisons, it was incumbent on the analyst to restore such amounts to net income.

Example 1: Homestake Mining, the leading gold producer, deducted tax-allowed depletion in its statements through 1956 and cost depletion thereafter. The change increased the 1957 earnings about 50 percent.

Example 2: Potash Company of America still charges substantial amounts for depletion in its statements. The figure for the June 1960 year was 94 cents per share, and reduced the reported earnings from $2.40 to $1.46 per share.

It is the practice of most financial services to state the per-share earnings of mining companies "before depletion."[18] This is inherently logical, since the only depletion calculation which would have real significance for the investor would be one related to the valuation of the ore reserves implicit in his own cost or to some assumed market value for the shares. We think it would be equally logical for the earnings of oil and gas producers to be shown before the companies' allowance for their *cost* depletion, and subject to a similar calculation by the analyst *and the investor.*

AMORTIZATION OF INTANGIBLE ASSETS

Intangible assets fall into various classes, depending on the way in which they may or must be amortized in the tax returns and on the varying treatment accorded them in corporate accounts. These items usually have a small effect on reported earnings. But there are exceptions, as already shown in our previous discussion of "intangible drilling costs." (These are not really intangible and are invariably carried in the balance sheet as part of the tangible property account.)

1. Items Which May Be Either Expensed or Amortized. Besides intangible drilling costs, these items include exploration costs, mine-development expense, and other research and development ("R&D"). They are almost always written off for taxes, but their treatment on the books varies. Productive exploration and development expense is regu-

---

[18] However, the *Financial World Stock Record* gives Homestake's per-share earnings after tax-allowed depletion through 1958 and before depletion in 1959. The rise shown from $0.96 to $2.20 per share in these two years is entirely misleading.

larly capitalized and amortized over the life of the property. The increasingly important item of R&D of industrial companies has been just as regularly charged to current expense, in part for conservative accounting, in part because of the difficulty of setting up a logical rate for future amortization. But in the case of numerous small concerns engaged in technological areas, it has become customary to capitalize all or part of R&D in the accounts while charging it off for taxes. The effect on reported earnings may be appreciable.

Examples: Lynch Communication Systems in its 1960 year reported net income of $276,000, or 86 cents per share. Of this, 27 cents per share was represented by "deferred R&D costs" less the related tax saving.

Similar items will be found in the 1960 statements of Dynacolor, Avien, and many others.

Comment: The write-off in full of current R&D by most companies undoubtedly serves to understate their profits, since a good part of these often substantial expenditures will have earning-power value in the future. However, the analyst would find it difficult to restate earnings by ascribing a suitable capitalized value to each year's R&D expense, less a suitable rate of amortization of previously capitalized R&D. It seems more practicable to accept the earnings on the conservative basis of treating all R&D as fully chargeable to expense in each year, but to reflect the expected benefits therefrom in the projection of future earnings and in the rate of capitalization thereof.

Looking forward to the future, we might envisage a change in standard corporate accounting for this major item. Most R&D expenses could be allocated to specific projects and products; the unsuccessful outlays could be charged off and the successful ones capitalized and amortized over the conservatively estimated "life" of the related income producer. This would place R&D on a basis fairly close to the exploration and development expense which is generally capitalized by mining, and oil and gas companies. The result might well be a fairer and more informative picture of many companies' results.

2. Items Which Must Be Amortized on Tax Returns. These intangibles include patents, licenses, and costs of leases. (Leasehold improvements—typically buildings erected on leased land—should best be considered the equivalent of a tangible asset, with life coterminous with the lease.) In the past most companies "conservatively" wrote off the cost of patents against *surplus* and thus relieved future earnings of the (usually small) amortization charge.[19] Accounting rules no longer permit this, and the cost of patents is regularly amortized against income.

3. "Development Items" Which Must Be Expensed on the Tax Returns. These include advertising, start-up costs, early deficits, and the

---

[19] Similarly, Empire Trust Company of New York charged the substantial remaining *cost of a lease* against surplus in 1940, in order to "spare the income account the heavy burden of amortizing the leasehold." See our 1951 edition, p. 143.

like. In some rather varied cases these have been capitalized in the accounts, with resultant benefit to the reported earnings.

Example 1: In 1959 Eastern Airlines reported net of $2.24 per share (before "Special Credit"). About one-quarter of this was made possible by entering as a deferred asset $4,015,000, representing "the cost of introducing new types of flight equipment, less amortization to date."

Example 2: Seaboard Finance Company began in 1959 to capitalize the first 12-months losses of new credit-card offices and new loan offices. At the end of 1960 these losses were carried as "deferred development" in the sum of $6,930,000 for the credit-card, and $555,000 for the loan offices. In 1960 the reported common-stock earnings were $1.40 per share; had the losses been written off, as is customary, the earnings would have been only 80 cents. The major item (less tax credits) is to be written off over a six-year period.[20]

Example 3: Empire National Corporation (lumber products) capitalized part of its 1960 advertising outlays. The amount added to earnings was small.

Comment: These assorted examples are cited to indicate what appears to us to be a new tendency to look for plausible means of bolstering up the reported per-share earnings, even though this involves changing former accounting methods and departing from customary practice.

Purchased Goodwill. The fourth group of intangibles comprises those which may be neither expensed nor amortized on the tax returns. Chief of these is goodwill, especially the important element of "purchased goodwill," which arises when a business is acquired at a cost exceeding its net tangible assets.[21] This is the one area where there is a wide tendency to make reported earnings *less* than the taxable earnings. Perhaps a majority of companies taking over purchased goodwill write it off against profits over a period between three and ten years, without any tax benefit therefrom. Sometimes the effect on earnings is appreciable.

Example 1: Gillette (Safety Razor) charged 1957 income with $2,628,000 for amortization of the excess cost of its Paper-Mate acquisition. This was being written off over three years, indicating a total cost of $7,884,000 for the purchased goodwill. The 1957 per-share earnings were reduced about 11 percent by this charge—which we deem entirely unnecessary.[22]

Example 2: McLean Trucking Company acquired Hayes Freight Lines

---

[20] In 1961 the company revised its accounts to eliminate the deferred-development items. See Appendix Note 5, p. 730, for a discussion of some implications of such revisions of past years' statements.

[21] Formerly organization expenses were in the same category, but since 1953 they may be written off for tax purposes in not less than five years.

[22] Zenith Radio reduced its reported earnings in 1950 substantially, from $14.05 to $10.70 per share, by a similar arbitrary write-off. See our 1951 edition, p. 143.

in December 1959 and carried almost its entire cost as an intangible asset of about \$3.2 million. Its statement for the June 1961 year shows the following:

(000 omitted)

Net before taxes	\$1,273
Income taxes	216
Net before amortization of intangibles	\$1,057
Amortization of intangibles	391
Net income	686
Per share on 1,238,000 shares	53 cents

(The *Wall Street Journal* reported the earnings as 53 cents per share, with a footnote referring to the earnings before amortization of goodwill as 82 cents.)

In view of the numerous acquisitions of one company by another in recent years we might expect to see many instances of large payments in excess of book value, which would then appear as an intangible asset on the balance sheet of the acquiring company. This in turn could produce significant deductions from earnings to write off such intangibles. But in fact this situation has not arisen; where such amortization has taken place the amounts involved have usually been of small moment. This has happened because in the more significant cases the acquisitions have been arranged either through merger or through the issuance of common stock, with low stated value, for the assets taken over. Such procedures permit the excess of the true consideration paid over the tangible assets acquired to be disregarded in the accounts.

The difference between traditional accounting concepts and recent investment attitudes is pointed up sharply by the tendency of most companies which have an item of "purchased goodwill" to write this sum off rapidly by charges to earnings.[23] Retention of this figure in the balance sheet is considered as a kind of "blot on the 'scutcheon." The investor might ask himself how his common-stock holdings would show up in terms of net-earnings yield, if he charged off the excess he paid over the underlying tangible assets of his shares against the earnings of, say, the next ten years. This is another aspect of the question of "amortization on the basis of cost to the investor," which will be discussed in the next chapter.

A Bizarre Example. The heavy going in this lengthy chapter tempts us to end it on a lighter note. The reader may be as amazed as we were to discover that a company listed on the New York Stock Exchange is currently practising amortization of goodwill *in reverse.* (Should it be called

---

[23] There are many exceptions. For example, Bristol-Myers does not amortize the \$10.8 million it paid for the goodwill of Clairol in 1959. Pittsburgh Brewing revised its property account in 1949 to show \$2 million of goodwill, which it has been writing off at the rate of \$100,000 per annum by charges to *surplus.* This is an innocuous practice.

"amortization of bad will"?) Since it bought an interest in other concerns at a cost *less* than their applicable tangible assets, it decided to *credit* income with a portion of the difference—apparently one-eleventh —in each future year. The name of the company is American Consumer Products (formerly American Ice) Company. Having acquired control of two ice and cold-storage concerns, it consolidated their accounts with its own in 1960. The excess of assets values acquired over cost thereof was $2,232,000. Instead of merely adding this amount to its "capital surplus," the company set it up as a kind of "deferred-profits" item to be taken into *income* over an arbitrarily selected period in the future.

By this interesting device the company was able to increase its "other income" in 1960 by $218,000, free of tax, thus upping its reported per-share earnings from an actual $1.10 to a somewhat imaginary $1.76. Since control of numerous not very successful enterprises can be acquired at discounts from book values, this procedure opens up appealing vistas to companies that might like to increase their reported per-share earnings by 50 percent or more.

CHAPTER THIRTEEN

THE CONCEPT OF CASH FLOW. AMORTIZATION

CHARGES FROM THE INVESTOR'S STANDPOINT

In the preceding chapter we discussed a number of aspects of depreciation, depletion, and other amortization, as these items appear, either actually or ideally, in the company's accounts. We are now ready to extend the discussion into two related areas. The first embraces the concept of "cash flow," which now plays an important part in Wall Street's thinking. The second considers amortization in terms of the market price of the shares—or the "investor's cost" thereof—insofar as this may require allowances different from those appropriate for the company itself. (This latter question has received virtually no attention from the financial community. Its implications will be found to be generally the opposite of those drawn from the cash-flow idea.)

The New Concept of "Cash Flow." The term "cash flow" is used to refer to the net earnings plus depreciation and other charges, often called "earnings before depreciation." It appears under these and other names in annual reports and in analyses by advisory services and brokerage firms.[1] This figure is generally presented on a per-share basis, often with the strong intimation that it is as important as, or even more significant than, the net income after depreciation (and taxes).

The cash-flow figures have always received some attention in security analysis, but until recent years it was usually confined to their use in comparative analyses of companies in the same industry. The oil industry has been considered especially suited to such treatment. The cash-flow item undoubtedly has good uses of a special sort. It indicates the total funds available to the company from the period's operations for replacements, expansion, reduction of debt, increase in working capital, and dividends. Its importance in comparative analysis would derive from

---

[1] Glickman Corporation, a real estate company, uses the term "cash-flow income" to mean "net taxable profit plus allowable depreciation less mortgage-debt reduction." Apparently this assumes that ordinary income will not be subject to income tax because of liberal depreciation allowed. (Bulletin of the company, dated Jan. 10, 1962.)

those instances in which the amortization allowance of certain companies are much higher or lower than the average of the industry. We might add that the companion figure of "cash throw-off" has always been a central point in the calculations of real estate investors.

It is only recently—say from 1959—that the cash-flow concept has been given importance in common-stock analysis generally—for example, as shown by the Value Line calculation of "cash earnings" for the Dow-Jones Industrial Average, first published in 1960. On what is this new emphasis based? Was cash flow always a major determinant of security values, but was its importance largely overlooked in former years? Or have new operating or financial conditions justified the shifting of emphasis from earnings after, to those before depreciation? We think that the explanation of the new vogue is somewhat different from either of the above and derives from the following facts:

1. Amortization changes are on the whole more liberal than they were a decade ago. This is due chiefly to the use in most annual reports of the accelerated depreciation rates permitted by the tax law on property acquired after 1953. For certain comparative purposes, therefore, earnings before depreciation may supply the more useful guide to performance.

2. Earnings before amortization have in fact grown at a much faster rate than those after amortization. This is shown by the following comparison, taken from the Value Line compilation:

Table 13-1. Dow-Jones Industrial Average

	1950	1960	Increase
Earnings (after amortization).................	$30.70	$33.30	8.5%
Amortization.............................	10.15	24.35	140.0
Earnings plus amortization—"cash earnings" ...	$40.85	$57.65	41.0

3. The rise in average stock prices has so greatly outstripped the increase in reported earnings that Wall Street has been constrained to look elsewhere for a justification of the market level. Much of it has been found in confident hopes of future expansion and in confident hopes or fears of future inflation. But the substitution of the much lower ratio of market price to "cash earnings" for the old price-earnings ratio has brought additional comfort to investors and financial analysts.

If these statements present fairly the reasons for the new importance of cash flow, we should examine them with a critical eye. The last reason can hardly be taken seriously as a matter for logical argument, although its influence on the future course of the stock market should not be ignored. Since the first two reasons relate to a change in the amount of the depreciation deducted from earnings, they suggest only that some adjustment needs to be made, either by decreasing the amortization now being taken or by increasing—for comparative purposes—that taken in the past. We have already discussed (Chapter 12) the amount of increase made in the ratio of depreciation to gross plant by the Dow-Jones companies and have found that an adjustment to the 1949 rates would raise the 1959 earnings by about 4½ percent. But in our subsequent consideration of depreciation we expressed the view that the present "post-1953" basis used by most concerns could not properly be said to be unduly conservative and to understate the true earnings.

The reader is free, of course, to disagree with this conclusion and to substitute lower depreciation charges for those now taken. But if he does so he should recognize that he is not adopting "cash flow" as a measure of earnings; he is merely adjusting the earnings to a "proper" amortization charge. The present cash-flow concept seems to go far beyond such an adjustment and to argue that the "true earnings" are those before depreciation. This contention would be based on the asserted fact that a company's depreciation charge is a "bookkeeping item" and does not represent any actual cash expense.

Is Depreciation an "Actual Expense"? The fraction of truth in the above assertion is just large enough to cause much confusion and misunderstanding. Depreciation and similar charges range in their nature from those which come very close to a current "out-of-pocket" expense to those that can be related only theoretically to either past or future outlays. The following list will illustrate the variety of amortization types, considered in terms of cash expenditures:

1. *Cost of dry holes drilled.* This item is included in amortization and therefore in the cash-flow figures of oil companies (e.g., Sinclair Oil, Texas Pacific Coal and Oil). But it represents for the most part money spent and lost in the current year.

2. *Amortization of special tools.* General Motors charged no less than $425,000,000 for this purpose in 1959, leaving an unamortized balance of only $318,000,000. This suggests that the average life of such tools is not much more than a year and that their cost is largely equivalent to ordinary operating expenses.

3. *Autos and trucks.* These are generally written off over a four- or five-year period and replaced at some such interval. The depreciation fund does not stay very long in the company's coffers.

4. *Machinery and equipment.* The depreciable life appears to average about 15 years. With technological change growing ever more rapid, the expectable disposal date of such assets could scarcely be placed much later. The depreciation money—and more—will be needed for their replacement.

5. *Factory buildings.* These are generally given a life of from 30 to 40 years for depreciation purposes. They are not replaced, as is most machinery, when their useful life expires. Generally the entire plant is eventually abandoned for a more efficient one, and the basic factor involved is obsolescence rather than normal depreciation. For this reason the depreciation taken on this important class of asset cannot be said to measure accurately the passing of its useful life, or the required rate of gradual return to the owner of the price he paid

for it. But it would be a greater mistake to assume that no provision for depreciation need be made out of earnings; the loss of value is very real, even though difficult to ascertain precisely in any year.

6. *Office and apartment buildings.* These are major assets, but only for a limited group of real estate companies. In their case the annual depreciation represents a return of a small part of the book cost, in an amount which is only theoretically related to the wearing out or other loss of value of the buildings. The depreciation money is in no sense set aside for the replacement of the asset, though usually the greater part of it is employed to pay down debt against it. For most such buildings, over most periods of time, the economic value of the land and buildings together has increased over the years; in any event, a loss of value, if it occurs, is only rarely related to the depreciation taken on the books.

This presentation suggests that only in the rather specialized sixth class of assets can we consider that depreciation constitutes a proper component of earnings from the standpoint of the stockholder. Let us approach the matter from another angle. If earnings before depreciation were the *true* earnings, then the amounts deducted for amortization would be really added to equity and reinvested in the business in the same way as undistributed profit. They should then generate a corresponding increase in subsequent cash-flow earnings. There is certainly no evidence over the long-term past that depreciation charges have been equivalent to earnings and equity, and have either been available for distribution to stockholders or have contributed to the growth of earnings. To test this hypothesis as applied to the last decade, let us first examine the figures of a company which has emphasized the cash-flow figure in its report for 1960—Sinclair Oil.

Table 13-2. "Cash Income" and Net Income of Sinclair Oil, 1950–1960

(in millions, except per share)

	Ten years 1951–1960	Year 1960	Year 1950
"Cash income"................................	$1,593	$166.3	$113.2
Depreciation, depletion, amortization............	....	85.6	33.1
Leases canceled, dry holes, property retired......	....	28.2	9.9
Total amortization, etc........................	$ 889	$113.8	$ 43.0
Net income....................................	$ 704	$ 52.5	$ 70.3
"Cash income" per share......................	$114.57	$10.83	$9.40
Net income per share..........................	50.47	3.42	5.81
Stockholders' equity...........................	....	940	485
Equity per share..............................	....	62.05	40.12
Gross property account........................	....	1,799	845
Accumulated depreciation, etc..................	....	897	470
Net property account..........................	....	$902	$375
Sales (excluding purchased products)............	....	979	606
Total daily production (1,000 bbl)..............	....	182.8	112.4

Comment: The company's comparative showing on a cash-income basis is much better than on the customary net-income basis. The earnings before depreciation and other charge-offs show a slight increase per share from 1950 to 1960, while the conventional net income per share declined over 40 percent. Is there any reason to believe that the company's "cash income" supplies the better guide to the company's profitability?

The only sound reason for considering amortization charges as a part of earnings would be the fact that they were equivalent to reinvested profits, which in turn would produce higher sales and net income in the future. However, from 1950 to 1960 the increase in Sinclair's physical output, dollar sales, and earnings before amortization all failed to keep pace with the stockholders' equity as shown on the books. There is thus no sign of any "hidden equity" having been developed for the owners by reason of reinvested amortization money. The net property account, now much higher than before in relation to the business done, suggests that the depreciation allowances were the reverse of unnecessary or excessive.

The use of the "cash-earnings" or the "cash-flow" figure in this case is particularly objectionable because a good part of such amounts is in the nature of ordinary expense. The cost of dry holes is a current, nonrecoverable outlay. The write-offs of leases and other property represent cash previously spent and now recognized as lost. (It will be noted that only three-fifths of the ten-year deductions show up as an increase in accrued depreciation; the other 40 percent—or $365 million—has disappeared from the accounts entirely.)[2]

The results of the Dow-Jones Industrial group, if worked out on the same basis as the above table, would also throw grave doubt on the hypothesis that all or even a large part of the amortization charges have been equivalent to reinvested profits. In sum, we must express the view that the transfer of emphasis from the net earnings to the cash flow is not warranted by the underlying facts or by logic; that it has been inspired largely by the high price-earnings ratios created by the great stock-market advance; and that if persisted in or extended, it can introduce highly unsound concepts and practices into security analysis.

Two Recent Cash-flow Calculations. To reinforce our criticism of the cash-earnings vogue, let us consider in some detail the 1960 reports of two companies which emphasized this calculation. They illustrate also some of the more complex features involved in the cash-flow concept.

[2] Cf. the statement made by the treasurer of du Pont in September 1961, as follows: "Our annual write-off of plant now approximates about 25% of construction expenditures. However, that figure is based on book values, and if we factor up the exits from the plant account to express them in terms of current dollar values, this relationship would be more in the neighborhood of 40 to 45%." A study of the retirements charged by U.S. Steel Corporation as compared with plant expenditures made 25 years earlier indicates that as a whole its capital assets have not long outlived their depreciable lives.

Example 1: Georgia Pacific Corporation.

The annual report for 1960 of this lumber producer presents among its "Highlights" the following:

Net income..............................	$15,210,000
Per share...............................	2.45
Net cash generated from operations........	40,031,000
Per share...............................	6.66
Property additions.......................	16,117,000

In a subsequent chart the above figure of $40,031,000 appears again under the title of "Net Cash Flow."

The impression conveyed to stockholders by this presentation is that the "net cash flow" of $6.66 per share is of about equal significance to them as is the conventional figure of $2.45 per share of net income. Also, the property additions are stated as much less than the $25,000,000 indicated charge for amortization—the statement indicating that the company has actually gained from these items a substantial amount of net cash, which may thus be thought of as accruing in some way to the stockholders.

The fact was that the "property additions" stated did *not* include $12,800,000 spent on timberland additions. Hence the company's additions to fixed assets exceeded the amortization charges. Furthermore, the company reported total long-term debt and notes payable of some $150,000,000, which made up more than half of the total capitalization. The annual installments payable on this debt more or less absorbed all the large depletion charge.

We consider the term "net cash flow," as used by the company, quite misleading, even though usually qualified by the additional phrase "generated from operations." For good semantics we suggest that earnings plus amortization be designated as "cash flow" or "*gross* cash flow," and that "*net* cash flow" should stand for the gross amount less additions to fixed assets. (That would be in most cases a *negative* figure.)

Example 2: Tishman Realty and Construction.

This company does not, like Georgia Pacific above, use the term "cash flow" in its 1960 report and calculate it on a per-share basis. But it does give great prominence to an equivalent figure, which it calls first "income from operation of properties—net (before depreciation)" and later "recurring income." Recurrently in its report the company refers to this figure as "all-important." Its statement of "financial highlights" includes the following:

(000 omitted)

Income	1959	1960
Net—before depreciation......................	$3,027	$3,495
Profit on disposition of real estate, etc., net......	3,172	659
Net income after depreciation and taxes.........	3,344	1,035
Net earnings per share of common stock........	$1.59	$0.50

In its report the company stresses the steady increase in its "recurring income" over the years, suggesting that this is of more importance than the decline in net income (after depreciation) registered in 1960. At first reading an analyst might be inclined to accept this point of view, in part at least, since depreciation on buildings for general rental purposes is considered to differ from that on other assets. Such real estate depreciation is included in the cash "throw-off" from the property; it is used ordinarily to pay down mortgage indebtedness, which in turn is considered to build up the owner's equity in some corresponding amount.

But the interesting aspect of the Tishman report is that all (and more) of the 1960 increase in "recurring income" came from the addition of depreciation of "rental equipment"—meaning television sets rented to hotels, etc.,—which became part of the company's business for the first time in 1960. Such TV depreciation (on $7,500,000 of cost) apparently accounted for the increase of $700,000, or nearly 60 percent, in amortization for 1960 against 1959. Depreciation on television sets is an entirely different matter from that on apartment houses or office buildings; it is, in fact, quite closely allied to ordinary expenses of operation.

Here again, in our view, the transfer of emphasis in a corporate report from earnings as traditionally calculated to "recurrent income" (a pseudonym for "cash flow") has a basically misleading effect. Two additional facts relating to the above examples may be worthy of comment. In both cases the provision for income tax is considerably lower than that indicated by the reported net income. Georgia Pacific deducted $7,000,000 for tax from pretax income of $22,200,000.[3] Tishman Realty deducted $290,000 from pretax income of $1,325,000. Thus the real question may be whether the reported net income *after depreciation* has been in some degree overstated. The second point is that both companies paid periodic stock dividends in 1960 and previous years. The market value of these stock dividends exceeded the available earnings after cash dividends—in the case of Georgia Pacific by a moderate amount, but in the case of Tishman by a large percentage. This suggests that the "cash flow" concept may have influenced the stock-dividend policy of at least one of the companies.[4]

AMORTIZATION FROM THE INVESTOR'S STANDPOINT

We turn now to the other aspect of the amortization question included in our chapter heading. The theory of amortization is that it should return over the life of a wasting or depreciating asset enough to repay the

---

[3] However, lumber companies are allowed to pay the 25 percent capital-gain rate on part of their profits.

[4] In Appendix Note 6, pp. 730–733, we discuss the concept of "net-worth accounting," set forth at length in the 1961 Annual Report of Sheraton Corporation of America. This purports to replace "ordinary" or "depreciation" accounting.

cost to the owner. Only after this is provided for can the remaining earnings be considered a true profit on the investment. A company's annual depletion charge is based on its own cost of the ore or oil deposit. But if the investor in the company's stock pays more or less than its net asset value he can usually be considered to be buying his share of the wasting asset at a higher or lower figure than the company's book cost. In calculating the true profits and the return on his investment, he should allow for its amortization over a suitable period of time—presumably the same span as used by the company—but the dollar amount per share may be considerably higher or lower than the company's figure. (At this stage of the discussion we are dealing with the typical producer of raw materials—a company whose earnings are derived almost solely from its wasting assets and which does not possess a separate goodwill or going-concern value.)

This consideration should mean that variations in the price paid for shares of a mining, oil producing, or similar company should have a *double effect* on the investor's expectable return. Not only will the stated profits per share give a lower or higher yield on his price, but the profits themselves should, in theory at least, be reduced or increased to take care of his particular amortization requirement.

We have used the phrase "in theory at least," because in a great many cases the actual experience of the investor will not be determined by this kind of reasoning, however correct in principle, but rather by fortuitous developments of one kind or another which invalidate any exact calculations. The chief development in practice is the acquisition at relatively low cost of additional reserves which extend the life of the stockholder's investment and thus raise his actual return above his expectable return.

Nevertheless, we believe that the analyst should familiarize himself with the theoretical concept involved. As we shall point out, in a variety of instances this concept has had important practical applications.

An Illustrative Calculation. Let us illustrate our point by returning to the 1959 report of Texas Pacific Coal and Oil. Since this is solely a producer of oil and gas (no coal), its results over the years may be expected to be, first, from the extraction of its reserves already developed, and second, from the addition of new reserves through the successful drilling of undeveloped acreage. (It may also acquire developed properties from others, but this has been a minor part of its past activities.)

The net income in 1959 was $7,200,000, or $1.85 per share, after amortization charges of, say, $4,500,000 on about $52,000,000 of net investment in producing properties, including wells and equipment. Large expenditures were also charged in connection with undeveloped leaseholds, carried at $12,500,000 cost. The book value of the stock was about $20 per share; its low market price in 1960 was about the same; and its high that year was close to $30.

These figures enable us to make certain somewhat theoretical calculations as to the expectable return to the investor who bought either at the high or the low price for 1960. They are based on the assumptions that: (1) the earnings of $1.85 fairly represent expectable future profits, except as the equity is built up through reinvestment; (2) the investor's cost of the producing properties should be written off over the same time span as is the company's cost—about 9 percent annually; and (3) the investor's cost of the shares (above working capital) is allocated proportionately to producing and undeveloped properties.

Table 13-3. Texas Pacific Coal and Oil Company: Calculation of Amortization Based on Per-share Cost

	Purchase at $20	Purchase at $30
Paid for producing properties............................	$13.00	$20.50
Paid for undeveloped properties.........................	4.00	6.50
Paid for working capital.................................	3.00	3.00
Total...	$20.00	$30.00
Earned before amortization..............................	3.02	3.02
Amortization of producing properties (9 percent)..........	1.17	1.85
Balance earned on investment...........................	$ 1.85	$ 1.17
Earned on cost of producing properties...................	14.2%	5.6%
Earned on total cost of shares	9.3	3.9
Earned on total cost of shares (reported basis)............	9.3	6.2

On the basis of the assumptions made we think this is a valid calculation. It illustrates arithmetically the twofold effect on the expectable return arising from a change in the price paid for properties with limited life. But how good are our assumptions? The chief unknown quantity in the picture probably lies in the undeveloped properties. These represent only one-fifth of the company's net assets as cost, but their contribution to future earnings may conceivably be very large. A second unknown quantity may lie in the future income tax situation, which could be less favorable than at present. Conceivably, continued inflation could raise the earnings at 1959 production rates. (The price received for crude oil rose about 20 percent from 1950 to 1959; that for natural gas more than tripled.)

The figures seem to warrant the conclusion that at the book value of $20 per share the investor could count fairly confidently on full amortization of his purchase price plus an attractive average earnings return. At an appreciably higher price—e.g., $30—the conclusion is not necessarily that the shares are overvalued, but rather (1) that a more comprehensive study of the company's holdings may be necessary to justify the commitment, or (2) that an essentially speculative component has been introduced into the purchase, an addition which may or may not turn out successfully.

An important technical point should be made relative to the above calculations. Amortization is taken in the usual fashion, on a straight-line basis, without allowing for earnings on the capital returned each year. This is done both to simplify the process and to introduce a factor of safety. On the basis of the declining cost of the stock, through the annual amortization, the earnings yield on the average investor's cost of the producing properties would be about twice that shown above for both the $20 and the $30 price.

Sequel to Past Illustrations. Most of the techniques used in this volume have proved more useful in establishing that a common stock is under-valued or reasonably valued, than that it is overvalued. This would naturally be true during a period such as 1949–1961, in which the stock market enjoyed a spectacular advance. The limitations of the amortization approach, described above, as applied to producing oil companies in a bull market, may be demonstrated by giving the price history of three such enterprises mentioned in this section of the 1951 edition as selling above a price justified by this type of calculation.

	Kern County Land	Southland Royalty	Louisiana Land & Exploration	Standard & Poor's Ind. Index
Average price:				
1949	22*	32	14*	15
1959	55	63	54	61
Reported earnings per share:				
1949	$3.11*	$3.44	$0.92*	$2.44
1959	3.86	4.88	2.16	3.26

* Adjusted to 1959 shares.

Investor's Amortization of Plant and Equipment. To what extent does our concept of "investor's amortization" apply to other than wasting assets? If an investor pays more than book value for the shares of a manufacturing concern, should he assume that the cost *to him* of the company's plant is correspondingly higher than the book cost, and that he must therefore deduct a larger depreciation charge from the earnings than is required to be taken on the books? If the question is relevant it is important, since for many years past the shares of most important industrial companies have been selling far above their book value.

These premium prices may properly be said to represent two com-ponents, although the stock purchaser rarely if ever recognizes the fact. The first is paid for the fair or going value of the company's tangible assets; the second is paid for the company's excess earning power, present and/or prospective, above that needed to support the tangible asset values. The second, or "goodwill," component need not be amortized in the investor's calculation on the accounting ground that it has a limited life and must eventually be replaced if the business is to continue.[5] But if it is assumed that the investor pays more than book value for the company's fixed assets—in particular, that his price includes a valuation of the plant at reproduction cost less accrued depreciation—then it would seem logical for the investor to provide annual amortization out of earnings at a rate higher than the company's own depreciation allowance.

This reasoning brings us back to the controversy which has raged around the use of reproduction cost as the proper basis for depreciation charges. If he is not too confused, the reader will note that we have made a distinction between amortization suitable for the company's accounts and that required for the investor's calculation, which is related to the cost of his shares. In each case, the implied cost of the fixed assets should determine their depreciation base. The two situations converge when one company buys out another and enters the latter's fixed assets on the new books at their current value. Then the depreciation rate must be raised to the reproduction-cost basis.[6] The same result would follow if companies marked up their fixed assets on their books to the reproduction-value basis, with a corresponding increase in the indicated stockholders' equity. This was widely done in the 1920's, to reflect the inflationary results of World War I, but is unlikely to happen now unless the higher depreciation rates are recognized for tax purposes.

Our conclusion from the above discussion is that in the great majority of common-stock investments the depreciation base used by the company is below that required by the stockholders. Hence, if the allowance made by the company is needed to show its true earnings, then a larger allowance is needed in the investor's calculations to show *his* true earnings on his investment. The current situation, if measured by the suggestive figures of Bristol-Myers (page 157) would require an increase of at least one-quarter. We consider this an added reason for favoring the more liberal "post-1953" basis of computing depreciation over the older straight-line rate. It does not really strengthen our former argument against using the "cash flow" as a measure of true earnings, except in pointing out that more rather than less conservatism is needed in interpreting earnings statements.

The Opposite Case. Suppose an investor pays substantially less than

---

[5] The conservative investor might well be justified in amortizing the cost to him of the goodwill factor against the expectable earnings, simply to be on the safe side in his calculations. But this would probably be merged into an amortization requirement for his entire stock investment. See the method of A. Wilfred May, described in Appendix Note 16, p. 748.

[6] For an example see Needham Packing Company, Appendix Note 7, p. 733.

book value for a company's shares. Would that justify his reducing his calculated depreciation of the fixed assets below the company's figure? If he bought the shares for no more than their working-capital value, may he assume that he has paid nothing for the plant and thus needs no depreciation charge against the profits? Would the much misused "cash-flow" figure be really applicable in his case?

These are interesting questions. They do not seem to be very relevant to the situation in the early 1960's, where so few important enterprises—other than the railroads and some insurance companies—sell below their net asset value. But at the time of our previous edition a large proportion of all companies sold at discounts from book value, and many hundreds could be bought on a basis representing no market value whatever for their fixed assets. Even at what seemed a high market level in 1957–1958 there remained many instances of the latter sort. What the reader of this book is destined to find in the future we cannot prophesy.

The Concept of Unexpended Depreciation. In our view the plausible answer to the questions above raised will depend upon an additional factor, namely, what has been happening to the sums charged by the company for depreciation. If the money has gone into plant replacements and additions, it cannot be conceived as accruing to the stockholder as earnings just because he has paid little or nothing for his share of the plant. The money may be considered rather as the equivalent of out-of-pocket operating expenses, or perhaps as a "defensive or non-profit-increasing investment," similar to the defensive additions to surplus which we shall discuss in Chapter 35.

But where a good part of the depreciation money has not been expended on new fixed assets over the years but has been added to working capital or used to retire debt, it would seem proper for the buyer of the stock on a "bargain basis" to consider that these sums contribute to the true return on his cost.

Illustrations of this situation were reasonably plentiful prior to 1950,[7] but they have disappeared during the last decade along with the "bargain opportunities" themselves.

[7] For examples see pp. 147–149 of our 1951 edition.

CHAPTER FOURTEEN

ALLOWANCE FOR RESULTS OF SUBSIDIARIES, AFFILIATES, AND FOREIGN OPERATIONS

A subsidiary is generally defined as a company controlled by a "parent" company which owns more than half the voting stock. (Most subsidiaries, however, will be found to be 100 percent owned by the parent.) Affiliate is a more indefinite term. An affiliate may be a company effectively controlled—perhaps jointly with others—though ownership is less than 50 percent. Or the relationship may exist through control of both companies by the same owning group or "parent," with resultant close commercial or operating ties. In some cases a company may be called an affiliate al though it really is a subsidiary.

The great majority of companies publish consolidated reports which include in the balance sheet and income statement the results and financial position of their subsidiaries. The earnings or net equity applicable to other stockholders, if any, are shown as a deduction for minority interests. In such consolidated reports there is generally no reason to distinguish between that portion of the results attributable to one corporate unit or another. The matter may become important, however, when a company elects to publish an unconsolidated (or "parent company only") statement, or when a so-called "consolidated statement" excludes certain important subsidiaries or affiliates.

The largest area for variation in reported results—and for possible correction or adjustment by the analyst—lies in the field of foreign operations, including those of subsidiaries and branches. For a number of our larger corporations such foreign operations are of major consequence, and their proper evaluation presents a challenge both of technique and of judgment to the securities analyst. We shall first discuss the treatment of domestic subsidiaries and affiliates, and then pass over to the foreign field.

DOMESTIC SUBSIDIARIES AND AFFILIATES

A. The Standard Procedure

Example 1: Gulf Oil Corporation. This company includes the results of all its subsidiaries, with provision for minority interests, as follows:

1960 Income Account

(In millions)

Net before minority interest	$348.1
Minority interest	17.8
Net income	$330.3

The balance sheet shows the minority interest in the net assets as $189 million against the Gulf stockholders' equity of $1,860 million. "Parent-company only" figures for this and other companies can be found in the 10-K reports filed annually with the SEC and the New York Stock Exchange, but such data are rarely of importance.

Example 2: American Tel. and Tel. This huge enterprise reports to the public both on a parent-company-only, and on a consolidated basis. For 1960 it showed consolidated earnings of $1,250 million, less minority interest of only $37 million, the balance equaling $5.53 per share on the average outstanding in the year. The parent-company-only report showed earnings of $4.08 per share. The analyst, of course, will consider only the consolidated figures in his work.

B. Exclusion of Subsidiaries' Results. Except in the railroad field it is rather rare to find annual reports which fail to include the full earnings of wholly owned or majority-owned domestic subsidiaries.

Example: An industrial example is provided by Kaiser Industries Corporation, which consolidates only its wholly owned subsidiaries. Its reports exclude the results of its important "affiliate," Kaiser Steel, 80 percent owned, except as to dividends received therefrom. The analyst clearly should adjust the published results to reflect the parent's full interest in Kaiser Steel's operations, and probably also in its other major affiliates, even though they are not majority owned. An illustrative adjustment of this kind would be shown in Table 14-1.

It would be particularly necessary to make an adjustment of this kind in analyzing the Kaiser Industries' results for 1960, since practically all its reported net income came from dividends paid by affiliates.

If the balance sheet were similarly adjusted to reflect the net asset value of the holdings in affiliates (instead of their cost) there would be only a minor change in the book value of Kaiser Industries' shares. However, a footnote indicates that the *market value* of these holdings in December 1960 was $370 million against a cost of $174 million. The analyst would have some difficulty in reconciling the indications given by the market quotations with the affiliates' *past* results.

C. Inclusion-Exclusion of Finance Company Subsidiaries. Large makers and sellers of durable goods often have subsidiary finance companies to handle installment sales of such items. It is customary to include the full results of such operations in the reported earnings but not to consolidate them into the balance sheet. The reason is that the finance companies have relatively huge liabilities to banks and others; their inclusion in the financial statement of the parent would distort the normal credit ratios for manufacturing and distributing concerns. Examples: Ford Motors, General Motors, American Motors, Caterpillar Tractor, and International Harvester.

Table 14-1. Kaiser Industries Corporation, 1960

(000 omitted)

Net income as reported:

Sales...	$191,200
Net income, excluding dividends received.......	1,330
Dividends from affiliates......................	7,493
Total income................................	$ 8,823
Income taxes..................................	2,300
Net after taxes...............................	$ 6,523
Earned per share of common....................	21 cents

Undistributed earnings of affiliates

Affiliates	100 percent basis	Kaiser Industries owns	Kaiser Industries' share
Kaiser Steel............................	−$11,560	79.9%	−$9,237
Kaiser Aluminum and Chemical..........	+ 4,487	43.8	+ 1,965
Permanent Cement.....................	+ 2,076	39.9	+ 810

Adjustment of reported earnings:

Net after taxes, as reported...........................	$6,523
Adjustment for Kaiser Steel...........................	− 9,237
Net, including controlled affiliates.....................	−$2,716
Adjustment for other affiliates........................	+ 2,775
Over-all result.......................................	+$ 59

D. Treatment of Noncontrolled Affiliates. Where a company does not own a majority of the voting stock of an affiliate, it is standard procedure to include in the accounts only the dividends received from it. This is on the theory that the affiliate represents only an ordinary stock investment. The theory is contrary to actual fact, since in most cases there is a common or interlocking directorate and also business relationships of considerable importance. The analyst should make allowance for the full equity in affiliates where the amounts involved are significant.

Example 1: An interesting example of this kind has long been afforded by Universal Leaf Tobacco, an important factor in the tobacco-leaf market. The company publishes a "consolidated statement," which includes the full results of 8 wholly owned subsidiaries. However, it excludes undistributed earnings of some 20 other partly owned subsidiaries and affiliates, in some of which Universal shares voting control equally with the managers. A footnote to the balance sheet each year shows the company's equity in the total undistributed profits of the affiliates. By comparing these annual equity figures the analyst can and should compute the amounts which should be added to each year's reported earnings to provide a more appropriate measure of the stockholders' position.

The adjustment for 1960, 1950, and the decade 1951–1960 is shown below. (Years end June 30; shares were adjusted for doubling in November 1960.)

Universal Leaf Tobacco Co.	1960	1950	Average 1951–1960
Earnings per share as reported................	$ 2.51	$ 1.28	$1.76
Earnings adjusted for nonconsolidated affiliates..	3.43	1.39	2.72
Net asset value as reported..................	19.60	15.47	
Net asset value as adjusted..................	33.40	17.55	
Average market price (calendar years)..........	28½	11½	18

Comment: The excluded results are important here, and would add more than 50 percent to the average earnings. The market has apparently ignored this fact, as is shown by the consistently low multiplier of adjusted earnings and average prices below book value each year. It might be added that the results since World War II show both excellent growth and good stability.

Example 2: In the railroad field the most striking consequences of the exclusion of affiliates' results was supplied by Northern Pacific and its interest in the Burlington. For the 10 years 1938–1947, Northern Pacific's earnings as reported averaged $3.80 per share, but its 48.6 percent equity in the undistributed income of Burlington Railroad (CB & Q) averaged an additional $2.40 per share.

In a very few cases a company may show its equity in a noncontrolled affiliate directly in its accounts. The only available example of this has been an outstanding one.

Example: The du Pont Company has held a substantial interest in General Motors since 1917. It was once as high as 37 percent but has stood at 22 percent since 1935. However, at this writing, du Pont is under orders to dispose of the shares. Through 1960 the company has shown its equity in the undistributed earnings of General Motors by a special procedure, viz.: it has credited surplus each year with the increase in the book value of its General Motors holdings and has marked up the carrying value accordingly.

The analyst might have presented the profit picture of du Pont somewhat as follows:

Earnings per share	1950	1960	Average 1951–1960
Excluding General Motors........	$3.92	$5.34	$4.41
Including GM dividends..........	6.58	8.09	7.18
Including full equity in GM.......	8.07	9.73	8.45

(For greater accuracy a small addition could be made to the top line to add back the 7.8 percent tax on the GM dividends received.)

EARNINGS OF FOREIGN SUBSIDIARIES, AFFILIATES, AND BRANCHES

The accounting for foreign operations of American corporations is remarkably varied. Dividends and other remittances received from these sources are, of course, reflected in the accounts; but the undistributed earnings may be shown in the income account and balance sheet, in the income account only, in the form of notes to the balance sheet, or not at all. Distinctions have often been made in the treatment of foreign earnings free from and subject to exchange controls. Provision sometimes appears for a possible U.S. tax on the future transmission of earnings retained abroad; in other cases, all earnings are included in the published results without such provision.

In the following discussion and examples we shall try to limit ourselves to instances that should be of importance in an analysis.

A. Full Inclusion of Foreign Earnings

Example: Chas. Pfizer (pharmaceuticals) includes its foreign subsidiaries' operations in full on the same basis as those of its domestic subsidiaries. A footnote states that "no provision is made for dividend tax with respect to subsidiaries' retained earnings inasmuch as it is considered that such earnings are essential to the continued operation of the subsidiaries' business." It should be borne in mind that remittances received from abroad are in general subject to a United States income tax equal to the difference between our 52 percent rate and that imposed on the earnings by the foreign government.[1] This difference will vary widely between different countries.

The following figures show the overshadowing importance of foreign operations to Pfizer in the year 1960:

(000,000 omitted)

	Domestic	Foreign	Total
Net before tax	$ 9.2	$29.7	$ 38.9
Income tax	6.9	5.8	12.7
Net after tax	$ 2.3	$23.9	$ 26.2
Net assets	76.1	94.4	170.5
(Net earnings per share on 16.8 million shares)	($0.14)	($1.43)	($1.57)

The "domestic" income tax includes that on $4.2 million of dividends received from foreign subsidiaries. The indicated amount of such tax is about $2 million, which is undoubtedly too high. However, the analyst may assume that were the remaining foreign profits to be remitted, there would be a substantial tax deduction against them.

[1] In accordance with the terms of the tax treaties.

The earnings of the foreign subsidiaries are not stated directly in the annual report, but they may be calculated from other available data, as follows:

(000 omitted)

Equity in undistributed earnings of foreign subsidiaries:

1960	$98,115
1959	78,485
Increase in 1960	$19,630
Add dividends to parent	4,236
Indicated foreign earnings after tax	$23,866

The foregoing figures would raise some questions in the mind of the analyst. The foreign earnings supply an extraordinarily large percentage of the total—quite out of line with the net assets at home and abroad. May expenses be allocated with an eye to lower taxes in foreign countries? The domestic profit plus dividends received from subsidiaries, minus tax, was only $6.6 million as against $13.3 million of dividends paid to stockholders. This suggests that larger transfers of foreign profits may be necessary in the future, subject to additional U.S. tax.[2] (The overall tax rate paid by Pfizer in 1960 was about 33 percent.)

B. Provisions for Possible Dividend Tax, etc.

Example 1: Merck & Company. This competitor of Pfizer included all its foreign operations in its consolidated statement for 1960, except comparatively small ones in the Philippines subject to exchange restrictions. The foreign subsidiaries and branches accounted for $10.5 million net after taxes (of which only $4 million was unremitted), out of a total of $28.3 million. From this sum $500,000 was subtracted to increase the "reserve applicable to foreign operations," relating to possible additional taxes thereon and to possible losses.

The company's balance sheet and appended notes showed that foreign net assets totaled $40 million (before reserve of $3 million) out of a total of $190 million. Of these foreign assets $18.2 million was said to be "subject to exchange fluctuations." Evidently the foreign interests of Merck do not present the same problems that the analyst finds in the Pfizer reports.

Example 2: Ford Motor Company estimates (but does not deduct) the tax on the future transfer of unremitted profits of its finance company and foreign subsidiaries. The figures for 1960 are as follows:

(000,000 omitted)

Equity in earnings of unconsolidated subsidiaries	$71.7
Of which remitted	27.5
Unremitted	$44.2
Estimated tax on future distribution	7.4
Over-all rate of added tax	16.7%

C. Exclusion of Unremitted Foreign Profits. Some important examples of excluded profits are discussed below. It will be noted that in recent

[2] In 1962 legislation was pending to tax most of such foreign earnings as if distributed.

years a number of companies have changed from an excluded to an included basis, sometimes with favorable effect on the market price of their shares.

Standard Exclusion Method

Example 1: International Business Machines since 1954 has excluded the sales and profits of its foreign subsidiaries from its accounts, but indicates the amount of such earnings in a footnote.[3] The results of IBM both with and without these undistributed earnings may be summarized as follows:

	Per share (adjusted to 27,516,000 shares)		
	1960	1954	Average, 1954–1960
Net as reported....................	$6.12	$1.87	$3.79
Foreign earnings unremitted.........	.92	.47	.84
Over-all earnings..................	7.04	2.34	4.63

Example 2: Hoover Company (vacuum cleaners). This company's showing at the end of 1957 was given in our second chapter (page 32) as an example of analytical work resulting in a confident conclusion. The undistributed earnings of its English subsidiary (if valued at 100 percent) would have added more than 40 percent to the reported profits for 1957 and 1948–1957, and a corresponding amount to the stockholders' equity.

An Unusual Exclusion Method

Example: National Cash Register combines its domestic and foreign operations in its reports—thus providing a fully consolidated statement—but deducts the unremitted foreign earnings at the end of its income account. The significance of its foreign business is shown in the following data for 1960:

(000,000 omitted)

	Domestic	Foreign	Combined
Sales........................	$271.7	$187.1	$458.8
Net before tax...................	20.6	30.7	51.3
Income tax....................	12.7	14.7	27.4
Combined net income............	7.9	16.0	23.9
Less unremitted foreign...........			3.9
Reported net income.............			$ 20.0
Net income per share.............	$1.00	$2.00	$3.00
Less unremitted foreign...........			.42
Net per share as reported.........			$2.58

[3] In 1961 the company changed its reporting of undistributed earnings of an intermediate holding company—IBM World Trade Corporation—but this step was of minor significance.

D. Change in Reporting Method

Example: International Harvester. Prior to 1940 this company consolidated its domestic and foreign results. Because of war conditions it excluded its foreign operations in 1940 and continued this policy for 20 years. In 1960 it returned to a fully consolidated basis (except for exclusion of finance-company details). The effect of the exclusion and the change is shown in the following data:

(000,000 omitted)

	1959		Average, 1950–1959	
	Unconsolidated	Consolidated	Unconsolidated	Consolidated
Sales......................	$1,363.2	$1,726.0		
Net before tax............	140.2	172.6		
Income tax...............	63.8	88.3		
Net after tax.............	76.4	84.3		
Per share of common......	$5.10	$5.66	$3.60	$4.49

Analyst's Treatment of Unremitted Profits. The diversity in treatment of this item by corporations presents a problem of security analysis. It is clear that unremitted foreign profits should not be left out of the figures merely because the company does not put them in its reported net income. But should they be counted at full value, regardless of possible tax liability and transfer difficulties? We think not. We might suggest that such profits be taken in at from one-half to three-quarters of their total, depending perhaps on their location and the general foreign-exchange situation. (Canadian profits might well be valued in full.) Such adjustments should be made, of course, only when appreciable amounts are involved. In the case of Pfizer, the consequent reduction in 1960 earnings would be considerable; but such a step should be taken only after further detailed study of the picture.

In general, the analyst should adopt a consistent method of treating such unremitted profits, which would not depend on the company's reporting procedure.

Broader. Significance of Subsidiaries' Losses. The matter of subsidiaries' losses raises a special question which may be worth dwelling upon, to illustrate some of the finer logical points involved in security analysis. We have asserted that both the profits and losses of subsidiaries should be taken fully into account in stating the parent company's earnings. But the question may well be raised: Is the loss of a subsidiary necessarily a direct offset against the parent company's earnings? Why should a company be worth *less* because it owns something—in this case, an unprofitable interest? Could it not at any time put an end to the loss by selling, liquidating, or even abandoning the subsidiary? Hence, if good management is assumed, must we not also assume that the subsidiary losses are at most temporary and therefore to be regarded as nonrecurring items rather than as deductions from normal earnings?

There is no one simple answer to the questions that we have raised. Actually, if the subsidiary could be wound up *without an adverse effect upon the rest of the business*, it would be logical to view such losses as temporary—since good sense would dictate that in a short time the subsidiary must either become profitable or be disposed of. But if there are important business relations between the parent company and the subsidiary, e.g., if the latter affords an outlet for goods, or supplies cheap materials, or absorbs an important share of the overhead, then the termination of its losses is not so simple a matter. It may turn out, upon further analysis, that all or a good part of the subsidiary's loss is a necessary factor in the parent company's profit. It is not an easy task to determine just what business relationships are involved in each instance. Like so many other elements in analysis, this point usually requires an investigation going well beyond the reported figures.[4]

Divisional Losses vs. Subsidiary Losses. This subject could lead us into a much wider field—namely, that of losing divisions, departments, or products. The distinction between a subsidiary, with a separate corporate name and accounts, and a not-so-separated division is likely to be one of convenience and form rather than of essence. When the subsidiary is not 100 percent owned, the presence of the minority interest requires the publication of its separate results. Hence the analyst is made directly aware of the existence of losses from such a source. Much more frequent, however, are losses from a wholly owned subsidiary or from a company division; the extent of such losses is usually only hinted at by the management, if revealed at all. However, a competent analyst, by inquiry and probing, can in most such cases obtain a fairly accurate idea of the drain on the company's profits. The possibility of terminating the drain should not be lost sight of in his analysis. Action of this kind is clearly called for; it is usually taken sooner or later—though a management shake-up may first be necessary; when taken, it may transform the earnings picture and the value picture of the company's stock.

Example 1: What may be called the classic sequence of events in this area may be traced through in the case of Philadelphia & Reading Corporation (formerly Philadelphia & Reading Coal & Iron), up to 1956 almost exclusively a producer of anthracite. Its earning power dwindled and turned to "losing power" in 1954 and 1955. In the latter year change of top management produced a policy of wide diversification, plus improvement in the coal results. When losses reappeared in 1960, the coal busi-

---

[4] For a discussion of two older examples illustrating this point (Purity Bakeries and Barnsdall Oil in the 1930's), see the 1951 edition of this book, pp. 159–160.

ness was disposed of completely. These moves resulted in a spectacular gain in the price of the shares from a low of $7.50 in 1954 to an equivalent of 169 in 1961.

Example 2: Chickasha Cotton Oil Company announced in 1961 that it had decided to sell its feed and poultry division, because these operations had been losing money constantly. The statement indicated that without such losses the results for the year ending June 30, 1961 would have been about 40 percent higher than the expected $1.40 per share (actual $1.90).

Summary. To avoid leaving this point in confusion, we shall summarize our treatment by making the following suggestions:

1. In the first instance, subsidiary or divisional losses are to be deducted in every analysis.

2. If the amount involved is significant, the analyst should investigate whether or not the losses may be subject to early termination.

3. If the result of this examination is favorable, the analyst may consider all or part of such losses as the equivalent of a nonrecurring item.

CHAPTER FIFTEEN

REPORTED EARNINGS AND TAXABLE EARNINGS

Tax Deduction a Check on Reported Earnings. A necessary step in the scrutiny of an earnings statement is a rough comparison between the reported earnings and the income tax deduction. In the standard case there is, or should be, a fixed relation between the two amounts, as follows:

Under the income tax law operative from 1953 through 1961, the corporate tax has been 52 percent of net income or 54 percent if a consolidated return is made. Thus the income after tax during those years should have been slightly less than the tax deduction.

Many annual reports show a significant variance from these ratios. The analyst will want to understand the reasons for such a variation because they may have a bearing on the dependability of the published income.[1]

SPECIAL PROVISIONS OF THE TAX LAW

Let us deal with the second situation first, in terms of the 1960 tax regulations.

There are five main reasons why a given amount of corporate income, accepted as such for tax purposes, may bear less than 52 or 54 percent tax rate. (There are no present reasons why the rate should be higher.)

1. *The first $25,000 of net income* is subject only to the 30 percent normal tax and exempt from the 22 percent surtax. This exemption will reduce a corporation's tax by not more than $5,500. It is rarely a matter of importance to the security analyst.

2. *Income received on state, municipal, and similar bonds* is tax-exempt and is thus eliminated entirely from taxable income. (Certain Federal bonds are also exempt from the 30 percent normal tax.) This item is of importance chiefly in the case of banks and insurance companies.

[1] For a more complete discussion of this question, the student is referred to *Taxable and Business Income* by D. T. Smith and J. K. Butters, published by the National Bureau of Economic Research, New York, in 1950; and also to *Differences in Net Income for Accounting and Federal Income Taxes* by C. T. Reimer, published in 1950 by Commerce Clearing House, New York.

3. *Dividends received from domestic corporations* are taxable only upon 15 percent thereof. The effective tax rate against them in 1953–1961 was thus 7.8 percent or 8.1 percent on a consolidated return.

When a company has a large dividend income, its tax accrual will be substantially less than 52 percent of its income before tax. This is regularly true of fire and casualty insurance companies and of certain holding companies.

4. *Gains realized on the sale of capital assets* held more than six months (in excess of corresponding "long-term capital losses") are subject to a tax rate of 25 percent. Capital assets are chiefly securities, land, and depreciable property, e.g., plant and equipment. The sale of such fixed assets at a net profit is taxed as a long-term gain (after six months' holding), but a net loss therefrom is deductible from ordinary income.

In most cases capital gains and losses are segregated from the year's earnings, either by the company or by the analyst. When this is done, it is important that the corresponding tax debits or credits be similarly segregated with them.

NET LOSS CARRY-BACKS AND CARRY-FORWARDS

5. *A net loss from operations* sustained in any year may be applied to offset profits in the three preceding or five succeeding years. This provision often has considerable significance in the analysis of the results shown for any one year. When a current year's loss is carried back against previous profits, the result is a tax refund which properly serves to reduce the impact of the loss by as much as one-half. The effect of such losses preceded by profits may be shown graphically by the income accounts of Douglas Aircraft for 1957–1960.

Table 15-1. Douglas Aircraft

	1957–1958 (in thousands)	1959–1960 (in thousands)	1957–1960
Net before tax.......	$104,073	loss *$108,779*	loss *$5,017*
Income tax..........	56,250	cr. 55,527	723
Net after tax........	47,512	loss *53,252*	loss *5,740*
Per share...........	$12.29	loss *$13.95*	loss *$1.66*

These results are appropriately stated, since each year's profit was subject to a corresponding tax charge and each year's losses to a corresponding tax credit. The situation is very different, however, when losses are carried forward and serve to reduce the tax against later profits. Let us first give some illustrations of this frequent occurrence:

Example 1: American Motors

(000 omitted)

	1958	1959*	1960
Net before Federal taxes on income............	$25,570	$101,342	$100,843
Federal income taxes.....	cr. 515	41,000	52,600
Net earnings............	26,085	60,342	48,243

* A footnote states that carry-forward of losses from the years before 1958 reduced Federal and state income taxes by approximately $10,800,000. This accounts for virtually all the difference between the 52 percent rate and the Federal tax actually paid. In 1959, the loss carry-forward was exhausted.

A company may get a carry-forward benefit through acquisition and thus show a tax saving without having reported any previous net loss.

Example 2: Foote Brothers Gear & Machine paid only $832,000 tax on $2,174,000 of net before tax in 1959. It saved $325,000 of tax by acquiring Whitney Chain Company in that year and using its loss carry-forward.

Example 3: United Whelan Corp. escaped all taxation on its own earnings in 1959 and 1960 by acquiring, at very low net cost, Crawford Clothes, a losing enterprise which it soon disposed of. A large over-all gain was made on the transaction, ascribable solely to the tax saving. The whole transaction was an unusual one, and is worth studying.

Comment. A major reform is called for in corporate reporting and in security analysis in this highly important area of loss carry-forward. There is no justification for considering the tax saved by reason of a past loss as part of the current year's earnings. The tax-credit portion of reported income does not reflect in any sense the "normal results" of the year; obviously it cannot be projected indefinitely into the future as part of the company's "earning power." Such a tax saving should be treated by the company—and certainly by the security analyst—as a "special credit," similar in its import to the various nonrecurring gains already treated in this fashion in most statements. This has been done in a very few corporate reports:

Example: Southern Nitrogen Company (in its "data file for analysts") showed its 1959 results first on the basis of a full tax charge and then canceled the charge by adding back the tax reduction from carry-forward of previous losses. Its annual report for 1959 and 1960 states the amount of income tax "eliminated due to past years' losses."

The loss carry-forwards remaining available at any date do, of course, have significance in the analysis, but not really as part of the future earning power. They represent a special or "windfall" value factor, which can add no more than the *total possible tax saving* to the value found without benefit of such saving. In other words, the earnings should be projected without any credit from the loss carry-forward, and the stock's value "ex-carry-forward" determined therefrom. To such a value may be added a realistic figure—say, 50 percent to 75 percent of the maximum tax saving, to reflect the carry-forward factor properly discounted.

Reconcilement of Net Income and Income and Income Tax. As an exercise in reconciling the actual tax paid with the basic 52 percent rate, we present in Table 15-2 such a calculation applying to all corporations

Table 15-2. Reconcilement of Net Profit and Income Tax Paid. All Corporations with Net Profit, July 1958–June 1959

(In millions of dollars)

A. Pro-forma disparity

Compiled net income before tax	$43,716
Tax thereon at 52%	22,732
Actual tax paid	18,659
Disparity	4,073

B. Explanation of disparity

	Rate of tax imposed	Saving in tax below 52%
First $25,000 of net income	30%	$1,300*
Tax-free interest	zero	335
Normal-tax-free interest	22%	16
Domestic dividends	7.8%	1,200
Long-term capital gains	25%	665
Net-loss carry-forward (a deduction)	(zero)	540
Total tax saved		4,056
Less 2% extra on consolidated-return net income		100
Net difference accounted for		3,956
Difference unaccounted for†		117

* Partly estimated from income-bracket and other data.
† Attributable to partial deduction of utility preferred dividends, exemption of distributed income of most investment companies, etc.

with net income for the year 1958–1959, i.e., for fiscal years between July 1958 and June 1959. (The data needed for this table is supplied in the valuable United States Treasury publication, *Statistics of Income: Corporation Income Tax Returns.*) It will be noted that the initial discrepancy of $4 billion, or about 18 percent, is virtually all accounted for by the tax provisions discussed above.

Percentage Depletion. Let us add the percentage-depletion deduction as a special status in our classification. It is basically not intended as a necessary and proper charge against earnings—as are other amortization provisions of the law—but purely as a means of reducing the tax rate. The difference between annual-report depletion and income tax depletion does not call for study and possible correction by the analyst. He may be concerned, however, by the possibility of some adverse change in this tax privilege.

Industries with a Special Tax Status. We have already pointed out the advantage enjoyed by industries which have depletable assets, by reason of the option to use percentage depletion. Certain other industries have the benefit of special provisions of the tax law. These include the following:

1. *Savings and Loan Companies.* Their privilege of setting up general reserves, sufficient to absorb all their otherwise taxable income, was commented on in Chapter 10.

2. *Subsidized Shipping Lines.* The amended Merchant Marine Act of 1936 both requires and permits the transfer of tax-free earnings to reserve funds, subject to possible later tax.

Example: Lykes Brothers SS. Company so deposited nearly all its net earnings above dividends in the ten years, 1951–1960. The amount involved aggregated over $90 million, and the tax saved thereon, at present rates, would be $46 million, or over $12 per share. This tax saving would account for more than 40 percent of the average earnings of $2.89 per share reported for the decade.

3. *Life Insurance Companies.* These companies are subject to special income tax provisions, which have resulted in their paying considerably less than the regular 52 percent on their reported net income.

General comment: Tax advantages of this type are extremely important to the companies benefiting therefrom, but they involve the hazard of adverse changes in the future. Some unfavorable developments of this type have occurred in recent years. They include (*a*) a change in the tax law affecting life insurance companies in 1959, which increased their income tax bill considerably, and (*b*) a Supreme Court decision which reduced greatly the depletion allowances formerly claimed by cement manufacturers. The present emphasis on "closing loopholes" in the tax laws may result in a further scaling down of these advantages.

MANAGEMENT-DETERMINED DIFFERENCE BETWEEN TAXABLE INCOME AND REPORTED INCOME

There are six chief ways by which management may at its option produce a difference between reported income and taxable income. The first is by charging depreciation in its income statement at a rate different from that taken on the tax return. The second is by writing off certain outlays for taxes which may be capitalized in the statements. The third is by reporting as profits to stockholders certain items which may be excluded from current taxable income. The fourth is by placing certain debits or credits in the surplus account but including the tax results therefrom (usually a credit) in the income account. The fifth is by the use of voluntary reserves or by special deductions or credits equivalent thereto. The sixth is by writing off purchased goodwill against income. The first four differences generally serve to reduce the tax paid below that indicated as due; the fifth usually and the sixth always result in an increased tax payment as against reported income.

Each of these divisions has been previously discussed and its tax effects referred to. We shall repeat some of the tax material here, in highly summarized form, in order to present a unified survey of the tax consequences of corporate accounting methods.

1. The differences between reported and tax-return depreciation have been an important element in income-account analysis. Formerly they were due to a variety of arbitrary practices by corporations. At present they are pretty well confined to the use of the straight-line method in published figures as against an accelerated method used on the tax return.

2. In our chapter on amortization we have already discussed the tax effect of various amounts written off on tax returns but capitalized on the statements. These include: intangible drilling costs of oil and gas producers; exploration and development expenses of mines; and—in a growing number of cases—R&D expenditures of smaller concerns. The two matters that the analyst must attend to are, first, to see that a deferred-tax equivalent is set up against a benefit so obtained, and second, that companies' accounts are placed on the same footing in these matters (where significant) for purposes of comparison.

Additional items of this kind are interest and miscellaneous taxes charged to construction. There is at least a technical similarity between these expenditures and intangible drilling costs. In both cases the amounts are charged off in full on the tax returns, with resultant tax saving of about one-half, but are capitalized in the accounts. In theory a deferred-tax reserve should be charged to income in the amount saved and amortized over the life of the construction, in the same way as bond discount, and the related tax saving should be amortized by charges to income during the life of the issue. Apparently this is rarely if ever done. The annual amounts of amortization involved are bound to be small, and this aspect of the matter may be ignored. However, in years of large expansion—particularly by public utility companies, including pipe lines—the tax saving through interest charged to construction may be appreciable. For proper analysis it should be charged back against net income.

Example 1: An old but striking example of the possible misleading effect of standard treatment of "interest charged to construction" is found in the 1949 statement of Texas Gas Transmission Company. We reproduce our discussion of this case from the 1951 edition.

Table 15-3. Earnings of Texas Gas Transmission Company, 1949

(000 omitted)

Item	1949	1948
Operating revenues...................	$9,981	$9,529
Net before interest and income tax.......	1,801	2,168
Interest paid.........................	2,307	202
Less interest received.................	cr. 427	
Less interest charged to construction.....	cr. 1,856	cr. 222
Balance before income tax.............	1,777	2,187
Income tax..........................	None	736
Balance for common...................	1,777	1,451
Earned per share.....................	$0.81	$0.66

The report (and press release) state that net income shows an increase of 22 percent over the previous year. A footnote in the report explains that no income tax was accrued because interest charged to construction was deducted from taxable income. It is clear that the company actually earned *less* in 1949 than in 1948. It cannot properly exclude its interest charges from income without also excluding the tax saving therefrom. Conversely, in order to take credit in income for the tax saving, it would have to charge income with its interest cost—thus wiping out the reported earnings.

In this case the analyst should have accrued tax at the rate of 38 percent upon the reported net income *before income tax,* thus producing an adjusted net-income figure of $1,102,000 for 1949 and $1,356,000 for 1948.

The annual report of Texas Gas Transmission Company contains an accountant's certificate warranting that the statements were prepared "in accordance with generally accepted accounting principles." In spite of the great progress made by the accounting profession in recent years toward the goal of fully informative and nonmisleading financial statements, it is evident that present-day practice still leaves room for certain kinds of questionable reporting. The security analyst must still carry on this work independently of the accountant's certificate.

3. The chief source of deferred profits for tax purposes is in installment sales. The law permits the profit to be taken in proportionately with the receipt of payments; but it is almost the invariable practice for companies *to report the full profit in their statements* at the time of sale.[2] The large difference between indicated and actual tax is disposed of by the standard deferred-tax procedure.

Example: Spiegel, Inc., reported net income of $23.0 million before tax in 1960, against which it deducted income tax of $11.3 million. It actually paid only about $800,000 of this, the remainder being represented by an increase in its reserve for deferred taxes from $27.3 million to $37.9 million. Something similar to these deferred profits occurs when untaken security gains or a fraction of unearned-premium reserves are considered to be part of a year's profits or of the stock equity. Allowance should be made in the first case for a 25 percent tax and in the second case for a 52 percent tax payable if and when these gains are realized.

4. The taking of tax credits to income against losses charged to surplus, while prevalent in the past, has virtually ceased, except perhaps in railroad accounts. However, there are still instances of losses being reported as a "special item" in the income account—and thus presumably excludable from the year's results—while the tax benefit has been absorbed in ordinary income. This would call for correction by the analyst.

---

[2] An exception is supplied by City Investing Company, which treats its installment sales of real estate in the same way for taxes and for its reports.

Example: This type of entry played a part in the extraordinary reports of Lehigh Valley Railroad for 1954–1956. In each of these years it reported both a substantial net *income,* and an income tax *refund* instead of payment.

Similarly, in 1960 Baltimore & Ohio Railroad reported net before taxes of $14,809,000 and a tax *refund* of $3,456,000. In addition to the usual differences in depreciation rates, the company gave as explanation "a loss on retirement due to special obsolescence." Obviously this loss was not charged to income, but the tax saving was so credited. The figures as published must be termed entirely misleading.

5. In Chapter 11 we discussed certain reductions of inventory values which did not produce a corresponding decrease in the year's taxes. These included the "LIFO-equivalent" adjustment made by Stewart-Warner and the "base-stock" adjustment made by Endicott-Johnson. Formerly there were numerous more or less arbitrary inventory reserves —actually contingency reserves—which carried no tax credit.

Similarly, some of the annual reserve charges made for "past-service liability" under pension plans have exceeded the 10 percent maximum allowed as tax-deductible. This has usually resulted in a small overstatement of taxes, unless offset by a "reverse deferral."

Example: Joseph Bancroft & Sons (textiles) reported as follows for June 1959:

(000 omitted)

Net before tax		$2,331
Income tax paid	$1,450	
Less future reduction a/c excess retirement reserve	174	1,276
Net after tax		$1,056

6. The effect of write-offs of goodwill against income is to understate the income in relation to tax paid, and—we think—to understate the true income. Examples of this were given on pages 169–171.

Unexplained Discrepancies. Every now and then the analyst will find a discrepancy between reported income and tax deduction, for which no ready explanation is at hand.

Example: Dura Corporation reported as follows for its July 1961 year:

Earnings before minority interest and Federal tax	$ 122,000
Minority interest in operating loss of subsidiary net, etc....cr.	1,137,000
Earnings before Federal tax	$1,259,000
Federal income tax (estimate)	1,014,000
Net earnings	$ 245,000

The tax here is evidently out of line with earnings, whatever be the taxable nature of the minority-interest adjustments.

In cases such as these the analyst interested in a thoroughgoing presentation should address an inquiry to the company's treasurer. In the majority of cases an explanation will be forthcoming, which will indicate whether or not an adjustment of the reported net after taxes is called for.

CHAPTER SIXTEEN

BALANCE-SHEET ANALYSIS

Six Types of Information in the Balance Sheet. The balance sheet deserves more attention than Wall Street has been willing to accord it for many years past. By way of introduction to this section of our work, let us list six types of information and guidance that the investor may derive from a study of the balance sheet:

1. It shows in nearly all cases how much capital is actually invested in the business and how the capital structure is divided between senior issues and common stock.

2. It reveals the strength or weakness of the working-capital position.

3. It provides a check upon the validity of the earnings reported in the income account.

4. It supplies data to test the true success or prosperity of the business, the amount earned on invested capital.

5. It supplies the basis for analyzing the sources of income.

6. It supplies the basis for a long-term study of the relationship between earning power and asset values and of the development of the financial structure over the years.

Presentation of the Balance Sheet. The conventional balance sheet lists all the assets on the left-hand side and the liabilities, capital, and surplus on the right. (In England the two columns are reversed.) New and more informing methods of presentation are gradually becoming popular in corporate statements. These seek to develop the figure for capital and surplus by subtracting the true liabilities from the assets; they also supply a better picture of the working-capital position by listing current liabilities directly below current assets. In many corporate reports this presentation appears under the title of Statement of Financial Condition and is given in addition to the conventional balance sheet.[1]

We recommend that the analyst follow this procedure in his work. We shall illustrate the method by restating the December 1960 balance sheet of Schenley Industries, Inc., in the newer manner, including therein our

[1] U.S. Steel Corporation, Burroughs Adding Machine Company, and others have published such a statement of financial condition in lieu of a balance sheet for many years. The auditors certify the accounts in this form.

recommended treatment of the liability for preferred stock (Table 16-1). Detailed items in the various categories are omitted.

Table 16-1. Recast Balance Sheet of Schenley Industries, Inc.,
December 31, 1960

(000 omitted)

Capital funds:

Funded debt..		$159,500
50¢ div. preferred, par 35¢; 950,450 shares valued at $10......		9,500
Total senior claims.......................................		$169,000
Common-stock equity (5,913,000 shares, par $1.40)...........		252,200
Total capital funds......................................		$421,200

Represented by:

Current assets.............................	$392,900	
Less current liabilities..........................	31,100	
Working capital...............................		$361,800
Intermediate assets, net...........................		18,700
Fixed assets, gross................................	$ 90,900	
Less depreciation.................................	50,200	
Fixed assets, net................................		40,700
Total...		$421,200

DISCUSSION OF BALANCE-SHEET ITEMS

Since the reader is assumed to be familiar with elementary accounting, we shall not discuss all the items in the balance sheet in detail but shall consider merely those aspects that may require special knowledge by the analyst.

Cash Items. Current assets include cash and cash equivalents, receivables, and inventories. Certain cash items, usually in the form of government bonds, are sometimes segregated by the company and shown elsewhere than in current assets. On rare occasions they are being held to meet liabilities not shown as current. In some instances they are appropriated for future expenditure on plant; in other cases they are arbitrarily separated from the current assets.

Examples: U.S. Steel showed $530 million held for plant additions at the end of 1958. Smaller items of this kind were shown on the balance sheets of Ohio Oil, Allied Kid, and Real Silk Hosiery in former years. Stewart-Warner showed $3,185,000 in government bonds carried as noncurrent "investments" at the end of 1949.

Most of the railroads make an arbitrary division of their government-bond holdings between Temporary Cash Investments, shown in current assets, and Other Investments, shown as an intermediate item. There was a shift by Northern Pacific of $11 million from the first to the second category in 1949.

From the analyst's viewpoint it is best to include in the current assets all cash items that are within the company's control, including those which it does not show as current but *could show* if it so elected. This would apply to most cash funds segregated for plant additions. A company without such a segregated fund may be just as likely to add to its plant by use of its ordinary cash.

Cash-surrender value of life insurance policies—at times a sizable item —was formerly shown as a current asset in most cases, but now it is almost always shown as an intermediate item.[2] We think the analyst may properly include such an amount, if important, in the current assets for the purpose of certain calculations, e.g., to find the current-asset value of the stock.

Inventories. It is now becoming the custom to separate from current assets certain slow-moving inventory items. Formerly it was considered sufficient to mark them down to estimated realizable value.

Example: Autocar showed $843,000 of "inventory in excess of one year's estimated requirements" as a noncurrent item at the end of 1949.[3]

A question of more general current importance is the basis of valuing inventory, especially as between the FIFO and LIFO methods. This was discussed in detail above in Chapter 11.

In some cases inventories are carried as current assets even though they will be realized upon over a period of years.

Example: Desilu Productions, in April 1961, carried "deferred show costs" of $4,266,000 as a current asset, equivalent to inventory, although stating that it may be amortized over "an indefinite period." The year before, the corresponding item was carried as a deferred asset.

Receivables. Trade or customer receivables, less allowances for losses, are shown as current assets, even though the period of payment may run well beyond a year in the case of installment notes. Such installment notes are often sold to finance companies or banks, on a "recourse" basis; i.e., the seller is responsible for nonpayment. The amount of such repurchase obligation will be shown in a footnote as a contingent liability. The analyst would be best advised, we think, if he added these amounts to both the receivables and the current liabilities, in order to get a clearer view of the company's financial position.

Examples: At the end of 1959 White Motors showed a contingent liability, amounting to about $119 million, to repurchase installment contracts or to reacquire vehicles sold under such contracts. Receivables

[2] As an exceptional case, C. E. Hires & Company included $425,000 of cash value of life insurance in its total current assets of $3,926,000 on Sept. 30, 1949.

[3] One of the few serious problems in this field was presented by R. G. Le Tourneau, Inc., in 1948. The auditors stated that "the inventories include substantial amounts in respect of slow-moving and possibly obsolete items, and equipment requiring further engineering and development." There was also a possible large liability for servicing products in the field. Because of the materiality of those two uncertain factors, the auditors did not express the usual opinion on the company's financial position at the year end or on the results of the operations for 1948.

Subsequently revised figures were presented showing a write-down of inventory values by $2 million and an increase in accrued liabilities of $500,000. As a result the company was compelled to suspend dividends on a recently sold issue of preferred stock.

retained amounted to about $46 million. Sears Roebuck and Company, in order to finance its aggressive expansion policy, sold the greater part of its installment receivables to banks, limiting its liability or potential loss therein to 10 percent of the amount sold. In January 1961 it sold the entire amount remaining, the total exceeding $1 billion.[4]

Where receivables play a large part in the company's business, special care should be given to the examination of the treatment of the item on the balance sheet. The reserve for losses and collection expense must be adequate. Comparisons should be made with other companies in the same field. In extreme cases, the true value of the receivables can prove to have been badly overstated.[5]

Tax on Installment Profits Should Be Deducted from Receivables. Installment-selling concerns have a peculiar accounting situation. They report profits to stockholders on the basis of each year's sales, making allowance for costs and losses incurred in collecting receivables. But for tax purposes they can defer accounting for profits until the installments are actually paid. As a result, these companies show large "contingent liabilities" for income tax, to be paid as the receivables are collected. Such reserves are not reserves at all but liabilities directly related to the accounts receivable. If the latter are good, the taxes will have to be paid as the accounts are collected. The analyst should deduct the tax "reserve" directly from the receivable figure itself, in the same way that the allowance for future losses and collection expense is deducted by the company. All these items are of the same kind and belong together.

Current Liabilities. This category should include all liabilities due within a year. Consequently it will show the current year's installment of a serial bond or note issue and, in some cases, the portion of a long-term bond issue due to be retired by sinking-fund operation within the year.

The large income tax liabilities that became the rule since 1940 have given rise to a new device, designed to improve the ratio of current assets to current liabilities. Companies purchase large quantities of United States Treasury tax anticipation notes bearing low rates of interest, which they are then permitted to deduct from the total of their tax liability.

Example: General Motors deducted $1,328 million of such notes from its current liabilities at the end of 1955, thus improving its current ratio from 1.8:1 to 2.5:1.

We consider this appropriate accounting because the notes are exact offsets to the tax liability.

[4] The complete disposal was made in order to permit the company thereafter to use the installment method of accounting for income tax purposes, instead of the full-profit-at-date-of-sale method, formerly followed. Such a change could be made only if it followed a change in the method of doing business.

[5] See on this score the example of Manufacturers Trading Corporation on p. 178 of the 1951 edition. The concern went into bankruptcy in 1948. Although the company claimed that its receivables were secured by collateral "valued" at twice its own debt, it appears to have dropped completely from view in 1950.

Include True Liability Reserves with Current Liabilities. From the analytical standpoint, reserves of any type that represent a fairly definite liability may best be included with the current liabilities thus reducing the net current assets. This has the advantage of simplifying the balance-sheet picture by dividing all liabilities into either current items or funded-debt items. In any case, the reserve liabilities are likely to be payable in a fairly short time.

Intermediate Assets. Intermediate items generally consist of noncurrent receivables, investments not treated as marketable securities, cash-sur-render value of life insurance, and deferred assets. The majority of companies include claims for tax refunds as an intermediate asset, but a good proportion show this item as a current receivable. The noncurrent receivables are generally due from officers, employees, or affiliated com-panies. Most investments in subsidiaries are eliminated from the balance sheet by the use of a consolidated statement, but there are various types of exceptions to this rule. Some companies do not consolidate foreign sub-sidiaries; others do not consolidate those less than 100 percent owned.[6] In some cases these investment items may represent the ownership of a substantial amount of current assets.

Example: Universal Leaf Tobacco, discussed on page 186. While the working capital of its affiliates is not stated separately, it may be assumed to constitute at least 75 percent of their net assets, since this is true for the parent company in the same business. Universal's share therein would add at least 50 percent to its own working capital of $20.3 million in June 1960.

Security Investments. A number of balance sheets show stock holdings of various size in other companies as intermediate assets. These may have active markets, in which case their market value is generally given in a footnote. Such holdings may come very close to being ordinary market-able securities, classifiable with the current assets by the analyst. This would be particularly true if the holdings are of relatively moderate size and do not constitute working control.

Example: At the end of 1960 Bishop Oil Company owned 88,000 shares of Flintkote Corporation (1.6 percent of the total) carried at cost of $164,000 but worth $2,550,000 at market. For analytical purposes, these shares should be considered as current assets at their market value less capital-gain tax on the indicated profit, i.e., at $1,955,000 net.[7]

Where working control is involved it is doubtful whether the market value of the shares should enter directly into a balance-sheet analysis of the owning company. In effect such a procedure would substitute earn-ing-power value for asset values with respect to an important part of the company's business—and thus vitiate the purpose of balance-sheet

[6] See Chap. 14, p. 184.
[7] Bishop Oil subsequently sold all its assets and distributed the Flintkote shares to its stockholders, thus avoiding its own tax thereon.

analysis, which deals with asset values as a separate factor in a company's valuation. An allocation of the underlying asset values—corresponding to an allocation of the controlled companies earnings—would appear to be more logical.

Example: In December 1960 Kaiser Industries showed Investments in Affiliated Companies of $182.0 million, with a footnote indicating that their market value was $388 million. This market appreciation of $206 million is relevant to an analysis of Kaiser Industries shares, but it does not contribute directly to the "asset value" of the common. That might best be determined as follows:

Table 16-2. Kaiser Industries

(000,000 omitted)

	Kaiser Industries excluding 3 affiliates	Kaiser's share of 3 affiliated companies*	Kaiser Industries adjusted
Net current assets....................	$ 45	$109	$154
Intermediate assets, less intermediate liabilities............................	42	−45‡	−3
Fixed assets, net......................	30	550	580
Total..............................	$117	$614	$731
Less debt and preferred stock...........	91	441	532
Balance for common..............	$ 26†	$173	$199
Equity per share (22.9 million shares)....			$8.69

* For list of three major affiliates and percentage holdings, see Table 14-1, p. 186.
† Excluding investment in the three affiliates carried at $164 million.
‡ The companies had large deferred-income tax reserves.

Comment: The above distribution of assets and liabilities brings out clearly the top-heavy capital structure of the Kaiser complex.

Fixed Assets. The fixed assets are also referred to as the "plant account" or the "property account." In nearly all companies they are now carried at a conservative figure. The usual basis is actual cost less depreciation. Important amounts of new plant were written off completely by the accelerated amortization permitted under the tax laws during and directly after World War II. (In many cases also, plant accounts had been written down in the depression of the 1930's to figures well below their cost.)

Stockholders and security analysts should be supplied with more information regarding the present value of the property account than is contained in the ledger figures, which reveal only original cost or a substitute value selected many years ago. A few companies have given an estimate of replacement value less depreciation—generally for the purpose of justifying a higher depreciation rate than is allowed for tax purposes. One or two also supply figures as to the insurance value of their building and machinery.

Examples: Equitable Office Building stated that as of April 30, 1949, the building and its contents were insured against fire for $18 million, but that the book value net was $5.4 million. It also stated that the land and building were assessed for $27,750,000 against a combined net book value of $19.9 million. Diamond T Motor reported the insured value of its buildings and machinery to be $4,878,000 on December 31, 1949, against a book value of $939,000.

If figures such as these were required to be supplied by all companies as a footnote to the balance sheet, a much more informative picture of the plant account would be available to those who really own the assets.

Prepaid Expense and Deferred Charges. Prepaid expense represents amounts paid to other parties for services to be rendered by them in the future—such as rent and insurance paid in advance. The accounting profession (AICPA) has suggested that such prepaid-expense items be included in the current assets—as the equivalent of accounts receivable—and they are now treated largely in this fashion.

Deferred charges, in contrast to prepaid expense, represent amounts paid or payable for which no specific services will be received in the future but which are considered properly chargeable to future operations. These include bond discount, which is logically amortized over the life of a bond issue, pensions "paid in advance," and other items. The cost of tools and dies for models not yet on the market, or similar items, is sometimes carried in this account. It is customary to charge off such items rather rapidly against actual sales.

Examples: In this general category belong deferred assets such as the following: Eastern Airlines in 1960 showed $4,015,000 as the cost of introducing its new jet planes. Seaboard Finance showed $5,871,837 in 1959–1960 as the expense of opening new offices.

In sum, the prepaid-expense and similar items are extremely varied in their character and their validity. The analyst may fortunately ignore most of them as unimportant; the larger ones may require rather careful scrutiny.

Unamortized Bond Discount. When companies receive less than par on the sale of bonds, the discount may either be charged off against surplus or carried as an asset to be amortized over the life of the issue. The latter is the more usual practice, so that it is customary to see an asset entitled Unamortized Bond Discount in the balance sheet of companies with funded debt. Some authorities treat this as an intangible item and deduct it from the book value of the stock. Generally the matter is not important enough to make much difference whichever way it is handled.[8]

---

[8] An interesting item appeared in the 1949 statement of Transcontinental Gas Pipe Line Company. About $3 million of bond discount was written off the balance sheet in that year by being added to construction account. In this way the bond discount was transformed into an indistinguishable part of the fixed assets.

Intangible Assets. The familiar types of intangible assets include good-will; patents, copyrights, and trademarks; franchises and licenses; organization and development expense. There are also many special items—for instance, subscription lists or "circulation" bulk large on the balance sheets of newspaper and magazine publishers.

Example: Hearst Consolidated Publications at the end of 1954 showed $81.5 million for "circulation, press franchises, and reference libraries" out of total assets of $161 million.[9] The following year $61.6 million of these intangible assets were removed from the books by being charged to earned surplus.

Leaseholds. A leasehold is the right to occupy premises for a stated period of time subject to payment of rent therefor. Such a right may be considered a valuable asset if the current rental value of the leased property is much greater than the rent called for in the contract. In past years, companies have sometimes set more or less arbitrary figures on such leasehold values and carried them as an asset. An asset of that type must of course be considered entirely intangible.

In many cases, however, companies have erected buildings on ground leased to them for a long period of years. At the expiration of the lease (and stipulated renewals) the building becomes the property of the lessor (the owner of the land). Technically the tenant (the lessee) does not own the building; it is part of his leasehold interest. To that extent such buildings, often designated in the balance sheet as "leasehold improvements," might accurately be called intangible assets; but it is more in accordance with practicality to consider them as a tangible investment by the lessee and therefore as a tangible asset.

Example: Hotel Waldorf Astoria erected its building above ground leased from a subsidiary of New York Central Railroad. In the balance sheet of the hotel its interest in the building is carried under the title of "leasehold." The net figure after amortization at the end of 1952 was $6.2 million.

The treatment of intangibles in the calculation of asset values is dealt with later in this chapter.

Proper Statement of Liabilities. The analyst's problems in dealing with the amount of liabilities are limited pretty much to two categories: treatment of reserve items and proper valuation of the preferred-stock liability.

As we explained in Chapter 10, it is desirable to apply all reserve items to the extent practicable (1) to reduce asset accounts, (2) to increase current liabilities, and (3) to increase the surplus account. Some reserve items may remain as true intermediate liabilities, e.g., reserve for injury and damage claims of a transportation company. In many cases these intermediate liabilities are minor in relative amount, in which event the balance sheet may be further simplified by grouping them with the current liabilities in a single total.

[9] See Appendix Note 18, p. 690 of the 1951 edition for details of the unusual intangible items in the balance sheet of American District Telegraph Company.

Other Liability Reserves or Provisions. Reserves for workmen's compensation and other insurance benefits are growing in importance. Apparently such benefits, along with pensions, are becoming a standard part of the wage structure. It may be assumed that the calculations approved by the accountants fairly represent the liability under these headings. The same will be true of provisions for profit sharing and bonus. However, most sums for the latter purposes are disbursed soon after the close of the accounting period, and they should be considered as equivalent to accounts payable.

Contingency and general reserves are regularly considered part of the surplus account. There may be some doubt on this score at times. In the Celanese report for 1949, for example, a footnote stated that there were back taxes in dispute, but that the final liability, if any, would be covered by the contingency reserve of $3,461,000. Some analysts would prefer to include a reserve of this sort among intermediate liabilities. Fortunately, these ambiguous items are rarely large enough to make much difference in balance-sheet analysis.

When a reserve is tagged in the balance sheet as for "possible additional tax" the analyst would do well to include it among Current Liabilities, even though the company places it elsewhere—unless he has strong reason to believe the reserve is largely unnecessary.

Example: Dynamics Corporation of America. This company showed an Income Tax Contingency Reserve in 1957 as a noncurrent liability. In 1958 it appeared as a current liability with the same title. In 1959 it was included with other Federal income taxes. (For the extraordinary reporting of this company in 1951–1960, see later in this chapter.)

Reserves for Foreign Assets. Where such reserves reflect a shrinkage sustained to date, they should be deducted from the related asset account. Where they anticipate future losses, they should be treated as a contingency reserve and equivalent to surplus.[10] Generally the sums involved are not large. Some exceptional cases may require special attention by the analyst.

Examples: In 1949 Vick Chemical Company (now Richardson-Merrell, Inc.) set up a reserve of $2.7 million out of surplus to offset its foreign assets in full. This was almost 10 percent of its total assets and would presumably be regarded by the analyst as part of the surplus account. The company subsequently changed its policy, and now the reserve is equal to the unremitted foreign profits. A similar item appears on the balance sheets of Coca-Cola Company. National Cash Register deducts this reserve from its foreign assets—listed in a footnote—and carries the net amount as a balance-sheet asset.

Preferred-stock Liability. Conventional balance sheets show preferred stock as part of capital and surplus. Thus it is placed with the common

[10] General Motors has held intact for many years a General Reserve for Foreign Operations amounting to $141.7 million. This belongs with surplus.

stock, as if sharing in the ownership of the business, and is sharply separated from funded debt and other liabilities. This traditional practice does not conform to the realities of corporate finance. In the usual case—where there is no conversion or similar right—preferred stock does not represent ownership but only an imperfect creditorship position. (Its sole effective value, on a going-concern basis, lies in its right to receive a stipulated annual dividend before anything may be paid on the common.) The most useful balance-sheet analysis will place preferred stock with the funded debt, as making up the total prior claims against the capital fund. Bonded debt and preferred stocks may be designed together under the name of "senior issues."

The proper calculation of the preferred-stock liability often presents the analyst with a problem. The simplest rule for the analyst to follow is to value stocks with preference claims at the highest of par value (plus any dividend arrears), call price (plus arrears), or average market price. In some instances a "synthetic par value"—e.g., the equivalent of a 5 percent or 6 percent dividend rate—may be more appropriate than any other measure. A figure of $100 per share may often be used for convenience instead of a more precise figure not greatly different from 100. The following discussion will illustrate the application of this rule.

In nearly all balance sheets the preferred stock is listed as a liability at its par amount if it has a par value. However, such par value may be unrealistic and therefore misleading.

Example: Island Creek Coal Company has a preferred stock of $1 par, which is entitled to annual dividends of $6 and to $120 per share in the event of dissolution. In 1960 the price of this issue averaged $120. In the calculation of the asset value of Island Creek Coal common, the preferred stock should be deducted not at $1 per share but at $120, which is its true or "effective par."

If the preferred stock is a no-par issue, it is often carried at an arbitrarily low figure which has no relationship to the true amount of its claim.

Example: Champlin Oil & Refining Company has 100,000 shares of $3 cumulative convertible preference stock, no par, callable at 65. It is carried as a liability at $25 per share.

In any statement or calculation purporting to show the equity for the common stock, it would be misleading not to deduct the preferred in an amount reasonably close to the true amount of its claim. There is no problem here if the preferred has a representative par value, carries a dividend rate of, say, not over 5½ percent, and has no arrearages. In such instances, which are numerous, the preferred stock may properly be deducted at the amount listed in the balance sheet.

Example: Associated Dry Goods Corporation has a 5.25 percent first preferred, callable at 110. Its average price in 1960 was 103. For practical purposes the analyst could accept the company's liability figure of $100 per share.

If the preferred stock has a dividend rate above, say, 5½ percent, and is callable, the call price is usually a more suitable value than par.

Example: Dennison Manufacturing Company has an 8 percent debenture (actually preferred) stock issue, callable at 160. Its average price in 1960 was 139. It would be best to value it at its call price.

If the preferred issue has a high dividend rate and is not callable, it may sell regularly far above its par value. No single figure for the liability is entirely satisfactory. We favor either of two alternative methods: (1) a round figure fairly close to the prevailing price of the issue or (2) a capitalized figure equivalent to a 5 percent dividend rate.

Examples: U.S. Steel 7 percent noncallable preferred might best be valued at 140. (Its average price in 1960 was 144.) Similarly, National Lead $7 and $6 preferred might be valued at 140 and 120, respectively, somewhat below their 1960 average prices.

Certain stock issues, called "class A stock" or by other names, have dividend claims prior to the common stock and should be evaluated accordingly in a balance sheet presentation. Even though they may have no preference as to assets in liquidation, their prior right to dividend should be considered the major factor. For under all but the most exceptional conditions, a business should be analyzed on a going-concern basis, i.e., on the assumption that it will continue operations indefinitely.

Example: Curtiss-Wright class A shares have a par of $1, are entitled to a noncumulative preferential dividend of $2 per annum, and are redeemable at 40. In 1960 their average price was about 34. For balance-sheet analysis, a valuation of 40 for the class A shares, while high, would not be inappropriate.

We believe that entirely too much confusion and misapprehension is caused by the frequent practice of stating preferred stocks at a completely unrepresentative figure in the balance sheet. A worthwhile improvement would be effected if all balance sheets were required to show in parenthesis, immediately below the carrying value of the preferred, the full dollar amount of the liability either at call or in liquidation.

We suggest, further, that where there are accumulated preferred dividends, this amount be shown clearly in the balance sheet and not buried in a footnote as it usually is. A good arrangement would be to place the amount of such accumulation in parenthesis immediately below the earned surplus figure, or else to allocate the latter figure directly between the amount needed to pay accumulations and the balance presumably available for the junior equity.

Computation of the Equity or Book Value per Share. The book value per share of a common stock is found by adding up all the assets (generally excluding intangibles), subtracting all liabilities and stock issues ahead of the common, and then dividing by the number of shares.

Our balance-sheet presentation, as given on page 203 will lead readily to the book value per share. All that is necessary is to divide the number of shares into the indicated equity. In the case of Schenley Industries, the figure works out at about $42.60 per share at the end of 1960.

Treatment of Intangibles in Computing Asset Values. It is customary to eliminate intangibles in the computation of the net asset value, or "equity," per share of common stock. The phrase "book value" is a little ambiguous; it is sometimes used to include all the assets shown on the books and sometimes to exclude the intangibles. Formerly the chief objection of analysts to counting the intangible items was not that they were unreal but that they had usually been carried on the books of arbitrary and meaningless figures. However, while this situation was characteristic of pre-SEC days, it is no longer true. In fact, the once-familiar item of "goodwill"—which was the basis of "stock watering" in the old days— has all but disappeared from the balance sheet, except in the special form of "purchased goodwill." In former years a large goodwill item was often shown as a separate asset—usually at some large and round amount—but perhaps equally often it was concealed in the total of the fixed assets.

Example: When United States Steel Corporation was organized in 1902 it showed no goodwill or other intangibles in its balance sheet. Thus all its capitalization was ostensibly covered by its property account and working capital. Many years later, it was revealed that no less than $769 million of the plant account was a written-up item, popularly known as "water." Thus all the initial common stock and surplus, amounting to $533 million, was represented by intangibles and a good part of the preferred stock as well. U.S. Steel wrote off all the intangibles in its balance sheet by the following procedures: (1) Between 1901 and 1929 it made annual sinking-fund appropriations to retire parent-company bonds, charging these amounts to earnings as additional "depreciation"; (2) in the same period it made special write-offs, charged both to income and surplus; and (3) in 1938 it made a final charge-off of $260 million, chiefly through decrease in the stated value of the common stock from $100 to $75 per share.

An Effect of the Securities Exchange Act of 1934. The U.S. Steel example illustrates what may be called the standard process of dealing with goodwill since the Securities Exchange Act of 1934 was passed. (This Act gave the Commission power to require full disclosure of balance-sheet and income-account items by all listed companies.) The first step was to separate the intangibles from the plant account. Later the intangibles were usually written off by a charge to some surplus account. Very few if any companies still retain the original large figure for goodwill or "water" among their listed assets. In the industrials, the intangible assets seen on the balance sheet nowadays consist mainly of patents, presumably carried at actual cost, and "purchased goodwill," which is the cost of acquisition of another concern in excess of its tangible assets. These latter goodwill items are usually written off in installments at some arbitrary rate.

Example: See our reference to Gillette Radio and McLean Trucking on page 167 above.

Although most of the intangible assets shown in present-day balance sheets are legitimate enough, we think that consistency requires that they be eliminated in the analyst's calculation of asset values per share, unless they are too small to be worth deducting. For this calculation is not intended to show the "true value" of the shares; if it were, the intangibles of many companies would have to be appraised at a very high figure. The "asset value" or "net worth," discussed in this section, is merely a single factor—usually an unimportant one—in the entire value picture. For this limited purpose it is better to confine oneself to the various categories of tangible assets. In nearly every case the true value of *intangible* assets is indistinguishable from the value of the earnings which they produce.

Asset Values and Investment Values. This may be a good place for some semiphilosophical observations about the historical relationship between asset values and investment values. Fifty years ago it was customary to attach considerable importance to the asset value of a common stock. But in those days the balance-sheet figures of the typical industrial and public utility concern were far from dependable, because the valuation shown for the fixed assets was likely to bear no relationship to actual cost or to any rational appraisal. Now that asset values are clearly stated—generally at depreciated cost for fixed assets, which is below present-day replacement value—practically no attention is paid to this figure in security analysis or in the calculations of investors.

Somewhat the same anomaly applies to the goodwill term itself in its accounting treatment by corporations. Woolworth originally carried its goodwill at $50 million. That was considerably above its true value at the time. (The common stock sold in the market in 1912 at the equivalent of $20 million for the goodwill.) Later when it was written down to $1, by several installments, "for the sake of conservatism," the goodwill was actually worth by the market's own calculation several hundred million dollars, or many times the original book figure.

In this and in other areas of finance, the development of accounting practice, corporate policies, and investment principles has been along separate and often contradictory lines.

Alternative Computation of Book Value. In most cases the book value may be computed readily from the liability side of the conventional published balance sheet. It is sufficient to add together common stock, at par or stated value, the various surplus items, and the voluntary reserves. (However, any arbitrary item for intangibles must be subtracted from this sum.) This will give the total common-stock equity, which is then divided by the number of shares. Adjustments may be made, if desirable, to correct the stated liability for preferred stock.

Example:

Table 16-3. Goodyear Tire & Rubber Company, December 1957

(000,000 omitted)

Common stock...........................	$ 53.0
Capital surplus.........................	76.2
Earned surplus..........................	326.8
Contingency reserve......................	28.9
Foreign and miscellaneous reserves........	31.3
Total net assets for common.............	$516.2
Per share on 10,590,000 shares...........	$48.74

Comment: Excluding the last reserve figure—treatment of which is optional—the net asset value would be $45.80 per share. The financial services, however, unaccountably excluded the contingency reserve as well, giving the figure as $43.10 per share. (The shares were split 3 for 1 in 1959.)

Calculation of Book Value of Preferred Stock. The standard calculations made in the financial manuals give the net asset value of preferred stock as so many dollars per share. At this point in previous editions we indicated how this should be done. (See 1951 edition, page 189.) We believe, however, that such per-share calculations tend to be misleading more often than helpful, unless the analyst is dealing with a single issue of preferred not preceded by funded debt. Otherwise, the per-share figure for a relatively small preferred issue may work out better than that for a senior preferred or for the bond issues. The arithmetical pitfall here is similar to that encountered in calculating earnings per share or times dividend earned of preferred stock by itself, without taking into account the requirements of issues senior to it. (See discussion in Chapter 24.)

In this edition we prefer to limit the asset-value factor for a preferred stock to a calculation of the number of times the net assets available will cover the claims of the issue plus all senior and equivalent claims. The following illustration will indicate how this should be done.

Example:

Table 16-4. Asset Coverage for the Senior Securities of J. I. Case, October 1960

(Dollar figures in millions)

Funded debt...	$ 42.2
$7 1st preferred (noncallable) at $120.......................	11.1
6½ percent 2d preferred (par $7) at par.....................	8.4
Common stock and surplus, less premium on 1st preferred.......	57.3
Total..	$119.0
Less "excess of asset cost over value".......................	11.5
Net tangible assets for senior issues.......................	$107.5

Coverage of funded debt (108 ÷ 42) = 4.76 times
Coverage of 1st preferred {108 ÷ (42 + 11)} = 2.04 times
Coverage of 2d preferred {108 ÷ (42 + 11 + 8.4)} = 1.74 times

Comment: In accordance with our standard procedure we value the $7 preferred as a liability at $120 per share instead of par and reduce the common equity accordingly. The equity is reduced also by an intangible item of $11.5 million. The conventional calculations show asset values of $2,820 per $1,000 of debt, $827 per share of first preferred, and $56.30 per share of second preferred. We doubt if these figures for the preferred issues have any real meaning.

Where a preferred stock has no bonds or other preferred ahead of it, the net asset value in dollars per share will give the same indication as the above coverage ratio. Also, where a preferred issue is selling at so low a price as to be partially equivalent to a common stock, its net asset value may be calculated in dollars per share as is done for common issues.

Current-asset Value and Cash-asset Value. In addition to the well-known concept of book value, we wish to suggest two others of similar character, viz., current-asset value and cash-asset value.

The current-asset value of a stock consists of the current assets alone, minus all liabilities and claims ahead of the issue. It excludes not only the intangible assets but the fixed and miscellaneous assets as well. It appears to be a common practice in Wall Street to state the "net-current-asset value" of a common stock without deducting the senior securities from the working capital. We consider such a figure relatively meaningless and potentially misleading.

The cash-asset value of a stock consists of the cash assets alone, minus all liabilities and claims ahead of the issue. Cash assets, other than cash itself, are defined as those directly equivalent to and held in place of cash. They include certificates of deposit, call loans, marketable securities at market value, and cash-surrender value of insurance policies.

An alternative calculation of the cash-asset value would assume that the current assets other than cash items are applicable to meet the liabilities ahead of the common. The cash assets are then reduced only by the amount needed to meet the balance of senior claims. The remainder of the cash may be considered as available for the common stock. This remainder may be called the "free cash," and the amount thereof per share of common may be called the "free-cash-asset value" of the common.

Table 16-5 shows an example of the computation of the four categories of asset value for a common-stock issue. Since the current assets exceed all liabilities ahead of the common, all the cash assets are "free cash."

Practical Significance of Book Value. The financial services regularly calculate the book value of common stocks from the published balance sheets. Presumably it is a figure of some importance. Yet it would be difficult to find any practical work in investments where a significant degree of attention is paid to the asset value of a common-stock issue—with two important generic exceptions. The first is the field of public utility stocks. Here the rates allowed by regulatory bodies, and the resultant earning power, may be largely governed by the value of the assets, calculated either at original cost or at "fair present value." The second field is that of financial companies, i.e., banks, insurance companies, investment funds, etc. Since the assets of such concerns are nearly all of a liquid nature, their value enters—to a varying extent—in investment decisions relating to their shares. (However, it was formerly not too unusual for the stock of a financial company to sell in the market for less than half its indicated asset value.)

Asset Value and Earning Power Apparently Unrelated. For the great category known as "industrial companies" and for the railroads, the book value appears to be of minimal importance to investors. Common stocks sell freely either at high multiples or at small fractions of book value,

Table 16-5. Calculation of Various Asset Values of Burton-Dixie Corporation Common Stock, November 1961

	Amount (in thousands)	Per share on 209,447 shares
1. Book value.	$10,614	$50.70
2. Current-asset value.	7,257	34.50
3. Net-cash-asset value		
Cash assets.	4,269	
Less all liabilities.	874	
Net cash assets.	$ 3,395	16.20
4. Free-cash-asset value.	4,269	20.30

with scarcely any notice being taken of the fact. For example, the average price of Texas Instruments common in 1960 was 200 against net asset value of 17, while the price of New York Central Railroad averaged 23 vs. net asset value of 146.

There is good reason for not taking the asset-value factor seriously. The average market price of a common stock over the years depends chiefly on the earning power and the dividend payments. These, in turn, usually do not bear any close or reasonably consistent relation to the asset value. (While such a relation may possibly be traced for corporations as a whole, the range in the case of individual companies is virtually unlimited.) Investors and speculators have found that the asset value is typically no guide at all to earning-power value or average market price. Hence they have gradually come to give the asset-value factor practically no weight.

We agree with the prevailing viewpoint that asset values are not a major factor in determining investment values. (We repeat that asset values are more important in public utility investment than elsewhere.) But this does not mean that it is wise or safe to lose sight completely of this element in the analytical picture. Discussion of this point belongs in our later section on bond selection and on the valuation of common stocks. But let us indicate here, briefly, the part which, in our opinion, should properly be played in investment by asset-value considerations:

1. A safe bond or preferred stock almost always requires an ample margin of tangible assets over the senior claim, together with adequate earning power.

2. There is a hazard of sorts in paying many times the asset value for a common stock—a point which the careful investor should take into account. Similarly, the purchase of a common stock at only a small fraction of asset value carries with it certain speculative possibilities—especially so, if there is no substantial debt.

3. The technique of valuing or appraising common stocks becomes more dependable in the formerly frequent cases where the indicated earning-power value is not more than the book value. Consequently, when shares can be purchased at a figure which is well below (*a*) earning-power value, (*b*) book value, and (*c*) average market quotation in the past, the combination of elements holds good promise for the investor.

4. A market quotation well under the *current-asset value alone* has potential significance in every case and real significance in many. It is almost an axiom that when this occurs, either the price is too low or the management should change its policies in some respect.

The Capital Structure. Our suggested balance-sheet presentation shows a total for Capital Funds and then the division of this fund among bonds, preferred stock, and common-stock equity. This division is referred to as the "capital structure" or "capitalization structure." It is usually summarized by stating the percentage of the total represented by each category. The effect of varying capital structures upon the earning power and stability of the common-stock issue will be dealt with in Chapters 40 and 48.

The Working-capital Position. Careful buyers of securities scrutinize the balance sheet to see if the cash assets are adequate, if the current assets bear a suitable ratio to the current liabilities, and if there is any indebtedness or near maturity that may threaten to develop into a refinancing problem.

Nothing useful can be said here on the subject of how much cash a corporation should hold. The investor must form his own opinion as to what is needed in any particular case and also as to how seriously an apparent deficiency of cash should be regarded. A real shortage of cash rarely occurs unless the working-capital position as a whole is poor. With a good ratio of current assets to current liabilities a corporation can get the cash it needs by bank borrowing.

On the subject of the working-capital ratio, a minimum of $2 of current assets for each dollar of current liabilities was formerly regarded as a standard for industrial companies. But since the later 1920's a tendency toward a stronger current position developed in most industries, and we find that the great majority of industrial corporations show a ratio well in excess of 2 to 1.

There has been some tendency to hold that a company falling below the average of its group should be viewed with some suspicion. This idea seems to us to contain something of a logical fallacy, since it necessarily penalizes the lower half of any group, regardless of how satisfactory the showing may be, considered by itself. We are unable to suggest a better figure than the old 2-to-1 criterion to use as a definite quantitative test of a sufficiently comfortable financial position. Naturally the investor would favor companies that well exceed this minimum requirement, but the problem is whether or not a higher ratio must be exacted as a condition for purchase, so that an issue otherwise satisfactory would necessarily be rejected if the current assets are only twice current liabilities. We hesitate to suggest such a rule, nor do we know what new figure to prescribe.

A second measure of financial strength is the so-called "acid test," which requires that current assets *exclusive of inventories* be at least equal to current liabilities.[11] Ordinarily the investor might well expect of a company that it meet *both* the 2-to-1 test and the acid test. The failure to meet either of these criteria would in most instances reflect strongly upon the investment standing of a common-stock issue—as it would in the case of a bond or preferred stock—and it would supply an argument against the security from the speculative standpoint as well.

For general information we supply, in Tables 16-6 and 16-7, figures of working capital and sales of manufacturing companies generally in 1939, 1949, and 1959.

Table 16-6. Working Capital of Listed Manufacturing Companies

(SEC figures; dollar figures in billions)

Item	1939	1949	1959*
Inventory	$ 6.1	$15.1	$ 57.9
Total current assets	13.1	34.2	130.9
Current liabilities	3.0	11.5	52.2
Net current assets	10.1	22.7	78.7
Current ratio	4.4:1	3.0:1	2.5:1

* For all manufacturing corporations. Taken from FTC-SEC *Quarterly Financial Report for Manufacturing Corporations*, first quarter 1960.

Table 16-7. Sales and Inventories of All Manufacturing Companies

(Department of Commerce figures, dollar figures in billions)

Item	1939	1949	1959
Sales	$61.3	$213.3	$356.4
Average inventory	11.5	28.8	52.4
Ratio of sales to inventory	5.3×	7.3×	6.8×

[11] The term "acid test" is now used by some authorities to require that "cash equivalents" alone, excluding both inventories and receivables, be equal to current liabilities. Our acid test above is then called the "quick-ratio test." See J. F. Weston, *Managerial Finance,* Holt, Rinehart & Winston, New York, 1962, p. 57.

Large Bank Debt Frequently a Sign of Weakness. Financial difficulties are almost always heralded by the presence of bank loans or of other debt due in a short time. In other words, it is rare for a weak financial position to be created solely by ordinary trade accounts payable. This does not mean that bank debt is a bad sign in itself; the use of a reasonable amount of bank credit—particularly for seasonal needs—is not only legitimate but even desirable. But, whenever the statement shows Notes or Bills Payable, the analyst will subject the financial picture to a somewhat closer scrutiny than in cases where there is a "clean" balance sheet.

Bank Loans of Intermediate Maturity. Since the early 1940's the "term loan" has developed as an important medium of financing by corporations. Such loans run generally from five to fifteen years, and they are repayable in installments over their life—often with a larger than average maturity at the end (called the "balloon"). The lender is usually a bank, but sometimes an insurance company.

Examples: These term loans have been made for a variety of purposes, such as, (1) to retire bond issues (Commercial Investment Trust Company in 1939) and even preferred stock (Guantanamo Sugar in 1950); (2) for additional working capital (Manhattan Shirt in 1946) or (3) to finance acquisitions of property or stock control (Beaunit Mills in 1948).

Debts and Dividends. In most cases term loans, as well as other forms of borrowing, involve an agreement by the borrower to maintain working capital at a prescribed figure, and also not to pay dividends except out of future earnings plus some limited figure. In effect, the greater part of the earned surplus is frozen until the loan is paid off. These provisions may result in disappointment for the company's stockholders in the event of even temporary loss of earning power.

Example 1: Northwest Air Lines sold $9,750,000 of 4.6 percent preferred at par ($25) in 1947. In 1948–1949 it borrowed up to $15.1 million from banks. In March 1950 it suspended the preferred dividend because of restrictions imposed by the bank-loan agreements relating to working capital and to earnings since March 1949. The price of the preferred declined to 13⅝ in 1949. Late in 1950 preferred dividends were resumed.

In 1958–1959 Northwest Air Lines again borrowed $40 million on term loans, due serially in 1966–1978. Cash dividends are limited to 70 percent of available consolidated net earnings since 1957, plus $2 million.

Example 2: In 1948 Kearney & Trecker (machine tools) borrowed $2 million, repayable over 15 years, to finance an acquisition, and thereby froze its entire earned surplus of $11.5 million. In October 1960 only $312,000 of the term loan was still outstanding, but by its provisions all of the then $10.3 million adjusted surplus, except $1,280,000, was restricted. Dividends were passed in 1959, when the company sustained its first loss since the borrowing.

From the standpoint of security analysis, term loans resemble the short-term notes that used to be sold to the public as a familiar part of corporate financing. They must be considered partly equivalent to current liabilities and partly to early maturing debt. They are not dangerous if either the current-asset position is so strong that the loans could readily be taken care of as current liabilities, or the earning power is so large and dependable as to make refinancing a simple problem. But if neither of these conditions is present, the analyst must view the presence of a substantial amount of intermediate bank debt as a potential threat to dividends or even to solvency.

CALCULATIONS OF EARNINGS VIA THE BALANCE SHEET

In many cases the true earnings over a period of years may be established more reliably by comparing the change in surplus and reserve accounts than by adding up the reported profits. The simple equation is as follows:

Earnings for period = Increase in earned surplus
(and surplus reserves) + dividends paid

In an uncomplicated case an equivalent calculation may be made by comparing the net assets per share at the beginning and end of the period and adding back the dividends paid.

The advantage of using the change in the earned-surplus account as the basic guide to earnings over the period is that all the gains and losses are reflected therein, whereas some of them may have been excluded from the annual income statements. (The analyst may sometimes find it advisable to exclude substantial debits or credits that relate to years before the period under review.) It is essential for this technique that all voluntary reserves be treated as part of the earned surplus. Fortunately, it is becoming accepted and even compulsory accounting procedure to show such reserves as part of the surplus, or stockholders' equity, accounts.

There are certain changes in the stockholders' equity which are not caused by earnings and cash dividends. These result mainly from (1) sale or repurchase of shares of stock by the company, (2) extraordinary write-downs or write-ups of assets. In most, but not all, such cases the transactions are cleared through the capital and capital-surplus accounts and do not affect the earned surplus. In a few cases, dividends which should be charged to earned surplus are charged to capital surplus.

Stock dividends may be charged to earned surplus in whole or in part. In comparing balance sheets over a period the analyst must, of course, make a suitable adjustment of the effect of any stock dividends.

In rare cases amounts are transferred from earned-surplus account to capital account without a stock-dividend declaration. Chrysler did this in 1949 when it increased the par value of its share from $2.50 to $25. In all balance-sheet comparisons over a period of time, the analyst must trace through the charges and credits to earned surplus to see what items, if any, are to be excluded from the record of over-all earnings.

The examples given in Tables 16-8 and 16-9 illustrate the two methods of checking on earnings for a period by balance-sheet comparisons. The first must be viewed as an extreme (and complicated) case of overstatement of income; the second is simpler than the average.

Table 16-8. Reported Earnings vs. Balance-sheet Changes (Earned-surplus Method) for Dynamics Corporation of America, 1951–1960

(000 omitted)

1. Reported net income.. $ 15,776
   Less preferred dividends..................................... 2,274
   Reported balance for common................................ $ 13,502
   (Average shares outstanding)................................ (2,700)
   Average annual earnings per share.......................... 50 cents
2. Earned surplus:
   December 1960... $ 8,022
   December 1950... *234 (d)*
   Increase in earned surplus for period...................... $ 8,256
   Deduct:
   Preferred dividends charged to capital surplus............. 883
   Miscellaneous nonincome credits, net of debits............. 527
   Adjusted increase in earned surplus = indicated earnings for common. (No common dividends were charged to earned surplus).. $ 6,846
   Adjusted average annual earnings per share................. 25 cents
3. Explanation of difference:
   Earned surplus in period was charged with following amounts, not deducted from the income account:
   Provision for additional taxes............................. $3,800,000
   Provision for development expense.......................... 1,252,000
   Provision for investment reserve, later used............... 1,027,000
   Loss on liquidation of subsidiary.......................... 576,000
   Total.. $6,655,000

This company pursued "unorthodox" accounting, not only by charging important items to earned surplus that should be deducted from the income account but also by charging all its common dividends and some of its preferred dividends to capital surplus instead of to earned surplus. In effect, its true earnings per share for the decade were only half the reported earnings. Nonetheless, the price advanced from a low of 2½ in 1957 to a high above 20 in 1961. The reader should take another warning here that *speculative market action* pays no attention whatever to past history (with or without the analyst's corrections) and very little heed to the *sober* possibilities of the future. The analyst's work will help to identify the situation as extremely speculative and thus constitute a guide of sorts to those seeking such enlightenment; but it has little relevance to the price fluctuations of issues such as Dynamics Corporation of America.

This more representative example—though simpler than most to calculate—indicates a close correspondence between the earnings as reported and those deduced from balance-sheet changes plus dividends added back.

Table 16-9. Reported Earnings vs. Balance-sheet Changes (Equity-per-share Method) for American Radiator & Standard Sanitary Corporation, 1951–1960

1. Reported earnings per share.................... $16.44
2. Net assets per share:
   December 1960............................. 23.79
   December 1950............................. 14.82

   Increase.. $ 8.97
   Less accumulated earnings of foreign subsidiaries,
      credited in 1957 to surplus.................... 3.80

   Adjusted increase in equity..................... $ 5.17
   Add dividends paid in period................... 11.22

   Indicated earnings per share................... $16.22

LONG-TERM STUDIES OF INCOME AND BALANCE-SHEET POSITION

In our next two chapters we shall consider the key relationships among invested capital, earnings, dividends, and market price that underlie our judgments as to the quality of a company's performance and the attractiveness of its securities. A comprehensive study of a common stock might well include comparisons of absolute amounts and key ratios that go back many years. Figures of this sort can give the analyst a long perspective and an adequate conception of both the company's vicissitudes and its rate and direction of change. Balance sheets and income accounts for selected years, spaced, say, ten years apart, will do this job quite well for most purposes, especially when comparisons are to be made between two or more enterprises. A more complete type of study will include the aggregate earnings for the decades between the balance-sheet dates, so that a few key ratios can be computed on the basis of successive ten-year performances rather than for the single years a decade apart.

In Appendix Note 8, page 733, we supply examples of both types of long-term study. They may best be considered after the next two chapters have been read.

CHAPTER SEVENTEEN

INTERPRETATION OF THE FINANCIAL DATA:

PER-SHARE FIGURES AND KEY RATIOS

The study of a given company's financial statements should proceed in a number of steps, in the following logical sequence: First, the analyst should determine the true operating earnings for the period under review. Next, he should examine the balance sheet and establish the working-capital position, the capital structure, and the amount of invested capital per share. He should then develop a number of key ratios, which will throw light on the company's over-all performance, on the safety of its senior securities and on the attractiveness of its common stock for investment.

PER-SHARE FIGURES

In Wall Street it is customary to sum up the statistical data about a common stock in three salient figures. These are the earnings per share, the dividend rate, and the price. However, in the last year or two, some services have also been reporting the cash flow per share.[1] Dividing earnings into price produces the much-emphasized "price-earnings ratio." Dividing the price into the dividend produces the often equally important "dividend yield" or "dividend return." For example, if a company earns $5, pays $3, and sells at 75, its price-earning ratio (or "earnings multiplier") is 15 and the dividend yield is 4 percent.

Per-share Data Defective in Two Ways. The convenience of per-share earnings figures leads inevitably to their widespread use. They have two drawbacks, however, which make them somewhat of a hindrance to serious analysis. The lesser defect is that they draw the investor's attention away from the enterprise as a whole—involving certain magnitudes of sales, profits, invested capital, and aggregate market value—and concentrate it too much on the single share of stock. The greater defect is that a figure of earnings per share, accepted and emphasized without

[1] See, for example, the Value Line *Investment Survey* and Studley Shupert & Company, *Analyses of Corporate Securities.*

regard to the details of the income account from which it is derived, may easily give rise to misleading inferences. Too much may therefore depend on arbitrary choices made by management as to the mere form in which the income statement is published—as, for example, whether major nonrecurrent items are taken in before or after the figure of net income from which the per-share calculation is made.

A significant statement on this subject was made by the American Institute of Accountants, through its Committee on Accounting Procedure, in Accounting Research Bulletin No. 32, published in December 1947. Paragraph 13 of the Bulletin reads as follows:

> In its deliberations concerning the nature and purpose of the income statement, the committee has been mindful of the disposition of even well-informed persons to attach undue importance to a single net income figure and to "earnings per share" shown for a particular year. The committee directs attention to the undesirability in many cases of the dissemination of information in which major prominence is given to a single figure of "net income" or "net income per share." However, if such income data are reported (as in newspapers, investors' services, and annual corporate reports), the committee strongly urges that any determination of "income per share" be related to the amount reported as net income, and that where charges or credits have been excluded from the determination of net income, the corresponding total or per share amount of such charges and credits also be reported separately and simultaneously. In this connection the committee earnestly solicits the cooperation of all organizations, both governmental and private, engaged in the compilation of business earnings statistics from annual reports.

Restatement of Earnings. No similar objection applies to the use of per-share figures for the cash dividends paid in a given year. This can hardly be open to any misconception. There is frequently some doubt as to what the current dividend rate really is—mainly because of variations between regular and extra disbursements—but that is a difficulty of another sort.

The analyst's intensive study of the income account will lead him on occasion to *restate* the reported profits on what may be called "a current-operating-performance basis," i.e., to reflect the "true" operating earnings. These adjusted figures will lead to a corresponding adjustment of the per-share earnings. Where the difference between the two amounts is substantial, it is one of the important functions of the analyst to call attention to the fact that his corrected calculation presents a more serviceable picture of the results from operations.

Allowances for Changes in Capitalization. In dealing with the past record of earnings, when they are given on a per-share basis, the analyst must follow the elementary practice of adjusting the figures to reflect any important changes in the capitalization which have taken place during the period. In the simplest case the changes will be only in the number of shares of common stock resulting from stock dividends, split-ups, etc. All that is necessary, then, is to restate the capitalization throughout the period on the basis of the current number of shares. (Such recalculations are made by some of the statistical services but not by others.)

When the change in capitalization has been due to the sale of additional stock at a comparatively low price (usually through the exercise of subscription rights or warrants) or to the conversion of senior securities, the adjustment is more difficult. In such cases the earnings available for the common during the earlier period must be increased by whatever gain would have followed from the issuance of the additional shares. When bonds or preferred stocks have been converted into common, the charges formerly paid thereon, less any related tax credit, are to be added back to the earnings and the new figure then applied to the larger number of shares. (Such recalculations need not be made unless the changes indicated thereby are substantial.)

A corresponding adjustment of the per-share earnings must be made at times to reflect the possible *future* increase in the number of shares outstanding as a result of conversions or exercise of option warrants. When other security holders have a choice of any kind, sound analysis must allow for the possible adverse effect upon the per-share earnings of the common stock that would follow from the exercise of the option.

Example: In July 1960, Northrop Aircraft had convertible issues which could effect an increase of over 23 percent in the outstanding common stock. The effect of the required adjustment in per share earnings is shown as follows:

	As reported	Adjusted for conversion
Net Income...................	$7,740,000	$7,740,000
Add interest saved less tax.....		329,000
Common shares...............	1,836,000	2,265,000
Earned per share.............	$4.22	$3.56

A striking example of the effect of adjustment for a conversion privilege was afforded by Studebaker (Packard) in 1959, as set forth on p. 320.

The effect of adjustments for both stock splits (or stock dividends) and conversion privileges is shown by the data for Collins Radio in Table 17-1.

Of the adjustments indicated here, that for 1951 is clearly needed. The others would be optional with the analyst under our "10 percent rule." Conversion is not allowed for if the results would *increase* the earnings per share, since the assumption of conversion would then be unrealistic. (This would have applied to Collins Radio in 1958.) In general, also, adjustment for conversion may be omitted if the conversion price is far higher—say 50 percent or more—than the market price of the stock. For such assumed conversion would carry with it the assumption of a large price advance in the shares, which, in turn, would make a detailed examination of the figures unnecessary

Allowance for Outstanding Warrants and Stock Options. Where substantial amounts of warrants are outstanding, giving the holders the right to purchase shares below or not far above the current market price, the consequences are basically similar to those resulting from the conversion privileges just discussed. Neither the past nor the future earnings can be said to belong unqualifiedly to the outstanding common shares in the same way as they would if there were no dilution through option warrants. However, it is not possible to make a precise calculation of the effect of the warrants upon the per-share earnings, as one adjusts for convertible issues by simply assuming a *pro forma* conversion. The warrants, if exercised, will bring in additional funds from which certain earnings would have to be conjectured.

Table 17-1. Collins Radio Company

(Number of shares and earnings in thousands)

Year (July 31)	Earnings for common as reported			Adjustment *A* for stock changes*		Adjustment *B* for possible conversions		
	Amount	Number of shares	Per share	Number of shares	Earned per share	Amount	Number of shares	Earned per share
1960	$6,525	2,149	$3.04	2,149	$3.04	$6,658	2,405	$2.77
1957	1,948	1,504	1.29	1,627	1.20	2,383	2,153	1.11
1951	692	310	2.23	1,590	0.44			

* Stock dividends of 25 percent were paid in 1952, 10 percent in 1953, 15 percent in 1954, and 4 percent in 1959 and 1960; plus a three-for-one split in 1955.

If the warrants are comparatively few in number, the analyst may consider their effects unimportant and ignore them. If their amount appears significant to the analyst, he can make a reasonably good adjustment for them by assuming that they are equivalent to additional outstanding common shares with the same aggregate market value as that of the warrant issue. This method of calculation is illustrated as follows:

Example: Del E. Webb Corporation (contracting, etc.) in June 1961 had outstanding 4.4 million shares of common stock and 800,000 warrants (running to 1975) to buy common stock, one for one, at $6\frac{1}{4}$. The common was selling at about $10\frac{1}{2}$ and the warrants at $6\frac{1}{2}$.

Calculation:

Market value of warrant issue............................. $5.2 million
Equivalent shares of common stock at $10\frac{1}{2}$................   495,000 shares
Adjusted common capitalization........................... 4,895,000 shares
Resultant dilution of earnings and assets = 495:4,895, or about 10 percent.[2]

[2] Where the asset value is important, as in the case of an investment company, the adjustment may be made by merely assuming exercise of the warrants. See discussion of the Tricontinental Corporation warrants below, p. 660.

Stock options granted to company employees and others have the same theoretical consequences as the option warrants just discussed, but they do not have a market price. Although their merits and demerits have been a subject of active controversy, they are seldom large enough to require a *pro forma* adjustment of past or expected earnings. However, should this need to be done, the analyst might be able to make a calculation analogous to the D. E. Webb one above by assigning to the options an estimated market value based on the current prices of various quoted warrants.

Allowance for Conversion of "Class B" into Publicly Held Shares. In recent years a considerable number of privately owned companies have gone public through the sale of "class A" common stock, while the interest of the former sole owners has been vested in "class B" (sometimes plain "common") shares. Though the respective dividend rights of the two classes vary from company to company, usually they give some priority to the public shares. However, in virtually all cases the other issue has the right of conversion—share for share—into class A stock. Occasionally the conversion right is immediate and complete—e.g., Max Factor common into class A—but more often it can be done only in blocks over a period of several years.

Example 1: Salant & Salant, Inc. (apparel manufacturers). The owners sold 100,000 class A shares to the public in 1959. The 625,000 class B shares were made convertible into class A, share for share, after September 30, 1962, "generally at the rate of 100,000 shares per year."

Example 2: Tip-Top Products Company (hair curlers, etc.) sold 266,-000 class A shares to the public in 1959, with control remaining in 402,000 class B shares. The latter were held by one person and were convertible in their entirety on his death. Otherwise, subject to certain earnings and dividend restrictions, they were convertible in various amounts between September 1961 and November 1962 (and subsequently).

The companies' reports follow various practices in stating earnings per share on the class A stock. In the above examples, Salant & Salant reported 1960 earnings as $3.74 on the class A and $0.93½ on the class B. Tip-Top Products gave its earnings as $1.15 per share "based on full conversion of class B into class A."

In the Salant case and all similar ones the analyst must obviously make his calculation on the basis of full conversion—i.e., assuming only one class of stock outstanding. This would reduce the 1960 earnings on Salant class A to only $1.28 per share (adjusted for a 3 percent stock dividend paid against such earnings)—a very considerable change from the figure given in the company's report.

Allowances for Participating Interests. In calculating the earnings available for the common, the analyst must give full recognition to the rights of holders of participating issues, whether or not the amounts involved are actually being paid thereon. Table 17-2 illustrates for the

1947–1956 period the adjustments which would have been in order to allow for the 213,000 outstanding shares of 6 percent cumulative participating preferred stock ($100 par value) of the Virginia-Carolina Chemical Company.[3] The preferred is entitled to $6 dividends per share, and after the common receives $3 participates equally with the common, share for share.

General Rule. The material in the last few pages may be summarized in the following general rule:

The intrinsic value of a common stock, preceded by convertible securities or subject to dilution through the exercise of stock options or through participating privileges enjoyed by other security holders, cannot reasonably be appraised at a higher figure than would be justified if all such privileges were exercised in full.

Table 17-2. Virginia-Carolina Chemical Corporation, 1947–1956

(Number of shares and earnings in thousands)

Year	Earnings for common after allowing a $6 dividend on the preferred*	Number of shares of common	Earned per share	
			Ignoring participating feature of preferred	Adjusted for participating feature of preferred
1947	$2,780	486	$5.72	$4.89
1951	3,776	486	7.76	6.31
1956	101	509	0.20	0.20
10-year average......	2,414	489	4.96	4.25

* Disregarding payments for accumulated preferred dividends.

PRICE-EARNINGS RATIOS

The main purpose of calculating earnings per share, aside from indicating dividend protection, is to permit a ready comparison with the current market price. The resultant "price-earnings ratio" is a concept that the working analyst will have to deal with extensively. The question of what price-earnings ratios are, and what determines them, must now be considered. Our treatment of the subject will fall into two parts. The first deals with the actual behavior of the market—i.e., of investors and speculators—in respect to price-earnings, ratios. The second, reserved for a later chapter on valuation methods, will venture some thoughts on what the price-earnings ratio *should be.*

[3] Earnings on the common since 1956 have been below $3 a share; accordingly, the participating feature would have had no effect.

The statement that a common stock "is selling at N times earnings" is not without some ambiguity. The earnings referred to may be those of the past year; or of the current year, partly estimated; or even of the latest three months, multiplied by four. The phrase is sometimes amplified to read "N times anticipated earnings" for a stated period in the future or "N times average earnings" for a stated period in the past. For the most part, however, the concept of the price-earnings ratio is applied to what is considered a current or quite recent full year's figure.

When the student compiles a large assortment of price-earnings ratios, he is likely to be bewildered by their diversity and inconsistency. Since many stocks cover a wide price range within a single year, this would mean that their ratios will vary correspondingly in that year. The average annual ratio for nearly every stock is likely to differ widely from one year to another. Finally, the ratios of different stocks when observed at the same moment could readily range from less than 7 times to more than 70 times current earnings.[4]

It seems almost impossible to make any degree of order out of this chaos. Nevertheless, one may discern some fairly well-defined and not irrational patterns in the price-earnings ratios, when they are viewed from the proper vantage. An effective way of doing this would be by comparing average price over a representative period of years with the average earnings during the same time. In Table 17-3 we show the resultant average ratios for each of the 30 stocks in the Dow-Jones Industrial list, taking the two 5-year periods 1950–1954, 1955–1959, and 1960. The range in 1950–1954 is found to be from 4.7 times for Bethlehem Steel to 17.9 times for Union Carbide; in the 1955–1959 span, from 9.5 times for Anaconda to 26.1 times for Aluminum Company of America; and in 1960 from 10.8 times for Standard of California to 48 times for Alcoa. For the vast majority of common stocks the average relationship between price and earnings—as shown by this kind of computation—may be said to reflect the views of investors and speculators as to the "quality" of the issue. A strong, successful, and promising company usually sells at a higher multiplier of current or average earnings than one that is less strong, less successful, and less promising.

The chief analytical elements governing the price-earnings ratio may be listed as follows:

1. Those factors that are fully reflected in the financial data (tangible factors)
   a. *Growth* of earnings and sales in the past
   b. *Profitability*—rate of return on invested capital
   c. *Stability of past earnings*
   d. The *dividend* rate and record
   e. Financial *strength*, or credit standing

---

[4] For example, in 1960 Atlantic Refining sold as low as 6.2 times and Automatic Canteen sold as high as 67 times that year's earnings.

2. Those factors that are reflected to an indefinite extent in the data (intangible factors)
    a. Quality of management
    b. Nature and prospects of the industry
    c. Competitive position and individual prospects of the company

The five factors listed in the first group may be studied by the analyst in the financial statements. The three in the second group do not, of course, admit of the same type of definite, quantitative calculation. A highly important point to bear in mind in this connection is that, typically, the incalculable factors have already exerted a strong influence upon the reported results. In other words, the figures themselves will show, fairly clearly and comprehensively, how good a business and how good a management the company has. This will not be true if the incumbent management has recently taken over, or if there have been major new developments in the industry or in the concern that make the past results irrelevant to the future. In the early stages of a highly dynamic industry —as in electronics (instrumentation and communication), business machines, drugs, etc.,—expectations of future profits are often divorced completely from the actual accomplishments of the past. But those are not the usual cases.

KEY RATIOS IN SECURITY ANALYSIS

The tangible factors affecting the quality of a company may be measured by the use of certain key ratios. Other key ratios measure the relationship between *price* and the analytical factors such as dividends, earnings, assets, sales. These should prove useful in every full-scale analysis. They fall under six general headings, as follows:

1. Profitability ratios
2. Growth ratios, or progress ratios
3. Stability ratios
4. Payout ratio (dividend policy)
5. Credit ratios
6. Price ratios

The first five groups measure the performance and financial strength of the enterprise, considered apart from the valuation placed upon it in the market. The sixth group will indicate what the investor *is getting for his money* if he buys, or had bought, at some specified price. Let us first discuss these various ratios in their proper sequence and then illustrate their use by applying them to a pair of comparable companies.

1. Profitability Ratios. The best gauge of the success of an enterprise is the percentage earned on invested capital,[5] i.e., on the long-term (non-

---

[5] "Invested capital," "capital funds," and "total capital" may be used interchangeably to denote the sum of the senior securities and the common-stock equity.

Table 17-3. Individual Stocks Constituting Dow-Jones Industrial Average. Average Earnings, Prices, and Price-Earnings Ratios 1950–1954, 1955–1959 and 1960

Component Stock†	Average earnings 1950–1954	Average* price 1950–1954	Price-earnings ratio	Average earnings 1955–1959	Average* price 1955–1959	Price-earnings ratio	Earnings 1960	Mean price 1960	Price-earnings ratio
Allied Chemical	$ 2.18	$ 33.1	15.2	$ 2.28	$ 48.7	21.4	$ 2.57	$ 52.5	20.4
Aluminum Co.	2.47	24.0	9.7	3.29	85.9	26.1	1.76	84.5	48.0
American Can.	2.65	32.8	12.4	2.77	44.2	16.0	2.06	37.5	18.2
American Tel. and Tel.	3.96	52.7	13.3	4.59	64.9	14.1	5.43	94.2	17.3
American Tobacco	2.96	32.5	11.0	4.11	40.5	9.9	4.56	58.5	12.8
Anaconda Co.	4.47	40.9	9.1	6.66	63.3	9.5	4.30	55.0	12.8
Bethlehem Steel	2.90	13.7	4.7	3.57	43.6	12.2	2.52	47.0	18.7
Chrysler	8.54	74.4	8.7	4.82	67.6	14.0	3.61	55.0	15.2
du Pont	5.64	97.8	17.3	8.42	205.3	24.4	8.10	223.0	27.5
Eastman Kodak	1.43	20.3	14.2	2.60	55.8	21.5	3.30	115.0	34.9
General Electric	1.93	24.2	12.5	2.72	65.7	24.2	2.26	85.1	37.7
General Foods	1.07	13.3	12.4	2.03	28.9	14.2	2.69	62.5	23.2
General Motors	2.47	19.6	7.9	3.87	44.4	11.5	3.35	48.0	14.3
Goodyear	1.33	7.4	5.6	1.99	28.3	14.2	2.10	40.5	19.3
International Harvester	3.71	31.7	8.5	3.49	38.3	11.0	3.40	44.4	13.1
International Nickel	1.92	20.0	10.4	2.71	44.0	16.2	2.76	53.5	19.4
International Paper	1.66	13.5	8.1	2.06	33.5	16.3	1.74	36.5	21.0
Johns-Manville	3.36	31.7	9.4	3.35	46.7	13.9	3.12	53.6	17.2
Owens-Illinois Glass	3.12	39.3	12.6	4.50	71.2	15.8	4.10	99.5	24.3
Procter & Gamble	2.58	35.1	13.6	3.39	59.9	17.7	4.72	109.0	23.1
Sears, Roebuck	1.70	19.0	11.2	2.67	33.9	12.7	2.55	51.5	20.2
Standard Oil of Calif.	2.85	24.1	8.5	4.11	49.9	12.1	4.21	45.5	10.8
Standard Oil of N.J.	2.81	22.7	8.1	3.49	53.0	15.2	3.18	44.5	14.0
Swift & Co.	3.47	38.6	11.1	2.68	40.7	15.2	3.09	45.0	14.6
Texaco, Inc.	3.24	25.4	7.8	5.36	64.0	11.9	6.34	74.0	11.7

232

Component Stock†	Average earnings 1950–1954	Average* price 1950–1954	Price-earnings ratio	Average earnings 1955–1959	Average* price 1955–1959	Price-earnings ratio	Earnings 1960	Mean price 1960	Price-earnings ratio
Union Carbide	$ 3.59	$ 64.2	17.9	$ 4.80	$ 112.8	23.5	$ 5.25	$ 127.5	24.3
United Aircraft	2.98	22.0	7.4	5.92	56.3	9.5	1.95	39.5	20.3
U.S. Steel	3.19	21.4	6.7	5.83	69.0	11.8	5.16	86.0	16.7
Westinghouse Electric	2.32	22.3	9.6	1.42	34.2	24.1	2.22	55.0	24.8
Woolworth	3.22	45.5	14.1	3.58	48.3	13.5	4.84	67.0	13.8
Total	$89.72	$963.20	10.7	$113.08	$1,742.80	15.4	$107.24	$2,090.3	19.5
Dow-Jones Industrial average (as actually reported) ‡	27.53	270.71	9.8	33.44	505.42	15.1	32.21	628.1	19.5

* Average of annual mean prices.
† Adjusted for splits and stock dividends through 1960.
‡ There is some discrepancy between the actually reported figures for the DJIA and the averages for the individual shares as a result of changes in the composition of the DJIA.

current) debt and preferred stock plus the book value of the common stock. This percentage, or rate of return, is the ratio to total capital of the *final* net profit available for capital funds. Thus it reflects all recurrent items of profit and loss, including income tax, but not deducting interest on funded debt. The fundamental merit of return-on-invested-capital ratio is that it measures the *basic* or over-all performance of a business in terms of the total funds provided by all long-term investors— rather than a single class.

The importance of depreciation has increased significantly in the postwar period, and at the same time marked differences in depreciation policies exist among companies. (See our discussion in Chapter 19 for specific illustrations, also Chapter 12.) Thus, in making a comparative analysis of a number of corporations within an industry, it will be helpful to give consideration to the depreciation factor. This may be done in a number of different ways, such as the well-known ratio of depreciation to gross plant or to sales. A somewhat different—but quick and effective— method for determining the influence of this factor on earnings is to compute a predepreciation return on total capital. (This is a legitimate use of the cash-flow concept.) For ease of tabular arrangement, we begin with this computation:

Ratio I—Earnings before depreciation per dollar of capital funds ("predepreciation return on capital")

It is a question of individual preference as to how the rate of return *after* depreciation is obtained. It may be either computed directly as follows:

Ratio II—Earnings per dollar of capital funds ("return on capital")

or it may be derived by multiplying the following two ratios:

Ratio III—Sales per dollar of capital funds ("sales ratio")
Ratio IV—Earnings per dollar of sales ("earnings margin")

Note that the "earnings margin" in these ratios is not the same as "margin of profit" as it is ordinarily used in accounting. The latter phrase refers to the direct operating results only; it is figured before the income tax deduction and also excludes nonoperating income and charges. Our figure is the ratio to sales of the *final* net profit available for the capital funds.

If there is only common stock outstanding, the earnings per dollar of capital are the same as the earnings per dollar of common-stock equity. But if there are senior securities, a separate calculation of Ratio II is necessary for the common stock.

The profitability ratios should be examined in terms of both period averages and individual years. In this manner the year-by-year fluctuations, as well as the level of performance over a span of time may be appraised.

Growth Ratios. The figures usually compared over time for company growth rates are:

Ratio V—Dollar sales
Ratio VI—Net profit for total capital in dollars
Ratio VII—Earnings per share

The tests of growth are most informative when they are made between years representing about the same phase of successive business cycles.

The absence of *major* cycles since 1949 has practically ruled out this desirable technique for recent analytical work. Instead the analysts have had to make their comparisons over some convenient period—say ten years. To diminish the effect of single-year variations we recommend that such a comparison be made between three-year averages—e.g., 1960–1962 versus 1950–1952.

The annual growth rates of various industries may be compared by a similar method, using a suitable group of companies as a sample of each industry. A study of this kind made by Stanford Research Institute covering the annual growth of sales for 32 industries from 1947 to 1957 showed variations from a high of 26.1 percent for the aircraft industry to a low of *minus 0.1 percent* for meat packing; and a mean annual growth rate of 7.23 percent for all divisions.[6]

3. Measures of Stability. It is possible to develop arithmetical indexes of the stability of earnings over a given period of years. One such might be the following: Select the lowest net income in, say, a given five- to ten-year period and calculate the ratio of such earnings to the average of the preceding three years. This will indicate fairly well how serious was the effect of any temporary setback.[7]

In the last two decades there has not been a year of general business recession sufficiently marked to test out the inherent stability of all enterprises. But this does not mean that some industries may not have had severe changes in profitability. In some instances, the decline represents a drop from unusually high levels immediately after World War II or in 1955; in other instances, it represents a true cyclical decline in demand. The following data illustrate the amplitude of the postwar fluctuations for some industries: The composite return on total capital for the major

---

[6] The valuable compilations made annually by First National City Bank of New York, in its April *Monthly Letter*, show composite dollar earnings, profit margins, and rate of return on stock equity for a large number of industry groups.

[7] We believe the effect of a "poor year" on earnings should always be measured against some preceding period and not against an average that includes subsequent years. If the later years show a large increase in profits, their effect (if used in such an average) would be to make the earnings appear arithmetically unstable, when in fact they are forging ahead.

units in the distilling industry dropped from 27 percent in 1946 to 6 percent in 1955; in automobiles it dropped from 32 percent in 1949 to less than 10 percent in 1958; in agricultural machinery from 13 percent in 1950 to 5 percent in 1954; in nonferrous metals (excluding copper) it went through two cycles—from 15 percent in 1948 to 10 percent in 1949 and from 18 percent in 1956 to 7 percent in 1958; and in steel it declined from over 10 percent in 1955 to less than 6 percent in 1959. Textile fabrics had the most violent swing; the return dropped from 29 percent in 1948 to less than 5 percent in 1954 and, after a modest recovery, dipped down to less than 4 percent in 1958.

Thus in some companies and industries the postwar fluctuations have supplied a reasonably good test of the relative soundness or competitive position of the individual firm. However, for some companies (and industries) the analyst in 1961 would need to go back as far as 1937–1938 for a comparable test. The remoteness of the 1937–1938 figures substantially reduces their usefulness but in some cases may not have destroyed it.

In determining the quality of a bond or preferred stock, the factor of earnings stability plays a large part. This may be handled in a simple manner by calculating the *minimum* coverage of charges or of prior charges and preferred dividends shown during a substantial number of years in the past.

In many cases the *minimum dividend* paid on the common stock over, say, a ten-year period will give a valuable clue to inherent stability, as well as to management's attitude on this factor—which is of major importance for all but the acknowledged "growth companies." (The dividend paid by a growth company in the past may have little bearing on minimum dividend expectations in the future or other determinants of its value.) Consequently, we suggest only two standard measurements of stability, viz.:

Ratio VIII—Minimum coverage of senior charges (See Ratio XIII below)
Ratio IX—Maximum decline in earnings rate on total capital

The latter ratio may be supplemented by measuring the maximum decline in the return earned on common-stock capital and/or in per-share earnings.

4. Payout Ratio. The percentage of available earnings paid out in common dividends often has a most important effect upon the market's attitude toward those issues not in the "growth-stock" category. This may be calculated, quite simply, by dividing the earnings into the dividend, yielding

Ratio X—Payout Ratio

In the case of issues paying stock dividends as well as cash, the computation is not so simple. As we explain in detail in Chapter 36, we are inclined to the view that—when stock dividends are declared out of *current* earnings—the investor, in computing the actual dividend rate, and therefore the payout ratio, should include these dividends at some figure between 50 and 100 percent of the per-share amount at which they are charged against surplus by the issuing corporation.

Inclusion of stock dividends in the payout is debatable. The logic in its favor turns on the contention that the investor, in a sense, has received a readily salable certificate representing a portion of the issuing corporation's current earnings. The logic against it rests on the argument that a stock dividend does not give a shareholder anything which he does not already possess. The reader must decide between these conflicting opinions—but not, we hope, before considering our later discussion (Chapter 36). From the realistic point of view something may be said for valuing periodic stock dividends at one-half their current market value. This compromise position may reflect reasonably well the stock market's own appraisal of such dividends in 1961.

5. Credit Ratios. These are of two kinds, relating to working-capital position and to capital structure.

Ratio XI—Working-capital ratio

The significance of this ratio was discussed in Chapter 16, pages 218 to 220.

If there are senior securities, their effect in relation to the balance sheet may be measured by Ratio XII and their effect on the earnings statement by Ratio XIII.

Ratio XII—Common-stock ratio

This is found by dividing the total capital fund, at book figure, into the common-stock component thereof. If there is only common stock, the ratio is 100 percent.

Ratio XIII—Coverage of senior charges

This is found by dividing the balance available for senior charges by (1) the fixed charges, or (2) the fixed and contingent charges, or (3) total prior charges, if any, plus preferred dividends. Separate ratios may be computed for each type of coverage. These are key figures in determining the quality of a bond or preferred-stock issue. Their calculation and significance will be discussed in detail in Part III, "Fixed-income Securities." The quality of a common stock, and its resultant price-earnings and price-dividend ratios, are also influenced strongly by the margin of safety shown above senior charges.

It is taken for granted in most financial discussions that the stronger a company's credit indexes are, the better it is for all concerned. This plausible view ignores some real problems relating to the most advantageous corporate policies from the standpoint of its equity owners—i.e., the common stockholders. A company may have more cash than it needs; while this condition makes for an impressive working-capital ratio and for excellent credit, it may result in a relatively unprofitable or inefficient use of the stockholders' capital.[8]

Similarly, the best capital structure, in terms purely of credit standing and financial strength, is one without any senior securities—i.e., with a "common-stock ratio" of 100 percent. But this would imply that no company, if it had a choice, should ever issue bonds or preferred stock. This simply is not true. There are obvious advantages to common stockholders in having the use of senior capital at low interest or dividend costs; those advantages must be weighed against the business risks involved, and a balance struck on some sound and common-sense basis. Thus in many cases it will be found that what we shall call an "optimal capital structure" will not consist exclusively of common stock.

6. Price Ratios. We suggest as a basic principle of finance that no investment decisions regarding a common stock can properly be made except in the light of a specific price—which is usually the current market but may be some anticipated or calculated figure. The security analyst should compare the price with earnings, dividends, asset value, and also —for a valuable additional insight—with sales. Thus we have a final set of four ratios, as follows:

Ratio XIV—Sales per dollar of common, at market
Ratio XV—Earnings per dollar of common, at market (earnings yield)
Ratio XVI—Dividends per dollar of common, at market (dividend yield)
Ratio XVII—Net assets (equity) per dollar of common at market (asset ratio)

These ratios are ordinarily calculated on the basis of the last full year's figures and the latest balance sheet. However, the earnings yield should always be computed also in relation to average earnings for some suitable period of years.

---

[8] In recent years, corporations have been subjecting their cash (and cash equivalents) to increased scrutiny. For a number of reasons, corporations make their cash work "harder" than ever before. As a result, the turnover of cash for a group of major manufacturing corporations has risen from about 8.7 times in 1950–1954 to 9.9 times in 1955–1959.

CHAPTER EIGHTEEN

A COMPARISON BASED ON KEY RATIOS.
PHYSICAL DATA USED IN ANALYSIS

CALCULATION OF KEY RATIOS FOR TWO CHEMICAL COMPANIES

To illustrate the key-ratio technique, we have selected two chemical companies of substantially different quality—Union Carbide and Koppers (Tables 18-1 and 18-2). The calculations are based, in separate columns, on the averages of 1950–1954 and of 1955–1959, and also on the results of the single year 1960. All of the market-value ratios are based on an average of the high and low price for each year. However, in the text is included a tabulation showing the comparative market-value ratios for Union Carbide and Koppers based on the price prevailing in May 1961. (This month was selected on the assumption that by that time the analyst would have received the annual reports and have had the opportunity of analyzing the data.)

It is to be pointed out that in computing the return on common stock capital the analyst is concerned with the "earning-capital" base as distinguished from the equity or "ownership" base. That is, the analyst is measuring the return on all of the capital directly at work for the common stockholder, and whether or not the stockholder actually has legal title to all of this capital is somewhat beside the point. In this sense, the common stockholders' "earning-capital" base may be defined as total tangible assets less current liabilities and *interest-bearing* non-current debt. (It would thus include reserve for deferred income taxes and similar items.) Or, if approached from the right-hand side of the balance sheet, the "earning-capital" base would consist of the common stock capital, earned and capital surplus, and all reserves not related to a specific asset. In the following computations this definition has been employed.

Adjustments of the kinds suggested in Chapters 9–15 have been made in the income of Koppers and Union Carbide. In this analysis, the earnings available for total capital are taken to be net income after taxes (subject to the above adjustments) plus interest on non-current

Table 18-1. Koppers Company, Inc.

(Large figures in millions)

	Data and ratios	1950–1954	1955–1959	1960
	Basic data:			
	Sales.....................................	$256.1	$271.9	$302.5
	Depreciation and amortization................	6.2	11.4	12.1
	Net for total capital (after tax)..............	10.0	9.6	8.4
	Interest and preferred dividends..............	1.4	1.4	1.5
	Net for common..........................	8.6	8.2	6.9
	Common dividends.........................	4.4	5.0	4.3
	Total capital (book value)*...................	124.0	164.1	174.2
	Common-stock equity (book value)*...........	83.8	124.1	137.0
	Common stock at market value...............	67.6	110.4	89.1
	Number of shares of common.................	(1.8)	(2.2)	(2.2)
	Current assets............................			$110.4
	Current liabilities..........................			37.2
	Ratios:			
	A. Profitability:			
I	Earned per dollar of total capital—before depreciation and amortization..........	13.1%	12.8%	11.8%
II	Earned per dollar of total capital—after depreciation and amortization..........	8.1%	5.9%	4.8%
III	Sales per dollar of total capital...........	$2.06	$1.66	$1.74
IV	Earnings margin (ratio net for total capital to sales)............................	3.9%	3.5%	2.8%
IIa	Earned per dollar of common equity.......	10.3%	6.6%	5.0%
	B. Growth:			
V	Ratio of sales to 1950–1954..............	100.0%	106.2%	118.1%
VI	Ratio of net for total capital to 1950–1954..	100.0%	96.0%	84.0%
VII	Ratio of net per share of common to 1950–1954	100.0%	74.9%	61.9%
	C. Stability:			
VIII	Minimum coverage of senior charges......	5.2×**	4.3×**	5.6×
IX	Percent decline in earnings rate on capital (lowest year vs. average of 3 previous years)	−40.2%**	−43.5%**	
	D. Payout ratio:			
X	Percent of earnings paid on common......	51.2%	61.0%	62.3%
	E. Credit:			
XI	Current assets to current liabilities........	3.5×**	3.3×**	3.0×
XII	Common equity as percent of total capital..	67.6%	75.6%	78.6%
XIII	Times senior charges were earned (after tax)	7.1×	6.9×	5.6×
	F. Per-share figures:			
	Price of common......................	37½	49	40½
	Sales.................................	$142.28	$123.59	$137.50
	Earned...............................	4.94	3.70	3.06
	Dividends.............................	2.50	2.23	1.90
	Book value............................	46.55	56.41	62.27
	G. Market-price ratios:			
XIV	Sales per dollar of common at market.....	$3.79	$2.52	$3.40
XV	Earned per dollar of common at market....	13.2%	7.6%	7.6%
XVI	Dividend yield.........................	6.7%	4.6%	4.7%
XVII	Net assets per dollar of common at market.	$1.24	$1.15	$1.54

* Based on average of book value at the beginning and end of each year.
** These figures cannot be computed from the basic information given.

Table 18-2. Union Carbide Corporation

(Large figures in millions)

Data and ratios	1950–1954	1955–1959	1960
Basic data (in millions):			
Sales...............................	$ 918.4	$1,346.9	$1,548.2
Depreciation and amortization..........	59.8	117.3	129.3
Net for total capital (after tax)..........	112.7	158.9	174.6
Interest and preferred dividends........	7.7	15.5	16.6
Net for common......................	105.0	143.4	158.0
Common dividends....................	69.2	101.3	108.4
Total capital (book value)*.............	828.1	1,231.4	1,421.1
Common-stock equity (book value)*.....	597.1	809.5	955.5
Common stock at market value.........	1.853.7	3,373.2	3,838.0
Number of shares of common...........	(28.9)	(29.9)	(30.1)
Current assets......................			$688.4
Current liabilities....................			245.9
Ratios:			
A. Profitability:			
I Earned per dollar of total capital—before depreciation and amortization......................	20.8%	22.4%	21.4%
II Earned per dollar of total capital—after depreciation and amortization	13.6%	12.9%	12.3%
III Sales per dollar of total capital.....	$1.11	$1.09	$1.09
IV Earnings margin (ratio net for total capital to sales)................	12.3%	11.8%	11.3%
IIa Earned per dollar of common equity.	17.5%	17.7%	16.5%
B. Growth:			
V Ratio of sales to 1950–1954.........	100.0%	146.6%	168.5%
VI Ratio of net for total capital to 1950–1954......................	100.0%	140.9%	154.9%
VII Ratio of net per share of common to 1950–1954....................	100.0%	133.7%	146.2%
C. Stability:			
VIII Minimum coverage of senior charges.	8.7×**	9.2×**	10.5×
IX Percent decline in earnings rate on capital (lowest year vs. average of 3 previous years)...............	−23.7%**	−16.7%**	
D. Payout ratio:			
X Percent of earnings paid on common.	66.0%	70.6%	68.6%
E. Credit:			
XI Current assets to current liabilities..	2.5×**	2.9×**	2.8×
XII Common equity as percent of total capital......................	72.2%	65.5%	67.2%
XIII Times senior charges were earned (after tax)....................	14.6×	10.2×	10.5×
F. Per-share figures:			
Price of common.................	64	113	128
Sales...........................	$31.78	$45.05	$51.44
Earned.........................	3.59	4.80	5.25
Dividends.......................	2.39	3.39	3.60
Book value......................	20.66	27.07	31.74
G. Market-price ratios:			
XIV Sales per dollar of common at market	$0.50	$0.40	$0.40
XV Earned per dollar of common at market	5.6%	4.3%	4.1%
XVI Dividend yield....................	3.7%	3.0%	2.8%
XVII Net assets per dollar of common at market.......................	$0.32	$0.24	$0.25

* Based on average of book value at the beginning and end of each year.
** These figures cannot be computed from the basic information given.

debt. This is in accord with prevalent practice. (However, because interindustry comparisons are involved in Chapter 19, the interest on noncurrent debt is adjusted for the tax factor in deriving the earnings available for total capital. This adjustment eliminates most of the effect of capital structure differences on the rate of return on total capital.)

The growth factor is measured by comparing 1960 and 1955–1959 with 1950–1954. The data and ratios for the full analysis are presented in seven sections. Seventeen key ratios, distributed in five of the sections, are marked by Roman numerals. In addition, one common-stock performance ratio is given as an alternative or equivalent of the corresponding capital-fund ratio. In this connection it is to be pointed out that should a substantial proportion of senior securities exist in the capital structure—so that the common-stock equity is, say, in the 50 to 60 percent range—the analyst may well find it desirable to compute all of the first four ratios on a common-stock, as well as a total-capital, basis.

Discussion of Data. It will be noted that the figures and ratios in sections A to E of the comparison relate to the performance and position of the two companies. Thus they supply indications of the quality of the enterprise, and presumably of its management. In nearly all the ratios developed in the first three sections, the showing of Union Carbide is superior to that of Koppers. In the fifth (credit ratios), Union Carbide has a clear-cut advantage in terms of earnings coverage of interest requirements but not in the other ratios. In section G the ratios depend upon the market price of the common stock. All these favor Koppers by a wide margin. This means that, at its *average* price in all three periods, Koppers offered more for the money than Union Carbide in terms of sales, net earnings, dividends, and assets. It will also be seen from Table 18-3 that the same held true at the market price for each stock in May 1961, related to 1960 data.

Table 18-3. Market-value Ratios. Union Carbide Corporation and
Koppers Company, Inc.

	Koppers	Union Carbide
Market price—May 1961....................	$43.00	$135.00
Sales per dollar of common at market........	3.20	0.38
Earned per dollar of common at market.......	7.1%	3.9%
Dividend yield.............................	4.4%	2.7%
Net assets per dollar of common at market....	$1.84	$0.24

Our key-ratio technique can carry the analyst up to the point of demonstrating that Union Carbide has undoubtedly a more profitable and more dynamic business than Koppers, but that this advantage *may be* offset by Koppers' lower price. Whether the advantage is in fact offset cannot be demonstrated by any mathematical operations. The answer must be given in the form of an opinion emanating from the informed judgment and perhaps the prejudices of the analyst. The determination of the respective merits or attractiveness of the two common stocks *at their prevailing market prices* is the final and most difficult stage of a full-scale comparative security analysis. This is a matter of common-stock valuation, and our observations on the subject belong to a later section of this book. But prior to reaching a conclusion as to value in relation to price, the analyst will draw a number of deductions from the key ratios developed in our comparative table. Let us discuss these in some detail, to illustrate what we may call the intermediate or "dissective" stage of security analysis.

A. *Profitability Ratios.* The substantially higher return on total capital for Union Carbide is the result of the marked superiority of its earnings margin. In fact, Union Carbide has a significantly lower turnover of capital than does Koppers—approximately one-third less in recent years. But this is much more than offset by an earnings margin which is 3½ times that for Koppers Company. This earnings margin is also excellent in terms of the average experience of the industry.

Table 18-4 shows the wide differences between the operating ratios of the two companies both before and after depreciation, as well as the differences in earnings margins. It is to be noted that the after-depreciation operating ratio for Union Carbide is well over three times that for Koppers in 1955–1959 in spite of the much higher ratio of depreciation and depletion to sales.

Table 18-4. Comparative Profit Ratios. Union Carbide Corporation and Koppers Company, Inc.

	Union Carbide		Koppers	
	1950–1954	1955–1959	1950–1954	1955–1959
Operating profit ratio before depreciation.....	30.2%	29.2%	11.6%	10.5%
Depreciation and depletion to sales..........	6.5	8.7	2.4	4.2
Operation profit ratio after depreciation......	23.7	20.5	9.2	6.3
Earnings margin........................	12.2	11.8	3.9	3.5

A prime consideration in the difference in profitability of the two companies lies in the product mix. Chemicals and plastics—which are in the better profit-margin area—constitute about three-fourths of Union Carbide's sales but about one-fourth of Koppers'. Moreover, something like one-half of Koppers' sales are in the more basic and less profitable tar-product, wood-preserving, and gas and coke products. In addition, over the 1950–1959 span, an average of more than one-fourth of Koppers' sales came from the engineering and construction division, which is engaged primarily in the construction of chemical recovery coke ovens and related equipment. The cyclical nature of this business is indicated by the drop in volume from $102,000,000 in 1957 to $27,000,000 in 1959.

At the same time, it is to be pointed out that Koppers has been placing increasing emphasis on its participation in chemicals and plastics, and that as a result, the sales of these two divisions in 1960 constituted nearly 23 percent of sales vs. 14 percent in 1950. This changing emphasis in product mix may—in time—bring a responsive shift in profitability and growth for the company as a whole.

B. Progress Ratios. Union Carbide has shown a substantially better growth rate in both sales and earnings. It may be seen from Tables 18-1 and 18-2 that Koppers' net earnings available for total capital in both 1955–1959 and 1960 were below those for 1950–1954, whereas Carbide's were 41 percent and 55 percent, respectively, over those for 1950–1954. Because of the leverage, the decline in the per-share earnings for Koppers Company was even heavier; in 1960 earnings were less than two-thirds of the 1950–1954 volume in contrast to Union Carbide's increase of more than 45 percent.

C. Indexes of Stability. The superiority of Union Carbide here is impressive. This fact may be seen from Section *C* of Tables 18-1 and 18-2 and from data for single years. In addition, in 1954 Koppers' sales declined 30 percent from the 1953 level compared to 10 percent for Carbide. In 1958 the respective declines were approximately 21 and 7 percent. In the same two cyclical downturns, the return on total capital for Koppers dropped 32 and 30 percent from the return for the preceding year, whereas Carbide's return dropped 18 and 9 percent. Again the differences in product mix would need to be considered. At the same time, it is quite probable that the better earnings stability for Union Carbide is also tied in with its much higher profit margin. It is almost a universal law of security analysis that, within any industry, the units with better profit margins show smaller percentage declines in recession years.

D. Payout Ratio. The percent of earnings paid out in the form of cash dividends is higher for Union Carbide in all periods. This difference in payout would appear to be primarily the result of fundamentally different financing policies. Undoubtedly, the policies are influenced substantially by the contrasting earnings performance—in terms of both level and stability. The marked difference in the manner in which each company has financed its expansion is shown in Table 18-5. It will be noted that the entire increase in Koppers' total capital came from an increase in common stock and retained earnings. In fact, the long-term debt was less in 1960 than at the end of 1949. In marked contrast, Union Carbide secured 41 percent of its increased capital in the form of debt financing.

At the same time, note that Carbide's capital in 1960 was about 130 percent above the 1949 figure, whereas Koppers' increase over the same span was less than 75 percent. By coincidence, if both corporations had had the same dollar amount of debt in 1960 as in 1949, their percentage increases in total capital would have been nearly identical.

Table 18-5. Sources of Increase in Total Capital. Union Carbide Corporation and Koppers Company, Inc., 1949–1960

(000,000 omitted)

	Koppers			Union Carbide		
	1949	1960	Difference	1949	1960	Difference
Common stock and capital surplus...............	$ 41.4	$ 72.0	+$30.6	$197.0	$ 247.6	+$ 50.6
Earned surplus*..........	18.9	65.3	+ 46.4	285.7	735.1	+ 449.4
Common-stock equity..	$ 60.3	$137.3	+$77.0	$482.7	$ 982.7	+$500.0
Preferred stock...........	15.0	15.0	....	....	....	....
Debt—noncurrent........	26.5	23.5	− 3.0	150.0	484.3	+ 334.3
Total capital..........	$101.8	$175.8	+$74.0	$632.7	$1,467.0	+$834.3

* Plus net-worth type reserves and less prepaid items.

E. Credit Ratios. The credit ratios show both companies in relatively strong positions. Their current ratios were different in 1950–1954 but closely comparable in the other two periods. Koppers has a higher common-stock equity to total capital ratio in every period, but Union Carbide has a much higher coverage of senior charges. In 1960 Union Carbide earned its interest requirements on long-term debt about $10\frac{1}{2}$ times on an after-tax basis, whereas Koppers earned its interest and preferred-dividend requirements approximately $5\frac{1}{2}$ times. Thus Union Carbide's substantially higher earning power much more than offsets the larger proportion of senior securities in the capital structure.

F and G. Per-share Figures and Price Ratios. If reference is again made to Tables 18-1 and 18-2, it will be seen that the higher earnings of Union Carbide were much more than offset by the higher price. In 1950–1954 the earnings yield on the market price of Carbide's common stock was 5.6 percent; i.e., stock was selling at 17.8 times earning. In the same period the earnings yield on Koppers' shares was 13.2 percent, or well over twice that for the Carbide shares. (Conversely, the price-earnings ratio was close to 7.6 times, which is less than one-half that for Carbide.)

The dividend yield and both sales and net assets per dollar of common stock at market value were also much higher for Koppers than for Union Carbide.

Since Union Carbide offered the buyer a great deal less *per dollar of price* than did Koppers Company, the question immediately arises as to whether this meant that—for the period under analysis—Koppers represented the more attractive opportunity. As a rough check, let us assume that at the beginning of 1950 an investor had purchased both shares at their *1950–1954 average price* and that he had sold out as of the end of 1960. The following tabulation shows the results:[1]

	Koppers	Union Carbide
Price per share (at the end of 1960)...........	$37.00	$118.00
Dividends—1950–1960.....................	26.05	33.05
Total.....................................	$63.05	$151.05
Price paid per share (average 1950–1954)......	37.50	64.00
Dividends plus realized appreciation:		
Dollar amount........................	$25.55	$ 87.05
Over-all gain on cost..................	6.8%	13.6%
Average annual dividend yield on cost......	4.9%	3.8%

The much superior over-all return for Union Carbide is attributable to the substantially greater growth in earnings, which for the common-stock investor has a threefold result. First, it usually means increased dividends and thus a rising yield on cost. Second, if the multiplier (capitalization rate) remains constant, the increase in earnings plus larger dividends means a higher price per share. However, in this instance the multiplier *rose* from 17.5 times in 1950–1954 to 24.4 times in 1960, and this factor *alone* would have pushed up price by nearly 40 percent. The multiplier for Koppers' earnings, however, rose even more—from 7.6 to 13.2 times—but the drop in per-share earnings from $4.94 in 1950–1954 to $3.06 in 1960 almost nullified this higher capitalization rate. (Actually, both stocks had slipped below their 1960 mean prices by the end of the year, and Koppers was selling at less than the 1950–1954 average.)

Emphasis Is on Quality. The foregoing analysis of key ratios has shown that the qualitative factors clearly favored Union Carbide and that the much lower relative prices for Koppers' stock made it quantitatively decidedly more attractive. However, the comparative results clearly establish for the periods of the analysis that—in spite of its higher price —Union Carbide was by far the better buy. This conclusion would confirm the accepted views in the market with respect to the purchase of *quality* shares. Nevertheless, we want to reemphasize (1) that at some

[1] If the two issues had been purchased in January 1950 and sold at the end of 1960, the relative performance of Union Carbide would have been even more pronounced.

point even the best quality common stock can be overpriced, and (2) that if an improvement in the quality of a *below-average* share can be anticipated, this can provide an excellent investment opportunity. In the latter instance, the investor is certain to enjoy the advantage of an increase not only in earnings and dividends but in the capitalization rate as well.

Improved quality can be the result of numerous factors; changes in management and in product mix are among the most prominent. It is no easy task—at an early stage in the proceedings—to anticipate with reasonable accuracy either the results of such changes or the length of time that may be required to bring them to fruition. But the rewards for successfully doing so can be substantial.

ANALYSIS RELATED TO PHYSICAL DATA

Analysis of the company's results should not be confined to dollar figures but should extend also to such physical data as lend themselves to analytical study. The material usually considered, whenever it is available, includes the following:

1. Physical Reserves. This matter is significant for all companies dependent on a wasting asset, such as oil and gas producers and mining companies. It could be important also for a transportation concern which depends on the reserves of its main shippers or suppliers—e.g., a railroad transporting chiefly timber, also an oil- or gas-pipe line.

In most cases the published figures of reserves represent a minimum total, which is likely to be increased by further development or new discoveries on the property.

Example: At the end of 1952, Climax Molybdenum Company reported reserves of 240 million tons of proved and provable ore containing about 1,475 million pounds of recoverable molybdenum. At the end of 1960, the reserves of the company (now American Metal Climax, Inc.) were reported to be 451 million tons of ore, containing over 2,000 million pounds of recoverable molybdenum.

Many companies limit their development to only a few years' reserves because local taxes would be largely increased if they reported that more ore was being developed.

In addition, companies with wasting assets generally anticipate the exhaustion of present bodies by property purchases or leases. Thus it is quite unusual for an important company of that type actually to go out of business because its reserves have been exhausted.

Example: Freeport Sulphur Company provides an example of a company with a wasting asset making various acquisitions. In 1951 the company acquired from Texaco rights to Lake Pelto dome—which was under water off the Louisiana coast—and established existence of substantial sulphur deposits. In 1956, similarly, it acquired rights from

Humble Oil & Refining Company to sulphur discovery at Grand Isle in the Gulf of Mexico. Other properties have also been acquired, such as the purchase of iron sulfide ore property from Virginia Iron Coal & Coke Company.

In estimating reserves, the analyst should consider the quality as well as the quantity. If a mining company has mainly low-grade ore in reserve while it is presently mining high-grade ore, its future earning power must be viewed conservatively.

There is similar significance in the ownership of less valuable low-gravity oil reserves as against the more valuable high-gravity types.

The figures of reserves must therefore be treated with circumspection. They do, of course, have some informative value. Other things being equal, a company with large developed reserves is preferable to another with small reserves. The calculation of oil reserves (including the liquid content of gas reserves) has made a great deal of technical progress in recent years, and most companies now supply estimates by their own staff or by consulting geologists. It is becoming customary to use these reserve figures in analyses and comparisons of oil companies—generally by setting a certain dollar value on the oil in the ground and then adding to it the book figure for the other assets, net, to find a total valuation. It is interesting to observe that, in the field of oil and mining companies, more emphasis is placed on appraised value of the assets than in the area of manufacturing and trading concerns.

2. Capacity. Most producers and processors of basic materials have a definite capacity expressible in physical units—e.g., tons of steel ingots; bags of sugar, both raw and refined; barrels of oil put through refineries; barrels of cement. The capacity figure changes, of course, through plant additions or abandonments, but it is useful in describing the position of the company at the time of analysis. The weight to be ascribed to this datum will vary greatly with circumstances, and we must leave it to the analyst's judgment.

3. Production in Units. Wherever available, this is a basic figure for intensive analysis. It is compared with capacity to indicate the possibility of future expansion.

When a company produces a homogeneous product—e.g., copper, sugar, or cement—and when unit figures of production are published, it becomes possible to calculate the selling price, cost of production, and margin of profit per unit. These are useful for comparative analysis and for calculating the effect of price changes on the individual company.

4. Production by Divisions. Many manufacturers turn out a variety of products, which fall into several categories or industrial divisions. If the company is to be studied from the standpoint of industry analysis, it is clearly necessary to know how its products are divided, either in unit terms or by dollar value. In Chapter 6, page 82, we discussed the degree to which such information is available.

5. Concentration and Geographical Location of Sales. Businesses dependent on one or two major customers are considered to be in a somewhat more vulnerable position than those with a large number of important accounts. The former situation is found often among the makers of automobile parts, and also in companies manufacturing almost exclusively for a large mail-order or chain-store organization. It is normal for a large, successful company to have a substantial foreign business in addition to its domestic sales; but a heavy dependence on exports—especially to a single geographical area—must be viewed as involving an added hazard. These matters will be considered by the analyst and given whatever weight in the valuation his judgment will dictate.

CHAPTER NINETEEN

ANALYSIS OF SPECIFIC INDUSTRIES.

RAILROAD AND CHEMICAL INDUSTRY ANALYSIS

GENERAL COMMENTS

Industry Background for Company Analysis. The analysis of an individual company is usually carried on against the background of the industry to which it belongs, and consequently, the form taken for its analysis will be governed in part by the special characteristics of the industry. The prospects of the company are generally, though not always, identified with those of its industry. Hence the development of demand and supply in the past is often studied in great detail, with a view to forecasting the relationship of these factors in years to come. Also major emphasis is often placed on the physical and operating factors; for example, on the underground reserves, productive capacity, and unit costs. In industries such as oil and steel the degree of integration—in particular, the extent to which raw materials are produced directly rather than purchased will play an important role. Attention is given to geographical location of plants and markets; to the character of competition both within the industry and from products outside of the industry; to labor costs and labor supply; and to the industry's problems of government regulation, government control, and special taxation.

In this chapter we shall deal with two important industries, each in a somewhat different manner. First we shall consider, in some detail, the elements that enter into a reasonably adequate railroad analysis. We shall then supply a detailed comparison of a group of chemical companies, prefaced by a foreshortened outline of factors entering into. the analysis of the industry as a whole. The next two chapters will contain Chas. Tatham's full analysis of the electric and gas utility industry.

FACTORS IN RAILROAD ANALYSIS

The key ratios which we have developed for companies generally may be applied to railroads with useful results. However, it is customary to analyze the reports of railroads in a somewhat specialized fashion, with emphasis upon elements that are peculiar to railroad operations. The presence of an enormous body of financial and operating statistics pertaining to railroad operations provides a wealth of information for the analyst to work with, which at times may embarrass by its very abundance.

In this section of the chapter we shall start with the more or less conventional elements in railroad analysis and then suggest some alternative techniques which we regard as more useful than the standard ratios.

Key Ratios Compiled by Financial Services. There are three ratios to which most prominence is given in the financial analysis of railroad results. These are (1) the operating ratio, (2) the coverage of fixed charges, of fixed and contingent charges, and of charges plus preferred dividends, (3) earnings per share of preferred and of common stock. The standard presentation of railroad results is illustrated in Table 19-1, which covers the Class I carriers as a group and the Chicago, Burlington & Quincy Railroad as an individual road.

Table 19-1. Condensed Income Account of All Class I Railroads and of Chicago, Burlington & Quincy Railroad, Year Ended December 31, 1960

	All Class I railroads* (in millions)	Chicago, Burlington, & Quincy R.R. (in thousands)
Freight revenue..............................	$8,025	$202,493
Passenger revenue...........................	640	21,431
Total operating revenue (including other)........	9,514	251,136
Maintenance of way and structure..............	1,192	34,085
Maintenance of equipment.....................	1,760	46,415
Transportation expenses.......................	3,833	103,168
Federal income taxes.........................	203	3,271
Other taxes.................................	796	21,907
Net railway operating income..................	584	16,632
Other income...............................	346	3,796
Total income...........................	$ 930	$ 20,428
Miscellaneous deductions......................	62	323
Available for fixed charges....................	868	20,106
Rents for leased roads, etc....................	51	57
Interest....................................	317	7,486
Other deductions............................	4	69
Total fixed charges......................	$ 373	$ 7,612
Contingent interest charges....................	50	
Net income.................................	445	12,493
Capital stock—earned per share................	......	$7.31
—number of shares................	......	1,708
Times charges earned, before Federal income taxes..	2.86×	3.07×
Times charges earned, after Federal income taxes...	2.33×	2.64×

* *Moody's Transportation Manual*, 1961, p. 8a.

1. *The Operating Ratio.* The operating ratio is an official figure computed in accordance with ICC requirements. It represents the ratio of expenses (down to, but not including, taxes) to operating revenue or "gross." The balance after such expense is called "net revenue from railway operations." Thus if this balance is 20 percent of revenue, the operating ratio is the supplement of that figure, or 80 percent.

The operating ratio is useful for purposes of comparing the performance of various railroads in a given year and of the same railroad in different years. However, we consider that other ratios computed somewhat differently will shed a better light on the operating position of a railroad.

2. *Coverage of Fixed Charges, Coverage of Contingent Interest, and Coverage of Preferred Dividends.* The calculation here is made in the standard manner. The amount available for fixed charges is divided by the charges, to give the "times earned," or coverage. Since Federal income tax appears with other taxes in the railroad reports, the coverage of fixed charges is most often stated on an after-tax basis. We point out later that it is more logical to calculate coverage of interest charges before deduction for income tax. In most cases a given result or coverage on one basis may be converted into an equivalent result or standard on the other. However, for a number of reasons the tax allowance made by railroads have almost uniformly been lower than that called for by their taxable income as reported by them, and in many instances the discrepancy has been extreme and largely unexplained. We recommend, therefore, that the analyst regularly compute the coverage of fixed charges on a before-tax basis and apply thereto his before-tax requirement.

The manuals and financial services show the coverage of fixed charges; and they also compute the coverage of interest on funded debt, taken alone, as distinct from the fixed charges which include such additional items as rent for leased lines, interest on unfunded debt, and amortization of debt discount. We see no reason for separating funded debt interest from other charges equivalent thereto, and so we recommend that the supplemental figure of coverage of funded interest alone be ignored.

Moreover, fixed charges, as defined, fail to take into account deductions which have some of the characteristics of fixed charges or are in substitution therefor. Chief of these are joint facility rents and net equipment rents. We shall suggest an alternative coverage test which will take these elements into account.

In addition, railroad analysts have used a "margin-of-safety" factor, derived quite differently from fixed-charge coverage, to indicate how much decline in business a road may stand. This consists simply of the balance after fixed charges, with income tax added back, expressed as a percentage of "gross." To avoid confusion with our "margin-of-safety" concept, used with other applications, we prefer to call this ratio the *factor of safety*. The factor of safety for the Burlington in 1960 is calculated from the preceding table as follows:

$$\text{Factor of safety} = \frac{12,493 + 3,271}{251,136} = 6.3 \text{ percent}$$

We come next to coverage of contingent interest. Nearly all the reorganized railroads have income-bond issues, interest on which is payable only if earned and to some extent also only if declared. Interest charges on these bonds are called "contingent charges" or "contingent interest." The coverage of charges on such bond issues is properly computed by adding the contingent interest to fixed charges and computing the number of times the total of both is covered. The same procedure applies to computing the coverage of preferred dividends, where the issue is analyzed for investment purposes. However, in Chapters 29 and 30 we suggest some adjustments to be made in the contingent-interest and the preferred-dividend figures when applying our recommended tests of adequate coverage.

3. *Earnings per Share of Common*. This calculation is ordinarily quite simple, but in the case of many of the reorganized railroads it presents special complications. The reorganization structure usually provides for specified deductions from annual income to take care of bond sinking funds and so-called "capital funds." The latter are intended to make sure that the needs of the road for additions and betterments will be taken care of before any dividends are paid.

It is customary to deduct these mandatory sinking funds and capital-fund provisions before showing the amount earned per share of preferred and common stock, and in most cases also before showing the amount earned on income-bond issues. However, such deductions are not in the nature of operating expenses or fixed charges, but are rather appropriations of surplus to pay off debt or to add to the property. Thus it would be accurate to measure the earnings for the stock issues and for the income bonds without such deductions, and in a separate calculation to show the *distributable portion* of the earnings after the required reservations for sinking fund and capital funds.

Additional Ratios Used in Railroad Analysis. The more detailed study of a railroad's performance is carried on in two areas—the financial and the physical. On the financial side the figures that receive most attention are the "maintenance ratio"; the "transportation ratio"; and the ratio of fixed charges to gross, to maintenance, and to working capital.

The Maintenance Ratio. The amount spent on maintenance is studied to determine whether the roadway and equipment are being kept in good condition, or are being "starved," or possibly are being rehabilitated at the temporary expense of reported net income. A subnormal maintenance ratio was a not infrequent occurrence among railroads with heavy fixed charges which had to reduce expenditures to a minimum in order to find the money for bond interest. (In some cases also they were pressed to report the bond interest covered by a 50 percent margin in order to keep their bonds legal for investments by life insurance companies, trust funds, and savings banks.) In most of these instances the road eventually went into bankuptcy, following which the receiver or trustees usually spent abnormally large amounts on maintenance to bring the property back into excellent condition.

The logical procedure in scrutinizing the maintenance expenditures of a given road is to compare its ratio with that for its geographical region or for all Class I railroads.

If the ratios shown by the road under study depart widely from the over-all figure, the analyst should inquire into the reasons for the divergence. It may be a justifiable reflection of special physical or operating conditions confronting the carrier. But to some extent, at least, it is likely to be the result of a temporary weather situation or of a temporary policy of overmaintenance or undermaintenance which cannot be expected to continue. If the latter circumstances hold, the analyst may make a *pro forma* adjustment of the maintenance ratio to bring it in line with his concept of a reasonable rate of upkeep. (He should be sure to allow for the tax effect of any such adjustment.)

Example: The variety of maintenance expenditures of individual roads is illustrated in Table 19-2, which compares 1960 figures for eight carriers.

Table 19-2. Ratio to Operating Revenues, 1960

Railroad	Maintenance of way	Maintenance of equipment	Total maintenance
Atchison, Topeka & Santa Fe.....	13.0%	20.5%	33.5%
Atlantic Coast Line.............	12.7	22.9	35.6
Chicago, Burlington & Quincy.....	13.6	18.5	32.1
Denver & Rio Grande Western....	10.4	15.1	25.5
Great Northern.................	16.0	18.4	34.4
Illinois Central.................	14.6	18.8	33.4
Kansas City Southern...........	6.9	14.0	20.9
Seaboard Air Line..............	13.0	19.4	32.4

The reader will observe the wide disparity between the maintenance ratio shown by Kansas City Southern and that shown by all the other roads, except the Denver & Rio Grande. These differences would not necessarily prove that the KCS or the Denver have been undermaintained; but they would call for further examination into the physical and operating conditions of both lines to determine whether their main-tenance expenditures have been adequate under their special circum-stances. (The fact that the two carriers have been able to maintain their operating-ratio advantage over a long span of years would indicate *prima facie* the adequacy of the maintenance provisions.)

The Transportation Ratio. The figure is found by dividing "operating revenue" into "transportation expenses." It is a good measure of the operating efficiency or the natural operating advantages of a railroad. (As pointed out before, the maintenance expenditures are largely con-trollable by management, while the other items of operating expense—traffic, miscellaneous, and general—are relatively minor.)

Physical Ratios and Factors. The main physical measure of operating performance is "net ton-miles per train-hour." The train-hour can be taken as a convenient measure of cost, while the ton-miles are of course the basic units for revenue. A large number of ton-miles will be put into a train-hour by good performance with respect to the following elements: (1) tons per car; (2) cars per train (the two producing the figure of trainload); and (3) miles per car-hour, or average freight-train speed. A contributing factor to general efficiency is a long "average haul," i.e., the distance for which the average shipment is carried on the line; it is found by dividing tons carried into revenue ton-miles.

One of the chief items of transportation expense is fuel. Consequently, analysts pay some attention to fuel cost per train-mile and per ton-mile. The detailed operating statistics submitted to the ICC supply quite a number of such unit calculations, which can be used to determine just where a given railroad shows strength or weakness in its operations.

Suggested Techniques for Railroad Analysis. Some of the foregoing observations have been mildly critical of the standard railroad accounting and the traditional ratios which have developed out of it. We should like to suggest a somewhat different method of presenting the basic operating results and also a different method of measuring the coverage of safety for fixed charges.

The first idea is illustrated in Table 19-3, which sets forth in a con-densed manner the 1960 income accounts of all Class I railroads, and also of Chicago, Rock Island & Pacific Railroad and Atchison, Topeka & Santa Fe Railroad.

"Intermediate items—debits or credit" comprise (1) equipment rents and joint facility rents, which include both debit and credit items; (2) other income, which includes dividend and interest income, profits from miscellaneous operations, and certain other items; (3) miscellaneous deductions, generally of minor character. These intermediate items, along with the important element of taxes other than income taxes, are left out of account in the conventional calculation of the operating ratio. On the other hand, it is useful to separate the maintenance expense from the less

controllable operating costs, and it is even more logical to exclude Federal income tax from any analysis of operating results.

Our primary operating ratio, derived from the primary operating expenses, we consider a somewhat better measure of the basic operating position of a railroad than the standard operating ratio, because it includes the general taxes and excludes the maintenance accounts. With the maintenance added in, we have what may be called the "total operating ratio" or the "primary-plus-maintenance ratio."

The proper treatment of intermediate items presents a difficulty to the security analyst. The debits partake somewhat of the nature of fixed

Table 19-3. Suggested Presentation of Railroad Income Account, (1960 figures)

	Chicago, Rock Island & Pacific R.R. (in thousands)	Atchison, Topeka & Santa Fe R.R. (in thousands)	All Class I railroads (in millions)
Railway operating revenue (gross).	$211,776	$614,017	9,514
Primary operating expense........	122,698	325,570	5,410
(Primary operating ratio)........	(57.9%)	(53.0%)	(57.0%)
Maintenance...................	63,673	205,978	2,951
Intermediate items, net..........	dr. 12,827	cr. 5,716	dr. 83
Balance for charges.............	12,578	88,185	1,071
Fixed charges..................	3,979	6,395	373
Contingent charges.............	2,566	1,623	50
Balance before income tax.......	6,033	80,167	648
Income tax.....................	18	28,571	203
Balance for dividends and reserve funds........................	6,015	51,596	445
Preferred dividends.............	....	6,209	....
Balance for common............	6,015	45,387	....

charges and somewhat of operating expense; the credits may be considered in part an offset to operating expense, in part an offset to fixed charges. It would be possible to allocate each of the various items to either expenses or fixed charges with a rough degree of accuracy, but that would involve more labor than is necessary for ordinary purposes.

We should like to suggest the following as a simple and a reasonably accurate method of dealing with all the intermediate items taken together. (This net figure may be found readily by deducting Available for Fixed Charges from Railway Operating Income, often called Net after Taxes.) One-half the net debit or net credit is apportioned to operating expenses and one-half to fixed charges, to give Adjusted Operating Expenses and Adjusted Fixed Charges. Table 19-4 shows the 1949 adjusted figures for Class I railroads and for the two individual roads covered in the preceding table.

Calculation of Adjusted Ratios. After these adjustments are made, the analyst can calculate the following significant ratios to indicate the performance of the road:

1. *Primary Operating Ratio.* Not materially changed from Table 19-8.

2. *Total Operating Ratio Adjusted.* This will include one-half the intermediate items, as credits to or deductions from operation expenses.

Table 19-4. Calculation of Adjusted Expenses and Charges, 1960

	Chicago, Rock Island & Pacific R.R. (in thousands)	Atchison, Topeka & Santa Fe R.R. (in thousands)	All Class I railroads (in millions)
Amount of adjustment (½ of net "intermediates")..............	dr. $ 6,413	cr. $ 2,858	dr. $ 42
Adjusted primary expenses (add ½ of intermediate debit or deduct ½ of intermediate credit).......	129,111	322,712	5,452
Adjusted total expenses (add maintenance to preceding figure).....	192,784	528,690	8,403
Adjusted balance for charges (add or subtract ½ of intermediate debit or credit)...............	18,991	85,327	1,112
Adjusted fixed and contingent charges (add or subtract ½ of intermediate debit or credit)....	12,958	5,159	464
Balance after fixed and contingent charges, before income tax......	6,033	80,168	648
Adjusted primary operating ratio..	61.0%	52.6%	57.5%
Adjusted total operating ratio.....	91.0%	86.1%	88.3%
Adjusted coverage of fixed charges (before tax)..................	1.82×	23.56×	2.68×
Adjusted coverage of fixed and contingent charges (before tax).....	1.47×	16.54×	2.38×
Factor of safety*...............	4.1%	13.3%	7.3%

* Before deducting contingent interest.

3. *Coverage of Adjusted Fixed Charges (before Taxes).* This is found by dividing the adjusted charges into the balance available for them.

3a. *Similarly Calculated Coverage of Adjusted Charges Plus Contingent Charges.*

4. *Factor of Safety.* This is an unchanged figure, found by dividing operating revenue into balance after fixed charges, but before income tax deduction.

Table 19-4 sets forth these key ratios for 1960 as derived from the adjusted figures. It will be observed that the intermediate items have a substantial impact on the showing of individual carriers.

The proper calculation of the coverage of preferred-stock dividends is a rather complicated matter. We shall deal with this in our section on investment-grade preferred stocks (Chapter 28). The application of suitable tests to the coverage of fixed and contingent charges in order to determine the investment merit of railroad bond issues will be discussed in Part Three, "Fixed-income Securities."

OUTLINE OF AN ANALYSIS OF THE CHEMICAL INDUSTRY

To save space we have decided to omit a comprehensive analysis of the chemical industry, covering the period 1939–1957,[1] prepared for inclusion at this point. Instead, we shall merely list the subheadings of that analysis, to indicate the scope of such a detailed study.

I. Economic analysis of the industry.

Its diversification. Industrial inorganic chemicals. Industrial organic chemicals. Industrial end-use chemicals.

II. Comparative analysis with other industries.

The industry sample used.
Growth in (*a*) sales, (*b*) capital, (*c*) dollar earnings.
Profitability: Earnings rate on total capital. Maintenance of return through time. Earnings margin (profit on sales). The depreciation factor. Capital turnover. Profitability factors compared with those of other industries. Earnings rate on common stock capital.
Stability of earnings.
Summary of earnings analysis.
Market valuation. Price-earnings ratios compared with other industries.
Conclusions.

COMPARATIVE COMPANY ANALYSIS

This sketched-out study of the chemical industry leads us now to a summary analysis of the comparative performance of the seven firms constituting the industry sample. If space permitted, each would be subject to the type of detailed analysis illustrated in Chapter 18. Of necessity, we confine the present review principally to tabular comparisons of the sales, capital, earnings, and market-value data for each company. A prime fact in each instance is the wide difference in the individual company performances. The period covered is mainly 1947–1957, with some figures carried back to 1935.

Sales. The composite postwar growth rate in sales for the Chemical Industry Sample excluding du Pont[2] is nearly 10 percent. The experiences of the individual companies (Table 19-5) depart substantially from this composite rate. The growth ranges from a high of 14.3 percent per

---

[1] The original study was made by Stanford Research Institute and kindly made available to us.

[2] Du Pont's holdings of, and income from, General Motors have been excluded from all of the du Pont data.

annum for Dow Chemical to a low of 7.1 for Allied Chemical. The rate of 9.3 percent for du Pont is a little below the composite for the other six companies.

Marked variations in growth rates have occurred over the entire 1935–1957 span, as well as in the postwar period. As a result, the proportions which the sales of the individual companies constitute of aggregate sales for the Sample, excluding du Pont, have changed substantially. For example, Allied Chemical's sales dropped from 32 percent of the aggregate in 1935–1939 to 18 percent in 1953–1957, whereas Dow Chemical's share jumped from 6 percent to 16 percent.

Total Capital. There are also significant differences in the growth rates in total capital for the seven firms. The range was from over 12 percent for American Cyanamid to under 7 percent for du Pont. The manner in

Table 19-5. Sample Companies' Comparative Postwar Growth in Sales: Annual Average Rate, 1947–1957

Dow Chemical	14.3%
Monsanto*	13.0
Union Carbide	10.0
Chemical Industry Sample, excluding du Pont	9.9
American Cyanamid	9.7
du Pont	9.3
Hercules Powder	7.2
Allied Chemical	7.1

* Adjusted for the acquisition of Lion Oil Company in September 1955.

which the increase in total capital was financed varied from solely retained earnings (du Pont) to 50 percent senior securities (Allied Chemical). Because of the different financial policies employed, the percent which common-stock equity constitutes of total capital changed significantly in some instances over the postwar span.

Earnings. The earnings performances of individual companies are compared in terms of both the rate of return on total capital and of per-share earnings.

Return on Total Capital. In Table 19-6 the annual data and period averages for the composite group and the individual companies are set forth. The companies are in the order of their 1953–1957 average returns on total capital. The differences in the rates earned are striking—ranging from nearly 21 percent for du Pont to 8.4 percent for both Allied Chemical and Monsanto. If Table 19-6 is examined closely, it will be seen that for the most part the individual rates of return tend to cluster around the composite relatively well in both the prewar and postwar spans. The notable exceptions are the substantially higher return of Dow—and to a lesser extent Monsanto—in 1935–1939 and the remarkable comparative performance of du Pont since 1951.

For the student analyzing du Pont, Table 19-6 raises this basic question: Can a major corporation, in a highly dynamic industry characterized by a *number* of large, aggressive competitors, outdo by a wide margin the average experience of the other important units in the industry for an *extended* period?[3]

Depreciation. Significant differences also exist in the depreciation policies employed by the several companies. Consequently, if depreciation

Table 19-6. Sample Companies: Comparative Earnings Rates on Total Capital, 1935–1957

(Companies in order of 1953–1957 average return)

Year	Industry (excluding du Pont)	du Pont	Hercules Powder	Union Carbide	American Cyanamid	Dow Chemical	Allied Chemical	Monsanto Chemical
1935	11.6 %	12.1 %	9.7 %	11.5 %	10.4 %	20.5 %	9.6 %	18.5 %
1936	13.4	12.7	13.0	14.6	10.6	15.2	12.5	13.4
1937	11.8	12.1	10.4	11.5	11.6	12.3	12.4	13.1
1938	6.7	7.9	8.3	5.6	5.7	12.4	7.0	7.2
1939	11.1	12.9	13.8	10.7	9.0	18.2	10.3	11.5
1940	12.0	12.5	14.6	12.4	12.2	14.4	10.2	11.0
1941	12.6	13.6	15.9	13.0	10.5	13.7	11.7	13.2
1942	11.6	9.6	16.7	12.3	8.2	12.7	11.3	9.2
1943	11.1	10.0	12.4	13.0	8.2	11.0	10.2	8.4
1944	9.7	9.7	9.5	11.6	7.4	9.5	8.7	7.4
1945	8.3	8.5	7.9	9.4	5.6	13.0	5.8	7.8
1946	11.9	16.3	16.6	14.2	7.6	8.9	11.7	11.3
1947	14.5	17.1	23.1	16.9	7.1	9.9	13.3	13.8
1948	14.3	15.4	15.8	18.8	7.5	10.6	12.9	13.6
1949	13.3	17.2	13.3	15.6	9.5	12.9	12.7	11.1
1950	16.8	21.3	18.1	19.5	16.1	13.9	13.9	16.7
1951	13.3	15.1	15.6	14.9	13.7	9.9	13.1	12.6
1952	10.6	17.2	11.9	12.8	9.0	8.2	10.9	9.4
1953	9.6	14.4	11.9	11.8	8.3	6.7	9.9	8.7
1954	8.6	21.8	13.7	9.7	7.5	7.3	8.0	7.7
1955	11.6	25.6	16.9	13.3	9.7	11.6	9.3	10.6
1956	10.6	21.1	14.0	13.0	10.3	10.3	8.1	8.0
1957	9.8	20.6	12.8	11.5	11.5	7.8	7.3	7.3
1935–1939	10.9	11.5	11.0	10.7	9.3	15.5	10.3	12.0
1947–1957	11.4	19.1	14.8	13.7	10.0	9.4	10.1	9.8
1953–1957	10.1	20.8	13.9	11.9	9.6	8.7	8.4	8.4

Source: Stanford Research Institute.

is added back, some changes occur in the rankings of the companies. As may be seen from Table 19-7, the principal change is in the case of Dow.

Earnings Margin and Capital Turnover. Since the return on total capital is the product of the earnings margin and capital turnover, the

[3] The ratio of du Pont's rate of return to the return for the Chemical Industry Sample (excluding du Pont) for the 1950–1957 period, and as a short sequel, for 1958 and 1959, was as follows:

1950	127%	1955	221%
1951	114	1956	199
1952	162	1957	217
1953	150	1958	176
1954	253	1959	174

next step is to examine these two ratios. Table 19-8 provides a summary comparison of these two ratios.

Two primary facts stand out in Table 19-8: the marked decline in earnings margin and the pronounced rise in capital turnover. From the examination of the individual company data, it may be seen that only American Cyanamid had an increase in earnings margin.

Table 19-7. Comparative Returns on Total Capital Before and After Depreciation, 1953–1957

Company	Return on total capital	
	Before depreciation	After depreciation
du Pont......................	30.6%	20.8%
Hercules Powder..............	24.4	13.9
Dow Chemical................	21.9	8.7
Union Carbide...............	21.3	11.9
American Cyanamid...........	16.3	9.6
Monsanto....................	16.0	8.4
Allied Chemical..............	15.5	8.4

Table 19-8. Sample Companies: Comparative Earnings Margins and Capital Turnover, Selected Periods

Earnings margin

Period	Industry excluding du Pont	du Pont	Hercules Powder	Union Carbide	American Cyanamid	Dow Chemical	Allied Chemical	Monsanto Chemical
1935–1939	14.9%	18.4%	10.4%	19.4%	7.8%	19.6%	14.4%	13.1%
1947–1957	10.0	12.7	7.7	12.3	8.3	10.1	8.5	8.8
1953–1957	9.3	13.3	7.4	11.1	8.7	9.1	8.0	7.7
1957	8.8	13.6	7.4	10.1	10.0	7.9	6.9	6.9

Capital turnover

Period	Industry excluding du Pont	du Pont	Hercules Powder	Union Carbide	American Cyanamid	Dow Chemical	Allied Chemical	Monsanto Chemical
1935–1939	73%	62%	106%	55%	120%	79%	73%	92%
1947–1957	114	151	193	111	121	94	118	112
1953–1957	108	156	187	107	110	95	105	109
1957	112	151	174	114	116	99	106	106

In terms of those with declines, du Pont had the smallest and showed by far the highest earnings margin in 1953–1957. In contrast, Dow had the most severe decline but, in this connection, the analyst would need to consider Dow's heavy depreciation charges.

As in the case of profit margins, wide variations exist in both the turnover of total capital and in the changes in turnover between periods. Hercules Powder had the highest turnover in 1953–1957 and—next to du Pont—the greatest improvement between the prewar and postwar periods. Du Pont stood second in turnover in 1953–1957. Dow Chemical had the lowest turnover. American Cyanamid was the only firm to show no increase in turnover but it will be seen that it still stood third in 1953–1957 and that it had an extremely high turnover in 1935–1939.

Clearly, the analyst cannot take all of the foregoing ratios (or any others) at face value. These ratios serve to indicate where further research needs to be done; thus he must dig beneath them and seek explanations.

In connection with his examination of the growth and profitability of the individual companies, he will want to examine as fully as possible the product mix of each firm. The industry review—only outlined above— noted important differences in growth rates of the major chemical products, and also compared the capital investment required and the profit-margin factor with those of other industrial groups. These facts must be brought fully into play in considering the profitability and the growth of individual firms. Only in this manner can an adequate appraisal be made of company performance.

Per-share Earnings. To reduce distortions arising from cyclical fluctuations, growth in per-share earnings is measured by taking the 1947–1951 span as the base and then computing the average increase in terms of the five-year span, 1953–1957. For comparative purposes, the increase for the last year (at the time of the original study—1957) is also shown as a percent of the 1947–1951 base. Derived in this manner, it may be seen from Table 19-9 that the increase in per-share earnings has ranged from 18 percent for Allied Chemical to 83 percent for du Pont (chemical earnings only).

Table 19-9. Comparative Postwar Increase in Per-share Earnings: °
1953–1957 and 1957 as Percent of 1947–1951

(Companies in order of 1953–1957 increase)

Period†	Industry (excluding du Pont)	du Pont‡	Dow Chemical	American Cyanamid	Hercules Powder	Union Carbide	Monsanto Chemical	Allied Chemical
1947–1951		$2.81	$1.33	$1.46	$1.50	$3.48	$1.34	$1.98
1953		3.19	1.29	1.58	1.40	3.55	1.48	2.34
1954		5.17	1.49	1.47	1.70	3.26	1.32	2.14
1955		6.30	2.33	2.03	2.30	4.83	1.83	2.64
1956		5.41	2.03	2.05	2.10	4.86	1.70	2.37
1957		5.66	1.71	2.42	2.13	4.45	1.62	2.18
1953–1957		5.15	1.77	1.91	1.93	4.19	1.59	2.33
1953–1957 as percent above 1947–1951..	23.3	83.2 %	33.0 %	30.8 %	28.7 %	20.4 %	18.6 %	17.7 %
1957 as percent above 1947–1951..	27.8	101.4	28.5	65.8	42.0	27.9	20.9	10.1

* Data adjusted for subsequent stock splits and stock dividends.
† On a calendar year basis. If the company has a fiscal year ending before June 30, its fiscal year is included in the preceding calendar year. For example May 31, 1954 earnings for Dow Chemical are put into calendar year 1953.
‡ Chemical earnings only.

Market Valuation. To complete our comparative analysis of the individual companies, the percentages which the price-earnings ratios (Table 19-10) and dividend yields (Table 19-11) constitute of the respective industry composites in selected postwar periods have been developed. Because of the impact of the General Motors holding on market price, price-earnings ratios and dividend yields are not included

Table 19-10. Price-Earnings Ratios as Percent of Chemical Industry Composite Data Excluding du Pont

(Companies ranked according to 1953–1957 average)

	P-E ratio for industry (excluding du Pont)	Dow Chemical	Union Carbide	Allied Chemical	Hercules Powder	Monsanto Chemical	American Cyanamid
1947–1951 average...	12.5	102 %	102 %	99 %	98 %	115 %	81 %
1953	18.6	146	104	74	86	96	82
1954	22.0	113	111	87	75	97	76
1955	19.6	105	104	102	90	106	73
1956	24.2	135	100	95	86	94	71
1957	23.0	143	105	83	85	93	75
1953–1957 average...	21.6	127	105	88	85	85	75

Table 19-11. Dividend Yields as Percent of Chemical Industry Composite Data Excluding du Pont

(Companies ranked according to 1953–1957 average)

	Industry (excluding du Pont)	American Cyanamid	Allied Chemical	Union Carbide	Hercules Powder	Monsanto Chemical	Dow Chemical
1947–1951 average...	4.2 %	100 %	117 %	105 %	112 %	81 %	67 %
1953	3.5	117	123	103	126	83	74
1954	3.1	129	110	100	116	87	81
1955	2.8	150	93	111	96	82	71
1956	2.5	152	108	104	100	96	68
1957	3.1	123	116	110	84	87	65
1953–1957 average...	2.9	138	110	107	103	86	72

for du Pont. It will be seen from the tables that Dow Chemical, which enjoyed the highest growth rate for sales and—excluding du Pont—for per-share earnings, had the highest price-earnings ratio and the lowest dividend yield relative to the group.

The reader has the right to ask us several questions about the foregoing analysis: (1) What definite conclusions for investment choices can properly be drawn therefrom? (2) How would such choices have fared in the ensuing period, say to the end of 1961? (3) What is the bearing of this stock-market experience on the practical utility of security analysis? We shall endeavor to answer these questions in Chapter 52, devoted to "Security Analysis in Action."

CHAPTER TWENTY

FACTORS IN PUBLIC UTILITY ANALYSIS:

INTRODUCTION. BALANCE-SHEET ANALYSIS

Public utility companies have certain special characteristics, both eco-nomic and financial, which justify their separate treatment at some length. Perhaps the most outstanding is their subjection to comprehensive and highly developed regulation by special government agencies.

Regulation by Government Agencies. These agencies include both state public utility, or public service, commissions, whose jurisdiction covers virtually every phase of the individual company's activities; and Federal agencies, such as the Federal Power Commission and the Securities and Exchange Commission, which exercise certain regulatory powers that are generally outside the purview of state jurisdiction.

The genesis of regulation lies in one of the industry's economic characteristics: .The most satisfactory service to the public requires individual company monopoly within its own area. Competition, which in other fields of corporate enterprise protects the consumer from exorbitant prices, has little or no place in public utility services, and its substitute is regulation by government commissions. From the viewpoint of the investor and consequently of the security analyst, this factor of regulation is extremely important, since to a considerable extent it actually determines a company's earnings.

The scope of regulation includes the prescribing of a uniform account-ing system, jurisdiction over rates charged for the service rendered, jurisdiction over the issuance of securities, acquisition or sale of property, standards of service, etc. In regard to most of these matters the jurisdic-tion is vested in the state public utility commission.[1]

Uniform Accounting an Aid in Analysis. From the analyst's viewpoint, the most direct impact of regulation, apart from control over rates, is seen in the adoption by the various utility industries of uniform account-

[1] All the 50 states and the District of Columbia now have public service commis-sions with power to regulate one or more of the public utility industries. In certain states, however, the extent of regulatory jurisdiction is limited. For example, the following states, at the end of 1960, were without commission regulation of electric and gas rates: Alaska, Iowa, Minnesota, Nebraska, and South Dakota. In Texas there is commission regulation of gas utilities only.

ing systems, applicable both to the balance-sheet presentation and to the reporting of earnings. This uniformity of corporate accounting substantially facilitates comparative analysis.

The present uniform system of accounts for electric and gas utilities was adopted in 1936 and revised in 1958 by the National Association of Railroad and Utilities Commissioners and is presently prescribed by virtually all state commissions. Effective January 1, 1937 and revised as of January 1, 1961, the Federal Power Commission prescribed an almost identical accounting system for companies operating hydroelectric plants under Federal licenses and electric systems operating across state lines. The gas, telephone, and water industries are subject to similar accounting requirements as well as to other aspects of regulatory supervision. In this chapter, while we shall confine ourselves primarily to a discussion of the electric industry, many of our comments will have equal applicability to the others.

Production Simultaneous with Use. A second important characteristic that is peculiar to the electric industry—a fundamental difference between it and practically every other type of business—is that electricity, except in relatively small quantities, cannot be stored. Production has to be simultaneous with use, and electricity exists only while it is being consumed. This fact explains the typical high ratio of capital investment per dollar of revenue, and from it stem practically all the financial and operating characteristics of the industry.

Necessity of Meeting the Demand. A third fundamental point is that electric utilities are required to furnish their service to anybody who asks for it, in as great or small quantities as the user desires. They have to forecast, and be prepared to meet, the demand for their product well in advance of the development of the demand, and they have to take every reasonable step to maintain themselves in a position instantly to satisfy this demand irrespective of its fluctuations. This also has a bearing on the large capital investment that has to be made in production, transmission, and distribution equipment. As a result, a utility must make every effort to keep its investment working as many hours and days of the year as it can, so that the fixed capital and operating costs can be distributed over as many units of output as possible. This necessity explains the declining price characteristics of electric rate structures; the object is to encourage increased use so as to reduce the time when the investment is idle and so to arrange the charge for the product that each consumer pays his proportionate share of the cost to serve him.

THE IMPACT OF REGULATION

Essentially, public utility analysis requires a study of factors that logically fall under two separate headings: (1) economic and (2) political, i.e, regulatory. Security analysis generally tends to concern itself primarily with the economic determinants, an entirely correct approach in the case of industrial securities. In the case of utilities, however, the political factors, which come alive in the impact of regulation, are frequently of even greater significance in the determination of what a company can and will earn.

The Return and the Rate Base. As generally conceived, the theory of public utility regulation is to permit the subject company to earn no more than a fair and reasonable return on its investment in facilities used and useful in the service of the public. The earnings which represent the return are net operating income after all expenses, including taxes and depreciation, but before capital charges such as interest and associated items and dividends. The investment in facilities, commonly called the "rate base," embraces the company's fixed capital, or plant account, to the extent that it represents facilities used in the public service, minus the reserve for depreciation, plus an allowance for materials and supplies used in operations and sometimes for cash working capital.

The basic regulatory attitude toward the permissible return has not essentially changed over the years. In 1898 the United States Supreme Court stated, in Smyth v. Ames, "What the company is entitled to ask is a fair return upon the value of that which it employs for the public convenience. On the other hand, what the public is entitled to demand is that no more be exacted from it . . . than the services rendered . . . are reasonably worth."

A more comprehensive pronouncement was made by the Supreme Court in 1923, in the Bluefield Water Works case. In this opinion the Court stated in part:

A public utility is entitled to such rates as will permit it to earn a return on the value of its property which it employs for the convenience of the public equal to that generally being made at the same time and in the same general part of the country on investments in other business undertakings which are attended by corresponding risks and uncertainties; but it has no constitutional right to profits such as are realised or anticipated in highly profitable enterprises or speculative ventures.

The return should be reasonably sufficient to assure confidence in the financial soundness of the utility, and should be adequate, under efficient and economical management, to maintain and support its credit and enable it to raise the money necessary for the proper discharge of its public duties.

The Rate Base at Fair Value. Prior to 1944 it was widespread practice to compute the rate base at its current fair value, i.e., the fair value of the property at the time of inquiry into the reasonableness of the rates, irrespective of the balance-sheet figures or the amount at which the plant account was carried on the books. This procedure recognized the fact that it was *property* that the owners devoted to the public service and that the compensation to which they were entitled should be based upon a reasonable return on the *value* of that property. When the value was in dispute it should be determined by competent engineering appraisal.

In January 1944, however, the Supreme Court, in its historic Hope Natural Gas decision, largely freed the regulatory bodies from adherence to any rate-base formulas and stated:

> The rate making process . . . involves a balancing of the investor and consumer interests. . . . The investor has a legitimate concern with the financial integrity of the company whose rates are being regulated. From the investor or company point of view it is important that there be enough revenue not only for operating expenses but also for the capital costs of the business. These include service on the debt and dividends on the stock. . . .
>
> By that standard the return to the equity owner should be commensurate with returns on investments in other enterprises having corresponding risks. The return, moreover, should be sufficient to assure confidence in the financial integrity of the enterprise, so as to maintain its credit and to attract capital.

Original Cost and Reproduction Cost. Following this decision there was a considerable movement on the part of state regulatory commissions to adopt a "net-investment" rate base, i.e., the actual amount at which plant and facilities are carried on the books, less the depreciation reserve and plus, of course, working capital. This trend has not, however, been universal, and the analyst should familiarize himself with the practice of the state in which any company under survey operates. In Ohio, for example, the state commission has followed for years the policy of using a reproduction-cost rate base, a practice of considerable help to the local companies during periods of rising construction costs. In a number of other states, including Arizona, Delaware, Illinois, Missouri, and Pennsylvania, the commissions still adhere to a "fair-value" approach.

The Spread in Allowable Returns. Since 1930, and until 1947, the regulatory concept of what constituted a reasonable return trended generally downward, largely reflecting the decline in interest rates and, perhaps of even greater significance, the lack of need on the part of the industry to raise any substantial amounts of new capital. During the years 1927–1931 a return of 7 percent was allowed in numerous rate cases; by the early 1940's a return of $5\frac{1}{2}$ percent, and in some instances lower, was found not to be unreasonable. In 1948, however, the downward trend appeared arrested. The industry was engaged in the largest expansion program in its history, and the necessity of raising large amounts of new capital, particularly common-stock capital, was clearly apparent. As a result of rapidly rising costs in the postwar period, operating profits had declined materially, and for many companies this had sharply reduced the over-all return. Higher earnings were clearly necessary in order to sell common stock at prices fair to the existing stockholders. Rate increases were widely asked for and were generally granted with reasonable promptness.

As a practical matter, the generally accepted attitude toward rate of return will vary somewhat in different parts of the country, a lower return being viewed as reasonable in the older and more thickly settled areas in the East, and a more liberal attitude prevailing in the more sparsely settled and growing sections of the West and Southwest. Thus, in states such as Arizona, Nevada, and New Mexico returns of 6½ and 7 percent have been considered reasonable by the commissions, while in New York 5 percent may be prescribed under temporary rates pending final determination.

Generally speaking, however, we believe that a rate of return in the area of 6 to 7 percent is as much as can be looked forward to with any confidence under present and foreseeable conditions. In terms of dollars of income, of course, variation in the type of rate base used will be highly important. A 6 percent return upon a fair-value or reproduction-cost rate base will, under present conditions, produce considerably more dollars than a similar return related to an original cost base. It is important, therefore, to be familiar with the practice of the state utility commissions on this point.

In those cases where a net-investment rate base is used, the analyst's problem is facilitated in respect to forming an opinion as to the adequacy of the earned return or the vulnerability of rates to reduction by regulatory action. The necessary data on which to base judgment can, to an informative degree, be obtained directly from the reported figures.

Because of the part played by the accounting factor in the regulatory determination of allowable earnings, it is important for the analyst to be thoroughly familiar with this aspect of utility operations. For this reason we believe that the following somewhat extended discussion of the principal balance-sheet and income-account items is justified.

BALANCE-SHEET ANALYSIS

Substantially the larger part of a utility's capital is invested in fixed, immovable property, land, buildings, large structures, bulky and expensive machinery, dams, etc. This heavy investment in permanent property is one of the characteristics of the industry and differentiates it from the majority of commercial enterprises. For the typical company the plant and property account will commonly aggregate between 80 and 90 percent of total assets.

The plant account, moreover, is unusually large, as compared with most other businesses, in relation to annual revenue and income. Many commercial concerns will turn over their capital a number of times a year, but the average electric or gas utility will require a property investment of several times its annual operating revenue. This reflects, of course, the fact that, although but intermittent use is made of the service by the consumers, the facilities and investment must be adequate to

handle their maximum requirements with due consideration to the variation in the incidence of peak demands.

Table 20-1 shows, in a condensed presentation, the composite balance
sheet as of December 31, 1949 and 1959, of all privately owned Class A

Table 20-1. Electric Utility Industry Balance Sheet, December 31, 1949 and December 31, 1959

	Dec. 31, 1949 Amount (000,000 omitted)	Percent	Dec. 31, 1959 Amount (000,000 omitted)	Percent
Electric utility plant..............	$17,325	75.1	$42,322	82.5
Other utility plant..............	2,302	10.0	4,531	8.9
Total utility plant..............	$19,627	85.1	$46,853	91.4
Investments and funds............	1,272	5.5	1,058	2.1
Current assets...................	1,899	8.2	2,943	5.8
Deferred debits..................	176	0.8	230	0.5
Other assets.....................	95	0.4	106	0.2
Total..........................	$23,069	100.0	$51,190	100.0
Long-term debt..................	$ 8,572	37.2	$19,834	38.7
Preferred stock..................	2,392	10.4	4,115	8.0
Common stock....................	4,623	20.0	8,520	16.6
Premiums, assessments, etc.........	240	1.0	1,464	2.9
Surplus..........................	1,552	6.7	3,711	7.3
Current liabilities................	1,359	5.9	2,966	5.8
Reserves for depreciation and amorti- zation.........................	4,069	17.7	8,978	17.5
Other reserves...................	99	0.4	107	0.2
Deferred income taxes.............	—	—	1,158	2.3
Other liabilities..................	163	0.7	337	0.7
Total..........................	$23,069	100.0	$51,190	100.0

Ratios

Total utility plant per dollar of revenue......................	$3.87	$4.21
Electric utility plant per dollar elec- tric revenue..................	3.95	4.45
Current assets times current liabili- ties.........................	1.40×	0.99×
Long-term debt		
Percent total utility plant.......	43.7%	42.3%
Percent net utility plant........	55.1%	52.4%
Percent total capitalization and sur- plus		
Long-term debt................	49.3%	52.7%
Preferred stock...............	13.8%	10.9%
Common stock and surplus......	36.9%	36.4%
Depreciation reserve, percent of utility plant...........................	20.7%	19.2%

SOURCE: Federal Power Commission.

and Class B electric utilities in the United States. These companies include those with annual revenues in excess of $250,000 and represent in
excess of 98 percent of the privately owned electric utility industry. The
data can be considered representative of the industry as a whole.

Over this ten-year period, the industry's investment in utility plant (fixed capital) has increased by 139 percent, an average compounded rate of growth of about 9.1 percent per year. It is pertinent to note that this substantial expansion has been financed in a manner so as to maintain sound capital-structure ratios, with little change in the proportions of senior capital and common-stock equity over the period.

In the typical balance sheet, utility plant is usually shown as a single figure; or, in the case of a combination company—i.e., one rendering more than one type of service, such as electricity and gas, water, heating, etc.—the plant account may be further segregated to show the investment in facilities used to provide each service. This segregation is important to the analyst since, from a regulatory viewpoint, departmental earnings are commonly related to the investment made to furnish the particular service, and if the latter is not revealed, a correct evaluation of reported earnings is difficult if not impossible.

A similar breakdown of the depreciation reserve is likewise desirable, since it is invariably in relation to the net investment that the adequacy of the return is judged.

Utility Plant. The present uniform system of accounts, which is now prescribed by virtually all the state commissions, requires that utility plant be carried on the books at original cost, defined as the cost of such property to the person first devoting it to public service. Any excess over original cost must be separated into other accounts for such disposition as the regulatory authorities may require.

In the case of property constructed by the utility and still owned by it, routine procedure calls for its recording at original cost. In the case of property purchased, however, the buying company frequently paid prices that were considerably higher than the seller's own construction costs. When the transaction reflected arm's-length dealing, the difference between the cost to the purchaser and the original cost of the property is to be classified in a special account entitled Plant Acquisition Adjustments.

For the great majority of companies, amounts in this account, which were frequently sizable ten years ago, have been largely written off and are no longer a significant factor in the analysis of plant account.

As a general guide to the accounting conservatism in the recording of the property investment, the ratio of *plant per dollar of operating revenue* is widely used. For the electric utility industry as a whole, at the end of 1959, the investment in plant account per dollar of revenue was $4.21. The increase in this figure during the preceding decade reflects primarily the rise in construction costs resulting from the country's experienced inflation. Typically the ratio is lower for a company whose generating facilities consist wholly or primarily of steam electric stations, and higher for a company with a large investment in hydro plants. For example, a group of predominantly hydroelectric companies had an average plant-to-revenue ratio of $6.73 at the end of 1959, while a group of steam-generating companies had a comparable ratio of $3.99.

Depreciation. In the last edition of this book, published in 1951, we stated that few phases of public utility accounting had been surrounded by more controversy than that of providing for depreciation. In recent years, however, the subject has been considerably less a matter for dispute, as more uniform methods of depreciation accounting have been adopted. Prior to 1937 the majority of companies used what was then called the "retirement-reserve" method of providing for property retired from service. Under this method appropriations were made from earnings (charged to operating expense) and/or surplus to provide for current retirements and to build up a reserve for future retirements. The reserve was in no sense intended to be a measure of the actual depreciation that had occurred, but was an amount which in the management's judgment would be sufficient to equalize the burden of retirement losses from year to year, with due regard to the amount of earnings available each year for this purpose.

The present uniform system of accounts, however, calls specifically for depreciation accounting and requires that each utility shall record at the end of each month the estimated amount of depreciation accrued during the month on depreciable plant. This is to be deducted as an operating expense and credited to the reserve for depreciation. The purpose of the depreciation reserve is to reflect the accumulated charges made during the useful life of the property for the purpose of writing off the book cost, plus cost of removal, less salvage, of all classes of depreciable property. Credits to the reserve are to be made in such way that the operations of each year shall bear a proportionate share of the burden.

"Depreciation" is defined in the uniform system of accounts as

. . . the loss in service value not restored by current maintenance, incurred in connection with the consumption or prospective retirement of utility plant in the course of service from causes which are known to be in current operation and against which the utility is not protected by insurance. Among the causes to be given consideration are wear and tear, decay, action of the elements, inadequacy, obsolescence, changes in the art, changes in demand, and requirements of public authorities.

"Service value" is defined as the difference between original cost and the net salvage value. "Original cost" means the cost of the property to the person first devoting it to public service.

Present practice is generally to provide for depreciation either on a straight-line or on a sinking-fund basis, with the great majority of companies following the former method. The *straight-line* method presupposes that the service life of the property can be estimated with reasonable accuracy and that uniform annual accruals should be made for its

ultimate retirement. For example, if a piece of equipment has an estimated life of ten years, the annual provision for depreciation would be
one-tenth of its cost, less net salvage value. This method has the advantage of simplicity and of harmonizing the annual charge for depreciation
with the reserve that is being built up.

Sinking-fund methods (or interest methods) of depreciation accounting are also based upon an estimate of service life; but only such amount
is set aside (charged to operating expense) each year as will at compound interest provide the necessary reserve at the time of retirement.
The accumulating reserve can be invested either in income-paying securities or in the utility's own property, the latter being the usual practice.
In this event it must, of course, earn a return; and therefore an unde-
preciated rate base is used. In effect the deduction of the depreciation
reserve is accomplished by impounding the return on that portion of the
property representing the reserve investment.

Today we believe that the analyst can generally accept as authoritative
and realistic the annual accrual for depreciation as reported. Similarly,
in the case of the accumulated reserve, the reported figures can usually
be taken in good faith as representing the cost of property recovered
through charges to the consumer. While this may well differ from the
amount of physical depreciation that might be determined by an engineering appraisal, it is significant that to an increasing extent regulatory
procedure is leaning in the direction of accepting the accounting provision as the amount to be deducted in arriving at the rate base.

Provision for Deferred Income Taxes. The uniform system of accounts,
adopted by the Federal Power Commission, provides for a special
balance-sheet account, shown on the liability side and entitled Accumulated Deferred Income Taxes.[2] This account is to be credited with the
amounts by which income taxes are reduced because of the use of accelerated (five-year) amortization of certified defense facilities and/or the
use of liberalized depreciation, as compared to the depreciation deduction otherwise allowable based on a straight-line, or another appropriate,
method applied to the estimated useful life of the property.

Accelerated amortization refers to a provision in the Internal Revenue
Code which permitted a company to amortize over a five-year period
for Federal income tax purposes the cost of facilities for which a certificate of emergency had been issued as necessary to national defense. In
1957, the Code was amended to exclude from emergency certification
facilities constructed for providing electric service. As of the end of 1960,
a number of companies, however, still had sizable property investments
which were being written off, for tax purposes, over this short period,

[2] The Revised Uniform System of Accounts recommended for adoption by the
NARUC omits all reference to deferred-tax accounting, and the various state regulatory commissions are presently permitting or prescribing a variety of methods of
treatment.

with a consequent result of reducing the income tax that would otherwise be payable. In reporting to stockholders, the usual practice has been to charge against income an amount equivalent to the reduction in Federal income taxes which results from the excess of such amortization over normal depreciation, and credit the amount to the balance-sheet account, "accumulated deferred taxes on income." At the end of the five-year period, when these facilities are fully amortized for tax purposes, a proportionate increase results, of course, in the income tax payable, which is met by debiting the tax reserve and crediting the income account by the amount of the increase.

Liberalized depreciation refers to a provision of Section 167 of the Internal Revenue Code of 1954 which permits larger depreciation allowances for tax purposes during the early years of property life than does the straight-line method. The intent of the law was to stimulate investment and encourage economic growth by accelerating tax-free recovery of capital investment. The effect is to shift the timing of allowable depreciation for tax purposes, by increasing the permitted deductions in the early years of service, without changing the total amount of tax depreciation that may be claimed over the entire life of the facility. In its reports to stockholders, a company may or may not "normalize" its annual income tax provision, i.e., charge income with an amount equivalent to the tax reduction resulting from the use of liberalized depreciation. When it does so, the amount of the normalizing charge is also credited to the balance-sheet account, Accumulated Deferred Income Taxes, with subsequent charges being made against this account, and commensurate credits made to income, when the annual depreciation charge becomes less than it would under the straight-line method. A further discussion of the impact of liberalized depreciation on earnings is presented in Chapter 21, which deals with the analysis of utility income statements.

Provision for Deferred Taxes Not to Be Included in Capitalization. For a number of years following the Revenue Code provision permitting the use of liberalized depreciation, there was considerable variation of opinion as to whether the accumulated deferred taxes should be credited to a restricted earned-surplus account, and considered as part of equity capital, or carried to a reserve for future taxes. Initially, a large number of companies contended for the former treatment, generally in conformity with an accounting practice approved by the state public service commission. In some states this accounting treatment is still in accord with state regulatory requirements.

In February 1960, the Securities and Exchange Commission issued a statement of administrative policy regarding the balance-sheet treatment of credits equivalent to the reduction in income taxes.[3]

---

[3] Securities Act of 1933, Release No. 4191; Securities Exchange Act of 1934, Release No. 6189; Holding Company Act, Release No. 14173; Investment Company Act of 1940, Release No. 2977; Accounting Series, Release No. 85.

The statement was not intended to establish accounting methods or to specify the manner in which tax deferrals should be recorded on the books of a company, but dealt rather with "the presentation in financial statements filed with the Commission of the credit arising when deferred tax accounting is employed."

As to companies which have adopted accelerated amortization and/or liberalized depreciation for tax purposes, but not for book purposes, the Commission stated:

> In a year in which costs are deducted for tax purposes in amounts greater than those used for financial statement purposes, then, unless corrected, there is a failure properly to match costs and revenues in the financial statements by the amount of the tax effect of the cost differential. To correct the resultant distortion in periodic net income after taxes, it is therefore necessary to charge income in earlier years with an amount equal to the tax reduction and to return this amount to income in subsequent years when the amount charged for financial statement purposes exceeds the amount deducted for tax purposes. It is our understanding that such deferred tax accounting is in accordance with generally accepted accounting principles.

> With specific reference to depreciation, since the total deduction allowed over the life of the asset is limited to its cost and hence is not affected by the method by which it is deducted from income, acceleration of tax deductions in earlier years results in deferring to later years the payment of taxes on an amount equivalent to the cost differential. Because of the interrelationship between income taxes and depreciation, the Commission is of the view that in the earlier years the charge equivalent to the tax reduction should be treated either (1) as a provision for future taxes in the income statement with a corresponding credit in the balance sheet to a non-equity caption such as a deferred tax credit, or (2) as additional depreciation in the income statement with a corresponding addition to the accumulated provision for depreciation in the balance sheet. In the Commission's view it is improper to charge income with an item required for the proper determination of net income and concurrently to credit earned surplus. . . .

> For the foregoing reasons, on and after the effective date of this statement (April 30, 1960) of administrative policy, any financial statement filed with this Commission which designates as earned surplus (or its equivalent) or in any manner as part of equity capital (even though accompanied by words of limitation such as "restricted" or "appropriated") the accumulated credit arising from accounting for reductions in income taxes resulting from deducting costs for income tax purposes at a more rapid rate than for financial statement purposes will be presumed by the Commission to be misleading or inaccurate despite disclosure contained in the certificate of the accountant or in footnotes to the statements, provided the amounts involved are material.

However, the SEC recognized that many state public service commissions permitted recognition of deferred income taxes for accounting and/or rate-making purposes, whereas some did not, and that where charges for deferred income taxes are not allowed for rate-making purposes, accounting recognition need not be given to the deferment of taxes. Thus the Commission accepted the fact that some state regulatory agencies permitted public utilities to deduct only the actual taxes payable in a given year, and it raised no question as to the propriety of this treatment. Similarly, the SEC stated that "it is entirely appropriate that (public utility) regulatory agencies treat the accumulated credit arising from deferred tax accounting in whatever manner they deem most relevant to their purpose."

The SEC, of course, has no jurisdiction over public utility rate making, and it has no authority to prescribe to the state commissions how items shall be treated either for accounting or rate-making purposes. However, in the same statement of policy it said:

So far as this Commission is concerned, since it believes that classifying this item as a component part of common stock equity is misleading for financial statement purposes, it does not intend to consider the item as part of common stock equity for analytical purposes, although it may give consideration to the item as one of a number of relevant factors in appraising the overall financial condition of a company.

From the standpoint of security analysis, we agree with the position taken by the SEC and we think that when accruals for future taxes are charged as an operating expense against earnings, the accumulated balance should not be considered as part of equity capital.

Working Capital. As indicated above, a utility is permitted to earn a fair and reasonable return on its investment in facilities used to serve the public. This includes not only the investment in plant and property, but also the necessary working capital used in carrying on the business. From a regulatory viewpoint, working capital may be briefly defined as the funds necessarily provided in order to conduct the business until the company is reimbursed through the amounts paid for the service. It includes the cash required to meet current operating outlays and necessary materials and supplies. It may bear little or no relation to the current assets shown in the corporate balance sheet.

Commissions have generally ruled that the amount of working capital to be allowed in a rate case must depend upon the facts in each instance. While no hard and fast rule can be laid down, it was formerly frequent practice to allow a sum equivalent to operating expenses, excluding taxes and depreciation, for a period of forty-five days to two months. In recent years however there has been a tendency on the part of regulatory commissions to reduce the cash working-capital allowance by a portion or all of Federal income tax accruals, and sometimes other tax accruals, on the grounds that these represent funds contributed by the customers which are available to the company for working-capital purposes.

It will be readily seen that "net working capital," or net current assets, as derived from the balance sheet, is a very different thing from the above concept. Current assets will frequently include substantial amounts of cash or construction funds that may be in the form of short-term or temporary investments. Similarly, current liabilities may include loans or notes payable and large amounts for tax accruals. Under normal operating conditions a utility, unlike most industrial concerns, seldom maintains a large net-current-asset position; it is not generally necessary, in view of the monthly receipts for the service rendered and in view of the relatively minor inventory requirements.

Despite the variance between the regulatory concept of working capital and net current assets as revealed by the balance sheet, we believe that, as a practical matter, the latter should be added to net plant in the analyst's determination of estimated earnings base. (Incidentally, we believe that this phrase is preferable in security analysis to the technical and legal term "rate base.") When net current assets include construction funds, these will in time be transformed into productive plant and become part of the earnings base and will thus be available both to produce and to support future income.

Only in those instances where current liabilities exceed current assets would we suggest that the analyst add an amount for working capital computed in the regulatory manner, in order to arrive at the earnings base.

Alternative Approach to Estimated Earnings Base. As a measure of the over-all rate of return being earned by a company, it is frequent practice to show gross income (i.e., income available for charges) as a percentage of total capitalization and surplus. While total capitalization and surplus will not usually be identical with the rate base, nevertheless it represents the total capital invested in the business and generally approximates very closely the figure for net plant plus net current assets. Divergence will occur, of course, when a company has substantial assets other than its investment in plant, such as securities or other investments. But since gross income includes the income from these assets, the ratio still measures the over-all return.

When the measure of rate of return is computed on this basis, however, we believe, that interest charged to construction (for a further discussion of this item see Chapter 21), which is usually shown as a credit against fixed charges, should be added to reported gross income. The reason for this is that total capitalization and surplus usually reflects amounts for property under construction, which is not currently in operation and thus not contributing to earnings. Since it can be confidently assumed that this property will become productive of earnings, some recognition should be given to this probable productivity, and the most practicable method, we think, is as suggested above.

Capitalization Ratios. In Chapter 25, in our discussion of fixed-income securities, we suggest that the maximum desirable debt ratio for utilities should be set at 60 percent of the net plant account in the case of a company that has debt and common stock outstanding, but no preferred stock. When preferred stock is included in the capital structure, the debt ratio should be somewhat lower in order to give the preferred stock an investment rating.

Expressed in terms of total capitalization and surplus, the debt ratio would automatically be somewhat lower since, for a typical company, capitalization and surplus (which reflects the inclusion of net current and other assets) will aggregate about 10 percent higher than the figure for net plant. This suggests that the maximum amount for debt expressed in terms of total capitalization and surplus should be about 55 percent if the company has no preferred stock outstanding. It is prevailing practice, however, for utility companies to issue preferred stock, and when this is done, we would suggest that the optimal capital structure would consist of

Bonds...........................	50%
Preferred stock...................	15
Common stock and surplus.........	35
Total........................	100%

In setting up a standard such as this, however, we do not mean to propose it as an inflexible rule. A company's financial policy must be governed by many considerations, of which some may be peculiar to its own operations and others may reflect existing economic circumstances. Under certain conditions a considerably higher debt ratio may be justified, but in this event provision should be made for its subsequent reduction, either through the operation of a sinking fund or by financing further property expansion with equity capital.

The SEC, in its administration of the Public Utility Holding Company Act, consistently indicated that 25 percent should be considered a *minimum* acceptable ratio for the common-stock equity to bear to total capitalization and frequently imposed restrictions on dividend payments when the ratio was less than this. That the Commission did not consider this a satisfactory ratio per se, however, was indicated in an opinion issued in December, 1949, in which it said:

We have never regarded a 25% common stock equity ratio as being anything other than a floor below which existing common stock equity ratios should not drop, or to which existing lower ratios should, as a minimum, increase. We have continuously striven to have common stock equity ratios maintained at, or increased to, levels substantially above 25% of capitalization and surplus.

As indicated above, the SEC has taken the position that when a company uses liberalized depreciation for income tax purposes, any accumulated provisions for deferred taxes are not to be included as part of common-stock equity or as part of capitalization and surplus. The Commission has, however, stated that it will give "due weight" to the existence of such accumulated tax reserve in determining appropriate capitalization ratios and that it would give consideration to this item as one of a number of relevant factors in appraising the over-all financial condition of a company.

The matter came up as an important issue in a proposed bank financing by Kentucky Power Company, a subsidiary of American Electric Power Company. Both Kentucky Power and American Electric carried significant amounts on their balance sheets designated as "Earned Surplus Restricted for Future Federal Income Taxes," and the Commission's staff claimed that this was not consistent with the SEC's stated policy. In a ruling dated January 13, 1961 (HCA Release No. 14,353) the Commission approved a settlement proposal which provided that the tax accumulations be carried under a designation: "Accumulated Amount Invested in the Business Equivalent to Reduction in Federal Income Taxes Resulting from Accelerated Amortization and Liberalized Depreciation, Which is Recorded as Earned Surplus Restricted for Future Federal Income Taxes in Accounts Maintained Pursuant to State Regulatory Requirements."

As part of the settlement, the Commission also approved certain ratio tests concerning the capital structure of the various companies in the American Electric holding-company system. It stated that in future financings by companies in the system, it would give due weight to the existence of the accumulated tax reduction and its size in determining appropriate capitalization ratios, and that when the consolidated balance sheet of American Electric and its subsidiaries, or the corporate balance sheet of any subsidiary, included a substantial amount of accumulated tax reduction, the Commission would not take any adverse action in respect to capitalization ratios where, upon completion of the financing:

a. Common stock equity is not less than 30% of total capitalization and surplus.

b. Mortgage debt is not in excess of 60% of total capitalization and surplus.

c. Long-term debt is not in excess of 65% of total capitalization and surplus.

For the purpose of these tests, the terms "common-stock equity" and "total capitalization and surplus" are not to include any accumulated tax reduction resulting from charges against income as an operating revenue deduction in respect of accelerated amortization or liberalized depreciation for Federal income tax purposes.

While these standards seem somewhat at variance with those which we have suggested above, we think that they are designated by the SEC, not as ideal or necessarily desirable, but rather as indicating the limits beyond which a company cannot go without risking terms and conditions being imposed in respect to new financing. It is in this area that the jurisdiction of the SEC lies rather than that of setting up standards for the guidance of security analysts.

One result of the Commission's ruling may well be to encourage debt financing by utilities in lieu of preferred stock. The tax advantages to a company are obvious, and the issuance of a reasonable amount of debentures should be feasible without impairing the quality and bond ratings of mortgage obligations. In fact, not long after the SEC findings in the Kentucky Power case, Pennsylvania Electric Company, a subsidiary of General Public Utilities Corporation, stated in connection with the sale of a debenture issue that it proposed to abandon preferred stock as a financing medium, unless conditions, not then contemplated, should change radically in the future. At the same time, General Public Utilities, in a statement filed with the SEC in March 1961, said that, "it is the hope of GPU and its subsidiaries that, after the securities market has become accustomed to GPU subsidiaries' debentures, it may be possible to retire outstanding GPU subsidiary preferred stock. While no definite program to that end is now in process, GPU and its subsidiaries would expect to give early consideration to the possible feasibility of initiating such a program."

Any judgment as to the adequacy of the common-stock equity must, of course, take into consideration the quality of the assets which it represents, including the integrity of the property account and the adequacy of the depreciation reserve.

If the plant account still includes significant amounts of inflationary or doubtful items, there is introduced the possibility of write-offs required by regulatory action and the likelihood that such write-offs may be charged against surplus or, if the latter is inadequate, against the capital-stock account. Under these conditions the reported equity may be vulnerable or even fictitious. Similarly, if the depreciation reserve is found by the regulatory authorities to be too small, they may require that it be built up by transfers from surplus.

As we have indicated earlier, a situation of this sort is the exception rather than the rule, but the fact that it may exist indicates the necessity of alertness in utility balance-sheet analysis.

An interesting example of a case in which a depreciation reserve deficiency might have a significant effect on the reported equity ratio as well as on the book value of the common stock was seen in the case of Consolidated Edison Company of New York at the end of 1960. At that date the total consolidated capitalization and surplus, as shown on the balance sheet, was $2,276,661,577. Of this amount, common stock and surplus aggregated $766,688,753, or 33.7 percent, and indicated a book value of $49.41 per share for the 15,517,723 common shares outstanding. The surplus account, however, included $163,552,590 which was designated as "unearned surplus—special" and which had been transferred from the stated value of the common stock in 1946 to make provision for estimated depreciation reserve deficiencies that had been indicated by a witness for the New York Public Service Commission. If this amount were eliminated from the capitalization structure, the resultant common-stock equity at the end of 1960 would have been reduced to 28.5 percent and the book value of the common to $38.87 per share. In its 1960 annual report the company pointed out that subsequent testimony by Commission witnesses indicated a substantially lesser amount for the alleged depreciation shortages; but until the matter is settled the true equity ratio and book value of the stock must remain uncertain.

CHAPTER TWENTY-ONE

FACTORS IN PUBLIC UTILITY ANALYSIS:

INCOME STATEMENT ANALYSIS

The typical utility income account generally sets forth the results of operations with substantial clarity and usually lends itself to satisfactory analysis. This general statement, however, must be made with certain important reservations.

Importance of Having a Departmental Breakdown of Earnings. In the case of combination companies it is almost universal practice to report a departmental breakdown of revenue, i.e., to show how much was derived from the sale of electricity and how much from the sale of gas and other services. A similar segregation of operating expenses is not usually given, and net operating income from all sources is commonly shown as a single figure.

The drawback to this presentation should be apparent. Under typical regulatory procedure each service is commonly required to be self-supporting, and in the event that one department does not earn a satisfactory return, it is seldom permissible to offset the deficiency for any length of time by higher than normal earnings from the other types of service.

Unless a departmental breakdown of net operating income is reported, it is not possible for the analyst to tell whether or not such a situation exists. The over-all return might appear no more than reasonable, but it might in fact reflect excessive earnings in one department and a deficiency in others.[1]

Under other circumstances one department might be operating at a loss, with a resultant understatement of potential over-all earnings. In this case the analyst, if he were guided solely by the reported earnings, might seriously undervalue the common stock. This would be particularly true if there were any likelihood that the unprofitable business might be disposed of. An interesting example of this ambiguous situation arose in

---

[1] Institutional Utility Service, Inc., gives a complete breakdown of the income account in this respect for all companies covered in its service.

connection with the sale of Birmingham Electric Company in 1950. While instances of this sort have been rare in recent years, we think that the transaction is still worth discussing. It may well be that, looking ahead, further consolidations and mergers of utility companies will take place, perhaps to a considerable degree. In this event, the following discussion may be helpful to the analyst.

Example: In August 1950, the SEC approved a proposal by the Southern Company and its subsidiary, the Alabama Power Company, to acquire the common stock of Birmingham Electric Company.[2] Approximately 46.6 percent of Birmingham's common was owned by Electric Bond & Share Company, and the balance was owned by the public. Southern Company's offer was in the form of a proposed exchange of $1\frac{1}{2}$ shares of its own common stock for each share of Birmingham common. The first public announcement of the terms of the exchange offer was made in June 1950.

For some months prior to this, Birmingham common had sold at approximately the same level as Southern Company common and in January and February 1950 had actually sold at a somewhat lower figure. (During these two months Southern's common had a price range of $11\frac{5}{8}$ to $13\frac{1}{4}$, while the range of Birmingham's stock was $9\frac{1}{2}$ to $12\frac{7}{8}$.) For the year 1949 the reported earnings of Birmingham Electric amounted to 48 cents per share, while the consolidated earnings of Southern Company were $1.27 per share. On the basis of these figures it would appear incongruous to accord a 50 percent higher value to Birmingham's common than to the stock of Southern Company.

But the reported figures were wholly misleading. Birmingham Electric, in addition to its electric business, operated a street-railway and motor-coach transportation system in the city of Birmingham and its suburbs. For some years these operations, which accounted for 33.3 percent of total revenue in 1949, had been conducted at a loss, and Southern Company proposed to dispose of the transportation properties as soon as possible. As stated above, Birmingham's reported earnings for 1949 were 48 cents per share, and for the 12 months ended May 31, 1950, they were 42 cents. Obviously, on the basis of these earnings, a value in the neighborhood of 18 or 19 could hardly be given to the stock. Estimated *pro forma* earnings, however, for the 12 months ended May 31, 1950, from the electric and (very minor) steam-heat departments alone, after the company's full income deductions and preferred-dividend requirements, on the assumption that the transportation operations had been divested, amounted to $2.03 per share, thus justifying the price proposed to be paid by Southern Company.

Structure of Operating Revenue. Although an electric utility company has but a single commodity or service to sell, the usage characteristics of different types of consumers will vary widely. This variation has a

[2] Holding Company Act Release No. 10,055.

direct impact on the cost to serve and consequently on the rates charged for the service. A typical company, for example, serves a wide diversity of customers, who can, however, be classified in a limited number of groups, each with certain common characteristics. In practice these groups are classified as residential or domestic, commercial (small light and power), industrial (large light and power), street and highway lighting, sales to other companies for resale, etc. Generally the first three groups account for 80 percent or more of total sales and revenues.

The different groups have varying characteristics. Stability and sustained growth are typical of the residential segment of the load. Residential customers are commonly there to stay; their demand for service persists in bad times as well as good; residential sales and revenues reflect the steadily growing electrification of American home life.

The commercial load has similar elements of stability, although it is vulnerable to the effects of a serious depression. This customer classification includes stores, office buildings, restaurants, hotels, theaters, hospitals, garages, filling stations, etc. This is largely a lighting and small motor load, since if the demand gets large enough it will result in the customer coming into the industrial classification. Air conditioning is more used by commercial customers than by any other class, although both residential and industrial air conditioning are becoming increasingly important. The commercial load has similar, although somewhat less pronounced, growth characteristics than does the residential.

A company's large light and power load will essentially reflect the industrial make-up of the service territory. It will be the most vulnerable to business depression, fluctuating largely with the economic activity and prosperity of the area. Rates for service are comparatively low, primarily reflecting the large volume of sales and the part played by this type of business in improving the system load factor. If the customer is large enough, moreover, the rates are effectively held down by the possibility of his installing his own electric generating equipment. Because industrial rates appear low, analysts frequently fall into the error of assuming that they are unprofitable. In times of normal cost relationships the assumption is not warranted; utility companies are almost always in a position to supply power to industrial customers at rates that are both reasonable to the user and directly profitable to the supplier. A large portion of the business is off-peak and subject to low incremental costs.

Analyzing Consumption by Categories. In addition to a breakdown of operating revenue according to customer classification, the analyst should also have a similar breakdown of kilowatt-hour (or, for gas, thousands of cubic feet) sales and customers in order to compute average rates for the service and average customer use. In respect to domestic service, for example, low average annual consumption indicates that the possibility may exist of expanding this portion of revenue by successful promotional efforts. Low average industrial use per customer, combined with a large number of customers, indicates that the company serves small, usually diversified industrial users.

Table 21-1 represents for the electric utility industry as a whole a breakdown of operating revenue, sales, and customers, together with average revenue per kilowatt-hour, average use per customer, and average annual bill for the years 1949 and 1959.

Table 21-1. Electric Utility Industry, 1959

	Revenue (000 omitted)	Percent	Kwh sales (000,000 omitted)	Percent	Customers (000 omitted)	Percent
Residential.....	$3,327,266	35.0	125,765	22.5	38,266	83.1
Rural..........	349,182	3.7	15,032	2.7	2,160	4.7
Commercial....	2,322,494	24.5	92,839	16.6	5,143*	11.2
Industrial......	2,461,222	24.9	230,304	41.2	295*	0.6
Street lighting..	155,486	1.6	4,832	0.9	41	0.1
Resale.........	531,026	5.6	71,101	12.7	4	—
Other..........	350,989	3.7	18,687	3.4	128	0.3
Total........	$9,497,664	100.0	558,560	100.0	36,037	100.0

	Average annual rate, cents		Average annual use, kwh		Average annual bill	
	1949	1959	1949	1959	1949	1959
Residential......	3.01	2.64	1,636	3,287	$ 49.21	$ 86.95
Rural..........	2.16	2.32	4,270	6,959	92.05	161.70
Commercial.....	2.84	2.50	8,877	18,050	252.00	452.00
Industrial......	1.17	1.07	201,351	780,700	2,348.00	8,343.00

* Approximate.
Source: Federal Power Commission.

Operating Expenses. The typical utility income statement, as reported in the annual reports to stockholders, usually segregates operating expenses under the following headings:

> Maintenance
> Depreciation
> Federal income taxes
> Other taxes
> Other operating expense

In some instances the cost of purchased power or gas is also shown separately. The total of these expenses, expressed as a percentage of revenue, is commonly called the "operating ratio."[3]

[3] Standard & Poor's Corporation defines operating ratio as the ratio of operating

Newer Concept of Operating Ratio. In our view, the "operating ratio" described above is almost meaningless and serves no useful purpose, either in comparing one company with another or as an indication of the trend of the actual operating results. In computing a ratio that is indicative of operating results, we believe that both depreciation and Federal income taxes should be excluded from expenses. Depreciation represents a non-cash-accounting expense, the function of which is to recover the net cost of depreciable property over its service life. It is thus more correctly related to capital investment than to expenses involved in operation. Federal income taxes, although a recognized item of operating expense from a regulatory standpoint, are levied against earnings after debt service and in effect represent a splitting of profits with the government. Their impact, in relation to revenue, varies widely from company to company; to include them in a determination of operating ratio produces wholly noncomparable results, both in a long-term trend analysis and in comparing one company with another. In our opinion, a much more illuminating and satisfactory ratio is that which relates what might be called the "operating profit" to revenue. This will be discussed below.

Concept of Operating Profit. The above expense breakdown, although it represents standard practice, does not reveal the basic cost elements involved in operations, and does not show what might be called the homogeneous cost factors. A certain amount of rearrangement of operating expenses by the analyst will greatly help to bring out the important cost relationships and trends. A more informative presentation is as follows:

> Wages and salaries
> Cost of fuel
> Cost of purchased power
> Operating taxes
> Other direct operating expense

The balance remaining after deducting these direct costs of doing business might be called the "operating profit." While this is not a term either used or recognized in the uniform system of accounts, we believe that it is useful for the analyst. It represents the profits from operations, before making provision for depreciation and before Federal income taxes. Over a period of years the ratio of this balance to revenue is the most revealing index of a company's success in controlling expenses, and thus indicates the degree of continuing basic profitableness of operations.

---

costs, including maintenance-depreciation allowances and taxes, to gross revenues. Moody's Investors Service excludes income taxes from operating expenses in computing the ratio, but includes depreciation.

The deduction of depreciation and Federal income taxes from the operating profit leaves *net operating income,* or the amount available from operations to meet the capital costs, interest and dividends, etc., of the enterprise. ("Other direct operating expenses," as classified above, include rents, insurance, cost of materials and supplies other than fuel, legal expense, etc. While the number of items included is considerable, the aggregate dollar figure is usually not large.)

It seems to us that this method of operating-cost presentation segregates expenses into their more basic elements and thus permits more satisfactory analysis. For the electric industry as a whole, the composite income statements for 1949 and 1959, including operating expenses segregated as above, are shown in Table 21-2.

During this ten-year period the electric industry continued the strong growth trend that has persisted since its inception. Operating revenues in 1959 showed an increase of 117 percent over 1949, indicating an average compound rate of growth of about 8.1 percent per year. Something close to this growth rate is expected to continue almost as far ahead as we care to look. The many uses for electric service in just about every area of our economic lives are far from reaching saturation levels, and the record to date has been one of constantly developing new applications. We see no reason why this should not continue. During the past decade, also, the industry has maintained its strong financial characteristics, as shown by the ratio tabulations in Table 21-2.

If a company generates a large portion of its power in hydroelectric plants, its fuel bill will, of course, be correspondingly reduced. Wages and salaries would also be somewhat lower, since fewer operating employees are commonly required in water-power plants than in steam-generating stations. The increased operating profit, however, would be offset by the higher capital costs usually involved in hydroelectric operation.

Additional cost breakdowns which the analyst should have at hand for a complete study are those which show in detail production, transmission, distribution, customers' accounting and collecting, sales-promotion expense, and administrative and general expense. For example, sales-promotion expense, which includes the cost of advertising, canvassing, and soliciting new business, is largely subject to managerial control and is frequently a significant item on a per-share of common stock basis. This provides a certain cushion of reserve earning power which should be taken into consideration by the analyst. In addition to the dollar amounts, the appropriate unit figures should be available for comparative purposes, such as production cost per kilowatt-hour sold, sales-promotion expense per customer, etc. Since all security analysis involves some study of trends, it is necessary to have this information covering a period of years. "A little knowledge is a dangerous thing," and data for a single year, no matter how detailed and comprehensive, may reflect temporary

Table 21-2. Electric Utility Industry, 1949 and 1959

	1949		1959	
	Amount (000 omitted)	Percent	Amount (000 omitted)	Percent
Operating revenue*.............	$4,381,849	100.0	$9,497,664	100.0
Wages and salaries*..........	$ 853,744	19.5	$1,545,577	16.3
Cost of fuel*.................	698,765	15.9	1,447,105	15.2
Purchased power*............	343,651	7.9	407,994	4.3
Operating taxes*†............	438,781	10.0	955,820	10.0
Other operating expense*.......	423,766	9.7	888,538	9.4
Total direct operating expense*...	$2,758,707	63.0	$5,245,034	55.2
Operating profit*...............	$1,623,142	37.0	$4,252,630	44.8
Depreciation*................	385,418	8.8	994,475	10.5
Federal income taxes*.........	347,668	7.9	1,218,215	12.8
Net operating income*..........	$ 890,056	20.3	$2,039,940	21.5
Other income................	131,694	3.0	245,766	2.6
Gross income.................	$1,021,750	23.3	$2,285,706	24.1
Charges.....................	264,491	6.0	629,870	6.6
Net income...................	$ 757,259	17.3	$1,655,836	17.5
Preferred dividends...........	103,484	2.4	186,089	2.0
Balance for common............	$ 653,775	14.9	$1,469,747	15.5
Common dividends...........	456,365	10.4	1,031,737	10.9
Balance to surplus..............	$ 197,410	4.5	$ 438,010	4.6

	Ratios	
	1949	1959
Operating profit..	37.0%	44.8%
Gross income, percent capitalization and surplus‡.............	6.1%	6.3%
Times charges earned (before taxes).........................	5.17×	5.56×
Times charges and preferred dividends earned (after taxes)......	2.78×	2.80×
Earnings for common, percent common equity.................	10.2%	10.7%
Common dividends, percent earnings for common (payout)......	69.6%	70.2%
Earned surplus times common dividends.....................	2.62×	3.25×

* Electric operations only.
† Includes all taxes other than Federal income taxes.
‡ For the purpose of computing this ratio, interest charged to construction has been added to gross income. Capitalization and surplus represent year-end figures.
SOURCE: Federal Power Commission.

distortions that might be highly misleading if the data were used as a basis for future projections.[4]

Table 21-3 shows, for the electric industry as a whole, the detail of these direct operating expenses for the years 1949 and 1959.

Table 21-3. Electric Industry Operating Costs

Item	1949		1959	
	Amount (000 omitted)	Percent revenue	Amount (000 omitted)	Percent revenue
Production expense:				
Steam generation................	$ 949,733	21.7	$1,908,436	20.1
Per kwh generated............	5.11 mills		3.93 mills	
Hydro generation................	$ 48,520	1.1	$ 55,221	0.6
Per kwh generated............	0.99 mills		0.98 mills	
Other generation................	$ 11,375	0.2	$ 5,709	0.1
Purchased power................	343,651	7.9	407,994	4.3
Other, net.....................	(1,239)		(4,201)	
Total.....................	$1,352,040	30.9	$2,381,561	25.1
Per kwh sold.................	5.27 mills		4.26 mills	
Transmission expense.............	$ 71,558	1.6	$ 144,762	1.5
Per kwh sold..................	0.28 mills		0.26 mills	
Distribution expense..............	$ 393,102	9.0	$ 720,419	7.6
Per customer served............	$11.66		$15.65	
Customers' accounting and collection				
expense.....................	$ 148,646	3.4	$ 285,253	3.0
Per customer served............	$4.41		$6.20	
Sales promotion expense...........	$ 69,937	1.6	$ 159,400	1.7
Per customer served............	$2.07		$3.46	
Administrative and general........	$ 284,643	6.5	$ 597,819	6.3
Taxes (excluding Federal income tax)	438,781	10.0	955,820	10.0
Total.......................	$2,758,707	63.0	$5,245,034	55.2

SOURCE: Federal Power Commission.

Maintenance and Depreciation. In the above tables it will be noted that maintenance expense is not shown separately, although it is almost universally so reported in the published income statement. By this omission we do not mean to decry its importance, and the analyst will certainly want to have the figure for this item of expense. Actually, the bulk of maintenance expense consists of wages and salaries, the other principal item being materials and supplies used for maintenance purposes.

---

[4] This statement applies, of course, both to individual company analysis and to industry analysis. Perhaps we should emphasize that we show industry tables for the years 1949 and 1959, not because they serve as a basis for analysis, but rather because they indicate the prevailing financial relationships.

As a practical matter, utility properties are almost always maintained in a high state of operating efficiency; the public requirement to provide service of certain standards necessitates this unless the company is to run into trouble. For the electric industry as a whole, maintenance expense averaged about 6.7 percent of operating revenue for the 11 years 1949–1959, but it will vary considerably from company to company. Comparisons between companies have thus less significance than a study of a company's own record over a period of years. If the ratio of maintenance to revenue shows a marked increase in any one year, it calls for an investigation by the analyst, since it usually means that abnormal circumstances, such as unexpected storm damage, may be causing an understatement of what would otherwise be normal earnings.

Example: In 1954 Narragansett Electric Company's maintenance expense, which had averaged about 8.1 percent of revenue for the previous seven years, increased to 12.7 percent of revenue, reflecting a substantial amount of hurricane repair costs. While the effect on earnings was significant, it was mitigated by a reduction in income taxes as a result of hurricane losses. In 1955 maintenance expense declined to 8.6 percent of revenue.

In the past it was common practice to associate maintenance and depreciation and to express the sum of the combined provisions as a percentage of revenue. A rule-of-thumb measure of the adequacy of the combined amount was to accept 15 percent of revenue as generally satisfactory. This percentage was frequently required as a minimum in bond indentures, and resulted in a provision of about 3.7 percent of the plant account where the latter was four times operating revenue. It corresponds closely to the experience of the electric industry as a whole over the past 12 years.

Depreciation Related to Plant, Not to Revenue. In our opinion, however, depreciation should be considered separately, and a more realistic approach is to show it as percentage of plant. The function of depreciation expense is to recover the cost of plant over the period of its service life. By expressing the annual accrual as a percentage of plant, the analyst can probably more easily form an opinion as to its adequacy. In the previous chapter we said that we felt that today the analyst can generally accept as authoritative and realistic the annual accrual for depreciation as reported. This reflects the fact that the great majority of companies now provide for depreciation on a service-life basis accrued in accordance with actual studies made of their own properties.

For the entire electric industry the annual provision for depreciation nas averaged approximately 2.2 percent of gross utility plant over the past 11 years. In the case of a hydroelectric company, with a large investment in dams and other relatively long-lived property, a somewhat lower percentage of plant, say from 1¾ to 2 percent, might be viewed as satisfactory.

Income Tax Depreciation. In the 1951 edition we stated that as a general guide to the adequacy of the reported accrual for depreciation the provision made for Federal income tax purposes could be used. However, because of changes in the income tax laws this is no longer the case in respect to the great majority of utility companies. As mentioned in Chapter 20, the Revenue Code of 1954 was amended to provide for what is now generally called "liberalized" depreciation. This permits the taxpayer to claim larger depreciation allowances for tax purposes during the early years of property life than does the straight-line method. (See Chapter 20, p. 273.) Since most companies are continuing to use straight-line depreciation for corporate reporting purposes, the book provision may vary substantially in any one year from the depreciation accrual claimed for tax purposes.

Example: For the year 1959 the Montana Power Company showed in its annual report to stockholders the amount of $4,008,766 as provision for depreciation and depletion. In a footnote to its financial statements, the company mentioned that it had adopted liberalized depreciation for tax purposes in respect to certain property additions made after December 31, 1953, and that it was also using accelerated amortization in respect to certain facilities that had been certified as attributable to national defense. Thus its depreciation and amortization for tax purposes aggregated $6,940,800, of which $4,227,200 represented straight-line depreciation on property installed prior to 1954 which was being depreciated on this basis, $1,403,600 represented liberalized depreciation on those property additions being depreciated on this basis, and $1,310,-000 represented accelerated amortization.

The two principal methods permitted by Section 167 of the 1954 tax law for accelerating depreciation are (1) the declining-balance method and (2) the sum-of-the-years-digits method. These methods were made available in respect to property additions made after December 31, 1953. In addition, of course, a company, may, if it so elects, continue to use straight-line depreciation.

The Straight-line Method. Under this method, the cost less net salvage value of depreciable property is charged as depreciation expense in equal annual amounts over its useful life. For example, if a property item has a cost, after net salvage, of $100 and a five-year service life, depreciation expense would be $20 per year.

The Declining-balance Method. This method permits the tax payer to use a depreciation rate not exceeding twice the straight-line rate. This rate, however, is applied not to the original cost of the facility, as in the case of straight-line depreciation, but to the declining balance of cost. In the above example, which assumed a 20 percent depreciation rate each year, the declining-balance method would permit a 40 percent rate, applied to the $100 of cost in the first year, to $60 of cost in the second year, and to $36 of cost in the third year, etc. Under this method there will always remain some balance of cost which is not recovered. Consequently the Internal Revenue Code permits a company which adopts this method to change to a straight-line depreciation at any time.

The Sum-of-the-years'-digits Method. Under this method, the digits represent the remaining property life to the beginning of each year. Thus, the digits for property with a five-year life are 5, 4, 3, 2, 1, the sum of these numbers being 15. Depreciation expense for the first year is five-fifteenths of the cost of the property, for the second year four-fifteenths of cost, and for the third year three-fifteenths of cost, etc.

A comparison of the way in which the three methods recover cost is shown in the following table:

Annual Depreciation Expense for Property with Five-year Life and Cost after Net Salvage of $100

Year	Straight-line method	Declining-balance method	Sum-of-years'-digits method
1	$ 20.00	$40.00	$ 33.33
2	20.00	24.00	26.67
3	20.00	14.40	20.00
4	20.00	8.64	13.33
5	20.00	5.18	6.67
Total.......	$100.00	$92.22	$100.00

Provision for Future Income Taxes. When a company adopts liberalized depreciation for income tax purposes the effect is to reduce taxable earnings and consequently the amount of the income tax payable in respect to the year's operations. Considerable divergence of opinion has developed as to whether the *reduced* tax is all that should be treated as expense in the year's income statement, or whether an additional provision, equal to the amount by which the tax is reduced, should also be treated as expense for income reporting purposes.

The first procedure has come to be called the "flow-through," or "actual-tax," method, while the second is designated as "normalization." As of the date of this writing (the summer of 1961) both the Federal Power Commission and the Securities and Exchange Commission have taken a position in favor of "normalization," with the provisions for future taxes to be carried to a special balance-sheet account, as discussed in Chapter 20.

The state regulatory commissions are widely split as to the proper accounting treatment for calculating expenses for rate-making purposes. A survey of cases involving the rate and accounting treatment of income tax deferrals, made as of June 1, 1961, showed that twenty state commissions favored "normalization" for accounting purposes, while seven commissions favored "flow-through." For rate-making purposes, however, sixteen commissions approved or prescribed "flow-through" vs. fifteen permitting "normalization."

This poses, unfortunately, a difficult problem to analysts and one to which we have no satisfactory answer at this time. If a company is using liberalized depreciation for tax purposes and is following deferred-tax accounting, i.e., normalization, reported earnings will be lower than if it were using flow-through. If at any time it decides to adopt flow-through, this may result in a sharp increase in reported earnings, which is a result merely of a change in accounting treatment rather than an improvement in the company's business.

Example: For the year 1958 Long Island Lighting Company reported earnings of $1.62 per share. Net income as shown was after a provision for deferred Federal income tax, due to liberalized depreciation, of $2,281,240, equal to almost 31 cents per share. In its report for the first quarter of 1959, the company stated that it had adopted flow-through accounting in accordance with a requirement by the New York Public Service Commission, and this resulted in a sudden jump in earnings reported for the twelve months ended March 31, 1959 to $1.99 per share. Of this increase, an amount equal to 31 cents per share was wholly due to the changed accounting treatment. The higher reported earnings also caused a significant rise in the market price of the stock.

A contrary action was taken by Montana Power Company in 1960. This company had been using flow-through accounting, and earnings for the common stock were shown in its 1959 annual report at $1.36 per share. In December 1960, however, the Montana Public Service Commission ordered "normalization" accounting. The change in accounting practice was retroactive, and in its 1960 annual report the company showed restated earnings for 1959 at $1.32 per share. While the difference here was not large, under other circumstances it might well be.

In view of the variations in accounting treatment and consequently the manner in which different companies report their earnings, it is apparent that a comparison of price-earnings ratios between companies which use divergent tax treatment is difficult to make with any logic. As mentioned above, the problem is not easy to solve. As long as one or the other tax treatment is prescribed by the public service commissions for rate-making purposes, the analyst is hardly on firm ground if he decides arbitrarily to adjust earnings so as to conform to some other company's method of treatment.

It is to be hoped that in time a general uniformity of treatment will be adopted. In the meantime, we think that when a company practices tax normalization, the analyst should recognize that flow-through accounting may be adopted at any time, and he should be prepared for the higher reported earnings that may result.

Charges in Lieu of Taxes. It occasionally happens that a company will have special and nonrecurring charges during the year that serve to reduce Federal income taxes sharply. These charges are usually not of an operating-expense nature, but generally result from the writing off of unamortized debt discount and expense, redemption premiums and expenses in connection with bond refunding, special property write-downs, or the like.

The SEC has taken the stand that when charges of this sort are incurred, the provision for Federal income taxes included as an operating expense deduction should represent no more than the tax believed to be actually payable and should not be increased by an amount, even though separately shown, designed to reflect what the tax would have been had the special transactions not occurred.

In the Commission's view, any reduction in taxes occasioned by refunding expense or similar transactions may, however, be appropriately recognized by a special charge deducted from gross income (balance available for charges) provided that the caption for the item indicates clearly the nature and amount of the item charged off. Company practice is in accordance with this policy.

From an accounting standpoint we are in full accord with this method of presentation. From the viewpoint of income-statement analysis, however, we think it is plain that this special charge should not be included with interest and other items used in computing fixed-charge coverage. We believe, rather, that irrespective of the strictly correct accounting procedure, it should be considered as part of Federal income taxes that would normally be payable on the basis of the year's operating results and as such should be deducted before arriving at gross income.

Composition of Fixed Charges. Fixed charges normally include those items of capital expense which are of a fixed, recurring nature and which must be deducted from gross income before arriving at the balance of earnings available for dividends. They include, of course, all interest requirements on outstanding debt, as well as various other cash or book-keeping obligations of a periodic nature. A list of these charges (or credits thereagainst), as usually itemized in public utility income statements, includes the following:

Interest on long-term debt, representing the interest payable on outstanding bonds and other funded debt

Other interest charges, including interest on notes payable, advances and other unfunded debt, such as customers' deposits, open accounts, claims and judgments, assessments, etc.

Amortization of debt discount, premium, and expense, representing the portion of unamortized debt, discount, premium, and expense chargeable to the period

Taxes assumed on interest, representing amounts paid to bondholders or to government agencies in their behalf in respect to income taxes when these taxes are assumed by the company

Other income deductions, including miscellaneous charges to income not provided for elsewhere, such as donations, decline in the value of investments chargeable to income, etc. (these are of minor importance)

Interest charged to construction (credit), representing credits for interest charged to construction and capitalized

With the exception of the last item, which is discussed at some length below, we do not believe that the above charges require additional comment.

Interest Charged to Construction. The Uniform System of Accounts provides that this item shall be included as a credit among gross income deductions, i.e., deducted from interest charges, amortization of debt discount and expense, etc. Interest during construction represents a component of construction costs and includes the net cost of borrowed funds used for construction purposes and a reasonable rate upon the utility's own funds when so used. The period for which interest may be capitalized is limited to the period of construction and ceases as soon as the plant or portion of plant is placed in operation or is completed.

The theory of this charge is that during the construction period the capital involved is earning no return, although it has to be paid for, and that its cost or "hire" is therefore a true part of the cost of constructing the facilities. The rate of interest will vary from company to company, depending upon the type of facilities under construction and the character of the funds, i.e., borrowed or equity capital, being used. The usual practice is not to charge interest during construction on small expenditures or on facilities that will be completed in a short period of time.

Effect of Interest Charged to Construction on Fixed-charge Coverage. During periods of rapid expansion and heavy construction this item may become sizable and have a marked effect on the fixed-charge coverage ratio. In the case of Idaho Power Company, for example, total fixed charges for 1958 amounted to $2,164,417 and were covered 6.44 times by gross income (before tax) of $13,915,101. Fixed charges, however, included a credit item of $3,057,583 for interest charged to construction. The actual interest and other net deductions paid totaled $5,222,000 and were covered 2.67 times by available gross income. In a situation of this sort the higher coverage figure does not give an accurate indication of the true measure of earnings protection for the bonds. The lower figure, however, tends to understate the true coverage and an adjustment of the figures should appropriately be made by the analyst. The suggested adjusted coverage would be determined as follows.

Rather than treat interest charged to construction as a credit among gross income deductions, as is called for by the accounting regulations, we believe that in a situation of this sort it should be treated as additional earnings and added to gross income. Actually, Idaho Power Company had a substantial amount of construction work in progress during the year which was contributing nothing to the earnings of the enterprise. The most practical measure of "earnings" of this nonproductive investment is that amount determined by the management as appropriate to be capitalized, viz., the interest charged to construction. With the inclusion of this amount, gross income would have been increased to $16,972,684 and the actual interest and other charges would have been covered 3.25 times.

This ratio, based on the 1958 rate of earnings, would appear to indicate the coverage protection more satisfactorily than either of the ratios based on the figures as reported.

Effect of Interest Charged to Construction on Over-all Coverage for Preferred Dividends. The distortion indicated above will be equally marked in respect to the over-all coverage for fixed charges and preferred dividends. In addition to Idaho Power's reported charges of $2,164,417, preferred dividends amounted to $860,000. The sum of these divided into gross income (after tax) indicated a coverage of 3.39 times. However, actual interest and other requirements plus preferred dividends amounted to $6,082,000, for which reported gross income provided a coverage of only 1.69 times. If gross income were increased to include interest charged to construction, the over-all coverage for preferred dividends and actual charges would have been 2.19 times.

As in the case of the coverage for fixed charges, we believe that this latter ratio more correctly indicates the earnings protection for preferred dividends than either the 3.39 or the 1.69 times coverage arrived at on the basis of the reported figures.

Effect of Interest Charged to Construction on Earnings for the Common Stock. A moment's thought will reveal that the accounting treatment of this item has no effect on the earnings available for the common. Treating it as a credit against gross income deductions results in the same equity earnings as though it were added back to gross income.

A Suggested Rearrangement of the Income Account. Methods of financial presentation that have been developed by the accounting profession do not always set forth the data in the manner most helpful to security analysis. The purpose of the annual income statement, for example, is to give the financial results of the year's operations, but the form of reporting does not permit a quick comprehension of those factors which have a determinative effect on the balance coming through to the common stock. The analyst, therefore, should not hesitate to explore new methods and techniques of presentation.

With this in mind, we have used for a number of years what might be called an analytical arrangement of the income account, which, we believe, presents the record of operations in a considerably more informative manner. It embodies the inclusion of certain key ratios that indicate at a glance whether or not the various items are "normal" in their relationships. This is particularly important under present-day conditions of rapid expansion and constant new financing.

The reported earnings for any period may fail to reflect the full impact of items that would have a significant bearing on earnings if operations should stabilize at the current level. The principal items and the questions concerning them are the following:

1. Is the operating profit ratio at approximately normal levels?
2. Is the depreciation provision adequate or reasonable?
3. Is the Federal income tax accrual normal in relation to earnings, or does it reflect any nonrecurring factors?
4. Is the over-all return reasonable, excessive, or deficient in relation to the estimated base?
5. Do fixed charges reflect the full service requirements of existing debt?
6. Do preferred dividends represent the full requirements of the outstanding preferred stock?

Each of these factors has an important bearing on the validity of the reported earnings. If, for example, fixed charges or preferred dividends do not reflect the full requirements of the existing capitalization, the earnings as shown for the common stock will be overstated *on the basis of the period's volume of business,* and it will require an increase in volume to maintain the common-stock earnings at the reported level. It may be, of course, that there is every reason to expect this increase, since the very fact that the income statement does not reflect the full impact of senior charges indicates that a portion of the capitalization, and therefore the investment which it represents, has not been outstanding for a full year and is not making its full contribution to earning power.

On the other hand it may be that the company is earning what appears to be close to a maximum permissible return in relation to the total current investment. In this event, no increase in the ratio of gross income to the earnings base can be expected, and the mounting impact of senior charges will serve gradually to reduce per-share earnings.

Example: The following method of income presentation helps to point out a company's earnings position in regard to these factors. Pacific Gas and Electric Company provides an interesting case (Table 21-4). We offer this example as it was presented in the 1951 edition of this book. While the period covered is now somewhat remote in time, the case illustrates a technique of analysis which is equally applicable today.

The first column shows the company's average revenue, expenses, and earnings for the three-year period 1946–1948, together with the key ratios measuring the impact of the six items listed above. Over this three-year period, per-share earnings on the common stock averaged $2.60, based on the average number of shares outstanding. The second column similarly presents the results of 1949 operations.

Table 21-4. Pacific Gas and Electric Company

(Dollar figures in thousands)

	Average 1946–1948	1949	1949 adjusted	
			Basis *A*	Basis *B*
Operating revenue.................	$185,480	$217,225	$217,225	$234,437
Operating profit...................	$ 74,611	$ 72,665	$ 72,665	$ 89,877
Percent revenue................	40.3%	33.5%	33.5%	38.2%
Depreciation....................	$ 23,912	$ 24,982	$ 24,982	$ 24,982
Percent plant..................	2.4%	2.0%	2.0%	2.0%
Charges........................	10,243	12,348	$ 16,759	16,759
Percent year-end debt...........	2.6%	2.2%	3.0%	3.0%
Balance.........................	$ 40,456	$ 35,335	$ 30,924	$ 48,136
Federal income tax.............	$ 14,786	8,017	9,737	17,600
Percent balance before tax.......	36.5%	22.7%	31.5%	36.5%
Balance.........................	$ 25,670	$ 27,318	$ 21,187	$ 30,536
Other income...................	353	285	285	285
Net income......................	$ 26,023	$ 27,603	$ 21,472	$ 30,821
Gross income (net plus charges).....	$ 36,266	$ 39,951	$ 38,231	$ 47,580
Percent of capitalization.........	4.6%	3.9%	3.7%	4.7%
Net income......................	$ 26,023	$ 27,603	$ 21,472	$ 30,821
Preferred dividends.............	8,561	10,582	10,582	10,582
Percent preferred stock..........	5.6%	5.1%	5.1%	5.1%
Balance for common..............	$ 17,462	$ 17,021	$ 10,890	$ 20,239
Common dividends.............	$ 13,466	$ 16,191		
Percent pay-out.................	77.1%	95.0%		
Average number of common shares outstanding...................	6,733,000	8,095,597		
Earned per share...............	$2.60	$2.10	$1.34	$2.50
Common shares outstanding at end of period.....................	....	8,280,780		
Earned per share...............	....	$2.06	$1.31	$2.45
Dividend per share...............	$2.00	$2.00		

The principal observations in regard to the 1949 income statement would appear to be

1. The operating profit ratio has declined sharply.
2. Charges appear understated in relation to the year-end outstanding debt.
3. The Federal income tax provision appears decidedly low.
4. The over-all return, as measured by the ratio of gross income to total capitalization and surplus, is very low.
5. If revenue should stabilize at the 1949 level and there should be no improvement in the operating-profit ratio, earnings for the common stock would fail by a wide margin to cover the dividend.

The basis for this last observation is shown in the third column, in which certain adjustments are made to the reported 1949 earnings. In this column (Basis *A*), charges are adjusted to eliminate a credit item of

$4,411,889 representing interest charged to construction. As we mentioned earlier, this is a bookkeeping item and does not actually reduce interest requirements that have to be met. The Federal income tax provision is increased by $1,719,857, to offset a reduction of this amount representing a previous year's accrual to cover tax deficiencies in prior years not subsequently considered necessary. This special tax credit was authorized by the California Public Utilities Commission in partial compensation for the increase in the cost of providing gas service. It results, however, in an overstatement of earnings for 1949. The effect of these adjustments, as shown in the column entitled Basis A, results in per-share earnings being reduced to $1.34 based on average shares outstanding, and to $1.31 based on the number of shares outstanding at the end of the year.

This, of course, represents rather drastic treatment and is not indicative of the reasonably expectable earning power of the company. In his approach toward a determination of the latter, the analyst would make certain other adjustments on the basis of information available to him. In recognition of the low rate of over-all return, the company in November 1949 was granted an increase in gas rates of approximately $4,000,000 on an annual basis, and in October 1949 it applied for (and was subsequently granted) an $8,800,000 increase in electric rates. The fourth column, Basis B, again restates 1949 earnings: (1) to increase operating revenue and operating profit by $12,800,000 on the assumption that the higher rates had been in effect throughout the year and had increased earnings before income taxes by this amount; (2) to increase revenue and operating profit by $4,411,869, the amount of interest charged to construction, on the assumption that the inoperative investment had earned this amount during the year. The only other change made in this column is to adjust Federal income taxes to the same level in relation to earnings that prevailed during the 1946–1948 period as shown in the first column. As will be seen, these adjustments restore earnings to approximately the level that prevailed in the 1946–1948 period.

The conclusion to be drawn is that earnings in 1949 were clearly inadequate and that, unless a sharp improvement could be assured, the mounting impact of senior charges would soon reduce the balance for common to a point where the dividend would not be earned. It soon became apparent, moreover, that the rate increases which were granted would be insufficient to provide a satisfactory return, and the company consequently applied for a further increase in gas rates to become effective January 1, 1951, estimated to increase operating revenue for the year 1951 by $15,600,000.

Sequel: Earnings in 1950 showed a sharp improvement, rising to $2.51 per share. While they declined again in 1951 because of the impact of higher senior charges and the issuance of additional common shares, they subsequently recovered to $2.82 in 1953 and have shown a generally rising trend since.

Common Dividend Payout. Generally speaking, the electric utility industry has followed the practice of paying out in dividends on the common stock a relatively high proportion of available earnings. This policy, we believe, has been thoroughly justified by the financial and economic characteristics of the business and by the restrictions on earnings imposed by regulation. The industry's persistent growth trend has constantly required large increments of investment capital, and the closely regulated return is insufficient to permit the retention of large amounts of earnings for the purpose of financing property expansion.

Additional capital has been regularly sought from investors, and in respect to equity capital, it is essential that it be obtained at a cost that does not cause any dilution in the existing common stockholders' investment. In fact, we would go further than this and say that when common stock is issued for new capital it is of major importance that it be sold at a price significantly higher than the book-value figure of existing shares. As will be discussed later in Chapter 43, this is a factor of major importance in contributing to an upward trend of per-share earnings.

In our 1951 edition we stated that the dividend payout was one of the important factors influencing the level of market price in relation to earnings. During a period following World War II and continuing until about 1955 there was a clear tendency for utility common-stock prices to be influenced by the dividend payout, with higher prices and higher price-earnings ratios tending to be associated with high payout ratios. This, we believe, reflected doubt in investors' minds as to how successful companies would be in earning a satisfactory return on retained earnings and whether or not retained earnings (earned surplus) might not be vulnerable to required accounting charge-offs. Since about 1955 this attitude on the part of investors has largely changed, no doubt helped by the present high personal income taxes.

Presently there is little evidence that the dividend rate exerts an independent influence on price, as distinct from the earnings rate. In fact, many investors who are principally interested in earnings growth prefer stocks of companies which pay out a relatively small portion of earnings. As long as investors have confidence in regulatory fair treatment of capital we think that, in theory at least, there should be no price discounting of retained earnings vs. earnings paid out in dividends.

In our opinion a conservatively capitalized company which has provided adequate reserves for depreciation and any other necessary purposes, whose income statement correctly reflects earnings, and which is experiencing a growth rate approximating the industry's long-term average, can reasonably pay out in dividends about 75 to 85 percent of the earnings available for the common stock. This presupposes, of course, that gross income reflects no more than a full permissible return and is not vulnerable to adverse regulatory action.

No single figure, however, can be selected as universally appropriate or desirable for all companies or at all times. The actual payout, expressed as a percentage of the balance available, will be largely controlled by two factors, the company's growth rate and the degree of leverage caused by the capital structure.

In respect to leverage, the larger the portion of gross income that is absorbed by senior charges, the smaller the percentage of balance available for the common stock that should be paid out in dividends. This is an obvious corollary of the factor of leverage; as senior fixed charges increase, any variation in gross income becomes increasingly magnified in terms of change in the balance for common. In order to assure a suitable earnings coverage for the common dividend, therefore, the payout ratio should bear an appropriate relationship to senior capital requirements.

In our 1951 edition we suggested that, as a method of correlating this relationship, the appropriate payout should equal the balance for common less 10 percent of gross income (amount available for charges).

The selection of 10 percent as the proportion of total earnings to be retained in the business, carried to surplus, reflected the average practice of independent operating electric utilities over a period of years. For example, the average carry-through to surplus of 10 leading independent electric utility companies over the twenty-year period 1929–1948 was 9.94 percent of gross income. For the five-year period 1935–1939, it was 9.8 percent.[5]

Using 10 percent of gross income, moreover, automatically compels the percentage payout to adjust for the impact of senior charges. This is revealed in Table 21-5, which shows how common dividends decline in relation to available earnings as prior charges increase.

Table 21-5

Gross income....................	$100	$100	$100	$100	$100
Prior charges....................	30	40	50	60	70
Balance for common..............	$ 70	$ 60	$ 50	$ 40	$ 30
Less 10 percent of gross income...	10	10	10	10	10
Common dividends................	$ 60	$ 50	$ 40	$ 30	$ 20
Percent balance for common.....	85.7%	83.4%	80%	75%	66.6%

Since the end of World War II, however, the electric-power industry has been engaged in an accelerated expansion program, and this more rapid rate of growth, with its attendant equity financing and consequent increased dividend requirements, has resulted in a larger retention of earnings and a somewhat lower payout.

[5] The companies used in determining these averages are Boston Edison Company, Cleveland Electric Illuminating Company, Commonwealth Edison Company, Consolidated Edison Company of New York, Consolidated Gas, Electric Light & Power Company of Baltimore, Detroit Edison Company, Central Hudson Gas & Electric Company, Pacific Gas & Electric Company, Southern California Edison Company, and Tampa Electric Company.

This is shown in Table 21-6, which gives the record for the electric utility industry as a whole since 1937, the first year of compilation by the Federal Power Commission.

Table 21-6. Electric Utility Industry: Dividend Payout and Earned Surplus

Year	Percent dividend payout	Balance to surplus, percent of gross income	Earned surplus times common dividends
1937	80.3	9.1	2.62
1938	81.3	8.3	2.67
1939	78.5	10.2	2.53
1940	76.7	11.2	2.65
1941	78.3	10.3	2.80
1942	78.0	9.7	3.09
1943	76.9	10.5	2.96
1944	73.5	12.0	3.08
1945	73.5	12.2	2.60
Average....	77.5	10.4	
1946	66.9	19.6	2.36
1947	72.8	16.8	2.23
1948	70.7	18.3	2.63
1949	69.6	19.3	2.62
1950	71.4	18.4	2.65
1951	76.6	14.5	2.71
1952	72.9	17.5	2.76
1953	72.0	18.2	2.90
1954	73.1	17.4	2.83
1955	72.4	17.9	2.76
1956	73.5	17.2	2.81
1957	72.4	17.9	3.01
1958	71.3	18.5	3.19
1959	70.2	19.2	3.25
Average....	71.6	17.9	

SOURCE: Federal Power Commission.

For the nine-year period, 1937–1945, the dividend payout averaged 77.5 percent and approximately 10 percent of gross income was carried through on average to earned surplus. Over this period, earned surplus remained fairly stable in relation to common dividends, averaging about 2.7 times the annual payment. Since 1945, the payout has been lower, averaging about 72 percent of available earnings; the carry-through has been higher; and earned surplus has been increased to (at the end of 1959) 3.25 times that year's dividends.

If we accept the concept that a major purpose of earned surplus in a regulated industry is to act as a dividend stabilization reserve and that no unusual or substantial charges, other than dividends, are apt to be made against it, then it would seem logical to gear dividend payments to that percentage of earnings which will permit a carry-through of such magnitude as will maintain surplus in some desired ratio to the annual common dividend requirements. What this precise ratio should be cannot be worked out on the basis of any mathematical formula, since in actual practice there are too many variables, but an interesting hypothetical support can be developed for the "10 percent formula" mentioned above. This is shown in Table 21-7.

Table 21-7. Common Dividends and Earned Surplus

Gross income	Balance for common	Common dividends	Percent payout	Balance to surplus	Percent of gross income	Earned surplus	Times common dividends
$100	$ 60	$50	83.3	$10	10.0	$150	3.00×
107	64	53	82.8	11	10.3	161	3.03×
114	68	56	82.4	12	10.5	173	3.09×
123	74	61	82.5	13	10.6	186	3.05×
131	79	65	82.3	14	10.7	200	3.08×
140	84	69	82.1	15	10.7	215	3.12×
150	90	74	82.3	16	10.7	231	3.13×
161	97	80	82.5	17	10.5	248	3.10×
172	103	85	82.5	18	10.5	266	3.13×
184	111	92	82.9	19	10.3	285	3.10×

In this example, we are assuming a rate of growth of 7 percent annually in gross income and a dividend payout of approximately 83 percent. As shown in the table, this results in a carry-through to surplus which maintains the latter at about three times the annual dividend requirement. In our opinion, this would seem to be a desirable relationship.

In the case of more rapidly expanding companies, a lower payout is normally to be expected, since total dividend requirements increase at a faster pace. Moreover, in actual affairs, it is distinctly theoretical to assume that a company's earned surplus may not be subject to unforeseen charges.

In estimating the possible payout in relation to future earnings, the analyst should make sure whether or not there are any restrictions on the payment of common dividends. Such restrictions have been frequently imposed when the ratio of the common-stock equity to the total capitalization is unsatisfactory. The restriction may exist either under the terms of the charter or bond indentures or as a result of action by the SEC. General practice has been to limit the payment to not more than 50 percent of the earnings available when the ratio of common stock equity is less than 20 percent, and to not more than 75 percent of such earnings when the equity ratio is between 20 and 25 percent, with the restriction removed when the ratio exceeds 25 percent. These restrictions are generally inoperative today, but this is not to say that they may not become operative in the future.

Operating and Financial Ratios. A number of operating and financial ratios are commonly used in public utility analysis, most of which are unique in that they reflect factors peculiar to the industry. Some of these have been discussed already; while we shall include them in the following list, we shall not repeat our previous comments.

Operating Profit Ratio. This ratio of net operating income before depreciation and Federal income taxes to operating revenue is the most significant single index for the analyst to follow in studying the trend of a company's operations. Changes therein usually occur slowly and reflect a certain momentum or inertia that provides a valuable guide to the future trend of earnings.

For the electric industry as a whole and for most individual companies, this ratio has shown a remarkable stability over the years, although it declined sharply during the years 1946–1948 as a result of the substantial increase in operating costs of all kinds. This decline, however, was arrested by the end of 1948, and since then the ratio has trended upward, to close to its earlier level. This is shown in Table 21-8.

Table 21-8. Electric Utility Industry: Operating Profit Ratio

1937	45.3%	1949	37.0%
1938	45.3	1950	38.5
1939	46.6	1951	39.2
1940	46.8	1952	41.2
1941	46.0	1953	41.9
1942	46.5	1954	43.1
1943	45.9	1955	44.1
1944	44.8	1956	44.0
1945	44.7	1957	43.3
1946	42.0	1958	44.2
1947	37.5	1959	44.8
1948	34.5	1960	45.1

Maintenance and Depreciation, Percentage of Operating Revenue. For the electric industry as a whole the aggregate of these charges has averaged 15.9 percent of operating revenue over the twenty-three year period 1937–1959, with negligible variation from year to year.

Depreciation Provision, Percentage of Plant. The annual provision for depreciation for the industry as a whole has averaged 2.2 percent over the 1937–1959 period.

Gross Income, Percentage of Capitalization and Surplus. This ratio, which may be used to measure the earned return on the investment, has shown considerable stability, as indicated by Table 21-9.

During periods of rapidly growing plant and recurrent new financing, a company will have large amounts of construction work in progress that are not contributing to earnings, although the investment (or funds marked for construction purposes) will be reflected in the outstanding capitalization. Under these circumstances gross income for the period will not reflect what could be considered the normal earning power of the total capital investment, and the indicated earned return will in effect be understated.

The most practicable correction for the analyst to make under these circumstances is to add back interest charged to construction to gross income, as we suggested earlier in computing fixed-charge coverage.

Example: At the end of 1958 Idaho Power Company had an aggregate capitalization and surplus of $247,474,037, and gross income for the year was $10,249,701. The indicated earned return was thus 4.1 percent, a de-

Table 21-9. Ratio of Gross Income to Sum of Capitalization and Surplus for Electric Utility Industry*

1946	6.75%	1953	6.22%
1947	6.54	1954	6.32
1948	6.19	1955	6.39
1949	6.41	1956	6.41
1950	6.30	1957	6.40
1951	5.92	1958	6.47
1952	6.19	1959	6.55

* In computing this ratio, capitalization and surplus represents the average of year-end figures, and gross income includes interest charged to construction.

cidedly low figure. Average capital investment for the year, however, (based on the average of year-end figures) was $219,562,273, and the credit for interest charged to construction for 1958 was $3,057,583. If this is added to gross income, the indicated return on average capital was 6.1 percent, a more reasonable rate.

Average Residential Rate, Use, and Bill. The cost of electric service, particularly to the residential or domestic consumer, measured on a unit basis, has shown a persistent decline over the years, primarily reflecting the steady growth in per-customer use. In estimating the vulnerability of rates to reduction by regulatory action, the analyst should take into consideration the level of the rates of the company under review, as compared with other companies in the same general area and with the same general operating characteristics. The commonly used measure of the rate is based on the average revenue per kilowatt-hour sold. This figure should be considered in conjunction with the average use, or average kilowatt-hour sold per customer served, since, because of the declining unit price characteristics of electric rate structures, a low average rate in part reflects high average use.

Low rates and high use are also a direct result of successful promotional efforts on the part of the company, a measure of which is indicated by sales-promotion expense shown on a per-customer basis. This figure is given above (page 288) for the electric industry as a whole in Table 21-3, showing the breakdown of electric operating costs. For the year

1959 it was $3.46 per customer. Variations in this item among companies will be considerable, since it will largely depend upon managerial policy.

Success in the design of the rate structure from the standpoint of producing revenue is indicated by the trend of average revenue per customer. Declining rates and increasing use obviously do not benefit a company unless they are accompanied by an increase in revenue.

For the electric industry as a whole these averages have shown, in recent years, the trends indicated in Table 21-10.

Table 21-10. Residential Electric Service

Year	Average rate, cents	Average annual use, kwh	Average annual bill
1948	3.01	1,563	$47.05
1952	2.77	2,169	60.08
1956	2.60	2,969	77.19
1960	2.47	3,790	93.61

Average Monthly Residential Bill. Residential rate comparisons among companies, on a cost-to-customer basis, can also be studied on the basis of average monthly bills.[6] In doing this, care should be taken to compare companies with generally similar operating and service characteristics and usually in the same general area. Many factors operate to cause differences in the level of rates and they should be taken into consideration by the analyst.

Table 21-11 shows the average monthly bill for residential service in all cities with a population of 2,500 or more, as reported by the Federal Power Commission as of January 1, 1935, 1940, 1955, and 1960. Prior to 1950 there had been a steady downward movement in the level of rates for residential service. Subsequently, this downward trend was arrested, and a slight upward movement in the averages has continued since 1951.

Table 21-11. Average Monthly Residential Electric Bill, All Cities of 2,500 Population or More

Date	100 kwh	250 kwh	500 kwh
Jan. 1, 1935.......	$4.67	$8.91	$13.87
Jan. 1, 1940.......	4.06	7.37	10.55
Jan. 1, 1950.......	3.76	6.98	10.11
Jan. 1, 1955.......	3.86	7.18	10.30
Jan. 1, 1960.......	4.04	7.44	10.62

[6] These data are published annually by the Federal Power Commission and are also reported by Institutional Utility Service, Inc.

System Peak and Load Factor. A characteristic of the electric utility industry is the hourly and seasonal variation in the demand for, and consequently output of, electric energy and the fact that it is not feasible to store electricity in amounts sufficient to meet the demand during the relatively short periods when consumption is heaviest.

"System peak" means the highest combined demand upon the system that occurs during the year; it is expressed in kilowatts (kw) for a limited period of time, generally one hour. Not only the installed generating capacity but also the transmission and distribution facilities must be adequate to handle this maximum demand for power from all the connected customers, with a reasonable reserve to take care of emergency breakdowns or outages and some provision for normal growth. System peak, therefore, rather than the number of kilowatt-hours (kwh) which are produced or sold, determines the capital investment required.

Since the capital charges, including interest, dividends and depreciation, etc., constitute a large part of the over-all cost of electricity, it is important that the investment, represented by property, be kept as productive as possible in order that these costs be spread over as large a volume of output as possible, thereby lowering them per unit of sale. It follows that there is every incentive to *maintain* the consumer demand at as high a level as possible. This will be done by encouraging off-peak sales; the measure of success will be the system load factor.

"Load factor" means the relation of the average load to the peak load over a certain period of time and is usually figured upon an annual basis. If during a year a company has a peak load of 100,000 kw and a total output of 500,000,000 kwh, its annual load factor is

$$\frac{500,000,000 \text{ kwh}}{8,760 \text{ hours}} \div 100,000 \text{ kw} = 57,000 \text{ kw} \div 100,000 \text{ kw} = 57 \text{ percent}$$

Annual load factor will, of course, vary considerably among companies, depending upon the type of territory and customers being served. In a well-developed system with an average volume of industrial business it will range from 55 to 65 percent, with the upper range being attained or exceeded as the relative volume of wholesale or industrial business increases. An improvement in the load factor almost always results in higher net earnings for the company.

Generating Plant Efficiency. Since the cost of fuel is one of the heavy items of operating expense in steam electric-plant generation, an important ratio to watch is that measuring the "heat rate" or thermal efficiency. A frequently used index is the amount of coal required to produce 1 kwh of electricity. For the electric industry as a whole in 1959, the average requirement was 0.89 pounds. Coal, however, may vary substantially in heat content, and a more appropriate ratio, therefore, is the number of British thermal units (B.t.u.) required to generate 1 kwh of electricity. For the industry as a whole in 1959 the average was approximately 10,880 B.t.u. per kwh generated. (This compares with 15,738 B.t.u. in 1948.)

Modern steam electric stations, however, have a thermal efficiency considerably higher than this, the "heat rate" in some of the newest and most efficient plants getting down to the range of 8,500 to 9,500 B.t.u. per kwh. This increased fuel efficiency means an important savings in operating expenses and is one of the factors that has helped to offset the burden of rising costs.

PART THREE

FIXED-INCOME SECURITIES

CHAPTER TWENTY-TWO

THE SELECTION OF FIXED-INCOME SECURITIES

We are now ready to turn from the technique of analyzing financial statements to the more advanced work of the security analyst in the selection of securities for investment. Our attention will be directed first to the more conventional and conservative area of fixed-income securities. It will be recalled that in our chapter on classification we grouped together all issues, whatever their title, which the investor may purchase with the expectation of receiving a steady and unchanging income, and with the further expectation that their principal value will not be subject to wide fluctuations (except possibly, as related to the basic interest rate). The correct name for this group should be "investments of the fixed-income, stable-value type." For ease of reference, we use the alternative short title of "fixed-income investments."[1]

Basic Attitude toward High-grade Preferred Stocks. By placing gilt-edged preferred stocks and high-grade bonds in a single group,[2] we indicate that the same investment attitude and the same general method of analysis are applicable to both types. The very definite inferiority of

---

[1] Certain types of securities that purport to carry fixed incomes are excluded from this group because they do not promise reasonable stability of value. These are senior issues whose character is speculative, either because there is doubt as to their underlying safety or because they have conversion or other privileges that may substantially affect their market price. At the same time, it is to be stressed that assurance of income does not in itself guarantee a stable market price. In fact, the marked advance in interest rates in recent years has brought a marked decline in the prices of top-quality bonds.

[2] Say, bonds in the top three grade ratings of either Standard & Poor's or Moody's, and preferred stocks in Standard & Poor's top ratings of AAA and AA.

the preferred stockholders' legal claim is here left out of account, for the logical reason that the soundness of the best investments must rest not upon legal rights or remedies but upon the ample financial capacity of the enterprise.[3]

Preferred Stocks Not Generally Equivalent to Bonds in Investment Merit. But it should be pointed out immediately that really first-grade preferred issues—e.g., those of General Motors—make up only a small percentage of all preferred stocks. Hence, we are by no means asserting the investment equivalence of bonds and preferred stocks *in general*. On the contrary, we shall in a later chapter be at some pains to show that the average preferred issue deserves a rank lower than that of the average bond, and furthermore that preferred stocks have been much too readily accepted by the investing public. The majority of these issues have not been sufficiently well protected to assure continuance of dividends *beyond any reasonable doubt*. They belong properly, therefore, in the class of speculative senior issues (Group 11*B*), and in this field the contractual differences between bonds and preferred shares are likely to assume great importance. A sharp distinction must, therefore, be made between the typical and the exceptional preferred stock. Only the latter deserves to rank as a fixed-income investment and to be viewed in the same light as a good bond.

Bond Form Inherently Unattractive: Quantitative Assurance of Safety Essential. Allusion has already been made to the dangers inherent in the acceptance of the bond *form* as an assurance of safety or even of smaller risk than is found in stocks. Instead of associating bonds primarily with the presumption of *safety*—as has long been the practice—it would be sounder to start with what is not presumption but fact, viz., that a (straight) bond is a security with *limited return*. In exchange for limiting his participation in future profits, the bondholder obtains a prior claim and a definite promise of payment, while the preferred stockholder obtains only the priority, without the promise. But neither priority nor promise is itself an assurance of payment. This assurance rests in the ability of the enterprise to fulfill its promise, and must be looked for in its financial position, record, and prospects. The essence of proper bond selection consists, therefore, in obtaining specific and convincing factors of safety in compensation for the surrender of participation in profits.

Major Emphasis on Avoidance of Loss. Our primary conception of the bond as a commitment with limited return leads us to another important viewpoint toward bond investment. Since the chief emphasis must be placed on avoidance of loss, bond selection is primarily a *negative art*. It is a process of exclusion and rejection rather than of search and acceptance. In this respect the contrast with common-stock selection is fundamental in character. The prospective buyer of a given common

---

[3] This inferiority is recognized, however, in setting minimum standards to determine whether an issue truly falls in this select category (see Chap. 28).

stock may be influenced more or less equally by the desire to avoid loss and the desire to make a profit. The penalty for mistakenly rejecting the issue may conceivably be as great as that for mistakenly accepting it. But an investor may reject any number of good bonds with virtually no penalty at all, provided he does not eventually accept an unsound issue. Hence, broadly speaking, there is no such thing as being unduly captious or exacting in the purchase of fixed-income investments. The observation that Walter Bagehot addressed to commercial bankers is equally applicable to the selection of investment bonds: "If there is a difficulty or a doubt the security should be declined."[4]

Four Principles for the Selection of Issues of the Fixed-income Type. Having established this general approach to our problem, we may now state four additional principles of more specific character which are applicable to the selection of individual issues:

I. *Safety is measured not by specific lien or other contractual rights, but by the ability of the issuer to meet all its obligations.*[5]

II. *This ability should be measured under conditions of recession or depression rather than of prosperity.*

III. *Deficient safety cannot be compensated for by an abnormally high coupon rate alone.*

IV. *The selection of all senior securities for investment should be subject to rules of exclusion and to specific quantitative tests.*

The ensuing discussion is designed to make clear both the nature and the justification of these ideas.

I. SAFETY IS MEASURED NOT BY LIEN BUT BY ABILITY TO PAY

The basic difference confronts us at the very beginning. In the (now distant) past the primary emphasis was laid upon the specific security, i.e., the character and supposed value of the property on which the bonds hold a lien. From the newer standpoint this consideration is quite secondary; the dominant element must be the strength and soundness of the obligor enterprise. There is here a clear-cut distinction between two points of view. On the one hand the bond is regarded as a claim against *property*, on the other hand, as a claim against a *business*.

The older view was logical enough in its origin and purpose. It sought to make the bondholder independent of the risks of the business by giving him ample security on which to levy in the event that the enterprise proved a failure. If the business became unable to pay his claim, he could take over the mortgaged property and pay himself out of that. This arrangement would be excellent if it worked, but in practice it

---

[4] Walter Bagehot, *Lombard Street*, New York, 1892, p. 245.

[5] This is a general rule applicable to the majority of bonds of the fixed-income type, but it is subject to exceptions which are discussed later.

rarely proves to be feasible in corporate affairs. For this there are three reasons:

1. The shrinkage of property values when the business fails
2. The difficulty of asserting the bondholders' supposed legal rights
3. The delays and other disadvantages incident to a receivership or bankruptcy

Lien Is No Guarantee against Shrinkage of Values. The conception of a mortgage lien as a guaranty of protection independent of the success of the business itself is in most cases a complete fallacy. In the typical situation, the value of the pledged property is vitally dependent on the earning power of the enterprise. The bondholder usually has a lien on property which is not adaptable to uses other than that for which it was constructed. Hence if the enterprise proves a failure, its fixed assets ordinarily suffer an appalling shrinkage in realizable value. A striking illustration of this point is afforded by Seaboard-All Florida Railway First Mortgage 6s which sold in 1931 at 1 cent on the dollar *shortly after completion of the road.*

Sequel: The lack of earning power is emphasized by subsequent developments. The railroad went into receivership in 1931, and in 1944 the properties were sold to Seaboard Air Lines Railroad. For each $100 of principal amount the first mortgage bondholders received in 1946 and 1947 as full settlement a total amount of $20.06. (It is an interesting aside to note that, in anticipation of the sale of the properties, speculators bid the issue up to 62 in 1941.)

Difficulty of Enforcing Legal Rights of Lien Holder. In cases where the mortgaged property is actually worth as much as the debt, the bondholder is rarely allowed to take possession and realize upon it. The procedure following default on a corporate bond differs materially from that customary in the case of a mortgage on individually owned property. The basic legal rights of the lien holder are supposedly the same in both situations. But in practice we find a very definite disinclination on the part of the courts to permit corporate bondholders to take over properties by enforcement of their lien if there is any possibility that the pledged assets may have a fair value in excess of their claims.[6] Apparently it is considered unfair to wipe out stockholders or junior bondholders who have a potential interest in the property but are not in a position to pro-

---

[6] This point is illustrated by the inability of holders of Interborough Rapid Transit Secured 7s, due 1932, for seven years after default of principal to foreclose on their collateral. (The collateral was worth, at market prices, well over the face of the notes shortly after default.) Indeed, it may be said that for practical purposes foreclosure with respect to railroad obligations has been abolished by Sec. 77 of the Bankruptcy Act, and the same is largely true of bonds of other types of corporations under Chap. X. Actual foreclosure is encountered in these times only in the relatively rare case where a reorganization plan is not feasible under Sec. 77 or Chap. X of the Act. (Appendix Note 9, p. 737.)

tect it. As a result of this practice, bondholders rarely, if ever, come into actual possession of the pledged property unless its value at the time is substantially less than their claim. In most cases they are required to take new securities in a reorganized company after a long and vexing delay.

Troublesome Delays. This delay constitutes the third objection to relying upon the mortgaged property as protection for a bond investment. The more valuable the pledged assets in relation to the amount of the lien, the more difficult it is to obtain legal possession of them, and the longer is the time required to work out an "equitable" division of interest among the various bond and stock issues. Let us consider the most favorable kind of situation for a bondholder in the event of default. He would hold a comparatively small first mortgage followed by a substantial junior lien, the requirements of which have made the company insolvent. It may well be that the strength of the first-mortgage bondholder's position is such that at no time is there any real chance of eventual loss to him. Yet the financial difficulties of the company usually have a depressing effect on the market price of all its securities,[7] even those presumably unimpaired in real value. As the bankruptcy proceedings drag on, the market decline becomes accentuated, since investors are constitutionally averse to buying into a troubled situation. Eventually the first-mortgage bond may come through the reorganization undisturbed, but during a wearisome and protracted period the owners have faced a severe impairment in the quoted value of their holdings and at least some degree of doubt and worry as to the outcome.

Example: St. Louis Southwestern Railway First Mortgage 4s, due 1989. The road was petitioned into bankruptcy in December 1935 and dismissed therefrom in July 1947, no reorganization then being necessary. With the exception of a delay of less than three months in paying each of the 1938 coupons, there was no interruption in the regular payment of interest on the issue, and it emerged from the bankruptcy undisturbed. Nevertheless, the price of the issue declined to 38 in the third year of bankruptcy.

Basic Principle Is to Avoid Trouble. The foregoing discussion should support our emphatic stand that the primary aim of the bond buyer must be *to avoid trouble rather than to protect himself in the event of trouble.* Even in the cases where the specific lien proves of real advantage, this benefit is realized under conditions which contravene the very meaning of *stable-value* investment. In view of the severe decline in market price almost invariably associated with receivership or bankruptcy, the mere

---

[7] W. B. Hickman, in his monumental bond study, *Corporate Bond Quality and Investor Experience,* Princeton University Press, Princeton, N.J., 1958, pp. 19–20, states: "One of the most persistent and most pronounced phenomena observed in the data is the propensity of the market to undervalue corporate bonds at or near the date of default."

fact that the investor must have recourse to his indenture indicates that his investment has been unwise or unfortunate. The protection that the mortgaged property offers him can constitute at best a mitigation of his mistake.

Corollaries from This First Principle. From Principle I there follow a number of corollaries with important practical applications.

1. *Absence of Lien of Minor Consequence.* Since specific lien is of subordinate importance in the choice of high-grade bonds, the absence of lien is also of minor consequence. The debenture (i.e., unsecured) obligations of a strong corporation, amply capable of meeting its interest charges, may qualify for acceptance almost as readily as its bonds secured by mortgage. Furthermore, the debentures of a strong enterprise are undoubtedly sounder investments than the mortgage issues of a weak company. No first-lien bond, for example, enjoys a better investment rating than Standard Oil Company of New Jersey Debenture 2⅜s, due 1971, or the 2¾s, due 1974. The fact is that only a very few *mortgage* bonds of industrial companies can be found in the comprehensive "Bond Guide" published monthly by Standard & Poor's Corporation. The prevailing form of new issue by such concerns is now the "subordinated debenture," which ranks junior to bank debt.

2. *The Theory of Buying the Highest-yielding Obligation of a Sound Company.* It follows also that if any obligation of an enterprise deserves to qualify as a fixed-income investment, then all its obligations must so qualify. Stated conversely, if a company's junior bonds are not safe, its first-mortgage bonds are not a desirable fixed-income investment. For if the junior obligation is unsafe, the company itself is weak, and generally speaking there can be no high-grade obligations of a weak enterprise. The theoretically correct procedure for bond investment, therefore, is first to select a company meeting every test of strength and soundness, and then to purchase its highest-yielding obligation, which would usually mean its junior rather than its first-lien bonds. Assuming no error were ever made in our choice of enterprises, this procedure would work out perfectly well in practice. The greater the chance of mistake, however, the more reason to sacrifice yield in order to reduce the potential loss in capital value. But we must recognize that, in favoring the lower-yielding first-mortgage issue, the bond buyer is in fact expressing a lack of confidence in his own judgment as to the soundness of the business—which, if carried far enough, would call into question the advisability of his making an investment in *any* of the bonds of the particular enterprise.

3. *But Senior Liens Are to be Favored, Unless Junior Obligations Offer a Substantial Advantage.* Obviously a junior lien should be preferred only if the advantage in income return is substantial. Where the first-mortgage bond yields only slightly less, it is undoubtedly wise to pay the small insurance premium for protection against unexpected trouble or market

changes. This point is illustrated by the relative market prices of Atchison, Topeka and Santa Fe Railway Company General (first) 4s and Adjustment (second-mortgage) 4s, both of which mature in 1995. In April 1961 the Generals were selling at 93 and the Adjustments at 90½, causing a yield differential of only ⅐ percent. This spread did not, in our opinion, warrant giving preference to the junior issue.

A junior lien of Company X may be selected in preference to a first-mortgage bond of Company Y, on one of two bases:

a. The protection for the total debt of Company X is adequate, and the yield of the junior lien is substantially higher than that of the Company Y issue; or

b. If there is no substantial advantage in yield, then the indicated protection for the total debt of Company X must be considerably better than that of Company Y.

Special Status of "Underlying Bonds." In the railroad field an especial investment character is generally supposed to attach to what are known as "underlying bonds." These represent issues of relatively small size secured by a lien on especially important parts of the obligor system and often followed by a series of "blanket mortgages." The underlying bond usually enjoys a first lien, but it may be a second or even a third-mortgage issue, provided the senior issues are also of comparatively small magnitude.

Bonds of this description have been thought to be entirely safe, regardless of what happens to the system as a whole. They have usually come through reorganization unscathed; and even during bankruptcy, interest payments are customarily continued as a matter of course, largely because the sum involved is proportionately so small. They are not exempt, however, from fairly sharp declines in market value if insolvency overtakes the system.

Example 1: Pacific Railroad Company of Missouri First 4s and Second 5s and Missouri Pacific Railway Third 4s, all extended from their original maturities in 1938, were underlying bonds of the Missouri Pacific system. They continued to receive interest and were left undisturbed in the receivership of 1915. Following the second bankruptcy in 1933, they continued to receive interest until their maturity date. At that time payment of principal was defaulted, but interest payments were continued. In spite of the continuance of interest payments, the prices of these three issues dropped as low as 65, 60, and 53, respectively. Principal and interest on each of them were paid in full under court order on November 1, 1943.

Example 2: The somewhat contrasting experience of first-mortgage bonds on a less important part of the Missouri Pacific system—thus not a true underlying issue—is to be noted. The First Gold 5½s, Series A, due 1954, of New Orleans, Texas & Mexico Railway Company (93.15 percent owned by Missouri Pacific) held a first lien on 1,581 miles of main line from New Orleans to Brownsville, Texas. The interest was not paid for nearly four years in the 1930's, and all arrearages were not cleared up until December 1947. As a result the price fell to a low of 17 in 1934—which was substantially below that for the underlying bonds discussed above. However, under the reorganization plan finally approved by court decree in March 1956, the issue received per bond $1,000 Missouri Pacific 4¼ percent Collateral Trust Notes, due 1976. The Notes represented a senior issue of the Missouri Pacific and were secured by a pledge of first-mortgage bonds.

Other bonds, however, once regarded as underlying issues, have not fared so well following insolvency.

Example: Milwaukee, Sparta, and Northwestern First 4s, due 1947, ranked as underlying bonds of the Chicago and North Western Railway, and for many years their price was not far below that of the premier Union Pacific Railroad First 4s, due the same year. Yet the receivership of the Chicago and North Western was followed by default of interest on this issue in 1935 and the collapse of its price to the abysmal low of 8 as late as 1940. In the reorganization consummated in 1944 this issue received less favorable treatment than did the General Mortgage Bonds of the company.

Regardless of the ultimate vindication of underlying bonds as well-secured investments, their price declines during a period of receivership would disqualify them as sound investments at full prices—unless the obligor itself made a strong over-all showing.

II. INVESTMENT ISSUES SHOULD BE BOUGHT ON A RECESSION OR DEPRESSION BASIS

The rule that a sound investment must be able to withstand adversity seems self-evident enough to be termed a truism. Any bond or preferred stock can do well when conditions are favorable; it is only under the acid test of depression that the advantages of strong over weak issues become manifest and vitally important. For this reason prudent investors have always favored the obligations of old-established enterprises which have demonstrated their ability to come through bad times as well as good.

Presumption of Safety Based upon Either the Character of the Industry or the Amount of Protection. Confidence in the ability of a bond or preferred-stock issue to weather depression may be based on either of two reasons. The investor may believe that the particular business will be immune from a drastic shrinkage in earnings or else that the margin of safety is so large that it can undergo such a shrinkage without resultant danger. The bonds of light and power companies have been favored principally for the first reason, the bonds of companies such as the United States Steel Corporation for the second. In the former case it is the *character* of the industry, in the latter it is the *amount* of protection, which justifies the purchase. Of the two viewpoints, the one which tries to avoid the perils of recession appeals most to the average bond buyer. It seems much simpler to invest in a depression-proof enterprise than to have to rely on the company's financial strength to pull its bonds through a period of poor results.

No Industry Entirely Depression-proof. The objection to this theory of investment is, of course, that there is no such thing as a depression-proof industry, meaning thereby one that is immune from the danger of *any* decline in earning power. It is true that the electric utilities have shown themselves subject to only minor shrinkage in profits, as compared, say, with the steel producers. But even a small decline may prove fatal if the business is bonded to the limit of prosperity earnings. Once it is admitted—as it always must be—that the industry can suffer *some* reduction in profits, then the investor is compelled to estimate the possible extent of the shrinkage and compare it with the excess above the interest requirements. He thus finds himself in the same position as the holder of any other kind of bond, vitally concerned with the ability of the company to meet the vicissitudes of the future.

The distinction to be made, therefore, is not between industries which are *exempt* from and those which are *affected* by depression, but rather between those which are *more* and those which are *less* subject to fluctuation. The more stable the type of enterprise, the better suited it is to bond financing and the larger is the portion of the supposed normal earning power which may be consumed by interest charges. As the degree of instability increases, it must be offset by a greater margin of safety to make sure that interest charges will be met; in other words, a smaller portion of total capital may be represented by bonds. At the extreme, if there is such a lack of inherent stability as to make solvency of the enterprise doubtful under continued unfavorable conditions (a question that has arisen frequently in the case of industrial companies of secondary size), then the bond issue cannot meet the requirements of fixed-income investment, even though the margin of safety—measured by past performance—may be exceedingly large. Such a bond will meet the quantitative but not the qualitative test; but both are essential to our concept of investment.

Investment Practice Recognizes the Importance of the Character of the Industry. This conception of diverse margins of safety has been solidly grounded in investment practice for many years. The threefold classification of enterprises—as railroads, public utilities, or industrials—reflects inherent differences in relative stability and consequently in the coverage to be required above bond interest charges.

Some radical changes have occurred over the years in the comparative quality and yields of these three groups. Once railroad bonds enjoyed the top position in the opinion of investors. As our Table 22-1 shows, between 1900 and 1925 high-grade rail issues sold at lower yields than those of public utilities. However, the steady progress of the utility group in the 1920's and, in the ensuing depression, the fact that the shrinkage in its gross and net earnings was so much smaller than that in the transportation industry, resulted in the bonds of soundly capitalized light and power companies replacing high-grade railroad bonds as the favored type of corporate investment.

It will be seen that in the more recent periods the yield on high-grade industrial bonds has been slightly lower than that on like-quality public utility bonds. It is doubtful, however, that this represents the market's

Table 22-1. Comparative Yield on High-grade Railroad, Public Utility, and Industrial Bonds, Selected Annual and Period Data

Year	Railroads, percent	Public utilities, percent	Industrials, percent
1900	4.05	4.54	4.86
1905	3.89	4.43	4.53
1910	4.16	4.80	4.83
1915	4.64	4.88	4.97
1920	5.79	6.73	6.01
1925	4.67	5.06	5.06
1925–1929	5.10	5.07	5.30
1930–1934	5.94	5.65	5.58
1935–1939	4.66	3.92	3.57
1940–1944	3.85	3.09	2.93
1945–1949	3.13	2.85	2.71
1950–1954	3.30	3.14	2.99
1955–1959	4.09	3.95	3.85
1960	4.92	4.69	4.59

SOURCES: Standard & Poor's High-grade Corporate Bond Yields, 1900–1925; Moody's Composite Bond Yields, 1925–1960.

estimate of the comparative investment risk involved in each class. For it is generally considered that the risk factor is somewhat higher in the case of industrial bonds. Moreover, the following evidence developed by Hickman as to the default rate for bonds would support this opinion, at least insofar as the 1900–1943 span is concerned:[8]

Bonds	*Life-span default rate**
Railroad	28.1%
Industrial	14.8
Public utility	10.6

* The life-span default rate is the proportion of the total amount of bond offerings in each group that went into default at any time between offering and extinguishment. Note that the 1900–1943 period includes the Great Depression of 1929–1932.

Quite probably the slightly lower yield on industrial than on public utility bonds is attributable to the moderately shorter maturities—which are further reduced by sinking-fund provisions—of industrial bonds than

[8] W. B. Hickman, *op. cit.*, p. 10.

of utilities, and to the fact that—in their quest for diversification—large institutional investors in particular are competing for the relatively limited supply of high-grade industrial bonds.

Minimum Standards of Safety Should Vary with Relative Stability of Earnings. We shall use the phrase "margin of safety" or "interest coverage" to represent the ratio of available earnings to total interest requirements.[9] Since the margin of safety is needed primarily to protect the bondholder against a possible future decline in profits, it follows that an industry or enterprise with high inherent *stability* requires an interest coverage smaller than is needed by one subject to wider earnings fluctuations.

Considered as groups, both the railroads and industrial enterprises have manifested noticeable irregularity in annual earnings throughout the various phases of past business cycles. For example, there was a cyclical decline of 37 percent in net railway operating income in the 1935–1939 span, and the two postwar declines have amounted to 31 and 34 percent. The amplitude of cyclical fluctuations in individual manufacturing industries is indicated by the data in Table 22-2. It is to be noted that—measured in terms of the return on total capital—the earnings of the 14 major industries declined an *average* of 64 percent in the 1935–1939 span and 46 and 40 percent in two postwar fluctuations.[10] The range of the fluctuations was from a low of 34 to a high of 93 percent in the 1935–1939 period, and in two postwar fluctuations from 31 to 76 percent and from 8 to 63 percent, respectively.

Based on past fluctuations in the earnings of corporations in the transportation and industrial sectors of the economy, the conclusion is inevitable that for such enterprises the downside of a pronounced business cycle may carry a real threat of financial discomfort and in some instances even of insolvency. The buyer of fixed-income securities should take this fact into account in his qualitative as well as his quantitative study of issues in those major groups. His minimum required margin of average earnings over fixed charges, as well as other tests of financial soundness, must be such as to give assurance that the enterprise can successfully weather the degree of adversity that it is likely to meet.[11]

---

[9] "Interest" is used here and elsewhere to connote total fixed charges.

[10] The median for the 14 industries was close to the average in each instance.

[11] Some aspects of the record of issues under conditions of severe adversity may be developed from data compiled in W. B. Hickman, *Statistical Measures of Corporate Bond Financing since 1900*, Princeton University Press, Princeton, N.J., 1960 (derived from his Tables 1 and 13*b*). For example, in the period 1931–1934 the following percent of the average par amount of bonds outstanding went into default in each group:

All Industries	12.8%
Railroads	15.6
Public Utilities	8.6
Industrials	17.2

Table 22-2. Selected Prewar and Postwar Cyclical Fluctuations in Earnings Based on Return on Total Capital of 14 Major Industries, 1935–1939; 1947–1959

Industry	1935–1939 fluctuations			Selected postwar fluctuations, 1947–1959					
	High	Low	Percent decline	High	Low	Percent decline	High	Low	Percent decline
Agricultural machinery and equipment	12.5%	3.3%	74	13.2%	5.3%	60	6.7%	5.4%	19
Automobiles	28.9	11.3	61	34.5	19.6	43	26.3	9.6	63
Electrical supplies and equipment	14.8	6.4	57	17.9	12.0	33	13.8	9.3	33
General industrial machinery and equipment	16.2	4.8	70	18.1	10.7	41	14.3	9.5	34
Corn products	10.6	2.6	75	18.5	10.5	43	14.5	13.3	8
Building materials	9.9	4.8	52	17.5	11.3	45	15.1	10.9	28
Toilet preparations and soap	15.3	10.1	34	23.5	11.9	49	21.4	10.9	49
Nonferrous metals, excluding copper	16.7	11.1	34	18.2	11.1	39	18.1	7.3	60
Oil	9.6	4.9	49	15.9	10.0	37	13.7	8.7	36
Paper and allied products	6.6	2.8	58	15.4	10.7	31	12.6	7.7	39
Automobile parts and accessories	19.2	2.4	87	19.9	12.1	39	15.9	7.4	53
Radio and television	18.9	6.9	63	32.9	8.0	76	9.8	4.9	50
Steel	6.0	0.8	87	12.3	7.0	43	12.6	7.8	38
Textile fabrics	6.9	0.5	93	14.1	4.6	67	6.9	3.6	48
Average decline—14 industries			64			46			40

SOURCES: Cottle and Whitman, *Corporate Earning Power and Market Valuation*, Duke University Press, Durham, N.C., 1959; and Stanford Research Institute.

Judging from all indications, including the record of the past, the impact of a depression upon the profits of utility companies may be expected to be less severe than for most other lines of business. This fact should justify less stringent requirements (i.e., a lower minimum margin of safety) for utility bonds than for those of railroads or industrials.

III. IT IS UNSOUND TO SACRIFICE SAFETY FOR YIELD

In the traditional theory of bond investment a mathematical relationship is supposed to exist between the interest rate and the degree of risk incurred. The interest return is divided into two components, the first constituting "pure interest"—i.e., the rate obtainable with *no* risk of loss—and the second representing the premium obtained to compensate for the risk assumed. If, for example, the "pure interest rate" is assumed to be 3 percent, then a 4 percent investment is supposed to involve one chance in a hundred of losing the entire principal in one year, while the risk incurred in a 7 percent investment would be four times as great, or one in twenty-five.

This theory implies that bond-interest rates are closely similar to insurance rates and that they measure the degree of risk on some reasonably precise actuarial basis. It would follow that, by and large, the final return from high- and low-yielding investments should tend to equalize, since what the former gain in income would be offset by their greater percentage of principal losses, and vice versa.

No Mathematical Relationship between Yield and Risk. This view, however, seems to us to bear little relation to the realities of bond investment. Relative bond yields usually do reflect the rating of the market as to the relative degrees of risk involved in the investments; but these yields have not been computed by means of mathematical equations involving chance of loss on the one hand and required income on the other.

It may be pointed out further that the supposed actuarial computation of investment risks is not a practicable undertaking. It is true that we now have a comprehensive record of investors' bond experience covering the years 1900–1943. (This is the extensive study by Hickman already cited.) But it is doubtful whether this experience could be relied on implicitly as a guide for the future. In life insurance the relation between age and mortality rate is well defined and changes only gradually. The same is true, to a much lesser extent, of the relation between the various types of structures and the fire hazard attaching to them. But the relation between different kinds of investments and the risk of loss is entirely too indefinite and too variable with changing conditions to permit of sound mathematical formulation. This is particularly true because investment losses are not distributed fairly evenly in point of time, but tend to be concentrated at intervals, i.e., during periods of marked decline in general business activity.[12] Hence the typical investment hazard is roughly similar to the conflagration or epidemic hazard, which is the exceptional and incalculable factor in fire or life insurance.

Self-insurance Generally Not Possible in Investment. If we assume a precise mathematical relationship between yield and risk, then the result of this premise should be inevitably to recommend the lowest-yielding—and therefore the safest—bonds to all investors. For the individual is not qualified to be an insurance underwriter.[13] It is not his function to be paid for incurring risks; on the contrary, it is to his interest to pay others for insurance against loss. Let us assume that a bond buyer has his choice of investing $1,000 for $30 per annum without risk, or for $80 per annum with one chance out of twenty each year that his principal would be lost. The $50 additional income on the second investment is mathematically equivalent to the risk involved. But in terms of *personal requirements,* an investor cannot afford to take even a small chance of losing $1,000 of principal in return for an extra $50 of income. Such a procedure would be the direct opposite of the standard procedure of *paying* small annual sums to protect property values against loss by fire and theft.

The Factor of Cyclical Risks. The investor cannot prudently turn himself into an insurance company and incur risks of losing his principal in exchange for annual premiums in the form of extra-large interest coupons. One objection to such a policy is that sound insurance practice requires a very wide distribution of risk, in order to minimize the influence of luck and to allow maximum play to the law of probability. The investor may endeavor to attain this end by diversifying his holdings, but as a practical matter he cannot approach the division of risk attained by an insurance company. More important still is the danger that many risky investments may collapse together in a depression period, so that the investor in high-yielding issues will find a period of large income (which he will probably spend) followed suddenly by a deluge of losses of principal.

Hickman states that his findings indicate "a clear-cut, long-run relationship between bond quality at offering and the yields actually obtained by investors. On the average and over long periods, the life-span yields realized on high-grade bonds were below those on low-grade bonds, with the result that investors, in the aggregate, obtained better returns on the low grades."[14] This higher return can be viewed simply as appropriate compensation to those investors who accepted the hazards of

[12] For example, based on the data developed by Hickman, the following percentages of the total par amounts of all defaults which occurred in the 44 years 1900–1943 took place in the four years 1931–1934: all industries 33.4 percent, railroads 30.0 percent (if 1935 were added it would jump to 41.1 percent), public utilities 35.2 percent, and industrials 38.9 percent. (*Ibid.*)

[13] As we note later on this page, Hickman's study indicates that in reality there is more-than-offsetting compensation for the additional risk undertaken. Our argument will take this fact into account.

[14] W. B. Hickman, *Corporate Bond Quality and Investor Experience,* p. 14.

low-grade bonds. In other words, investors—in return for taking the greater risk involved in lower-quality bonds—in the long run obtained a *profit* over and above the losses in principal suffered. Yet even assuming that the record of the past is a true indicator of the future and that high coupon rates will, in the great aggregate, more than compensate on an actuarial basis for the risks accepted, low-grade bonds are still undesirable investments from the standpoint of the *average* investor.[15] Thus our arguments against the investor turning himself into an insurance company remain valid even if the insurance operations, all told, may prove profitable. The bond buyer is neither financially nor psychologically equipped to carry on extensive transactions involving the setting up of reserves out of regular income to absorb losses in substantial amounts suffered at irregular intervals.

Risk and Yield Are Incommensurable. The foregoing discussion leads us to suggest the principle that income return and risk of principal should be regarded as *incommensurable*. Practically speaking, this means that acknowledged risks of losing principal should not merely be offset by a high coupon rate but can be accepted only in return for a corresponding opportunity for *enhancement of principal,* e.g., through the purchase of bonds at a substantial discount from par, or possibly by obtaining an unusually attractive conversion privilege. While there may be no real *mathematical* difference between offsetting risks of loss by a higher income or by a chance for profit, the *psychological* difference is very important. The purchaser of low-priced bonds is fully aware of the risk he is running; he is more likely to make a thorough investigation of the issue and to appraise carefully the chances of loss and of profit; finally—most important of all—he is prepared for whatever losses he may sustain, and his profits are in a form available to meet his losses. Actual investment experience, therefore, will not favor the purchase of the typical high-coupon bond offered at about par, wherein, for example, a 6 percent interest return is imagined to compensate for a distinctly inferior grade of security.[16]

[15] Hickman, also, has serious reservations as to the advisability of the individual's acquiring low-grade bonds. He states, "The major conclusion that investors obtained higher returns on low-grade issues than on high-grades should not be accepted without proper qualification. For it cannot be emphasized too strongly that this finding emerges only when broad aggregates of corporate bonds are considered over long investment periods, and given the price and yield relationships that existed during those periods. In effect, the aggregate results reflect the experience of all investors over long periods, rather than that of any particular investor over any given short period. Another qualification is that realized yields and loss rates were not nearly so regularly related to quality as were promised yields and default rates. Because of the disparity in the performance of low-grade bonds, small investors (and many large investors that may have been inhibited from practicing the broadest type of diversification) would frequently have fared best by holding only the highest grade obligations." *Ibid.,* pp. 14–15.

[16] Conceptions of what constitutes a *high* coupon rate vary with the times. In

Fallacy of the "Businessman's Investment." An issue of this type is commonly referred to in the financial world as a "businessman's investment" and is supposedly suited to those who can afford to take some degree of risk. Most of the foreign bonds floated between 1923 and 1929 belonged in that category. The same was formerly true of the bulk of straight preferred-stock issues. According to our view, such "businessman's investments" are an illogical type of commitment. The security buyer who can afford to take some risk should seek a commensurate opportunity of enhancement in price and should pay only secondary attention to the income obtained. It seems a bit paradoxical that the ability to withstand a *loss* of money should somehow become an *investment* criterion.

Reversal of Customary Procedure Recommended. Viewing the matter more broadly, it would be well if investors reversed their customary attitude toward income return. In selecting the grade of bonds suitable to their situation, they have been prone to start at the top of the list, where maximum safety is combined with lowest yield, and then to calculate how great a concession from ideal security they are willing to make for the sake of a more attractive income rate. From this point of view, the ordinary investor becomes accustomed to the idea that the type of issue suited to his needs must rank somewhere below the very best, a frame of mind which is likely to lead to the acceptance of definitely unsound bonds, either because of their high income return or by surrender to the blandishments of salesmanship.

It would be sounder procedure to start with minimum standards of safety, which all bonds must be required to meet in order to be eligible for further consideration. Issues failing to meet these minimum requirements should be automatically disqualified as straight investments, regardless of high yield, attractive prospects, or other grounds for partiality. Having thus delimited the field of eligible investments, the buyer may then apply such further selective processes as he deems appropriate. He may desire elements of safety far beyond the accepted minimum, in which case he must ordinarily make some sacrifice of yield. He may also indulge his preferences as to the nature of the business and the character of the management. But, essentially, bond selection should consist of working upward from definite minimum standards rather than of working downward in haphazard fashion from some ideal but unacceptable level of maximum security.

1921 the yield on Standard & Poor's A1⁺ bonds was 6.0 percent; thus strongly entrenched bonds were offered yielding at least this rate. In contrast, the comparable S&P yield in 1946 was 2.4 percent, and an offering of top-rated debentures of Standard Oil (New Jersey) sold to yield almost exactly that rate. In 1960 the interest rate was substantially higher, and the high-quality bonds of Cincinnati Gas & Electric sold to yield 4.375 percent to maturity.

CHAPTER TWENTY-THREE

SPECIFIC STANDARDS FOR BOND INVESTMENT

In Chapter 22 we discussed three of the four principles for the selection of fixed-income securities. Let us now consider the fourth principle.

IV. DEFINITE STANDARDS OF SAFETY MUST BE APPLIED

Since the selection of high-grade bonds has been shown to be in good part a process of exclusion, it lends itself reasonably well to the application of definite rules and standards designed to disqualify unsuitable issues. Such regulations have in fact been set up in many states by legislative enactment to govern the investments made by savings banks and by trust funds.

It is our view that the underlying idea of fixed standards and minima should be extended to the entire field of straight investment, i.e., investment for income only. These legislative restrictions are intended to promote a high average level of investment quality and to protect depositors against losses from unsafe securities. If such regulations with respect to fixed-income investment are desirable in the case of institutions, it should be logical for individuals to follow them also. We have previously challenged the prevalent idea that the ordinary investor can afford to take greater investment risks than a savings bank and need not therefore be as exacting with respect to the soundness of his fixed-income securities.

When we wrote in 1950—and looked back over the amplitude of the 1920–1921, 1929–1933, 1937–1938 depressions—it was in order to conclude, "The experience of the last thirty years undoubtedly emphasizes the need for a general tightening of investment standards, and a simple method [for individuals] of attaining this end might be to confine all straight bond selections to those which meet tests of eligibility similar to those prescribed for the investments of savings banks."[1] Today, in reviewing the much more moderate post-World War II cycles, we see no reason for suggesting a further tightening of our 1951 standards. However, as we noted in Chapter 22, improved over-all economic stability does not in itself guarantee only moderate fluctuations in the earnings of individual companies or, as a matter of fact, in entire industries. Ac-

---

[1] 1951 edition, p. 297.

cordingly, we question the desirability of any significant easing of the tests of eligibility. (However, we shall suggest later in this chapter— only because of the increase in the corporate-income tax ratio since our last edition—a minor reduction in *after-tax* earnings coverage.)

Thus, to repeat, we consider that the individual investor should set his *bond-investment* standards by those of conservative financial institutions, such as the savings banks. Such a procedure would appear directly consonant with our fundamental principles that straight investments should be made only in issues of unimpeachable soundness and that securities of inferior grade must be bought only on an admittedly speculative basis.

As a matter of *practical policy,* an individual bond buyer is likely to obtain fairly satisfactory results by subjecting himself to the restrictions which govern the investment of savings banks' funds. But this procedure cannot be seriously suggested as a *general principle of investment,* because the legislative provisions are themselves far too imperfect to warrant their acceptance as the best available theoretical standards. The acts of the various states are widely divergent; most of them are antiquated in important respects; none is entirely logical or scientific. The legislators did not approach their task from the viewpoint of establishing criteria of sound investments for universal use; consequently they felt free to impose arbitrary restrictions on savings banks which they would have hesitated to prescribe for investors generally.

Specific Criteria for the Selection of Investment Bonds. In earlier editions of this work we discussed criteria for the selection of fixed-income securities by using as a frame of reference the provisions of the New York statute governing the investments of savings banks. This procedure is abandoned here in the interest of brevity and with a view to emphasizing more directly the standards which we deem essential. We shall discuss criteria for bond selection under the following general headings:

1. The *nature and location* of the business
2. The *size* of the enterprise, or the issue
3. The *terms* of the issue
4. The *record* of solvency and dividend payments
5. The relation of *earnings* to interest requirements
6. The relation of the *value* of the property to the funded debt
7. The relation of *stock* capitalization to the funded debt

The first four of these will be discussed in this chapter, the fifth in Chapter 24, and the last two in Chapter 25.

NATURE AND LOCATION

An especially striking feature of some legal regulations governing savings-bank investments has been the complete exclusion of bonds in certain broad categories, such as street-railway bonds, water bonds, public utility debentures, industrial bonds, and bonds of financial companies.[2] It is no longer necessary to argue, as we did in former editions, against the application of such blanket prohibitions. The highest-rated industrial bonds now sell at lower yields than similarly rated public utility and railroad issues. Industrial debentures as a class yield less than industrial mortgage bonds as a class (of different obligors), and some of the Commonwealth Edison debenture issues actually yield less than the first mortgage bonds *of the same company*. It is clear that the blanket preferences and prohibitions that governed a good part of the old-time investment have pretty well disappeared from the financial scene. All that should remain is a more stringent requirement for quantitative measures of safety in the selection of industrial bonds as against public utility bonds, to reflect the lower inherent stability of the former group.

Obligations of Foreign Governments. In dealing with foreign-government debts we are confronted with a different situation. Such issues respond in but small degree to financial analysis, and investment therein is ordinarily based on general considerations, such as confidence in the country's economic and political stability and the belief that it will faithfully endeavor to discharge its obligations. To a much greater extent, therefore, than in the case of other bonds, an opinion may be justified or even necessitated as to the *general desirability* of foreign-government bonds for fixed-income investment.

A foreign-government obligation is in theory a claim against the entire resources of the nation, but the extent to which these resources are actually drawn upon to meet an external debt burden depends in good part upon political expediency. In final analysis, a foreign-government debt is an unenforceable contract, whose destiny in times of stress is dominated by willingness to pay, even if specific revenues or assets are pledged as security.

At one time, the record of foreign-bond investment in this country was far from encouraging. In 1934, 33 percent of foreign dollar bonds were in default. The more recent experience, however, is in marked contrast. In 1958, the Foreign Bondholders Protective Council wrote, "Defaults arising out of the Great Depression have left the scene."[3] The postwar period has seen a significant volume of dollar-bond flotations of foreign governments in the United States.

---

[2] Although the specific provisions of the New York statute still exclude bonds in the broad categories mentioned above, the Legislature amended the law in 1938 in such a way as to permit exceptions to all the blanket exclusions. About 20 percent of the issues "legal" in New York in 1959 consisted of bond issues, otherwise proscribed, which had been added to the list on application of 20 savings banks and approved by the Banking Board.

[3] Foreign Bondholders Protective Council, Inc., *Report 1955 through 1957*, p. xxvi.

At the same time, we must not lose sight of the recent experience of the holders of Cuba's 4½s of 1977. It is indicative of the hazard to which foreign bonds are subjected. These bonds, which have the first preferential right and lien on 90 percent of the revenue collected from certain specified taxes, sold at a high of 105¼ in 1959. But interest and sinking-fund payments were defaulted in 1960, and the bonds fell as low as 33½ in 1961. It may thus be seen that the purchase of foreign-government bonds is subject to an objection which is generic in character: The basis for the credit is fundamentally intangible.

Canadian issues may undoubtedly be exempted from this blanket condemnation, both on their record and because of the closeness of the relationship between Canada and the United States. Individual investors, for either personal or statistical reasons, may be equally convinced of the high credit standing of various other countries, and will therefore be ready to purchase their obligations as high-grade investments. Such commitments may prove to be fully justified by the facts; but it would be well if the investor approached them in the light of *exceptions* to a general rule of avoiding foreign bonds, and required them accordingly to present exceptionally strong evidence of stability and safety.

Bonds of Foreign Corporations. In *theory*, bonds of a corporation, however prosperous, cannot enjoy better security than the obligations of the country in which the corporation is located. The government, through its taxing power, can take the property away from the private bondholder and utilize it to discharge the national debt. But in actuality, distinct limits are imposed by political expediency upon the *willingness* of governments to meet their obligations through taxation or expropriation. Accordingly, there have been numerous instances of corporations meeting their dollar obligations even when their government is in default.[4]

Although the holder of foreign-corporation bonds has specific legal remedies, such as the right of foreclosure, and the obligor may, therefore, be under greater compulsion to meet its debt than is the sovereign nation, conditions resulting in the default of government obligations are certain to affect adversely the position of the corporate bondholder. Restrictions on the transfer of funds have frequently prevented the payment of interest in dollars even though the company has remained amply solvent.[5]

Accordingly, it is to be seen that certain hazards existent in foreign-government obligations as fixed-income investments also attach themselves to foreign-corporation bonds.

In summary, it may be stated that the typical holder of foreign securities inevitably faces risks not involved in domestic issues. That the

[4] For examples, see Appendix Note 15, p. 738, in the 1951 edition.
[5] For examples, see Appendix Note 16, p. 739, in the 1951 edition.

situation with respect to foreign investment has become more favorable in recent years is unquestioned—although there is a wide variation between countries and parts of the world. Nevertheless, the individual investor will need to exercise considerable discretion in the purchase of foreign fixed-income obligations.[6]

SIZE

The bonds of exceptionally small enterprises are subject to objections which disqualify them as media for conservative investment.[7] A company of relatively minor size is more vulnerable than others to unexpected happenings, and it is likely to be handicapped by the lack of strong banking connections or of technical resources. Very small businesses, therefore, do not obtain public bond financing but rather depend on private capital, those supplying the funds being given the double inducement of a share in the profits and a direct voice in the management.[8]

The establishment of such minimum requirements as to size necessarily involves the drawing of arbitrary lines of demarcation. There is no mathematical means of determining exactly at what point a company becomes large enough to warrant the bond investor's interest. The same difficulty will attach to setting up any other quantitative standards, as for example, the margin of earnings above interest charges or the relation of stock or property values to bonded debt. It must be borne in mind, therefore, that all these "critical points" are necessarily rule-of-thumb decisions, and the investor is free to use other amounts if they appeal to him more. But, however arbitrary the standards selected may be, they are undoubtedly of practical utility in safeguarding the bond buyer from inadequately protected issues.

We believe that the requirements for minimum size proposed in the following table, although by necessity arbitrarily taken, are in reasonable accord with the realities of sound investment.

---

[6] The essential analytical techniques cannot readily be reduced to workable rules of thumb and minimum standards. Considerable factual data regarding budget balance, population, national production and income, balance of trade, and the like can be assembled. But such data lend themselves readily neither to analysis regarding ability to pay in the case of foreign government issues nor to indications of willingness to pay with respect to any foreign bonds—public or private.

[7] Our discussion is confined to corporate bonds. For a consideration of municipal and other obligations, we suggest that the student examine Chap. 22 of Dowrie, Fuller & Calkins, *Investments*, 3d ed., John Wiley & Sons, Inc., New York, 1961, and other well-known texts.

[8] Both loan and stock capital are now being supplied to small businesses by "Small Business Investment" companies, organized under the Small Business Investment Act of 1958. In turn, the public has been offered shares in the "SBICs."

Issuer	Minimum requirement of size
Public utility enterprises	$4,000,000 total operating revenues[9]
Railroad systems	5,000,000 total operating revenues[10]
Industrial companies	15,000,000 sales

Industrial Bonds and the Factor of Size. The experience of the past indicates that substantial size affords an element of protection against the hazards of instability to which industrial enterprises are subject.

Hickman's bond study shows, by size of obligor, the following proportions of industrial bond offerings of the 1900–1943 period that went into default before 1944:[11]

Asset size of obligor	Percent of offerings defaulted
Under $5 million	38.0
$5–99 million	25.3
$100–199 million	17.2
$200 million and over	3.4

The substantial difference in results is impressive and argues strongly for giving careful consideration to the size of the enterprise in appraising an industrial bond issue.

It may well be that the amplitude of future cyclical fluctuations will be significantly less than in the 1900–1943 period. Nevertheless, the fact apparently remains that small firms are prone to greater instability than large ones. This is indicated by the following tabulation, which shows the average annual fluctuations in the return on net worth over the 1951–1960 period for manufacturing corporations by size groups.[12]

Asset size	Average annual fluctuations in return on net worth, 1951–1960
Less than $1 million	31.7%
$1–5 million	27.8
$5–10 million	19.0
$5–100 million	16.3
$100 million and over	10.9

The results of Hickman's study and the foregoing data suggest that *large size* is a trait of considerable advantage in dealing with exceptionally unfavorable developments in the industrial world. As a corollary, a

[9] In 1959 there were 125 utility holding companies and operating electric companies in the United States with operating revenues in excess of $4 million. The aggregate revenues for these 125 companies amounted to 97 percent of the operating revenues of all privately owned Class A and B electric utilities in the United States.

[10] Out of 110 Class I railroads, 91 had operating revenues of $5 million or more in 1959.

[11] W. B. Hickman, *Corporate Bond Quality and Investor Experience,* Princeton University Press, Princeton, N.J., 1958, p. 495.

[12] Derived from data in *Quarterly Financial Report for Manufacturing Corporations,* Federal Trade Commission–Securities and Exchange Commission.

cautious investor would apparently be justified in deciding to confine his bond purchases to the leading companies in an industry.[13] The investor may also wish to add the suggested minimum requirement of $15 million of annual sales for individual companies.

Such minimum standards may be criticized as unduly stringent, in that if they were universally applied (which in any event is unlikely) they would make it impossible for sound and prosperous businesses of moderate size to finance themselves through straight bond issues.[14] But, until the expected greater cyclical stability in the economy is reflected more generally in the experience of individual industries, we favor an exacting attitude toward the purchase of straight industrial bond *at investment levels.*

Large Size Alone No Guarantee of Safety. These recommendations on the subject of minimum size do not imply that enormous dimensions are in themselves a guarantee of prosperity and financial strength. The biggest company may be the weakest if its bonded debt is disproportionately large. Moreover, in the railroad and public utility groups no practical advantage attaches to the very largest units as compared with those of medium magnitude. Whether the gross receipts of an electric company are $20 million or $100 million has, in all probability, no material effect on the safety of its bonds. It is only in the industrial field that we have suggested that the bonds of a very large enterprise may be inherently more desirable than those of rather small companies; but even here a thoroughly satisfactory statistical showing on the part of the large company is necessary to make this advantage dependable.

No Minimum Size of Issue Prescribed. There is a certain logical fallacy in the prescription found in some savings-bank statutes and in the counsel of investment advisers that a bond issue itself be of a certain minimum size. If the enterprise is large enough, as measured by its gross business, then the smaller the bond issue, the easier it will be to meet the requirements for interest and principal. The legislators and advisers probably desire to avoid the inferior marketability associated with very small issues. In our view, the element of marketability is generally given too much stress by investors, and accordingly we do not think it desirable to specify a minimum size of issues as a general rule for bond investment.

[13] This will range from two or three major units in some industries (e.g., automobiles) to at least a dozen in other industries (e.g., paper).

[14] Since small and medium-size industrial concerns are an essential feature of a free-enterprise system as it has been traditionally operated in this country, and since concerns of such magnitude will frequently desire to do business in part on borrowed funds, we suggest that their borrowing be primarily in the form of term loans from banks and insurance companies. Their bonds ordinarily are not suited to the requirements of ordinary fixed-income investment by *laymen.* On the other hand, institutional lenders are equipped to appraise the risks of such loans and to watch over and advise the borrowers on a continuing and fully informed basis.

THE PROVISION OF THE ISSUE

Under this heading come the terms of the issue, including such features as the security pledged to assure payment of bonds, the conditions affecting interest payments, the date of maturity, and various provisions often made to protect the rights of bondholders (and preferred stockholders) against impairment of their position. The latter include the prohibition of, or restrictions upon, the creation of prior liens; safeguards against the creation of additional amounts of the same issue; certain prohibitions against dividends and other reductions of equity capital; requirements as to net current assets; and provision for a sinking fund. Preferred stockholders generally obtain special voting rights if dividends are suspended for a stated period.

Conversion and similar privileges are, of course, important in themselves, but they do not enter into the determination of standards for the selection of *fixed-income* investments.

Secured vs. Unsecured Obligations. In view of our emphatic argument in Chapter 22 against attaching predominant weight to specific security, it must be clear that we do not favor the exclusion of any group of *unsecured* bond issues per se, or even the establishment of any *sharply defined* standards or requirements which favor secured bonds over debentures.

If a company has only one bond issue, it would seem to make little difference whether this is a first mortgage or a debenture, provided the latter is protected against the placing of future issues ahead of it. Needless to say, a debenture bond preceded by a first mortgage is not so attractive as the first-mortgage bond itself, even though the investor's chief reliance in both cases must be the same—i.e., the ability of the company to meet all its obligations. But this distinction would be equally applicable to a second-mortgage issue and hence is not concerned with debentures as such. We have already discussed the practicalities of selection as between senior and junior liens (pages 313 to 315) and shall refer to this point again when we consider interest coverage.

Conditions Affecting Interest Payments. The typical corporation bond provides for the payment of interest at a fixed rate on fixed dates. This is true whether the bond is secured or unsecured. Income bonds, on the other hand, usually provide for the payment of such interest (up to a stated maximum) as is earned under stipulated accounting rules. Although unpaid interest on them usually accumulates, the recent fashion has been to limit accumulation to a sum equal to three times the annual coupon. The provisions of income bonds vary greatly among the different issues, the basic distinction being between those on which interest *must* be paid if earned and those over which the directors have a greater or lesser measure of discretion. Generally speaking, income bonds are allied more closely to preferred stocks than to ordinary fixed obligations. We shall consider them, accordingly, in Chapter 29 after our discussion of preferred stocks, at which point we shall set forth the need for especial caution and strictness in the selection of this type of security for *straight investment*.

Standards of Safety Should Not Be Relaxed because of Early Maturity. Investors are inclined to attach considerable importance to the *maturity date* of an issue, because of its bearing on whether it is a short- or long-term security. A short maturity, carrying with it the right to repayment fairly soon after purchase, is considered an advantageous feature from the standpoint of safety. Consequently, investors have been prone to be less exacting in their standards when purchasing notes or bonds due in a short time (say, up to three years) than in their other bond selections.

In our opinion this distinction is unsound. A near maturity means a problem of refinancing for the company as well as a privilege of repayment for the investor. The bondholder cannot count on the mere fact of maturity to assure this repayment. The company must have either the cash available (which happens relatively seldom) or else an earning power and financial position which will permit it to raise new funds. Corporations have frequently sold short-term issues because their credit is too poor at the time to permit of a long-term flotation at a reasonable rate. Such a practice has often resulted in trouble for the company, and therefore for the investor, at maturity.

For these reasons we advise against the drawing of distinctions between long- and short-term issues which result in any relaxation of standards of safety in the selection of issues of the latter type.[15] Preference may properly be given to short maturities at times as a matter of *investment policy*—but not to the extent of accepting inadequate measures of safety.

Protective Provisions for Senior Issues. Although the holder of senior securities must rely primarily upon the earning power of the issuer to provide the element of safety and must insist upon adequate margins of safety in the financial exhibits at the time of initial commitment, the obligor should also be bound by reasonable rules of financial housekeeping designed to prevent corporate acts injurious to his status, to strengthen his position as time goes on, and to afford remedies in case of certain unfavorable developments. It is not feasible or even desirable in every case to reduce these matters to quantitative formulation or precise rules, but they undoubtedly tend to safeguard the position of the senior-security holder and are therefore desirable from his point of view.

1. *Prohibition of Prior Liens.* Other things being equal, a provision in a mortgage-bond indenture prohibiting the placing of any new prior lien on the property is desirable as well as of common occurrence.

---

[15] In an exceptional case a short-term issue may be bought at an investment price, even though the earnings exhibit is inadequate, provided the working-capital position is so strong as to assure payment without difficulty. Such an investment would correspond to a loan by a commercial bank.

2. *Equal-and-ratable-security Clause.* When a bond issue is unsecured, provision is ordinarily made that it shall share equally and ratably in any mortgage lien later placed on all or certain of the company properties.

3. *Purchase-money Mortgages.* It is customary to permit without restriction the assumption of *purchase-money mortgages.* These are liens attaching only to new property subsequently acquired, and their assumption is not considered to affect the position of the other bondholders.[16] The latter supposition is not necessarily valid, of course, since it is possible thereby to increase the ratio of total debt of the enterprise to the total shareholder's equity in a manner which might jeopardize the position of the existing bondholders.

A great deal of industrial-company bond financing is now done by the issuance of "subordinated debentures," which give unsecured bank loans a prior claim against the issuer. This is done to make bank borrowing easier for the issuer, but it undoubtedly detracts from the bondholders' position. Nearly all such subordinated debentures are made convertible into stock, or are sold with attached warrants or in units with stock. When they are later dealt in separately, as straight bonds, they are likely to sell on a high-yield basis, unless the company is unusually strong and stable.

Example 1: Teleregister Subordinated Debenture 6s, due 1980, sold in 1961 ex-warrants at 70, yielding over 8 percent. (In the meantime the common stock and warrants sold for an aggregate value of nearly $100 million against $13 million of debt.)

Example 2: By contrast, the $4\frac{5}{8}$ percent subordinated debentures, due 1983, of Corn Products Company (a straight bond) averaged above par in 1960.

4. *Safeguards against Creation of Additional Amounts of the Same Issue.* Nearly all bonds and preferred-stock issues enjoy adequate safeguards in respect to the creation of additional amounts of the issue. The customary provisions require a substantial margin of earnings above the requirements of the issue as thus enlarged. Earnings-coverage provisions of this sort are not common in the railroad field, however. Blanket open (or "open-end") mortgages of railroads more commonly restrict the issuance of additional bonds through a provision limiting the emission of new bonds to a certain percentage of the cost or fair value of newly acquired property (75 or 80 percent being the typical figures). The corresponding figure in the case of public utility bond indentures is usually 60 percent.

These safeguards are logically conceived and almost always carefully observed. Their practical importance is less than might appear, however,

[16] Somewhat in contrast, debenture issues, in recent years, commonly contain an indenture provision requiring that the cash proceeds from a sale-and-lease-back arrangement with any company other than a subsidiary be applied to the reduction of the funded debt (sometimes to the reduction of a specific issue). Examples: American Can debenture $4\frac{3}{4}$s, due 1990; and Riegel Paper debenture $5\frac{1}{4}$s, due 1985.

because in the ordinary instance the showing stipulated would be needed anyway in order to attract buyers for the additional issue.

5. *Working-capital Requirements.* Provisions for maintaining working capital at a certain percentage of bonded debt are by no means standardized and appear only in industrial bond issues. The required percentages vary, and the penalties for nonobservance vary also. In most cases the result is merely the prohibition of dividends until the proper level or ratio of working capital is restored.[17] Occasionally the principal of the bond issue may be declared due.

It would appear to be sound theory to require regularly, for industrial bonds, some protective provisions on the score of working capital. We suggest that a ratio of 100 percent in net current assets to funded debt be considered one of the specific criteria in the selection of most types of fixed-income industrial bonds. It would be well if this criterion were set up in the indenture itself, so that the bondholder will be entitled to the *maintenance* of a satisfactory ratio throughout the life of the issue and to an adequate remedy if the figure declines below the proper point. (Term loans made by banks almost universally embody provisions of this type.)

The prohibition of dividend payments under such conditions is sound and practicable. But the more stringent penalty, which terms a deficiency of working capital "an event of default," is not likely to prove effective or beneficial to the bondholder. The objection that receivership or bankruptcy harms rather than helps the creditors applies with particular force in this connection.

We suggest, therefore, that if a more stringent remedy than mere prohibition of dividends is desired in the event of working-capital impairment, this remedy might consist of a transfer of voting control from the stockholders to the bondholders. In fact, we think that there is much to be said for the suggestion that the bondholders' right to the appointment of trustees in the event of *any* default might well be replaced by a right to receive voting control over the enterprise. Whatever the reader's view as to the soundness of this suggestion as applied to default in payment of interest or principal, we imagine that he will agree with us that it has merit in the case of "secondary" defaults, e.g., failure to maintain working capital as agreed or to make sinking-fund payments; for the present alternatives—either to precipitate insolvency or to do nothing at all—are alike completely unsatisfactory.

6. *Protective Provisions for Investment-company Issues.* Investment-company bonds belong in a special category, we believe, because by their nature they lend themselves to the application of stringent remedial provisions. Such bonds are essentially similar to the collateral loans made

[17] Most debt issues include a provision freezing nearly all the surplus at time of issuance; that is, dividends may not be declared except mainly out of earned surplus subsequently attained.

by banks on marketable securities. As a protection for these bank loans, it is required that the market value of the collateral be maintained at a certain percentage in excess of the amount owed. In the same way the lenders of money to an investment company should be entitled to demand that the value of the portfolio continuously exceed the amount of the loans by an adequate percentage, e.g., 200 percent. If the market value should decline below this figure, the investment company should be required to take the same action as any other borrower against marketable securities. It should either put up more money (i.e., raise more capital from the stockholders) or sell securities and retire debt with the proceeds, in an amount sufficient to restore the proper margin.

The disadvantages that inhere in bond investment generally justify the bond buyer in insisting upon every possible safeguard. In the case of investment-company bonds, a very effective measure of protection may be assured by means of the covenant to maintain the market value of the portfolio above the bonded debt. Hence investors in investment-company issues should demand this type of protective provision, and—what is equally important—they should require its strict enforcement. Although this stand will inflict hardship upon the stockholders when market prices fall, this is part of the original bargain, in which the stockholders agreed to take most of the risk in exchange for the surplus profits.

7. *Sinking Funds and Serial Maturities.* In its modern form a sinking fund provides for the periodic retirement of a certain portion of a senior issue through payments made by the corporation. The precise manner of acquiring the bonds for retirement varies and is not of material significance to the present discussion.

The benefits of a sinking fund are of a twofold nature. The continuous reduction in the size of the issue makes for increasing safety and the easier repayment of the balance at maturity. Also important is the support given to the market for the issue through the repeated appearance of a substantial buying demand. Nearly all industrial bond issues have sinking funds; the public utility group shows about as many with as without; in the railroad list sinking funds are exceptional, except for the bonds of roads reorganized since the 1930's. But in recent years increasing emphasis has been laid upon the desirability of a sinking fund, and few long-term senior issues of any type are now offered without such a provision.

Under some circumstances a sinking fund is absolutely necessary for the protection of a bond. This is true in general when the chief backing of the issue consists of a wasting asset. Bonds on mining properties invariably have a sinking fund, usually of substantial proportions and based upon the tonnage mined. A sinking fund of smaller relative size is regularly provided for real estate-mortgage bonds. In all these cases the theory is that the annual depletion or depreciation allowance should be applied to the reduction of a funded debt.

When the enterprise may be regarded as permanent, the absence of a sinking fund does not necessarily condemn the issue. This is true not only of most high-grade railroad bonds and of many high-grade utility bonds, but also of most of the select group of old-line industrial preferred stocks which merit an investment rating, e.g., National Biscuit Preferred, which had no sinking fund. From the broader standpoint, therefore, sinking funds may be characterized as invariably desirable and sometimes but not always indispensable.

The general object sought by a sinking fund may be obtained by the use of serial maturities. The retirement of a portion of the issue each year by reason of maturity corresponds to the reduction by means of sinking-fund purchases. Such retirement of debt, however, does not assure market support for the unretired balance through the repeated appearance of buying demand, as do sinking-fund operations.

The enforcement of sinking-fund provisions of a bond issue presents the same problem that is involved in covenants for the maintenance of working capital. Failure to make a sinking-fund payment is regularly characterized in the indenture as an event of default, which will permit the trustee to declare the principal due and thus bring about receivership. The objections to this "remedy" are obvious, and we can recall no instance in which the omission of sinking-fund payments, unaccompanied by default of interest, was actually followed by enforcement of the indenture provisions. When the company continues to pay interest but claims to be unable to meet the sinking fund, it is not unusual for the trustee and the bondholders to withhold action and merely to permit arrears to accumulate. More customary is the making of a formal request to the bondholders by the corporation for the postponement of the sinking-fund payments. Such a request is almost invariably acceded to by the great majority of bondholders, since the alternative is always pictured as insolvency.

The Call Provision. Our observations on this important matter, which belong at this point, have (by inadvertence) been relegated to Appendix Note 20, p. 753.

Preferred-stock Protective Provisions. Preferred stocks are frequently accorded certain safeguards against impairment of their position, similar in spirit, though not in detail, to those provided on behalf of bondholders. While this chapter and the next two are devoted primarily to a discussion of standards of safety for the selection of fixed-income bonds, and a later chapter deals with similar criteria for the selection of high-grade preferred stocks, it is convenient at this point to comment briefly upon protective provisions for preferred stocks.

1. *Protection against Creation of Senior Claims.* Preferred stocks are almost always accorded certain safeguards against the placing of new issues ahead of them. The standard provision prohibits either a prior stock or a mortgage-bond issue except upon approval by vote of two-

thirds or three-fourths of the preferred stock.[18] The prohibition is not made absolute, because conditions are always within contemplation under which the preferred stockholders may find it to their advantage to authorize the creation of a senior issue. In an extremity this may be done because new financing through a bond issue is necessary to avoid receivership.

2. *Protection against Creation of Unsecured Debt.* It is common practice to give preferred stockholders no control over the creation of *unsecured debt.* This distinction appears to us to be unsound, since unsecured debt is just as much a threat to preferred stock as is a mortgage obligation. It does seem illogical to provide, as is usually done, that preferred stockholders may forbid the issuance of new preferred shares ranking ahead of or equivalent to theirs, and also of any *secured* indebtedness, but to give them no voice in the creation of a *debenture* bond issue, however large.

Presumably this exclusion arose from the desire to permit bank borrowing for ordinary business purposes; but this point may be taken care of by a specific stipulation to that effect—just as the standard provision now used permits the pledge of assets to secure "loans made in the ordinary course of business" without preferred stockholders' consent.[19]

3. *Preferred-stock Sinking Funds.* Relatively few public utility or railroad preferred-stock issues have a sinking-fund provision.[20] But in the case of industrial preferred-stock offerings, sinking funds have become the general rule. The advantages which bonds derive from a sinking fund are equally inherent in preferred stocks. Furthermore, in view of the weak contractual position of preferred stocks as contrasted with bonds, there is the more reason for the buyer to insist on special protective arrangements of this kind. But while a sinking fund is thus a highly desirable feature of a preferred issue, its presence is no assurance of adequate safety nor is its absence a negation thereof.

4. *Net-current-asset Requirement.* A small number of preferred stocks are protected by an agreement to maintain net current assets, usually at

[18] There are various departures from this 2/3–3/4 range. For example, Diamond National Corporation can increase its funded debt with the approval of a majority of the $1.50 cumulative preferred-stock issue. Various issues provide that it is not necessary to secure the consent of the preferred stock to create additional debt if certain standards with respect principally to earnings coverage and net-asset coverage are met. In this connection, see St. Regis Paper 4.40 percent cumulative first preferred, Series A. The provisions of Macy's 4 1/4 percent cumulative preferred, Series A (as reported in Moody's *Industrial Manual*) are silent in regard to the creation of additional debt.

[19] It should be noted, however, that there is a growing tendency in recent years to protect preferred stockholders against the creation of debenture bonds by requiring their approval of the issuance of any "bonds, notes, debentures or other evidence of indebtedness maturing later than one year from the date of their issue."

[20] However, many pipe-line company preferred stocks have sinking funds.

100 percent of the preferred issue or 100 percent of the preferred stock plus bond issues. Sometimes the penalty for nonobservance is merely a prohibition of common dividends; sometimes voting control passes to the preferred stock. Where found, these provisions may well be advantageous to the holder.

5. *Voting Power in the Event of Nonpayment of Dividends.* It is fairly common among industrial preferred issues for voting power to accrue to the holders in the event of nonpayment of dividends. As far as we know, these stipulations apply only to cumulative issues. The arrangement varies with respect to the time when the voting power becomes effective and to the degree of control bestowed. On the first point, the range of variation extends from voting power becoming effective upon the passage of *one* quarterly dividend to the passage of the *eighth* quarterly payment. The more customary periods are four or six quarters. Giving the right to vote upon the passage of, say, *four consecutive* quarterly dividends has led to the fancy artifice of paying less than regularly but with such frequency that no voting power has actually passed to the preferred holders.

The right conferred upon the preferred stock may be (1) to vote exclusively for the directors; (2) to elect separately a majority of the board; (3) to elect separately a minority of the board; or (4) to vote share for share with the common stock.

Example 1: The voting provision of National Gypsum's $4.50 cumulative preferred stock is as follows: "When six or more quarterly dividends (whether consecutive or not) are unpaid in whole or in part, the number of members of the Board of Directors shall be increased by one-half and the additional directors shall be elected by the holders of the preferred stock, as a class."

Example 2: Virginia-Carolina Chemical preferred votes share for share with the common under all circumstances. Its total vote is only 40 percent of that of the common. Thus, although dividend arrears were $90 per share in 1961, it was unable to elect any directors or to obtain any dividends in 1959–1961, despite earnings of $2\frac{1}{2}$ times the $6 dividend in the June 1960 year.

Noncumulative Issues Need Greater Protection. The practices outlined above merit certain other criticisms of a more general nature. In the first place, while it is taken for granted that these special voting provisions should apply to cumulative preferred stocks only, the exclusion of noncumulative issues seems to us to be most illogical. Their holders have certainly a greater reason to demand representation in the event of nonpayment, because they have no right to recover the lost dividends in the future. In our view it should be established as a financial principle that *any* preferred stock which is not paying its full dividend currently should have some separate representation on the board of directors.

On the other hand we do not consider it proper to deprive the common stock of all representation when preferred dividends are unpaid. Complete domination of the board by the preferred stockholders may lead to some practices distinctly unfair to the common stock, e.g., perpetuation of preferred-stock control by unnecessarily refraining from paying up back dividends in full. An alert minority on the board of directors, even though powerless in the actual voting, may be able to accomplish a great deal in preventing unfair or unsound practices.

A General Canon regarding Voting Power. From the foregoing discussion, a general canon with respect to voting power may readily be formulated. The standard arrangement should give every preferred and every common issue the separate right to *elect some directors under all circumstances* unless the investment status of the preferred issue is maintained in accordance with rather stringent standards. It would be logical for the common stock to elect the majority of the board as long as preferred dividends were regularly paid; and equally logical that, whenever the full dividend was not paid on either a cumulative or noncumulative preferred issue, the right to choose the majority of the board should pass to the preferred stockholders.

Adequate protection for preferred issues should require that voting control pass to the holders in the event not only of default in dividends but also of nonpayment of the sinking fund or the failure to maintain working capital as stipulated.[21]

Value of Voting Control by Preferred Stock May Be Questioned. Viewing the matter realistically, we must admit that the vesting of voting control in holders of a preferred issue does not necessarily prove of benefit to them. Perhaps the holders cannot always make effective use of this privilege; or perhaps they are sometimes too inert—or too poorly advised—to protect their interests even though they have power to do so.

The preferred stockholders individually have no satisfactory means of going about the nomination and election of directors to represent them. This duty should devolve upon the financial houses that originally offered the issue, and they should discharge it conscientiously. They should (1) obtain a list of the preferred stockholders of record, (2) advise them of their new voting rights, and (3) recommend to them a slate of directors and request their proxies to vote for these nominees. The directors suggested should, of course, be as well qualified as possible for their posts. They must be free from any large interest in, or close affiliation with, the common stock, and it would be desirable if they were themselves substantial owners of preferred shares.

It is quite possible, nonetheless, that the directors chosen by the pre-

---

[21] Corporations which, pursuant to the provisions of Chap. X of the Bankruptcy Act, issue stock that is preferred as to dividends are required to include provision in their charters for the election of directors representing such preferred shareholders in the event of default in the payment of preferred dividends. See Chap. X, Art. X, Sec. 216(12) (*a*) of the Bankruptcy Act.

ferred stockholders will be incompetent or will for other reasons fail to represent their interests properly. But this is not a valid argument against the possession and the exercise of voting power by preferred stockholders. The same objection applies to voting rights of common stockholders—and of citizens. The remedy is not disfranchisement but education. A combination of adequate voting-control provisions for preferred shares with their prompt and effective use could largely overcome the disadvantages inherent in the absence of an unqualified legal right to receive dividends. But until *both* these conditions are fulfilled, we must continue to stress the practical superiority for investors of the bond form over the preferred-stock form.

6. *Maintenance of Adequate Junior Capital.* An adequate amount of junior capital is an indispensable condition for any sound fixed-income investment. In earlier times it was common for senior issues to permit withdrawal of junior capital by action of the common stockholders. This could, and did on occasion, leave the senior-security holders in the absurd position of having provided all or practically all the actual capital of a business, thereby assuming all or most of the risk of loss, without any share in the profits above ordinary senior-security yields. Fortunately, most new senior-security agreements contain provisions prohibiting dividends or other distributions to the junior stockholders (including repurchase of common shares), unless an adequate margin of resources above the claims of senior-security holders remains.

Concluding Caveat concerning Protective Provisions. The emphasis we have laid upon the proper kind of protective provisions for industrial bonds and preferred stocks should not lead the reader to believe that the presence of such provisions carries an assurance of safety. This is far from the truth. The success of a bond or preferred-stock investment depends primarily upon the success of the enterprise, and only to a very secondary degree upon the terms of the indenture or character provisions. Hence the seeming paradox that the senior securities that fared best in the 1932 depression had, on the whole, quite unsatisfactory indenture or charter provisions. The explanation is that the best issues as a class have been the oldest issues, and these date from times when less attention was paid than now to protective covenants.

A *Contrary Example:* Cudahy Packing 4½ percent cumulative preferred stock, which was publicly offered in 1945, has all of the typical protective covenants. However, the price of the shares dropped from 101 in 1947 to 48 in 1954—after dividend payments were omitted in 1953 and 1954.[22] Thus, those who purchased the shares at an investment level

---

[22] The after-tax coverage of interest and preferred dividend requirements was reported to be 2.48 times in 1945 but jumped to 6.90 times in 1946. Apparently, the buyer at 101 in 1947 was either giving great weight to the 1946 coverage or basing his decision on the questionable use of per-share earnings figures, which were $25.05 in 1945 and $67.21 in 1946.

found that all the standard protective provisions failed to safeguard them against a loss of substantial proportions. But while the protective covenants we have been discussing do not *guarantee* the safety of the issue, they nevertheless *add* to the safety and are therefore worth insisting upon.

RECORD OF INTEREST AND DIVIDEND PAYMENTS

Solvency Record. Investment bonds should have behind them a sufficiently long record of successful operation and of financial stability on the part of the issuer. New enterprises and those recently emerged from financial difficulties are not entitled to the high credit rating essential to justify a fixed-income investment.[23] Savings-bank statutes recognize the past-solvency criterion by providing that issuers shall not have defaulted on principal or interest for stipulated periods if their issues are to be eligible for investment of savings-bank funds. Our view is that an appropriate *fixed-charge-coverage* requirement should adequately take care of the question of past record without a separate past-solvency test.

The Dividend Record. Since private business corporations exist primarily to earn money and pay dividends to their owners, it might at first glance seem reasonable to require a record of dividend payments as a condition for investment in corporate bonds, and a record of such payments to *junior* stockholders in the case of commitments in high-grade preferred stocks. Such a requirement would be based on the theory that fixed-income commitments should be made only in securities of successful concerns and that the dividend record affords a useful clue on that point.

Dividend Record Not Conclusive Evidence of Financial Strength. It may not be denied that dividend-paying concerns as a class are more prosperous than those which pay no dividends. But this fact would not in itself justify the summary condemnation of all the bonds of non-dividend-paying enterprises. An exceedingly strong argument *against* such a rule lies in the fact that the payment of dividends is only an indication of financial strength; and not only does it fail to afford any *direct advantage* to the bondholder, but it may often be injurious to his interests by reducing the corporation's resources. In actual practice the dividend provisions of the statutes governing legal investments have at times had consequences directly opposite to those intended. Railroad companies in a weak financial position have improvidently continued dividend payments for the particular purpose of maintaining their bonds on the eligible list, so that

---

[23] An exception to this statement is justified in those cases in which the financial difficulties were due to an excessive debt burden which reorganization has reduced to a figure that would have been amply taken care of by the previous earnings. Thus the fixed-interest bonds of some railroads reorganized since 1940 appeared sound enough to qualify as fixed-income investments, especially since reductions in fixed charges had been so drastic.

the very practice supposed to indicate strength behind the bond has in reality undermined its safety.

The Role of the Dividend Record in Bond Investment. The evidence given by the balance sheet and income account must be regarded as a more dependable clue to the soundness of an enterprise than the record of dividend payments. It seems best therefore to dispense with all hard and fast rules on the latter point in determining the suitability of bond and preferred-stock issues for straight investment. But the failure of a (nongrowth)[24] company to pay dividends when the earnings appear satisfactory should properly cause an intending bond buyer to scrutinize the situation with more than usual care, in order to discover whether the policy of the directors is due to weak elements in the picture not yet reflected in the income account. We might also point out incidentally that the bonds and preferred stocks of dividend-paying companies possess a certain mechanical advantage in that their owners may receive a definite and perhaps timely warning of impending trouble by the later passing of the common dividend. Being thus placed on their guard, they may be able to protect themselves against serious loss. Bonds of non-dividend-paying concerns are at a certain disadvantage in this respect; but in our opinion this may be adequately offset by the exercise of somewhat greater caution on the part of the investor.

[24] In recent years a number of rapidly growing companies have followed a policy of not paying cash dividends. See Chap. 36.

CHAPTER TWENTY-FOUR

SPECIFIC STANDARDS FOR BOND INVESTMENT

(*Continued*)

RELATION OF EARNINGS TO INTEREST REQUIREMENTS

The present-day investor is properly accustomed to regard the ratio of earnings to fixed charges as the most important specific test of safety. This attitude is the logical consequence of the fact that on a going-concern basis, interest charges are met from earnings and business values are in the last analysis dependent upon earning power. It is a thesis of our earlier discussion that the buyer of fixed-income securities should place primary reliance upon the ability of the issuer to meet all its charges—an ability which cannot be sustained without earning power and which at bottom cannot be measured dependably except in terms of earning power.

Three Phases of Earnings Coverage. Three phases of determining earnings coverage for fixed charges deserve consideration. The first considers the *amount* of fixed charges to be covered; the second, the *method* of computing coverage; and the third proposes the *standards* to be applied in determining whether the coverage is adequate for the purpose of fixed-income investment.

What Is the Amount of the Fixed Charges? In the ordinary case fixed charges and interest charges are identical.[1] However, certain important exceptions to this statement deserve notice:

1. *Interest on income bonds* is not a fixed charge from the point of view of the holder of *fixed-interest* bonds of the issuer. This follows from the fact that, at most, interest on income bonds must be paid only if earned. However, from the point of view of the buyer of the income bond for fixed-income investment, the interest thereon must be regarded as equivalent to a fixed charge, since it is mainly to receive this interest regularly that such a bond is bought at a full or standard price.

[1] Included as a part of bond interest are charges for the amortization of bond discount and expense incidental to the borrowing of funds, since these costs are a part of interest cost on capital borrowed. Amortization of bond premium is an offset to interest charges for the opposite reason.

2. *Rentals paid or accrued* for the use of leased lines should be included among the fixed charges in the case of railroads, since in actuality they are substitutes for interest charges on funded debt that would have been made had the properties been acquired outright rather than leased.

3. Similarly, as is pointed out in Chapters 25 and 26, a part of the *rent paid for building space* by retail chains, department stores, and similar enterprises should be included among the fixed charges if a realistic view of the relationship between available earnings and fixed charges is to be attained. Our investigations indicate that it is reasonable to include one-third of such rentals among fixed charges.

4. In the case of holding-company bonds, the *dividend requirements* on underlying preferred-stock issues, as well as the fixed charges on subsidiary debt, must ordinarily be included in the over-all fixed charges when computing coverage from a consolidated statement. This follows from the fact that these underlying issues have a prior claim to the earnings of the subsidiaries ahead of that of the bonds of the parent company.

5. Finally, there are many instances in which railroads will be obligated to pay *net rentals for the hire of equipment and joint facilities* which are not fully offset by interest, dividend, and other income. It is our conclusion that one-half of any *net debit* for intermediate items (mainly hire of equipment and joint facilities minus other income) should be *included* with fixed charges when computing coverage for railroad bonds, and that one-half of any *net credit* for these items should be treated as an *offset* to fixed charges. Unless an adjustment of this type is made, many roads will present coverage exhibits which inadequately reflect a burden of costs which are substantially in the category of fixed charges.[2]

Coverage Before or After Income Taxes? The *method* of calculating earnings coverage is complicated by the question whether earnings *before* or *after* deducting income taxes should be used. In the case of bonds of operating companies the logic of the matter is clear. Income taxes are imposed upon profits after subtracting interest paid. The probability that a bondholder will receive his interest from earnings is not impaired by the need for paying income taxes on the balance of those earnings left after deducting the interest charges. Hence earnings available for interest charges should properly be shown *before* deducting income taxes and the coverage calculated from that figure. In corporate reports to stockholders it is customary to reverse this order and to show the amount of earnings available for interest charges *after* deduction of income taxes. But the income tax figure is usually shown or easily determinable, and the proper adjustment can readily be made by adding back the tax figure before computing coverage.

The logic of computing coverage before income taxes is by no means so clear in the (now rare) cases of holding-company bonds where the impact of income taxes is divided. Moreover, the calculation after taxes

[2] See Chap. 19 for a discussion of the analysis of railroad securities.

in *all cases* has the virtue of being convenient, as well as being the method uniformly employed by the financial services. (Usually they calculate coverage before taxes as well.) The after-tax coverage can normally be used—on a basis equivalent to a before-tax coverage—by taking a correspondingly lower minimum requirement, after making allowance for the income tax factor at the appropriate rate. An exception to this statement is noted in the next paragraph with respect to fixed-interest bonds of companies having large income-bond issues outstanding. Moreover, when the company's income tax allowance for a period does not roughly correspond to the balance after fixed charges, it would be preferable to calculate coverage before income taxes to eliminate distortions due to special income tax debits or credits not related to normal earning power.

A Technicality of After-tax Coverage. When computing coverage for fixed-interest bonds, interest charges on income bonds are not included among the fixed charges. Yet if the issuer has income bonds outstanding and has paid the interest thereon, it will have received a tax benefit which will be reflected in the tax accrual deducted on the income statement. The result will be that, if a company has a large income-bond issue outstanding and has paid the charges on it, the fixed-interest bonds will show a *relatively* better coverage on an after-tax basis than on a before-tax basis (as compared with a fixed-interest bond issue with the same charges not followed by income-bond interest charges), since the tax accrual is held down by the payment of contingent interest.

This matter is not important except in the case of reorganized railroads with large income-bond issues—a limited situation. We suggest that the before-tax test recommended below be used in the case of fixed-interest bonds of such roads.

Example: In 1957 the Chicago, Milwaukee, St. Paul and Pacific Railroad Company reported fixed charges as earned 4.33 times before taxes and 4.06 times after taxes. Income taxes were reduced, however, by about $3,400,000 (assuming the 52 percent rate) by reason of the deduction of $6,562,000 for contingent interest. If the tax saving on contingent interest were excluded from the computation of fixed-charge coverage, the latter figure would be reduced to 3.34 times after adjusted income taxes.

The foregoing figures are based on reported charges, without adjustment for intermediate items. On the basis of our suggested procedure of adding one-half the net intermediate debits to fixed charges, the latter figure would be increased from $4,731,000 to $8,018,000 for 1957. The coverage before taxes would be reduced to 2.80 times, and after taxes (excluding the tax credit for contingent interest) it would be 2.38 times.

Three Methods of Computing Coverage for an Individual Bond Issue. Whether the calculation is made on the basis of earnings before or after deducting income taxes, and whether computed from the earnings of a single year or their average for a period of years, various methods are in common use for computing and stating the relation of earnings to fixed charges.

1. *The Prior-deductions Method.* One of these (which may be called the prior-deductions method) is thoroughly objectionable. Nevertheless, it was once followed by the majority of issuing houses in their circulars offering junior bonds for sale, because it makes for a deceptively strong exhibit.

The procedure consists of first deducting the prior charges from the earnings and then calculating the number of times the junior requirements are covered by the balance. The following illustration will show both the method itself and its inherent absurdity:

Company *A* has $10,000,000 of first-mortgage 4 percent
  bonds and $3,200,000 of debenture 5 percent bonds.
Its average earnings are...... .... $2,000,000
Deduct interest on first 4s.........................   400,000, earned 5 times
Balance for debenture 5s........................... $1,600,000
Interest on debentures.............................   160,000, earned 10 times

Years ago a circular offering the 5 percent debentures was likely to state that "as shown above" the interest charges are covered ten times. It should be noted, however, that the interest on the first 4s is covered only five times. The implication of these figures would be that the junior issue is better protected than the senior issue, which is clearly absurd. The fact is that the results shown for junior bonds by this prior-deductions method are completely valueless and misleading.

One of the favorable results of the Securities Act of 1933 has been the abandonment of this indefensible method of stating interest coverage in new bond offerings. This change has been due, apparently, not to any specific prohibition by the statute or the SEC regulations, but rather to the desire to avoid risking penalties for deceit. But the possibility of the same type of deception is implicit in any statement of *earnings per share* on preferred-stock issues which are preceded by bonds or other obligations requiring the payment of fixed charges. Such per-share earnings figures are usually computed by the financial services (accompanied by the more significant figure showing the number of times fixed charges and preferred dividends *combined* are earned) and in brokerage-house analyses.

2. *The Cumulative-deductions Method.* The second procedure may be called the cumulative-deductions method. Under this method, interest on a junior bond is always considered in conjunction with prior and equivalent charges. In the previous example, the interest on the debenture 5s would be earned 3.57 times, found by dividing the combined charges of *both* issues, viz., $560,000, into the available earnings of $2,000,000. The first-mortgage interest, however, would be said to be earned five times, since bond interest *junior* to the issue analyzed is left out of considera-

tion in this method. The majority of investors would regard this point of view as entirely sound.

3. *The Total-deductions or "Over-all" Method.* In a previous chapter, however, we have emphasized the primary importance of a company's ability to meet *all* its fixed obligations, because insolvency resulting from default on a junior lien invariably reacts to the disadvantage of the prior-mortgage bondholders. An investor can be sure of his position only if the total-interest charges are well covered. Consequently, the conservative and therefore advisable way of calculating interest coverage should always be the total-deductions method; i.e., the controlling figure should be the number of times that *all* fixed charges are covered. This would mean that the *same earnings ratio would be used in analyzing all the fixed-interest bonds of any company,* whether they are senior or junior liens. In the example above, the ratio would be 3.57 as applied to either the first 4s or the debenture 5s. This method is now commonly referred to as the "over-all basis" for computing coverage.

There is no reason, of course, why the coverage for a senior bond should not be computed by the cumulative-deductions method also, and if this coverage is very large it may properly be regarded as an added argument in favor of the issue. But our recommendation is that in applying any *minimum* requirement designed to test the company's strength, the total fixed charges should always be taken into account.

Current Charges vs. Actual Charges. Another problem of *method* used in calculating coverage grows out of the fact that at the time a bond issue is being analyzed the new or current fixed charges may differ substantially from those of a past representative period chosen for study. This has been true in recent years, largely because of the substantial increase in the rate of interest on new bond flotations.

The rate of interest on new bond issues declined from 5.73 percent in 1932 to 2.75 percent in 1946, and has since advanced to 4.82 percent in 1960. Where bonds have matured and been refunded in recent years the new interest charges are higher than the old. In appraising the current bond issue it would be sound practice to apply the former earnings to the new interest charges, rather than to accept the past interest coverage based on lower charges.

This approach would necessarily exclude bonds of new enterprises—such as pipe-line and chemical concerns, which in recent years sold large debt issues to finance plant construction—and of some older ones which embarked on large-scale expansion projects. We think that the *individual* investor would simplify his problem along logical lines by avoiding the bonds of all issuers that would depend on expected future earnings *alone* to create the required margin of safety. Large institutional investors are much better qualified than the individual or the small institution to make the requisite study of the company's propects. Both the investigation and the investment had best be left to them.

What Standards of Coverage Should Be Applied? Minimum required coverage for total fixed charges should be set high enough to provide a persuasive assurance of safety. They should reflect variations in the inherent stability of earnings of the several major types of enterprise—public utilities, railroads, and industrials. The following is a summary of the tests recommended for this purpose.

1. *Average earnings* for a period of from seven to ten years should equal at least the following multiple of fixed charges:

Type	Before taxes	After taxes*
Public utilities...........	4×	2.4×
Railroads.................	5×	2.9×
Industrials..............	7×	3.8×

* Based on an assumed tax rate of 52 percent. The actual figures are 2.44×, 2.92×, and 3.88×. We have chosen to round in each instance to the lower number.

2. Alternatively, *the earnings of the poorest year* during the period should equal at least the following multiple of fixed charges:

Type	Before taxes	After taxes
Public utilities...........	3×	1.9×
Railroads.................	4×	2.4×
Industrials..............	5×	2.9×

3. Supplemental test (in addition to either 1 or 2 above): *Average available income before income taxes* should equal at least the following percentage of funded debt:

Type	Ratio, percent
Public utilities..............	18
Railroads..................	22
Industrials.................	30

The Period to Be Used for the Test. The usual period taken would run from seven to ten years preceding the date of the study. The suggested span should be sufficient to cover both prosperity and recession. For example, the seven years, 1954–1960, encompass practically two complete business cycles. While the downswings were small in contrast with earlier depressions, they did give evidence as to the relative vulnerability of various industries and of individual companies.

The Minimum Coverage Required. The coverage figures suggested in our table may be more stringent than those employed by some investors. We recommend them, nevertheless, because experience demonstrates that investors in high-grade securities have suffered losses in the past which can be traced to the acceptance of inadequate earnings protection.

The "Poorest-year" Test. If the period used is long enough to include the variations of a business cycle, the results shown in the poorest year should indicate how well the company can fare under unfavorable conditions. Such poorest-year results will, of course, be less than the average for the period. If they come reasonably close to the minimum requirement for the entire period, that fact should indicate a high level of stability for the company, and should carry perhaps a better assurance of safety for the bonds than a somewhat better average figure comprising wider fluctuations.

Thus we suggest a "poorest-year" test as an alternative to the average. The requirements are less than, but related to, those for average earnings. This alternative test has an advantage of simplicity. In the typical case the analyst can tell quickly by inspecting the coverage figures supplied by the financial services (or the net available for interest) whether the poorest year's results exceed the requirement.

Other Aspects of the Earnings Record. There are, of course, a number of other aspects of the earnings picture to which the investor would do well to pay attention. Among these are the *trend* and the *current figure*. Their importance cannot be gainsaid, but they do not lend themselves effectively to the application of hard and fast rules.

In dealing with factors of this sort the investor must *demand* an average or a minimum at least equal to the standard recommended. In addition, he will be attracted by (1) a rising trend of profits,[3] (2) an especially good current showing, and (3) a combination of a high average and a good minimum figure. If a bond is deficient in any one of these three aspects, the result should not necessarily be to condemn the issue, but rather to exact an average-earnings coverage well in excess of the minimum and to require closer attention to the general or qualitative elements in the situation. If the trend has been unfavorable or the latest figure alone has been decidedly poor, the investor should certainly not accept the bond unless the average earnings have been substantially *above* the minimum requirement—*and unless also he has reasonable grounds for believing that the downward trend or the current slump is not likely to continue indefinitely.* The *amount* by which the average must be advanced in order to offset an unfavorable trend or current exhibit is a matter within the discretion of the investor to determine and cannot be developed into any set of mathematical formulas.

[3] In cases of unusually pronounced upward trends in earnings, the proposed test based on the *average* may seem rather severe. However, the analyst who accepts as a high-quality bond one which has ample coverage only in the last few years is faced with the problem not only of distinguishing between trend and cyclical moves in earnings but also of convincing himself that the competitive and other factors are such that there will be no falling back from the recently attained high level of earnings.

The Relation of the Coupon Rate to Earnings Coverage. The theory of earnings coverage is complicated by the arithmetical fact that this coverage varies inversely with the rate of interest. Given the same earnings, interest on a 2½ percent bond issue would be earned twice as many times before taxes as it would be if the rate were 5 percent. Consider the comparison shown in the accompanying table, covering two companies each with $10,000,000 of debt:

	Utility Co. *A* (1946), interest rate 2½%	Utility Co. *B* (1961), interest rate 5%
Average earnings for interest (before taxes)........................	$1,190,000	$1,850,000
Earnings for interest (after taxes)*...	700,000	1,150,000
Interest charges.....................	250,000	500,000
Times interest earned (before taxes)..	4.8×	3.7×
Times interest earned (after taxes)...	2.8×	2.3×

* Assuming a 52 percent tax rate.

The difference in coupon rates alone makes Company *A* pass our earnings-coverage test, whereas Company *B*'s coverage falls below it. This point may well raise several questions, viz: (1) Can a bond be considered "safe" merely because it carries a low coupon rate? (2) What would be the effect on this safety of a rise in the general rate of interest? (3) Are the bonds of Company *A* a sounder purchase for investment than those of Company *B*? Let us attempt to answer these questions briefly in their order.

1. *Effect of Coupon Rate on Safety.* Safety, in the technical sense of assurance of continued payment of interest, can certainly be created or destroyed by varying the coupon rate. It is not feasible to think of a 5 percent bond as being safe as to 2½ percent interest and unsafe as to the additional 2½ percent. Safety of interest is an indivisible concept and must apply to the entire interest charge, the reason being that inability to pay part of the contractual interest—or even junior interest—will result in financial difficulties. These in turn mean the destruction, at least temporarily, of the investment status.

Safety in the sense of maintenance of principal value can also be "created" by a low rate of interest, provided this rate is considered to be permanent—i.e., lasting either through maturity or for a great many years in the future. If the 2½ percent rate proved to be permanent, the after-tax earnings of $700,000 ($1,190,000 pretax) should enable Company *A* to refund its bonds at maturity, and they should also maintain the market price of the bonds not far from par. Let us emphasize that it is questionable to accept as permanent interest rates which are at or near *historically low* levels—even though they may remain there for a number of years. In the 18 years from 1938 through 1955 the annual rate on Standard & Poor's A1+ bonds exceeded 3 percent only in one year, and the period average was 2.65 percent. However, in 1960 the average annual rate was 4.41 percent.

Allowance must be made for the fact that the rate of interest tends to vary inversely with the ability of the company to pay it. A strong company borrows at a low rate, although it could afford to pay more than could a weak company. This means that "good credit" itself produces "better credit" through its own saving in interest charges, whereas the opposite is equally true. Although this may seem paradoxical and unfair, it must be accepted as a fact in security analysis.

2. *Effect of a Rise in Interest Rates on Safety.* A general rise in interest rates would not affect the ability of a company to meet its interest charges during the life of its low-rate bond issue. But if the bonds mature in a short time, the company will be faced with the problem of refunding at a higher rate, to effect which its earnings must show an adequate margin above this higher rate. On the other hand, if the maturity is distant, the market price of this and other bonds will decline substantially, should the general rate of interest experience a considerable rise. (Note that, as a result of substantial increases in interest rates, Standard & Poor's Composite Index of High-grade Bond Prices fell 22 percent between 1905 and 1919 and dropped 24 percent between 1946 and 1960.)[4]

It follows, therefore, that safety of principal, in the sense of maintenance of market value, is certain to be affected adversely in the case of long-term bonds by a sharp rise in the rate of interest.[5] Safety of principal of short-term debt *may* also be affected adversely by such a rise in interest rates, if the earnings coverage does not exceed our minimum by a comfortable margin.

The practical conclusion must be that, if the investor considers a rise in interest rates probable, he should not buy long-term bonds no matter how strong the company; and he should buy short-term issues only if earnings would cover a higher coupon rate with an adequate margin. If, however, he is convinced that a (historically) low interest rate is here to stay, he may accept it in the same way in which the higher rates were formerly accepted. If he is undecided as to the future of interest rates, the best policy might seem to be to confine purchases to bonds of fairly

---

[4] Norfolk & Western first consolidated gold 4s, due 1996, and rated Aaa, fell from a high of 143 in 1946 to a low of 90 in 1960. This is equivalent to the loss of more than 13 years' interest.

[5] An exception would be high-coupon bonds whose prices had been held down by a callable feature; but most of these would have been refunded at lower coupon rates.

short maturity (say not longer than ten years) and also to increase his earnings-coverage requirement to offset the low coupon rate.[6]

3. *Relative Attractiveness of the Two Bonds.* Our third question relates to the comparative attractiveness of the 2½ percent bonds of Company A and the 5 percent bonds of Company B. In strict logic the 5 percent bond must certainly be more desirable than the 2½ percent bond, since the 5 percent bondholder could always place his claim to the extra 2½ percent on a contingent basis and thus make his company's margin above *fixed* charges better than Company A's. But in practice such a reduction of fixed interest is likely to be made only after the issuer has fallen into financial difficulties, which in turn would cause a substantial decline in the market price of the issue. Hence, as a practical matter, it is possible that the holder of the 2½ percent bond may fare better than the owner of the 5 percent.

It should be clear, however, that there are limits to the bootstrap operation of creating safety for a bond by means of a low coupon rate and consequent high earnings coverage. To set up a formal safeguard against this possibility, we have suggested a separate requirement of earnings which is related solely to the principal amount of the debt, as indicated earlier in this chapter.

This test should be applied for the same period as the earnings covered. It will be noted that Company A, in the table on page 350 will fail this test, since before a 52 percent tax it earns 11.9 percent on the principal of its debt. Company B would pass the test, with an 18.5 percent figure, but it fails to show the minimum after-tax coverage of 2.4 times interest, because of the high coupon rate. Hence, neither company passes both tests; by our severe criteria neither is eligible for conservative investment.[7]

The "funded debt" which is used for this supplemental test in the case of railroads and industrials should be the same as that used for the stock-equity ratio. In other words, it should correspond to the actual fixed charges, and thus should include an allowance for the capitalized value of rentals. This matter is discussed further in Chapter 25.

---

[6] Note that this discussion applies directly to the low interest rates prevailing at the time of the 1940 and 1951 editions. The situation in 1961, with its much higher rates, does not pose the same problems that the investor faced in 1936–1956.

[7] Note that if Company A's 2½ percent bonds have a near maturity it might be faced with serious refinancing difficulties because its earnings coverage at a 5 percent rate would be inadequate.

CHAPTER TWENTY-FIVE

SPECIFIC STANDARDS FOR BOND INVESTMENT

(Continued)

THE RELATION OF THE VALUE OF THE PROPERTY TO THE FUNDED DEBT

In our earlier discussion (Chapter 22) we pointed out that the soundness of the typical bond investment depends primarily upon the ability of the obligor corporation to take care of its debts, rather than upon the value of the property on which the bonds have a *lien*. This broad principle naturally leads directly away from the establishment of any *general* tests of bond safety based upon the value of the mortgaged assets, where this value is considered apart from the success or failure of the enterprise itself.

However, we do believe that the possession of assets in substantial amount by issuers has some significance for the buyers of fixed-income securities. For, in the normal case, assets costing well in excess of funded debt or other senior securities are essential to supply earning power at a sufficiently high level and with sufficient dependability to make these senior securities safe. Instances will be rare in which securities otherwise eligible for fixed-income investment will be disqualified because of a minimum-asset requirement such as we suggest below. It is nevertheless desirable to safeguard the buyer of such securities (who has everything to lose by making errors in the measurement of risk and little to gain by taking chances) against the exceptions where the issues should either be rejected because of apparent asset deficiency or else be subjected to unusually searching analysis in order to warrant commitment in them.

Minimum Asset Requirements. Accordingly, we recommend the following maximum ratios of funded debt to net tangible assets (or the indicated substitutes therefor) for issues which are otherwise eligible for fixed-income investment:

	Maximum ratio of debt to
Type	*net tangible assets, percent*
Public utility bonds...................	60*
Investment-company bonds..............	33⅓†

* In the case of public utility bonds this ratio is generally computed against net-plant account, thus excluding working capital. (This is equivalent to a ratio of net-plant account to debt of 1.7 times.) A 60 percent bond component, while theoretically permissible, would not leave room for a sound preferred-stock issue. Since the typical utility company has a three-class capitalization structure, its bond component is normally less than 60 percent. For most companies the figure runs between 50 and 55 percent. In practice the ratio is sometimes based on the sum of capitalization and surplus, in which case 55 percent ratio would be a suitable maximum, as explained on page 277. (In other words the above sum must exceed 1.8 times the debt.)

† Assets to be valued at current market, or fair value when market quotations are not readily available.

For railroad and industrial bonds we believe the better test is that of stock equity at market (see pages 359 to 363 below). Hence we do not suggest a net-tangible-asset test for these categories. However, as noted on page 372, industrial bonds should normally be protected by at least 100 percent in net working capital.

Charges-to-property Ratio for Public Utility Bonds. A useful additional test in the case of public utility bonds is the ratio of *fixed charges* to the minimum value of the property that might be used for rate-making purposes. For practical purposes the latter may be taken in most cases at total capitalization, including surplus. For high-grade, fixed-income commitments this ratio should not exceed 2½ percent, in order to afford adequate protection against a severe decline in earnings which might be remedied by rate relief only after a lapse of time.

The logical justification for setting up this maximum ratio stems from the legal regulation of public utility earnings. If existing rates for service do not produce a reasonable return, the company is entitled to increase its rates; but in times of adversity it might well find difficulty in obtaining permission to do so unless the return being earned is so low that confiscation clearly results. Moreover, a considerable delay in time might be involved. Let us assume a company is allowed a return of 6¼ percent on its rate base. If a company has a ratio of funded debt to rate-base property at 55 percent and the funds are borrowed at 4½ percent, the charges on the debt work out at about 2½ percent of the rate base. Under normal conditions 6¼ percent earnings on the rate base will cover these charges, after income taxes, over 2.4 times—which is our minimum standard after taxes.[1] Meeting this 2.4 standard assures the bondholder that if earnings decline to virtually confiscatory levels (say 4½ percent on rate base) the interest charges on his bonds will still be protected by sufficient earnings to assure continued payment and reasonable stability in market price. It will be noted that this ratio combines our fixed-charge-coverage

---

[1] The pretax rate would be equivalent to 13.02 percent (assuming an effective tax rate of 52 percent) and the coverage of interest charges would be 5.2 times.

test and our ratio-of-debt-to-property test and is consistent therewith.[2]

Special Types of Obligations. There are various special types of obligations, the safety of which is in much greater measure dependent upon the assets securing them, as distinguished from the going-concern value of the enterprise as a whole. In these categories investments are often made primarily on the basis of the specific security pledged or held and with smaller attention to the coverage of fixed charges.

1. *Equipment Obligations.* The most characteristic of these, perhaps, is the railroad equipment-trust certificate, secured by title to locomotives, freight cars, or passenger cars and by the pledge of the lease under which the railroad is using the equipment. The investment record of these equipment obligations is very satisfactory, particularly because even the most serious financial difficulties of the issuing road have very rarely prevented the prompt payment of interest and principal. The primary reason for these good results is that the specific property pledged is removable and usable by other carriers. Consequently, it enjoys an independent salable value, like that of automobiles, jewelry, and other chattels on which personal loans are made.

Even where great difficulty might be encountered in actually selling the rolling stock to some other railroad at a reasonable price, this mobility still gives the equipment obligation a great advantage over the mortgages on the railroad itself. Both kinds of property are essential to the operation of the line, but the railroad bondholder has no alternative save to permit the receiver to operate his property, while the holder of the equipment lien can at least threaten to take the rolling stock away. The certificate holders have the legal right (acting through the trustee for the certificates) to take the equipment from the road if payments under the lease agreement fail to be made promptly; the road pays in an initial margin (usually 25 percent) of original cost of the equipment over the amount borrowed against it; and ordinarily the certificates are paid off at a rate exceeding the rate at which the rolling stock depreciates in value.

It follows that the holder of equipment-trust certificates has two separate sources of protection—one, the credit and success of the borrowing railway and the other, the value of the pledged rolling stock. If the latter value is sufficiently in excess of the money loaned against it, he may be able to ignore the first or credit factor entirely, just as a pawnbroker ignores the financial status of the individual to whom he lends money and is content to rely exclusively on the pledged property.

The over-all financial record of equipment-trust obligations has been exceedingly good, especially when contrasted with the numerous defaults

[2] For more detailed comment on the charges-to-property ratio and its usefulness, see Charles Tatham, "Two Useful Ratios in Public Utility Bond Analysis," *Analysts Journal,* April 1945, pp. 29–32.

and losses experienced by holders of other types of railroad bonds.[3] Equipment-trust certificates have become an increasingly important segment of railroad debt. The outstanding amount has grown from $774 million in 1943 to $2,804 million in 1960, and their percentage to total carrier debt from 7.4 to 28.3 percent in the same years.

2. *Investment-company Bonds.* Bonds of investment companies derive their major security from the value of the assets applicable thereto. These assets may be pledged to secure an issue, or they may be general (unpledged) security for debt. It makes little practical difference whether the portfolio is physically pledged with a trustee, as under a collateral-trust indenture, or whether it is held by the corporation subject to the claim of the debenture bondholders. In the usual case the debentures are protected by adequate provisions against increasing the debt and frequently also by a covenant requiring the market price of the company's assets to be maintained at a stated percentage above the face amount of the bonds.

Example: The following is an old but excellent illustration. The Reliance Management Corporation Debenture 5s, due 1954, proved an instance of the working of these protective provisions. The enterprise as a whole was highly unsuccessful, as is shown vividly by a decline in the price of the stock from 69 in 1929 to 1 in 1933. In the case of the ordinary bond issue, such a collapse in the stock value would have meant almost certain default and large loss of principal. But here the fact that the assets could be readily turned into cash gave significance to the protective covenants behind the debentures. It made possible and compelled the repurchase by the company of more than three-quarters of the issue, and it even forced the stockholders to contribute additional capital to make good a deficiency of assets below the indenture requirements. This resulted in the bonds selling as high as 88 in 1932 when the stock was sold for only 2½. The balance of the issue was called at 104¼ in February 1937. (A 1961 example of investment company debentures protected by similar provisions is the Tri-Continental Corporation 3⅞ percent debentures, Series A, due 1966.)

Under Section 18 of the Investment Company Act of 1940, bonds of investment companies may not be issued unless the net assets at current market value (or fair value as determined in good faith by the board of directors with respect to issues for which market quotations are not readily available) are at least 300 percent of the debt. We have adopted this ratio as a criterion of soundness for high-grade bonds of this type. All investment-company bonds issued since 1940 have given an excellent account of themselves—a fact not characteristic of many of their earlier issues.

[3] For reference to embarrassments affecting holders of certain equipment trusts in the 1930's see our 1951 edition, pp. 328–329.

REAL ESTATE MORTGAGES AND REAL ESTATE BONDS

Real estate financing is done mainly by the issuance of first mortgages on the property, which are now purchased chiefly by institutional investors. In this form they should not be called "marketable securities," and thus they lie outside the scope of our book. But they could come into our purview indirectly, when considered as the main asset of savings and loan associations, the *shares* of which are now a popular form of security.

Real estate mortgage *bonds* are generally marketable securities. They are created in the form of participating interests (in the usual $1,000 denominations) in one or more larger mortgages held by a trustee to secure the bonds. Some decades ago such bonds or certificates were created in huge amounts and widely held by the investing public. Many of them were "guaranteed," generally by an affiliated real estate concern, but in some cases by independent surety companies. This form of financing suffered from gross abuses in the 1920's; most of the real estate bonds went into default; the guarantees proved relatively valueless; and heavy losses were suffered by the holders.

Real Estate Mortgages in Recent Years. Since World War II the amount of real estate mortgages created has completely dwarfed the upsurge of the 1920's. (In 1959 total mortgage debt reached $191 billion, against $41.4 billion in 1930 and only $32.5 billion in 1940.) These mortgages are now of two principal kinds. "Conventional," or unguaranteed, mortgages are generally issued for not more than 75 percent of the cost (or other "value") of the property. The second group includes (1) FHA mortgages, which are insured by the Federal Housing Administration, an agency of the United States government, and which may be issued in amounts up to 90 percent of appraised value of the property; and (2) VA mortgages, which are issued to ex-servicemen in amounts which, with prior debt, may represent 100 percent of the property's value. These are guaranteed by the Veterans Administration and if defaulted may be turned over directly to it for payment. If default occurs on FHA mortgages, the mortgagee must foreclose and then claim reimbursement for any ultimate loss from the government.[4]

The most important difference between present-day and earlier types of real estate mortgages lies in the terms of payment. Virtually all of those created since the 1930's have provision for annual or more frequent repayments of principal, sufficient to discharge the debt in full within 15 to 25 years. This has undoubtedly added greatly to the underlying

---

[4] Insured mortgages are issued mainly under Secs. 203, 603, and 608 of the Federal Housing Act. Guaranteed mortgages are issued mainly under Secs. 501 and 505a of the Servicemen's Readjustment Act. There are also minor issues under Title I ("Class 3") of FHA and Sec. 502 of VA.

soundness of the mortgage investments. Whether the mortgage structure as a whole is now depression-proof—or whether depression and deflation need no longer be considered as even outside possibilities of the future— must be a matter of diverse opinion.[5]

Real Estate Bonds. The chief medium for bond financing of real estate —i.e., for the creation of marketable debt securities in this field—has been through the so-called "New Housing Authority" or "Public Housing Administration" bonds. These are issued in the first instance by "local public agencies," to finance construction of large-scale housing projects, generally for lower-income tenants. They are secured by the pledge of net income from the structures, and in addition are backed by the equivalent of a United States government guarantee to make good any deficiency in funds needed to meet interest and principal payments on the bonds. They are free from Federal income tax and generally from other taxes in the state of issue. They mature serially, over a period of some 40 years from issuance. In a 1961 offering the yields on the 1971 maturities were 2.65 percent; on the 1981 maturities, 3.15 percent; and on the 1991 maturities, 3.38 to 3.50 percent. They are not callable for 15 years after issuance.

The total amount of "New Housing" bonds outstanding in September 1961 was $2.9 billion out of original issues totaling $3.3 billion. The combination of net-rental pledge, United States government guarantees, and tax exemption appears to make these an unusually attractive bond. Their net yields would be larger for high-bracket investors than those obtained from the direct obligations of the United States government with comparable due dates.[6]

RELATION OF STOCK CAPITALIZATION TO FUNDED DEBT

The plant account of a public utility company, as valued on the books, affords a significant indication of the protection existing for the bond issues. This is hardly true in the case of railroad and industrial concerns. For the latter categories one should use a different measure of the "junior equity," or "cushion," on which the bondholders may rely, to absorb the shocks of adversity. This equity is based on the going-concern value of the enterprise rather than the book value of the assets. A substantial margin of *going-concern value* over funded debt is not only important but even vitally necessary to assure the soundness of a fixed-income investment. Before paying standard prices for bonds of any enterprise,

---

[5] In recent years the general public's interest in real estate financing has been confined largely to equity-type securities, such as the stock of real estate companies and real estate participation certificates in various kinds of syndicated operations. The growth in popularity and volume of these securities is a virtual guarantee that sizable losses will ultimately be sustained in the field.

[6] In September 1961, the corresponding yields of United States Treasury taxable bonds were about 3.90 percent, 4.00 percent, and 4.10 percent, respectively.

whether it be a railroad, a telephone company, or a department store, the investor must be convinced that the business is worth a great deal more than it owes. In this respect the bond buyer must take the same attitude as the lender of money on a house or a diamond ring, with the important difference that it is the *value of the business as an entity* which the investor must usually consider and not that of the separate assets.

Going-concern Value and Earning Power. "The value of the business as an entity" is most often dominated by its earning power. This explains the overshadowing significance that has come to be attached to the income exhibit, for the latter reveals not only the ability of the company to meet its *interest* charges, but also the extent to which the going value of the business may be said to exceed the *principal* of the bond issue. It is for this reason that most investors have come to regard the earnings record as the *only* statistical or quantitative test necessary in the selection of bond issues. All other criteria commonly employed by them are either qualitative or subjective (i.e., involving personal views as to the management, prospects, etc.).

While it is desirable to make the tests of safe bonds as simple and as few as possible, their reduction to the single criterion of the margin of earnings over interest charges would seem to be a dangerous oversimplification of the problem. The earnings during the period examined may be nonrepresentative, either because they resulted from definitely temporary conditions, favorable or the reverse, or because they were presented in such a way as not to reflect the true income. These conditions are particularly likely to occur among industrial companies, which are subject both to greater individual vicissitudes and to a somewhat smaller degree of accounting supervision than is exercised over railroads and utilities.

Shareholders' Equity Measured by Market Value of Stock Issues: A Supplemental Test. We believe, therefore, that it is essential, in the case of *railroad and industrial bonds* at least, to supplement the earnings test by some other quantitative index of the margin of going-concern value above the funded debt. The best criterion that we are able to offer for this purpose is the ratio of the *market value* of the capital stock to the total funded debt. Strenuous objections may, of course, be leveled against using the market price of stock issues as proof of anything, in view of the extreme variations to which stock quotations have been notoriously subject. Nevertheless, with all its imperfections, the market value of the stock issues is generally recognized as a better index of the fair going value of a business than is afforded by the balance-sheet figures or even the ordinary appraisal.[7]

---

[7] The liquidating value, as measured conservatively by the working capital, may—under very unusual circumstances in today's market—exceed the market price, but this point is seldom of significance in the selection of *high-grade* investments.

The utility of the market-price test in extreme cases is unquestionable. The presence of a stock equity with market value many times larger than the total debt carries a strong assurance of the safety of the bond issue; and conversely, an exceedingly small stock equity at market prices must call the soundness of the bond into serious question. The determination of the market value of the stock equity and its comparison with the total amount of funded debt are well-established features of bond analysis. We recommend that this calculation be made a standard element in the procedure of bond selection for industrial and railroad issues, and that a minimum requirement under this heading be set up which will serve as a secondary quantitative test of safety.

Application of the Stock-equity Test to Industrial Bonds. Let us assume that in selecting a sound industrial bond the investor should require that the value of the enterprise be at least three times the amount of the debt. On the basis of our requirement that interest charges be earned 3.8 times after tax, it would appear that the normal or average market price of the stock issues should equal twice the face amount of the bonds, thus giving a total ratio of enterprise value to debt of about 3 to 1. This is shown by the accompanying tabulation, which assumes a 4½ percent interest rate applicable to $10 million of bonds and a multiplier of 15 for the earnings available for the stock.

Earnings before income taxes (7.0 times $450,000)	$3,150,000
Less taxes at 52 percent on $2,700,000 (after interest)	1,400,000
Balance after taxes (3.8 times fixed charges)	$1,750,000
Less fixed charges	450,000
Balance for stock	$1,300,000
Balance capitalized at 15 times earnings, about	20,000,000
Ratio of stock at market to debt at par	2.0 times
Ratio of total capitalization to debt at par	3.0 times

However, market prices are constantly fluctuating, and they are often far out of line with real value as the analyst would determine it. If we are to set up a *minimum* requirement governing market values of stock issues to be applied under all market conditions, we should allow considerable leeway for the vagaries of Wall Street.

Making arbitrary decisions here, as we must everywhere when quantitative tests are devised, we should recommend that the minimum stock equity at market prices for industrial bonds be set at 125 percent of total debt. As a partial offset to the rather *low* figure recommended, we would require that this equity be shown *both* currently and by the average over a past period—say the preceding five calendar years. (This calculation may be facilitated by adding up the five annual highs and lows, as shown in the manuals, and dividing by 10.)

Comprehensive data would show, we think, that nearly all well-regarded industrial bonds would pass this supplemental stock-equity test by a comfortable margin, except in periods of severely depressed market prices.

Capitalization of Rentals in Computing Stock-value Ratios. If, in addition to charges on funded debt, a company pays rentals on building space or incurs other fixed charges which are not reflected on its balance sheet in the form of funded indebtedness, all or a part of those charges should be capitalized at an appropriate rate to arrive at a fair estimate of total debt. For here the balance sheet does not tell the whole story. The sum thus derived, plus the funded debt (if any), rather than the funded indebtedness per balance sheet, should then be used to compute the stock-value ratio.

For example, many chain-store enterprises rent some or all of their store locations. Others own them outright by having purchased them with the proceeds of bond issues. No valid comparison can be made between the bonds of the owning and those of the renting enterprises without a capitalization of all or some portion of the rentals paid. We suggest that one-third of the annual rentals for building space paid by chain and department stores be regarded as fixed charges (the balance being regarded as operating expenses).[8] Correspondingly, the capitalized value of these rentals (say at $4\frac{1}{2}$ percent) should be regarded as funded debt in the computations of stock-equity ratios.

The Stock-equity Test for Railroad Bonds. The critical financial problems of the railroads have grown out of capitalization structures in which bonded debt played too large a role. Nearly all the roads that failed have had heavier than average fixed charges. Conversely, the prosperous roads have held their bonded debt within moderate limits. Those who buy railroad bonds of investment grade must make sure that there is a really substantial cushion behind them. As in the case of industrial bonds, this cushion cannot be measured dependably by property values per books. If it is to be measured at all by tests other than the earnings record, the investor must use the stock market's valuation of the junior equity.

We recommend a requirement that the junior equity have both a current and an average market value of not less than 50 percent of the adjusted debt. If the test is being applied to the fixed-interest bonds of a road with income bonds outstanding as well, it is permissible to regard the income issues as part of the junior equity. (However, if the income bonds are being analyzed as investment issues, they must then be considered as part of the total debt, and only the preferred and common stock may be considered junior equity.)

---

[8] The Securities and Exchange Commission has adopted a definition of "fixed charges" which includes one-third of all rentals reported in Schedule XVI (Form S-9), or such other portion as can be demonstrated as representative of the interest factor in the circumstances of a particular case, and requires an explanation to be set forth if any other proportion of rentals is used. See Act of 1933 Release No. 4245, dated June 30, 1960.

Under normal stock-market conditions, a railroad showing its fixed charges covered at least 2.9 times after taxes should also show a stock equity considerably higher than 50 percent of the bonded debt. Assuming a 4½ percent interest rate and an average price-earnings ratio of 10 to 1 for the stock issues, the calculations would work out as follows:

Bond issues at par.....................................	$100,000,000
Interest charges*.....................................	4,500,000
Earnings available after taxes (2.9 times charges)......	13,000,000
Balance for stock.....................................	8,500,000
Market value of stock at 10 times earnings.............	85,000,000
Stock-equity ratio.....................................	85%

* Here assumed about equal to adjusted fixed charges.

Our minimum stock-equity ratio of only 50 percent, as in the case of industrial bonds, is intended to allow considerable but by no means unlimited leeway for the imperfections of stock-market appraisals. While our requirement may appear to be unduly lenient in theory, it has in the past excluded issues that have been well regarded.

Example 1: Illinois Central bond issues were rated Baa (lowest bank-quality grade) at the end of 1960. The year-end market price for its 3.1 million shares of common stock was $99.1 million against $206.5 million of stated funded debt, a ratio of slightly less than 50 percent. Thus, while the bonds would pass the average-earnings test for 1954–1960 (the actual after-tax coverage was 3.44 times), a prudent investor might well have preferred some other railroad bond issue at the time.

Example 2: Pennsylvania Railroad. At the end of 1960 its 13.2 million shares of common stocks sold for $151.4 million, whereas the road's bonds and equipment debt totaled $550 million; in addition there were bonds and guaranteed stocks of leased lines and subsidiaries. The Pennsylvania bonds carried a rating of Ba. Over the 1954–1960 span interest was covered an average of only 1.67 times after taxes. In this case the bonds failed to meet both the interest-coverage and the junior-equity tests, and so had doubtful attraction for the bond investor.

Significance of Unusually Large or Small Stock-value Ratio. If the stock-value ratio were always proportionate to the interest coverage there would be no reason to apply both tests, since passing one would assure passing the other. Such is not the case, however, and we must accordingly consider what is implied when the stock-value ratio gives a substantially different indication from that given by the interest coverage.

Let us assume that the earnings picture reveals that the minimum standard is barely met, but that the stock-value ratio is considerably higher than our minimum requirement on that score. This evidence of strength might well dispel any doubt arising from the marginality of the earnings-coverage ratio.

The opposite case is that in which the interest coverage is ample, but the stock-value ratio is substantially below the minimum required. The purchaser of bonds on such an exhibit would have to assume that the price of the stock is too low; but, as a general rule, no straight bond investment should be made if it requires such an assumption. If the investor is right in that judgment of the stock value, it would certainly be more profitable to buy the stock than the bonds. If he is wrong as to the stock value, he runs great risk of having made a poor bond purchase. Bond investment is a negative art, and the investor should never lose sight of that fact. A low stock equity not only indicates quantitative deficiency of the issue, it usually implies qualitative inferiority as well and at times casts doubt upon the accuracy of the reported earnings.

CHAPTER TWENTY-SIX

ADDITIONAL FACTORS IN BOND ANALYSIS

Railroad Bond Analysis. Because of the wealth of statistical data available for the railroads, it is customary to develop correspondingly elaborate material in analyzing their bonds. This relates not only to financial and physical information concerning the road as a whole, but also to the traffic density—and sometimes the estimated gross and net earnings—of the mileage which constitutes the specific security for the bond issue in question.[1]

Elaborate Technique of Analysis Not Necessary for Selection of High-grade Bonds. This emphasis upon operating and financial details runs counter to our whole concept of investment in high-grade bonds as a comparatively simple procedure, turning upon the application of a few rigorous standards. An understandable reason for the elaborateness of railroad-bond analysis is that these issues are often bought in large blocks by major financial institutions; the size of the commitment would seem to justify an intensive study of all aspects of the bond, and the per-unit cost of such study may not be excessive.

The history of railroad bonds is marred by defaults. Twenty-eight percent of all the railroad bonds offered between 1900–1943 went into default between offering and extinguishment.[2] Moreover, at the end of 1939, there were 108 steam railroads in the hands of receivers or trustees. These roads had outstanding nearly $4 billion in funded debt at that time and operated nearly one-third of the total railroad mileage in the United States. In addition, most of the companies that preserved their solvency appeared at times to be in a precarious position, and their bonds sold at speculative prices. For only a small minority of cases could it be said that the safety of the entire debt structure was never in doubt.

---

[1] Elaborate graphic portrayal of railroad mortgage liens, the specific trackage covered, etc., together with supporting data and descriptions are provided by White and Kemble's *Atlas and Digest of Railroad Mortgages,* covering all the railroads of major importance in the United States. In our view, this sort of information is useful primarily, if not exclusively, in the analysis of defaulted railroad bonds and bonds of roads in a marginal earnings position, rather than in the analysis of high-grade bonds of the fixed-income type.

[2] W. B. Hickman, *Corporate Bond Quality and Investor Experience,* Princeton University Press, Princeton, N.J., 1958, p. 10.

In the post-World War II period the situation has been materially different. At the end of 1948, 46 roads were in the hands of receivers or bankruptcy trustees. These involved only 13,280 miles of operated road, or about 5.6 percent of the total operated mileage in the country. By the end of 1959, completion of reorganization proceedings had reduced the number of railroads in the hands of receivers and trustees to 8. Moreover, they operated only about 1,000 miles of road, or less than ½ of 1 percent of all the road operated by railways. Nevertheless, it is to be pointed out that on July 7, 1961, the New York, New Haven & Hartford Railroad filed a petition for reorganization under Section 77 of the National Bankruptcy Act. The New Haven operates 1,700 miles of road and had $199,000,000 of debt outstanding at the end of 1960.

Once a railroad's financial position becomes uncertain, the analyst must study all the major phases of its operations with care if he wishes to form a reasonably dependable view of the value of any of its securities. This study will include the matter of the specific liens protecting the various bond issues. The analyst can draw valuable conclusions from such intensive work; but as far as railroad bonds are concerned, its value should lie exclusively in the field of issues selling at depressed prices.

The widely held notion that a railroad bond can both require intensive study and deserve to be bought at a high price and low yield is at bottom a logical contradiction. The history of investment in low-yielding railroad bonds bears us out. Nearly all those which turned out well, without intervening headaches, could have been selected by the application of simple tests of over-all safety. Nearly all those which would not have passed such tests proved disappointing investments to those who bought them at full prices. The rule is basic, and it should hold as well for the future as it has for the past.

The "Factor-of-safety" Test. The five tests suggested for the analysis of investment-grade bonds of railroads are brought together in our summary at the end of this chapter. They include one criterion which we do not *require* in the case of utility or industrial bonds. This is the "factor of safety"—used here in a special sense—which represents simply the percentage of operating revenue left over after payment of fixed charges, with income taxes added back. We suggest that a margin of not less than 12 percent of "gross" be required for the period used for the earnings test. In theory this would mean that revenues could decline 12 percent with no offsetting saving in expenses, before the margin of earnings above fixed charges would disappear. In practice, however, this would permit a much larger possible decline in revenue, because the major portion of such loss would be recouped by a curtailment of expenses. We believe that in the case of a typical railroad with adequately protected bonds, in which expenses down to fixed charges and income taxes take about 85 percent of gross and fixed charges are 3 percent of gross, revenue could decline by about 25 percent before coverage would fall below twice the after-tax charges.[3] A coverage of this character will be necessary to protect the investor against a serious price decline.

It is important to understand the reason for adding the factor-of-safety requirement to those for the coverage of fixed charges and for the relationship between available income and the principal amount of debt. The last two criteria can be met by a railroad with high operating costs and a very small bonded debt—e.g., with a 95 percent over-all operating ratio and fixed charges of only 1 percent of total operating revenues. But such a road would be quite vulnerable to any untoward development, from the direction either of declining revenues or increasing expenses. The low charges would not guarantee safety if the company could not meet its operating expenses.

A low factor of safety may prove a serious weakness not only in the event of a falling off in revenues but also in case of a disproportionate increase in operating expenses, taxes, or rentals. If this increase should add only a small percent of gross to the operating ratio, the balance available for fixed charges would shrink rapidly and even disappear.

Example. The significance of the factor of safety as a separate criterion is shown by the comparison of Chicago & North Western Railway and the Kansas City Southern, based on the average results for 1948 and 1949, which we made in our 1951 edition (Table 26-1). In the table the coverage of adjusted fixed charges is somewhat better for Chicago & North Western than for Kansas City Southern. However, the factor of safety shown by Chicago & North Western was inadequate by our standards, whereas that of Kansas City Southern was unusually high. (The difference between the adjusted charges used in this calculation and the reported charges is explained in Chapter 17.)

Sequel: Chicago & North Western had inadequate coverage from 1951 on, and reported deficits after charges in several years. Rather exceptionally, its troubles were due in good part to a large increase in the equipment rentals. The apparently strong position of the first-mortgage bonds was impaired, and their price suffered a severe shrinkage. In contrast, Kansas City Southern continued to show good results, and its bonds have retained a satisfactory investment quality.

Additional Factors in the Analysis of Utility Bonds. Most of the special factors to be considered in the analysis of public utility bonds have been covered in our chapters immediately preceding and in our chapters on the analysis of financial statements of utility companies. The ensuing discussion in this chapter, although not confined exclusively to public

---

[3] This is based on the assumption that expenses will decline by a percentage equal to three-fourths of the percentage by which revenues decline. In other words, if gross declines 25 percent, expenses are expected to decline by about 19 percent of expenses. Charles Tatham recommends the use of an historical approach to measurement of probabilities in this area of analysis as applied to individual *utility* companies. Presumably this would be equally logical in railroad analysis. See his "Two Useful Ratios in Public Utility Bond Analysis," *Analysts Journal,* April 1945, pp. 31–32.

utilities, is more largely relevant to bonds of such concerns than to those of other types of enterprise.

"Factor of Safety" for Public Utility Bonds. Utility bonds meeting our minimum-fixed-charge-coverage test will in practically every case show a factor of safety of not less than 13½ percent. For this reason, perhaps, it is customary for institutional investors to require a factor of safety of that magnitude or larger in selecting utility bonds for investment. We offer no objection to such a requirement, but we believe that for utility companies it is a criterion not essentially distinct from fixed-charge coverage, because the relationship between the two elements tends to be fairly constant for all companies. A margin of 13½ percent and coverage of 4 times before income taxes would permit a 20

Table 26-1. Factor of Safety for Two Railroads

Item	Average of 1948 and 1949	
	Chicago & North Western Railway	Kansas City Southern (including Louisiana and Arkansas)
(1) Operating revenue	$184,000,000	$60,300,000
(2) Available for adjusted charges before income tax	11,487,000	21,602,000
(3) Adjusted charges	1,900,000	4,104,000
(4) Balance	9,587,000	17,498,000
(5) Times adjusted charges earned (before tax)	6.05×	5.26×
(6) Factor of safety = (4) ÷ (1)	5.2%	29.0%
(7) Fixed charges unadjusted	$2,524,000	$2,586,000

percent decline in revenues, accompanied by a 15 percent decline in operating expenses before income taxes, and still leave coverage of 2.3 times before income taxes and 1.6 times after income taxes of 52 percent. The large majority of utility companies are able to meet such a test.

"Parent Company Only" vs. Consolidated Basis. Both prospectuses and annual reports almost invariably present the earnings statement of a public utility holding-company system in a *consolidated* form; i.e., they start with the gross revenues of the operating subsidiaries and carry the figures down through operating expenses, depreciation, fixed charges, and preferred dividends of subsidiaries, until they arrive at the balance available for the parent company's interest charges, and finally at the amount earned on its common stock. There is also published the income account of the parent company only, which starts with the dividends received by it from the operating subsidiaries and therefore does not show the latter's interest and preferred dividend payments to the public. The interest coverage shown by the income account of the parent com-

pany only is an example of the prior-deductions method, and consequently it will almost always make a better showing for the parent company's bonds than will be found in the consolidated report. The investor should pay no attention to the "parent-company-only" figures and should insist upon a completely consolidated income account.[4]

Example. The example shown in Table 26-2 will illustrate the point. The parent company did not receive in dividends the full amount earned by its subsidiaries, but even with this smaller income, the prior-deductions method resulted in much larger indicated coverage for the parent-company bond interest on the basis of its own results than on a consolidated basis.

Table 26-2. American Telephone and Telegraph Company, 1960

(Dollar figures in millions)

Item	Parent company only	Consolidated results
Gross operating revenues...............	$ 599.0	$7,920.5
Balance for fixed charges...............	1,001.0	1,451.7*
Fixed charges........................	105.5	258.3
Balance for parent company stock......	895.5	1,193.4*
Fixed charges earned after taxes........	9.49×	5.62×

* After deducting $38.0 million net income applicable to minority interests and excluding $56.5 million interest in undistributed earnings of unconsolidated subsidiaries. Adjustment for rentals would not affect the conclusion.

Dividends on Preferred Stocks of Subsidiaries. In a holding-company system the preferred stocks of the important operating subsidiaries are in effect senior to the parent company's bonds, since interest on the latter is met chiefly out of the dividends paid on the subsidiaries' common stocks. For this reason subsidiary preferred dividends are always included in the fixed charges of a public utility holding-company system. In other words, these fixed charges consist of the following items, which are listed here in order of seniority.[5]

1. Subsidiaries' bond interest and other fixed charges
2. Subsidiaries' preferred dividends
3. Parent company's bond interest and other fixed charges

[4] Prior to the enactment of the Public Utility Holding Company Act of 1935 and its vigorous enforcement by the SEC, holding companies were much more numerous than they are today.

[5] This order of priority is not strictly valid to the extent that the parent company has operating income of its own, income from investments outside the system, or income from *senior* securities of subsidiaries which it happens to own. This is true of American Telephone and Telegraph Company. The parent company's net operating income in 1960 was approximately 11 percent of the net available for its own fixed charges. It also owned over $519 million in notes and advances to subsidiaries, on which it received large interest income.

This statement assumes that all the subsidiary companies are of substantially the same relative importance to the system. An individual subsidiary which happens to be unprofitable may discontinue preferred dividends and even bond interest, while at the same time the earnings of the other subsidiaries may permit the parent company to continue its own interest and dividend payments. In such a case, which is somewhat exceptional, the unprofitable subsidiary's charges are not really senior to the parent company's securities. This point was discussed in Chapter 14.

The fixed charges should also properly include any annual rentals paid for leased property which are equivalent to bond interest or guaranteed dividends. On the other hand, "interest charged to construction" is a credit against the fixed charges (which include such construction interest in their total). The item usually represents a temporary expense not offset by normal earnings from the properties under construction. As explained on page 294, we consider that in treating interest charged to construction (when the amount is substantial) in the calculation of fixed-charge coverage, the preferable method is to add this item to gross income,[6] which is in turn divided by the total of fixed charges without benefit of any credit for interest charged to construction. (This method is not used by the financial services.)

The holder of preferred shares of an important operating subsidiary has, to all intents and purposes, a claim against system earnings which is as likely to be met as that of the parent company's bonds. But if the parent company becomes insolvent, then the owners of the underlying preferred issues no longer occupy the strategic position of bondholders, since they cannot compel the operating subsidiary to continue paying its preferred dividends.

Minority Interest in Earnings of Subsidiaries. The earnings applicable to minority stock are usually deducted in the income statement *after* the parent company's bond interest, and hence the former item does not reduce the margin of safety as generally computed. We prefer to subtract the minority interest *before* calculating interest coverage. We do not favor inclusion of the earnings applicable to the common-stock minority interest among the fixed charges, as is sometimes done; this represents carrying conservatism to an unreasonable extreme.

Exact treatment would require a prorating of revenues and deductions based upon the parent company's proportionate interest in the common stock of each subsidiary, but this involves needlessly burdensome calculations.[7] When the minority interest is small, as it usually is, the difference between the various methods is inconsequential. When the minority interest is fairly large, analysis will show that the customary

---

[6] This method is followed by American Telephone and Telegraph Company in its recent reports to stockholders. See, for example, the Annual Report for 1960, pp. 27–28.

[7] This method is known as "proportional consolidation."

procedure gives a margin of safety somewhat higher than is strictly accurate, whereas our method errs moderately in the opposite direction and hence should be preferred by conservative investors.

Undistributed Earnings of Subsidiary and Affiliated Companies, Not Consolidated. In Chapter 14 we suggested that security analysts should take such profits into account (after provision for possible related tax) in calculating the true earnings for any period. Since the choice of high-grade bonds should rest on the *obvious* presence of an ample margin of safety, it is not ordinarily desirable to increase the reported earnings by these undistributed equities in calculating fixed-charge coverage. In special cases a calculation of this sort may prove useful, perhaps to indicate that the true coverage is very large and that the bond is therefore unusually attractive at its price.

Capitalization of Fixed Charges. As we pointed out in our earlier discussion of the composition of fixed charges, the latter are not confined solely to interest on funded debt. All or some part of annual rental obligations, interest and dividends guaranteed under lease or otherwise, and dividend requirements on subsidiary-company preferred stocks constitute fixed charges in computing over-all coverage. Similarly, for the purpose of comparing "funded debt" with tangible-asset values, net current assets, and stock equity at market, it is important to recognize that debt may be represented not only by bond issues but also by guaranteed stocks, by annual rental obligations, and effectively also by nonguaranteed preferred stocks of operating subsidiaries.

The principal amount of its obligations is usually stated quite adequately in the consolidated balance sheet of a public utility enterprise; but this may not be true of a railroad company or an industrial or commercial concern, chiefly because its rental obligations are not likely to be reflected in its balance sheet. We suggest, therefore, that the "effective debt" of a railroad may be calculated by multiplying the "adjusted charges" by an appropriate figure, say 22. This is equivalent to capitalizing the adjusted charges at an assumed rate of $4\frac{1}{2}$ percent—in other words, to assuming that the true debt is that figure of which $4\frac{1}{2}$ percent will equal the adjusted charges.[8]

In the previous chapter we suggested that one-third of building-space rentals be considered the equivalent of fixed charges, and that this amount be capitalized at our standard $4\frac{1}{2}$ percent rate (multiplier of 22) to determine their principal equivalent. However, in considering the obligations of retail establishments (chain stores, department stores, etc.), we recommend that the minimum coverage required for interest plus one-third of rentals be reduced from the 3.8 times for other industrials to 2.9 times after taxes and from 7 times to 5 times before income taxes.

---

[8] Moody's *Railroad Manual* makes a similar calculation on a per-mile basis only. However, it adjusts fixed charges by the full amount of the net "intermediate items," while we prefer to give them 50 percent weight.

This reduction recognizes the relative stability of retail business, after allowance is made for the special burden attaching to the rental factor.

Example: The effect of capitalizing chain-store rentals is illustrated in Table 26-3 by the examples of Neisner Brothers and G. C. Murphy Company—two variety chains. The capitalization of rentals transforms

Table 26-3. Effect of Capitalizing Chain-store Rentals

(000 omitted)

Item	Neisner Brothers, 1960	G. C. Murphy Co., 1960
Funded debt, as reported......................	$ 3,200	$ 8,143
Rentals..	4,174*	7,453
One-third rentals, capitalized at 4½ percent.......	30,890	55,200
Effective debt................................	34,090	63,343
Common stock at book value..................	17,340	83,963
Common stock at market value†..............	7,867	107,540

* Moody's *Industrials* reports that "minimum annual rentals at December 31, 1960, on 166 leases expiring after December 31, 1963, totaled $4,173,646 plus real estate taxes, etc."

† Mean price, 1960.

Table 26-4. Effective Debt of Two Railroads

(000 omitted)

Item	Atchison 1960	Chicago, Rock Island & Pacific 1960	Chicago, Rock Island & Pacific 1960, fixed interest debt only
Funded debt, as reported......	$198,726	$158,407	$101,800.0
Fixed and contingent charges..	8,017	6,545	3,979.0
Intermediate items, net........	cr. 5,716	dr. 12,827	dr. 12,827.0
Adjusted fixed and contingent charges (charges plus ½ intermediate debit or minus ½ intermediate credit)........	5,159	12,958	10,392.0
Effective debt (adjusted charges capitalized at 4½ percent)...	115,000	288,000	231,000.0
Junior issues at market value...	704,000	73,000	116,000.0

the financial structure of Neisner from an apparently strong to a weak one. The same procedure does not affect the financial picture of Murphy to any similar degree. In Table 26-4 the "effective-debt" technique is illustrated for two railroads, Atchison and Chicago, Rock Island & Pacific. This technique reduces the "effective debt" of Atchison and, in contrast, increases very substantially that of Rock Island. Obviously it is not necessary to make this calculation where the net intermediate items represent a comparatively small figure.

Comment: The purpose of the calculation in Table 26-4 is mainly to test whether a railroad meets our requirement with respect to the junior equity or "cushion." The results herein indicate an ample protection for the Atchison debt, including its 4 percent adjustment (i.e., income) issue. However, on the basis of 1960 average prices, the total adjusted debt of the Rock Island, including its Income 4½s, would have an insufficient cushion. When the income bonds are treated as a junior, non-fixed charge, the fixed-interest debt structure is found to have the required 50 percent equity protection.

The Working-capital Factor in the Analysis of Industrial Bonds. For reasons already explained, a company's statement of its *fixed assets* (other than in the case of public utilities) will not ordinarily carry much weight in determining the soundness of its bonds. But the *current-asset position* has an important bearing upon the financial strength of nearly all industrial enterprises, and consequently the potential bond purchaser should give it close attention. It is true that industrial bonds which meet the stringent tests already prescribed will in nearly every instance be found to make a satisfactory working-capital exhibit as well; but a separate check is nevertheless desirable in order to guard against the exceptional case.

Three Requisites with Respect to Working Capital. In examining the current-asset situation an industrial bond buyer should satisfy himself on three counts, viz:

1. That the cash holdings are ample.
2. That the ratio of current assets to current liabilities is a strong one.
3. That the working capital bears a suitable proportion to the funded debt.

It is not feasible to fix definite minimum requirements for any one of these three factors, especially since the normal working-capital situation varies widely with different types of enterprises. It is generally held that current assets should be at least double the current liabilities, and a smaller ratio would undoubtedly call for further investigation. We suggest an additional standard requirement for the ordinary industrial company, viz., that the *net* working capital be at least equal to the amount of the bonded debt. This is admittedly an arbitrary criterion, and sometimes it may prove unduly severe. But it is interesting to note that the criterion was met by every one of the industrial issues which maintained their investment rank on the market throughout our year of extreme test, 1932: for every issue the net working capital exceeded the total of bonds.[9]

[9] For details, see the 1940 edition of this work, pp. 97 and 182n, and the 1934 edition, pp. 81–82 and 152. See also, O. K. Burrell, *A Study in Investment Mortality*, Bureau of Business Research, University of Oregon, Eugene, Ore., 1947, pp. 28–29.

Table 26-5. Minimum Quantitative Requirements for Investment Grade Bonds

1. Size of obligor:

Public utilities, total operating revenues......................... $ 4,000,000
Railroads, total operating revenues............................. 5,000,000
Industrials, sales.. 15,000,000

2. Earnings test:

   a. Average fixed-charge coverage (alternative to 2*b*):

Type	Before income taxes	After income taxes (rounded)
Public utility............................	4×	2.4×
Railroad (adjusted charges)...............	5×	2.9×
Industrials in general....................	7×	3.8×
Retail concerns..........................	5×	2.9×

   b. Fixed charge coverage in "poorest year" (alternative to 2*a*):

Type	Before income taxes	After income taxes
Public utility............................	3	1.9×
Railroad (adjusted charges)...............	4	2.4×
Industrials in general....................	5	2.9×
Retail concerns..........................	4	2.4×

   c. Average available income before income taxes as a percentage of funded debt (or "capitalized fixed charges"):

Type	*Ratio, percent*
Public utility..............	18
Railroad..................	22
Industrial................	30

   d. Additional test for railroad bonds—"factor of safety":

   Average ratio of net income after fixed charges, with income taxes added back, to total operating revenues.................................... 12%

3. Value of the property:

   a. Public utilities:

   Ratio of net plant account to debt*.............................. 1.7×

   or

   Ratio of sum of capitalization and surplus to debt*................. 1.8×
   Also:
   Ratio of sum of capitalization and surplus to fixed charges........... 40×

   b. Industrials:

   Ratio of net current assets to funded debt........................ 100%

   c. Investment company bonds:

   Ratio of net assets at market to funded debt at par................. 300%

Table 26-5. Minimum Quantitative Requirements for Investment Grade Bonds
(*Continued*)

4. Stock equity or "cushion":

   a. Industrials:

      Equity at market as percentage of total debt (to be shown currently and
      by average over preceding five years)............................ 125%

   b. Railroads:

      Equity at market as percentage of total debt (to be shown currently and
      by average over preceding five years)............................ 50%

  * These ratios are based on an assumed debt bearing 4½ percent interest and
selling at about par. Actually, many public utility bonds carry lower interest rates
and sell below par. In applying these tests, the par amount of the low-coupon-debt—
not of short maturity—may be reduced in some marginal cases to a 4½ percent
coupon equivalent.

Exceptions. Certain types of industrials—e.g., baking, ice, and restaurant concerns—normally require a relatively small amount of working capital in relation to total assets and business volume. For such enterprises the 100 percent net-current-asset coverage requirements for bonds would be overstringent. But it would be well if bond investors in these enterprises would insist upon indenture provisions requiring the maintenance of a ratio of working capital to funded debt which is reasonable in terms of the nature of the business. Another exception might be some of the chemical companies. For example, Dow Chemical and Diamond Alkali Company reported more debt than working capital throughout the 1950's. (In 1960, both had reversed the situation by a very slight edge.) In view of the strong earnings picture and large common stock equity shown by these companies, the working-capital requirement need not be taken too seriously. The point here is that some chemical companies have a particularly large plant account per dollar of sales; consequently, for them, a moderate debt in relation to total assets may exceed working capital. In most manufacturing lines a debt of, say, 50 percent of plant would be well under normal working capital.

In contrast with the emphasis laid upon the current-asset position of industrial concerns, relatively little attention is paid to the working capital shown by railroads, and none at all to that of public utilities. The reason for this is twofold. Neither railways nor utilities have the problem of financing the production and carrying of merchandise stocks or of extending large credits to customers. Furthermore, the utility companies, at least, have been accustomed to raising new capital periodically for expansion purposes, in the course of which they readily replenish their cash account if it is depleted. Because new financing is easily obtainable by prosperous companies of this type, even an excess of current liabilities over quick assets has not been considered a serious matter.

In Table 26-5 we summarize our various quantitative tests applicable to the selection of bonds for fixed-income, stable-value investment.

CHAPTER TWENTY-SEVEN

PREFERRED STOCKS

GENERAL POSITION OF PREFERRED STOCKS

We have pointed out previously that *legally* a preferred stock represents a portion of the *ownership* of the company, and thus is classed in balance sheets with the common shares as making up the capital stock or equity interest. In investment practice, however, the typical preferred stock has a *claim* rather than an interest, and as such it really ranks with the creditors in *genus*, though below them in *species*. The most definite claim of the preferred holder is the right to receive a stipulated amount of dividends before anything is paid on the common. His companion right to receive his principal ahead of the common in the event of liquidation becomes important only in exceptional cases.

The preferred-stock *form* is fundamentally unsatisfactory, since it gives the holder neither the enforceable claim to interest (and principal at maturity) that attaches to a standard bond nor the right to all residual profits that inures to common shares. Nevertheless, preferred stocks can constitute sound and well-protected investments of the fixed-income type if their contractual weakness is offset by the strength of the issuing company. Basically, the same elements of protection which assure the safety and relative stability of a high-grade bond can do the same for a strongly entrenched preferred issue. But as a class, preferred shares are distinctly more vulnerable to adverse developments than are bonds. Hence investor experience with them *as a whole* over past decades has undoubtedly been less satisfactory than with bonds.

An important consequence of the difference in legal position of bonds and preferred stocks has been a corresponding difference in their *tax status*. Preferred dividends do not carry a commensurate income tax saving to the paying company. But if *received* by a corporation they can be excluded from its taxable income to the extent of 85 percent—i.e., they are subject to an effective tax rate of only 7.8 percent against 52 percent for most other types of corporate income. However, they carry no similar tax advantages if received by individuals. With the increase in corporate income tax rates from 11 percent in 1929 to the present 52–54 percent burden, these tax provisions have become of major importance. They make a preferred-stock issue more than twice as expensive to the issuer as a bond with the same annual charge. Conversely, they make preferred-dividend income almost twice as attractive to a recipient corporation as the same amount of bond interest.

Price-and-yield History of Preferred Stocks vs. Bonds. A comparative picture of the price-and-yield record of high-grade bonds and high-grade preferred stocks appears in Table 27-1. We add the price record of two representative preferred issues now rated as of "medium-grade" and

Table 27-1. Prices and Yields of Preferred Stocks and Corporate Bonds, Selected Years, 1929–1959

Dates	High-grade corporate bonds (Standard & Poor's)		High-grade noncallable preferred stocks (Standard & Poor's)[1]		Prices of lower- and medium-grade preferred stocks	
	Price	Yield	Price	Yield	American Sugar Refining*	U.S. Rubber†
1929 high	90.87	4.71%	138.1	5.07%	28	93
1932 low	81.73	5.49	101.8	6.88	11	3
1937 high	111.40	3.22	167.6	4.18	36	118
1938 low	109.90	3.32	154.3	4.54	20	46
1939 high	116.10	2.93	172.8	4.05	24	115
1942 low	117.00	2.88	154.8	4.19	20	57
1946 high	124.60	2.44	204.9	3.42	40	187
1949 low	119.80	2.71	171.4	4.09	30	112
1955 high	116.70	2.90	176.7	3.96	37	172
1959 low	92.37	4.59	146.0	4.85	27	143

* Originally 7 percent cumulative preferred $100 par; split 4 for 1 in 1959, price adjusted for split; dividends continuous since 1891. Rated BB by Standard & Poor in 1961.

† 8 percent noncumulative preferred $100 par. Dividends irregular 1893–1928. No dividends 1929–1937. Regular dividends since 1943. Rated BBB by Standard & Poor's in 1961.

"lower-grade" quality. It will be noted at once that the two added issues have been subject to extremely wide price fluctuations, part of which is accounted for by the variations in the basic interest rate, part by the extreme severity of the post-1929 depression, and part by the inherent vulnerability of all but the highest-grade preferreds to adverse developments of any sort.

The price-and-yield comparisons between high-grade preferred stocks and high-grade bonds—brought out in Table 27-2—has some interesting features. The price index of the bonds varies considerably less than their yield index, because of the moderating effect of the maturity factor—not present in preferred stocks. The yield variations were distinctly greater for the preferreds than for the bonds in the earlier years, and the bonds benefited more than the preferreds from the fall in interest rates between 1929 and 1949. However, the reverse situation has held true since 1949. Bond yields have increased considerably more than preferred-stock yields, with the result that the 1949 yield ratio of 1.5 to 1 fell to only 1.06 to 1 in 1959.

Present Status of Preferred Stocks. The near equalization of the yields of high-grade bonds and preferreds reflects chiefly the gradual (and belated) influence of the tax factor referred to above. On the one hand, it has drastically reduced the supply of new straight preferred stocks of prime investment quality. Few have appeared amid the vast outpouring of securities of many types in recent years; these few seemed required by

Table 27-2. Comparative Fluctuations in Prices and Yields of High-grade Preferred Stocks and Corporate Bonds, Selected Years, 1929–1959

Dates	Prices		Yields	
	Bonds	Preferreds	Bonds	Preferreds
1929 high–1932 low...............	−10%	−26%	+17%	+36%
1932 low–1937 high...............	+36	+65	−41	−39
1937 high–1938 low...............	− 1	− 8	+ 3	+ 9
1938 low–1939 high...............	+ 6	+12	−12	−11
1939 high–1942 low...............	+ 1	−10	− 2	+ 3
1942 low–1946 high...............	+ 6	+32	−15	−18
1946 high–1949 low...............	− 4	−16	+11	+20
1949 low–1955 high...............	− 3	+ 3	+ 7	− 3
1955 high–1959 low...............	−21	−17	+58	+22

the standard capital-structure patterns of public utility and pipe-line companies.

Most corporations have ceased to issue prime preferred stocks because, financially, they do not make sense. If such an issue would be really prime, the company must be strong enough to assume a debt obligation of equivalent amount, with consequent large saving in net annual cost. The device of the "subordinated debenture" will give whatever flexibility is needed in respect to present or future bank borrowing.[1] The existing supply has been considerably diminished, also, by the operation of sinking funds attached to most of the preferred stocks created since 1929. Quite a number of preferred issues have been retired and replaced by bond issues.[2] Conversely, corporations having investment portfolios— chiefly insurance companies of various types—are attracted to the existing preferred issues of good quality because of their tax advantage to

[1] The more radical device of the income bond is also beginning to be used for new financing as a substitute for preferred stocks. See below, p. 395.

[2] The replacement of this type made by Commonwealth Edison in 1961 is especially significant, as it appeared to initiate a movement away from the traditional preferred-stock component in utility capital structures.

corporate owners. This combination of diminished supply and increasing demand no doubt accounts for the unprecedentedly narrow spread in 1961 between the yields of high-grade preferreds and bonds.[3]

Corporate financing in recent years has included a fairly large number of preferred issues ranking below prime grade which have been made attractive by the addition of "sweeteners," such as a conversion privilege or attached warrants to buy common stocks. These types of senior issues will be discussed in Chapters 45 to 47.

The over-all situation with respect to preferred stocks as a medium of corporate finance is summarized in Table 27-3, which shows the

Table 27-3. Dollar Amount of Long-term Debt, Preferred Stock, and Common-stock Equity for All United States Corporations, Selected Years, 1926–1958

(In billions)

Year	Long-term debt*	Preferred stock	Common stock and surplus†
1926	$31.8	17.1	$102.1
1934	48.6	20.0	121.7
1945	48.2‡	14.8	139.7
1958	132.1	16.3	352.9

* Bonded debt and mortgages; after 1940 includes bonded debt and mortgages with maturity of one year or more.
† Includes surplus reserves, surplus, and undivided profits (retained earnings).
‡ Bonds, notes and mortgages payable.
Sources: U.S. Bureau of the Census, *Historical Statistics of the United States*, 1926, 1934, 1945; U.S. Internal Revenue Service, *Statistics of Income*, 1958.

amount of preferred and common stock of all United States corporations outstanding on various dates since 1926. In this connection it must be borne in mind that many enterprises of all types and sizes have been originally capitalized on the basis of issuing preferred stock to represent the tangible assets and common stocks to represent goodwill and earning power. While the 1958 total of $16.3 billion of preferred stock outstanding is far from negligible, the figure denotes a tremendous falling-off in the importance of preferred stock in relation to total corporate capital.

PREFERRED STOCKS VS. BONDS IN THEORY AND PRACTICE

The legal position of a preferred stockholder is always inferior to that of a bondholder, but his practical status is another matter. The holder of the usual bond can sue to compel payment of his interest or principal on

[3] The trend away from straight preferred-stock issues was illustrated rather spectacularly in September 1961 when Fairmont Foods Company called its 4 percent preferred at 103. At the time of the announcement its market price was only 82.

their due dates; the preferred holder has his enforceable right of priority against the common and nothing more. But if the company is very strong and common dividends are sure to be paid, then this limited claim is sufficient to give the preferred issue ample protection and to make unnecessary the addition of the bondholders' remedies in the event of non-payment. At the opposite extreme are the cases in which corporations are *unable to pay anything*, whether on bonds or on preferred stock. In such situations the bondholder's legal right to receive interest results not in payment but in bankruptcy or receivership. The practical value of these remedies is doubtful, and in most instances it may fairly be said that the position of a bond in default is little better than that of a non-dividend-paying preferred stock without bonds ahead of it.

At both extremes, therefore, the contractual superiority of bonds over preferred stocks is not of substantial value. This fact has led many investors to believe that *as a general rule* the bond form has no real advantage over the preferred-stock form. Their line of reasoning runs: "If the company is good, its preferred stock is as good as a bond; and if the company is bad, its bonds are as bad as a preferred stock."

Weakness because of the Discretionary Right to Omit Dividends. This point of view is highly inexact, because it fails to take into account the wide middle region occupied by companies neither unqualifiedly "good" nor unqualifiedly "bad," but subject to variations and uncertainties in either direction. If it could be assumed that directors will always pay preferred dividends when *possible* (and hence will suspend payment only under conditions which would compel default of interest if the issue were a bond), then even in the intermediate situations the preferred stockholder's status would not be greatly inferior to the bondholder's. But in actual fact this is not the case, because directors frequently exercise their discretion to withhold preferred dividends when payment is by no means impossible but merely inconvenient or inexpedient. It is considered an approved financial policy to sacrifice the preferred stockholder's present income to what he is told is his future welfare; in other words, to retain cash available for dividends in the treasury to meet future emergencies or even future expansion.[4]

Even if we concede that such a practice may ultimately be advantageous to the preferred stockholder, the fact remains that it subjects

[4] The financial press of July 12, 1950, carried the following item, evidently based on an official "release": "Gar Wood Industries voted to omit the regular quarterly dividend of 56¼¢ on the $50 par 4½ percent cumulative convertible preferred in view of capital requirements connected with the expansion program at Wayne, Mich., and the acquisition of National Truck Equipment Co. of Waukesha, Wis." The uncertainty involved in this discretionary feature may be illustrated by a contrary situation. Publicker Industries has paid the regular quarterly dividend on its $4.75 preferred since its issuance in 1945. But the company suffered operating losses in 1954–1955 and earned little more than its preferred dividend in 1956. As a result, the price of the preferred dropped from 95 in 1951 to 64 in 1956.

his income to a hazard not present in the case of a similarly situated bond. If such a hazard is at all substantial, it automatically disqualifies the preferred issue as a fixed-income investment, because it is the essence of such investments that the income must be considered highly dependable. Stating the point more concretely, we may say that any preferred stock subject to a real danger of dividend reduction or suspension will fluctuate widely in market value. It is a point worth noting that whenever a dividend which *could* be continued is instead withheld "for the sake of the stockholders' future advantage," the quoted price suffers a severe decline, indicating that the investment market does not agree with the directors as to what is really in the best interests of the preferred stockholders. As we shall point out below, the reduction or passing of the dividend on a noncumulative preferred issue means irrecoverable loss to the holders.

Form of Preferred Contract Often Entails Real Disadvantage. Whatever the reason or justification may be, the fact remains that preferred stockholders are subject to the danger of interruption of dividend payments under conditions which would not seriously threaten the payment of bond interest. This means that the *form* of the preferred stockholder's contract will often entail a real disadvantage.

Example: A classical illustration of this fact is afforded by our old example of United States Steel Preferred. Its $360 million size makes it probably the largest senior stock issue in the world, and it was for many years thoroughly representative of those preferred shares which enjoyed a high investment rating. In 1931—although the Depression was well advanced—this issue sold at a price to yield only 4.6 percent, and it was thought to occupy an impregnable position as a result of the accumulation of enormous sums out of the earnings during the preceding 30 years and their application to the improvement of manufacturing facilities, the enlargement of working capital, and the retirement of nearly all the bonded debt. Yet immediately thereafter, a single year of operating losses jeopardized the preferred dividend to such an extent as to destroy nearly two-thirds of its market price and undermine completely its standing as a prime investment. In the following year the dividend was reduced to $2 annually.

Weakness of Contractual Position Illustrated. These disastrous developments were due, of course, to the unprecedented losses of 1932–1933. But if it had not been for the weakness of the preferred-stock *form*, the holder of United States Steel Preferred would have had little reason to fear the discontinuance of his income. In other words, if he had possessed a *fixed* claim for interest instead of a contingent claim for dividends, he could have relied with confidence on the corporation's enormous resources to take care of its obligations.

In support of this contention we give, in Table 27-4, a brief comparison of the market action of Inland Steel 4½s with that of United States Steel

Preferred. Both these issues were subject to the same adverse business conditions, but the *contractual* weakness of United States Steel Preferred was responsible for the loss of an investment position which the Inland bonds were able to retain without serious difficulty (except for a brief period of utter demoralization in the bond market).[5]

Voting Rights a Potential Safeguard but Generally Ineffective. The contractual weakness of preferred stocks as compared with bonds might be greatly reduced if preferred stockholders were to exercise *effective voting control* over the enterprise as soon as either dividends or sinking-fund payments were suspended. Such voting control, properly exercised, might constitute the best protective and remedial arrangement for *both*

Table 27-4

Item	U.S. Steel preferred		Inland Steel 4½% bonds, due 1978	
	Price	Yield, percent	Price	Yield, percent
High price, 1931............	150	4.67	97¾	4.62
Low price, 1932............	51½	13.59	61	7.54
High price, January 1933.....	67	10.45	81	5.67

bonds and preferred stock. This would imply that, *given suitable protective provisions intelligently utilized,* the practical positions of bondholders and preferred shareholders would not be significantly different. In our opinion, a good part of the present very real inferiority of preferred stocks to bonds is ascribable to the failure of preferred stockholders either to obtain voting control promptly or to exercise it intelligently, after dividends are suspended. However, our analysis of the investment status of preferred stocks must be predicated on the undoubted fact that, with conditions as they are, the individual holder of preferred shares cannot rely upon his voting rights to achieve full protection of his interests.

Preferred-stock Sinking Funds. The general advantage to preferred-stock investors of having a liberal sinking-fund provision was discussed above (page 337). In particular cases such a feature may prove espe-

---

[5] The Inland Steel bonds were later called at a premium. Although this example is now a part of the history of the distant past, it illustrates very well a common occurrence. For examples of a similar phenomenon during the 1937–1938 and 1939–1942 declines, the reader is referred to the price and dividend records of preferred-stock issues of Cities Service Company, West Penn Electric Company, and Pacific Power & Light Company in contrast with bonds similarly situated as to earnings coverage. It will be found that the preferred stocks suffered greater declines in price and longer terms of distress, even though in the end arrearages were made good and the issues retired.

cially helpful; in others it may operate as a slight disadvantage because of the call feature associated with it.

Example 1: FMC Corporation (formerly Food Machinery & Chemical) issued a 3¾ percent preferred stock in 1948. The sinking fund provides that annually, beginning in 1949, the greater of $145,000 or 5 percent of consolidated net income available for dividends for preceding fiscal-year shares be set aside to purchase preferred stock. In 1960 the sinking fund exceeded $1 million and retired over 20 percent of the outstanding shares. In consequence, the issue sold at 97½ in 1961, to yield only 3.8 percent. At the same time, the company's 3.80 percent debentures, due 1981, which were offered at 100 in 1956 and are provided with a less liberal sinking fund (not yet in operation), were quoted at only 90, to yield 4.54 percent.

Example 2: Cluett Peabody & Company has a 7 percent cumulative preferred, noncallable except at 125 for the sinking fund. The sinking fund provides for an annual cumulative sum sufficient to purchase 2 percent of the largest amount of preferred outstanding at any time or to redeem preferred when available funds equal at least 10 percent of the preferred outstanding. In most years the issue has sold regularly above 125, the high being 165 in 1946. Those holders who have some of their shares called by lot for the sinking fund thus suffer a market loss.

Yield and Risk. What yield advantage should the investor demand to compensate him for the contractual weakness of preferred stocks against bonds? We are inclined to think that an *individual* should not buy any preferred stock unless he is able to obtain *both* adequate safety and a differential of, say, 1 percent in the yield over that afforded by a bond of similar safety. It is clear that the present virtual equality of yield of high-grade preferreds and high-grade bonds precludes such purchases by the individual investor. This means, in essence, that under present tax laws high-grade preferred stocks are not logical investments for individuals. They *are* logical investments for corporations, which can obtain a much higher net return from them than from corporate bonds of comparable quality. There is a close analogy here between preferred stock and tax-free (municipal, etc.) bonds. The latter are not logical investments, as against United States government securities, except for those who pay income taxes and thus would benefit from the tax exemption.

What of preferred stocks of secondary or inferior grade which can be bought at tempting yields? Our attitude toward them is the same as that toward high-coupon bonds. (See pages 320–323.) It is unsound to accept inadequate security to obtain a higher income, *unless* the buyer obtains also an opportunity for a substantial increase in principal value and *unless also* he is prepared to take the speculative risk of loss involved in the transaction.

Qualifications of High-grade Preferred Stocks. What must be the qualifications of a well-protected preferred stock? In the first place, it must meet all the minimum requirements of a safe bond. In the second place, it must exceed these minimum requirements by a certain added margin to offset the discretionary feature in the payment of dividends; i.e., the margin of safety must be so large that the directors may always be expected to declare the dividend as a matter of course. Third, the stipulation of inherent stability in the business itself must be more stringent than in the case of a bond investment, because a company subject to alternations between large profits and temporary losses is likely to suspend preferred dividends during the latter periods even though its *average* earnings may far exceed the annual requirements.

CHAPTER TWENTY-EIGHT

TECHNIQUE OF SELECTING PREFERRED

STOCKS FOR INVESTMENT

Our discussion of the theory of preferred stocks led to the practical conclusion that an investment preferred issue must meet all the requirements of a good bond, with perhaps an extra margin of safety to offset its contractual disadvantages. In analyzing a senior stock issue, therefore, the analyst should apply the same types of tests that we have previously suggested and described with respect to bonds, and presumably he should set the various minimum requirements at a higher figure than for bonds. In computing all ratios based on capitalization, he should substitute the senior obligations, down to and including the preferred stock under study (at its market value), for the funded-debt or senior-capitalization figure alone. For example, in the case of public utility preferred stocks preceded by bond issues, net tangible assets of 1.7 times the bond issues alone will not be sufficient to qualify the preferred-stock issue on that score. They must be at least 1.7 times the *sum* of the preferred stock at market value and the par value of the securities senior thereto.

Difficulty of Applying More Stringent Requirements. The presumption that the minimum requirements for preferred stocks should be more stringent than those for bonds creates a very real difficulty in investment practice. Our standards for bonds are high; to make them higher for preferred stocks would seem to make them prohibitive. Investors have been accustomed to requiring lower standards of safety for preferred stocks than for bonds, on the theory that—at least in the past—the higher yields on preferred stocks compensate for a lower degree of protection. We are opposed to any such sacrifice of safety for the sake of yield, for reasons we have developed elsewhere.

As a concession to practicality, *we suggest that the same minimum standards be required for the total of preferred stock plus any bonded debt as are now required for a bond issue alone.*

Allowance for Differences in Tax Status of Bonds and Preferred Stock. In order to cover a preferred dividend with the same margin that would apply to a similar amount of bond interest, larger earnings are required before income taxes. The reason (as noted in Chapter 27) is that bond interest is a charge before any income tax accrual, whereas preferred dividends can be regarded as earned only after the full income tax is provided for. This tax disadvantage of preferred stocks may be allowed for arithmetically by adding to the preferred dividend the amount of related tax—i.e., the tax the company would save if the charge were bond interest but does not save on the dividend charge. For convenience, the tax rate may be assumed at 52 percent (under 1961 conditions) thus making the enlarged dividend-plus-tax requirement equal to more than twice the actual dividend.[1] The addition of such a tax component will then give the same basic coverage for a preferred stock as the coverage before taxes for a corresponding bond. This point is demonstrated by Table 28-1 covering three industrial-company situations.

Table 28-1

Item	Company A	Company B	Company C
Bond interest............................	$ 300,000	....	$ 180,000
Preferred dividend........................	....	$ 300,000	120,000
Tax related to preferred dividend (108.3 percent of dividend)......................	....	325,000	130,000
Total senior charges plus related tax....	$ 300,000	$ 625,000	$ 430,000
Earnings required before taxes, viz., 7 times sum of interest and 208 percent of preferred dividends.............................	$2,100,000	$4,375,000	$3,010,000
Corresponding earnings after tax, but before interest................................	1,165,000	2,100,000	1,540,000
Senior charges earned before tax...........	7.0×	14.6×	10.0×
Senior charges earned after tax............	3.8×	7.0×	5.1×
Check (assume shrinkage of ⁵⁄₇ of earnings):			
Earned before tax (⁵⁄₇ of above)..........	300,000	625,000	430,000
Bond interest........................	300,000	....	180,000
Balance before tax....................	zero	625,000	250,000
Tax................................	....	325,000	130,000
Balance after tax.....................	....	300,000	120,000
Preferred dividend....................	....	300,000	120,000
Remainder...........................	zero	zero	zero

In the case of companies having only preferred stocks (with no bonds) in their capitalization structures, our test may be applied in a simple

[1] The fraction by which preferred dividends should be stepped up to correspond to any given tax rate may be derived by the following equation:

$$\text{Step-up fraction} = \frac{\text{tax rate}}{100 - \text{tax rate}}$$

For example, by this equation, when the tax rate is 52 percent the step-up fraction is actually 108.3 percent, and preferred dividends should be multiplied by 2.083 for the purpose of computing coverage. For convenience, a multiplier of 2 may be used without ill effect.

manner merely by requiring that the coverage *after* taxes be as large as that required for a bond issue *before* taxes. Note that Company *B* in our table shows a coverage of 7.0 times after taxes, while Company *A* shows the same figure before taxes. Where the company has both bonds and preferred stock, it is necessary to increase the preferred dividends by the tax equivalent and then to apply the standard "before-taxes test" to the total of bond interest plus the stepped-up preferred dividend.

Mere Presence of Funded Debt Does Not Disqualify Preferred Stocks for Investment. It is proper to consider whether an investment rating should be confined to preferred stocks not preceded by bonds. That the absence of funded debt is a desirable feature for a preferred issue goes without saying; it is an advantage like that of having a first mortgage on a property instead of a second mortgage. It is not surprising, therefore, that preferred stocks without bonds ahead of them have *as a class* made a better showing than those of companies with funded debt. But from this rather obvious fact it does not follow that *all* preferred stocks with bonds preceding are unsound investments, any more than it can be said that *all* second-mortgage bonds are inferior in quality to *all* first-mortgage bonds. Such a principle would entail the rejection of all public utility preferred stocks (since they invariably have bonds ahead of them) although these are generally better regarded than are the "nonbonded" industrial preferreds. Furthermore, in the extreme test of 1932, a substantial percentage of the preferred issues which held up were preceded by funded debt.[2]

To condemn a strongly entrenched security such as American Radiator & Standard Sanitary preferred in 1961 because it was preceded by an inconsequential funded debt would be absurd. This example should illustrate forcibly the inherent unwisdom of subjecting investment selection to hard and fast rules of a *qualitative* character. In our view, the presence of bonds senior to a preferred stock is a fact which the investor must take carefully into account, impelling him to greater caution than he might otherwise exercise; but if the company's exhibit is sufficiently impressive, the preferred stock may still be accorded an investment rating.

Total-deductions Basis of Calculation a Necessity. In calculating the earnings coverage for preferred stocks with bonds preceding, it is absolutely essential that the bond interest and preferred dividend be taken *together*. The almost universal practice of stating the earnings on the preferred stock separately (in dollars per share) is exactly similar to, and as fallacious as, the prior-deductions method of computing the margin above interest charges on a junior bond. If the preferred-stock issue is much smaller than the funded debt, the earnings per share will indicate that the preferred dividend is earned more times than is the

[2] Of 21 such issues, 11 were preceded by bonds (5 public utilities, 1 railroad, and 5 of 15 industrials). For details, see the table on p. 191 of the 1940 edition of this work.

bond interest. Either such a statement must have no meaning at all, or else it will imply that the preferred dividend is safer than the bond interest of the same company, which is self-contradictory. (See Table 28-2, in which coverage is computed on an after-tax basis.)

Table 28-2. Example of Correct and Incorrect Methods of Calculating Earning Coverage for Preferred Stock. Southern California Edison Company, 1960

Earnings available for charges (after income taxes)......	$71,172,441
Fixed charges..	20,192,909
Net income..	$50,979,532
Original (first) preferred dividends*....................	415,771
Balance...	$50,563,761
Preferred (second) dividends..........................	6,165,075
Balance...	$44,398,686
Convertible (third) preference dividends...............	417,097
Balance for common.................................	$43,981,589

* Includes participating dividends properly deductible with common dividends.

Incorrect statement

Item	Times charges or dividends earned (after taxes)	Earned per share
Fixed charges..............	3.5×	
First preferred.............	122.5×	$318.62
Second preferred...........	8.2×	9.07
Third preferred............	106.5×	124.65

Correct statement

Item	Times earned (after taxes)
Fixed charges...	3.53×
First preferred and prior charges......................	3.45×
Second preferred and prior charges....................	2.66×
Total preferred and prior charges.....................	2.62×

Southern California Edison Company, in effect, had outstanding at the end of 1960 three classes of preferred in the following amounts and ranking:

(1) Five percent original cumulative participating prior preferred.... $ 4,000,000
(2) Five issues of cumulative (second) preferred.................... 139,361,000
(3) Two issues of cumulative convertible (third) preferred.......... 8,904,000

Consequently, in this instance, the use of the prior-deductions method would make the most junior preferred appear to be a much stronger issue than the second-ranking preference shares. Also, the first preferred dividends would seem to be many times safer than the bond interest. This, of course, results from the wide disparity in the size of the three groups of preferred stocks. The correct statement shows that the total preferred dividends and bond interest were earned 2.62 times, which is quite a contrast to the 106.5 times—under the prior-deductions method—for the most junior preferred issue.

An Apparent Contradiction Explained. Our principles of preferred-dividend coverage lead to an apparent contradiction, viz., that the preferred stockholders of a company should logically require more stringent coverage than they require for bonds of the same company; yet by the nature of the case the actual coverage is bound to be smaller. For in any corporation the bond interest alone is obviously earned with a larger margin than the bond interest and preferred dividends combined. This fact has created the impression that the tests of a sound preferred stock must necessarily be less stringent than those of a sound bond. But this is not true at all. The real point is that where a company has both bonds and preferred stock, the latter can be safe enough *only if the bonds are much safer than necessary.* Conversely, if the bonds are only just safe enough, the preferred stock cannot be sound.

"Dollars-per-share" Formula Misleading. When a preferred stock has no bonds ahead of it, the earnings may be presented either as so many dollars per share or as so many times dividend requirements. The second form is distinctly preferable, for two reasons. The more important one is that the use of the "dollars-per-share" formula in cases where there are no bonds is likely to encourage its use in cases where there are bonds. Security analysts and intelligent investors should make special efforts to avoid and decry this misleading method of stating preferred-dividend coverage, and this may best be accomplished by dropping the dollars-per-share form of calculation entirely.

For example, a financial-services report shows for Worthington Corporation the data in the first two columns of Table 28-3. We have added the third (times dividends earned).

Table 28-3

Year	(1) Times charges and preferred dividends earned (after taxes)	(2) Earned per share of preferred	(3) Times preferred dividends earned
1960	5.02×	$108.99	24.2×
1959	6.35	118.25	26.3
1958	5.67	111.87	24.9
1957	5.91	140.20	31.1
1956	6.30	116.63	25.6
1955	6.15	88.28	19.3
1954	5.68	80.53	16.2

Worthington has $21,550,000 of long-term debt outstanding, in addition to 70,774 shares of cumulative prior preferred, 4½ percent series ($100 par value). Both column (2) and column (3) in the above table are equally meaningless or misleading.

As a second point, it should be noted that the significance of the dollars earned per share is dependent upon the market price of the preferred stock. Earnings of $20 per share would be more favorable for a preferred issue selling at 80 than for a preferred selling at 125. In the one case the earnings are 25 percent, and in the other only 16 percent, on the market price. The dollars-per-share figure loses all comparative value when the effective par value of the preferred issue is less than $100. Norfolk and Western Railway and Union Pacific Railroad have 4 percent preferred-stock issues outstanding with $10 par value. Earnings of $6 more per share on such issues would, of course, be far more favorable than earnings of $28 a share on some 5 percent preferred stock with a $100 par value.

Calculation of the Stock-value Ratio. The technique of applying this test to preferred stocks of industrial companies is in all respects similar to that of the earnings-coverage test. The bonds, if any, and the preferred stock must be taken together and the total compared with the market price of the common stock only. When calculating the protection behind a bond, the preferred issue is part of the stock equity; but when calculating the protection behind the preferred shares, the common stock is, of course, the only junior security.[3] An example is shown in Table 28-4.

Table 28-4. Example of Calculation of Stock-value Ratios for Preferred Stock. The Celotex Corporation

Capitalization Oct. 31, 1960	Face amount	Price Dec. 31, 1960	Value at Dec. 31, 1960
4⅛ convertible sub. debentures, 1976..	$10,000,000	*	$10,000,000
Term loans.........................	9,500,000	*	9,500,000
5 percent preferred stock (par $20)....	5,137,250	17¼	4,431,000
Common stock, shares...............	1,028,651	24½	25,202,000

* Debt taken at par.

1. Stock-value ratio for bonds:

$$\frac{4,431,000 + 25,202,000}{19,500,000} = 152 \text{ percent}$$

2. Stock-value ratio for preferred:

$$\frac{25,202,000}{4,431,000 + 19,500,000} = 105 \text{ percent}$$

Should the market value of the common stock be compared with the *par* value or the *market* value of the preferred? In most stocks—as in

[3] In cases where there are both a first and second preferred issue, the second preferred is added to the common stock in calculating the equity behind the first preferred.

our Celotex example—it will not make a serious difference which is used. However, in some long-outstanding noncallable issues, the choice could be of some significance. To illustrate: The following firms have 7 percent cumulative noncallable preferred stocks outstanding, and the high price in 1960 was as follows:

International Harvester.......... 153
National Biscuit................ 158
U.S. Steel..................... 148
National Lead................. 160

There are also those few instances in which the real par is entirely different from the stated par. An outstanding illustration here is Island Creek Coal, which has a $6 cumulative preferred issue with a stated par of $1; this was discussed on page 211. Where the market value differs materially from the par or stated value, it would seem the better rule to use the *market price* of preferred stocks regularly in computing stock-value ratios. On the other hand, we recommend the regular use of the *face value* of bond issues rather than the market price, because it is much more convenient and does not involve the objections just discussed in relation to preferred shares.

NONCUMULATIVE ISSUES

The theoretical disadvantage of a noncumulative preferred stock as compared with a cumulative issue is very similar to the inferiority of preferred stocks in general as compared with bonds. The drawback of not being able to compel the payment of dividends on preferred stocks generally is almost matched by the handicap in the case of noncumulative issues of not being able to receive in the future the dividends withheld in the past. This latter arrangement is so patently inequitable that new security buyers (who are often far from exacting) balk at noncumulative issues, and for many years new offerings of straight preferred stocks have almost invariably had the cumulative feature.[4]

Noncumulative issues have generally come into existence as the result of reorganization plans in which old security holders have been virtually forced to accept whatever type of security was offered them. But in recent years the preferred issues created through reorganization have been preponderantly cumulative, though in some cases this provision becomes operative only after a certain interval. Erie Railroad Company 5 percent Preferred, Series A, for example, was issued in the 1941 reorganization of the road. The dividend was cumulative only to the ex-

[4] Perhaps the only important "straight" noncumulative preferred stock sold to stockholders or the public since World War I was St. Louis-San Francisco Railway Company Preferred. This was offered at $100 in 1928. It was wiped out in the 1947 reorganization.

tent earned until January 1, 1944, becoming cumulative thereafter whether earned or not; but cumulation is limited to a maximum of $14 a share.[5]

Chief Objection to Noncumulative Provision. One of the chief objections to the noncumulative provision is that it permits the directors to withhold dividends even in good years, when they are amply earned, the money thus saved inuring to the benefit of the common stockholders. Experience shows that noncumulative dividends are seldom paid unless they are necessitated by the desire to declare dividends on the common; and if the common dividend is later discontinued, the preferred dividend is almost invariably suspended soon afterward.[6]

Example: St. Louis–San Francisco Railway Company affords a typical example. No dividends were paid on the preferred issue between 1916 and 1924, although the dividend was fully earned in most of those years. Payments were not commenced until immediately before dividends were initiated on the common; and they were continued (on a new preferred) less than a year after the common dividend was suspended in 1931.

The manifest injustice of such an arrangement led the New Jersey courts (in the United States Cast Iron Pipe case) to decide that if dividends are earned on a noncumulative preferred stock but not paid, then the holder is entitled to receive such amounts later before anything can be paid on the common.[7] This meant that in New Jersey a noncumulative preferred stock was given a cumulative claim on dividends to the extent that they were earned. The United States Supreme Court, however, handed down a contrary decision (in the Wabash Railway case) holding that while the noncumulative provision may work a great hardship on the holder, he has nevertheless agreed thereto when he accepted the issue.[8] This is undoubtedly sound law, but the inherent objections to the noncumulative provision are so great (chiefly because of the opportunity

[5] For a discussion of the special characteristics of preferred stocks issued in railroad organizations, see *Transportation and National Policy*, House Document No. 883, 77th Congress, Second Session, 1942, pp. 191–192.

[6] Kansas City Southern Railway Company 4 percent Noncumulative Preferred, which paid dividends between 1907 and 1929 while the common received nothing, is an outstanding exception to this statement. St. Louis-Southwestern Railway Company 5 percent Noncumulative Preferred received full dividends during 1923–1929 while no payments were made on the common, but for a still longer period preferred dividends, although earned, were wholly or partially withheld (and thus irrevocably lost).

[7] Day v. United States Cast Iron Pipe and Foundry Company, 94 N.J., Eq. 389, 123 Atl. 546 (1924), aff'd. 96 N.J. Eq. 738, 126 Atl. 302 (1925); Moran v. United States Cast Iron Pipe and Foundry Company, 95 N.J. Eq. 389, 123 Atl. 546 (1924), aff'd. 96 N.J. Eq. 698, 125 Atl. 329 (1925).

[8] Wabash Railway Company, et al. v. Barclay, et al., 280 U.S. 197 (1930), reversing Barclay v. Wabash Railway, 30 Fed. (2d) 260 (1929). See discussion in A. A. Berle, Jr., and G. C. Means, *The Modern Corporation and Private Property*, New York, 1932, pp. 190–192.

it affords for unfair policies by the directors), that it would seem to be advisable for the legislatures of the several states to put the New Jersey decision into statutory effect by prohibiting the creation of completely noncumulative preferred stocks, requiring them to be made cumulative at least to the extent that the dividend is earned. This result has been attained in a number of individual instances through insertion of appropriate charter provisions.[9]

Matters of Form, Title, or Legal Right Not Always Immaterial. We are aware that some preferred stocks with excellent investment records (e.g., Norfolk & Western Preferred, U.S. Tobacco Preferred, G. W. Helme Preferred, American Snuff Preferred), listed on the New York Stock Exchange, are noncumulative issues. The fact merely affords evidence in support of our basic thesis that matters of form, title, or legal right are usually immaterial, and that the showing made by the individual issue is of paramount importance. If a preferred stock could always be expected to pay its dividend without question, then whether it is cumulative or noncumulative is an academic matter in the same way that the inferior contractual rights of a preferred stock as compared with a bond would cease to have practical significance. But the market's most confident judgment on this point may turn out to be ill-founded.

Example: The adverse possibility inherent in even a high-grade noncumulative preferred is well illustrated by Atchison, Topeka & Santa Fe Railway Company Preferred. Its 5 percent preferred is non-cumulative. It paid full dividends between 1901 and 1932 and was long regarded as a gilt-edged investment. As late as 1931 the price reached 108¼, *within a half point of the highest level in its history until that time,* and a yield of only 4.6 percent. The very next year the dividend was reduced to a $3 basis. It was later restored to 5 percent, but in 1938 the dividend was omitted entirely, and the price declined from 104 in 1937 to 40 in 1938. (It subsequently recovered to 125 and was later changed to a $10 par issue by a 10-for-1 split.)

Hence, as a point of practical investment policy, we suggest that no matter how impressive may be the exhibit of a noncumulative preferred stock, it would be better to select a cumulative issue for purchase in order to enjoy better protection in the event of unexpected reverses.

---

[9] The "earned cumulative" feature became the more usual practice as regards railroad preferred stocks issued in railroad reorganizations after the middle 1930's. See, for example, the preferred issues of Chicago & North Western, St. Louis–San Francisco, Wabash, and the class A stock of Chicago & Eastern Illinois.

CHAPTER TWENTY-NINE

INCOME BONDS AND GUARANTEED SECURITIES

I. INCOME BONDS

The contractual position of an income bond (sometimes called an "adjustment bond") stands midway between that of a straight bond and that of a preferred stock. Basically, the payment of interest on an income bond is dependent upon the availability of earnings therefor during a related accounting period. So far as we know, all income obligations have a definite maturity, so that the holder has an unqualified right to repayment of his principal on a fixed date.[1] In this respect his position is entirely that of a bondholder. However, we should point out that the greatest number of outstanding corporate income bonds are to be found among the railroads; and there they almost always have been given a long maturity date.[2] In contrast, the maturity of industrial income bonds tends to be substantially shorter than that for rails. For example, the average maturity—from date of issuance to designated maturity—for 16 income bonds in Moody's *Industrial Manual* for 1961[3] was about 25 years. Several would mature in the present decade. Consequently, the investor would need to give careful consideration to this factor in analyzing an industrial income-bond issue.

Interest Payment Sometimes Wholly Discretionary. In the matter of interest payments, some income bonds are almost precisely in the position of a preferred stock, because the directors are given practically complete discretion over the amounts to be paid to the bondholders. The customary provisions require that interest be paid to the extent that income is available, but some indentures have permitted the directors to set aside what-

[1] A possible exception (turning on definition) is the Atlantic Coast Line Company class A 5 percent irredeemable certificates of indebtedness issued in 1897 to provide for the reduction of capital stock. Interest is noncumulative and payable if earned. Bid-price range in 1960 was 99 to 100.

[2] Out of the 88 income issues listed in Moody's *Manual*, 1 issued in 1863 matures in 2862, and 38 others mature in 2000 or later. Although the passage of time has brought the maturity of two or three issues into the 1960's, most still have such distant maturities that the problem of repayment is not likely to be of practical importance in the typical case studied. (Many will be retired gradually over their life by operation of a sinking fund.) Moody's *Transportation Manual*, 1961, p. a105.

[3] Pp. a145–148.

393

ever portion of the income they please for capital expenditures or other purposes before arriving at the "available balance." In the case of Missouri-Kansas-Texas Railroad Company Adjustment 5s, due 1967, the amounts paid out between 1935 and 1944, inclusive, aggregated 5 per cent, although the earnings available were equal to over 90 percent.[4] In modern income-bond indentures (e.g., Denver and Rio Grande Western Railroad Income 4½s, due 2018, and Chicago, Milwaukee, St. Paul and Pacific Railroad Company General Income 4½s, Series A, due 2019) the manner of accounting and a specified order of priority of payments from available funds are usually prescribed. The bond indentures of many roads recently reorganized in part through the use of income bonds require the accumulation of capital funds of stipulated amounts out of net income before contingent interest.[5] However, it may be said that individual income-bond issues may be found illustrating almost every step in the range of variation between straight preferred stocks and ordinary bonds.

Low Investment Rating of Income Bonds as a Class. Since the contractual rights of income bonds are always more or less superior to those of preferred stocks, it might be thought that a greater proportion of income bonds than of preferred stocks would deserve an investment rating. However, they have not received it. Until recent years virtually all the outstanding income bonds were rated as speculative securities. We have here a contrast between theory and actuality, the reason being, of course, that income bonds in the past have been issued almost exclusively in connection with corporate reorganizations and have therefore been associated with companies of secondary credit standing.[6] The very fact that the interest payments are dependent on earnings implies the likelihood that the earnings may be insufficient. Preferred-stock dividends are equally dependent upon earnings, but the same implication is not as-

[4] The issue vanished in the subsequent reorganization. See also Baltimore Transit Company First 4s, Series A, due 1975, and Denver & Salt Lake Railway Company Income 6s, due 1960 (retired in the reorganization of the 1940's). Attention should also be called to the device of making interest payments discretionary with the directors for a period of several years, at the end of which they become compulsory if earned. See Norfolk Southern Railway Company, Income 5s, due 2014, on which interest was payable if earned and if declared until 1943 and payable if earned thereafter.

[5] See W. H. S. Stevens, "Railroad Reorganizations under the Bankruptcy Act," *Journal of Business of the University of Chicago*, July 1942, pp. 222–224; and *ibid.*, October 1942, pp. 361–364.

[6] An exception to this rule has been the Atchison, Topeka and Santa Fe Adjustment 4s, due 1995, issued in the reorganization of 1895. This road soon attained a strong position, and its Adjustment bonds have had investment status for a half century—except for a temporary lapse from grace in 1938. (See p. 314.) Some guaranteed income bonds of leased railroads have maintained a high investment standing, similar to that of guaranteed railroad stocks. *Example:* Elmira & Williamsport Railroad Income 5s, due 2862, guaranteed by Pennsylvania Railroad and by an important subsidiary. Also observe the superior treatment accorded Chicago, Terre Haute and South Eastern Income 5s, once guaranteed by Chicago, Milwaukee, St. Paul & Pacific Railroad, in the reorganization of that system. Part of the interest was placed on a fixed-charge basis in lieu of the former guaranty.

sociated with them. Hence the general investment status of income bonds as a class has been governed evidently by the circumstances under which they have been created rather than by the legal rights which attach to them. To use an analogy: If it had been the general practice here, as in England, to avoid mortgage-bond issues whenever possible, using them only where doubtful credit made this protection necessary, then we might find that mortgage bonds in general would occupy an investment position inferior to that of debenture bonds.[7]

Newer Developments in the Income-bond Field. In the 1950's a beginning was made in the issuance of income bonds under conditions more favorable to their status than those of corporate reorganizations. For the most part they have been created to replace existing preferred stocks, the chief objective being the large income tax savings derived from the substitution of an interest charge for a preferred dividend.

Example 1: In 1954 Western Pacific Railroad issued 5 percent income bonds, due 1984, in exchange for a 5 percent cumulative, participating preferred stock. Unexchanged shares were called at $106.67. The income-tax saving—equivalent to about $2\frac{1}{2}$ percent annually—readily permitted provision for a cumulative sinking fund of corresponding size, calculated to retire the entire issue by its maturity date. Similar exchanges were made by Virginian Railway, Chicago & Eastern Illinois Railroad, and other carriers.

Example 2: Armour & Company, also in 1954, issued $120 of subordinated income debenture 5s, due 1984, in exchange for each share of its $6 cumulative convertible prior preferred stock.

Other industrial companies effecting similar exchanges include American Hide & Leather, Curtis Publishing, and Utah-Idaho Sugar.

In a very few cases income bonds have been issued to raise new money rather than to replace preferred stock.

Example 1: Armour & Company sold privately at par in 1947 an issue of $35 million of cumulative subordinated debenture $3\frac{1}{2}$s, due 1972. (This sale points up dramatically the low interest rates prevailing at that time.) The income debentures are subordinated in claim to all other debt of the company, except that they rank ahead of the later-issued income debenture 5s.

Example 2: Sheraton Corporation of America sold at 96 an issue of "Income Subordinated Debenture" $6\frac{1}{2}$s in 1956, and at 100 an issue of "Capital Income" Debenture $7\frac{1}{2}$s in 1959.

Income bonds have not yet established themselves as a standard form of senior financing with public acceptance comparable to that of good preferred stocks.[8] Nevertheless, the tax saving on income bonds vis-a-vis preferred stock is so substantial that some day their use might spread to

---

[7] We have pointed out above (p. 313) that this is actually true with respect to industrial straight debentures as against industrial mortgage bonds. (Convertible debentures fall into a different category.)

[8] In 1961 only 7 of the 88 income bonds listed in Moody's *Transportation Manual* were rated as "bank grade" (Baa or better).

even the strongest companies. If such a development took place, a respectable number of income-bond issues might ultimately deserve to rank as fixed-income investments.

Income bonds have been favored over preferred stocks in railroad reorganizations because of legal restrictions on insurance companies and savings banks which would prohibit the railroads from holding preferred shares in place of their old bonds. Conceivably considerations of this kind, as well as the tax saving, could induce corporations to do *new* financing through income bonds in lieu of preferred stocks.

Advantages of Income Bonds over Preferred Stock. Theoretically, income bonds have advantages over preferred stocks and no important disadvantages. From the point of view of the purchaser, their form supplies greater assurance of continued income, assuming that the earnings situation is the same for an income bond as for a preferred stock issue. The same kinds of protective provisions could be set up in the event of nonpayment.

From the corporation's standpoint there is the advantage (as against the ordinary bond) that if the interest is not earned it need not be paid. If it is earned, we believe the issuer should have a definite obligation to pay it, especially if the issue is created otherwise than by reorganization after insolvency. Under present tax laws the saving of income tax through the use of the contingent-interest form is so substantial that it will provide money for a liberal sinking fund. Thus the issuer can look forward to retiring most of the principal through tax savings and probably to interest savings as well.

Split-coupon Bonds. A number of railroad and real estate bonds emerging from the reorganizations of the 1930's and 1940's bear interest that is partly fixed and partly contingent.[9] These are hybrid issues, and the type of analysis and minimum standards to which they should be subjected will depend largely upon their exhibits—mainly coverage, price, and yield. They can hardly be analyzed for *fixed-income investment* on the basis of the fixed portion of the interest alone, since insistence upon a substantial margin of earnings over charges would, if met, result in the payment of both the fixed and contingent interest. Coverage

---

[9] New York Athletic Club First and General 4–5s, due 1955, on which 4 percent interest was fixed and 1 percent additional was payable if earned, was typical of the first group. Typical of the railroad issues are Denver & Rio Grande Western First 3–4s, due 1993; Denver & Salt Lake Railway Income Mortgage 3–4s, due 1993; two issues of Chicago, Terre Haute & South Eastern Railway (assumed by the St. Paul); and Southern Indiana Railway First 2¾–4¼s, due 1994 (also assumed by the St. Paul). In addition, there are a number of split-coupon issues of railroads which emerged from voluntary recapitalizations under Chap. XV of the Federal Bankruptcy Act and Sec. 20b of the Interstate Commerce Act (the so-called "Mahaffie Act") and others issued in exchange for leased-line stocks in an effort to reduce income taxes. See, for example, the capital structure of Delaware, Lackawanna, & Western.

on them should therefore be analyzed in terms of the probability that the *entire* interest (fixed and contingent) will be paid, applying the standards for income bonds generally and insisting upon a higher yield than would be exacted for straight fixed-interest bonds of high grade.

The inherent undesirability of a hybrid bond issue is exemplified by the Chicago, Terre Haute & South Eastern securities, which carry fixed interest of 2¾ percent and contingent interest of 1½ percent. Since their creation in 1945 they have consistently sold well below their investment value as indicated by the prices of equivalent issues of the obligor (Chicago, Milwaukee, St. Paul and Pacific). This discrepancy is discussed below (page 400).

Calculation of Margins of Safety for Income Bonds. Computations of earnings on income-bond issues taken separately (prior-deductions method) must, of course, be rigorously avoided in the analysis of such issues for fixed-income commitment. In our judgment, the standards of safety for such issues as have *discretionary-payment* features should be more severe than the standards for fixed-interest bonds and less severe than the standards for straight preferred stocks. To accomplish this end in terms of the technique of analysis, we suggest that the interest charges on discretionary-payment income bonds be stepped up by 50 percent of the full contractual rate in the calculation of over-all coverage and that the minimum "before-tax" standards for fixed-interest bonds then be applied.[10]

Typical income bonds, on which interest is payable if earned and without intervention of discretion on the part of directors, are in a stronger contractual position than either preferred stocks or discretionary-payment income bonds. On the other hand, they are weaker, contractually, than fixed-interest bonds, and their record is one of considerable instability of price, even under conditions which result in the interest being paid with greater regularity than one could expect for the payment of preferred dividends. We accordingly recommend a compromise position for them, between the standards for fixed-interest bonds and those for discretionary-payment income bonds. This could be accomplished by stepping up the interest charges on them by 30 percent of their maximum contractual amount in the calculation of over-all coverage and by applying the "before-tax" standards for fixed-interest bonds of investment grade.[11]

[10] This represents a lower requirement than for preferred stocks, whose dividends are to be more than doubled to allow for the related income tax (52 percent rate).

[11] Appropriations for sinking funds on income bonds or on bonds senior thereto and appropriations to "capital funds" (to the extent that they appear as appropriations of income rather than as depreciation charges) should be regarded as appropriations of surplus in the analysis of income bonds for fixed-income investment. They should not, therefore, be included among the fixed and contingent charges in calculating coverage. It is quite proper, however, to regard them as prior charges when analyzing the probability of payment of interest on *low-priced* income bonds, whether they fall in the category of senior securities of questionable safety or in that of securities of the common-stock type.

Example: The following analysis of the Chicago, Rock Island & Pacific Railroad Company income account for 1960 (Table 29-1) will illustrate the proper method of dealing with all the senior securities of a company having income bonds.

Table 29-1. Chicago Rock Island & Pacific Railroad Company, 1960

(000 omitted)

Railway operating revenues................................	$211,775
Railway operating income (net after taxes)...................	25,387
Intermediate charges.....................................dr.	12,827
Gross income (net after rents, plus other income).............	12,560
Fixed charges (fixed interest and other deductions)............	3,979
Balance for contingent interest.............................	8,581
Contingent interest (payable if earned)......................	2,566
Balance for dividends (net income).........................	6,015
Supplementary data:	
Federal income tax deducted as operating expense...........	17
130 percent of the amount of contingent interest.............	3,336

$$\text{Adjusted charges} = \$3,979 + \frac{\$12,827}{2} = \$10,392$$

Amount available for adjusted charges before tax =
$$\$8,581 + \$10,392 + \$17 = \$18,890$$

$$\text{Times adjusted charges earned} = \frac{\$18,890}{\$10,392} = 1.8\times$$

Times adjusted charges plus 130 percent of contingent interest earned =
$$\frac{\$18,890}{\$10,392 + \$3,336} = 1.4\times$$

Note that the interest charges on income bonds are not part of the fixed charges when calculating the coverage for the *fixed-interest* bonds. In this respect the position of an income bond is exactly that of a preferred stock. But, according to our suggested techniques, 130 percent of the contingent interest becomes a fixed charge when computing over-all coverage on the income bonds with a view to fixed-income investment therein. It is clear that the fixed-interest bonds of the Rock Island would not meet our stringent requirements in 1960 (although they did in previous years); hence the income bonds would have to be rated as speculative.

II. GUARANTEED ISSUES

Guaranteed securities, other than mortgages guaranteed by government agencies, are more interesting with respect to the techniques of their analysis than they are significant numerically or in terms of their dollar magnitude. With the exception previously noted, they are now prevalent only in the railroad field, where the charges on them appear for the most part as rent for leased roads in the fixed-charges section of income accounts. We shall accord them only abbreviated treatment, in keeping with the minor role which they play in American private finance.

No special investment quality attaches to guaranteed issues as such. Inexperienced investors may imagine that the word "guaranteed" carries a positive assurance of safety; but, needless to say, the value of any guaranty depends strictly upon the financial condition of the guarantor. If the guarantor has nothing, the guaranty is worthless. In contrast with the attitude of the financial novice, Wall Street displays a tendency to *underestimate* the value of a guaranty, as is shown by the lower prices often current for guaranteed issues in comparison with the debentures or even the preferred stock of the guarantor. This sophisticated distrust of guaranties apparently dates back to the Kanawha and Hocking Coal and Coke Company case in 1915, when the guarantor railroad endeavored to escape its liability by claiming that the guaranty, made in 1901, was beyond its corporate powers and hence void. This attempt at evasion, encouraged by the outcome of antitrust suits in the Ohio and Federal courts, in the end proved completely unsuccessful; but it cast a shadow over the value of all guaranties, from which they have not completely emerged even after 45 years. We know of no important case in which a solvent company has escaped the consequences of its guaranty through legal technicalities.[12]

[12] However, the shadowy form of "insolvency" provided for in Chap. XI of the Chandler (Federal Bankruptcy) Act has been invoked to induce holders of guaranteed issues to modify their contracts without sacrifice by the guarantor company and to force minority holders to accept the modified terms. *Example:* Modification of the guaranty of Trinity Building 5½s by United States Realty and Improvement Company, proposed in March 1939.

Contrast this with the full payment in October 1932 of the unpurchased portion of Savoy Plaza Corporation Debenture 5½s, which had also been guaranteed by United States Realty and Improvement. At that time unguaranteed *First Mortgage* bonds of Savoy Plaza had been selling as low as 5. Note also the full payment in 1939 of Utica, Clinton and Binghamton Railroad First 5s through funds supplied by Delaware & Hudson Railroad, the guarantor, although Delaware & Hudson had not been operating the Utica line for a great many years.

Under Chap. XV of the Federal Bankruptcy Act, railroad corporations which are neither in receivership nor in bankruptcy may, in order to avoid temporary financial difficulty, compromise with their security holders without recourse to bankruptcy, under Sec. 77. In at least one such case (see the Debt Readjustment Plan of the Lehigh Valley Railroad Company in 1940) maturities of several underlying guaranteed bond issues were extended ten years. But the compromise involved no cessation of the regular payment of rent and of interest on the bonds.

The serious student is referred to the interesting history of the various securities of the Pittsburgh Railways Company which were guaranteed by the Philadelphia Company. Pursuant to the reorganization plan consummated in 1950 the guaranteed bonds were all paid off at a premium, and the guaranteed common stocks were paid off on a cash basis which compared very favorably with previous market prices. Monongahela Street Railway Company common stock, with a dividend of $2.25 guaranteed by Philadelphia Company, sold in the low 20s while still paying its dividend, because of doubt as to the future of the guaranty. In the reorganization completed in 1950, the holders received $48 per share, or payment on a 4.69 percent basis.

A Current Example: That some vestige of doubt as to the legal position of guaranteed issues still lingers in the securities markets is apparently demonstrated by the current price relationship between Southern Railway 5 percent noncumulative preferred stock (par $20) and the Southern Railway–Mobile & Ohio $4 Stock Trust Certificates (par $100). The $4 dividend on these certificates is guaranteed in perpetuity by Southern Railway. After making continuous payments between 1904 and 1940, the guarantor endeavored to void its obligation in 1941. This move was defeated in the courts, and the $4 annual rate has been paid without interruption since 1942. There is every reason to regard the Certificates as direct óbligations of the Southern Railway, without maturity.

In 1960 Southern Railway preferred sold at an average price of 17¾, to yield 5.64 percent, while the M. & O. Certificates averaged 66¾, to yield 6 percent. Clearly a noncumulative preferred should not yield *less* than the fixed obligations of the same company, especially if the latter returns as high as 6 percent. (In some previous years, e.g., 1956, the yield on Southern Railway preferred was considerably higher than that on the M. & O. Certificates.)

Technical Status of Guaranteed Issues. If a company guarantees interest, dividend, or principal payments, its failure to meet this obligation will expose it to bankruptcy. The claim against the guarantor ranks equally with any unsecured debt of the company, so that guaranteed issues deserve the same rating as a debenture bond of the guarantor and a better rating than its preferred stock. A guaranteed issue may also be entitled to an investment rating because of its own position and earning power independent of the guaranty. In such cases the guaranty may add to its security, but it cannot detract therefrom, even if the guarantor company itself is in bad straits.

Examples: The Brooklyn Union Elevated Railroad First 5s, due 1950, were guaranteed by Brooklyn Heights Railroad Company, which went into receivership in 1919; but the bond came through the reorganization unscathed because of its own preferred position in the Brooklyn Rapid Transit System. Similarly U.S. Industrial Alcohol Company Preferred dividends were guaranteed by Distilling Company of America; the latter enterprise became bankrupt, but the Alcohol Company was easily able to continue the dividend out of its own earnings and later to retire the preferred issue at 125.[13]

A common or preferred stock fully guaranteed by another company has the status of a bond issue as far as the guarantor is concerned. If the guaranty proves worthless, it would naturally return to the position of a stock—usually a weak issue, but possibly a strong one, as in the case of U.S. Industrial Alcohol Company Preferred just mentioned. A similar

---

[13] U.S. Industrial Alcohol (subsequently U.S. Industrial Chemicals, Inc.) was merged into National Distillers and Chemical Corporation in July 1951.

situation obtains with respect to income bonds of one company guaranteed by another (e.g., Elmira and Williamsport Railroad Income 5s, due 2862, guaranteed by the Pennsylvania Railroad and by an important subsidiary).

Terms of the Guaranty Are Important. The exact terms of a guaranty have obviously a vital influence upon its value. A guaranty of interest only is likely to be much less significant than a guaranty of principal as well, although guaranty of principal repayment at some very distant date will be of little current significance. The duration of a guaranty of interest or dividends is likewise of obvious significance and needs to be reckoned in the analysis of issues. These comments apply with equal force whether the guaranty is a *direct* one, by endorsement or otherwise, or *indirect* through the terms of a lease.

Joint and several guarantees are given by more than one company to cover the same issue, and each company accepts responsibility not only for its prorata share but also for the share of any other guarantor who may default. In other words, each guarantor concern is potentially liable for the entire amount of the issue. Since two or more sponsors are better than one, bonds bearing a joint and several guarantee are likely to have special advantages.

Example: The most familiar class of issues backed by such a guaranty are the bonds of union railroad stations. An outstanding example is supplied by Kansas City Terminal Railway Company First $1\frac{7}{8}$s to 3s, due at various dates to 1974, which are guaranteed jointly and severally by no less than 12 railroads, all of which use the company's facilities. The 12 guarantors are as follows: Atchison, Burlington, St. Paul, Great Western, Rock Island, Gulf, Mobile & Ohio, Kansas City Southern, M-K-T, Missouri Pacific, 'Frisco, Union Pacific, and Wabash.

The value of each of these individual guaranties has varied greatly from road to road and from time to time, but at least three of the companies have consistently maintained sufficient financial strength to assure a Terminal bondholder that his obligation would be met without difficulty. Investors have not fully appreciated the superior protection accorded by the combined responsibility of the 12 carriers as compared with the liability of any one of them singly. The price record shows that jointly and severally guaranteed Terminal bonds have frequently sold at no higher prices (in relation to interest payments) than representative issues of individual guarantor companies which later turned out to be of questionable soundness, whereas at no time was the safety of the Terminal bond ever a matter of doubt. (The Kansas City Terminal bonds are rated Aaa.)

It would seem good policy for investors, therefore, to favor bonds of this type, which carry the guaranty of a *number* of substantial enterprises, in preference to the obligations of a single company, when the former are obtainable at comparable yields.

INCLUSION OF GUARANTIES AND RENTALS IN THE CALCULATION OF FIXED CHARGES

All obligations equivalent to bond interest should be included with a company's interest charges when calculating the coverage for its bond issues. This point has already been explained in some detail in connection with railroad fixed charges. The procedure in this group offers no special difficulties. But in the accounts of certain types of industrial companies, the treatment of rentals and guaranties may show confusing variations. This question is of particular moment in connection with retail enterprises, theater companies, etc., in which rent or other obligations related to buildings occupied may be an important element in the general picture.

Example: A wide difference exists among the limited-price variety chains in regard to the extent to which stores are owned or leased. A rough indication of this fact may be seen from the following tabulation which shows the sales, rents,[14] and the ratio of the two for five different chains:

Company	Rents (in millions)	Sales (in millions)	Rents as percent of sales
F. W. Woolworth Company	$48.0	$1,035.3	4.6
W. T. Grant Company	21.4	512.7	4.2
S. S. Kresge Company	16.2	418.2	3.9
G. C. Murphy Company	7.5	245.6	3.1
S. H. Kress & Company	2.3	144.6	1.6

Let us compare the two companies at the extremes—Woolworth and Kress. Kress stated in its annual report for 1960 that it wholly owns 146 out of 258 stores. Similar information is not available for Woolworth, but the comparative data below may be taken as indicative.

Company	Land and buildings (net value) (in millions)	Sales (in millions)	Land and buildings as percent of sales
F. W. Woolworth	$203.3	$1,035.3	19.6
S. H. Kress	62.1	144.6	42.9

[14] The SEC Form 10-K groups rents and royalties together. We have assumed that the full amount represents rents, because royalties cannot be important for these companies.

Furthermore, if we employ our rule of capitalizing at 4½ percent one-third of the rentals, the resulting difference in the effect on the capital structures of the two firms is striking.[15]

(000,000 omitted)

	December 31, 1960	
	F. W. Woolworth	S. H. Kress
Long-term debt..............................	$130.6	$10.5
Capitalized rentals (⅓ at 4½ percent)..........	356.0	17.0
Common-stock equity (including reserves).......	478.2	96.4

Status of Guaranteed Obligations. Some additional observations may properly be made as to the computation of earnings coverage in the case of guaranteed obligations. In the typical case the properties involved in the guaranty form part of the whole enterprise; hence both the earnings therefrom and the guaranteed payments are included in a single income statement.

When the guaranteed security is outstanding against a separately operated property, its standing may depend either on its own results or on those of the guarantor. Hence the issue need be required to pass only one of three alternative tests, based on (1) earnings of the issuing company, independent of the guaranty, or (2) combined earnings and charges of the issuing and guarantor companies, or (3) earnings of the guarantor company applied to its own charges plus its guaranties.

Separate Analysis of Subsidiary Interest Coverage May Be Essential. The bonds of a subsidiary of a strong company are generally regarded as well protected, on the theory that the parent company will take care of all of its constituents' obligations. This viewpoint is encouraged by the common method of setting up consolidated income accounts, under which all the subsidiary bond interest appears as a charge against all the combined earnings, ranking ahead of the parent company's preferred and common stocks. If, however, the parent concern is not contractually responsible for the subsidiary bonds, by guaranty or lease (or direct as-

[15] As noted earlier, the SEC forms group "rents and royalties" together. In October 1949, the Committee on Accounting Procedure of the American Institute of Accountants released Accounting Research Bulletin No. 38, unanimously recommending disclosure in financial statements of the amounts of annual rentals to be paid under long-term leases, with some indication of the periods for which they are payable and any other important obligation assumed or guaranteed in connection therewith. The committee recommended that these disclosures be made in the annual report for the year in which the transaction originates and so long thereafter as the amounts involved are material. See *Journal of Accountancy*, November 1949, pp. 388–389.

sumption), this form of statement may turn out to be misleading. For if a particular subsidiary proves unprofitable, its bond interest may conceivably not be taken care of by the parent company, which may be willing to lose its investment in this part of its business and turn it over to the subsidiary's bondholders.

Just as investors are prone to underestimate the value of a guaranty by a strong company, they sometimes make the opposite mistake and attach undue significance to the fact that a company is controlled by another. From the standpoint of fixed-income investment, nothing of importance may be taken for granted. Hence a subsidiary bond should not be purchased on the basis of the showing of its parent company, unless the latter has assumed direct responsibility for the bond in question. In other cases the exhibit of the subsidiary itself can afford the only basis for the acceptance of its bond issues.

Example: Saltex Looms, Inc., was a wholly owned subsidiary of Sidney Blumenthal & Company, Inc., and prior to November 1939, the latter carried an issue of 6 percent first-mortgage bonds of Saltex on its consolidated balance sheet, accompanied by a denial of any liability therefor. At the same time the parent company had outstanding a 7 percent preferred-stock issue which was larger than the subsidiary bond issue. The subsidiary defaulted and went into bankruptcy in 1939. The preferred stock of the parent was retired, partly through sinking-fund operations and partly by redemption in 1946 at 110 percent of par with the proceeds of the sale of additional common stock of the parent. The holders of the subsidiary-company bonds suffered a heavy loss in the liquidation of the Saltex properties, receiving liquidation payments of about 50 cents on the dollar of their claims to principal, after the bonds had declined to as low as 5 cents on the dollar in 1940.

As a practical matter, the financial interest of a parent company in its subsidiary, and other business reasons, may result (in rare instances) in its protecting the latter's bonds even though it is not obligated to do so. This would be a valid consideration for an investor, however, only if he is deciding upon a purchase on a *speculative basis* (i.e., carrying a chance of principal profit), but it would not justify him in buying the bond at a full investment price.

If the above discussion is compared with that on page 367, it will be seen that investors in bonds of a *holding company* must insist upon a consolidated income account, in which the subsidiary interest—whether guaranteed or not—is shown as a prior charge; but that purchasers of *unguaranteed subsidiary bonds* cannot accept such consolidated reports as a measure of their safety and must require a statement covering the subsidiary alone. These statements may be obtainable with some difficulty, but they must nonetheless be insisted upon.

PART FOUR

THE VALUATION OF COMMON STOCKS

CHAPTER THIRTY

THE THEORY OF COMMON-STOCK INVESTMENT.

HISTORICAL SURVEY

The prevailing attitude toward common stocks as investment media has passed through a number of phases in the past half century. It is worth-while to summarize these variations, as part of the basic grounding of the student in the historical development of security investment.

Before World War I. At that time the distinction between investment-grade and speculative common stocks was quite clear in the minds of experienced investors. The chief characteristic of the former was a stable, and perhaps increasing, dividend rate, maintained in the face of panic and depression periods, such as 1907–1908. This dividend stability car-ried with it, as prerequisites, a reasonable stability of earnings, a sound financial structure, and ample working capital.

Listed common stocks of investment rank were found chiefly in the railroad field. (There were many weak railroads also—characterized by overheavy bonded debt—whose stocks were regarded as speculative.) Among public utility and industrial companies, the proportion of such investment issues was definitely smaller. The unlisted issues included quite a number of bank and insurance stocks that were investment favorites of wealthy men, who expected them to show a steady growth of value over the years.

One of the dependable signs of an investment issue was an average market price close to or exceeding the *par value*. Most of these stocks were understood to be backed by a real capital investment equal to their par value plus accumulated surplus—as contrasted with the fictitious or "watered" asset values shown on the balance sheets of many speculative enterprises. In Table 30-1 we list three investment issues which sold in 1913 at about their book value or higher; also two speculative common stocks which sold for much less than their par or their reported book value. In the latter cases the stated values included large amounts of intangibles, or "water," which were later written off.

Examples:

Table 30-1. Prices and Book Values in 1913 as Percentage of Par

Group *A*. Investment issues

	Book value	Average price
Consolidated Gas..................	129	134
General Electric...................	117	158
Pennsylvania Railroad............	128	115

Group *B*. Speculative issues

	Book value		Average price
	As reported	As adjusted*	
American Can......	110	1	34
U.S. Steel.........	141	†	59½

* Deducting intangibles later written off.
† Deficit.

World War I and Its Aftermath. The decade 1914–1923 was marked by a conspicuous improvement in the general position of *industrial* common stocks and at least a minor retrogression in that of the railroads. This point is illustrated by the comparison in Table 30-2.

Table 30-2. Year's Average of High and Low as Percentage of Par

	1913	1923
American Can (speculative)...........	34	91
National Biscuit (investment).........	117	333 (adjusted)
Pennsylvania Railroad (investment)....	115	89

Quite a number of successful industrial and mercantile enterprises had been introduced to public trading just before and during this decade, and many of them were rapidly acquiring an investment standing. Table 30-3 shows two examples.

The Big Bull Market. We come now to the "new-era" bull market of the late 1920's. This is now ranked in the history books, along with the Mississippi Bubble and the South Sea Bubble of the 1700's, as a classic example of mass speculation developing into mass mania, with catastrophic consequences extending far beyond the financial community.

At first the phenomenon took shape slowly. The first years of the 1924–1929 rise were hardly distinguishable from other bull markets. When stock prices had a severe setback in early 1926, it seemed to many that a normal bear-market sequel was at hand. Instead, the upswing was soon renewed, and it continued at an accelerating pace until the explosion of October 1929.

Table 30-3

	Year listed	Initial price	Average price, 1923
May Department Stores.......	1911	70	160
Woolworth.................	1912	97	245

During this period the course of business was by no means identical with that of the stock market. True, there was prosperity; but the indexes showed that at the top of the cycle in 1929 business failed to reach the percentage level (above "normal") of the preceding booms of 1916 and 1919. (As late as 1926 there had been complaints in Wall Street of "profitless prosperity.")

The real estate field constituted in these years a sort of connecting link between business and finance. It contributed, perhaps more than any other line, to general business activity by reason of the record high rate of construction of all sorts in the years 1922–1929. At the same time it developed into a leading area of "high finance." This embraced (1) speculation of huge dimensions by individual operators, (2) a large-scale involvement of banking resources through both loans and direct acquisitions by bank affiliates, (3) a far-flung investment-banking business devoted to the sale of the real estate-mortgage bonds or participation certificates to "prudent investors." A goodly proportion of these bore the guarantee of casualty insurance companies.

The Precursor from Florida. It is interesting to observe that a large-scale rehearsal of the whole spectacle of new-era boom and bust had already taken place in the Florida real estate annals before the stock market rise reached its zenith. Many fortunes had been made in Florida real estate by 1925; many more had been wiped out by a collapse of the familiar sort which began the next year. With that object lesson before its eyes, the public, one might have thought, would have taken warning against similar adventures in Wall Street. But a prime characteristic of speculative mania is its complete insulation from all the lessons of history, whether remote or directly at hand.

The last three years of the new-era boom were marked by several new or extreme pathological developments. The use of bank credit for marginal trading reached unheard-of totals, with brokers' loans rising from about $1 billion in 1921 to $8.5 billion in September 1929. Manipulation on the exchanges also set new records for its unscrupulousness and its blatancy. Brokers congregated daily in the office of a leading manipulator to be told what issues were to "move" the next day. Speculators were eager for market "tips"; these, in turn, were often passed on to them by brokerage employees who were paid for this service by the pool operators.

The boom of the 1920's operated in the field of corporation finance largely through two distinctive manifestations: the public utility holding company and the investment trust. Nearly all the holding-company structures had at their base a group of sound and growing operating utilities. But above them were reared fantastic pyramids, comprising as many as six successive layers of holding companies—each with its own complicated capitalization. These never-ending corporate developments added continuous fuel to the speculation of Wall Street. They also created huge amounts of inadequately secured bond and preferred-stock issues, together with a sad record of financial exploitation and malpractice.

The investment trust was an institution borrowed from Great Britain, where by the 1920's it was well established and favorably regarded. Its theory has always been that the lay investor will act wisely in turning over his funds to capable managers for placement in a diversified list of sound, shrewdly chosen securities. But in the climate of the new-era bull market, this logical idea was transformed into a noxious growth. The American "investment" trusts functioned as blind speculative pools, administered in many cases by men of reputation and ability who were carried away by the universal madness. These new "creations" played a double role in intensifying the speculative orgy, for they were themselves both active speculators and active media of speculation.[1]

Older Tenets Abandoned. Most important to our present study are the novel concepts of common-stock investment that developed during the new-era bull market. Wall Street has never paid much attention to theoretical thinking. The systematic studies and the elaborate controversies of the economists were rarely addressed to matters in the area of private finance, and the rather minor quantity of academic research in investment principles has generally passed unnoticed by the actual buyers and

---

[1] Let us emphasize here that the present-day "investment company" or "mutual fund," closely supervised by the SEC, is much different from and far sounder than its forebears of the late 1920's.

sellers of securities. Nevertheless, there have always been some theories to which Wall Street has paid lip service and which have exerted a traceable influence upon the actions of investors and speculators.

The earlier bull markets had been frankly speculative in their enthusiasm; they made no pretense to vindication by established investment principles. The carouse of the 1920's succeeded in mixing up speculative and investment viewpoints in inextricable fashion—nor have we yet been able to put asunder the approaches that were so undivinely joined together. The new concepts of common-stock investment rested on the twin bases of "historical optimism" and "growth selectivity." A study, published in 1924, of the price and dividend records since the Civil War had demonstrated that representative common-stock lists had consistently outperformed standard bond investments over any ten-year period, taking into account both income return and price changes.[2]

From these figures was born the new gospel that common stocks as a whole were not risky commitments, as we had always been taught, but rather sure-fire bearers of increasing dividends and ultimate price appreciation.

The principle of selectivity was an old and obvious guidepost in Wall Street. It was no more than the truism that some companies are better than others, and hence that some stocks will fare better than others in the market. In the 1920's, however, selectivity took on a new character by reason of the overshadowing emphasis placed on expected future growth as the prime criterion of an attractive investment. The unconscious reasoning probably ran as follows: "Since we favor common stocks as a whole because of their dynamic growth quality, we should use our intelligence as investors to pick out those individual companies which are most likely to grow rapidly, and we must avoid those which will stand still or retrogress."

Optimism and Price Level; Each Justifies the Other. There was nothing wrong with these ideas, except that it was almost impossible not to carry them too far. With encouragement from the past and a rosy prospect in the future, the buyers of "growth stocks" were certain to lose their sense of proportion and to pay excessive prices. For no clear-cut arithmetic sets a limit to the present value of a constantly increasing earning power. Such issues could become "worth" any value set upon them by an optimistic market. It is characteristic of all bull markets that speculative optimism increases with the price level and the price level with optimism. But in previous advances it was the selling of hardheaded and calculating investors, when stocks became clearly high by former standards, that kept the rise within bounds and helped finally to turn the tide. In 1928 the thinking of common-stock "investors" had become indistinguishable

---

[2] Tho study was contained in a small book by Edgar Lawrence Smith, entitled *Common Stocks as Long-term Investments* and destined to become the official "textbook" of the new-era stock market.

from that of speculators; the only practical difference between them was that the former may have paid cash for the same stocks that the latter carried on a thin margin.

The class of stocks continuously favored by investors were those whose "quality" had been established by a longish record of past success. These included old-time favorites, such as General Electric and National Biscuit, and many others—e.g., American Can, Corn Products—that had been transformed from second-grade into well-entrenched enterprises by the prosperity of World War I. These formed the aristocratic group admiringly referred to as the "blue chips"—a phrase appropriately borrowed from the poker or roulette table. To repeat our point, these stocks were bought with equal fervor and enthusiasm by both investors and speculators—and at the same exalted prices.

Table 30-4. Progress of Three Common Stocks, 1913–1929

(Data for later years converted to the 1913 basis of capitalization)

	1913	1923	1929
American Can:			
Earnings per share.........	$6.69	$19.64	$48.12
Dividend................	None	5.00	30.00
Average price............	34	91	810
National Biscuit:			
Earnings per share.........	$9.59	$35.42	$57.20
Dividend................	7.00	21.00	52.50
Average price............	117	319	1,316
Sears Roebuck:			
Earnings per share.........	$12.17	$28.70	$69.50
Dividend................	7.00	None	26.30
Average price............	185	210	1,370

In Table 30-4 we present data concerning three such issues. The reader should observe here that the price rises from 1913 to 1923, while impressive, were somewhat less proportionately than the increase in earnings. But from 1923 to 1929 the rate of price advance far outstripped that of earnings. Note that in 1923 National Biscuit averaged a price of 9 times its current earnings; at the *high* of 1929 (not shown in the table) this ratio was 28.9 times earnings.

The high price levels were by no means limited to the blue-chip aristocracy. Many common stocks of definitely speculative character also made sensational advances during this period. In the typical case we saw a manipulative price movement—which attracted the get-rich-quick trader—supported, for the record, by a sketchy history of increasing earnings for several years past, plus an airy promise of still better things to come. Certain newer issues, such as those of public utility holding companies, completely captured the imagination of experienced investors. In the semantics of the period, these were readily accepted as "quality stocks," a phrase which meant that they were to be regarded as sound and superior investments *regardless of price*. In actuality these issues were generally of poor investment quality, because the pyramiding of debt and preferred stocks in their financial structures made them vulnerable to any breath of adversity.

Summarizing again the "investment theory" of the new-era market, we can boil it down to the sentence: "A stock with good long-term prospects is always a good investment." This meant that the factor of future expectations had become the sole criterion of investment choice. The old quantitative safeguards that had been thrown around conservative common-stock selection were thus abandoned. Their original premise—that

Table 30-5. Earnings per Share

Year	Company A (Electric Power & Light)	Company B (Bangor & Aroostock R.R.)	Company C (Chicago Yellow Cab)
1925	$1.01	$6.22	$5.52
1926	1.45	8.69	5.60
1927	2.09	8.41	4.54
1928	2.37	6.94	4.58
1929	2.98	8.30	4.47
5-year average......	$1.98	$7.71	$4.94
High price, 1929....	86⅝	90⅜	35

the investment should be fully backed by real assets—lost all vestige of authority, and, indeed, was no longer valid. But the more basic concepts of an *"adequate* earning power" and an *"adequate* dividend return"—both tested over a period of years in the past—were similarly discarded.

The only quantitative factor that remained was the specific rate of growth, either historical or projected. But while this concept might lead the investor to the "best" companies, it could not possibly protect him against paying too much for their shares. On the contrary, the acceptance of the growth-stock principle as the only guide to investment made the payment of excessive prices its inevitable consequence.

The stock market of 1928–1929 was highly discriminating, in accordance with its single touchstone of value. Nearly all companies that had failed to expand their profits during the current period of good business were held to have mediocre prospects at best, and thus they sold at low multipliers of earnings. The three examples shown in Table 30-5 are rather typical of 1929 valuations in relation to the earnings trend on the one hand and the average earnings on the other.

The 1929 high prices for these three companies show that the new-era attitude was enthusiastically favorable to Company *A*, unimpressed by Company *B*, and definitely hostile to Company *C*. The market considered Company *A* shares worth more than twice as much as Company *C* shares, although the latter earned 50 percent more per share than Company *A* in 1929, and its average earnings were 150 percent greater.

The Stock Market between 1929 and 1949. As many people remember only too well, the unparalleled bull market of the 1920's was followed by a similarly unparalleled collapse in both the stock market and business during the early 1930's. The law of retribution worked with a vengeance. Many common stocks were as much underpriced in 1932–1933 as they had been overpriced in 1929. In the depths of the Depression many people believed that the whole idea of common-stock investment had

Table 30-6. Price Fluctuations of Eight Leading Issues, 1929–1949°

	1929 high	1932 low	1937 high	1942 low	1946 high	1949 average
American Can..................	46¼	7⅜	30¼	14⅛	26⅝	23½
Consolidated Gas (Edison)......	183¼	31½	49⅞	11⅜	36	25⅜
General Electric...............	31½	2⅞	21⅝	7⅛	17⅜	12¾
National Biscuit...............	94½	20¼	33⅜	13	37⅜	35¼
Pennsylvania Railroad..........	110	6½	50¼	18⅞	47½	15¾
Sears Roebuck.................	16½	2½	8⅛	3⅝	16½	13
U.S. Steel....................	44	3½	21	7⅜	16¼	23½
Woolworth................·....	103⅞	22	65⅜	21½	62½	46¾

* All issues adjusted for 1959 capitalization.

been a delusion, and that common stocks by their nature could not be other than speculative.[3]

With the advent of the New Deal, business and the stock market recovered from the Depression depths. As the price chart in Chapter 1 (Chart 1-1) shows, there were renewed fluctuations in stock prices on a scale comparable to those before 1927. The investor's philosophy changes with his psychological state, which in turn interacts with the market level. By the middle 1930's there had been a rebirth of confidence in the investment merits of "good common stocks." In 1936–1937 overconfidence was once more manifest, with an admixture of inflation fears or hopes. At the low market points of 1938 and 1942 this confidence appeared to be suspended, and in the milder bear years of 1947–1949 it was not much in evidence. But these might be called normal variations in the state of mind. The reader may obtain a concrete impression of the ebb and flow of enthusiasm for common stocks over the 1929–1949 span by the price fluctuations in the eight major issues shown above (Table 30-6).

[3] This was the view expressed by Lawrence Chamberlain in *Investment and Speculation* by Chamberlain and William W. Hay, New York, 1931, p. 8.

In this period the prevailing theory of common-stock investing represented a composite approach. Considerable emphasis was placed on future expectations, but attention was paid—much more than in the 1920's—to the longer-term past record and to the company's financial condition as warranties of a satisfactory future. Hence in this two-decade span, common-stock investment preferred a well-established company, with a long dividend record and a generally upward trend of earnings in the past. We had thus a combination of the old-time investment approach, with its almost exclusive emphasis on the past record, and the new-era attitude which looked only to the future. In other words, the pendulum had swung back, but only part way.

The Stock Market since 1949. At the beginning of 1950, neither the public nor the investment authorities suspected that a new bull market of unexampled duration had just begun. Most writers, including ourselves in the 1951 edition, anticipated some falling off in earnings from the then record figures of 1949. Our calculation of the Central Value of the Dow-Jones Industrial Average early in 1950 gave a figure of 270, against an opening level of 200. Thus stocks as a whole seemed quite reasonably priced, and there were a number of extraordinary bargains available in lesser-known issues. But there was no inkling of the spectacular rise to come, which resulted from (1) a combination of economic expansion and stability unmatched in our history and (2) a parallel growth of the public's enthusiasm for common stocks.[4]

The extent of the market's advance in the 1950's and its relationship to the accompanying rise in earnings and dividends, are illustrated in Table 30-7. This gives certain 1949 and 1959 data for two of the well-known stock averages, and also for General Electric and International Business Machines, two of the major companies in the "growth stock" group.[5] (For comparative purposes, we have subsequently added figures for 1961. It will be seen that the comments made with respect to 1959 are equally applicable to 1961.) These data show (1) a substantial rise in earnings and dividends during the ten years and (2) a much more than proportionate advance in the price level of the general market, and particularly of favored issues. In addition, there was a noteworthy rise in the basic interest rate, which might well have correspondingly offset, at least in part, the higher earnings and dividends.

By what seems an inevitable rule of the stock market, the prevalent theories of common-stock *values* have developed in rather close conjunction with the change in the level of prices. Just as the broad array of com-

---

[4] As late as 1948 a survey taken for the Federal Reserve Board had shown that the public's attitude toward common stocks for investment was in the proportion of 1 in favor to 13 against. Of those opposed, about half gave the reason "not safe, a gamble," and about half, the reason "not familiar with."

[5] The single-year figures for earnings and dividends are considered sufficiently representative in these comparisons.

Table 30-7. Comparative Price, Earnings, and Dividend Levels, 1949, 1959, 1961

	Standard & Poor's Composite (500 stocks)			Dow-Jones Industrial Average			General Electric*			IBM*		
	1949	1959	1961	1949	1959	1961	1949	1959	1961	1949	1959	1961
Closing price	16.79	59.89	71.55	200	679.4	731.1	14.4	99	75	24	292	579
Earnings	$2.32	$3.39	$3.21	$23.54	$34.31	$32.90	$1.52	$3.17	$2.71	$1.34†	$5.31†	$7.52†
Dividends	1.14	1.83	2.02	12.79	20.49	22.61	.67	2.00	2.00	.43	1.36‡	2.30‡
Price/earnings	7.2×	17.6×	22.2×	8.5×	19.8×	22.2×	9.5×	31.3×	27.7×	17.9×	55.0×	76.7×
Dividend yield	6.79%	3.06%	2.82%	6.40%	3.01%	3.09%	4.64%	2.02%	3.33%	1.75%	0.46%	0.40%
Increase:												
Price—over 1949	......	+258%	+426%	......	+245%	+266%	......	+584%	+421%	......	+1,216%	+2,412%
Earnings—over 1949	......	+ 46	+ 39	......	+ 46	+ 36	......	+110	+ 78	......	+ 297	+ 461
Dividends—over 1949	......	+ 61	+ 77	......	+ 56	+ 77	......	+200	+200	......	+ 217	+ 435
Bond yields (year-end)§	2.67%	4.61%	4.44%									
Ratio: stock yield to Aaa bond yield	256%	66%	64%	238%	65%	69%	172%	44%	75%	66%	10%	9%

* Adjusted for stock dividends and splits through 1961.
† Excluding unremitted foreign earnings.
‡ Plus stock dividend.
§ Aaa average.

mon stocks did not appear temptingly low at the end of 1949, when their dividend return was 2½ times the high-grade-bond yield, so they did not appear frighteningly high ten years later, when their yield was only ⅔ that obtainable from bonds—*a reversal of nearly 4 to 1*. The emphasis had shifted radically from the risks associated with common stocks to their *opportunities*. Investors were convinced that the same factors that produced the impressive growth of the 1950's would continue through the 1960's (and probably indefinitely), and that adequate action could be expected from the Federal government to prevent any downward spiral producing large-scale unemployment and a major slump in business activity and earnings. Furthermore, investment of most of one's funds in common stocks was regarded as virtually a necessity, to guard against loss of real value through continued inflation.

Along with this greater enthusiasm for common stocks as a whole went an expanded emphasis on the superior merits of "good stocks" and especially of "growth stocks." For some of the latter issues the ratio of price to current earnings may have appeared astronomically high; but the quotation was justified without too much difficulty by projecting recent growth rates far enough into the future. Clearly, during the 1950's the pendulum of common-stock theory once again reversed its swing, and its arc has carried investment modes toward an emphasis on the future somewhat reminiscent of the 1920's.

As we stated in our preface, the greatly enhanced investment standing of common stocks at the beginning of the 1960's presents us with vexing problems when we come to reformulate our criteria of value. In the ensuing chapters we shall do our best to cope with these problems.

CHAPTER THIRTY-ONE

STOCK-MARKET PHILOSOPHY AT THE BEGINNING

OF THE 1960's. ALTERNATIVE APPROACHES

TO COMMON-STOCK INVESTING

At this point in our previous editions we presented arguments for the inclusion of a common-stock component in standard investment portfolios. Briefly these were: (1) that, on the positive side, a representative group of common stocks bought at a *reasonable price level* could be counted on both to provide a higher income return than bonds and to appreciate in value over the years; and (2) that, on the negative side, the probability of continued inflation removed much of the inherent safeguards in bond investment and required a fair holding of common stocks as a protective measure. The reader will note the requirement of "a reasonable price level." It was part of our thesis that the safety and attractiveness of common-stock investing were jeopardized when the investor bought at an excessively high general market level—as in the upper reaches of a bull market—or when he paid too much in advance for the promising prospects of favored issues.

Our philosophy and its related standards of value were derived primarily from the actual experience of stock investors (and speculators) during many decades prior to the 1950's. They were consistent with stock-market conditions existing at the time our previous editions were published. We think they proved a useful guide to investors from 1934 through 1954. But, as pointed out in the closing paragraphs of Chapter 30, the latter half of the 1950's brought record high levels in stock prices and with them new points of view and standards of value. It is our difficult task to examine these new levels and standards as they exist at the beginning of the 1960's and to reach some conclusions as to their validity for investment purposes.

The actual level of stock prices at the beginning of the 1960's is indicated sufficiently in Table 30-7. It is not to be supposed that Wall Street authorities as a whole were concurrently justifying these quotations by detailed assumptions and calculations, for that has never been the accepted procedure. Investors and their advisers, for the most part, based

416

their confident appraisal of the market's future on the general expectation of continued prosperity and growth, with freedom from any serious cyclical downturns. Nearly all the published, detailed calculations by security analysts and investment writers which we have seen in 1959 and early 1960 have produced current valuations of the leading stock averages somewhat below the record level, but have indicated that the deficiency could soon be made up as earnings increased.

Predominantly, these recent valuations and conclusions reflect two departures from the older viewpoint. First, they assume a growth rate for stock prices in general exceeding the long-term historical rate of about 2.5 percent.[1] Second, they virtually rule out the possibility of an "old-fashioned bear market" succeeding the overenthusiasm of the current bull market. Instead, it is only a matter of holding through moderate declines and waiting "for the normal growth of the country to lift stock prices, in general, to new highs."[2] It is suggested, also, that even though the market as a whole may show only a modest advance in the sixties, the selective, well-counseled investor has a highly favorable potential before him.

It would be instructive to the reader to compare these newer appraisals with others based on methods developed before the 1950's and founded, therefore, on the former behavior of the stock market. One set of such calculations was made by Professor J. Fred Weston.[3] He derived the following estimates from historical data through 1953. 1954 was then taken as the base, and projections were made therefrom up to 1960. Some of the 1960 estimates for the Dow-Jones Industrial Average, developed in this manner, were as follows:

Arithmetic trend	460
Geometric trend	478
Warranted value (based on relationship between growth of the economy and Standard & Poor's index)	450
Central value (based on 10-year average earnings divided by 2 times Aaa corporate bond yield)	398
Dividend central value (current dividends divided by 10-year average dividend yield)	505
Intrinsic value (12.5 times 10-year average earnings plus 20 per cent of book value)	470

The average of Weston's several valuations of the Dow-Jones Industrial Average for 1960 is about 460, or about one-third less than the closing level for 1959. An investor who accepted this average appraisal as dependable would have to conclude that the stock market in early 1960 was dangerously high. If he accepted also the amplitude of past market swings as a guide to the future, he would have to prepare himself for the

[1] N. Molodovsky, "Stock Values and Stock Prices," *Financial Analysts Journal*, May–June 1960, p. 84.

[2] Quoted from a study issued by a leading investment-counsel firm in May, 1960.

[3] Subsequently published. See J. Fred Weston, "A Not-So-New-Era in the Stock Market," *Financial Analysts Journal*, November–December, 1960, pp. 59–60.

possibility of an ultimate decline of as much as 40 to 50 percent from the cyclical peak.

Against these figures, based on older approaches, we must set the calculations of investment authorities, as actually presented in early 1961. The following three estimates are illustrative:

	Current valuation		Projected valuation	
	Date	Amount	Date	Amount
Nicholas Molodovsky*.........	Mar. 1961	590	1970	765
Naess and Thomas†..........	Mar. 1961	515	1965	688
The Value Line‡.............	Jan. 1961	567	av. 1963–5	705

* *Financial Analysts Journal,* March–April 1961, p. 7.
† Supplied to the authors.
‡ Computed from individual valuations.

In seeking to arrive at our own opinion we must examine somewhat critically the principal arguments currently used to demonstrate that the economy and the stock market are in a basically different and better position than before 1950.

Support for the 1960 Level. Earlier in this chapter we indicated two respects in which present price projections typically represent departures from the past. Here we shall turn to the examination of the three views— generally accepted by security analysts and investment managers—which primarily explain the widespread lack of apprehension about the level of the market in early 1960. These views are much as follows: (1) The long-term prospects for both the growth and stability of corporate earnings are much better than they appeared to be in 1950;[4] (2) common stocks now are much more broadly accepted by not only the general public but, more importantly, by major investment institutions; and (3) the average market levels of the past greatly understated the true merits and values of common stocks, whereas the current bases of appraisal are fairer and more realistic.

The following comments occur to us as relevant and sound with re-

[4] The investment community nearly always expects that the general experience of the past decade will be continued in the next, and in this it has virtually always been wrong. An investment service made this point in late 1959 as applied to the three preceding decades. In 1929 there was unlimited optimism, but the 1930's brought the worst experience on record. In 1939 we were all deflation-minded and cautious, but World War II brought active business and much inflation. In 1949, after a rather modest bear market in stocks, economists were still looking for a postwar recession, but instead we experienced ten years of unparalleled prosperity. By the end of 1959 the numerous references to the "golden 1960's" implied that we had returned to the optimism of 1929. Would this, too, prove to be unfounded?

spect to the foregoing three arguments. First, the roseate view with respect to the future stability of earnings has a factual base in that the Federal government is committed to intervene massively in the economy to prevent a downward spiraling depression and large-scale unemployment. Both general business and corporate earnings may be expected to suffer less instability in the 1960's than in the pre-World War II period. At the beginning of the 1960's, the companion view to expected *stability* is the confident expectation of the maintenance of a high rate of *growth*. An analyst, however, might well question whether a high growth rate in earnings can be looked forward to with the same degree of assurance as improved stability. For example, he might doubt that the annual growth rates typified by the earnings of the Dow-Jones Industrial Average over the 1940–1959 or 1945–1959 periods—approximately 8 and 6¾ percent, respectively—could be projected into the 1960's.

What growth rate should be expected and used as a basis for investment decisions? This is a matter on which the analyst needs to arrive at his own conclusions. We shall reserve our opinion for Chapters 33 and 34, which deal in detail with the projection of earnings and dividends. The setting forth of our views is not essential to the present discussion. At this point our fundamental concern is with methodology and not with decisions as to the level of earnings. That is, we are seeking to consider here only the period of the projection and the appropriate capitalization rate.

The second point in support of the level of the market in early 1960 pertained to the broad acceptance of common stocks by institutional funds as well as by individuals. This fact undoubtedly explains in part the higher price-earnings ratios and lower yields of common stocks in 1960 as against 1949. However, one may wonder how much of this greater popularity of equity shares would remain if the bull market of the 1950's were followed by a bear market of major proportions. (We should not forget that the "investment respectability" of common stocks grew steadily with the market rise in the late 1920's, although logically they should have been viewed as increasingly speculative and dangerous.)

The third claim—that common stocks were generally undervalued in former markets—also has merit, in the sense at least that over the long-term past common stocks in general have proved far more profitable investments than bonds. To that extent it must be conceded that the average ratios of stock prices to earnings and to dividends have been lower than was necessary to justify the investment—at least with the benefit of hindsight. If we take the long period from 1871 through 1949, the record indicates that industrial common stocks yielded an average dividend return of more than 5 percent and in addition increased in price—quite irregularly, to be sure—at a compounded annual rate of 2.5 percent per annum. Thus we were able to point out in 1952 that common stocks, on their historical records, might be expected to grow in value at the same rate as the popular United States Savings Bonds Series E, and thus that all of the substantial dividend return (then averaging over 5½ percent) could be regarded as an additional reward for undergoing the trials and risks of a stock investor.[5]

At the end of 1949 the dividend yield on common stocks was unusually attractive relative to that for bonds. In fact, for the period 1938–1955 the returns on stocks tended to run about twice the yield on bonds. And for the historical span 1871–1938 it averaged about 1¼ times bond yield. Thus it is to be stressed that common-stock buyers have historically demanded an additional return *except* in the upper stages of bull markets, at which times the public apparently became fully conscious of the great intrinsic merits of common stock. When the bull market was over the public always returned to its perhaps unreasonable demand for a higher current income from representative stocks than from bonds. The additional prospect of long-term growth in earnings, dividends, and market value was taken for granted and not paid for.

Projections Implicit in the 1960 Level of the Market. From the foregoing, it would appear reasonable to conclude that those analysts who accepted the early 1960 stock-market level as appropriate quite probably did so—for the most part—by both projecting a higher and more stable growth rate for earnings and accepting a somewhat lower over-all return on common stocks than has existed over the long-term past. Let us test the reasonableness of that market level in terms of its implicit projections.

In Table 31-1 we seek to express arithmetically the expectations which might be considered implicit in the price level at the end of 1959. For the two stock series and for General Electric and IBM, we assume growth rates in the 1960's for earnings and dividends equivalent to those experienced in the 1950's. We assume, further, that the investor requires—including both dividends and price appreciation—the annual historic return of 7½ percent.[6] The table shows the annual rate of market appreciation needed to produce the over-all return of 7½ percent and the December 1969 price to be attained thereby. We add the implicit 1969 price-earnings ratio, which has been calculated by dividing the 1969 expected price by the 1969 expected earnings.

Many analysts would say that the foregoing earnings, dividend, and price projections represent modest enough expectations—especially for IBM and General Electric—and furthermore that the 7.5 percent over-all return required by these computations may be greater than investors may demand. Hence they would assert that the early 1960 prices could be justified by a realistic and fair appraisal of the future.

[5] Benjamin Graham, "Toward a Science of Security Analysis," *Financial Analysts Journal*, August, 1952. The annual rate of price advance was there taken at 2.9 percent.

[6] The return for the 1871–1959 span is 7.5 percent. See N. Molodovsky, "Stock Values and Stock Prices," *Financial Analysts Journal*, May–June 1960, p. 81.

We must express doubt as to the practical soundness of this reasoning. The crucial point, to our mind, is the reliance on *future increases* to vindicate so large a part of the current price. It is one thing to expect confidently that your companies will march forward in the future, and to look to this growth for a handsome profit on your stock investments. It is quite another thing to *pay in advance* for a substantial and long-continued rate of growth; to require, to come out whole, both that this growth be realized and that the public continue to look favorably on the company's still later prospects; and to have a really satisfactory profit on the investment only if either the growth proceed faster and longer or the

Table 31-1. Comparative Price, Earnings, and Dividend Projections, 1960–1969

	Standard & Poor's Composite, 500 Stocks	Dow-Jones Industrial Average, 30 Stocks	General Electric	IBM
Earned 1949	$2.32	$23.54	$1.52	2.01
Earned 1959	3.39	34.31	3.17	7.97
Projected 1969	4.95	50.00	6.63	31.64
Closing price 1959	60	680	99	438
Dividend yield	3.05%	3.01%	2.02%	0.46%
Needed annual appreciation for 7½ per cent over-all return	4.45%	4.49%	5.48%	7.04%
Needed appreciation in 10 years	54%	55%	70%	97%
Needed closing price 1969	92	1,054	168	863
Projected multiplier 1969	19	21	25	27

public's enthusiasm be still greater. That such favorable things *may* occur in a given case goes without saying. But in our view this approach to the purchase of sound and attractive common stocks is inherently a *speculative* rather than an investment operation. In this regard we must make two points. First, a speculator may be successful by being either knowledgeable and shrewd or by being lucky (or both), and a successful speculator makes more money faster than a successful investor. Second, speculating, as we call it, in high-grade stocks by paying hard-to-justify prices for them involves smaller ultimate risks than the ordinary speculation in doubtful issues, and in many cases even substantial paper losses can be recovered through patient holding.

Our deepest objection lies not so much against paying these "future prices" for companies with good growth prospects, but rather against the widespread belief that this represents sound investment policy. In fact we have the following semantic contradiction: Wall Street says, "The better the company's long-term growth prospects, the sounder *investment* are its shares, and therefore the higher the price justified in terms of its current earnings and dividends." Yet we say, "The higher this current price-earnings ratio, the greater the portion of the price represented by expectations and hopes for the future; consequently, the larger the *speculative* component in the price paid." As we see it, the chief dangers here lie in the gradual loss of all experience-based quantitative tests of sound common-stock investment and in the loss also of all worthwhile distinctions between investment and speculation in this area, with the result that the greater part of stock "values" will come to depend on the public's psychology. Under these circumstances the stock market loses its moorings, and the investing public is certain to find itself ultimately on stormy seas.

Conclusions: We believe it reasonable to adopt a somewhat more generous approach to the valuation of common stocks than appeared justified in our previous edition. This conclusion is based on the assurance—not formerly present—of massive Federal intervention to prevent a serious business depression. This appears now to be a basic tenet of both political parties. While one cannot yet be positive as to the effectiveness of Federal action, it seems logical to expect that deficit spending and possible renewed inflation will be found preferable to painful deflation.

OUR VALUATION OF THE DJIA

How much more generously should the earnings and dividends of, say, the Dow-Jones Industrial Average be valued now? We do not feel qualified to speak authoritatively on that score, because brief experience does not provide an adequate basis for determining how much to depart from long-run experience. Detailed treatment of this matter belongs in Chapters 37 and 38, on capitalization rates for earnings and dividends. But to round out the present discussion let us say that careful consideration of this problem in 1960–61 led us to increase our 1951 valuation standards by a largely arbitrary 50 percent. We now apply this increase to the two independent methods formerly used for valuing the DJIA, with the following results at the beginning of 1962.

(*A*)   Our Central Value method consisted of capitalizing the average earnings for the past ten years by twice the interest rate on highest-grade corporate bonds (now using a three-year moving average for the latter). The average earnings for 1952–1961 were \$31.18, the interest rate taken was 4.38 percent, and the resultant valuation would have been only 356. Our new and more generous formula is equivalent to capitalizing average earnings at $1\frac{1}{3}$ times the basic interest rate. It produces a valuation of 534 for the DJIA at the beginning of 1962.

(*B*)   Our more orthodox alternative method consisted of capitalizing expected *future* earnings at an appropriate rate. (We assumed a normal payout for the DJIA, and thus gave the dividend factor no separate consideration.) We now estimate average earnings for 1962–1968 at \$44, and have selected a multiplier of 13—i.e., a capitalization rate of 7.7

percent. The consequent valuation at the beginning of 1962 works out at 572.

In preparing this revision we originally reached somewhat lower valuations early in 1961. The text we then added could appear irrelevant to the more chastened stock market of mid-1962, but it may be worth retaining in quotation marks.

"On the basis of the foregoing estimates, for which we make no strong claims but which certainly do not seem unduly pessimistic in terms of the historic record, a value range of 500 to 550 results. This range—if it has any merit—raises serious doubts as to the early 1960 price of 685 for the Dow-Jones Industrial Average. Moreover, we should add that, based on the propensity of the stock market to decline percentagewise as far below normal as it formerly had advanced above it, a 500–550 value range against a record price of 685 suggests the possibility of an offsetting decline to as low as 365 to 400.

"The possibility that the bull market of the 1950's might be succeeded —some year, some day—by a bear market of corresponding proportions has been all but completely ignored in Wall Street. (One almost gets the impression from current literature that bear markets are no longer legal.) In this respect the attitude of 1960 appears identical with that of 1929, 1937, and 1946. If this view is now valid, at long last, it would imply that not only have our financial institutions changed radically but also human nature as well. We find this particularly hard to believe.

"To be quite frank, it seems to us that at the beginning of this decade everyone in finance—investor, security analyst, teacher, or student—faces a serious handicap. If there are to be new standards, they cannot be reliably established in advance but can be recognized as such only after they have been validated by fairly long experience. In the meantime nearly everyone seems to be taking his standards from the market itself —as most people have been wont to do in the past. This facile procedure, if carried sufficiently far, must inevitably lead to disappointment if not disaster. To us, the logic of the situation is in favor of conservatism."

BASIC METHODS OF COMMON-STOCK INVESTMENT

The purchaser of common stocks has had a fairly wide choice of basic approaches in his selection and his timing. Let us first list them and then discuss them in some detail.

1. The cross-section approach
2. The anticipation approach
   a. Short-term selectivity
   b. Growth-stock selection
3. The margin-of-safety approach
   a. "Buy low, sell high"
   b. Value approach

The Cross-section Approach. This method subordinates selectivity to *diversification*. Its object is to make sure that the investor fares as well as major American business units. The common stocks purchased are exclusively or mainly primary issues (or market leaders). A characteristic industrial-stock portfolio of this type would consist of the 29 components of the Dow-Jones Industrial Average, presumably excluding American Telephone and Telegraph as a nonindustrial issue.[7] A complete portfolio would doubtless include issues taken from the utility, financial, and railroad fields.

Although the Dow-Jones list is widely accepted as mirroring the major American industrials as a whole, it is a rare if not unheard-of phenomenon for an institution or individual to hold exactly that portfolio. The reason, evidently, is that everyone believes he can better the performance of the famous 30 stocks by injecting some element of selectivity into his portfolio. But when the large institutional holdings are scrutinized with an appraising eye, it will be noted that selectivity really plays a minor role as compared with the controlling objective of wide diversification among major units in most of the leading industries.

It is worth pointing out that when investment and investors are considered in the most comprehensive sense, the element of selectivity necessarily vanishes. Stockholders as a whole must prosper or suffer with the rise and fall of corporations as a whole. Nor is it likely that any large section of stock buyers, calling themselves conservative investors, would obtain over-all results of their holdings which would differ substantially from the aggregate performance of the entire group of primary issues.

An unabashed cross-section approach appears too simple to be sound, and it reduces the role of security analysis to a minimum. We suggest that the student should not dismiss it too contemptuously. It is by no means certain that the analyst will get better results from the type of selectivity most favored in Wall Street—viz., picking out the industries or individual companies that are likely to make the best comparative showing in the near future. In that activity it is difficult to determine the extent to which the present price may already discount, or even over-discount, the anticipated industrial performance. If we could assume that the price of each of the leading issues already reflects the expectable developments of the next year or two, then a random selection should work out as well as one confined to those with the best near-term outlook.

The Anticipation Approach. *Short-term Selectivity.* To a surprising degree the recommendation of common stocks in Wall Street, and pre-

[7] At mid-1962 these were Allied Chemical, Aluminum Company of America, American Can, American Tobacco, Anaconda Company, Bethlehem Steel, Chrysler, du Pont, Eastman Kodak, General Electric, General Foods, General Motors, Goodyear, International Harvester, International Nickel, International Paper, Johns Manville, Owens-Illinois Glass, Procter & Gamble, Sears Roebuck, Standard Oil of California, Standard Oil of New Jersey, Swift & Co., Texaco, Inc., Union Carbide, United Aircraft, U.S. Steel, Westinghouse Electric, Woolworth.

sumably their purchase by both investors and speculators, are based on near-term anticipations.[8] The stocks with the best outlook for the next six or twelve months are considered to be the best ones to buy. Much analytical effort goes into appraising these near-term prospects. Volume, selling prices, and costs are carefully estimated, often with the aid of studies "in the field." The concentrated attention paid to these short-period anticipations is often justified by the assertion that no really dependable forecasts can be made for more than a year in advance.

In spite of this plausible argument, we are still surprised at the weight so frequently accorded to the near term in Wall Street's calculations. The value of a stock does not depend on what it is going to earn this year or next, but on its expectable average earning power and dividends over a fairly long period of time and on its general prospects over the still longer future. The chief fallacy in buying stocks on the basis of their immediate prospects is that the price of the issue is usually left out of the calculation, whereas the price may already have advanced substantially in anticipation of the very improvement that the buyer is counting upon. If he is paying today, and perhaps overpaying, for this future improvement, how can he expect to profit from it when it comes?[9]

Investment-fund Methods and Results. In this connection we venture some observations on the policies followed by investment funds. It is our belief that in their earlier years they placed most of their emphasis on near-term anticipation both of the general market's behavior and of the earnings performance of individual industries and companies. The over-all results they achieved were far from brilliant. In the last two decades we think they have shifted at least part of their emphasis to more basic considerations of value—such as prospective average earning power in relation to current price. Their over-all results for 1940–1959 have been much better, relative to the course of the general market, than in the years preceding. Yet, as a whole, they have been unable to equal the performance of a comprehensive stock-market index.[10]

The Growth-stock Approach. Although selectivity based on near-term prospects is possibly still a dominant element in common-stock analysis by brokerage houses, it may be objected to as a criterion of common-

---

[8] "The most common type of stock forecast in Wall Street is that which derived from the mind of the chartist." A. Bernhard, *The Evaluation of Common Stocks,* Simon and Schuster, Inc., New York, 1959, p. 35. In this regard, Armand G. Erpf, in "The Stock Market: Thoughts and Observations," *Commercial and Financial Chronicle,* May 19, 1960, p. 3, after discussing a number of secular considerations, states, "These and other forces, such as the so-called $10 billion for research and development, the power of the unions to prevent downward spirals, and monetary management in the place of the mechanics of gold, all became subordinate to the trend of business over the next six months."

[9] We return to this point in Chap. 34 and also in the final chapter.

[10] See Appendix Note 10, p. 740, for material regarding the performance of investment companies for 1927–1935, 1936–1939, 1940–1949, and 1951–1960.

stock investment on the ground that it deals too much with the transient and superficial. But this criticism could not apply to the factor of long-term prospects. Not only are these relevant to the investment value of any security, but they may well embody the most important determinant of ultimate worth. We all know that in the past a number of favored concerns have grown and prospered far beyond the average. It is inevitable that such growth companies should come to be considered the most suitable media for long-term investment. Similarly, the identification and selection of this type of common stock is viewed by many security analysts as their most characteristic and valuable function.

This philosophy of investment was set forth at some length in the 1938 report of National Investors Corporation, an "investment trust," from which we quote as follows:

The studies by this organization, directed specifically toward improved procedure in selection, afford evidence that the common stocks of growth companies—that is, companies whose earnings move forward from cycle to cycle, and are only temporarily interrupted by periodic business depressions— offer the most effective medium of investment in the field of common stocks, either in terms of dividend return or longer term capital appreciation. We believe that this general conclusion can be demonstrated statistically and is supported by economic analysis and practical reasoning.

In considering this statement critically, we must start with the emphatic but rather obvious assertion that the investor who can successfully identify such "growth companies" when their shares are available at reasonable prices is certain to do superlatively well with his capital. Nor can it be denied that there have been investors capable of making such selections with a high degree of accuracy and that they have benefited hugely from their foresight and good judgment. But the real question is whether or not careful and intelligent investors as a class can follow this policy with fair success.

Three Aspects of the Problem. Actually the problem falls into three parts: First, what is meant by a "growth company"? Second, can the investor identify such concerns with reasonable accuracy? Third, to what extent does the price paid for such stocks affect the success of the program?

1. *What Are Growth Companies?* The National Investors Corporation discussion defined growth companies as those "whose earnings move forward from cycle to cycle." How many cycles are needed to meet this definition? The fact of the matter seems to be that prior to 1930 a large proportion of *all* publicly owned American businesses grew from cycle to cycle. The same has been true in the post-World War II period. It was only during the "stagnant" and depressed 1930's that business enterprises in general did not evidence secular growth. These facts may be established in various ways. We have selected two.

First, the per-share earnings of 202 of today's major industrial corporations which were in existence in 1929 were determined and compared as of the following dates: 1929, 1936–1937 (high), 1955–1956 (high), and 1958–1959 (high).[11] It was found that only 34 percent had larger per-share earnings at their 1936–1937 high than in 1929, but that 92 percent had better earnings at their 1955–1956 highs than in 1929, and 85 percent at their 1958–1959 highs, and that in nearly every instance they had better earnings at both postwar highs than at their 1936–1937 high.

Second, studies of the performance of 150 major corporations, grouped into 33 manufacturing and trade industries, establish the pronounced, post-World War II growth in the earnings of American business. For example, the average earnings for the 33 industries (arithmetic average of the earnings index of each industry) were 57 percent higher in 1953–1957 than in 1947–1949 and 382 percent higher than in 1935–1939. Although a few industries, e.g., textile fabrics, distilling, and meat packing, did not show improved earnings in 1953–1957 over 1947–1949, they represented the exception.

The view that "growth is inherent in the life of any well-managed corporation"[12] may represent somewhat of an overstatement, but it is indicative of the extent to which growth is an accepted fact today in American business. Consequently, in a period characterized by growth, the existence of earnings growth in a company or an industry does not in itself establish that either the company or the industry is in the so-called "growth" category. Moreover, there have been no really major business cycles in the last fifteen years. It is doubtful, therefore, whether the postwar period has provided a dependable "cyclical test" of growth stocks. Under these circumstances, what is the current definition of growth stocks?

We know of no universally accepted definition. One writer has stated, "A minimum definition of a growth corporation, which is about all the professionals can agree on, is a corporation whose earnings per share have shown an annual rate of increase, over several years, of more than 4 percent (in constant dollars) or 6.5 percent (in current dollars), which is about the annual growth rate of the U.S. economy during the postwar period . . . "[13] He then suggests that Wall Street is actually looking for companies with an 8 to 10 percent annual increase. Another has held that, to be significant from an investment standpoint, growth

---

[11] Derived from *Fortune* magazine's 1959 list of the 500 largest industrial corporations.

[12] "Those Delicious 'Growth Stocks,'" *Fortune*, April 1959, p. 130.

[13] *Ibid.* pp. 129–130. Perhaps the most realistic definition has been proposed by Howard Conklin in "Growth Stocks: A Critical View," *Analysts Journal*, February 1958, p. 49. "In the minds of the investing public, a 'growth stock' is a common stock which has recorded or gives promise of recording, a greater than average appreciation in market price over a span of several years."

stocks should be defined as "those growing about twice as much as a broad index of common stocks over a period of five to ten years."[14]

In general terms, growth stocks are those which have maintained a *pronounced* (substantially above average) rate of growth over a period of years and are expected to continue to do so. In our opinion, the past span ordinarily should be in excess of five years.[15]

In addition to the "growth-company" approach, there is a separate concept of growth stocks which is grounded on the expected expansion of the industry as a whole. Such "growth industries" in 1960 would include, for example, aluminum, electronics, drugs, office equipment, paper, and some branches of chemical manufacture.

2. *Can the Investor Identify Them?* Our natural enthusiasm for excellent records and for especially favorable industry prospects is tempered somewhat by a sobering consideration. This is the fact that, viewed historically, most successful companies of the past are found to have pursued a well-defined life cycle, consisting first of a series of struggles and setbacks; second, of a halcyon period of prosperity and persistent growth; this in turn passes over into a final phase of super-maturity—characterized by a slackening of expansion and perhaps an actual loss of leadership or even of profitability.[16] It follows that a business that has enjoyed a very long period of increasing earnings may *ipso facto* be nearing its own "saturation point."

---

[14] Harry C. Sauvain, *Investment Management*, 2d ed., Prentice-Hall, Inc., Englewood Cliffs, N.J., 1959, p. 404. Other points of view: " . . . a growth stock should be expected to grow significantly faster than the national economy." R. E. Kennedy, Jr., "Growth Stocks and the Chemical Products Industry," *Analysts Journal*, February 1959, p. 54. "A growth company's sales and earnings should be expected to show a rising trend, and the trend should climb more steeply than the average." P. L. Bernstein, "Growth Companies vs. Growth Stocks," *Harvard Business Review*, September–October 1956, p. 91. " . . . so-called growth stocks, that is stocks whose earnings and dividend payments on a per-share basis show an average long-term growth rate well in excess of the average 3 percent annual growth of our economy." R. A. Bing, "Can We Improve Methods of Appraising Growth Stocks" *Commercial and Financial Chronicle*, Sept. 13, 1956, p. 1.

[15] J. G. Buckley in "A Method of Evaluating Growth Stocks," *Financial Analysts Journal*, March–April 1960, p. 19, holds that "the growth rate of net income of a company should be calculated for a 10-year period." R. W. Anderson in "Unrealized Potentials in Growth Stocks," *Harvard Business Review*, March–April 1955, p. 52, suggests, "There must have been an actual historical growth over a period of years— say, three to five years for an older rejuvenated company, or seven to ten years for a new company under untried management."

[16] This characteristic pattern of successful enterprise is discussed at length in the 1938 report of National Investors Corporation, pp. 4–6. In addition, see "Why Companies Grow," *Nation's Business*, November 1957, pp. 80–87. Also under the same title by N. R. Maines, a Stanford Research Institute publication. Theodore Levitt, in "Marketing Myopia," *Harvard Business Review*, July–August 1960, p. 45, holds that "Every major industry was once a growth industry. But some that are now riding a wave of growth enthusiasm are very much in the shadow of decline. Others which are thought of as seasoned growth industries have actually stopped growing."

Hence the seeker for growth stocks really faces a dilemma; for if he chooses newer companies with a short record of expansion, he runs the risk of being deceived by a temporary prosperity; and if he chooses enterprises that have advanced through several business cycles, he may find this apparent strength to be the harbinger of coming weakness.

We see, therefore, that the identification of a growth company or a growth industry is not so simple a matter as it may at first appear.[17] It cannot be accomplished solely by an examination of the statistics and records but requires a considerable supplement of special investigation and of business judgment. Proponents of the growth-company principle of investment are wont currently to lay great emphasis on the element of industrial research. In the absence of general business expansion, exceptional gains are likely to be made by companies supplying new products or processes. These, in turn, are likely to emerge from research laboratories. The profits realized from cellophane, nylon, ethyl gas, and various plastics, and from advances in the arts of radio, photography, refrigeration, electronics, etc., have created a natural enthusiasm for research as a business asset and a natural tendency to consider the possession of research facilities as the *sine qua non* of industrial progress. Moreover, a detailed study by Stanford Research Institute of the relative postwar growth of 400 corporations disclosed that the high-growth companies were predominantly research- and development-oriented.[18]

Still here, too, caution is needed. If the mere ownership of a research laboratory could guarantee a successful future, every company in the land would have one.[19] Hence the investor must pay heed to the kind of

[17] One writer advances two points of view: " . . . (1) that growth companies constitute a very small and select rather than a broad and important roster of corporate enterprises; and (2) that growth stocks are a happy or haphazard category of investments which, curiously enough, have little or nothing to do with growth companies." P. L. Bernstein, "Growth Companies vs. Growth Stocks," *Harvard Business Review,* September–October 1956, p. 87. Another states, " . . . there exists a formidable array of problems which make growth stock analysis extremely complicated even when the growth industries seem properly identified for prospective investment." R. E. Kennedy, Jr., "Growth Stocks and the Chemical Products Industry," *Analysts Journal,* February 1959, p. 52.

[18] An unpublished study as of the date of this writing.

[19] In "Trends in Industrial R&D" (mimeographed material provided at a meeting at Stanford Research Institute), p. 22. Yale Brozen concludes that "research and development expenditures have grown rapidly because they have become increasingly profitable." Furthermore, he presents industry data indicating a correlation between research and development expenditures and the return earned on net worth. But what is true in general or for an industry, may not be true for a specific firm. Theodore Levitt, *op. cit.,* states, "Another big danger to a firm's continued growth arises when top management is wholly transfixed by the profit possibilities of technical research and development." A study by Merrill, Lynch, Pierce, Fenner & Smith, *R&D and the Investor,* 1960, p. 3, includes the statement, " . . . R&D has become an important factor in the appraisal of any company from an investment point of view. But just because a company has a research and development program is not enough. . . . "

facilities owned, the abilities of the researchers, and the potentialities of the field under investigation. It is not impossible to study these points successfully, but the task is not easy, and the chance of error is great.

3. *Does the Price Discount Potential Growth?* The third source of difficulty is perhaps the greatest. Assuming a fair degree of confidence on the part of the investor that the company will expand in the future, what price is he justified in paying for this attractive element? Obviously, if he can get a good future for nothing, i.e., if the price reflects only the past record, he is making a sound investment. But this is not the case, of course, if the market itself is counting on future growth. Characteristically, stocks thought to have good prospects sell at relatively high prices. How can the investor tell whether or not the price is too high?

A good answer to the foregoing question is difficult. The amount of attention which security analysts quite appropriately have devoted to this subject, particularly in the past ten years, is attested by the many articles on the subject which have appeared in professional journals and elsewhere. As is to be expected, the proposals are varied. Some suggest appraising growth stocks on an absolute basis and others on a relative basis.[20]

It is to be stressed that—irrespective of the analytical methodology adopted—the investor must be convinced that he is paying a fair price, considering the risks involved, for what he thinks he will receive. Clearly, he cannot successfully operate on the principle of "growth at any price."[21] We have already pointed out that an evaluation which rests heavily on future anticipations—in the form of the long-term continuation of a significantly above-average performance—inevitably embodies a wide possibility of error.

In marked contrast, assume that the investor tries to avoid paying a

---

[20] For several references, see Chap. 39, footnote 7.

[21] In "Unrealized Potentials in Growth Stocks," *Harvard Business Review*, March–April 1955, p. 64, R. W. Anderson draws two conclusions pertinent to this point: "The record seems to show that a portfolio of established, recognized growth stocks (even at relatively high price-earnings ratios) retained on a long-range basis will give investment results superior to those of the stable income stocks and the market averages. . . . However, growth stocks are by no means foolproof; and frequently they sell too high either in an absolute sense or in terms of comparative investment value. An intelligent and industrious analyst, or an investor who has access to such, should be able to find better investment value and to achieve better investment results over the long range by avoiding the "haloed" growth stocks, and by trying instead to find stocks now having substantial (though perhaps no better than average) growth prospects yet still selling at a sufficiently low price-earnings ratio to provide very clear evidence of strongly attractive investment value." In an article entitled, "Stock Market Outlook," *Commercial and Financial Chronicle*, Sept. 25, 1958, p. 11, D. Moreau Barringer stated, "As long as business volumes and profits seem to be on the increase, so long will people project the earnings of their favorite growth stock in the same direction—and, irrespective apparently of such things as P/E ratios, do the same with their estimates of future prices."

high premium for future prospects by choosing companies about which he is personally optimistic, although they are not favorites of the stock market. No doubt this is the type of judgment that, if sound, will prove most remunerative. But, by the very nature of the case, it must represent the activity of strong-minded and daring individuals rather than investment in accordance with accepted rules and standards.

May Growth-stock Purchases Form the Basis of Successful Investment? In this discussion we have laid emphasis more on the pitfalls of investing for future growth than on its advantages. Nevertheless, if the analysis of growth stocks is pursued with skill, intelligence, consistency, and diligent study, it should yield satisfactory over-all results.[22] Thus it can provide the foundation for successful common-stock investment—provided two basic cautions are observed. The first, already mentioned, is that the elements affecting the future be examined with real care and a wholesale skepticism, rather than accepted quickly via some easy generalization; the second, that the price paid be one which can be justified on a quantitative basis.

Selection Based on the Margin-of-safety Principle. The third approach to common-stock investment is based on the margin-of-safety principle. If the analyst is convinced that a stock is *worth more* than he pays for it, and if he is reasonably optimistic as to the company's future, he would regard the issue as a suitable component of a group investment in common stocks. This attack on the problem lends itself to two possible techniques. One is to buy *at times when the general market is low,* measured by quantitative standards of value. Presumably the purchases would then be confined to representative and fairly active issues. The other technique would be to discover *individual* issues which are under —or at least within—a conservative value range. Such stocks are presumably available even when the general market is not particularly low. In either case the "margin of safety" resides in the fact that the stock is satisfactorily priced in terms of its intrinsic value as measured by the analyst. That is, by conservative standards, the investor is getting his money's worth. But with respect to the hazards and the psychological factors involved, the two approaches differ considerably. Let us discuss them in order.

[22] It does not follow, however, that the results for a "growth stock" portfolio will necessarily be strikingly different from that for a well-diversified list of common stocks. In this connection a number of mutual funds were examined. The performance—appreciation (assuming capital-gains distributions were accepted in additional shares) plus dividends—of the so-called growth-stock fund exceeded that for the diversified common-stock fund but only by a modest margin. R. W. Anderson, in his analysis of the performance of 10 mutual funds of considerable repute, found that these professional investors had a tendency "to fail to hold growth stocks consistently, to consider them attractive at one time and then to drop them through lack of confidence or the lure of something better. . . . " "Unrealized Potentials in Growth Stocks," *Harvard Business Review,* March–April 1955, p. 58.

Exploiting General Market Swings. "Formula Timing." In Chapter 5, which deals with investment policy, market fluctuations and formula plans were considered at some length. There is no merit in a detailed repetition of our views here. But we should like to state, again, that we are favorably disposed toward the principle of formula timing. If the plan employed is carefully tailored to the specific needs and basic objectives of the investor and well tested, it should provide a satisfactory means for taking advantage of significant market swings. Moreover, a formula plan is particularly suited to investment portfolios which have a significant common-stock component consisting of a broad cross section of investment-quality issues. We should add, however, that bull markets of the magnitude and duration of the present one constitute stringent tests of the perspicacity, courage, and tenacity of the formula planner.

Buying on the Basis of Value. The security analyst may properly devote his energies to seeking out securities which are either undervalued or selling at a price which—in relation to a conservative value—provides the buyer certainly with his money's worth. Such seeking carries with it some correlative notion of the proper level of value or price, which we have characterized by the general term "intrinsic value." To do this work systematically the analyst would need some workable technique for determining or estimating the intrinsic value. His procedure would then be to recommend for investment a group of issues which were currently selling at prices preferably well under—or at the least within—his calculated range of value. The idea of formally appraising securities in order to arrive at their intrinsic value is no longer novel, but it is far from standard practice in the field of practical finance. We propose to develop this technique in some detail in subsequent chapters.

Values at Market Bottoms. At this point we shall limit our comment to the general place of undervalued—or satisfactorily valued—securities in the scheme of common-stock investment. At the low levels of swings in the general market it is usually possible to establish that the *primary issues* are undervalued, by applying the standard method of estimating average future earning power and capitalizing this figure by use of an appropriate multiplier. This method may be applied to individual stocks or to a composite group, such as the Dow-Jones Industrial list. Here we find that the cross-section approach, the value approach, and the buy-low, sell-high approach all converge; because at historically low market levels most common stocks prove to be undervalued when subjected to appraisal.

Values at Market Mid-levels. When the stock market is at more or less neutral levels it is rare to find any leading issues selling at demonstrably bargain prices. The field of undervalued securities would then be confined to certain depreciated bonds and preferred stocks and to certain secondary common stocks. In most cases the latter will appear cheap from the quantitative angle, but their prospects for the future will be no better than average. This combination of an attractive *quantitative* showing—in relation to price, of course—with a mediocre qualitative position has become a standard occurrence, because of the stock market's obsession with companies considered to have unusually good prospects of growth.

As a result of this emphasis on the growth factor, quite a number of enterprises that are long established, well financed, important in their industries, and presumably destined to stay in business and make profits indefinitely in the future, but lacking in speculative or growth appeal, tend to be discriminated against by the stock market—especially in years of subnormal profits—and to sell for considerably less than they would be worth to private owners.

We incline strongly to the belief that this last criterion—a price far less than value to a private owner—will constitute a sound touchstone for the discovery of true investment opportunities in common stocks.

SUMMARY

In this discussion we have described various current approaches to common-stock investment and have expressed our own views as to their relative possibilities and difficulties. Our preference is either for the simple purchase of a diversified list of primary issues at reasonable price levels—a task well within the competence of a defensive investor—or else for the effort, by means of skillful security analysis, to find common stocks selling well below their intrinsic value. The student has been sufficiently warned, we hope, that our judgment on these matters is not necessarily shared by the majority of experienced investors or practicing security analysts.

CHAPTER THIRTY-TWO

THE PROS AND CONS OF THE VALUATION

APPROACH. THE VALUATION FACTORS

The practical objective of security analysis in the common-stock field is to assist the investor in selecting attractive issues. How does the analyst conclude that a given stock is attractive?

At this point in our 1951 edition, we questioned seriously the logic behind the analytical approaches customarily employed by Wall Street. It is now our opinion that, while much progress has been made toward more effective security analyses in the last ten years, there still remain too many studies of individual companies which do not provide an adequate basis for investment decisions. Typically, these latter studies rest on a careful but too abbreviated forecast of probable future earnings for a company—covering generally only the next twelve months or less. Furthermore, the rest of the study is mainly qualitative in character. It leads to an over-all opinion, stated primarily in descriptive terms, about the standing and prospects of the enterprise. The opinion will thus be grounded in part on specific statistical data—relating to the dividend and earnings record and to the financial position—and in part on more impressionistic views as to the industry, the individual company, and its management.

Usually such studies do not arrive at a carefully calculated value or value range. Instead, the stock may be termed "cheap" or "attractive" solely because it is selling at what seems a low price in relation to current earnings or those about to be realized. While such a measurement is important, it is hardly sufficient for an investment recommendation, since value cannot soundly be established on the basis of earnings shown over a short period of time. Another type of recommendation is founded so emphatically upon the character and quality of the enterprise that very little attention is given to the effect of the *price* of the stock upon the attractiveness of the issue for investment. In many such analyses the price is hardly mentioned, and the general impression created is that, since the company is a good one, its stock should be bought regardless of price. Moreover, this favorable and optimistic attitude toward the better

434

type of company will naturally be confirmed rather than weakened as the market advances. As a consequence, analyses of this type will not indicate that good stocks are overpriced even in the upper ranges of bull markets.

Determining Intrinsic Value. The analyst could do a more dependable or professional job of passing judgment on a common stock if he were able to determine some objective value, independent of the market quotation, with which he could compare the current price. He could then advise the investor to buy when the price was at or below value—or, at least, when the current price lies within the indicated range of value—and to sell when the price was well above value. This is undoubtedly a good idea if it will work. Obviously it must have difficulties and limitations; otherwise it would have become standard practice long ago. We recognize these difficulties, but we believe that the valuation or appraisal idea is nevertheless basically sound. In this preliminary chapter on the subject we shall consider some of the broader aspects of common-stock valuation, passing on afterward to its technical details.

The Valuation Process Briefly Described. The standard method of valuation of individual enterprises consists of capitalizing the expected future earnings and/or dividends at an appropriate rate of return. The average earnings will be estimated for a period running ordinarily between five and ten years. In the case of an issue valued as a "growth stock" the projection may be of a terminal year—e.g., four to five years hence—rather than of a longer term average. The capitalization rate, or multiplier, applied to earnings and dividends, will vary with the quality of the enterprise and will thereby give recognition to the longer-term profit possibilities which cannot be established with precision. Asset values become a significant factor in the appraisal only at the extreme ranges, where either the tangible assets are very low in relation to earning power value or the net current assets alone exceed the earning-power value.

Practical Utility of the Valuation Method. How useful are the results obtained by the appraisal process? This question divides itself into several subquestions, viz.:

1. What kinds of valuations have been made in the past, and how dependable were they?
2. What kinds of common stocks lend themselves best, and what kinds least, to valuation?
3. To what extent is the utility of the valuation approach dependent upon the additional factors of diversification and margin of safety?
4. Is an imperfect valuation better or worse than none for the investor; and does valuation aid or interfere with successful speculation?

Legal Valuations. Up to the present the largest collection of formal and complete valuations of common stocks are to be found in legal proceedings. (Valuations for investment purposes are still in an early stage of development, but they have already become a factor of note in the public utility field.) Legal valuations may be divided into three classes: those made (1) for purposes of estate and gift taxes; (2) as a basis for reorganization, recapitalization, and (less frequently) merger or other intercompany plans; and (3) for the purpose of determining amounts payable to dissenting stockholders under the "appraisal statutes" of the various states.

It will be observed that legal appraisals are made not because the common stocks involved are best suited for valuation, but because some corporate or personal events makes a determination of value necessary. In fact, most of the legal valuations deal with rather unsuitable material. The typical gift- or estate-tax case involves shares in a "closed corporation," which is usually of less than major size and would be considered in Wall Street terms as being exposed to a more than average degree of future uncertainties. Corporate reorganizations grow out of insolvency, and this suggests considerable vulnerability to business vicissitudes. To some extent this is true also of recapitalization plans designed to clear up large amounts of preferred-dividend accumulations, which are in themselves a mark of subnormal past performance.

Fortunately, one important group of legal valuations has dealt with conditions of more than average suitability. These have been the valuations made by the SEC, and confirmed by the courts, under Section 11 of the Public Utility Holding Company Act (the "1935 Act"). The purpose of such valuations has been, typically, to allocate to the preferred and common stocks of a utility holding company their proper proportions of the stocks of the subsidiary operating companies. Public utility operations lend themselves especially well to projections of future earnings, since they appear to be subject only to a minor degree to fluctuations and other uncertainties. The work done by the SEC in the utility cases has produced useful material on valuation techniques, and it has set a pattern that has been gaining increasing acceptance in Wall Street investment analysis.

Value Based on Future Earning Power. In this review of valuation work done to date, we should point out that since the 1930's some important changes in the judicial view of "value" have brought it closer to the thinking of the experienced investor. The earlier valuations, made mainly for tax purposes, often followed a rigid formula based on past earnings and upon the balance-sheet equity. It was assumed either that future earnings would repeat those of the past or else—most impractically—that only the past earnings and the assets counted in finding value. In a series of Supreme Court decisions[1] the rule has now been laid

---

[1] Consolidated Rock Products Company et al. v. du Bois, 312 U.S. 510 (1941). Case v. Los Angeles Lumber Products Company, Ltd., 308 U.S. 106 (1939). Group of Institutional Investors and Mutual Savings Bank Group v. Chicago, Milwaukee,

down that the value of a company for purposes of reorganization depends primarily upon its expectable earning power.

Similarly, in tax and appraisal cases the standard of value is the price at which a willing and informed buyer would do business with a willing and informed seller. In the ordinary instances, where a business is to be valued primarily on a going-concern rather than on a liquidating basis, this criterion coincides with the judgment of the Supreme Court; and both would also represent the accepted view of sound value in investment circles.

Thus it may be said, in sum, that judicial valuations and investment valuations now follow the same principles and face the same problems. The security analyst has the advantage—denied the courts—of being able to choose pretty much the types of common stocks to which he will apply his valuation technique.

Issues Suited and Unsuited for Valuation. We have already pointed out that public utility common stocks appear to have qualities of stability and predictability which make them ideal for formal appraisal. In theory, the mere factor of variability in earnings would not be a bar to a worthwhile valuation, provided that we could be reasonably certain what the average earning power would prove to be. But in practice, we find that the more a company's results are subject to fluctuation, the less predictable becomes the future average. Thus the best industries for valuation are those which do not show large profit declines in periods of recession. Such industries would include, in addition to public utilities, the insurance companies, chain stores, chemical and pharmaceutical companies, cigarette makers, can manufacturers, and others.

Many rather unstable industries include a few favorably situated members which have a strategic or management advantage over the rest, and which turn in a good performance even in bad times. Such companies have a stability of their own that makes them suitable for valuation.[2]

Let us make the point here, however, that while the future earnings of the strong and stable companies (for, say, a seven-year average) may be estimated with some degree of confidence, the proper capitalization rate for those earnings may present a troublesome problem. Issues which combine resistance to depression with a good record of growth tend to become so popular with investors that they sell typically at uncomfortably high multipliers of their past earnings and dividends and even of any conservative projection of expectable earnings and dividends. Thus we face the familiar dilemma that common stocks of investment quality

---

St. Paul & Pacific Railroad Company, 318 U.S. 523 (1943). Ecker v. Western Pacific Railroad Corporation, 318 U.S. 448 (1943).

[2] In this connection, the student might compare the return earned on total capital by J. C. Penney with that for some of the other apparel and accessories chain stores.

often sell at speculative prices. This is one of the chief reasons why the successful choice of common stocks for investment is a much more difficult matter than the mere identification of the "good companies."

Margin of Safety and Diversification as Aids to Practical Valuation. If a high price can turn an investment issue into a speculation, can a low price turn a speculative issue (the shares of a secondary company) into an investment? What this question implies, in valuation language, is that even though a company may be subject to a more than average amount of uncertainty and fluctuation, its shares may still be found to have a minimum valuation which is so conservative as to be reasonably dependable, and which will often be significantly above the market price. We believe that this situation exists with respect to the great majority of issues when the market is at depression levels. It also exists at most other times with respect to a fair number of individual issues which are suffering from unpopularity or mere neglect.

When the price is well below the indicated value of a secondary share, the investor has a margin of safety which can absorb unfavorable future developments, and which can permit a satisfactory ultimate result even though the company's future performance may be far from brilliant. This margin of safety corresponds to that which we have found to be essential in the purchase of bonds and preferred stocks for investment. It serves the same purpose in common stocks as in bonds, but with the added advantage for common stocks that it will often permit a substantial profit to be reaped out of the initial discrepancy between price and indicated value.

In our opinion, a margin of safety—in the form of an excess of estimated intrinsic value over current market price—is prerequisite to investing in secondary shares. But, is it equally essential in the purchase of primary issues?

Obviously it is highly desirable to have a substantial "protective cushion" between the estimated intrinsic value and the price paid for an investment-quality stock. However, this may prove difficult to find except at low levels of the general market. Does this mean that the analyst must give up the margin-of-safety concept for standard issues? We think not. Rather he seeks it in a different form: in an excess of expected dividends for a period of years over the income which would result from a normal interest return. In the case of growth stocks this may be rather the attainment of an ultimate *earning power* sufficient to justify a value well above the price paid.

It is to be emphasized that a margin of safety—in the form of either a price or a yield differential (or both)—does not *guarantee* an investment against loss; it merely indicates that the probabilities are against loss. Therefore a single issue—whether a primary or secondary stock— purchased with a margin of safety may still "go sour" for some special reason and produce a loss. A group of, say, twenty or more common stocks will usually average out the individual favorable and unfavorable developments. For this reason, the diversification or group approach is an integral part of the valuation concept itself.

The fact that the analyst may have much more confidence in his projection of the future earnings and dividends of a representative list of common stocks, taken together, than in any of his individual estimates may be readily illustrated. The most obvious example would be an appraisal of the Dow-Jones Industrial unit as a whole—i.e., the composite of the 30 individual components. Such a valuation has been made at times to indicate whether the general level of industrial stock prices, which is fairly well reflected in the market price of the Dow-Jones unit, should be considered low or high. An example of such a group valuation is given in Table 32-1.

Note from the table that, although the earnings estimates were wide of the mark in several instances (e.g., Chrysler, National Distillers, U.S. Steel), the aggregate earnings estimate for the 29 stocks was very close to the actual. In fact, it missed by less than 6 percent. By contrast, the aggregate market value estimate for 1956–1958 was significantly less accurate—missing by more than 22 percent the three-year mean price. The extent of the discrepancy is indicated by the fact that for 14 stocks the estimated values did not fall within the three-year price ranges. (Observe, however, that the projected 1956–1958 prices were nearly all considerably above the 1955 levels, so that the conservative bias did no harm.) This tends to confirm our view that earnings can be predicted with more confidence than can the capitalization rate or multiplier, which to a major degree will reflect the market psychology existing at the time.

There is nothing to prevent the investor, whether an individual or an institution, from making actual investment purchases of a unit such as the Dow-Jones Industrial group when the composite valuation indicates he is getting good value for his money. Such a policy may be unusual, but it is not illogical.

Valuation vs. Alternative Procedures for the Analyst. Assume that a run-of-the-mine common stock is not particularly well suited to a formal appraisal, because there are too many uncertainties about its future to permit the analyst to estimate its earning power with any degree of confidence. (Probably that is the way that practicing analysts feel about most common stocks they examine.) Should the analyst reject the appraisal technique in such cases and form his opinion about the issue by some other approach? We are inclined to make the rash statement that a common stock that cannot be appraised with confidence cannot be analyzed with confidence. We mean by this that buying or selling recommendations that cannot be related to a reasonably careful valuation are not based on analysis proper but on what we call pseudo-analysis or quasi-analysis. In such situations the underlying interest in both the analyst's and the investor's mind is likely to be the probable market

Table 32-1. Stocks Comprising Dow-Jones Industrial Average: Value Line Estimates of 1956–1958 Earnings and Prices Compared with Actual Results

(Estimates made in 1953)

Company	1956–1958 earnings*		1956–1958 prices*			
	Value Line estimate	Actual earnings	Value Line estimate	Actual prices		
				High	Low	Mean†
Allied Chemical..........	$ 3.01	$ 3.09	43	63	34	46
American Can..........	3.65	2.79	48	52	37	44
American Smelting.......	4.00	4.38	39	64	35	49
American Tel and Tel....	3.95	4.46	55	76	53	60
American Tobacco........	4.20	4.06	41	49	34	39
Bethlehem Steel..........	2.40	3.62	19	55	33	43
Chrysler Corporation.....	12.00	4.21	103	87	44	64
Corn Products..........	2.17	2.59	28	55	28	35
du Pont................	9.00	7.98	150	237	161	194
Eastman Kodak.........	1.81	2.52	24	74	36	51
General Electric.........	2.55	2.69	30	79	52	63
General Foods..........	1.66	2.00	20	40	20	26
General Motors.........	2.50	2.74	24	52	33	43
Goodyear Tire..........	1.60	1.94	11	41	18	26
International Harvester...	4.70	2.90	42	44	25	35
International Nickel......	2.00	2.52	25	58	33	45
Johns Manville..........	4.10	3.11	40	59	34	46
Loew's.................		‡		‡	‡	‡
National Distillers.......	3.46	1.96	31	31	20	25
National Steel..........	7.30	6.01	68	80	47	66
Procter & Gamble.......	3.25	3.35	39	79	44	56
Sears, Roebuck..........	2.22	2.19	25	40	24	30
Standard Oil of California.	3.20	4.29	28	62	43	52
Standard Oil (N.J.).......	3.28	3.64	32	69	47	56
Texaco, Inc.............	3.85	5.44	35	89	53	66
Union Carbide..........	5.75	4.49	90	133	84	110
United Aircraft..........	4.67	6.74	28	81	42	62
U.S. Steel..............	3.62	6.16	29	98	48	66
Westinghouse Electric....	3.25	1.31	31	38	25	31
Woolworth.............	3.75	3.45	43	54	35	44
Total.................	$112.90	$106.63	1221			1573

* Adjusted for stock splits and stock dividends subsequent to 1953. Prices rounded to whole numbers.

† Average of annual highs and lows.

‡ Comparable actual data not available for 1956–1958; therefore stock excluded.

action of the stock in some relatively short period in the future. The analytical work done, which may be quite comprehensive, will thus serve as an adjunct to an essentially speculative decision—disguised though it may be under some other name.

The appraisal approach is still too new to permit us to dogmatize about its value either absolutely or in relation to other methods of analysis. What we are expressing here is more an opinion than a settled conclusion. But we suggest that the soundness of a common-stock investment, in a single issue or a group of issues, may well be dependent upon the ability of the investor or his analyst-advisor to justify the purchase by a process of formal valuation. In plainer language, a common-stock purchase may not be regarded as a proper constituent of a true investment program unless it is possible to show by some rational calculation that it is worth at least as much as the price paid for it.

What May Be Accomplished by Sound Appraisals. If the appraisal approach is to have practical value it must produce satisfactory investment results. How should such "satisfactory results" be defined? Various possible objective tests may be used for this purpose. In one of these we may take the central-appraised value—the center or midpoint of the appraisal range—as the "justified purchase price" and the top of the appraisal range—say, one-fourth above the central value—as the "justified selling price," which should be reached in the market within a reasonable period of time, such as the next four years. The success of the appraisal technique may then be judged by the percentage of issues that were selected or recommended for purchase at their central-appraised value and which actually attained a market price one-fourth above that value (their justified selling price) within the next four years.

Another test can be along comparative lines. Issues selling below appraised value may be placed in one group and those selling above in another group. The appraisals can be called successful if the first group turns in a better over-all return—measured by dividends, plus or minus price change—than the second. In this test, only those common stocks selling substantially lower or higher than their central-appraised value should be considered. Where the variations are small they should be disregarded, since our valuations at best can give us only rough approximations.

At this time sufficiently comprehensive data are not available to enable us to judge definitely the practical value of the appraisal approach by either of the above methods or by acceptable variants thereof.[3] We do have data, however, which indicate that the approach has real utility in locating groups of undervalued securities which will prove profitable

[3] The same may undoubtedly be said of other methods of common-stock selection. The performance records of investment funds do provide a mass of material available for study, but unfortunately these results cannot be related to clearly stated and imitable techniques of selection.

investments. We have used successfully a special application of this principle in investment-fund operations. In this form the criterion of undervaluation was a price below the net current assets available for the common stocks.[4]

Another simple application has been the use of the price-earnings ratio, in a group of fairly homogeneous stocks, as the chief criterion of relative value. Those selling at the lowest ratios are presumed to be undervalued as against the high-ratio fraction or the group as a whole. Various studies have been made of the results of annual selections along these lines, made among the 30 issues of the Dow-Jones Industrial Average. Since 1933 the low-price-earnings–ratio sextile has quite consistently outperformed both the 30-stock total and the five highest-ratio issues.[5] Tests of later years were made by students in our classes with corresponding results.

Two independent studies employing a similar principle of selection and covering numerous periods between 1937 and 1959 were reported on in 1960.[6] In the first of these studies, the selection was made among 100 common stocks which were "predominantly industrial issues of trust-investment quality." In the second, the group comprised 29 chemical stocks. The results were strikingly similar to our own indications, using the Dow-Jones list; the low-multiplier issues tend to show about twice as good results—in terms of percentage gain—as either the entire group or the high multiplier portion.

The practical application of the appraisal approach demonstrates that it is most useful in detecting instances of substantial undervaluation. It is not equally useful in determining overvaluations. Many such apparent overvaluations are shown by growth companies which are selling much higher than conservative projections and multipliers would warrant. As we have stated often in this revision, such issues are inherently speculative and as such are refractory material for analysis. To advise their sale may often prove as embarrassing as to advise their purchase. The appraisal technique is undoubtedly valid in showing that many of the *new stock offerings* in bull markets are priced much too high, and so also the prices attained by many secondary and cyclical common stocks under favorable market conditions.

From the most general standpoint we consider that common-stock

[4] Since Arnold Bernhard, in *The Evaluation of Common Stocks,* Simon and Schuster, Inc., New York, 1959, has set forth in detail the method employed by Value Line in estimating the value of individual stocks, we suggest that the student explore this alternative approach. The results of employing this approach in managing an investment fund are reported periodically in the *Value Line Investment Survey.*

[5] See article on this subject by H. S. Schneider in the *Journal of Finance,* June 1951, pp. 229–237.

[6] S. Francis Nicholson, "Price-Earnings Ratios," *Financial Analysts Journal,* July–August 1960, pp. 43–45, covers both studies.

valuations can help the investor choose issues that will yield satisfactory dividends and maintain an earning power commensurate with the price paid. If such results are obtained, the over-all experience in terms of stock-market behavior should not be unsatisfactory. But, as we noted earlier, the market-price factor is the hardest of all for the security analyst to foretell or to control. One basic trouble is that the shares which appear most attractive from the standpoint of value analysis usually do so precisely because they are relatively unpopular in the market. The market's "momentum" is against them, and there is no assurance that the unpopular will become popular within a measurable period of time.

Let us state our position in another way. The valuation approach cannot be counted upon for a quickly gained stock-market profit; but we doubt whether any other approach or method can deliver this brand of goods. Successful common-stock investment is a process extending over many years and usually involving many separate commitments. Its results are measured by the aggregate dividend return received and by the movement of aggregate market value, preferably from an earlier point to a later point similarly situated in the stock-market cycle. Common-stock investments based in the first instance upon the appraisal method, and if possible buttressed by a substantial indicated margin of safety, are more likely to work out well over the years than those based on superficial analysis or market popularity or business anticipations for the short term.

FACTORS IN THE VALUATION OF COMMON STOCKS

The basic components in a common-stock valuation are fourfold, viz.:

1. The expected future earnings
2. The expected future dividends
3. The capitalization rates—or multipliers—of the dividends and earnings
4. The asset values

It should be pointed out that these four factors include, by implication, a number of elements which enter into both the quantitative and qualitative analysis of a common stock. Chief of these are the past and expected rates of profitability, stability, and growth; the abilities of the management; and, the various underlying facts and hypotheses that will govern sales volume, costs, and profits after taxes. Each of the four elements in our list will be discussed in some detail in the following chapter. At this point let us make some preliminary observations about them.

Interrelationships of These Value Factors. When we attempt to discover the explanation for the wide variations that have always existed among the earnings multipliers for individual common stocks we find that many ascertainable factors have played a part, but often with an admixture of arbitrary psychological attitudes that cannot be related to the known facts. Insofar as the past and current record exerts an influence, we may say generally that the multiplier tends to vary in the same direction as (*a*) profitability, (*b*) stability, and (*c*) growth—all of which are susceptible of quantitative expression. It is also true that the *quality of management* is considered to be a primary determinant of value, and therefore of the appropriate multiplier of earnings. Yet for established managements their quality is presumably reflected in the record of profitability, stability, and growth achieved by their companies. As we have said elsewhere, it is difficult to justify logically a separate increase in the multiplier for a favorable component already accounted for in the reported results.

If the future is considered basically as a continuation of past performance, then the multipliers selected by the analyst should depend primarily upon the past record of profitability, etc. If the future performance is viewed as departing significantly from the past, then the analyst must construct new indexes for the three determinants in accordance with his detailed estimates or prophetic vision. (A relatively new management or a major change in the nature of the business affords a major reason for making such a break with the past.)

First, as to the growth element. A good part of this will be reflected in the projection of future earnings to which the selected capitalization rate will be applied. But the expected growth rates will have additional weight in determining the multiplier since it enters into the longer future beyond the period of the earnings projection. The diverse expectations for the longer future are the influences which lead to the choice of different multipliers for different stocks. In the case of a rapid-growth stock the factors of profitability and stability are generally assumed to be included in, or overshadowed by, the dominant expectation, of rising profits. Thus, as we shall develop in Chapter 39, the multiplier is almost always a function solely of the projected rate of growth, with some minor adjustment for the anticipated payout.

While we consider the factor of profitability—i.e., rate of return on capital—to lie at the core of a company's performance, it resembles the management factor in that its consequences are pretty fully reflected in the record of stability and growth, as well as in the per-share earnings themselves. It can be shown, quite simply, that in the standard case both stability and growth tend to vary with and thus to reflect the degree of profitability.

Assume that Company *A* earns 15 percent on its capital and Company *B* only 3 percent, with both paying out two-thirds of profits in dividends. Company *A* will reinvest the equivalent of 5 percent of its capital each year and Company *B* only 1 percent. If the rate of profit remains unchanged, Company *A*'s per-share earnings will grow five times as fast as those of Company *B*. Again, assume that the higher profitability of *A* is largely due to a higher margin of profit on sales—a likely reason—and that its margin is 10 percent against only 3 percent for *B*. If in a recession each company experiences a fall in earnings equal to 3 percent of prior sales, the result would be to reduce Company *A*'s profits by 30 percent, but to wipe out those of Company *B* entirely.

Stability as an Independent Factor. Stability of earnings may show itself independently of the rate of past growth, and it may be accompanied by slowly decreasing profitability. This would be likely to occur only in an industry of extremely stable customer or consumer habits.

Example: Perhaps the only really impressive illustration of this is the snuff industry, as exemplified by the 40-year record of U.S. Tobacco Company. Between 1922 and 1961 the net earnings never fell below $2.2 million or rose above $4.2 million. In 1922 they were $2,614,000, and in 1961 $3,430,000—representing a growth rate of less than 1 percent per annum.

The influence of stability alone on market multipliers is well shown by our U.S. Tobacco example. Despite the virtual absence of a growth trend, the shares sold in 1961 as high as 45½, or 26 times the current and average earnings of about $1.75. (The dividend was $1.35, returning a yield at the high price of just under 3 percent.)

Significant Elements. The valuation procedure we shall follow will take into account all the significant elements of financial analysis that engaged our attention in the earlier chapters on analysis of the income account and the balance sheet. The past-earnings record is drawn upon to help establish the expected future earnings and the multiplier applicable to such expectations. The dividend factor, stated historically in the form of the "payout ratio," is given a separate weight, exceeding—in all instances except the suggested maximum valuation formula applicable to high-growth stocks—that of the undistributed portion of the earnings. The balance-sheet factors enter into the valuation in two different ways: First, the indexes of financial strength—supplied by the working-capital ratio and the common-stock ratio—exert an influence upon the capitalization rate of earnings and dividends. Second, the asset value per share of stock—in terms both of all tangible assets and of net current assets alone —may, in somewhat exceptional cases, affect the final valuation.

In our theory of valuation, the expectations for a moderate term of years—generally the next five to ten—are formulated in a specific estimate of earnings and dividends. The longer-term expectations are taken into account in the capitalization rate or multiplier applied to the specific estimate. For example, we may project identical average earnings and dividends—say, for the next seven years[7] for Company *A* and Company *B*, but we may use a multiplier of 13 in one case and of 20 in the other. By so doing we are projecting a considerably better earning power in later years (after the span of the estimate) for the higher-valued con-

[7] It will be recalled that the end of the fourth year would be taken as representative of a 7-year average for a growth company.

cern, without actually calculating what these long-term earnings will be. The multipliers are influenced not only by the measurable factors which are dealt with in financial-statement analysis—profitability, growth, stability, and financial strength—but also by the highly important intangible elements which affect and perhaps control the longer-term expectations. Such intangibles may be considered under the three basic headings of (1) the character of the industry, (2) the position of the company in its industry, and (3) the quality of the management.

We shall try to develop in orderly fashion the various components of common-stock valuation listed above. Our attention will be directed first to the problem of estimating or projecting the average future earnings, with suitable emphasis upon the use of the past record as a guide to such projections. We shall then consider the capitalization rate for earnings. The third section of valuation theory will deal with the general significance of the dividend factor in investment and in the valuation technique. It will also take up separately the influence of capital structure on the final valuation.

The last part of our exposition will deal with the asset-value factor. In general terms, this factor will affect the valuation in two rather exceptional types of cases—first, when tangible assets are low in relation to earning-power value, and second, when working capital alone exceeds the earning-power value. However, we shall point out that in some individual instances the book value may itself qualify as the best figure for "intrinsic" or "normal value," because it is supported by dividend and earning-power considerations and by the past market-price record of the shares. We believe that some special degree of dependability attaches to valuations in which these various criteria can be brought together into a single figure.

THE ROLE OF THE VALUE APPROACH IN INVESTMENT TIMING AND INVESTMENT POLICY

The intrinsic-value approach proposed in this book is but one of several methods for determining both the absolute and the relative attractiveness of common-stock issues. Those who practice it will use their conclusions as a basis for selecting issues to make up a common-stock portfolio, and for recommending the sale of holdings that appear definitely overvalued or the replacement of less by more attractive stocks. Many of our readers would like as much guidance as we are able to give them in this highly important and intensely practical aspect of the work of the security analyst. Each senior analyst, however, will develop his own approach to these problems, in accordance with his investment philosophy, his interests and his individual capabilities. We have no desire to prescribe dogmatically any one course of procedure in this area. But it may be useful if we attempt to sketch out a "model investment policy" which is closely geared to the valuation process. In framing this policy, it is assumed that the fund is that of an individual and of sufficient size to make possible adequate diversification.

Such a policy would first determine what percentage of the liquid assets or portfolio fund is to be held in common stocks at varying levels of the stock market. It would then establish a procedure for making up a common-stock portfolio. Its third division would relate to rules for selling a security held or replacing one stock by another.

1. In establishing our model, we shall assume that the typical individual investor would always have a fixed-value component in his portfolio. Accordingly, we would set an upper limit of 75 percent to be held in common stocks and a lower limit of 25 percent. This minimum proportion, which would be kept in common stocks irrespective of the level of the market or the outlook for equities, is in accord with the view set forth early in this book regarding the inclusion of common stocks in the ordinary investment portfolio.[8] (These proportions are at market value.) The proposed common-stock proportions would be put into effect pursuant to a formula plan, which in turn would be geared to the analyst-investor's valuation of the DJIA, Standard & Poor's Composite Index, or some other measure of the market. Assume, for example, that the analyst accepts our unpopular valuation of the DJIA at between 540 and 570 at the beginning of 1962. The actual market level of 730 would then call for holding at or close to the minimum figure of 25 percent in common stocks. This percentage would not be increased until the level fell to the top of the *then* valuation range—not necessarily 570. It would be brought up to 50 percent of the portfolio within the new valuation range, and to the maximum of 75 percent at various levels below the range. We refrain from specifying the exact times and amounts of each purchase—or corresponding sale as the market advances—since these cannot be governed by any a priori principle.

Very few professionals or nonprofessionals in finance would at this time accept and follow the policy outlined above. Not only does it involve the use of a formula-timing approach—which has been steadily losing favor since its considerable vogue in the early 1950's—but it is also based on two underlying concepts, each of which is now widely regarded as obsolete. The first is that the market has recurrent wide swings above and below some central value which is susceptible to, at least, some broad appraisal. The second is that this broad appraisal may be based on relationships developed out of long-term past experience, but liberalized to reflect the better general standing of common stocks since 1949.

2. The choice of common stocks may be governed by the appraisal method even though the general investment policy is not similarly controlled as outlined above. However, one might argue that if it is feasible to classify individual stocks as selling above or below their value range,

[8] See our discussion under the heading "Long-term Trend Inflationary" in Chap. 1.

then the same should be true of the market as reflected in a comprehensive index. Hence the adoption of the appraisal philosophy for single
issues logically implies its application to the market as a whole, with
necessary consequences therefrom as to over-all holdings of common
stocks.

Those who prefer some other method of deciding how large a proportion of equities they should own may still wish to apply the appraisal
method to individual selections. The general approach we suggest for a
typical individual's portfolio is as follows:

The "basic portfolio list" should consist of a substantial number—say
not more than 100—of primary common stocks. (These companies are
large, prosperous, soundly capitalized, and well-known to investors.) The
actual portfolio would be constructed from between twenty and thirty of
those issues which, at the time of selection, showed the most favorable
relation between market price and the analyst's appraised value. Some
limitation as to the amount committed to any one industry would be
imposed to assure adequate diversification. If this process takes place at
a high level of the market, the issues selected may actually be selling
above their valuations; that would be the necessary penalty for making
commitments at what appears to be a basically unfavorable time. (No
doubt those who are convinced that the 1962 levels are *not* excessive will
in their individual valuations apply multipliers high enough to make
many issues appear absolutely as well as relatively attractive. Typically,
they will conclude that certain promising issues are "intrinsically" attractive at, say, twenty-five times earnings because most other promising
issues are selling at thirty or more times earnings.)

Our program would allow for the substitution of secondary issues in
place of primary ones—but only if the value conservatively found for a
secondary issue shows it to be *substantially* cheaper than the *most attractive* primary issue it would replace in the list. By "substantially cheaper"
we imply a required differential of at least 25 percent.[9]

3. The procedure for determining what and when to sell is logically
the converse or opposite of that for buying. The investor with a full 75
percent common-stock portfolio at a low market level[10] would begin to
sell, on some graduated basis, after the market has again advanced to at
least the upper limit of the (new) appraisal range.

If the analyst-investor is reducing his portfolio he could do so either
"across the board" or by selling those issues which at the time of sale

---

[9] In our vocabulary the words "attractive" and "cheap" are synonymous, since
both turn on the relationship between appraised value and current price. The
"attractiveness" of the business itself is fully reflected in the valuation, by way of
the estimated future earnings and the multiplier applied thereto.

[10] We must point out that a policy of large equity investment at low market levels
and small equity holdings at high levels is at the same time logical and in contradiction both with human nature and the essential character of stock markets. We
realize that it is a counsel of perfection.

bear the least attractive relation to their then appraised value. If a list is re-examined at intervals, one or more issues will usually be found to be candidates for replacement. The investor would be justified in making changes in his portfolio whenever a fairly substantial advantage is indicated by the switch. Under our method such advantage would again be measured entirely by the value-price test. In most cases the issues sold will be quoted above their valuation range. But in low markets it is conceivable that some issues which are not intrinsically dear may be replaced by others which are considerably cheaper. However we caution the analyst against recommending an exchange to an investor, entirely on the analyst's responsibility, unless the indicated price-value advantage is quite large—say, at least one-third. The reason for this caution is practical. A favorable outcome of such an exchange can never be guaranteed, and analysts' clients are notoriously more resentful of advice that turns out badly than grateful for that which turns out well.

CHAPTER THIRTY-THREE

PROJECTIONS OF EARNINGS AND DIVIDENDS.

SIGNIFICANCE OF THE EARNINGS RECORD

In the previous chapter we suggested that common-stock valuations be based ordinarily on projected earnings and dividends for the next five to ten years. This has not been standard Wall Street procedure, which has, in fact, tended either to shorten or to lengthen the period of earnings projections. For the usual company—i.e., one not designated as a "growth" enterprise—it is customary to estimate earnings only for the current or the coming twelve months. By contrast, in order to justify the high multipliers of current earnings commanded by many growth stocks, it becomes necessary to project the expanding earnings quite far into the future. The many analysts who favor companies of this type find no difficulty in making such far-reaching forecasts.

There is also a well-established financial principle which states that the investment value of a common stock equals the "present worth" of all its future dividends.[1] To apply this principle in practice would require dividend projections for, say, between 40 and 50 years.[2] We do not believe that estimates for so remote a future can be made with enough dependability to be really useful. The investor may, however, assume a permanent or "built-in" *growth rate* for common stocks in general, derived basically from the reinvestment of undistributed earnings and buttressed by the country's long-term financial history. Where significantly higher rates of growth are assumed for some favored enterprise, we think that the specific projections should be limited to, say, four years[3] and that the

---

[1] John Burr Williams, *The Theory of Investment Value*, Harvard University Press, Cambridge, Mass., 1938, p. 55.

[2] Beyond 40 to 50 years the present value of all future dividends becomes relatively inconsequential. The present worth of $1, discounted at 5 percent 50 years hence, is less than 9 cents. The marked decline in the present value of earnings to be received in the distant future is shown by the fact that—on a 5 percent basis—the present worth of an annuity of $1 per year for 25 years is 77 percent of the present worth of a like annuity for 50 years.

[3] Except in the case of very high assumed growth rates, a trend projection of

attractive longer-range prospects should be allowed for, less definitively, in a higher-than-average multiplier.

It is clear that an *actual* dollar of earnings of growth stocks is worth no more than an *actual* dollar of earnings of nongrowth stocks. Consequently, if it were possible to estimate with complete accuracy the total earnings (and dividends) of a growth and a nongrowth share over the life of each corporation, the *same* capitalization rate—or discount factor —would be appropriate for each. Thus the only justification for a difference in the multipliers of current earnings (or of the average of some limited future period, i.e., five to ten years) for a share of the common stock of two individual corporations is the *long-run earnings* and *dividend differential* which the analyst is assuming—but not attempting to estimate in specific terms—for the shares. Thus, if the analyst were willing to use a multiplier of 13 times the estimated average earnings for, say, the next seven years of an *average* company (one with a growth rate in earnings of about 3½ percent) and a multiplier of 20 times for a *high-growth* company, he would in effect be assuming that the earnings differential for as long a period as he considers to be of consequence will aggregate for the growth share in excess of one-half more than that for the average share.

The actual choice of the projection period must—of necessity—be arbitrary. The span of from five to ten years, which we have suggested, is based in part on the concept of including the good, bad, and average years of a full business cycle. Moreover, it is comparable to the period for which most intelligent business men are accustomed to look and plan ahead. And incidentally, it tends to correspond to the period of *past* earnings which the analyst ordinarily will scrutinize with particular care.

Although their number is decreasing rapidly, some analysts still hold that it is difficult enough to estimate the coming year's results with any accuracy, and that therefore to extend the forecast through the next five to ten years is foolhardy. The trouble with this approach is that it emphasizes the easier thing rather than the more important and more useful. For the investor, next year's profits are of real importance only if they can be viewed as indicative of the longer-term *earning power*. Thus to use one year's results intelligently, the investor and the analyst must have at least a background idea of the probable earnings level for a number of years.

PROJECTION OF EARNINGS

In recognition of the necessity of formulating as definitive an opinion as possible as to the *earning power* of a corporation, it is becoming increasingly the practice to make estimates or projections of the longer-

---

four years is representative of the *average* level for seven years. For example, assuming a 10 percent growth rate, a four-year projection would show an increase of 46 percent, which approximates the seven-year average of 49 percent.

term earnings as well as of the near-term earnings of companies under study. Typically, these estimates are for the current or coming year and for a "target date," such as five years ahead. In the latter projection the procedure often followed—and one which we approve—is first to formulate a view as to the general economic climate to be expected; next to determine therefrom the general picture of common-stock earnings, e.g., the anticipated earnings of the Dow-Jones Industrial Average or Standard & Poor's 500 Stock Composite; and finally—against this background—to calculate the earnings for individual companies.

The number of variables involved and their constantly shifting influence make it impossible to establish definitive, teachable techniques for forecasting successfully financial developments. Consistently successful work here must be attributable to superior ability to discern and appraise the key factors which determine earnings in any period. Nevertheless, in security analysis, projective work inevitably starts with an examination of the actual record of the past. The extent that the past average or trend may be counted on to continue determines the relative value and importance of such an examination. It is well known that, in general, the broader the segment of the economy analyzed, the more gradual will be the change and the closer the probable relationship between the past and the future. Thus a projection of Gross National Product—the basic measure of the nation's final output—is likely to prove closer to the mark than a projection of earnings of common stocks as a whole, and the latter forecast is likely to be more accurate than similar projections for individual stocks.

The Probable Range of Gross National Product. In 1960 the differences between the projections of GNP by four well-recognized organizations, as reported by *Business Record*, were modest:[4]

Organization	Annual rate of growth	
	1960–1965	1965–1970
National Planning Association	4.0%*	4.6%
U.S. Department of Labor	3.4	4.1
Stanford Research Institute	3.5	3.7
Fortune magazine	4.2	4.2

* 1955–1957 to 1965.

Subsequently, the Stanford estimates, which were initially published in 1957, have been revised upward and the National Planning Association

[4] National Industrial Conference Board, "Looking Ahead at the Nation's GNP," *Business Record,* June 1960.

estimates have been revised downward. Accordingly, at the time of this writing the four projections for 1965–1970 are nearly identical. Moreover, in 1960 the active controversy over GNP was fundamentally whether (1) the historic growth rate of 3 percent—in constant dollars— was inadequate,[5] (2) the 4 percent rate of the last decade was satisfactory, and (3) a 5 percent rate was feasible.[6]

Relying on the foregoing estimates, it is to be concluded that the growth rate for GNP will average in the neighborhood of 4 percent in the present decade, or approximately the same as in the 1950's. This estimate is in terms of constant dollars and does not allow for inflation. Prevalent opinion is that the price level will rise an average of 1 to 1½ percent per annum over the decade.[7] If the lower figure is taken,[8] the combined effect would be an increase in GNP in current dollars of 5 percent a year, or, say, 28 percent in five years and 63 percent in the full decade.

Projection of Aggregate Common-stock Earnings. A corresponding forecast of GNP for 1963–1965 made by Value Line, a prominent investment service, in early 1961 was $625 billion.[9] This figure represents an increase of nearly 43 percent over the 1955–1959 average of $437.2 billion and is equivalent to an annual growth rate of approximately 5.2 percent. On the basis of this projection for GNP, the service estimated the 1963–1965 earnings for a large number of common stocks. For those in the Dow-Jones Industrial Average, their aggregate figure worked out at slightly over $50, an increase of nearly 50 percent over the 1955–1959 average of $33.49, or an annual growth rate of 6 percent. In making these computations, we have assumed that the 1963–1965 estimates represent the median year, 1964.

An early 1961 forecast by the investment-counsel firm of Naess and

[5] See *The Growth Reckoner,* Committee for Economic Development, October 1959, for growth rates over selected periods since 1909.

[6] For a discussion of this subject, see Rockefeller Brothers Fund, *The Challenge to America: Its Economic and Social Aspects,* Doubleday & Company, Inc., New York, 1958.

[7] "The forecasts of the experts appear to embody a near-consensus in anticipating an upward trend of the price level of about 1½ percent per year for the coming decade." J. M. Clark, *The Wage-Price Problem,* American Bankers Association, 1960. Very probably this statement was written in 1959. Since then the growing opinion that the problem of inflation has been easing has led to some use of a 1 percent figure.

[8] Use of the lower figure is buttressed by the recent view expressed by Martin R. Gainsbrugh, "Inflation in the 1960's?" *Business Record,* National Industrial Conference Board, March 1961, p. 36. After discussing the fact that there would probably be no increase in prices in 1961, Gainsbrugh stated, "This picture of general price stability may well be the most likely pattern not only for 1961 but for much if not all of the 1960's."

[9] Value Line states that they "do not estimate or forecast" but rather "hypothesize" the 1963–1965 economy.

Thomas estimates the earnings of the Dow-Jones Industrial Average at $46.65 in 1965. In relation to the 1955–1959 actual level of $33.49, this represents an absolute increase of 40 percent, which is equivalent to an annual average rate of approximately 4.3 percent. This provides a 1964 projection of approximately $44.75.

Another forecast of the earnings of the Dow-Jones Average, which was published in an article in an early 1961 issue of the *Financial Analysts*

Table 33-1. Earnings of the Dow-Jones Industrial Average and Standard & Poor's 500 Composite Stocks as Percent of Each Billion Dollars of GNP, 1929–1960

Year	DJIA	S&P's 500	Year	DJIA	S&P's 500
1929	19.1%	1.5%	1950	10.8%	1.0%
			1951	8.1	0.7
1930	12.1	1.1	1952	7.1	0.7
1931	5.4	0.8	1953	7.4	0.7
1932	*	0.7	1954	7.8	0.8
1933	3.8	0.8			
1934	6.0	0.8	1955	9.0	0.9
			1956	7.9	0.8
1935	8.7	1.0	1957	8.1	0.8
1936	12.2	1.2	1958	6.3	0.6
1937	12.6	1.2	1959	7.1	0.7
1938	7.0	0.8			
1939	10.0	1.0	1960	6.4	0.7
1940	10.8	1.0	Averages:		
1941	9.2	0.9	1929–1931	12.9	1.2
1942	5.8	0.6	1933–1935	6.4	0.9
1943	5.0	0.5	1938–1940	9.4	0.9
1944	4.8	0.4	1943–1945	4.9	0.4
			1948–1950	9.6	0.9
1945	4.9	0.4	1953–1955	8.1	0.8
1946	6.5	0.5	1958–1960	6.6	0.7
1947	8.0	0.7			
1948	8.9	0.9			
1949	9.1	0.9			

* Deficit.

Journal, might also be cited. The author, Nicholas Molodovsky, estimates the growth rate for earnings over the 1961–1970 span at 5 percent. Correspondence with Molodovsky reveals that his 1964 trend value is $42.55, which actually represents a growth rate from the 1955–1959 base— $33.49—of 3½ percent per annum.

In our own thinking for this projection, we started with a review of past relationships between GNP and the earnings for the Dow-Jones Industrial Average and for Standard & Poor's 500 Composite Stocks. The percentage relationships per billion dollar of GNP for the period from 1929 through 1960 are set forth in Table 33-1. It will be noted that the ratio of common-stock earnings to GNP has trended definitely downward in the past 30 years.[10] (This would be particularly evident from the period averages if we eliminated the ratio for 1933–1935, which was low because of depression conditions, and that of 1943–1945, which was low because of war conditions.)

The following are the average percentage relationships between the earnings of the Dow-Jones stocks and GNP (per billion dollars) in five recent periods:

6 years, 1955–1960.	7.5%
5 years, 1956–1960.	7.2
4 years, 1957–1960.	7.0
3 years, 1958–1960.	6.6
3 years, 1957–1959.	7.2

These figures produce a range between 6.6 and 7.5 percent. In the absence of any strong reason to anticipate a marked reversal in this unfavorable trend, we should not be inclined to assume a better relationship between the Dow-Jones industrial earnings and GNP than that which obtained in the last five years, a ratio of 7.2 percent. If this figure were applied to an expected GNP of, say, $615 billion—based on the use of a growth rate of 5 percent per annum and the 1955–1959 average of $437.2 billion—the earnings for 1964 would work out at $44.[11] Entirely by coincidence, this figure is approximately the same as the Naess and Thomas estimate adjusted to a 1964 termination. Both are below the Value Line projection as we have derived it.

A different approach in forecasting earnings for the stock averages would seek to determine the future rate of growth from a study of their past record of increase. The annual growth rate for the longest historical period—1871 through 1959—was slightly over 2½ percent for Standard & Poor's 500 Stock Composite. The postwar growth rates for both Standard & Poor's Composite and the Dow-Jones Industrial Average are set forth in the following tabulation:

[10] If the student examines the ratio of all corporate earnings after taxes to Gross National Product and to national income, he will find that there has been a definite decline in the postwar period. For example, in the 1919–1930 span corporate profits averaged 7.1 percent of national income; in 1947–1959, 6.6 percent; and in 1955–1959 they were 6.2 percent. Preliminary estimates for 1960 indicate that corporate earnings were only about 5 percent of national income in 1960.

[11] It is of interest to note at this point that using the $44 and a multiplier of 13, the resulting *current* value estimate is 572. If the formula derived by J. Fred Weston in "The Stock Market in Perspective," *Harvard Business Review*, March–April 1956, p. 75, is applied to the GNP estimate of $615 billion, a 1964 value of 623 would be derived for the Dow-Jones group. If applied to an estimated "normal" GNP of $531 billion in 1961, the current value for the Dow-Jones Industrial Average would be 542.

Period	Annual growth rates*	
	DJIA	S&P's 500
1945–1959	6.8%	8.2%
1947–1959	4.0	4.6
1948–1959	3.3	3.4
1950–1959	2.4	3.2
1951–1959	3.6	4.1
1954–1959	0.8	1.0

* Based on trend computations for each period.

It will be noted that the annual increase averaged 6.8 and 8.2 percent for the two series over the 1945–1959 span. The greater part of this rather spectacular gain occurred in the immediate postwar years. In fact, for most of the 1950's—from 1951 on—the growth rate for the Dow-Jones shares was close to 3½ percent and for Standard & Poor's about 4 percent. Moreover, in each series there was a weakening tendency in the latter portion of the decade.

We have seen arguments advanced for growth rates ranging from a low of 2½ percent to a high in excess of 6 percent.[12] This range plus the foregoing discussion may assist the student in working out his own projection of common-stock earnings as a whole. But they cannot provide him with an *authoritative* figure. Our own estimate has no particular expertise behind it, and many readers may consider it vitiated by an undue tendency toward conservatism. We supply it here, nevertheless, for whatever our opinion may be worth.

We would prefer to assume a future growth rate toward the lower end of the 2½ to 6 percent "range of reason" and one closer to the rate for most of the decade of the 1950's. This is in accord with the prevalent view that the growth in GNP in the 1960's will be close to that for the 1950's. Therefore, we are inclined to accept a growth rate of 3½ percent for the earnings of both the Dow-Jones Industrial Average and Standard & Poor's 500 stocks.[13] Moreover, in making this choice we are following what in the past has always proved a sound principle of in-

[12] A number of estimates were made at the end of 1959. On the whole, they tended to exceed the actual performance for the decade of the 1950's. For the Dow-Jones Industrial Average the consensus appeared to project a growth rate of about 5 percent per annum. It is fair to add that these estimates were made at a time of great confidence in the future of business and of stock prices.

[13] While the growth-rate figures for several of the postwar periods show a rather surprising advantage for Standard & Poor's Composite over the Dow-Jones Industrial Average, there is no reason to believe this to be inherent. In some former years the smaller Dow-Jones list showed the better result.

vestment: "When in doubt be conservative." It seems to us that there are sufficient areas of uncertainty affecting the future of corporate profits to justify recourse to our maxim.[14]

Assuming an annual average increase of 3.5 percent, we would thus use the following basic estimates for the earnings of the two averages during the 1960's:

Actual and projected earnings	Dow-Jones Industrial Average	Standard & Poor's 500
Average for 1950's............................	$30.51	2.96
Average for the 1960's (midpoint 1964–1965)..	43.00	4.15
End of decade............................	51.00	4.95

It is interesting to note that the average earnings projections under the two independent methods are nearly the same—$43 and $44. (This differential would be increased a little if allowances were made for the slight difference in the projection periods.) The reader is not advised, however, to take too much comfort in the nearness of the results. It may simply mean that both will be wrong by about the same amount.

In this connection, the reader should be aware that in the previous (1951) edition of this work we took an even more conservative attitude, in that we expressed the opinion that the results of the postwar period, 1946–1950, were "too good to continue." Our estimate for the future earnings (say, 1951–1957) of the Dow-Jones Average was set at $15, which was about midway between those of 1936–1940 and of 1945–1949. The actual average earnings for 1950–1959 were double this projection. Because of the low level of stock prices at the beginning of the last decade, this conservative view probably did no harm, for it still led to appraisals in excess of the then market level and a generally favorable view toward stock purchases. At the present time we are estimating earnings for the 1960's at well in excess of those of the 1950's. This can hardly be characterized as pessimistic. But it is possible that our present projection, like its predecessor, will prove too low.

Our moderately hopeful estimate may be viewed from another standpoint. The average earnings for the Dow-Jones Industrial Average in

[14] In considering the growth rate for per-share earnings, it is to be pointed out that as the payout rate rises, this inevitably tends to dampen down the increase in per-share gains, since a smaller percentage is reinvested in the business. We anticipate a higher payout in the sixties than in the fifties. Thus to assume that the same increase in per-share earnings will prevail during the present decade as prevailed throughout most of the past may not be quite as conservative as would appear at first blush.

1955–1959 were about 22 percent above the 1950–1954 average. Measured in this manner, the growth rate between the two periods is approximately 4 percent per annum. This is not much above our preferred assumption of 3½ percent for the future. Thus it may be said that roughly we expect the same relative improvement in earnings during the 1960's that existed between the last half and the first half of the 1950's.

Projections of Earnings of Individual Stocks. In the more conservative stock markets of former years it was often possible to buy leading stocks at a standard multiplier—say 10 to 15—of their past average earnings. On such a basis the average earnings of the past generally supplied a sufficient guide to the expectable future, for—in the long run, at least —the changes were likely to be in the right direction. Hence it was not necessary to make any careful assumptions as to future rates of growth, and the investor was free to make his selections largely on a general belief that certain companies had better prospects than others. In recent years, however, the investor or analyst has been compelled to make significant assumptions as to future changes in earnings of the common stocks he studies, and the success of his investment program may depend to a large degree upon the accuracy of these forecasts.

The earnings estimates for most common-stock issues will, of course, be related to the growth rates assumed for the economy as a whole and particularly for common stocks in general. But no type of purely mechanical projection, or "formal approach," can be counted on to produce results sufficiently dependable to be made the basis of investment choices. If the analyst's work here is to have serious value it must be based on considerable knowledge of the profit-making factors present in the particular company. Of these we shall speak in a later section of this chapter.

Yet every projection has a mechanical basis in that it starts from a consideration of past results—including average, variance, and trend. A frequently employed shortcut method of projection is to estimate future growth at the same rate as was shown in some past period. How good is such an approach? Let us apply it to the stocks in the Dow-Jones Industrial Average in a manner permitting some evaluation of its usefulness. In Table 33-2 we show first the average earnings for 1947–1949 and again for 1952–1954. (Three-year periods are preferable to single years, since they reduce the impact of nonrecurrent conditions.) Next we project earnings for 1957–1959, assuming the same rate of change in the second as in the first five-year span. For contrast, we add a "naïve projection," which assumes the same 22 percent rate of growth *for each stock* as was recorded by the group as a whole from 1947–1949 to 1952–1954. Finally we list the actual earnings during 1957–1959. As it happened, the list as a whole almost exactly duplicated its previous 22 percent growth rate.

Two conclusions emerge from the figures in our table. The first is that neither the past rate of increase nor the flat application of a 22 percent growth factor produced sufficiently accurate estimates of 1957–1959 earnings to encourage reliance on this approach. The second is that in the majority of cases the across-the-board advance of 22 percent turned out

Table 33-2. A Test of Two Mechanical Estimates of Per-share Earnings°
for Individual Stocks in the Dow-Jones Industrial Average,† 1957–1959

(Based on growth between 1947–1949 and 1952–1954)

Company	Average earnings		Percent change, 1947–1949 to 1952–1954	Estimated 1957–1959 earnings, based on:		Actual 1957–1959 earnings	Percent change, 1952–1954 to 1957–1959
	1947–1949	1952–1954		Individual % change	Group change of 22 %		
Allied Chemical	$1.72	$2.22	+29	$2.86	$2.71	$2.27	+ 2
American Can	2.06	2.45	+19	2.92	2.99	2.64	+ 8
American Smelting	5.72	3.84	−33	2.57	4.68	2.74	−29
American Tel and Tel	2.91	3.69	+27	4.69	4.50	4.66	+26
American Tobacco	3.53	2.79	−21	2.20	3.40	4.35	+56
Bethlehem Steel	2.00	2.94	+47	4.32	3.59	3.16	+ 7
Chrysler	11.05	6.59	−40	3.95	8.04	3.08	−53
Corn Products	1.44	1.70	+18	2.01	2.07	2.82	+66
du Pont	3.42	5.66	+65	9.34	6.90	8.22	+45
Eastman Kodak	1.25	1.43	+14	1.63	1.74	2.78	+94
General Electric	1.34	2.02	+51	3.05	2.46	2.94	+46
General Foods	1.02	1.19	+17	1.39	1.45	2.23	+87
General Motors	1.70	2.45	+44	3.53	2.99	2.75	+12
Goodyear Tire	0.70	1.46	+109	3.05	1.78	2.08	+42
International Harvester	3.88	2.49	−36	1.59	3.04	3.56	+43
International Nickel	1.13	1.96	+73	3.39	2.39	2.41	+23
Johns-Manville	2.21	3.10	+40	4.34	3.78	3.01	− 3
Loew's‡							
National Distillers	3.66	1.23	−66	0.42	1.50	2.01	+63
National Steel	4.81	5.31	+10	5.84	6.48	6.07	+14
Procter & Gamble	2.20	2.35	+ 7	2.51	2.87	3.63	+54
Sears Roebuck	1.66	1.70	+ 2	1.73	2.07	2.33	+37
Standard Oil of California	3.11	4.74	+52	7.20	5.78	6.52	+38
Standard Oil of New Jersey	1.68	2.96	+76	5.21	3.61	3.16	+ 7
Texaco, Inc	2.47	3.64	+47	5.35	4.44	5.70	+57
Union Carbide	3.14	3.35	+ 7	3.58	4.09	4.77	+42
United Aircraft	1.47	3.53	+140	8.47	4.31	6.20	+76
U.S. Steel	2.22	3.12	+41	4.40	3.81	5.57	+79
Westinghouse Electric	2.07	2.26	+ 9	2.46	2.76	2.22	− 2
Woolworth	4.21	3.03	−28	2.18	3.70	3.60	+19

* Earnings adjusted for stock splits and stock dividends to the end of 1959.
† Because composition of the Dow-Jones Industrial Average was not changed until June 1, 1959, the stocks comprising the Average throughout most of the period were used.
‡ Comparable data not available for latest years.

to be nearer to actual earnings than the more sophisticated application to each company of its own past performance.

To pursue our investigation further, let us now examine the results of two other types of forecast of future changes in earnings. The first type we consider to be implicit in the stock market's valuations of different issues. It is fair to assume that, in general, the higher the market's multipliers of current earnings, the more optimistic its view as to expectable growth.[15] The second type includes forecasts of future earnings made by large investment-counsel and trust organizations, on the basis of a study of each company's potentialities.

In Table 33-3 we again list the companies in the Dow-Jones Industrial Average, this time in the order of their average market multipliers, in 1952–1954. We show also the actual percentage gain—or decline—in the per-share earnings for each company from 1952–1954 to 1957–1959. If the price-earnings ratio is an indication of expected future growth, the correlation between the *market's* growth expectations and the growth which actually occurred in the next five years appears—from this single test—to be very poor indeed.

The forecasts of future earnings by an investment advisory organization may be seen by referring again to Table 32-1. There we set forth the 1956–1958 earnings projections of the Dow-Jones shares made by Value Line in 1953 and compared them with the actual results. Their estimate of the group's earnings was close to the realized figure, but 13 of their estimates for individual companies missed the actual earnings by more than 25 percent. We cite this fact to emphasize again the problems involved in estimating the earnings of individual business enterprises.

Projection of Earnings by Analysis of the Business. The figures just given covering the projections and realizations from 1952–1954 to 1957–1959 point to two conclusions. The first is that even the most carefully worked out forecast may often be found quite wide of the mark, especially when it is confined to a single industrial corporation. The second is that to obtain creditable results in these endeavors, the analyst cannot follow mechanical methods but must bring specialized knowledge and skill to bear upon the problem. In other words, he must analyze the business *itself*. To do so, he must also probe carefully the performance and prospects of the industry (or in some cases the industries) of which it forms a part.

[15] It is possible to work out various theoretical equivalents between the market's multiplier's and assumed rates of earnings growth. For example, the following figures show that widely different prices may be paid for shares all with the same current earnings, yet with the result of paying for the same number of years of assumed future earnings:

Stock	Today's price	Current year's earnings	Assumed growth rate	Number of years assumed earnings purchased
A	13	$1.00	3½%	11
B	16	1.00	7	11
C	19	1.00	10	11
D	24	1.00	15	11
E	32	1.00	20	11

There are two technical approaches to a company analysis and projection, and they can be used separately or together. The first may be called the "scientific" method; the second, the "return-on-investment" approach.

The scientific method of projecting future earnings consists in developing the figure from estimates of sales, operating and nonoperating expenses, taxes, and senior charges. The sales figure is derived from estimated physical volume multiplied by the expected average selling price.

Table 33-3. Comparison of Average 1952–1954 Price-Earnings Ratios and Percentage Increase in Per-share Earnings 1952–1954 to 1957–1959 of Stocks in Dow-Jones Industrial Average

Company	Average price-earnings ratio, 1952–1954	Percent increase in per-share earnings, 1952–1954 to 1957–1959
Union Carbide	21.3	+ 7
du Pont	19.2	+65
National Distillers	18.7	+63
Allied Chemical	16.1	+ 2
Eastman Kodak	15.7	+94
Procter & Gamble	15.3	+54
Woolworth	15.1	+19
American Can	15.0	+ 8
Corn Products	14.6	+66
American Tel and Tel	14.5	+26
General Electric	14.1	+46
Sears Roebuck	12.1	+37
General Foods	12.0	+87
Johns-Manville	11.7	− 3
American Tobacco	11.4	+56
International Nickel	11.3	+23
Westinghouse	11.2	− 2
International Harvester	10.7	+43
American Smelting	10.7	−29
National Steel	10.0	+14
General Motors	9.2	+12
Standard Oil (N.J.)	9.2	+ 7
Standard Oil (Calif.)	9.1	+38
Texaco, Inc	8.3	+57
U.S. Steel	7.6	+79
Chrysler	7.3	−53
United Aircraft	7.1	+76
Goodyear	6.2	+42
Bethlehem Steel	5.2	+ 7
Loew's	*	*
Dow-Jones Industrial Average	10.9	+22

* Comparable data not available for latest years.

The expenses may be worked out by categories—labor costs, material costs, overhead, etc.,—or they may be covered by a single estimate of the profit margin.[16] This general procedure is now standard for estimating the future earning power of public utility companies, and it can be applied to any other type of enterprise for which the analyst is willing to make the necessary estimates.

Nearly all the large organizations doing this kind of analytical work place major reliance on direct contacts with company executives. This is usually done by personal interviews. Many opportunities are afforded to groups of analysts to obtain detailed information by field-trip visits to the plants. There has also been an extensive development of the "luncheon-meeting" system, at which executives of many companies have addressed security-analyst societies and answered searching questions.

The rapid development of technological innovations has made it increasingly important for analysts to go behind the dollar figures into analysis of product changes, improvements in manufacturing methods, and various types of competitive developments both interindustry and within the industry. The greater the price that the investor must pay for expected future growth, the more important it is to gain a comprehensive knowledge of, and to apply competent judgment to, the host of factors that have a major bearing on future earning power.

Personal contacts of various sorts are also important to the analyst through enabling him to form a first-hand opinion of the character and capabilities of the management of the medium-sized and smaller companies. The management factor is nearly always of prime importance in appraising an equity security, but because of the scope of the activities and the breadth of management of America's largest corporations, e.g., General Electric, du Pont, etc., we consider that in appraising such management the analyst will find it necessary to place major reliance on the performance record. For all corporations, the management factor enters into the picture in a special way when *major* changes have recently taken place in the top personnel. In such cases the past record of the company may afford little clue as to the quality of the new management, and thus it must be gauged in some other way—preferably by direct interview.

The Return-on-investment Method. In our opinion, the forecast of per-share earnings will usually be more accurate if derived from the estimated earning power of the enterprise as a whole, i.e., from its ability to earn on its total capital. Thus, we consider that the per-share estimate should be developed from an analysis and prediction of the earnings available to total capital rather than from an estimate only of the earnings available to the common-stock equity. In other words, the rate of

---

[16] This technique of analysis and projection, as applied to a very large enterprise, is illustrated by the section of *The Evaluation of Common Stocks*, by Arnold Bernhard, 1959, dealing with the future earnings of General Motors (pp. 61–72).

return earned on the total capital (book value of the common stock plus the preferred stock and the noncurrent debt) is the basic test of profitableness and the factor of primary initial concern.[17]

There are several reasons for employing the rate of return on total capital as the criterion of earning power. First, through the use of a *rate* of return—rather than actual dollar amount of earnings—we make allowance for changes in the capital investment and thus obtain a more satisfactory measure for reviewing the *long-run* earnings performance of a business. Second, because earnings on total capital are less affected by changes in capital structure than earnings on net worth or common-stock capital, they provide the most consistent long-run measure of performance. Third, because the earnings rate on total capital minimizes the influence of differences in capital structure,[18] its use provides a sound basis for comparative examination of the earning power of individual companies.

In dealing with a specific future span of years, the analyst's objectives are (1) to select that earnings rate which will be most representative of *average* performance and (2) to estimate the *average* total capital investment. In this connection, the return-on-total-capital technique may be used in either a broad-brush or a detailed manner in projecting future earnings. In the first approach, the analyst may derive his estimate of the average rate of return for a future period simply from an analysis of earnings rates for selected past periods, and his estimate of average total capital simply from the anticipated amount of retained earnings. In the more thorough approach the analyst would base his rate-of-return estimate on a careful investigation of the primary determinants of the rates of return in past periods. For example, since the earnings rate is a product of the earnings margin (earnings available for total capital divided by sales) and capital turnover (sales divided by total capital), a careful analysis should be made of the principal factors behind these ratios. Conversely, the analyst might base his estimate of total capital on a careful projection of sales and estimated capital turnover as well as on a projection of retained earnings.

It is our own experience that the use of both the scientific and the return-on-total-capital techniques—although they are not entirely independent throughout—provides a helpful cross-check on estimated earnings.

[17] Some compute the return on total operating assets. This is an excellent measure of earnings performance and even preferable to the return on total capital in comparing the operating performance of two or more companies. But it does not lend itself to the derivation of a return on the common-stock equity and thus provide the basis for determining per-share earnings—the final objective of the analyst. If the analyst has the time to compute this return as well as that on total capital and on the common stock, we recommend its use.

[18] The student may make his comparisons of operating performance more exact by deducting from reported earnings on total capital any tax saved because of funded debt.

Specific Reasons for Questioning or Rejecting the Past Record. The technique of forecasting future earnings includes—as we have pointed out—a careful study of the past record, with a presumption that this record is of substantial value for the subsequent projections. In this section we shall consider certain formal reasons which in various cases require the analyst to reject the past record as a guide to the future. The major elements that produce the operating results of an enterprise are (1) volume, (2) price received, and (3) costs. If developments have occurred or are to occur that will significantly change the company's position in any of these categories, the analyst must be sure to take them into account. For if they are likely to make the past record irrelevant for future prognoses, he must not hesitate to reject the past as his guide and to construct some more reliable basis for his estimate of value.

It is true, of course, that changes are constantly under way in all three of the major components of the earnings statement. But in the typical case these changes are not sufficiently drastic to break the continuity of the operations for purposes of analysis. The developments that we have in mind would fall under headings such as the following:

1. *A basic change in the line of products made.*

Example: Hupp Motor Car Company discontinued making automobiles during World War II and now—under the name of the Hupp Corporation—is engaged in the manufacture of a diversified line of products which includes electric window regulators, automobile heaters, plumbing and air-conditioning equipment and supplies, marine products, gas infrared generators for industrial heating, heat pumps, electric refrigerators, ranges and home freezers, missile and jet-engine components, and metal and plastic pipe.

2. *A basic change in the manufacturing or sales policy.* This could include the abandonment of highly unprofitable operations.

Example: Philadelphia & Reading Corporation was, for many decades, an anthracite-coal producer. Beginning in 1955, the firm diversified into several different lines and by 1961 had withdrawn entirely from the coal business.

3. *A drastic change in management,* where the analyst has reason to believe that such change will be followed by radical developments affecting the company's results.

Example: The most important change of management of which we know came about when W. P. Chrysler took over as the head of the then almost prostrate Maxwell Motors in 1921. The results he produced were phenomenal, especially in view of the competitive situation in the auto industry. In this case an observant and well-informed analyst might well have rejected the past record of Maxwell as a guide to its future; but we wonder if he could have developed any substitute measure of its future expectations. The deterioration in the relative position of Chrysler since World War II is one of countless illustrations of the variability of corporate fortunes. The forward surge of American Motors since 1958 under the presidency of George Romney affords an interesting parallel to the Chrysler story.

4. *The loss of some special advantage of great importance:* i.e., expiration of patents or sales contracts, exhaustion of ore bodies, and the like.

Perhaps the simplest example of a break with the past is found when a mining company which is nearing the exhaustion of its old mine is planning to transfer operations to another property. Here the former earnings are clearly irrelevant in the future, since the analyst is dealing virtually with a new and different enterprise. A similar effect appears when a mining company exhausts high-grade or low-cost ore, with a subsequent significant lessening in its profit margin.[19] Conversely, the development of a new ore body can move a mining company's basic position in the opposite direction.

Example: The exploration and development of the San Manuel ore body by Magma Copper Company.

The Newer Trend toward Diversification. During the 1950's a trend developed at an accelerated rate toward changing the complexion of many companies' operations, and thereby weakening and even breaking the chain that ties future prospects to past operations. In the broader sense this has been a trend toward diversification. In previous times diversification was considered a sound policy, provided the company kept its additional lines within the same or some related industry. But this traditional restriction has had less and less weight in recent years.

Companies have gone into fields completely foreign to their established business. For the most part, this has been done by the acquisition of existing concerns, so that experienced personnel was immediately available to carry on the new lines of business.

Striking Examples: Stanley Warner Corporation, which was formed in 1953 to take over the theater interests of Warner Bros. Pictures, Inc., acquired in 1954 International Latex Corporation and in early 1960 Sarong, Inc., and an affiliate, Dora Miles Company. As a result, in addition to being engaged in operating or holding 238 motion picture theaters and related commercial properties, Warner manufactures synthetic latex, undergarments and other latex and sewn products, and antiseptic products.

Textron, Inc., as a result of a series of acquisitions in unrelated fields, has changed in recent years from exclusively a textile company to a diversified manufacturing concern with a wide range of industrial and consumer products. In 1959 the sales of Textron and its subsidiaries were classified as follows: consumer and home-improvement products, 23 per-

---

[19] The student is referred to the long history of Calumet and Hecla Mining Company for at least two examples of this type of development. These are discussed in detail in the 1934 and 1940 editions of this book.

cent; automotive parts and supplies, 20 percent; textiles, 21 percent; general industrial metal products, 10 percent; electronic equipment, 10 percent; process machinery and machine tools, 8 percent; aviation, missile, and other products, 8 percent.

The argument in favor of such radical diversification of business operations is presumably similar to the one for wide diversification in the typical investor's portfolio. If the individual or an investment fund should spread the risk, why should not an individual or commercial corporation do likewise? With commitments in widely different industries, there is a fair chance that unfavorable developments in one will be offset or attenuated by better results in the others. Furthermore, the company will now be able to concentrate its attention and additional capital on the line or lines that show most promise for the future.

The principal argument against diversification in dissimilar fields is that top management cannot cope successfully with such a congeries of policy decisions and operating problems. Undoubtedly, it is more difficult to run a half-dozen businesses with maximum efficiency than to concentrate on one. How this works out in practice depends a great deal on the special capabilities of top management and more particularly on its ability to find the right people to put in charge of each of the different operations. It is too early to generalize about the net advantage or disadvantage of this recent movement.

The vogue of diversification has created some added difficulties for the security analyst. As we have already mentioned, the past results may appear of little value for study if the operations of future years will be radically different. However, if the acquisitions are long-established firms for which financial information is available, this obstacle may be overcome at least in part by combining the figures of past years to create a *pro forma* record of performance.[20] (This will not always be possible.) A separate problem of classification occurs when a company crosses industry lines so substantially that it can no longer be placed in the single category of "steel," "department stores," or some other grouping. Comparisons with other companies "in the same industry"—a favorite analytical tool—then become well-nigh impossible.

Caution regarding Temporary Factors in the Earning Power. A competent analyst is always alert to discover elements in the past earnings picture that are unlikely to continue in the future. These are similar in their significance to the nonrecurring gains and losses which we counseled the analyst to eliminate from his presentation of the "actual operating results" of a given year. But they differ from nonrecurring items, in the technical sense, because the latter represent transactions that

---

[20] *Example:* Data on American Can in Moody's *Handbook of Widely Held Common Stocks* for 1960 include in gross revenues and per-share earnings the *pro-forma* results of Dixie Cup and Marathon Corporation for the years 1952–1956 although the acquisition took place in 1956.

can and should be separated from the company's ordinary operations, while those we now consider are *temporary* rather than extraordinary.

Example: The earnings and market performance of Studebaker-Packard in 1959 is an illustration of the effects of such temporary factors—in this case chiefly the demand for compact cars in advance of their production by the larger companies. (And also by a timely strike in the steel industry which relieved S-P of a possible inventory burden.) The reader is referred to our earlier discussion of this situation, on page 31, as an example of dependable conclusions based on security analysis.

CHAPTER THIRTY-FOUR

PROJECTIONS OF EARNINGS AND DIVIDENDS.

THE CONCEPT OF EARNING POWER

The concept of *earning power* has a definite and important place in investment theory. It combines a statement of actual earnings performance —over a period of years—with a reasonable expectation that the past level or trend will be approximated in the future, unless extraordinary conditions supervene. This performance may be measured in terms of either (1) the earnings per share of common stock or (2) the rate of return earned on the common-stock equity. In fact, the analyst may find it desirable to use both methods to cross-check his results. It is our own inclination—when using the rate-of-return approach—to compute first the return on total capital, take this as the basic measure of performance, and then derive from it the return on the common-stock equity.

Irrespective of the earnings yardstick employed, the record must cover a number of years. This is essential for two reasons: first, because a continued or repeated performance is always more impressive than a single occurrence, and second, because the results for a fairly long period— either a trend or an average—will tend to absorb and equalize the distorting influences of the business cycle.

In our opinion the use of a period average is nearly always appropriate when the rate of return is being analyzed. Depending on the facts, it may or may not be appropriate in the analysis of per-share earnings. But whenever an average is used, it is essential that a distinction be drawn between an average that is the mere arithmetical resultant of an assortment of disconnected figures and an average that is "normal" or "modal," in the sense that the annual results show a definite tendency to approximate the average. The contrast between the two types of earning power may be clearly seen from the following examples (Table 34-1).

In the case of Young, Spring & Wire, the variance of the earnings figures in the individual years from the period-average is so great and so erratic that the 11-year average is of no practical assistance to the analyst in predicting the future *level* of earnings. From the standpoint of security analysis, the $3.31 figure constitutes a meaningless abstraction of eleven widely varying figures. In contrast note how closely in each year the per-share earnings for Peoples Drug Stores cling to the 11-year average of approximately $3.60. While such a consistent record is ordinarily of decided help in making earnings projections, it is not an infallible guide to the future. The present illustration proves our point. The per-share earnings for Peoples Drug Stores in 1960 dropped sharply to $2.39, or two-thirds of the 1949–1959 average, and thus constituted by far the widest departure from the general level in more than a decade.

The 1949–1959 records for Corn Products Company and Chrysler Corporation also illustrate our view as to the significance of averages. In

Table 34-1. Comparative Earnings Performance of Four Selected
Companies, 1949–1959

Year	Earnings per share		Return on total capital	
	Peoples Drug Stores	Young, Spring & Wire	Corn Products	Chrysler
1949	$3.95	$11.46*	11.3%	31.3%
1950	3.85	8.53	18.3	26.3
1951	3.45	2.42	11.4	14.1
1952	3.34	4.81	10.2	14.9
1953	3.50	3.32	11.5	13.6
1954	3.44	.42	10.9	3.2
1955	3.51	3.45	13.2	14.5
1956	3.61	2.79	13.9	2.8
1957	3.31	1.82	12.4	13.7
1958	3.85	2.01	13.7	−2.6
1959	3.61	4.61	12.6	−0.1
11-year average	3.58	3.31	12.7	12.0

* Years ending July 31, 1950, etc.

this instance, return on total capital is the measure of earnings performance. The 11-year average returns are closely comparable but here, again, one figure is truly indicative of the past level of earnings whereas the other is of very doubtful value. In five years the return on capital was close to the period average but the variations in the other six years make the entire picture highly confusing. Moreover, an average which includes deficits may be seriously distorted.

Quantitative Analysis Should Be Supplemented by Qualitative Considerations. In studying earnings records an important principle of security analysis must be borne in mind.

Quantitative data are useful only to the extent that they are supported by a qualitative survey of the enterprise.

In nearly all cases a long record of stable earnings, under varying economic conditions, will prove a good indication that the business is inherently stable. An examination of the nature of the business will usually indicate the qualitative factors on which such stability is based. There are a number of exceptions, of course. An example we gave years ago was that of Studebaker Corporation, which showed a deceptive stability in its results from 1922 through 1929 but was later forced by large losses into reorganization.[1] Two more modern-day illustrations would be Reed Roller Bit Company and Douglas Aircraft, as shown in the following table.

Table 34-2. Fluctuations in Per-share Earnings. Reed Roller Bit Company and Douglas Aircraft Company

Reed Roller Bit				Douglas Aircraft			
1947	$2.71	1954	$1.48	1948	$ 2.15	1955	$ 7.65
1948	3.91	1955	1.72	1949	1.53	1956	8.96
1949	1.86	1956	2.64	1950	2.00	1957	8.28
1950	2.78	1957	2.76	1951	1.92	1958	4.41
1951	2.78	1958	0.43 (d)	1952	3.00	1959	8.86 (d)
1952	2.91	1959	0.19 (d)	1953	5.15	1960	5.09 (d)
1953	2.60	1960	0.03 (d)	1954	9.80		

Reed Roller Bit in the 1947–1953 span enjoyed comparatively stable earnings, but in the last three years—1958–1960—it has operated at a deficit. Likewise, Douglas Aircraft had relatively stable per-share earnings over the five-year span from 1948 through 1952, but they were followed by marked fluctuations—reaching a peak of $9.80 per share in 1954 and a trough in the form of a loss $8.86 in 1959.

Trend vs. Average of Earnings. Earlier in this chapter we set forth our opinion that a *permanent* growth rate exists in investment-quality common stocks in general, and we further stated that this growth might be estimated conservatively at 3½ percent per annum. We, therefore, find ourselves in favor of the use of some kind of trend approach in projecting per-share earnings of the typical industrial concern. In adopting this approach, we feel called on to note two facts. First, in preceding editions of this book we suggested that the analyst use *averages* of per-share earnings for selected *past* periods as indicators of future earnings. Second, we suggested that he not use a projected per-share figure higher than that already achieved.

In accepting the trend approach, we are not suggesting the complete abandonment of the use of averages. A straight average has the obvious disadvantage that it fails to take into account what may be a significant trend in per-share earnings. But this does not mean that a growth

---

[1] For reference to Studebaker-Packard's highly variable recent earnings, see Chap. 2, pp. 31–33.

economy makes the use of averages obsolete. In fact, we believe the student may be surprised at the number of companies whose per-share earnings—principally as a result of cyclical fluctuations—do not readily lend themselves to "trend treatment." In those instances, he may find that a comparison of averages for selected periods (in the manner crudely employed by us in Chapter 33) may be a more effective tool—than fitting traditional trend lines—for arriving at growth rates and making earnings projections.

Moreover, the use of trends has difficulties and dangers of its own. Valuations based on trend projections of per-share earnings obey no mathematical rules and therefore may too easily be exaggerated. All too frequently a proposed trend—particularly if pronounced—proves deceptive, and the error then becomes the more costly because so much of the conclusion as to the value has depended on the trend projection. In addition, since earnings trends are typically computed from fairly short historical records—e.g., 10 or 15 years—the terminal dates selected become most important. To illustrate, if the reader refers again to page 456, he will see that the growth rate for the earnings of Standard & Poor's 500 stocks over the 1950–1959 span is 3.2 percent but over the 1951–1959 period is 4.1 percent. Note the effect of one year on the results.[2]

There is indeed a fundamental conflict between the concepts of the average and the trend, as applied to an earnings record. This may be illustrated by the simplified example in Table 34-3.

Table 34-3

Com-pany	Earned per share in successive years						7th (current)	Aver-age of 7 years	Trend
	1st	2d	3d	4th	5th	6th			
A	$ 1.00	$ 1.35	$1.85	$2.50	$3.30	$4.50	$6.00	$2.95	Excellent
B	6.00	6.00	6.00	6.00	6.00	6.00	6.00	6.00	Neutral
C	11.00	10.00	9.00	8.00	7.20	6.50	6.00	8.25	Bad

From Table 34-3 it may be seen that, although each firm had the *same earnings* in the current year (year 7), Company A had a pronounced upward trend and, in relation to current earnings, a low seven-year average. In contrast, Company C had a downward trend and a seven-year average much higher than the current earnings figure. Com-

---

[2] In the early 1960's earnings growth for a period as short as five years was generally considered sufficient to establish the enterprise as a growth company. This was notoriously true in the case of new offerings of shares of smaller companies. (A ¾-page advertisement in a well-known Eastern newspaper with the caption, "Our Approach to Growth Stock Investing," stated, "We project earnings on the basis of a 3- to 4-year historical trend.")

pany *B*, with constant per-share earnings—a horizontal trend—lay between the other two companies. These hypothetical figures bring out two important facts: (1) the better the trend in per-share earnings of a company, the lower will be the period average in relation to current earnings; (2) the poorer the trend, the higher will be the average in relation to current earnings.

The foregoing study raises an important question in regard to the theoretical and practical interpretation of earnings records. Is not the trend at least as significant for the future as the average? Concretely, in judging the probable performance of Companies *A* and *C* over the next five years, would not the analyst find more reason to think in terms of their trends—an increase of approximately 35 percent per year for *A* and a decline of about 10 percent for *C*—than in terms of past averages? In other words, *A*'s future earnings would be assumed to be $8.25, $11.00, $15.00, $20.00, and $27.00 rather than the seven-year average of $2.95, whereas *C*'s earnings would be taken at $5.50, $5.00, $4.50, $4.00, and $3.50 rather than the seven-year average of nearly $8.25.

The answer to the problem derives from common sense rather than from formal or a priori logic. The favorable trend of Company *A*'s results must certainly be taken into account, but not by a merely automatic projection of the 35 percent growth rate into the distant future. On the contrary, it must be remembered that the normal economic forces militate *against* the indefinite continuance of a given trend. Competition, regulation, the law of diminishing returns, etc., are powerful foes to unlimited expansion, and in smaller degree, opposite elements may operate to check a continued decline. Hence instead of taking the maintenance of a pronounced trend for granted—as the stock market is often inclined to do—the analyst must approach the matter with caution, seeking to determine the causes of the superior showing and to weigh the specific elements of strength in the company's position against the general obstacles in the way of continued growth.

Attitude of the Analyst When the Trend Is Upward. If such a *qualitative* study leads to a favorable verdict—as frequently it should—the analyst's philosophy should impel him to place some limitations on his enthusiasm. In this regard, we have three suggestions to make. First, the projected growth rate for earnings should not exceed that already achieved by the business—giving consideration to the years of abnormal and normal profits. We suggest this limitation because, in our opinion, investment values can be related only to demonstrated performance; so that neither an *expected* higher rate of increase nor even the past results under conditions of abnormal business activity may be taken as a basis. As we pointed out earlier in this chapter, because of the brevity of the period from which a trend of earnings is typically derived, the results for a single year—if abnormally good or abnormally bad—can distort the results. To the best of his ability the analyst seeks either to develop the trend from those earnings figures which he considers to be representative of the company's earning power, or to establish it by an independent appraisal of future prospects. Second, as set forth in Chapter 33, we propose that the projection for growth use be limited to four years. Third, and this is also of primary importance, we suggest that the growth rate assumed, except in the most extraordinary circumstances, *should not exceed 20 percent per annum.* Lest this seem unduly conservative, it is to be noted that a compound rate of 20 percent represents more than a doubling of earnings in a four-year span. Moreover, this aggregate growth for the four years exceeds by six times that which would result from the use of our conservative rate of 3½ percent for the over-all growth of industrial corporate per-share earnings. Finally, a check of the per-share earnings of more than 300 stocks listed in Studley Shupert's *Analyses of Corporate Securities* reveals that over the decade of the fifties less than 5 percent of the issues had growth rates in excess of 20 percent per annum.[3] A similar examination of nearly 600 common stocks contained in Value Line discloses that less than 8 percent had a growth rate in earnings of more than 20 percent annually. Thus the proportion of shares exceeding our maximum growth rate appears to be very small.

We have also suggested that if the valuation is to be kept within investment limits, the maximum multiplier be held to a generous but still limited figure of, say, 20 times the projected earnings four years hence. On this basis, the earning power of Company A (in Table 34-3) might be taken at a *maximum* of $12 per share, and its investment value might be set as high as 240. It is to be noted that this valuation is equivalent to a multiplier of 40 times the earnings of $6 in year 7.

The divergence in method between the stock market and the conservative analyst—as we define his viewpoint—would mean in general that the price-levels ruling for many of the so-called "growth stocks" will often appear far too generous to the analyst. This does not mean that he is convinced that the market valuation is wrong but rather that the price contains a substantial "speculative component." That is, the market appears to be basing today's price on the assumption that an extraordinary growth rate will be maintained for a remarkably long period of time.

Attitude of the Analyst When the Trend Is Downward. Where the trend has been definitely downward, as was that of Company C, the analyst will assign great weight to this unfavorable factor. He will not assume that the curve *must* turn upward, nor can he accept the past average—which is much higher than the current figure—as a normal index of future earnings. But he will be equally chary about any hasty conclusions to the effect that the company's outlook is hopeless, that its earnings are certain to disappear entirely, and that the stock is therefore

---

[3] The average growth rate for the companies was 3.3 percent, and the median was 4.4 percent. These growth rates have been computed by determining the increase in per-share earnings between 1950–1954 and 1955–1959. Interestingly, the growth rate for the Dow-Jones Industrial Average—computed on the same basis—lies in between at 4 percent.

without merit or value. Here, again, a qualitative study of the company's situation and prospects is essential to forming an opinion whether *at some price,* relatively low, of course, the issue may not be a bargain, despite its declining earnings trend. Once more we identify the viewpoint of the analyst with that of a sensible businessman looking into the pros and cons of some privately owned enterprise.

Examples: In former editions we gave detailed figures for Continental Baking Corporation and American Laundry Machine Company, covering the years 1925–1933. Both had shown a consistent decline in earnings—those of Continental from $8.8 million in 1925 to $2.8 in 1933; those of American Laundry from $5.1 to a *deficit* of $1.2 in the same period. The market price of both issues reflected the view that both enterprises were definitely on the downward path. We suggested that a study of the two businesses from the *qualitative* standpoint would have indicated that both industries were permanent and reasonably stable, and that each company occupied a leading position in its industry and was well fortified financially. The analyst might well have concluded that the earnings decline in both cases was due to accidental or temporary conditions, aggravated by the post-1929 depression. Hence at their very depressed prices both issues presented an attractive opportunity from the standpoint of security analysis. (These inferences were borne out by the earnings-and-market-price sequel.)

In the highly prosperous period since World War II certain companies have been characterized by a downward drift in earnings. Without attempting to determine whether any of them are in the Continental Baking and American Laundry Machinery category, we might mention the following as illustrations: J. I. Case, Admiral Corporation, United Fruit, Industrial Rayon, Pabst Brewing, and Montgomery Ward.

Example: To provide some illustrative data, the following are the 1950–1960 net-income figures as reported for the United Fruit Company:

1950	$66,159,000	1956	$30,283,000
1951	50,894,000	1957	31,455,000
1952	37,937,000	1958	22,742,000
1953	44,556,000	1959	12,088,000
1954	31,460,000	1960	2,171,000
1955	33,539,000		

Deficits a Qualitative, Not a Quantitative, Factor. When a company reports a deficit for the year, it is customary to calculate the amount in dollars per share or in relation to interest requirements. For example, it was reported that in 1959 Douglas Aircraft suffered a net loss after taxes of $33.8 million or $8.86 per share. The company was said to have "earned" the interest on its long-term debt a "deficit 8.2 times." It should be recognized that such figures, when taken by themselves, have no *quantitative significance,* and that their value in forming an average or a trend may often be open to serious question.

Let us assume that Company *A* lost $5 per share of common in the last year, and Company *B* lost $7 per share. Both issues sell at 25. Is this an indication of any sort that Company *A* stock is preferable to Company *B* stock? Obviously not; for assuming it were so, it would mean that the more shares there were outstanding, the more valuable each share would be. If Company *B* issues 2 shares for 1, the loss would be reduced to $3.50 per share, and on the assumption just made, each new share would then be worth more than an old one. The same reasoning applies to bond interest. Suppose that Company *A* and Company *B* each lost $1 million, and *A* had $4 million and *B* $10 million of 5 percent bonds. Company *A* would then show interest earned "deficit five times" and Company *B* would earn its interest "deficit two times." These figures should not be construed as an indication of any kind that Company *A*'s bonds are less secure than Company *B*'s bonds. For if so, it would mean that the smaller the bond issue, the poorer its position—a manifest absurdity.

While in general an average of past earnings must include deficits as well as income figures, the predictive value of an average containing deficit figures is necessarily less than in other cases. This is true because any average based on individual figures with wide variability must be viewed as an accidental rather than a descriptive figure.

Intuition Not a Part of the Analyst's Stock in Trade. In the absence of indications to the contrary, we accept the past record as at least a starting basis for judging the future. But the analyst must be on the lookout for any such indications to the contrary. Here we must distinguish between vision or intuition on the one hand, and ordinary sound reasoning on the other. The ability to see what is coming is of inestimable value, but it cannot be expected to be part of the analyst's stock in trade. (If he had it, he could dispense with analysis.) He can be asked to show only that moderate degree of foresight which springs from logic and from experience intelligently pondered. It was not to be demanded of the security analyst, for example, that he foretell the enormous increase in cigarette consumption since 1915 or the decline in the cigar business until recently or the surprising stability of the snuff industry. Furthermore, we doubt very much whether he could have predicted—to use another example—that International Business Machines' product-development and merchandising abilities would be of such amazing proportions that, in spite of greatly intensified competition, per-share earnings would increase 13 times in the two decades from 1937–1939 to 1957–1959, or 4 times in the decade from 1947–1949 to 1957–1959. Analytical reasoning with regard to the future is of a somewhat different character, being penetrating rather than prophetic.

We retain the example given at this point in our 1940 edition, and we shall later supply the sequel. This example includes certain material on the general process of common-stock valuation which lies outside a schematic arrangement of the subject. It is given here primarily because it was current at the time of selection and involved no advantage of hind-sight.

Example: Let us take the situation presented by Intertype Corporation in March–July 1939, when the stock was selling at $8 per share. This old, established company was one of the leaders in a relatively small industry (line-casting machines, etc., for the printing trade). Its recent earnings had not been favorable, nor did there seem to be any particular reason for optimistic expectations as to the near-term outlook. The analyst, how-ever, could not fail to be impressed by the balance sheet, which showed net current assets available for the stock amounting to close to $20 per share. The ten-year earnings, dividend, and price record of the common stock was as shown in Table 34-4.

Table 34-4. Intertype Corporation

Year	Earned per share	Dividend paid	Price range
1938	$0.57	$0.45	12¾–8
1937	1.41	0.80	26¼–9
1936	1.42	0.75	22¾–15
1935	0.75	0.40	16–6⅛
1934	0.21	. . . . .	10–5⅝
1933	*0.77(d)*	. . . . .	11¼–1⅞
1932	*1.82(d)*	. . . . .	7–2½
1931	0.56	1.00	18½–4⅝
1930	1.46	2.00	32–12
1929	3.05	1.75	38⅞–17
Average 1934–1938. . . .	0.87		
Average 1929–1938. . . .	0.68		

Certainly there is nothing attractive in this record, marked as it is by irregularity and the absence of a favorable trend. But although these facts would undoubtedly condemn the issue in the eyes of the speculator, the reasoning of the analyst might conceivably run along different lines.

The essential question for him would be whether or not the company can be counted on to remain in business and to participate about as be-fore in good times and bad. On this point, consideration of the industry, the company's prominent position in it, and the strong financial setup would clearly suggest an affirmative answer. If this were granted, the analyst would then point out that the shares could be bought at 8 with very small chance of ultimate loss and with every indication that under the next set of favorable conditions the value of the stock would double. Note that in 3 years out of the past 5 and in 6 out of the past 10 the stock had sold between two and four times the July 1939 price.

This type of reasoning, it will be noted, lays emphasis not upon an accurate prediction of future trends but rather on reaching the general conclusion that the company will continue to do business pretty much as before.

Wall Street is inclined to doubt that any such presumption may be applied to companies with an irregular trend, and to consider that it is just as difficult and hazardous to reach a conclusion of this kind as to determine that a "growing company" will continue to grow. But in our view the Intertype form of reasoning has two definite advantages over the customary attitude, which at the time (1939) preferred a company such as Coca-Cola, at 24 times recent earnings and 35 times its asset value, because of the virtually uninterrupted expansion of its profits for more than 15 years.

Sequel to the Intertype–Coca-Cola Example: It is interesting to note that (1) if Intertype had been purchased in 1939 at 8 and Coca-Cola at 142, (2) if stock dividends and splits had been held, and (3) if both issues had been sold out at the closing price on December 31, 1959, the comparative results would have been as follows:

	Harris Intertype*	Coca-Cola
Market price, Dec. 31, 1959	$ 98†	$150
Cost	8	142
Realized appreciation	$ 90	$ 8
Total cash dividends	35	102
Total return	$125	$110

* Intertype merged with Harris-Seybold Company in 1957 through an exchange of 6 shares of Intertype for 5 shares of Harris-Seybold. But see our reference to an apparent overvaluation of Intertype in 1950 (p. 691 below).

† After allowing for stock dividends and splits.

The return on the investment of $8 in Intertype is equivalent to a little over 74 percent per annum, whereas the return on the $142 invested in Coca-Cola is less than 4 percent per annum. These returns are not compounded.

Current Earnings as a Basis of Market Prices. In considering the role of current earnings in stock prices, our objective is not to undertake intensive research into stock-price formation but rather to set forth some general views on the subject. First, in our opinion, current earnings play neither a readily definable nor a constant role in stock prices. That is, the stock market does not always give the same weight to current earnings. (This is not to imply that it should. Current earnings should be valued in relation to whatever is considered to be "normal.") The contrasting experiences of the decades of the forties and of the fifties illustrate well this point.

The earnings of the Dow-Jones Industrial Average rose from $10.92 in 1940 to $23.54 in 1949, but the price-earnings ratio *fell* from 12.3× to

$7.6\times$ in the same years. The average for the decade was $11.8\times$. The reverse development in the 1950's is shown in Table 34-5. In the 12 years, 1950–1961, the earnings showed only a small over-all gain, but the market price advanced spectacularly and the price-earnings ratio rose from $6.4\times$ at the low point in 1950 to $23.4\times$ at the 1961 high.

Table 34-5. 1950–1961 Earnings, Dividends, Market Prices, and Price-Earnings Ratios of Dow-Jones Industrial Average

Year	Earnings	Dividends	Yearly range of price	Mean price-earnings ratio
1950	$30.70	$16.13	196.8–235.5	$7.0\times$
1951	26.59	16.34	239.0–276.4	$9.7\times$
1952	24.76	15.48	256.4–292.0	$10.9\times$
1953	27.23	16.11	255.5–293.8	$10.1\times$
1954	28.40	17.47	279.9–404.4	$11.9\times$
1955	35.78	21.58	388.2–488.4	$12.2\times$
1956	33.34	22.99	462.4–521.1	$14.9\times$
1957	36.08	21.61	419.8–520.8	$13.1\times$
1958	27.95	20.00	436.9–583.7	$17.2\times$
1959	34.31	20.74	574.5–679.4	$18.3\times$
1960	32.21	21.36	566.0–685.5	$19.4\times$
1961	31.83*	22.61	610.3–734.9	$21.1\times$

* Partly estimated.

If the historical record of price-earnings ratios is meaningful, there can be little doubt but that the market in neither 1949 nor 1961 considered current earnings closely indicative of expectable earnings over the years to come. In the first instance, it was too conservative—and we along with it. We now find ourselves unable to justify the high price-earnings ratio prevailing at the beginning of the 1960's. Accordingly, this time either we, once again, are too conservative, or the market is too optimistic. It is doubtful that we shall both be proved wrong.

So much for our first point: the varying role of current earnings in price. Our second point may seem somewhat contradictory. But in spite of the repeated disregard of current earnings in the course of the last two decades, as indicated by various stock-market averages, substantial *fluctuations* in numerous individual prices have often accompanied changes in *current* earnings and *current* earnings prospects. A considerable part of the activity of Wall Street analysts—as reflected in the advisory bulletins of financial services and in brokerage-house circulars—is constantly devoted to the effort to forecast near-term changes in earnings. Furthermore, many of their conclusions as to the dearness or cheapness of individual shares (other than "growth" stocks) appear to be based on a capitalization of the profits and dividends expected in the next twelve months.

If the current or immediately foreseeable earnings have a determining influence upon the price movements of most common stocks, it is natural that analysts should attach major significance to these figures and estimates. But it should be clear that current or near-term earnings *alone* are ordinarily a less reliable clue to the fundamental *value* of a security than would be a carefully formulated projection of the future level of earnings—i.e., average for a span of future years. Hence the analyst interested in *value* is likely to place only minor emphasis upon the short-term-earnings outlook; whereas the analyst who endeavors to anticipate the price movements of the near future will make such outlook his major concern.

The professional security analyst will have to make a personal choice between the two approaches. This decision is of vital importance to his career. Our own experience and observation lead us to recommend the *long-term-value* approach strongly, as by far the sounder and more rewarding of the two.

DIVIDEND PROJECTIONS

The estimate of expectable dividends is ordinarily related closely to the projection of earnings. This explains the paradox that, while for most companies the dividend payments may be basically more important than the earnings, the bulk of the analyst's attention is likely to be focused on earning-power factors. In considering the dividend question separately, he will be guided by the company's payout policy in the past, by consideration of its financial position, and by such allowance as he is able to make for the impact of new conditions.

We venture the hope that in future years both managements and stockholders may gain a better understanding of the merits of an over-all dividend policy geared in principle to the earning power and intrinsic value of the equity, rather than to the arbitrarily determined "needs of the business." (Such a policy should permit the legitimate needs of the business for *large* amounts of additional capital to be financed by sale of securities on satisfactory terms.) For growth companies the adoption of a clearly formulated and consistently followed *stock-dividend policy* would permit sufficient flexibility in the payout rate for cash dividends, without creating accompanying uncertainties and possible price instability. Were this realization to become widespread, the analyst would be able to project the dividend payout with more confidence, and the stockholders might be able to count on more equitable and favorable treatment.

At the present time, however, the dividend policy of many companies is not closely related to the past or estimated future earning power. Consequently the dividend factor, *as an element of value independent of earnings,* often plays a major role in common-stock valuation. In the next two chapters we deal with what at bottom may be called "the problem of disparities between earnings and dividends."

CHAPTER THIRTY-FIVE

THE DIVIDEND FACTOR IN COMMON-STOCK

VALUATION

Since our last edition, changes have been taking place in the thinking of theorists, in the attitudes of investors, and in corporate practices, with respect to the reinvestment of earnings as against the payment of dividends. On the one hand, the investment opportunities which exist in an expanding economy, coupled with the impact of personal income tax laws on cash dividends, create strong arguments in favor of the reinvestment of profits by prosperous and dynamic companies. On the other hand, long tradition and much disillusioning experience have produced in investors an ingrained sentiment in favor of liberal dividends. In consequence, the stock market's reaction to dividend policies now shows a somewhat confusing pattern, which is perhaps characteristic of a transition period. We must try in this chapter to shed light on the contradictory influences presently at work in this area and to supply some aid to the analyst in their evaluation.

Historical Primacy of Dividends. For the vast majority of common stocks the dividend record and prospects have always been the most important factor controlling investment quality and value. The success of the typical concern has been measured by its ability to pay liberal and steadily increasing dividends on its capital. In the majority of cases the price of common stocks has been influenced more markedly by the dividend rate than by the reported earnings. In other words, distributed earnings have had a greater weight in determining market prices than have retained and reinvested earnings. The "outside," or noncontrolling, stockholders of any company can reap benefits from their investment in only two ways—through dividends and through an increase in the market value of their shares. Since the market value in most cases has depended primarily upon the dividend rate, the latter could be held responsible for nearly all the gains ultimately realized by investors.

This predominant role of dividends has found full reflection in a generally accepted theory of investment value[1] which states that a common

---

[1] We use the term "generally accepted" because in recent years this view has

480

stock is worth the sum of all the dividends expected to be paid on it in the future, each discounted to its present worth.[2]

Because (1) dividends play a dominant role in the market price of the typical common stock and (2) the discounted value of near dividends is higher than the present worth of distant dividends, of two companies with the same earning power and in the same general position in an industry, that one paying the larger dividend will almost always sell at a higher price. Or, similarly, when a company raises its dividend, the price of its shares will also rise, even though there is no accompanying increase in earning power.

Examples: In 1939–1947 the Reading Railroad paid a dividend of $1, against average earnings of $4.25. Its average price was 18. In the same period, Pennsylvania Railroad earned only $3.54, but it paid an average dividend of $1.83. Result: Its average price was 26½. In 1945 alone, Reading earned $5.59, paid $1, and its average price was 24½. In that year Pennsylvania earned $3.72, it paid $2.50, and its price averaged 40. By contrast, when Reading's dividend was raised in 1948 and that of Pennsylvania was reduced, they promptly reversed their price relationship.

A second example is that of New Amsterdam Casualty Insurance Company vs. New Hampshire Fire Insurance Company. The figures are presented in Table 35-1. The relationships of these figures are surprisingly

Table 35-1. Ten-year Average, 1938–1947

	New Amsterdam Casualty	New Hampshire Fire
Average price..................	$22.00	$44.50
Average earnings per share*.....	4.04	2.04
Average dividends.............	0.89	1.74

* Calculated from the 10-year increase in liquidating value plus the 10-year dividend payments.

pat. New Hampshire paid *twice* the dividend of New Amsterdam and sold *twice* as high, although its earnings were just *half* as great. Incidentally, the price of New Amsterdam averaged about one-third less than

---

[2] been questioned. In particular, the student should read F. Modigliani and M. H. Miller, "The Cost of Capital, Corporation Finance and the Theory of Investment," *American Economic Review*, vol. 48, no. 3, June 1958. Other references are provided in connection with our discussion of "The Theory Favoring Reinvestment" later in this chapter.

[2] See John Burr Williams, *The Theory of Investment Value*, Harvard University Press, Cambridge, Mass., 1938.

book value, while that of New Hampshire was only 8 percent less—although average earnings on book value were 12.5 percent and 4.3 percent, respectively.

In 1948, after considerable prodding by stockholders, New Amsterdam Casualty began a gradual advance in its dividend from the $1 rate it had maintained for several years previously. In early 1950 the dividend rate had reached $1.40, and the price of the shares had risen to 42, within a few points of that of New Hampshire.

Tempering Considerations. Although investors have prized dividends, they have never expected companies to pay out the full amount of their earnings. It is considered sound corporate policy, and thus in the interests of the shareholders, to retain an appreciable part of an average year's earnings for various protective and constructive purposes. These include (1) strengthening the capital position—i.e., the ratio of current assets to current liabilities, or of stock equity to debt; (2) modernizing the plant for greater efficiency; (3) providing capital for expansion; and (4) building up a surplus for "rainy-day" contingencies, and to maintain the dividend rate in bad years. This heterogeneous list supplies no clue in itself as to what portion of the earnings of a given company should best be withheld from the stockholders.

The actual practice seems to have developed somewhat as follows: Over the six decades from 1871 to 1930, a ratio of roughly two-thirds payout and one-third retention became accepted as normal or standard; hence the directors of most companies tended to follow some such proportion in their dividend policy, and to depart from it only for rather compelling reasons. However, changes in economic conditions since 1929 have produced corresponding changes in over-all dividend policies. As the figures in Table 35-2 indicate, companies drew on accumulated surpluses to pay dividends in excess of earnings during the Depression of the early 1930's. During the war years the payout swung back toward the two-thirds "normal." In the period since 1945 the great need of funds for corporate expansion, accentuated dollarwise by price inflation, has held down dividend disbursements, and may have created a new "normal" payout of between 50 and 60 percent rather than the former 60 to 70 percent.[3]

---

[3] It is to be pointed out that in contrast, J. Lintner, in an extensive study entitled, "Distribution of Incomes of Corporations among Dividends, Retained Earnings, and Taxes," *American Economic Review*, vol. 46, no. 2, May 1956, p. 112, has stated, "This work . . . indicates that the common explanation of low payout ratios in the postwar period as being due primarily to *ad hoc* current allowance for spectacularly large investment outlays misses the essential point involved. The evidence available indicates that the lag in the adjustment to new higher levels of profits was no more sluggish than would have been expected on the basis of patterns of behavior established between World War I and World War II, nor is there evidence that the normal or target or equilibrium ratio of dividends to profits for corporations as a whole is any different in the postwar years than during the preceding quarter century."

These changed conditions and their effect on dividend policy were recognized explicitly in the 1949 annual report of General Motors Corporation, in the following words:

General Motors has always believed in a liberal dividend policy, and dividends in the pre-war years reflected this. During the years 1946–49 capital requirements increased greatly. The factors that were responsible for this were the inflation that had occurred since the war, the need for replacement and modernization of facilities for more efficient operations, and some expansion of facilities to take care of the high demand for goods. In order to meet the increase in capital needs it was necessary not only to obtain new capital but also to retain in the business a much higher percentage of earnings than pre-war.

A statement of both general and specific dividend policy appears in the 1960 annual report of American Brake Shoe Company, as follows:

The company's policy on dividend payments is to give shareholders reasonable dividend stability by relating the dividend rate to long-term trends in earnings, rather than allowing them to fluctuate annually. Within this context our policy is to pay out an average of 50% of long-term earnings as dividends. In years of relatively poor earnings the amount paid out may be greater than 50% as it was in 1958 and 1960. [The actual payout for 1951–1960 averaged 60 percent.]

Table 35-2. Payout Rates of Selected Corporate Groups, Five- and Ten-year Spans, 1871–1959

	Cowles Commission Standard & Poor's Composite Stocks, percent	Dow-Jones Industrial average, percent	Moody's 200 stocks, percent	All corporations, percent
1871–1880	68*			
1881–1890	75			
1891–1900	63			
1901–1910	58			
1911–1920	55			
1921–1930	63			
1931–1935	140	155	132	†
1935–1939	69	73	73	103
1940–1944	67	66	59	48
1945–1949	53	53	51	41
1950–1954	55	59	55	49
1955–1959	52	64	56	55

* The payout ratio is reduced by zero figures for non-dividend-paying stocks, which were numerous in earlier years.
† Deficit reported before dividends.

The Case for Liberal Dividends. Before adverting to certain newer concepts which favor low payout rates for successful and growing companies, we should develop at somewhat greater length the reasons behind the strongly held preference of investors for liberal dividends. This was based on more than the natural liking for goodly dividend checks, and on more than the down-to-earth concept that a corporation is in business to earn profits and to pay commensurate dividends to its stockholders. On the more negative side, long experience had taught investors to be somewhat mistrustful of the benefits claimed to accrue to them from re-tained and reinvested earnings. In very many cases a large accumulated surplus failed not only to produce a comparable increase in the earnings and dividends, but even to assure the continuance of the previously established rate of disbursement.

This important point will be illustrated by several examples taken from various periods during the past 30 years.

Example 1: U.S. Steel. The lack of relationship between retained earn-ings and dividend continuance is well summarized in the following fig-ures applying to the nation's largest steel company:

Profits available for the common stock, 1901–1930	$2,344,000,000
Dividends paid:	
Cash	891,000,000
Stock	203,000,000
Undistributed (and uncapitalized) earnings	1,250,000,000
Loss after preferred dividends,	
Jan. 1, 1931, to June 30, 1932	59,000,000
Common dividend passed June 30, 1932	

A year and a half of declining business was sufficient to outweigh the beneficial influence of 30 years of practically continuous reinvestment of profits. In 1933 the *preferred* dividend was reduced from the $7 to a $2 rate, and this lower payment was continued through 1935.

Example 2: Atchison, Topeka & Santa Fe Railroad. At the end of 1929, Atchison had reinvested earnings of almost $400 million. It had never failed to earn something for the stock issues since 1897. In 1931, it was paying dividends on the common at the rate of $10 per share. In 1932, although still earning something for the common, it passed the dividend entirely. After resuming common dividends in 1934, it again suspended them between 1938 and 1940, although it reported some earnings for the common in each year and still showed an accumulated surplus of over $100 per share. Dividends on Atchison Preferred may be paid only to the extent they are earned in each fiscal year ending June 30. Because of this provision, the preferred dividend was reduced in 1933 and again in 1938–1939.

Example 3: R. G. LeTourneau, Inc. This company was prosperous be-tween 1937 and 1946, during which years it earned $37 per share for the common and paid out about one-third. In 1947 it lost money and passed the common dividend. In 1946 it raised $5,100,000 by sale of a $4 pre-ferred stock at $104. In 1947 it borrowed $5,000,000 for additional working capital. In 1949, following two years of substantial losses, it passed the dividend on the preferred stock. At that time the earned surplus was considerably more than the entire preferred-stock issue, but the loan restrictions compelled suspension of the dividend.

Example 4: Douglas Aircraft Company. Over the 20-year span 1939–1958, Douglas earned a total of nearly $73 per share of common stock and paid out $34, or about 47 percent for the period. As of November 30, 1958, earned surplus exceeded $138 million. In 1958 earnings declined sharply, and in 1959 a substantial loss was suffered. As a result dividends were suspended in September 1959, although at the end of the fiscal year earned surplus still amounted to slightly over $100 million.

Retained Earnings Often Unreflected in Market Price. If reinvested earnings cannot be depended upon to increase or even to maintain dividends, it is obvious that they cannot be depended upon to reflect themselves in a corresponding increase in the average market price of the shares.

Example: This point can be illustrated from our comparison of New York Amsterdam Casualty and New Hampshire Fire, by adding figures showing the development of the average market price in relation to earnings paid and retained from 1938 to 1947 (Table 35-3). Only half

Table 35-3. Per-share Figures*

	New Amsterdam	New Hampshire
Earned, 1938–1947.............	$36.64	$18.48
Dividends.....................	8.98	19.40
Earnings retained.............	27.66	0.92(d)
Increase in average price........	13.25	0.75

* These calculations are from figures in Best's digest. They allow for the equity in unearned premiums on an overliberal basis which applies to both companies.

the reinvested earnings of New Amsterdam were reflected in an increased average price in 1947 against 1938. New Hampshire had no reinvested profits, but its market price did not decline. In fact, the over-all *realization for stockholders*—measured by dividends plus price change—was almost as great for New Hampshire as for New Amsterdam, although the latter's earnings were *twice as large.* Poor earnings and a good payout may do as well for stockholders as good earnings and a poor payout.

Some broad conclusions as to the value to stockholders in general of the earnings withheld from them can be drawn from the 68-year conspectus of corporate results in the elaborate and well-known Cowles Commission's study of common stocks. These show that between 1871 and 1938 the market price of common stocks as a whole tended to increase at a slower rate than the additions to capital by undistributed earnings.[4] Such figures supported the strongly held view that the typical dollar of reinvestment had less economic value to the stockholder than a dollar paid in dividends.[5]

Whether the same is still true is another one of the questions on which the analyst must make up his own mind. On one side, it is to be pointed out that in a large number of cases there is reason to think that the purpose of retaining earnings is primarily *defensive*—a matter of necessity impelled by competitive pressures rather than of free choice looking toward enlarged earning power. Such compulsory reinvestment cannot be expected to add much to the stockholder's real equity. Because of the prevalence of this experience, it has been natural to conclude that the only dependable earnings are those paid out in dividends, and that the retained portion should be valued at a greatly discounted rate.

On the other side, it is to be noted that the foregoing generalization implies that over the long term the return on common-stock capital as a whole should have declined gradually. Long-run data are sketchy, but our own research—involving the development of rate-of-return information for 150 major corporations over a 25-year span—and an examination of numerous studies by others do not indicate the existence of a *secular* decline in the composite experience of manufacturing corporations.[6]

At the same time, studies made by various analysts—including ourselves—have led to the somewhat surprising conclusion that for typical groups of stocks the weight in market price of $1 of distributed earnings tended to be about *four times* as great as that of $1 of retained earnings.[7]

---

[4] " . . . for the 68 years from 1871 to 1938, the average amount of earnings retained by corporations is 2.5 percent of the value of their common stocks. As previously noted, all stocks on the average advanced in price at the rate of 1.8 percent a year for the period under consideration. This means that every $2.50 of earnings retained by a corporation has, on the average, been associated with an increase of $1.80 in the value of its stock." Cowles Commission for Research in Economics, *Common-stock Indexes*, Principia Press, Inc., Bloomington, Ind., 1939, p. 42.

[5] The Cowles Commission study suggests (p. 43), as an alternative possibility, that the discrepancy was due to the undervaluation of common stocks in the market during 1871–1938. If average prices had been 39 percent higher, market values would have advanced proportionately with reinvested earnings. This view as to long-term undervaluation would find general acceptance in the early 1960's, but obviously it was not widely held in the earlier period.

[6] For example, see Machinery & Allied Products Institute, "Postwar vs. Pre-depression Profits of Manufacturing Corporations," *Capital Goods Review*, no. 25, February 1956. Calvin B. Hoover, in an article unpublished at the date of this writing, "The Marginal Efficiency of Investment, Rates of Profit on Corporate Investment and the Market Rate of Interest," holds that corporate management in making investment decisions keeps the marginal efficiency of investment relatively high. He states, "In summary, one may conclude that corporate investment decisions are not made in such a way that either the expected or the experienced rates of profit are customarily pushed to the point of equality with the market rate of interest. On the contrary, the corporate rate of profit return on investment is ordinarily maintained at more than twice the market rate of interest" (p. 24).

[7] See article by Hugh Pastoriza, "Valuing Utility Earnings Distributed and Re-

As will be explained in Chapter 37, our "standard valuation formula" reflects these relative contributions to fair value. It is still applicable, we think, to the large number of common stocks which are not considered to have significant growth possibilities.

The Dividend Record as a Qualitative Factor. The quality of a common stock, which reflects itself in the multiplier applied to current or prospective earnings and dividends, is in most cases largely determined by the dividend record. The monthly "Stock Guide" published by Standard & Poor lists as a salient item of information the year since which dividends have been continuously paid. The absence of rate reductions in the past record is perhaps as important as the presence of numerous rate advances.

The Theory Favoring Reinvestment. The emphasis on expansion of the American economy which accompanied the reduced payouts since World War II has tended to introduce some new thinking about the relative desirability of dividends vs. reinvestment.[8] In opposition to the theory that stock values are measured by expected future dividends is the "earnings theory." Two of its articulate exponents, Modigliani and Miller, hold that "as long as management is presumed to be acting in the best interests of the stockholders, retained earnings can be regarded as equivalent to a fully subscribed, pre-emptive issue of common stock. Hence, for present purposes, the division of the stream between cash dividends and retained earnings in any period is a mere detail."[9] Thus they hold that "the dividend payout would determine merely how a given return to

---

tained," in the July 1945 issue of the *Analysts Journal*. His conclusion was that undistributed earnings of utilities had a weight in relation to distributed earnings that varied with the credit of the company. In his list of 14 companies this weight ranged from 17 to 31 percent, and averaged 25 percent. The latter figure meant that $1 of retained earnings had an effect on market price equal to only 25 cents of earnings paid in dividends. An article by Harold H. Young, "Factors Influencing Utility Price Earnings Ratios," *ibid.*, January 1945, makes the same point in more general terms. For a critical view of this approach, see "Public Utility Price Earnings Rates," by H. A. Diamant, *ibid.*, first quarter 1946. Also F. P. Morrissey, "Dividend Payout and Utility Common Stock Value," *Public Utilities Fortnightly*, vol. 55, no 11, May 26, 1955.

[8] For an interesting discussion, read Philip A. Fisher, *Common Stocks and Uncommon Profits*, chap. 7, "The Hullabaloo about Dividends," Harper & Brothers, New York, 1958.

[9] Much controversy exists in regard to this concept, and the analyst and student will want to check carefully current literature. The following are some suggested references: F. Modigliani and M. H. Miller, "The Cost of Capital, Corporation Finance and the Theory of Investment," *American Economic Review*, vol. 48, no. 3, June 1958; "The Cost of Capital and the Theory of Investment: Comments and Replies," *American Economic Review*, vol. 49, no. 4, September 1959; F. Modigliani and M. H. Miller, "Leverage, Dividend Policy and the Cost of Capital," paper read at the 1960 meetings of the Econometric Society; J. Lintner, "A New Model of the Cost of Capital: Dividends, Earnings, Leverage, Expectations and Stock Prices," paper read at the 1960 meetings of the Econometric Society; and M. J. Gordon, "Risk, Debt and Share Prices," paper read at the 1960 meetings of the Econometric Society.

stockholders would be split as between current dividends and current capital gains and would not affect either the size of the total return or the current value of the shares." Basically, this theory holds that it is better—or at least as good—for the stockholder if the earnings are reinvested rather than paid out, *provided* such reinvestment can be expected to earn a rate of return as large as or larger than the earnings yield on the market price of its common stock. That is, if the corporation can earn more with retained earnings than the stockholder could earn with them in the form of dividends—which are subject in most cases to a substantial income tax—then a low payout rate (or a zero payout rate) would in theory be best for the stockholder.

For this discussion, let us define a successful company as one which has earned and is expected to earn a large enough return on the shareholders' equity to produce (or justify) an average market price for the shares in excess of their book value. Let us assume, further, that these "excess" or "premium" earnings can be maintained on a large amount of reinvested profits. The logical deduction from these assumptions is that *all* profits should be reinvested by such companies—at least up to the point, if any, where diminishing returns vitiate the premise of superior profitability. Quite a large proportion of our important companies have sold for many years substantially above their book values, and there has been no indication of inability to maintain premium market prices with respect to their reinvested profits.

Table 35-4 shows the relationship between changes in earnings, book value, and market price for the Standard & Poor's 425 Industrials between 1929 and 1959. During the 1940's earnings grew much faster than book value, but the market price lagged somewhat. During the 1950's the opposite phenomenon occurred. The rate of return on book value fell sharply, but the ratio of price to book value rose just as sharply.

Since many factors produce changes in earnings, such changes cannot fairly be divided by the increase in book value to calculate "the rate of return on reinvested profits." But our table does at least show a *lack of proof* that reinvestment by corporations *as a whole* during the "fabulous fifties" was highly profitable.[10]

On the other hand, two of our leading growth stocks—General Electric and IBM—yield much more favorable indications as to the desirability of reinvestment on their part. (Their data appear in Table 35-4.)

Our figures suggest that a fundamental difference may exist between the appropriate payout policy for average or subaverage companies and that for the exceptional growth issue. In theory, our conclusions should

---

[10] The actual average returns, by *five-year periods,* earned on their common-stock equity by the 425 industrial companies over the last three decades are as follows:

1930–1934	5.2%	1945–1949	13.8%
1935–1939	9.9	1950–1954	14.8
1940–1944	10.1	1955–1959	12.8

Table 35-4. Relationship between Earnings, Book Value, and Market Price: Standard & Poor's 425 Industrial Stocks, International Business Machines, and General Electric, Selected Dates and Periods, 1929–1959

Year	Standard & Poor's 425 Industrial Stocks					International Business Machines†					General Electric†				
	Year-end			Earnings rate on:					Earnings rate on:					Earnings rate on:	
	Earnings	Book value	Price	Book value	Price	Earnings	Year-end book value	Mean price for year	Book value	Mean price	Earnings	Year-end book value	Mean price for year	Book value	Price
1929	$1.30	$ 8.38	$16.99	15.5%	7.6%	$0.40	$ 1.22	$ 7.—	32.7%	5.7%	$0.75	$ 4.49	$23.50	16.7%	3.2%
1934	0.45	8.18	9.12	5.5	4.9	0.42	2.19	6.50	19.1	6.5	0.20	3.56	7.00	5.6	2.9
1939	0.79	8.31	12.17	9.5	6.5	0.55	2.87	8.50	19.2	6.5	0.48	3.67	12.50	13.1	3.8
1944	0.78	9.74	13.05	8.0	6.0	0.59	3.87	11.50	15.2	5.1	0.59	4.38	12.50	13.5	4.7
1949	2.42	13.74	16.49	17.6	14.7	2.01	7.76	30.50	25.9	6.6	1.47	7.11	12.50	20.7	11.8
1954	2.88	20.91	37.24	12.5	7.7	2.81	14.23	71.00	19.7	4.0	2.36	11.48	39.00	20.6	6.1
1959	3.52	30.56	64.50	11.2	5.4	7.97	45.95	408.50	17.3	2.0	3.19	16.09	87.00	19.8	3.7

Period	Standard & Poor's 425 Industrial Stocks					International Business Machines†					General Electric†				
	Increments			Ratio of increments		Increments			Ratio of increments		Increments			Ratio of increments	
	Earnings	Book value	Price	Earnings to book	Earnings to price	Earnings	Year-end book value	Mean price for year	Earnings to book	Earnings to price	Earnings	Year-end book value		Earnings to book	Earnings to price
1929–1949	$1.12	$ 5.36	*	20.9%	—%	$1.61	$ 6.54	$ 23.50	24.6%	6.8%	$0.72	$ 2.62	*	27.5%	—%
1939–1949	1.63	5.43	$ 4.32	30.0	37.7	1.46	4.89	22.00	29.8	6.6	0.99	3.44	$ 0.00	28.8	—
1949–1959	1.10	16.82	48.01	6.5	2.3	5.96	38.19	378.00	15.6	1.6	1.72	8.98	74.50	19.2	2.3
1949–1954	0.46	7.17	20.75	6.4	2.2	0.80	6.47	40.50	12.4	2.0	0.89	4.37	26.50	20.4	3.4
1954–1959	0.64	9.65	27.26	6.6	2.3	5.16	31.72	337.50	16.3	1.5	0.83	4.61	48.00	18.0	1.7

* Decrease.
† Adjusted for stock dividends and splits through 1960.

point to complete retention by expanding companies, since it would be hard to establish any percentage figure beyond which the payment of cash dividends becomes inherently more advantageous. It should be pointed out here that the undoubted need of some owners for cash income from their shares is not a valid argument against complete reinvestment of profits. For it is assumed that these dollars will have a premium value in the market when reinvested; hence a shareholder will fare better by selling off corresponding amounts of his holdings than by receiving the money in dividends—and he will have much more favorable tax effects as well. Such cashing-in where needed could be readily facilitated by the practice of paying periodic small stock dividends to represent the profits plowed back.

Application of the New Theory. The higher the average multiplier of earnings in the stock list, the greater the proportion of issues which presumably should retain all or nearly all their profits. For—presumably again—the rate of return on reinvestment will substantially exceed, in the typical case, what the stockholder could earn on the same money received in dividends. A good corporate-earnings picture and opportunities for profitable expansion generally go together. Thus the favorable business and stock-market developments of the 1950's have greatly extended the field of companies for which, in theory at least, low dividends and high reinvestment would appear the best policy for the stockholders. Carried to its logical conclusion, this analysis would suggest that nearly all really successful companies should follow a program of full reinvestment of profits, and that cash dividends should be paid only to the extent that opportunities for profitable expansion or diversification were not present.

The inferences drawn above are stated in a provisional and qualified manner. One reason is that we are by no means certain that the rate of future return on additions to capital can be equated with past returns or calculated by the investor with true dependability. This uncertainty, which is a very real one, will make it more difficult for stockholders generally—and their alter ego, "the stock market"—to abandon their ingrained preference for cash dividends in favor of the theoretical advantages of retained profits.[11] The security analyst, in turn, must give major weight to investors' partialities, as expressed in the market itself, in evaluating the dividend factor.

Low Payout Accepted in Some Areas. As might be expected, the low payout doctrine has received its first full acceptance by the stock market only in a rather limited number of cases. These belong in two quite different classes. The first comprises highly dynamic companies which are expected to show unusually high growth rates in the future and

---

[11] Note that one of the tests of a growth stock contained in *Fortune's* article of April 1959, "Those Delicious 'Growth Stocks'," is that the company should either be paying dividends or be expected to do so in two to three years and that dividends should increase with an increase in earnings.

which enjoy unprecedented price-earnings ratios. The second is a specialized group of Canadian investment companies or funds which have been sold to tax-conscious investors on the basis of the important tax advantages derived from a no-distribution policy.

Examples of the First Class: An outstanding example here is Superior Oil, which in 1957 sold at 2,000 per share on $44.71 of earnings and *no dividend*. In 1960 it sold at 2,165, paying $7.50 out of earnings of $51.19. Texas Instruments, similarly, advanced from 5 in 1954 to 256 in 1959, without ever paying dividends (and with earnings rising from 42 cents to $3.59), while Polaroid sold at 261 in 1960, with a dividend rate of only 5 cents quarterly and earnings of $3.

Some of the recognized growth companies have supplemented a low cash payout by more or less periodic stock dividends. IBM paid stock dividends of 5 percent in 1949–1953 and $2\frac{1}{2}$ percent in 1954, 1956, 1958, and 1959.[12] In 1959 the earnings were $7.97, the cash dividend $2.03, and the high price 488. Rohm & Haas sold at 780 in 1960, earned $18.47, and paid $3 in cash plus 2 percent in stock. In only a few cases have these stock dividends followed a clearly enunciated and well-understood policy. At a later point we shall give expression to our strong views about the desirability of a well-defined and consistently followed stock-dividend policy for growth companies.

Examples of the Second Class: There are at least nine "non-resident-owned," or "NRO," Canadian Investment Companies, the shares of which have been sold in the United States under special provisions of the Canadian tax law and special regulations by the SEC. The first of these was Scudder Fund of Canada, Ltd., organized in 1954. At the end of 1959 total assets of the nine funds aggregated $396 million, the largest being Investors Group Canadian Fund, Ltd., with $114 million of resources.

These companies have a favorable tax status in Canada with respect to their own investment income and security profits. They are not required to pay dividends to their shareholders. Consequently, they have been sold on the basis of an announced policy of no disbursements in the future. All the stockholders' gains will accrue to them in the form of an increased value for their shares and will be realized by redemption of shares at such increased value.

The typical stockholder is expected to retain his shares through the years and thus escape payment of all income taxes thereon. But it would be possible for a stockholder owning, say, 100 or more shares to cash in each year the equivalent of the year's increase in value (or investment income alone) by redeeming a proportionate small number of his shares. The income tax on such redemption would be quite negligible in the early years, and would slowly build up toward a maximum of 25 percent of the year's income—or half the holder's bracket rate, if lower.

[12] In addition, there was a series of stock splits: 5 for 4 in 1954 and 1956, 2 for 1 in 1957, and 3 for 2 in 1959.

It is somewhat anomalous that these shares could readily be sold to the public by pointing out the tax advantages of a no-dividend policy, whereas the suspension of a previously established cash dividend or even its replacement by an equivalent or better in stock will invariably have an unfavorable effect on the market price.[13] This contradiction illustrates the ambivalent and transitional attitude of the financial community on the dividend question.[14]

Dividend Policies of the Future. We expect that, little by little, progress will be made in the direction of dividend policies best suited to (1) our modern economic climate and our tax laws; (2) the type of company involved; and (3) the varying requirements of its large and small stockholders. In the case of companies with relatively mediocre or uncertain growth prospects—probably the majority of the thousands of publicly held concerns—the shareholders will continue to favor as liberal cash dividends as conditions will permit. To a great extent, therefore, earnings retention will be viewed as a *defensive* measure, designed to keep the company in the competitive running, and will not be expected to produce commensurate increases in earning power. But to the dynamic enterprises, which have a recognized ability to earn satisfactory amounts on increasing capital, the stock market will accord wide leeway in their choice between payout and retention. The judicious use of periodic stock dividends will make a low cash payout palatable to the stockholders who need cash income.

A significant area where a change in policy may eventually take place is that of the growing public utilities which constantly sell additional shares to their stockholders, thus taking back the money paid them in cash dividends. We expect that this unnecessary exposure to double income tax will gradually be eliminated through adoption of a suitable stock-dividend policy, assisted at the beginning perhaps by underwriting arrangements to cushion the market effect of the transition. We discuss this point in Chapter 36.

Security analysts should develop two related prima-facie tests to determine the companies for which a low cash payout is advantageous and those for which it is disadvantageous to the owners. These tests are first, the rate of return on the book value of the common-stock capital and second, the ratio of average market price to book value of the shares. Where these ratios are high, reinvestment of profits should generally be

[13] An example is Caterpillar Tractor, which in June 1953 reduced its cash dividend from a $3 to a $2 rate plus declaration of a 4 percent stock dividend. Despite the company's statement that the stockholders' position was thus improved, the price of the shares quickly fell about 10 percent.

[14] For other examples of an announced no-dividend policy by successful companies, the reader is referred to Ling-Temco and Tidewater Oil Companies in 1960. The latter first replaced its cash dividend by periodic stock dividends and then paid none at all. In each case it offered "outside" stockholders the option to exchange their common shares for the same amount of $1.20 preferred. Most of the outside stock was so exchanged.

welcomed by shareholders. Where low, it should be either objected to or accepted as compelled by competitive necessities—in either case recognized as a price-depressant factor. As we shall develop later (Chapter 50), it is on this point, as much as on any other, that stockholders are entitled to full and frank explanations from their managements.

TREATMENT OF DIVIDENDS IN THE VALUATION PROCESS

The transitional aspects of the dividend element in investment, discussed above, make it especially difficult to lay down hard and fast rules for evaluating the dividend factor at this time. We can identify two groups of common stocks about which fairly definite statements may be made. The first is that of recognized growth stocks, which have sold for some time at high multipliers of current earnings. In this group low payouts are customary and prove no handicap to the market price. Once an analyst has classified a given company in that select category he might best ignore the dividend factor entirely in his valuation—on the convenient theory that whatever payout the management elects to follow is presumably best suited to the stockholders' interests. Thus expected earning power would become the sole criterion of value of such concerns, perhaps tempered directly or indirectly by some consideration of the comparatively low asset values.[15]

For the fairly large section of the corporate list which does not earn a thoroughly satisfactory return on its capital—and which therefore tends to sell most of the time at a market-to-book-value ratio below the average for the major industrial shares (e.g., Standard & Poor's 425 industrial stocks)—the dividend rate should retain its traditional importance. The analyst should assume, as the stock market has always assumed, that the undistributed portion of the earnings of such "nonprosperous companies" has a much smaller value to the owners than the part paid in dividends. The formula, to be developed in detail in Chapter 38, will take this important relationship into account.

The "Middle Group." A large number of concerns do not fall readily into the classification of either "recognized growth companies" or "below-average companies." For such a typical middle-ground enterprise, theoretical considerations might justify a small payout and a large reinvestment, while the stock market continues to prefer as liberal a dividend as possible. In this area the analyst will have to work out some compromise position in his treatment of the dividend factor. It is doubtful whether any formula, simple or complicated, would prove of value here.

Still another problem is presented in the treatment of periodic stock dividends which purport to capitalize a portion of the past year's undistributed earnings. We shall treat this question in the next chapter.

---

[15] For our views of the theoretical relationship between this "earning-power" concept of value and the "discounted-value-of-future-dividends" theory of value, see Appendix Note 11, p. 741.

CHAPTER THIRTY-SIX

TECHNICAL ASPECTS OF THE DIVIDEND RATE.

STOCK DIVIDENDS

The method of paying dividends has a bearing on the investor's evaluation of the amount paid. What may be called the standard type of dividend is paid in cash at quarterly intervals, and no part is designated as an "extra." In a few cases dividends are paid monthly; while this appears to be welcomed by many stockholders, it is not likely to be asked for or adopted as general practice, because of the expense involved.[1]

A small number of companies pay semiannual dividends. This practice was formerly prevalent among insurance companies.[2] No basic objection can be voiced to semiannual payments, we believe, especially since they correspond to the standard interval for paying interest on bonds. However, a small number of companies pay their dividend only once a year. This is a definite drawback from the standpoint of stockholders, not only for the financial inconvenience involved, but more substantially because of the doubt it casts upon the dependability of the rate. An annual dividend is almost the same as a sporadic dividend, paid whenever the directors think it is time to do something for the lowly stockholder. Thus, in the case of companies paying once a year it becomes difficult for the analyst to give normal weight to the amount paid, and the valuation of the issue must suffer accordingly.[3]

The Extra Payment. In recent years the practice of paying part of the dividend in the form of an "extra" has become increasingly prevalent. This is considered a means of disbursing a fair portion of the unusually large profits, coupled with an implied warning that the extras will be discontinued if earnings decline. Extra dividends complicate the analyst's

---

[1] Wm. Wrigley Company, Inc., is the notable exponent of the monthly dividend, having paid not less than once in every month since the beginning of 1912, with the exception of about two years during World War II when the banks and fiscal authorities asked the company to make dividends bimonthly. In 1960 American Home Products and Colorado Central Power also paid monthly dividends.

[2] Examples of semiannual dividends in 1960 include Burry Biscuit, Canadian Bank of Commerce, and Camden Fire Association.

[3] Cf. the annual dividend of Northern Pacific Railway in 1943–1949 and its low average price in those years. For a number of years prior to 1962 Hygrade Foods, Inc., paid annual dividends.

494

task of determining and evaluating the dividend rate. This is particularly true if he places his main emphasis upon the current situation and upon expected near-term changes. The difficulty appears in the simple matter of showing in the newspapers or elsewhere what the "present dividend rate" is.[4] In our valuation approach, the emphasis is not placed on *current* earnings and dividends but upon those fairly expectable over a period of years in the future. While this requires more estimating or prediction than many analysts are willing to embark upon, it has the slight advantage of minimizing the confusion between regular and extra dividends. For the appraiser needs only to estimate the total disbursements expectable over the future period, without bothering to distinguish between a regular and an extra portion thereof.

A conspectus of dividend practices in 1960 may be gained from Table 36-1, which summarizes the types of payment made on the first 1,000 common stocks appearing in Standard & Poor's *Monthly Stock Guide.*

Table 36-1. Types of Dividends Paid in 1960

Regular cash dividends only..............	576 companies
Regular and extra cash dividends..........	104
Cash and stock dividends................	77
Stock dividends only....................	34
No dividend...........................	209
Total..............................	1,000 companies

Waiving of Dividends. One of the newer developments in corporate finance is the voluntary waiving of dividends that would normally be paid on shares owned by controlling interests. This phenomenon is a direct outgrowth of the heavy personal income tax on upper-bracket incomes, and is not without relationship to the broader, countertraditional movement away from cash dividends.

Example 1: Helene Curtis Industries, Inc., paid no dividends on its class *B* stock (held by the management) in 1956–1961, although it paid dividends on the publicly owned class *A* shares. Both classes are entitled to the same treatment.

Example 2: Max Factor Company paid larger dividends on its class *A* shares in 1950–1960 than on its management-owned common, although it could have required the class *A* shares to be converted into common stock after January 1, 1950—thus equalizing all rights of both classes.

Example 3: Directors holding about 40 percent of the stock of Air Control Products in April 1961 waived their rights to a 12½-cent quarterly dividend declared by the board. In this case the action grew out of dividend restrictions imposed by an insurance-company loan,

[4] On this point we suggest that the rate shown be the current regular rate on an annual basis, except where extras have been paid with no recent decrease in the regular rate. In the latter case, it would be preferable to show the total disbursed in the past twelve months, including extras, if such total is larger than the current annual regular rate. The amount shown should be marked as "including extras."

which otherwise would have compelled a reduction in the rate of dividend.

In some of these proceedings the arithmetic is interesting. It can be shown that a majority holder may gain more by waiving a dividend than by taking it. Take the hypothetical case of stockholders owning 80 percent of a company and belonging collectively in the 80 percent tax bracket, who would be entitled to $100,000 in dividends. If they took this sum, they would retain $20,000 after tax. If they waived it, it would be added to the company's surplus, their share therein being increased by $80,000. If this amount is realized later through a sale of shares, their gain after capital-gain tax would be $60,000. The important point here is that they retain control of the money left in the company, and in that sense it is equivalent to money paid out to the other shareholders.

STOCK DIVIDENDS AND SPLIT-UPS

In recent years an increasing number of companies have split their shares by one of several means, including the payment of a large stock dividend. In addition, many companies have followed the practice of paying small stock dividends—not equivalent to split-ups—with more or less regularity. Our Table 36-1 indicates that about one out of seven dividend-paying companies paid some dividend in stock in 1960. These practices involve a number of complicating features and also more than one controversial question of policy. We shall discuss these matters as briefly as their importance—and our strong views on some of them—will permit.

The Stock Split. The purpose of a stock split is to rearrange the common-stock issue by increasing substantially the number of shares outstanding through a free distribution to or exchange by each stockholder. The three ways of doing this are as follows:

A. By a reduction in par value. This involves no change in the total dollar value of the capital stock.

Example: Allied Chemical reduced its par from $18 to $9 in 1956 in order to effect a 2-for-1 split.

B. By issuing a larger number of no-par shares in place of either par-value or no-par shares. Normally this also involves no increase in the stated capital.

Example: Universal Leaf Tobacco split its no-par stock 2 for 1 in 1961 without changing its stated value.

C. By payment of a stock dividend. This usually involves an increase in the stated capital by transfer from earned surplus.

Example: Franklin Life Insurance Company made a series of six stock splits between 1944 and 1957, by paying stock dividends on its $4 par stock ranging from 25 to 100 percent. Each required a transfer from earned surplus to capital.

D. Combinations of par-value reductions and stock dividends occur from time to time.

Example: U.S. Playing Card Company made a 4-for-1 split in 1959 by both reducing the par from $10 to $5 and paying a 100 percent stock dividend, which doubled the stated capital.

One of the reasons for preferring a reduction in par value to a stock dividend may be that the earned surplus is insufficient for a large distribution on the order, say, of 300 percent of the stated capital. But the method used for making the split-up is of small practical importance, and we shall not dwell upon the various alternatives.[5]

The legitimate purpose of a stock split is to reduce the market price of the shares to a level more attractive to the investing public. There appears to be an optimal level of market price—perhaps in the range between 25 and 50, or thereabouts—which avoids, on the one hand, the stigma of a "low-priced, ergo, speculative issue" and on the other, the practical drawback of high-priced shares. This drawback relates chiefly, we think, to the amount of money required to buy a "round" (100-share) lot of the issue and thus to escape the slight extra expense and the sense of inferiority associated with odd-lot purchases.[6] The establishment of such an optimal price range for the shares is expected to increase the public interest therein, add to the number of shareholders, and raise to some degree the equivalent market price of the issue.

The announcement of a stock split is often followed or immediately preceded by increased trading and a quick advance in the shares. A good deal of this activity may be ascribed to the normal behavior of speculative elements in the stock market, who are on the lookout for some promising piece of news. Often the rise is associated with the declaration or the expectation of a higher aggregate cash-dividend rate, and this too may often have a very pronounced effect upon the market price.

Example: The outstanding illustration of this conjunction in recent years was the 3-for-1 split of American Telephone and Telegraph in 1959, accompanied by the first increase in its cash dividend since 1922—from $9 on the old shares to $3.30 on the new. By consequence, the price of the stock more than doubled between 1958 and early 1961, although the cash dividend advanced 10 percent and the earnings about 20 percent.

[5] Perhaps mention should be made here of the "reverse split," by which the number of shares is reduced prorata instead of increased. The purpose of this is usually to correct an unmanageably large number of shares selling at what is considered to be an undignifiedly low price. The celebrated example of this is the 1-for-4 reverse split of General Motors in 1924. Salem-Brosius, Inc. (steel mill equipment) reduced its shares from over 15 million to 631,000 by a 1-for-25 reverse split in 1953.

[6] It may be pointed out that 100 shares of each of a diversified list of 15 stocks selling at an average price of about 33 would represent an investment of some $50,000.

Questionable Stock Splits. The stock split as a vehicle for attracting speculative interest to an issue sometimes recommends itself to managements, although their shares are selling too low to qualify them for such treatment by logical standards.

Example 1: In 1955 Dejay Stores split its stock 3 for 2 when the shares were quoted at about 11. The new stock later fell below 2.

Example 2: Hytron Radio & Electronics doubled its shares in 1950 by a 100 percent stock dividend, when they were selling at about 8.

Recommended Policy on Stock Splits. The right kind of directorate will always seek to reduce to a minimum the purely speculative effects of any action taken by it. We think that the objectionable features of stock splits could be pretty well removed if each board would enunciate clearly at an appropriate time, the conditions under which it could be expected to split the shares. As an illustration, such a statement could read as follows:

The shares will be split at least 3 for 2 if (*a*) the price has ruled above $100 per share for more than a year, and if (*b*) the company can expect to pay a dividend of not less than $1 per share on the new shares.

The important point here is not the precise policy to be adopted, but rather the adoption of any policy which is clearly stated, is reasonable in its terms, and can be depended on by the public. Such a declaration should remove the elements of uncertainty and surprise which have invested the stock split with much of its speculative character.

The Nonsplit Stock Dividend. Stock dividends of relatively small size—say, under 20 percent—are not considered to represent a recapitalization or split-up. They are subject to special accounting rules, which we shall discuss later. Such small stock dividends have become increasingly frequent, and their vogue is indicated by our figures in Table 36-1. Their method of use has been anything but systematized. In most cases they supplement cash dividends; but the policy under which they are declared is rarely stated, and the practice is variable and often quite arbitrary. Often a growing company will pay nothing but stock dividends, as part of an announced policy of retaining all earnings for expansion. More often the substitution of stock dividends for cash dividends takes place when earnings have fallen off. The majority of companies that use small stock dividends declare them more or less regularly. In the cases where they have become annual or more frequent events, they are often referred to as "periodic stock dividends."

A Recommended Stock-dividend Policy. We believe that periodic stock dividends can contribute greatly to sound corporate finance and to satisfactory stockholder experience, *provided* that their use is properly conceived and applied by the management and is clearly understood by the owners. In our view, a policy of periodic stock dividends should meet the following four requirements:

1. The stock dividend should represent a stated amount of *recent earnings* which have been reinvested in the business.

2. The management should be confident that the reinvested earnings so capitalized will add about proportionately to the company's future profits.

3. The amount of such reinvested earnings should be measured by the market value of the stock dividend at the time of declaration.

4. The dividends should be declared in accordance with a clearly expressed statement of policy, repeated sufficiently often to be understood at all times by the shareholders. Any departure from the expressed policy should be adequately justified.

The typical stock-dividend policy of the kind recommended will involve a dividend declared at about the end of the year, with a market value not exceeding the undistributed earnings for such year. The declaration of an amount significantly lower than the undistributed earnings would indicate a cautious view of the directors as to the future earning power of the plowed-back profits. Small fractional amounts could be carried over to the next year, as could the entire dividend if it falls under, say, 2 percent.

Only a handful of companies, among the hundreds resorting to stock dividends, pursue a policy closely resembling the one we recommend. These include Commonwealth Edison, the Government Employees Insurance Group, Purex Corporation, Ltd., and the Franklin National Bank of Long Island.[7] The following is quoted from page 11 of the 1960 annual report of Government Employees Insurance Company, as a complete statement of cash dividend, stock dividend, and split-up policy:

Dividends. For more than a decade our Company has had a three-pronged policy with respect to the payment of dividends:

(1) To pay cash dividends to stockholders in an amount substantially equivalent to our annual net investment income after applicable taxes;

(2) To pay periodic stock dividends in an amount which, at market value, is generally equivalent to the undistributed earnings for the preceding year, thus providing a sound and steadily growing capital structure for expanding operations; and

(3) To split the capital stock of the Company when such action is deemed to be in the best interests of the stockholders and the Company, taking into account the market price of the stock, the cash dividend rate and other pertinent factors.[8]

[7] This banks states its policy as payment of dividends in cash and stock equal to about 70 percent of earnings (1961 report, p. 19). However, the net addition to reserves for possible loan losses is not deducted from the Net Operating Earnings. After such reserve addition the total payments in 1961 exceeded 90 percent of profits.

[8] The report adds that in accordance with the announced policy, the company split its stock 3 for 2 by a 50 percent stock dividend; raised the cash dividend by continuing the 25-cent quarterly rate on the new shares; and declared a stock dividend of 2½ percent in January 1961, which at the adjusted market price of $90.73 per share capitalized $4,632,000 of undistributed earnings for 1960. This sum slightly exceeded the reported net profit, less cash dividends but not counting important additional credits for the year.

Objections to Stock Dividends. Most academic writers on the subject appear opposed to stock dividends of any kind. They claim that such dividends are only pieces of paper which give the shareholders nothing they did not own before in somewhat different form; that they involve expense to the issuer, and inconvenience and possible added costs to the recipients; that they delude stockholders and create unwarranted speculative interest in the stock.[9] The subject is thus controversial. We have space only for a highly compressed statement of our views thereon.[10]

We agree that stock dividends can be and have been misused. The chief misdemeanor has been the continued payment of stock dividends with market value substantially greater than the reinvested earnings for the period. Shareholders have considered such market value equivalent to a current and continued dividend return, when, in fact, the dividends were largely a dilution of capital. This was one of the prevalent financial abuses of the 1920's.[11] To a great extent, although not entirely, dangers of this sort have been obviated by stricter accounting and Stock Exchange rules. The type of policy we have recommended should not give rise to any mistaken inferences as to what the stock dividend represents.

Items of expense and inconvenience are undoubtedly of minor importance in the context, and their weight should best be appraised in relation to the basic question—which is whether a stock dividend of any kind can serve a useful purpose. We agree that the stock dividend gives the shareholder only what he had before, but in a different form. To our mind "the different form" is the key to the matter. The form in which the stockholder holds his investment *through time* is of great importance to him. This may be shown easily by assuming an extreme case. Suppose that a company refused to alter the number of shares of stock outstanding under any circumstances which did not change the prorata interest of each stockholder. If it needed more money for the business, it would *assess* the owners—i.e., make them supply the funds without receiving additional shares therefor—or simply withhold all cash dividends until it accumulated all the money it wanted from earnings. Neither of these devices, while "logical" enough, would be satisfactory to most stockholders. As against the first, they would want additional shares to represent the additional money they put up. As against the second—suspension of all dividends—nearly all stockholders would prefer to receive regular cash dividends plus the right to subscribe to additional shares and thereby return the dividend money to the company.

[9] For expressions of these adverse viewpoints, see "Stock Dividends Are Lemons, Not Melons," by S. H. Sosnick, in *California Management Review*, Winter 1961; also, letter of Dr. Neil Carothers of Lehigh University, in *Commercial and Financial Chronicle*, Dec. 10, 1953, p. 2255.

[10] These appear at length in two articles by Benjamin Graham in *Barron's* for Aug. 3 and 10, 1953.

[11] See our discussion of the North American Company's policy in 1923–1932 on pp. 446–447 of the 1951 edition.

But here is the crucial factor in regard to periodic stock dividends. The combination of cash dividends plus subscription rights—which is the standard practice of most public utility companies—is actually almost identical in its consequences with the payment of periodic stock dividends equivalent in value to the shares otherwise offered for subscription. The "almost" refers to one important difference that greatly favors the stock dividends—namely, that no income tax is imposed on receipt of the latter, while stockholders must pay full tax on the cash dividends, even though they are turning the same money back to the company to pay for additional stock.

It is true, of course, that the stockholders have the option of selling their subscription rights if they do not want to buy the additional shares —i.e., if they need or want to retain the cash dividends for other purposes. Again, precisely the same consequences will follow from the *sale of the stock dividend,* except that such sale will be subject, typically, to a negligible income tax as compared with that involved in the receipt of cash dividends plus the sale of subscription rights.[12]

In theory, a stockholder receiving neither cash nor stock dividends could realize the same amount of cash by selling off a small part of his original shares, presumably at a price per share enhanced by the retained earnings. But in practice, this is usually highly inconvenient, if not downright impossible; and since the price of the shares is almost certain to be lower because of the absence of a dividend, instead of higher because of the increase in book value, stockholders generally find the sale of shares much less palatable than the sale of a stock dividend. Thus, while the prorata interest of a stockholder in the company would remain the same if he sold some of his old shares, as against receiving and selling additional shares on subscription or through a stock dividend, the *form* his investment takes under the first arrangement would be contrary to all his preferences.

If the above reasoning is correct, several consequences follow: First, a periodic stock dividend is shown to have virtually the same effect and justification as the issuance of additional shares to the stockholders for cash. This justification consists largely in the convenience and attractiveness of receiving additional shares to represent an additional investment, as against having to rely upon a greater underlying value for the original shares. Second, the periodic stock-dividend device has an important advantage over the subscription-rights device now in common use by most public utilities and many industrial companies. The latter could be characterized as an entirely unnecessary arrangement especially invented to subject earnings to a second (personal) income tax, even though they are needed by and returned to the business.

The investment community—which includes stockholders, their financial advisers, and corporate managements—is by no means prepared as

[12] See Appendix Note 12, p. 742, for illustrative calculations on this score.

yet to accept and to act on the above reasoning. Few appear to have thought the question through; most have let the issue go by default, for lack of attention. Those who might acknowledge that a straight stock-dividend policy is logically more advantageous than the cash-dividends-and-rights combination will still claim that it is impracticable, because investors prefer the old arrangement and would show their displeasure at the new one by selling their shares and depressing their price.

Commonwealth Edison Company was the first public-utility enterprise to make an explicitly reasoned, although partial, move in the direction of replacing cash dividends and rights by stock dividends. Prior to 1958, the company followed the standard policy of raising the cash dividend every two or three years and offering subscription rights from time to time. In 1958 it announced its new policy of keeping the cash dividend unchanged at $2 and supplementing it by annual stock dividends about equal in value to the year's undistributed earnings. Against 1960 profits of $3.86 per share, it paid $2 in cash and a 2 percent stock dividend, equivalent to about $1.85 per share. Thus the cash payout of 52 percent was far below the industry practice. However, investors have accepted this arrangement with satisfaction, as is shown by the comparatively high price-earnings ratio for the shares—which exceeded 20 times in early 1961.

The Optional Dividend. No doubt the most acceptable method of dealing with investor preference would be to give each stockholder the option of taking dividends either in cash or in stock of equivalent value, as he preferred. However, the income tax law states that any such optional dividend shall be taxable at its cash equivalent to all recipients, on the theory that those taking stock are first getting cash and then buying stock with it. Nonetheless, optional dividends are in effect, essentially, with many mutual funds, chiefly with respect to their capital-gain dividends but in some cases applying to their regular dividends as well.[13]

By means of a recapitalization plan in 1956, Citizens Utilities Company gave its stockholders the choice of taking a new class *A* common issue which would receive only stock dividends, or a class *B* issue which would receive cash dividends—both of equivalent value. The class *A* shares were made convertible, share for share, into class *B*. About 75 percent of the stock was exchanged for class *A*, indicating the strong preference of many investors for a nontaxable stock-dividend issue, if they could be sure that its market price would not suffer from the absence of cash dividends. Perhaps more impressive is the fact that the stock-dividend issue has sold regularly at a premium of about 10 percent above the cash-dividend issue. Up to the end of 1961 the United States Treasury succeeded in blocking other plans of the Citizens Utilities type.[14]

[13] In April 1961, City Stores Company declared such an optional dividend, payable either as 15 cents in cash or in one-ninety-fourth of a new share.

[14] A case study of the Graduate School of Business Administration of Harvard Uni-

Financial ideas and practices change much more slowly than those of industry. Many of our investment attitudes are preserved intact from the days of no SEC and no or small income tax. The development away from emphasis on cash dividends toward emphasis on expected growth of earnings has been an uneven one up to now and has shown itself chiefly—and at times unsoundly—in the more speculative area of the stock market. We are hopeful that the true function of periodic stock dividends will become more universally understood in future years, and that they will be adopted, *under proper conditions and in proper amounts,* by an increasing number of companies. For this to happen, the whole question of dividend policy will have to be approached in the same open-minded, unprejudiced fashion in which a good management approaches all other aspects of corporate policy. In addition, managements will have to take the lead in educating their stockholders on the subject of what policy is most in their interest.

We believe also that initial investor opposition to a soundly conceived stock-dividend plan, in place of cash dividends accompanied by subscription rights, could be readily overcome by a gradual transition, fortified by an underwriting or purchase offer for stock dividends which will give each holder the definite possibility of getting at least as much cash income as previously. Furthermore, there are additional ways of instituting a two-class capitalization scheme, which are not as likely to be opposed by Internal Revenue Service as was the Citizens Utilities model.

Stock-dividend Policies of the Present. In the light of the above extended discussion the student may be better able to consider and appraise the highly variable stock-dividend policies currently in use. We exclude herefrom the larger stock dividends which are equivalent to a stock split. The New York Stock Exchange, in its statement of July 21, 1955, set the dividing line at a 25 percent distribution. The revised Accounting Research Bulletins of AICPA, dated 1953, deal with the subject in Chapter 7, and set the demarcation line at "say, 20 percent or 25 percent." The common point of both pronouncements is that the payment of a non-split stock dividend should be accompanied by the transfer of an amount equal to the fair (usually market) value of such dividend from earned surplus to capital account. In addition, the New York Stock Exchange statement requires the following:

A notice should be sent to stockholders with the distribution advising them of the amount capitalized per share, the aggregate amount thereof, the relation of such amount to current undistributed earnings, the account or accounts to which such aggregate has been charged and credited, the reason for paying

---

versity, published in 1959, discusses the Citizens Utility two-series plan in great detail, including the controversy with the Internal Revenue Service, finally resolved in favor of Citizens as a unique case.

the stock dividend and that the sale of the dividend shares would reduce their proportionate equity in the company.

The reference to "the relation of such aggregate amount to the current undistributed earnings" might imply that such stock dividends are to be kept within the amounts available therefor out of "current" profits—presumably of the related fiscal year. But while listed companies now follow, as they must, the prescribed accounting procedure as to the balance-sheet treatment of those stock dividends,[15] they do not always observe the implied limitation with respect to current profits. In many cases the value of the stock dividend exceeds the earnings available from the current or preceding year.

Example: Automatic Canteen of America paid stock dividends of 5 percent in 1959 and 2 percent in 1960. Their value was $4,378,000 in 1959 and $4,673,000 in 1960. These amounts were properly charged to "retained earnings" and credited to capital accounts. However, the profits available for such stock dividends were $2,427,000 in 1959 and only $925,000 in 1960. Hence the earned-surplus account was reduced from $7,700,000 in October 1958 to $2,200,000 in October 1960. The greater part of the amount represented by the stock dividends was not currently earned.

Comment: We consider this practice, which is fairly widespread, to be basically harmful. It is either confusing or misleading, or both, and it offers good ammunition to the critics of stock dividends in general.

A number of companies consider a "regular" stock-dividend policy to be desirable, and accordingly they pay the same amount year after year.

Example 1: Universal Cyclops Steel has paid stock dividends of 3 percent a year in 1957–1961 in addition to cash dividends. The value of each stock dividend has been less than the available earnings of the year; in 1959 it was well under half such an amount.

Example 2: In 1960 Georgia-Pacific Corporation (plywood, etc.) initiated a regular dividend policy of 25 cents in cash and 1 percent in stock each quarter. The stock dividends in 1960 were valued at $11,288,000, while the earnings available were $9,560,000.

Example 3: Publicker Industries has paid stock dividends of 5 percent annually since 1947, without a single cash dividend. Its aggregate earnings in the period 1947–1960 have been quite negligible in relation to the market value of the stock dividends distributed. Hence its earned surplus was reduced from $67.0 million to $47.9 million at the end of 1960.

Example 4: Thiokol Chemical paid 5 percent in stock and no cash in 1954–1958. In the latter year the market value of the stock dividend was at least $4.50 per share, against available earnings of only 68 cents.

[15] Unlisted companies, such as Franklin National Bank of Long Island and Diebold, Inc., did not in 1961 make such transfers from earned surplus to capital or capital surplus account.

Comment: The last two examples illustrate the often strange earnings conditions under which a "consistent" or "regular" stock-dividend policy is currently followed. Needless to say, we think that in many of these cases the consistency is the opposite of a virtue.

Irregular Stock Dividends. Most stock-dividend policies appear to follow no plan at all. They neither are fixed in amount nor do they vary in accordance with an announced program.

Example 1: Texaco, Inc., paid 2 percent stock dividends in 1957, 1958, and 1960, but none in 1959. In 1959 it earned $5.24, paid $2.35 in cash, and could readily have continued the 2 percent stock dividend out of the year's retained profits.

Example 2: Ohio Oil declared a 2 percent stock dividend in 1961—its first of the kind—with the following explanation:

The stock dividend at this time gives recognition to the future earning potential resulting from the enlarged exploration program and from the company's growth and expansion in all phases of its operations which have been financed out of retained earnings in recent years.

Comment: The Ohio Oil stock dividend had a value of about 80 cents, against undistributed earnings of $1.24 in 1960 and $6.35 in the "recent years" of 1956–1960. If the stock dividend represented the beginning of a policy of capitalizing the retained earnings of *each year,* it would be meaningful to the shareholders. But the statement implies otherwise, and suggests that only a small part of the company's "growth and expansion" can properly be recognized by stock dividends.

The two examples just given, relating to important enterprises, illustrate the unsystematic and unsatisfactory present estate of stock-dividend policy, as followed by prosperous concerns.

Substitutional Stock Dividends. Many stock dividends take the place of former cash dividends under circumstances which tend to discredit stock dividends in general. When this is done—as when dividends are omitted entirely—reference is often made to the desirability of conserving cash for the company's expansion; but the true motive is usually a falling off in earnings.

Example 1: In February 1961, Continental Copper & Steel Industries initiated a new dividend policy by dropping its 15-cent quarterly cash payment and replacing it by a 1 percent quarterly stock dividend. The company's statement referred to a decline in earnings but emphasized that "the new policy of regular stock dividends is designed to give the stockholders a share in the company's growth while conserving earnings to protect and further that growth." The figures for the current nine months actually showed a small deficit.

Example 2: The earnings of Colorado Fuel & Iron declined from $4.04 per share in 1957 to a deficit in 1960. During this period the company switched from a $2 cash dividend to a 6 percent stock-dividend policy. This stock dividend's value exceeded the earnings in 1959 and, of course, in 1960. The shares declined sharply in 1960.

In the 1951 edition we expressed approval of a well-defined policy under which periodic stock dividends might be paid against accumulated surplus even though not covered by current earnings, in order to maintain a continuity of disbursements. Further thought on the matter leads us to abandon this view. In nearly all cases accumulated surplus does not constitute a special fund available for "rainy-day" dividends, in either cash or stock. It is an indistinguishable part of the total capital fund which is used to carry on the business. If the company is strong in cash it may be able to continue a cash dividend during a period of insufficient earnings—and this is often a praiseworthy policy. But the payment of periodic stock dividends against accumulated surplus has no sound relation to corporate realities. Instead of being helpful, its effect is apt to be misleading.

CHAPTER THIRTY-SEVEN

THE CAPITALIZATION RATE FOR EARNINGS
AND DIVIDENDS

The logical approach to the selection of a capitalization rate would seem to be the same as the approach to the estimation of future earnings and dividends; i.e., the analyst should study the past record and either accept or modify it as rational considerations would dictate. This examination in our opinion should involve a consideration of the price-earnings ratio or dividend yield of the specific share, not only in terms of its own historic record but also in terms of its relationship to that of the general market.

The Basic Multiplier. It is, therefore, our suggestion that the capitalization rate for a given company's common stock should be arrived at by two major steps. First, the analyst should establish for himself a *basic capitalization rate* which he will apply to common stocks generally—i.e., to a comprehensive group of companies, such as those in the Dow-Jones Industrial Average and in Standard & Poor's Composite Index of 500 companies. Second, he will develop, for the individual issue, a multiplier which is related to this basic or over-all rate but which also reflects his appraisal of the record, quality, and long-term prospects of the specific company.

This twofold approach is followed explicitly by a number of analysts, and implicitly, or perhaps unconsciously, by many more. It should be observed here, however, that in the early 1960's it had become rather fashionable in Wall Street to deny any value or significance to the level and movements of the "general market." Many leading authorities insisted that successful investment follows entirely from the choice of superior issues, and that a wise choice would bring satisfactory results to the purchaser regardless of what happened to the stock market as a whole or to any comprehensive index. Analysts wedded to this viewpoint would consider any process of valuing common stocks in general as irrelevant to their work. In our perhaps prejudiced eyes this dismissal of the general market level represents largely an effort to escape from some uncomfortable comparisons between the current and past bull markets.

507

Choice of the Market Averages. There are a considerable number of common-stock indexes or "averages," but most studies of the earnings, dividends, prices, and other market relationships of cross-sectional groups of stocks have used the data of the Dow-Jones Industrial Average. This Average comprises 30 issues, of which one—American Telephone and Telegraph Company—is, anomalously, a public utility. For many decades the price movements of this index have attracted more attention than any others, especially because of its intimate connection with the famous Dow theory.[1] Quarterly figures on the earnings and dividends of the various Dow-Jones Averages—rails and utilities as well as industrials—appear in *Barron's* (Weekly). However, similar data are available for a much more comprehensive sector of the stock market in the Standard & Poor's series. These comprise 425 industrials, 25 railroads, and 50 public utilities; together they constitute the Composite Index of 500 companies. (There are also supplemental indexes of banks, insurance companies, and investment funds.) In addition to earnings, dividend, and price data for each of these indexes, Standard & Poor supply an index figure for the book values of the industrial stocks.

The present Standard & Poor's Indexes go back to 1926, but they are linked to the Cowles Commission Indexes, which commence as early as 1871. It is possible, therefore, to make continuous studies of certain common-stock relationships extending over a 90-year span. (The data in the years prior to 1900 are much more fragmentary and less reliable than those for subsequent years.)

We consider Standard & Poor's Composite Index to be a preferable representative of the general market, but because of its wide acceptance and use, we shall employ also the Dow-Jones Industrial Average whenever available data permit. In addition, for certain purposes we shall refer to Standard & Poor's 425 industrial stock series.

The Historical Multipliers. Our objective at this point is to develop a *basic* multiplier for the "market" which can be considered appropriate for use in terms of the future. In seeking a guide to the future a prudent person always begins by consulting past experience. Therefore, in Table 37-1 we summarize a substantial amount of data bearing on the relationships between average earnings and average price for the Cowles Commission–Standard & Poor's Composite Index and the Dow-Jones Industrials. (Figures on dividend yields, dividend payout, and the interest rate for high-grade bonds are set forth in Appendix Note 15, page 747.)

At this point the alert student should raise a technical question. The ratios given in the tables, he would point out, show the prevailing relationships between *current* earnings and current price during the periods covered. But what we are seeking to establish is the proper relationship between present price and expected *future* earnings. How can the former aid in arriving at the latter? The answer is that a simple mathematical

[1] See Appendix Note 13, p. 743, for comments on the Dow theory.

connection can be established between calculated *normal current* earnings and expected average *future* earnings, based on the rate of growth assumed. Hence we pass readily from a multiplier related to current earnings to one related to future earnings, and vice versa. (We shall designate these as the "current multiplier" and the "future multiplier.")

To illustrate this point, assume (1) that we accept a current multiplier of 15, (2) that we anticipate a growth rate of 3½ percent per annum, and (3) that we use average earnings for the next seven years. That earnings average will then be about 115 percent of the current figure, if the latter is taken as normal, or "normalized" to place it on the earnings curve. Hence, if the multiplier chosen for *current* earnings is 15 times, the appropriate multiplier for expected *future* earnings is 15 divided by 115 percent or about 13 times. Conversely, if 13 had been selected as the normal multiplier of *future* earnings, the multiplier for current earnings could be found through multiplying 13 by 115 percent —which is 14.95 times or, say, 15 times.

The relationships shown by the historical record, summarized in Table 37-1, appear highly variable when studied in the form of 5-year averages,

Table 37-1. Average Multipliers (Price-Earnings Ratios) by 5-, 10-, and 20-year Periods. Cowles Commission–Standard & Poor's Composite Index, 1871–1960; Dow-Jones Industrial Average, 1926–1960

Period ending:	5-year period		10-year period		20-year period	
	Cowles–S&P	Dow-Jones	Cowles–S&P	Dow-Jones	Cowles–S&P	Dow-Jones
1880			11.2×			
1890			16.0×		13.6×	
1900			16.1×		16.1×	
1910			13.2×		14.7×	
1920			9.7×		13.5×	
1930	14.7×	14.7×	12.3×		11.0×	
1935	18.7×	31.7×	16.4×	17.2×	14.4×	
1940	13.9×	15.5×	16.3×	19.6×	16.4×	
1945	11.4×	13.2×	12.7×	14.3×	14.5×	15.9×
1950	8.0×	8.6×	9.7×	10.1×	11.2×	12.8×
1955	10.7×	11.1×	9.4×	10.0×	9.6×	11.2×
1960	15.5×	16.5×	13.2×	14.0×	11.3×	12.6×

and they would of course be much more so if considered by single years. As would be expected, the variations diminish somewhat as the period is lengthened, first to 10 years and then to a 20-year span. For the Cowles Commission–Standard & Poor's Composite series over the 85 years from 1871 to 1955, the mean of the ten 20-year averages works out as a multiplier of 13.5 times, or an earnings-price ratio (earnings yield) of 7.4 percent. Within the periods, the range is from 9.6 to 16.1 times. We shall reserve the 1956–1960 period for separate study. In the four 20-year periods for which there are data for both indexes, the mean multiplier for the DJIA works out at 13.1 times against 11.7 times for the Standard & Poor's Composite.

The dividend yields over the same periods show somewhat more stability than the earnings yields. A number of them are fairly close to the mean figure of 5.1 percent for the 85-year span. An average of the payout figures by 10-year periods produces a historic average of 66 percent.

Somewhat surprisingly, perhaps, this long (1871–1960) sequence of figures does not show any clear-cut *trend* in the capitalization rate of earnings or dividends. We might have expected the over-all returns on the market prices of common stocks to grow gradually lower through the years as the country's enterprises built up their financial strength and management skills and thus made their shares more attractive to investors.

Theoretical analysis suggests also that both the dividend yield and the earnings yield on common stocks should be strongly affected by changes in long-term interest rates. It is assumed that many investors are constantly making a choice between stock and bond purchases; as the yield on bonds advances, they would be expected to demand a correspondingly higher return on stocks, and conversely as bond yields decline. It must be admitted, however, that the figures in Table 37-1 do not lend much statistical confirmation to this universally held view. By one of those disconcerting coincidences, the five-year period of *lowest* bond yields (1946–1950) happens to be the period of *highest* common-stock yields. A study of other periods hardly discloses a consistent pattern of change of the two yield figures in the same direction. The variations in earnings-price ratios do not disclose any greater influence exerted by bond yields.

Nonetheless, in our calculations of a "central value" of the Dow-Jones Industrial Average for the period 1924–1955, we found that the simple formula of dividing the ten-year average earnings by twice the current high-grade-bond interest rate produced values which did correspond fairly well with the actual midpoints of successive market swings.[2] For this reason, we shall employ our former principle of relating the capitalization rate of common-stock earnings to the basic interest rate on bonds as one of the methods for arriving at a *basic* capitalization rate for earnings.

Let us now consider the ratios existing in the five years 1956–1960, and particularly those in 1959–1961, which gave the market at the beginning of a new decade its particular cachet. The spectacular advance in the level of stock prices produced a 1956–1960 price-earnings ratio of 15.5 for Standard & Poor's Composite and of 16.5 for the Dow-Jones

[2] See Appendix Note 14, p. 744.

group. These ratios are higher than that for any other five-year span except those in the 1930's which include the Great Depression.[3] The 1960 price-earnings ratio was 19.4. At the high price of 735 in 1961, the Dow-Jones Industrial Average was selling at 23.1 times the estimated earnings for the year.

Our Suggested Multipliers for Common Stocks as a Whole. We are now faced with the task of deriving from the foregoing figures and our best judgment some plausible basic multiplier for common-stock earnings, to be used as a guide to future investment. To do this we must take the past record into account but at the same time modify its findings to the extent deemed necessary to reflect the impact of new conditions. Schematically, this is the same procedure that the analyst must follow when he seeks to estimate the future earnings of a company, beginning from its past performance.

Our own choice is to select the multiplier from the cross-check which results from the use of two relatively independent methods: (1) consideration of the price-earnings-ratio record and (2) consideration of the relationship between the capitalization rate for earnings—and/or dividends—and the yield on high-grade bonds. This is somewhat comparable to our views as to the use of two methods (the "scientific" and the rate-of-return) as cross-checks in estimating earnings.

We have given this problem long and prayerful thought, as befits its primary importance. Considerations of space and ease of reading have decided us to transfer our detailed treatment to the Appendix Note 15, page 745, and to present our reasoning and conclusions here in sharply abbreviated form.

As indicated in Chapter 31, we suggest a future multiplier of 13—equivalent to a current multiplier of 15 (page 509)—for the earnings of both the DJIA and S&P's Composite. The values we found in January 1962 on this basis were about 55½ for the S&P stocks and 572 for the DJIA (13 times expected average future earnings of $44). Our revised central-value method provided an estimate of 534 for the DJIA.[4]

We consider that our appraisals are consistent with traditional relationships between stock-market movements and underlying values. If the 12-year advance in 1949–1961 constitutes a bull market in the historical sense, it must be expected that the high levels attained therein would be considerably above "central value" or "justified selling price." Our figure for the DJIA lies about midway between the mean valuation (of about 400) that would be reached by the various pre-1956 appraisal

---

[3] High multipliers are to be expected at such times because of the extremely low level of earnings. For example, earnings on the Standard & Poor's Composite Index fell from $0.94 in 1927 to $0.31 in 1932. Although the average price also declined from 12.53 to 5.37, the multiplier advanced from 13.3 times to 17.8 times.

[4] Our former "central-value" approach would have produced an evaluation of only 356 at the beginning of 1962. See this calculation in the Appendix Note 14, p. 744.

methods and the top level of 1961. This would indicate that about half of the spectacular rise of the market above its old normals could be ascribed to the advent of new and more liberal standards of valuation, and the other half to the speculative enthusiasm and excesses that have always been an inherent part of wide market fluctuations. Again we warn the reader that this is distinctly a minority view.

A Disclaimer. It is important that the reader understand just what we have and have not attempted to do in the preceding discussion. We do not present a mathematical or "scientific" calculation of the exact value of the two stock averages at the beginning of 1962. We are not qualified to do this, and we doubt if anyone else is so qualified. Nor do we claim that ours is an approximate value which has behind it the weight of superior authority. But we have said that a serious-minded analyst must seek to form some idea of the proper or justified level of common stocks in general. The reader has the right to ask us how we would go about determining such a level or valuation, and we have given him our best answer to that question. We need hardly urge him not to accept our conclusions as gospel; the dissent that they will provoke among leading Wall Street practitioners is sufficient to assure us against that embarrassment.

We face a further, more basic criticism of this part of our work. Many analysts claim that the whole idea of "valuing the averages is passé, and worse than useless." This is no longer a "stock market," they say, but a "market of stocks"—meaning by that word play that stocks in no sense act as a unit, but that each has its own performance and price path. Thus any view as to the proper level of the averages has no bearing on the valuation of an individual security and is irrelevant to the analyst's fruitful work. By selecting the better opportunities he can assure his clients of excellent results, no matter what happens to the averages. In the words of a leading analyst and financial philosopher: "Every day is a good day to buy a good stock."

We do not agree with this view. We think that the relation of the price action of individual issues to that of the averages is not essentially different now from what it has always been. Nor do we deem it possible for many security analysts to show good absolute results from their selective work during a period of substantial decline in the general market. (Nearly all of them constantly recommend issues which they term "reasonably priced in the current market.") Intelligent investors should have a smaller proportion of their resources in common stocks, however chosen, at ultra-high levels of the market than at low or normal levels. To implement such a policy—which runs counter to the instincts of the crowd—it is necessary for the analyst to form a carefully based view as to whether the market level is or is not excessive. As long as he is satisfied, upon such inquiry, that it is not excessive, he is free to follow selectivity as far as his talents will permit.

Selection of Price-Earnings Ratios for Individual Companies. By accepting in 1962 a *current* multiplier of 15 times as the normal capitalization rate for a representative group of investment-quality stocks we are in effect—as already noted—accepting the 1955–1959 price-earnings ratio for the Dow-Jones Industrial Average. It may be equally logical to accept the average 1955–1959 multiplier registered in the market for each component of the Dow-Jones group and, perhaps, for other common stocks outside the group as well. Undoubtedly, the analyst should determine what these historical multipliers have been and should give them respectful heed. But for several reasons he should not arbitrarily adopt them without very careful further thought. Two reasons particularly merit mention here. First, it is almost certain that in the present decade—as in past ones—changes will occur in the investment standing of industries as well as of companies. Second, the analyst can never accept unquestioningly the stock market's valuation or scheme of valuation for individual issues.

Defining the Range of Multipliers. We would suggest, in the first place, that the analyst confine his range of multipliers within somewhat narrower limits than the market has done. It is a basic assumption of this book that the processes of the stock market are psychological more than arithmetical. This produces the well-known tendency of stock prices as a whole to go to extremes in either direction, as optimism or pessimism holds sway. In the same way, we are certain, it produces a tendency for favored stocks to sell at unduly high prices at the same time that unpopular stocks are selling at unduly low prices. This characteristic shows itself in an extraordinarily wide dispersion of the market's capitalization rates when applied to current or past average earnings. Even if these relative multipliers are acceptable when applied to the past results, they would hardly be appropriate to use with future estimates, for these estimates will assume as realized some of the better prospects which are reflected in the liberal multipliers of the more promising companies.

For example, let us assume that Company *A* has sold at 30 times its five-year average earnings of $4, and Company *B* has sold at only 10 times its earnings of the same amount. We estimate future earnings—average of next seven years—of Company *A* at $8 and those of Company *B* at only $4. It would be unsound to apply the historical multiplier of 30 to *A*'s projected earnings of $8, because we should then be "double-discounting" its supposedly excellent prospects. In the parlance of bridge, we should be "counting the same trick twice"—once in the estimate of larger earnings and again in using the capitalization rate which was *anticipating* this increase.

If the range of multipliers is to be limited, these limits must be somewhat arbitrarily set. For reasons which can be explained in broad terms—but which are difficult to defend in detail—we favor a range from 7 to 20. These multipliers would be applicable to *projected* "normal" earnings.

As we have explained earlier, we should be inclined to use a four-year projection period, i.e., the average of the next seven years. Having selected 13 as the future multiplier for average shares of investment quality (e.g., Dow-Jones or Standard & Poor group), this figure could be taken as representative of the center of the valuation range. In Chapter 31 we suggested that, for a top-quality growth share, the analyst restrict the premium which he pays for the above-average growth potential to not more than about 50 percent of the price he would consider appropriate without it. Using 13 as his base, he would conclude that he would not pay more than about 20 times the estimated earnings four years hence—except under most unusual circumstances.

In theory the minimum multiplier could drop to practically nothing. However, we should question whether a stock which in the investment climate prevailing at the turn of the decade warranted a normal multiplier of less than 7 times *projected* earnings would come within the category of common stocks suitable for the *value* approach.[5] The use of a minimum multiplier of 7 would mean that approximately the same proportional difference would exist between the capitalization rate for the average investment-quality share and the lowest investment-quality stock that exists between the average and the top-quality growth share.

The choice of the specific multiplier will need to be made by the analyst without benefit of a definite formula from us. It will reflect the qualitative factors, discussed in previous pages, which are expected to influence the long-term prospects. It is possible, of course, to develop a rating system of sorts, which will convert "marks" given for growth prospects, inherent stability, quality of management, etc., into a final figure for the multiplier. We prefer not to suggest any specific way of doing this—even for purely illustrative purposes—because the reader may ascribe more authority to such a formula than we consider it would deserve.[6] (Basically, the use of the multipliers for growth stocks, to be suggested in Chapter 39, is equivalent to allowing for the continuation of the assumed rate for an additional three years beyond the fourth-year estimate, with an abrupt decline then to the estimated conservative average rate of $3\frac{1}{2}$ percent per annum.)

---

[5] Out of the above-referenced 1,000 shares listed in Value Line, only 13 in 1959 had price-earnings ratios of less than 7 (and only 16 had ratios in excess of 40) times actual 1959 earnings.

[6] See, for such an attack, "Two Illustrative Approaches to Formula Valuations for Common Stocks," by Benjamin Graham, *Financial Analysts Journal,* November 1957.

CHAPTER THIRTY-EIGHT

THE CAPITALIZATION RATE FOR EARNINGS

AND DIVIDENDS (CONTINUED). DIVIDENDS

AND THE MULTIPLIER

Dividends and the Multiplier. The fact that the influence of dividends on the price of some common stocks may have been changing in recent years was pointed out in Chapter 35.[1] We doubt that anyone at present has sufficient insight into these changes to determine with finality whether they will result in the establishment of a new, long-term pattern of capitalization rates. However, in this interim period of uncertainty—and probably of transition—the analyst cannot suspend his activities. He must cope with this problem as best he can. In Chapter 35 we suggested one possible approach, which is to classify common stocks into three broad groups for valuation purposes. The next step at this point is to review these groups in more detail and set forth our further views as

[1] This changing character of the role of dividends in some stock prices has been noted and examined by many. For example, F. P. Morrissey, in an article entitled "Current Aspects of the Cost of Capital to Utilities," *Public Utilities Fortnightly*, Aug. 14, 1958, p. 221, has fitted lines of regression for each year 1950–1956 relating the dividend-price and earnings-price ratios to the payout for 27 electric companies. He concludes that "it is unequivocal that the data . . . show a changing evaluation of earnings and dividends by investors of utility equities." At another point he states, "From this we might conclude that the market price of a utility stock is more a function of earnings per share than of the cash dividends paid." J. C. Bonbright, *Principles of Public Utility Rates*, Columbia University Press, New York, 1961, p. 251, also points out that "the common stocks by reference to total per-share earnings, with no clear consistent tendency to 'discount' retained earnings. Earnings-price ratios, therefore, deserve more attention than current dividend yields as evidence of capital-attracting rates of return." In contrast, W. F. Stanley, in "Impact of Dividend Pay-out on Price-Earnings Ratios," *Public Utility Fortnightly*, Feb. 2, 1961, p. 151, holds that "the trend of the survey seems to indicate that higher dividend pay-out is usually accompanied by higher price-earnings ratios, and, accordingly, by higher market prices, except in cases of extremely large utilities, where other factors overshadow the importance of dividend pay-out policy." Stanley's study covered 115 electric utility companies.

to the possible treatment of dividends in the capitalization rate for the shares of each group.

It will be recalled that the three general categories were termed the "growth-stock," "below-average," and "middle" groups. Since the nature of the middle group is less distinct than the others, it may be best indicated by defining the two groups which set its limits. Therefore we shall first describe as clearly as possible the determinants of the growth-stock and below-average groups. In this manner the broad nature of the middle group will be automatically designated.

According to the definition employed in Chapter 31, the growth-stock group would consist of those issues whose per-share earnings have increased at an average annual rate of at least 7.2 percent; i.e., earnings double in ten years. In addition, these stocks should have a demonstrated ability to earn an attractive return on their book value and to maintain this return on a rapidly expanding capital base. It is to be expected that ordinarily the rate of return on capital will be well above that for, say, Standard & Poor's 425 industrial stocks.[2]

The below-average group consists of those stocks which have (*a*) sold for some recent period of time, such as the average of the last five years, at less than approximately 1½ times their book value and (*b*) earned a return on book value for the same period below that for, say, Standard & Poor's 425 industrial stocks.

We hold no strong brief for the employment of a five-year test period in measuring the market-to-book ratio and the rate of return on the common-stock equity. If the analyst considers a longer or a shorter period desirable he is privileged to use it, but we think it should not be less than three years.

As determined by the foregoing definitions, the "middle" group will thus consist of those shares with the following characteristics: First, the growth rate in per-share earnings will have been less than 7.2 percent per annum—in the last decade quite probably closer to 4 percent. Second, the average return on the common-stock equity for, say, the last three years will have been above that for Standard & Poor's 425 industrial shares.[3] Third, the market-price-to-book-value ratio will have been above 1½ times but probably below 2½ times.

Having divided industrial common stocks into three broad groups, we

---

[2] Out of 300 industrial issues reviewed by us, those shares which—judged in terms of increase in average per-share earnings 1955–1959 over 1950–1954—had a growth rate of 7.2 percent or more in the decade of the 1950's earned a 1955–1959 average return on their common-stock equity of 15.6 percent. This compares with 12.8 percent for Standard & Poor's 425 industrials. The market-value-to-book-value ratio over the 1955–1959 period for these "growth" shares averaged 244 percent.

[3] The rate of return earned on the common-stock equity may or may not be below that for the growth shares. It is possible that the principal distinguishing feature of a growth share is that its book value is increasing much more rapidly than that of the middle-group share and not necessarily that the return is substantially higher.

must next arrive at some general conclusions as to the role of dividends in the valuation process of each group. The reader must allow for the difficulty of the problem here presented and be prepared to exercise caution and judgment in applying the following suggested techniques:

First, in valuing *growth shares* the dividends can be for all practical purposes ignored and sole reliance placed on expected earnings.[4]

Second, in valuing below-average shares, dividends are of paramount importance and should have the traditional weighting along the lines suggested in our 1951 edition and repeated later in this chapter.

Third, in valuing shares in the middle group, the role of dividends is still dominant, but the weighting will be less than in the case of the below-average shares. Since the shares in this group cover the broad gamut between the below-average and the growth-stock groups, we doubt that there is some formula or neatly arranged schedule that can be developed for treating the payout rate. Thus the analyst will need to take a compromise position in this regard, such as adopting something less than the suggested 4-to-1 weighting ratio for below-average stocks but something more than the proposed 1-to-1 weighting for growth stocks. It may also involve giving somewhat less consideration to changes in the payout rate as it fluctuates moderately about the typical norm of approximately two-thirds. Thus a change in the payout rate between, say, roughly one-half and three-fourths might modify only slightly the price-earnings ratio.[5] We believe that the more important consideration in valuing these shares lies in determining (a) whether a significant change in dividend policy is taking place and (b) if so, whether it may have a substantial impact on *expectable* dividends. For example, does an increase in the payout rate herald a slowing down in the growth rate for the company? Contrariwise, does a decrease in the payout rate indicate an attempt to accelerate the growth of the company by husbanding funds for a diversification or acquisition program?

Below-average Shares. As proposed in Chapter 35, we suggest for industrial common stocks in the below-average category and for railroad shares that dividends be given a specific weighting in relation to earnings in the valuation process. As it happens, this can be done in a very simple manner, and in one which will enable us to use the same sort of *earnings*

[4] Philip A. Fisher, *Common Stocks and Uncommon Profits*, Harper & Brothers, New York, 1958, p. 99, holds that "actually dividend considerations should be given the least, not the most, weight by those desiring to select outstanding stocks." In his approach, preponderant emphasis is laid upon prospects of future growth and especially on the prospects of a change in the growth rate.

[5] Some support for this point of view may be implied from the results of the already-cited article of Aug. 14, 1958, by Morrissey. For the 27 companies studied, he found that in 1956 the line of regression relating the earning-price and payout ratios "was almost perfectly horizontal." Thus in that year differences in payout had no practical effect on price. Examination of the payout ratio for each company disclosed that in 1956 the range was from a low of 47 to a high of 86 percent. Thus it might be conservatively said that the study indicates that the market was disregarding the payout ratio within a range of roughly ½ to ¾ for public utility companies.

multiplier that is customarily employed. Our suggested formula—excluding possible adjustment for asset values—is as follows:

Value = earnings multiplier × (expected
dividend + one-third expected earnings)

or

$$V = M(D + \tfrac{1}{3}E)$$

In this formula the multiplier taken is that which would be applied to the earnings alone if the expected dividend is at a "normal" payout rate of two-thirds of earnings. In that case the formula reduces to the conventional one

$$V = M(\tfrac{2}{3}E + \tfrac{1}{3}E) = M \times E$$

On the other hand, if the payout is more than two-thirds, the value will exceed $M \times E$; and conversely if the payout is below two-thirds.

If all the earnings are distributed, the value becomes

$$V = \tfrac{4}{3}M \times E$$

If nothing is paid out, it becomes

$$V = \tfrac{1}{3}M \times E$$

Examples: Assume Companies A, B, C, D, and E all have expected average earnings of $6 per share and a "normal" multiplier of 12. The expected average dividends, however, are respectively $4, $5, $2, $6, and zero—the latter a highly improbable assumption. Substituting 12 for M, 6 for E, and the various dividends for D, the formula will produce the following valuations for the five companies:

Company A: $V = 12 \times 4 + 12 \times 2 = 72$
Company B: $V = 12 \times 5 + 12 \times 2 = 84$
Company C: $V = 12 \times 2 + 12 \times 2 = 48$
Company D: $V = 12 \times 6 + 12 \times 2 = 96$
Company E: $V = 12 \times 0 + 12 \times 2 = 24$

Our formula involves the assumption that a dollar paid out in dividends has four times the weight in the valuation process as the same dollar retained in the business. (This is demonstrated by the ratio of the values derived in the two extreme cases of 100 percent and zero payouts, as in Companies D and E above.) While this may appear to exaggerate the importance attaching to the payout policy, the various tests that we and others have made of market-price behavior *in this context* give considerable support to that conclusion when applied to below-average companies.

Formula for Public Utility Common Stocks. Our valuation process for utility stocks will be developed in a separate section and in a more elaborate form than that for industrials and rails (see Chapters 42 and 43). The more dependable nature of utility operations and prospects permits of more refinements in the analyst's calculations than would be appropriate for enterprises in which the unpredictable factors bulk so large as to make close calculations rather absurd.

Evaluating Intangibles. Let us add some observations regarding the *qualitative* elements in security analysis, by way of a brief critique both of present Wall Street attitudes and of the valuation problem in itself. The factors that appear to influence most the attitude of security buyers and sellers toward any company are (1) industry prospects and (2) the quality of management. The vital importance of both factors cannot be gainsaid, but neither lends itself particularly well to the processes of security analysis. The problem of appraising the management factor in reaching an investment decision is twofold: First, how does the analyst form a dependable judgment of management's ability or lack of it apart from the actual results obtained in the past?[6] Second, assuming management may properly be considered a plus or minus factor, separately from the actual financial results achieved by it, how does the analyst or investor translate that factor into an appropriate price-earnings ratio?

A somewhat different hazard arises when the analyst endeavors to forecast the relative long-term prospects of one industry or another. It is easy to be wrong on this as on all matters of specific prophecy. Where the chance of error in the prediction appears to be least, the chance of profiting therefrom also may be least—because the current market prices are probably already reflecting (or "discounting") these confident expectations. Thus the investor may be right about the future but wrong about the price paid for the issue, and this can be bad. He may even be wrong about the future as well as about the price—which is much worse.[7]

A frequent procedure of the security analyst is to form a favorable opinion of the long-term prospects of a certain industry, because of his general knowledge and judgment, and then to make an intensive study of the available materials to find confirmation of his views. Research which (albeit unintentionally) represents "working backwards from the answer" is of questionable worth. One of the dangers is that the readily available and familiar figures will prove—at least at first blush—quite encouraging. This is to be expected since the analyst was very probably attracted to

---

[6] For a comprehensive approach to this problem, see Philip A. Fisher, *op. cit.,* Chap. 3. We have also commented on this matter in Chap. 33.

[7] See Table 7-1 for material relative to changes over the years in the percentage earned on total capital in different industries. Since the stock market almost always projects past trends into the future, it rarely shows any degree of anticipation of the reversals in performance that are constantly occurring.

the industry in the first place by optimistic on-the-surface indications. And as a consequence, there is a great inclination for the analyst to rest his case there without probing deeply below the surface.

Industry Studies. In Chapter 7 we set forth two basic points of view pertaining to industry studies. First, we stated that, in our opinion, information about industry has an essential role to play in the evaluation of individual companies. Second, we advanced some serious reservations as to that great mass of industry studies which represents primarily a "warm-over" of readily available data. As a result, all too frequently these studies present material with which the public is already fairly familiar and which has already exerted a substantial influence on market quotations. Therefore, to make a worthwhile contribution to security analysis— and in turn to common-stock investing—industry studies should be undertaken in sufficient depth to generate new information and to reveal more fully than before the anatomy of the industry. To the extent that such studies are productive of insights into important factors that will be operative in the future and are insufficiently appreciated by the current market, their value will, indeed, be substantial.

We are convinced that technological rivalry, particularly between major corporations, will intensify in the sixties. Along with manufacturing, marketing, and management skills, the area of research and development has become one of the major determinants of success in a number of industries. The increase in research and development expenditures from an aggregate of about $11 billion in all of the 1940's to an estimated $10 billion in the single year 1960 (and an anticipated increase to something like an annual expenditure of $20 billion by the end of this decade) is indicative of the rapidly expanding role of "R&D" on the industrial scene. Product life cycles are becoming measurably shorter in high-research industries, and, as a result, the sales of "new" products constitute a growing proportion of corporate sales. Thus R&D—through intensifying the technological obsolescence of both products and processes—has injected into business a dynamic element, for both good and ill, which will require the increasing attention of the analyst.

In Chapter 33 we referred to technological innovations, and we have discussed the matter more broadly here because, in our opinion, the typical industry study of the past must now become a much more penetrating techno-financial analysis. Financial projections will, of course, remain the all-important end product; but, to make such projections reliable, quite probably they will have to be based on a broader and deeper study of the company's position than formerly was necessary. In this connection, careful consideration will need to be given to such factors as (1) growth opportunities arising from product developments and process improvements and (2) threatening competition resulting from industry shifts and changes. Furthermore, widening diversification among corporations—which will also be accelerated by R&D—will force closer interindustry analysis in order to appraise more fully the possible attractiveness of significant corporate moves into different fields.

Counting the Same Tricks Over. Studies in depth cannot eliminate, though they should reduce, the hazards involved in forecasting the relative long-term prospects of an industry. Up to a point, the judgment factor in any long-term projection should become sharper and more dependable as it becomes better informed. Nevertheless, long-run industry prospects—like the caliber of management—must still be considered among the qualitative factors in security analysis.

In envisaging industry prospects the analyst must beware of worshiping what may prove to be, in Francis Bacon's phrase, the "idols of the market place." The payment of an exceedingly liberal price for expected future improvement—in the form of a very high multiplier of past or current earnings—is hardly a businesslike procedure. The investor should expect to be rewarded for his own good judgment when the improvement he anticipated is realized. But if the price he pays today already reflects tomorrow's performance, the best he can hope for is not to lose. In view of the hazards of the future, that would be a bad bargain.

Promising companies, mainly in promising industries, are bound to sell at more liberal prices than unpromising ones. The analyst, while accepting this fact, must be careful to set modest limits to the premiums paid for prospects. The market's general failure to do this has served at times to turn some of our best and strongest common stocks into speculative and risky vehicles.

Examples of Dangerously High Multipliers of First-grade Common Stocks. The hazards attaching to undue enthusiasm for the best-quality companies are illustrated by the recurrent overvaluations of General Electric common in the bull markets of the past three decades. The figures are summarized in Table 4-1, page 57. Since 1929 the declines in this high-grade issue have been on the order of 93 percent, 68 percent, 35 percent, and 39 percent. Equally significant is the fact that the 1929 high was not reached again until 25 years later. The high and low prices made by the DJIA as a whole during this period reproduce, within somewhat narrower limits, the behavior of investors toward General Electric.

OTHER METHODS OF VALUATION

The "Range-of-value" Approach. Those experienced in appraisal work prefer to consider the value of a common stock as falling within a certain band or range rather than as a single figure. The definiteness of a single figure is out of harmony with the essential indefiniteness of the concept of intrinsic value. If a range of value is taken, the practical implication is that the issue would be "cheap" at a price under the lower limit of value and "dear" at a price above the upper limit. For prices within the band of value the analyst would not use the term "overvalued" or "undervalued," but remark only that they fell above or below the mid-point of value.[8]

In our chapters on the appraisal of public utility common stocks we shall employ a uniform range of value in which the upper limit exceeds the low by 20 percent. The range for *industrial* companies would vary under different circumstances but in most cases would be wider than the 100-to-120 ratio. To simplify our exposition as much as possible we shall develop our technique around a single-figure appraisal, which should be viewed as the *midpoint of the appraisal range*. (For ease of reference, we shall term this the *central-appraised value* or *central value*.) The student should use his own judgment in setting the upper and lower limits of the appraisal band.

Growth Stocks. To judge by articles in financial journals and other financial literature, there has been great intensification in recent years of the endeavor to establish more or less definite valuations of common stocks by analytical approaches. These have been applied especially to the field of growth stocks and hinge primarily on the rate and period of expected growth. The subject is discussed in detail in Chapter 39.

Value Line Approach. The Value Line *Investment Survey* evaluates some 1,000 important common stocks, using a method developed gradually over many years. It derives a value figure for the next twelve months (formerly given more prominence in the *Survey*, now in a footnote), and another figure ("potential value") relating to a three-year period beginning about three years hence.[9] The future or potential value of a stock is determined, first, by making certain assumptions as to the economy in general and as to the probable average dividend yield and price-earnings ratio of the market in general. (For this purpose, the experience of 45 industrial stocks considered by Value Line to be "representative" is employed.) Second, a rather elaborate projection of the company's business results is made to arrive at its probable per-share earnings and dividends during the future period. Third, the historical relationships of the stock's price-earnings ratio and dividend yield to those of the general market are determined from the past record. Fourth, these relationships establish the expected future capitalization rates for earnings and dividends and hence the expected average market price or "potential." ("The two values,

---

[8] The "range-of-value" idea is given a practical application in the appraisals made by the SEC to determine the fairness of proposals for reorganization or of sale transactions requiring its approval. If the proposed price (or the values used for reorganization purposes) falls within the range of value found by the Commission's appraisal, no change in the figure will be required; if it falls outside the range, the proposal will be disapproved or modified. For an example see Holding Company Act Release No. 10740-A, dated Aug. 29, 1951; also see C. C. Bosland, "The Valuation of Public Utility Enterprises by the Securities and Exchange Commission," *Journal of Finance*, March 1961, pp. 52ff.

[9] For example, in the expository book *The Evaluation of Common Stocks*, Arnold Bernhard compares April 1959 prices with the "potential value 1962–1964."

the one obtained by capitalizing the expected dividend, and the other by capitalizing the expected earnings per share, [are] reconciled by simple averaging."[10])

The determination of the expected near-term value—as reported by Bernhard in 1959—is made in quite a different way. The factors involved are the combined estimated earnings and dividends, the "lagged price," and average stock yields; but the weight of these factors varies with the "quality group" to which the issue is assigned.[11] This assignment is based on the issue's past record of growth and price stability. The quality rating has independent value as a guide to investors.

The reader will note from this abbreviated presentation that the Value Line techniques are highly refined and complicated. Whether results of equal practical value may be achieved by simpler means must remain a controversial question. The serious student should investigate carefully as many approaches as possible to the valuation process, and select one that appears both theoretically promising and practically feasible in the light of his own resources.[12]

Practical Use of Common-stock Valuations. The purpose of formal valuations is, of course, to aid the analyst in his choice and recommendation of attractive common-stock purchases. Normally he will prefer an issue selling at a lower percentage of his derived value to one selling at a higher percentage. And normally he would compose an investment list of diversified issues giving the most "value" for the price paid—giving due consideration to the stability factor.

What appears to be the beginning of a new movement along these lines has it origins in a work done by H. M. Markowitz.[13] He posits expected over-all return and expected price stability (the opposite of "variability" or "uncertainty") as two independent criteria for satisfactory investment. Presumably the investor must to some degree sacrifice return to stability or stability to return. Markowitz has developed an interesting computing technique for arriving at what he calls "efficient portfolios"— i.e., those which will provide a maximum return for a given accepted degree of uncertainty, or a minimum degree of uncertainty with a given desired (and expected) return.

---

[10] *Ibid.*, p. 81.

[11] There may have been some subsequent changes in this methodology. Recent issues of Value Line *Investment Survey*, in discussing probable market performance in the next 12 months and explaining the ranking method, state, "The determination of rank is based upon an objective analysis of the dividend-paying ability of the stock in the future capitalized according to multipliers that have prevailed in the past, adjusted for the trend of these multipliers."

[12] A much more conservative approach to common-stock investing has long been used by A. Wilfred May, contributing editor of the *Commercial and Financial Chronicle*. See Appendix Note 16, p. 748, for a summary of his method.

[13] See his book, *Portfolio Selection,* prepared for the Cowles Foundation at Yale University, and published in 1959.

The analyst must be well aware of the two major limitations of this or any similar approach. The first limitation derives from the inherent unreliability of *all* investment decisions which are based largely on estimates of future earnings and on a more or less arbitrary choice of the multiplier to be applied to these expectations. In recent decades the scheme of valuation has been departing more and more from the use of factors which are knowable, correctable, and analyzable (such as the true earnings of the past, the dividend record, the asset value, and financial position) and has been becoming increasingly dependent on elements which must be estimated, conjectured, or prophesied—chief of which is the growth rate of net income in the future. This change in emphasis has largely offset the advantages that security analysis has been deriving from the availability of more comprehensive and reliable economic and corporate data and from increasing skill in their study and use. When the *quantities* that the analyst must use are largely "guesstimates" of future earnings and future market norms, he must recognize that his valuation process is far from being truly quantitative or scientific.

The second limitation is structural, and grows out of an inherent opposition between stock-market valuations and security-analysis valuations. The stock market tends to recurrent extremes, in its general bullishness and bearishness, in its marking-up of investment and speculative favorites and its marking down of unpopular issues. The analyst seeks for a middle ground in his view of common stocks in general, and he tends to narrow somewhat the huge spread which the market has established between the valuation rates for popular and unpopular issues. We recommend this attitude for the analyst; it provides what is, on the whole, a sound corrective for the excesses of the stock market; and it produces over the long haul a more satisfactory investment result than comes from "following the crowd."

But we must recognize that this attitude and the related valuation techniques tend to exclude from the analyst's investment list the shares of those companies with the most impressive record of past growth and the best promise of future growth. For it is precisely such shares that are valued most liberally by the stock market, and hence that in most periods command prices above the maximum value which the analyst could justifiably assign to them. But any one of such issues has within it the possibility of a substantial further advance in market price, either because its subsequent growth rate exceeds the analyst's conservative expectations, or because the market itself persists in an unrealistically high rating for its special favorites. Our contention here is that in such cases there occurs an essentially *speculative* corporate development and price advance, which the analyst is not equipped to foresee and foretell with a sufficient degree of confidence in such a recommendation. Others may, with greater or less justice, accuse our viewpoint of being shortsighted, unimaginative, or plain unintelligent.

We write of this problem of the analyst with a certain poignancy, because in our 1951 edition we were rash enough to make a "current presentation" of the records and market-price ratios of three leading issues as they appeared in 1949. These were the common stocks of the Atchison, Topeka & Santa Fe Railroad, Atlantic Refining, and International Business Machines. The record of IBM was by far the best, but its price appeared more than correspondingly high. Our concluding paragraph (pages 462–463) reads as follows:

From the qualitative standpoint, investors are clearly right in preferring I.B.M. to Atchison or Atlantic. Are they right in their quantitative decisions, as expressed in the relative multipliers and prices of the three issues? In our view, this is more than doubtful. Future developments *may* make a purchase of I.B.M. at 1949 levels turn out to be sounder and more profitable than an investment in either of the other companies. But we consider this essentially a speculative matter. The price itself of I.B.M. precludes the margin of safety which we consider essential to a true investment.

From 1949 to 1961 the price of IBM has had many times the market advance registered by the other two issues. Thus the only thing demonstrated by our comparative presentation was the fallibility of conclusions relating to individual issues, and particularly of a conservative approach applied to the valuation of a dynamic growth stock.

CHAPTER THIRTY-NINE

NEWER METHODS FOR VALUING GROWTH
STOCKS

Historical Introduction. We have previously defined a growth stock as one which has increased its per-share earnings for some time in the past at faster than the average rate and is expected to maintain this advantage for some time in the future. (For our own convenience we have defined a true growth stock as one which is expected to grow at the annual rate of at least 7.2 percent—which would double earnings in ten years, if maintained—but others may set the minimum rate lower.) A good past record and an unusually promising future have, of course, always been a major attraction to investors as well as speculators. In the stock markets prior to the 1920's, expected growth was subordinated in importance, as an *investment* factor, to financial strength and stability of dividends. In the late 1920's, growth possibilities became the leading consideration for common-stock investors and speculators alike. These expectations were thought to justify the extremely high multipliers reached for the most favored issues. However, no serious efforts were then made by financial analysts to work out mathematical valuations for growth stocks.

The first detailed basis for such calculations appeared in 1931—after the crash—in S. E. Guild's book, *Stock Growth and Discount Tables*. This approach was developed into a full-blown theory and technique in J. B. Williams's work, *The Theory of Investment Value*, published in 1938. The book presented in detail the basic thesis that a common stock is worth the sum of all its future dividends, each discounted to its present value. Estimates of the rates of future growth must be used to develop the schedule of future dividends, and from them to calculate total recent value.

In 1938 National Investor's Corporation was the first mutual fund to dedicate itself formally to the policy of buying growth stocks, identifying them as those which had increased their earnings from the top of one business cycle to the next and which could be expected to continue to do so. During the next 15 years companies with good growth records won

526

increasing popularity, but little effort at precise valuations of growth stocks was made.

At the end of 1954 the present approach to growth valuation was initiated in an article by Clendenin and Van Cleave, entitled "Growth and Common Stock Values."[1] This supplied basic tables for finding the present values of future dividends, on varying assumptions as to rate and duration of growth, and also as to the discount factor. Since 1954 there has been a great outpouring of articles in the financial press—chiefly in the *Financial Analysts Journal*—on the subject of the mathematical valuation of growth stocks. The articles cover technical methods and formulas, applications to the Dow-Jones Industrial Average and to numerous individual issues, and also some critical appraisals of growth-stock theory and of market performance of growth stocks.

In this chapter we propose: (1) to discuss in as elementary form as possible the mathematical theory of growth-stock valuation as now practiced; (2) to present a few illustrations of the application of this theory, selected from the copious literature on the subject; (3) to state our views on the dependability of this approach, and even to offer a very simple substitute for its usually complicated mathematics.

The "Permanent-growth-rate" Method. An elementary-arithmetic formula for valuing future growth can easily be found if we assume that growth at a fixed rate will continue in the *indefinite future*. We need only subtract this fixed rate of growth from the investor's required annual return; the remainder will give us the capitalization rate for the current dividend.

This method can be illustrated by a valuation of DJIA made in a fairly early article on the subject by a leading theoretician in the field.[2] This study assumed a permanent growth rate of 4 percent for the DJIA and and an over-all investor's return (or "discount rate") of 7 percent. On this basis the investor would require a current dividend yield of 3 percent, and this figure would determine the value of the DJIA. For assume that the dividend will increase each year by 4 percent, and hence that the market price will increase also by 4 percent. Then in any year the investor will have a 3 percent dividend return and a 4 percent market appreciation—both on the starting value—or a total of 7 percent compounded annually. The required dividend return can be converted into an equivalent multiplier of earnings by assuming a standard payout rate. In this article the payout was taken at about two-thirds; hence the multiplier of earnings becomes $\frac{2}{3}$ of 33 or 22.[3]

[1] *Journal of Finance*, December 1954.

[2] See N. Molodovsky, "An Appraisal of the Dow-Jones Average," *Commercial and Financial Chronicle*, Oct. 30, 1958.

[3] Molodovsky here assumed a "long-term earnings level" of only $25 for the unit in 1959, against the actual figure of $34. His multiplier of 22 produced a valuation of 550. Later he was to change his method in significant ways, which we discuss below.

It is important for the student to understand why this pleasingly simple method of valuing a common stock or group of stocks had to be replaced by more complicated methods, especially in the growth-stock field. It would work fairly plausibly for assumed growth rates up to, say, 5 percent. The latter figure produces a required dividend return of only 2 percent, or a multiplier of 33 for current earnings, if payout is two-thirds. But when the expected growth rate is set progressively higher, the resultant valuation of dividends or earnings increases very rapidly. A 6½ percent growth rate produces a multiplier of 200 for the dividend, and a growth rate of 7 percent or more makes the issue worth *infinity* if it pays any dividend. In other words, on the basis of this theory and method, no price would be too much to pay for such a common stock.[4]

A Different Method Needed. Since an expected growth rate of 7 percent is almost the *minimum* required to qualify an issue as a true "growth stock" in the estimation of many security analysts, it should be obvious that the above simplified method of valuation cannot be used in that area. If it were, every such growth would have infinite value. Both mathematics and prudence require that the period of high growth rate be limited to a finite—actually a fairly short—period of time. After that, the growth must be assumed either to stop entirely or to proceed at so modest a rate as to permit a fairly low multiplier of the later earnings.

The standard method now employed for the valuation of growth stocks follows this prescription. Typically it assumes growth at a relatively high rate—varying greatly between companies—for a period of ten years, more or less. The growth rate thereafter is taken so low that the earnings in the tenth or other "target" year may be valued by the simple method previously described. This target-year valuation is then discounted to present worth, as are the dividends to be received during the earlier period. The two components are then added to give the desired value.

Application of this method may be illustrated in making the following rather representative assumptions: (1) a discount rate, or required annual return of 7½ percent;[5] (2) an annual growth rate of about 7.2 percent for a ten-year period—i.e., a doubling of earnings and dividends in the decade; (3) a multiplier of 13½ for the tenth year's earnings. (This multiplier corresponds to an expected growth rate after the tenth year of 2½ percent, requiring a dividend return of 5 percent. It is adopted by Molodovsky as a "level of ignorance" with respect to later growth.

---

[4] David Durand has commented on the parallel between this aspect of growth-stock valuation and the famous mathematical anomaly known as the "Petersburg Paradox." See his article in *Journal of Finance,* September 1957.

[5] Molodovsky later adopted this rate in place of his earlier 7 percent, having found that 7½ percent per year was the average over-all realization by common-stock owners between 1871 and 1959. It was made up of a 5 percent average dividend return and a compounded annual growth rate of about 2½ percent in earnings, dividends, and market price.

We should prefer to call it a "level of conservatism.") Our last assumption would be (4) an average payout of 60 percent. (This may well be high for a company with good growth.)

The valuation per dollar of present earnings, based on such assumptions, works out as follows:

    A. Present value of tenth year's market price:
        The tenth year's earnings will be $2, their market price 27, and its present value 48 percent of 27, or about $13.
    B. Present value of next ten years' dividends:
        These will begin at 60 cents, increase to $1.20, average about 90 cents, aggregate about $9, and be subject to a present-worth factor of some 70 percent—for an average waiting period of five years. The dividend component is thus worth presently about $6.30.
    C. Total present value and multiplier:
        Components A and B add up to about $19.30, or a multiplier of 19.3 for the current earnings.

Valuation of DJIA in 1961 by This Method. In a 1961 article, Molodovsky selected 5 percent as the most plausible growth rate for DJIA in 1961–1970.[6] This would result in a ten-year increase of 63 percent, raise earnings from a 1960 "normal" of, say, $35 to $57, and produce a 1970 expected price of 765, with a 1960 discounted value of 365. To this must be added 70 percent of the expected ten-year dividends aggregating about $300—or $210 net. The 1960 valuation of DJIA, calculated by this method, works out at some 575. (Molodovsky advanced it to 590 for 1961.)

Similarity with Calculation of Bond Yields. The student should recognize that the mathematical process employed above is identical with that used to determine the price of a bond corresponding to a given yield, and hence the yield indicated by a given price. The value, or proper price, of a bond is calculated by discounting each coupon payment and also the ultimate principal payment to their present worth, at a discount rate or required return equal to the designated yield. In growth-stock valuations the assumed market price in the target year corresponds to the repayment of the bond at par at maturity.

Mathematical Assumptions Made by Others. While the calculations used in the DJIA example may be viewed as fairly representative of the general method, a rather wide diversity must be noted in the specific assumptions, or "parameters," used by various writers. The original tables of Clendenin and Van Cleave carry the growth-period calculations out as far as 60 years. The periods actually assumed in calculations by financial writers have included 5 years (Bing), 10 years (Molodovsky and Buckley), 12 to 13 years (Bohmfalk), 20 years (Palmer and

---

[6] "Dow-Jones Industrials: A Reappraisal," *Financial Analysts Journal,* March 1961.

Burrell), and up to 30 years (Kennedy). The discount rate has also varied widely—from 5 percent (Burrell) to 9 percent (Bohmfalk).[7]

The Selection of Future Growth Rates. Most growth-stock valuers will use a uniform period for projecting future growth and a uniform discount or required-return rate, regardless of what issues they are considering. (Bohmfalk, exceptionally, divides his growth stocks into three quality classes, and varies the growth period between 12 and 13 years, and the discount rate between 8 and 9 percent, according to class.) But the expected *rate of growth* will of course vary from company to company. It is equally true that the rate assumed for a given company will vary from analyst to analyst.

It would appear that the growth rate for any company could be established objectively if it were based entirely on past performance for an accepted period. But all financial writers insist, entirely properly, that the past growth rate should be taken only as one factor in analyzing a company and cannot be followed mechanically in setting the growth rate for the future. Perhaps we should point out, as a cautionary observation, that even the past rate of growth appears to be calculated in different ways by different analysts.[8]

Multiplier Applied to "Normal Earnings." The methods discussed produce a multiplier for a dollar of present earnings. It is applied not necessarily to the actual current or recent earnings, but to a figure presumed to be "normal"—i.e., to the current earnings as they would appear on a smoothed-out earnings curve. Thus the DJIA multipliers in 1960 and 1961 were generally applied to "trend-line" earnings which exceeded the actual figures for those years—assumed to be "subnormal."

Dividends vs. Earnings in the Formulas. A Simplification. The "modern" methods of growth-stock valuation represent a considerable departure from the basic concept of J. B. Williams that the present value of a common stock is the sum of the present worths of all future dividends to be expected from it. True, there is now typically a ten- to twenty-year dividend calculation, which forms part of the final value. But as the expected growth rate increases from company to company, the anticipated payout tends also to decrease, and the dividend component loses in importance against the target year's earnings.

---

[7] See R. A. Bing, "Can We Improve Methods of Appraising Growth Stocks?" *Commercial & Financial Chronicle,* Sept. 13, 1956; "The Growth Stock Philosophy," by J. F. Bohmfalk, Jr., *Financial Analysts Journal,* November 1960; J. G. Buckley, "A Method of Evaluating Growth Stocks," *Financial Analysts Journal,* March 1960; "A Mathematical Approach to Growth-stock Valuation," by O. K. Burrell, *Financial Analysts Journal,* May 1960; R. E. Kennedy, Jr., "Growth Stocks: Opportunity or Illusion," *Financial Analysts Journal,* March 1960; G. H. Palmer, "An Approach to Stock Valuation," *Financial Analysts Journal,* May 1956; and the various articles by Molodovsky.

[8] Note that the ten-year *past* growth rate of Dow Chemical was set at 16 percent by Kennedy, 10 percent by Bohmfalk, and 6.3 percent by Buckley, all writing in 1960. See previous footnote.

Possible variations in the expected payout will not have a great effect on the final multiplier. Consequently the calculation process may be simplified by assuming a uniform payout for all companies of 60 percent in the next ten years. If T is the tenth-year figure attained by $1 of present earnings growing at any assumed rate, the value of the ten-year dividends works out at about 2.1 + 2.1T. The present value of the tenth-year market price works out at 48 percent of 13.5T, or about 6.5T. Hence the total value of $1 of present earnings—or the final multiplier for the shares—would equal 8.6T + 2.1.

Table 39-1 gives the value of T and the consequent multipliers for various assumed growth rates.

Table 39-1

Growth rate	Tenth-year earnings (T)	Multiplier of present earnings (8.6 T + 2.1)
2.5%	$1.28	13.1×
4.0	1.48	14.8×
5.0	1.63	16.1×
6.0	1.79	17.5×
7.2	2.00	19.3×
8.0	2.16	20.8×
10.0	2.59	24.4×
12.0	3.11	28.8×
14.3	4.00	36.5×
17.5	5.00	45.1×
20.0	6.19	55.3×

These multipliers are a little low for the small growth rates, since they assume only a 60 percent payout. By this method the present value is calculated entirely from the current earnings and expected growth; the dividend disappears as a separately calculated factor. This anomaly may be accepted the more readily as one accepts also the rapidly decreasing importance of dividend payments in the growth-stock field.

An Apparent Paradox in Growth-stock Valuations. Let us return to the Molodovsky assumptions, used as our model and taken as representative. His method requires that all stocks be presumed to sell a decade hence at 13.5 times their earnings in that year. (Similarly, Bohmfalk assumes that all the 100 growth stocks he valued in his article will sell at between 11 and 12½ times their earnings 12 to 13 years hence.) It is obvious, however, that the 1971 multipliers will vary greatly as between different companies, and that those which have had good actual growth during the 1960's will sell at much higher multipliers than those showing small improvement.

Why should not the valuers make the more realistic assumption that their issues will sell in the target year at a multiplier more or less pro-

portionate to the assumed rate of growth? If a stock doubles its earnings
in 10 years, and is presumed to be now worth 20 times its earnings, why
should it not be expected to sell in 1971 as well at no less than 20 times
its earnings? But if this assumption is made, the present value of the
stock would have to be moved up to more than 20 times current earnings
to avoid exceeding the 7½ percent required return. This would then
suggest a higher multiplier than 20 for the 1971 earnings, and the adjustments would have to be repeated until the present value approaches
infinity.

The mathematical fact is that for any stock presumed to give a combined dividend return and growth exceeding the discount rate the assumed multiplier in the target year *must* be lower than the derived current multiplier. Otherwise we should be back to the infinite valuation
which made us discard the simple assumption of a combined perpetual
growth rate and dividend return exceeding 7 or 7½ percent.

The objection to assuming a 13.5 multiplier ten years hence for earnings considered to grow at, say, a 10 percent rate in the decade can be
overcome if the idea of conservatism and a safety factor are introduced
into the discussion. A valuation of the Molodovsky type should be viewed
not as that present price which will in fact produce an annual return of
7½ percent if the projected growth is realized, but rather as one which
will produce a return *higher* than 7½ percent under such conditions.
We consider it perfectly logical for the investor to require this mathematical result as compensation for the very large risk that the actual
growth realized will prove less than the estimates.

Two Supplementary Calculations Recommended. To give this point a
concrete expression for the investor, we suggest to analysts that their
valuations of the kind we have been discussing be supplemented by
either or both of two corollary calculations. The first would seek to
approximate the true probable rate of return to the investor if the projected growth rate is realized. The simplest assumption for this purpose
is that the shares will sell in 1971 at the same multiplier of their earnings
as is applied by the valuer to the 1961 earnings. Since this will invariably
exceed the 13.5 multiplier used in the first calculation, it will produce a
rate of return above the basic 7½ percent. The difference will indicate
either (1) the extra profit that may be expected from realization of the
growth prediction, or (2) the amount of the safety factor embedded in
the primary valuation. The second such calculation could determine, by
a similar method, how much *below* the estimate the actual growth rate
may fall and still produce the required 7½ percent return to the purchaser at the primary valuation.

Let us illustrate the derivation of these supplementary figures by using
an issue with an expected 7.2 percent growth rate. Its current multiplier,
shown in Table 39-1, worked out at 19.3—based on a 60 percent payout
and a 13.5 multiplier in 1971. Assume now that the actual multiplier
in 1971 will be the 19.3 found proper for 1961. This will add $11.60 to

the 1971 value of a $1 of present earnings. By adroit manipulation of the compound-interest tables we can establish that, on the new basis of 1971 value, the rate of return realized by the purchaser at 19.3 times 1961 earnings will be about 10 percent rather than the basic 7½ percent. Similarly, even if the actual growth rate averaged only 5 percent, but the multiplier were maintained at 19.3, the investor at this price would still obtain his target yield of 7½ percent.

These calculations are by no means free of mathematical taint—partaking a bit of the bootstrap character—but they are not far off the mark, we think, in their implication that the original valuation formula includes a factor of safety of about one-third.

Uses of Growth-stock Valuations. Obviously, the most direct and positive use of a set of growth-stock valuations made by any of the methods proposed would be for the selection of attractive (undervalued) issues and the identification of overvalued ones. The two techniques discussed above—those of Molodovsky and Bohmfalk—were applied in this manner in the respective studies. The former found an "investment value" for each of the stocks in the DJIA and compared it with the concurrent price. The February 1961 level of the unit as a whole (649) was found to be 10 percent above its investment value of 590; five of the components were selling between 75 percent and 95 percent of value, fifteen between 100 and 120 percent, and ten between 120 and 153 percent. These valuations, and the resultant indications of current cheapness or dearness in the market, depended both on the specific formula approach used by Molodovsky and on his choice of estimated annual growth rates. The latter varied between a nominal 1½ percent for United Aircraft to a maximum of 10 percent for Alcoa and Eastman Kodak.

Bohmfalk compares his valuations with current price in a different way. He calculates the growth rate implicit in the present price—i.e., that rate which, by his formulas, would produce a value equal to the July 1960 price. This is done for 93 stocks classed into three quality groups. (He uses moderately different discount rates and growth periods for each group.) For the most part his projected growth rates are quite close to those implicit in the market price. (He takes 6½ percent for the DJIA, which he found to be both its historic rate for 13 years past and the market-price rate.) But in two cases his rate is nearly three times the market rate; in one case the market rate is 40 percent above his own.

It may be interesting to compare the future growth rates selected by Molodovsky and Bohmfalk for the nine stocks appearing in both lists. We add the "historic" or 1946–1959 rate as found by Bohmfalk.

Table 39-2 indicates that historical growth rates play an important, though by no means determinative, part in the projection of future growth, and also that quite considerable differences of opinion on the rates to take for a given company may develop between highly competent analysts.

Other Uses of the Valuation Approach. A number of studies of the subject have been devoted to the various interrelationships between value (as a multiplier of current earnings or dividend), rate of growth, period of growth, and discount rate. If one starts with an actual or assumed dividend yield (or earnings multiplier) one can calculate alternatively (1) what rate of growth is necessary to produce a required over-all return within a given number of years, (2) how many years' growth at various rates would be needed to produce the required return, and (3) what actual returns would follow from given rates of growth proceeding over given periods.[9] These presentations are undoubtedly of value to the analyst in making him aware of the quantitative implications as to

Table 39-2. Comparative Historical and Projected Earnings Growth Rates of Nine Stocks

	Historic	Bohmfalk's projections	Molodovsky's projections
Allied Chemical & Dye..........	7.5%	10.0%	6.0%
Alcoa........................	12.0	13.0	10.0
du Pont......................	10.0*	10.0*	7.0
Eastman Kodak................	9.5	11.5	10.0
General Electric..............	9.0	10.0	10.0
Goodyear.....................	12.0	9.0	5.0
International Paper............	4.5	8.5	3.5
Procter & Gamble.............	6.0	9.0	8.0
Union Carbide................	9.0	9.5	5.0

* Excluding General Motors.

growth rates and periods that must be read into the current market price for a growth stock.

Lessons from Past Experience. A study of actual investment results in groups of popular growth stocks will point up the need for a substantial safety margin in calculating present values of such issues. We know, of course, that where high growth rates have been continued over long periods, investors have fared very well in such shares, even though they paid what seemed to be a very high multiplier of current earnings at the time. The outstanding example of such experience is International Business Machines. Its apparently high selling prices in the past have always turned out to be low in the light of subsequent growth of earnings and subsequent price advances. The 1961 multiplier of, say, 80 times current earnings could also prove to be an undervaluation if the rate of past growth is maintained sufficiently long in the future. Investors generally have been encouraged by the brilliant performance of IBM to think that

[9] An article by R. Ferguson in the May-June 1961 issue of *Financial Analysts Journal*, p. 29, contains an ingenious "nomograph," or arrangement of various figures in columns, which can be used for readily making a number of calculations of this type.

almost any company with a good record of recent growth and with supposedly excellent prospects for its continuance can be safely bought at a
correspondingly high multiplier.[10]

When growth-stock experience is viewed as a whole and not simply
in the blinding light of IBM's achievements, quite a different picture
emerges. One would have expected the general performance of growth
stocks in the past two decades to have been decidedly superior to that
of the market as a whole, if only because they have steadily increased
in market popularity, and thus have had an extra factor to aid their
market prices. Available data would indicate that the facts are different
from this plausible expectation. Let us refer to three studies or compilations on this point:

1. In an article on "The Investment Performance of Selected Growth
Stock Portfolios," by T. E. Adderley and D. A. Hayes (*Financial Analysts
Journal*, May 1957), the authors trace through annually to the end of
1955 the results of investment in each of five growth-stock portfolios
recommended in articles published in a financial magazine in 1939, 1940,
1941, 1945, and 1946. For each portfolio and each year the results, including and excluding dividends, were compared with the corresponding
results of the DJIA. In the aggregate the performances ran surprisingly
parallel. They may be summarized as follows:

Table 39-3. Over-all Gains, Including Dividends Received

Holding period	Recommended portfolios	DJIA
3 years............	26%	22%
5 years............	65	60
10 years...........	153	165

The average total gains for the varying periods (9 to 16 years) to the
end of 1955 were 307 percent for the portfolios and 315 percent for the
DJIA.

2. Bohmfalk's article gives an "Eleven-year (1946–57) Record of
Selected Growth Stocks," including 24 issues. Their annual results, com-

[10] The difference between hindsight and foresight in growth-stock selection is well
illustrated in this very instance of IBM. The SEC study of investment companies
(to be published in 1962) shows that at the end of 1952 the 118 funds covered had
only ½ of 1 percent of their common-stock holdings in IBM shares. This issue ranked
twenty-third in a list of 30 largest holdings. These institutional investors were made
cautious by the relatively high multiplier of IBM shares as far back as 1952. They
were unable to forecast *with sufficient confidence* its coming superior performance so
as to impel them to make a concentrated investment in its shares. While they participated to some degree in its later spectacular advance, this benefit was made relatively
unimportant by the small size of their holdings.

pounded, varied between 6 percent for Air Reduction and 25 percent for IBM. The author points out that the return averaged about 13 percent for the list—which compares with 13.4 percent shown in the same table for Standard & Poor's 425 industrials.

3. Wiesenberger's *Investment Companies 1961* has a separate analysis of the performance of "Growth-appreciation Funds." Results for 1951–1960 are available for 20 funds, on a basis assuming reinvestment of all distributions from security profits and other capital sources. The range of total gain for the 10 years is from 392 percent down to 127 percent, with a mean of 289 percent. The corresponding figure for S&P's 500 Stock Composite Average is 322 percent.[11]

Comment: The results of these three studies point up the basic problems involved in attempting to select securities in the stock market primarily on the basis of the expected rate of future growth. We do not know the extent to which mathematical valuation methods entered into the results we have compared with the market averages. It is possible, though by no means certain, that perfected techniques of the sort described earlier in this chapter may produce a better comparative performance in future years. However, we must express an ingrained distrust, on our part, of the employment of refined mathematical calculations to arrive at valuations which at bottom are based on inherently inexact projections or "guesstimates" of performance for many years in the future.

OUR APPROACH TO GROWTH-STOCK VALUATION

The authors of this book, separately and together, in working on this problem in recent years have developed several methods and formulas. Let us describe briefly three of these approaches. Somewhat to our surprise, the multipliers produced for given growth rates showed only narrow differences under the respective techniques.

Our first method endeavored to apply to growth stocks the same basic treatment that we have recommended for common stocks generally, except that we eliminate the dividend factor in the valuation. This means that the value would be found by applying a suitable multiplier to the average earnings for the next seven years. For any expected growth rate this average would be about equal to the middle or fourth year's earnings. (Note that this does not reduce our contemplated growth period below seven years: the multiplier for the fourth year could be mathematically converted into a smaller multiplier of the seventh-year figure.)

Our range of multipliers was established by two considerations. The first was a limitation of the seven-year growth rates to 20 percent per annum. This upper limit would envisage a 3½-fold expansion of earn-

---

[11] No deduction from these performance results is made for sales load on mutual-fund shares or commission cost on the S&P "portfolio." See also the third calculation in Appendix Note 10, p. 741.

ings in seven years—certainly enough for any investment expectations. Our second step was to establish a similar maximum multiplier of 20 times the average or fourth year's earnings. This maximum was arbitrarily taken as 150 percent of the 13 multiplier assigned to large and sound companies of medium prospects, such as the DJIA group in the aggregate, for which we project future growth at a $3\frac{1}{2}$ percent annual rate. These premises would suggest that the multipliers should advance proportionately from 13 to 20 as the expected growth rate rises from $3\frac{1}{2}$ percent to 20 percent. The resultant table would work out about as follows:

Table 39-4

Expected rate of growth (for 7 years)	Multiplier of average (fourth-year) earnings	Multiplier of current earnings
3.5%	13×	15×
5.0	14×	17×
7.2	15×	20×
10.0	16×	$23\frac{1}{2}$×
12.0	17×	27×
14.3	18×	31×
17.0	19×	$35\frac{1}{2}$×
20.0	20×	$41\frac{1}{2}$×

This schedule bears an accidental similarity to the Molodovsky technique, in that all the multipliers of the projected *seventh-year* earnings would fall within the narrow range of $11\frac{1}{2}$ to $12\frac{1}{2}$. However, the student should recall that Molodovsky's and most other methods discussed above involve a calculation of dividend income and a discount factor, neither of which we allow for here.

Our second approach was developed independently by Charles Tatham and was published by his firm in 1961.[12] It is set forth in this book in his chapter on "Valuation of Public Utility Common Stocks" (Chapter 43).

Finally, our study of the various mathematical processes used by others led us to formulate two highly simplified methods of attaining approximately the same results as those produced by more complicated calculations. The first was our "8.6T plus 2.1" multiplier, developed directly out of the Molodovsky concept and previously discussed. The second is even simpler and reads as follows:

Value = current "normal" earnings × (8.5 plus 2G), where G is the average annual growth rate expected for the next 7 to 10 years.

---

[12] *Price-Earnings Ratios and Earnings Growth,* Bache & Company, New York, Oct. 2, 1961.

The specific figures in this formula are derived largely from the concept that a multiplier of 8.5 is appropriate for a company with zero expected growth, and a current multiplier of 13.5 is satisfactory for one with an expected 2½ percent growth. (The latter is a Molodovsky assumption.) In addition, the resulting multipliers for various other assumed growth rates appear to be as plausible as those worked out more laboriously by others.

A comparison of our four separate multipliers for various growth rates, together with the typical results of the Molodovsky method, is given below:

Table 39-5

Expected growth rate	0%	2.5%	5%	7.2%	10%	14.3%	20%
Growth in 10 years		28.0%	63%	100.0%	159%	280.0%	519%
Multipliers by:							
Molodovsky's method*	11.5×	13.5×	16.1×	18.9×	23.0×	31.2×	46.9×
Tatham's table†			18		25		
"8.6T + 2.1" formula	10.7	13.1	16.1	19.3	24.4	36.5	55.3
"8.5 + 2G" formula	8.5	13.5	18.5	22.7	28.5	37.1	48.5
Our preferred method (7-year projection)	8.5	13.5	17	20	23.5	31	41.5

* Molodovsky's method bases these rates on the assumption that the projected 10-year growth rates are the same as the actual rates for the previous 5 years.

† From column for 7-year growth projections in Chap. 43, p. 591.

It will be noted that our preferred method, based on a 7-year projection of growth, yields current multipliers quite close to those from the other formulas for growth rates up to 10 percent. For higher rates our recommended multipliers are more conservative than the others. This follows in part from the great impact of the eighth- to tenth-year growth at such optimistic rates, and in part from our self-imposed limitation of 20 times fourth-year earnings. Since we have already expressed our lack of confidence in predictions of large percentage gains for many years in the future, we do not have to say more to defend our conservatism in this range.[13]

[13] The case for not paying extremely high multiples is most persuasive. In this regard, the student should read S. F. Nicholson, "Price-Earnings Ratios," *Financial Analysts Journal*, July-August 1960, pp. 43–45. In a study of 100 common stocks, principally industrial issues of investment quality, including many of the largest companies, over 11 selected time spans from 1939 to 1959, the author found that the stocks selling at the lowest multiples showed much more appreciation than the stocks selling at the highest multiples and that the individual issues which showed losses during these periods or which showed relatively little appreciation were predominantly in the high-multiple groups. A similar study of 29 chemical stocks produced comparable results. For example, "the 50 percent lowest price-earnings ratios averaged over 50 percent more appreciation than the 50 percent highest ratios." Among Nicholson's conclusions is the statement, "Many investors have apparently underestimated the importance of reasonable price-earnings relationships."

CHAPTER FORTY

CAPITALIZATION STRUCTURE

In our discussion of key ratios in statement analysis, in Chapter 17, we commented briefly on the significance of the "common-stock ratio," which shows the ratio of common-stock equity to total capital funds. We indicated that—other things being equal—the higher this ratio, the better the credit standing of the company; the higher in turn the "quality" of the stocks issue; and the higher—other things being equal—the multiplier to be applied to earnings per share. At the same time we commented that this did not necessarily mean that an all-common-stock capital structure was the most advantageous one for the owners of the business. We return to this subject now, as part of our discussion of factors governing the multiplier of per-share earnings and dividends.

The subject divides itself into two questions, viz: (1) What should be, in theory, the effect of variations in capital structure on the multipliers for earnings and dividends? (2) What relationship actually exists in the markets between one factor and the other? We have no doubt that the second question is more important to the analyst than the first. However, the theoretical aspects of the matter have received a great deal of attention in the financial and economic journals, and in recent years something of a controversy has raged on the subject. In the present chapter, we think it well to consider this highly debatable matter from the viewpoint of both theory and practice. For clarity of exposition we shall discuss first the theoretical issues, then present some relevant material drawn from the stocklist itself, and finally set forth our conclusions in terms of both valuation procedure and corporate policy.

Possible Results from Variations in Capital Structure. Let us begin by assuming three similarly situated industrial companies, A, B, and S— each of which has $10 million of capital funds and earns $1.5 million before income taxes. Company A's only securities are 100,000 shares of common stock, without par value. Company B has the same stock issue, plus $3.5 million of 5 percent bonds. Company S has the same common stock, plus $10 million of 6 percent bonds. For our first approach let us assume that regardless of capital structure the market is willing to pay 13.9 times earnings for each common stock, and that the bonds would be worth par. The figures would work out as shown in Table 40-1.

These results, if actually realized in the market, would be extraordinary. Company A would sell for the amount invested, Company B, for 23.4 percent more, and Company S, for 60 percent more. These wide differences in the enterprise value would be due solely to variations in the capital structure, including the differing tax burdens flowing therefrom. If our postulates as to price relationships were valid it would be obvious that stockholders would gain most by issuing the largest possible amount of bonds, and that the much-praised "clean" capital structure would be a costly mistake.

Table 40-1

Capital structure	Company A	Company B	Company S
Bonds:			
5 percent.............................	....	$ 3,500,000	....
6 percent.............................	....	....	$10,000,000
Book value of common...............	$10,000,000	6,500,000	0
Total capital fund.................	$10,000,000	$10,000,000	$10,000,000
Net before taxes and interest.........	1,500,000	1,500,000	1,500,000
Interest...........................	....	175,000	600,000
Balance...........................	$ 1,500,000	$ 1,325,000	$ 900,000
Income tax (52 percent).............	780,000	689,000	468,000
Balance for common................	$ 720,000	$ 636,000	$ 432,000
Value of common at 13.9 times earnings......	10,000,000	8,840,000	6,000,000
Value of bonds at par...............	....	3,500,000	10,000,000
Total value of enterprise...........	$10,000,000	$12,340,000	$16,000,000
Times interest earned before taxes....	....	8.5×	2.5×

Of course, our assumptions are not correct. The common stocks of all three companies would *not* sell at the same multiplier of earnings, nor would both the bond issues necessarily be quoted at par.

Let us now make an alternative assumption. This is that since all the companies are in exactly the same position as to capital invested, earnings before taxes, and prospects, they should all sell at the same aggregate or enterprise valuation, except to the extent that interest charges reduce the tax burden. In other words, we assume in these examples that they would all sell in the aggregate at the same 13.9 multiplier of earnings on capital after income tax. For simplicity, we assume further that the bond issues would sell at par. The resultant enterprise valuations and common-stock valuations are shown in Table 40-2. In accordance with our assumptions, the enterprise value increases as the bond component rises, by reason of the tax saving. But the multiplier of the common stock declines, as required to offset the "leverage" advantage from the use of bonded debt.

Two Schools of Thought. The foregoing hypothetical illustrations somewhat roughly depict the two broad theoretical points of view which presently exist. In essence, one group (represented—and also exaggerated

—by Table 40-1) holds that capital structure can affect the aggregate market valuation of a firm's securities, even apart from the tax impact, whereas the other group (represented by Table 40-2) considers that—except for the tax factor—capital structure has *no* effect on the aggregate market valuation of a company's securities.

Table 40-2. Effect of Differences of Capital Structure, Assuming a Constant Multiplier for Total Earnings after Tax and Par Value of Bonds

	Company *A*	Company *B*	Company *S*
Earnings after taxes................	$ 720,000	$ 636,000	$ 432,000
Interest...........................	....	175,000	600,000
Earnings after taxes before interest...	$ 720,000	$ 811,000	$ 1,032,000
Assumed multiplier................	13.9×	13.9×	13.9×
Value of enterprise.................	$10,000,000	$11,270,000	$14,340,000
Less par value of bonds............	....	3,500,000	10,000,000
Resultant value of common.........	$10,000,000	$ 7,770,000	$ 4,340,000
Resultant multiplier of common earnings...........................	13.9×	12.2×	10.0×

The fundamental differences between these two schools of thought have been aptly set forth by David Durand.[1] He treats them in reverse order to that employed above. Durand points out that the proponents of the second, or "entity," approach, "argue that the totality of risk incurred by all security holders of a given company cannot be altered by merely changing the capitalization proportions. Such a change could only alter the proportion of the total risk borne by each class of security holder." In regard to the first, or "optimal," approach he states, "Those who adhere strictly to this method contend: first, that *conservative* increases in bonded debt do not increase the risk borne by the common stockholders; second, that a package of securities containing a conservative proportion of bonds will justifiably command a higher market price than a package of common stock alone." (Certainly, insofar as Companies *A* and *B* are concerned, Table 40-1 is representative of this point of view.)

We do not propose here to enter into the details of the controversy,[2]

[1] David Durand, *The Cost of Debt and Equity Funds for Business,* National Bureau of Economic Research.

[2] The following are some of the writings on this subject which the student will find it desirable to review: E. Solomon, *The Management of Corporate Capital,* University of Chicago, Free Press of Glencoe, Ill., 1959; F. Modigliani and M. H. Miller, "The Cost of Capital, Corporation Finance and the Theory of Investment," *American Economic Review,* June 1958; by the same authors, "Leverage, Dividend Policy and the Cost of Capital," paper read at 1960 meetings of the Econometric Society; John Lintner, "A New Model of the Cost of Capital: Dividends, Earnings, Leverage, Expectations and Stock Prices," paper read at 1960 meetings of the Econometric Society; C. W. Howe, "Corporate Savings Behavior: A Theoretical and Empirical Investigation of Internal Financing," unpublished doctoral dissertation, Stanford University, Stanford, Calif., 1959.

with its elaborate mathematical calculations; we seek rather to point up some of the practical implications of the question.

Our Own View. Let us call attention first to a significant fact which appears to have been given too little consideration in the theoretical discussions. This is that a good part of *any* suggested gain in enterprise value through creating or increasing the debt component will be accounted for (under existing legislation) by the factor of tax savings—a benefit apparently conceded by those who deny the other claimed benefits. Thus we find that having the bond issue raises the total value of Company B 23.4 percent over that of Company A in our Table 40-1—which illustrates the "optimal" theory—but it also raises the value by 11.3 percent under our Table 40-2—which presents the "entity" theory. In other words, the tax saving *alone* resulting from the use of debt was sufficient to increase the value of Company B by about as much as could be expected from the leverage factor. Since the tax saving is not in dispute, the great controversy—from a practical standpoint—seems to reduce to a calculation of the amount by which a given *acceptable* bond component will raise the total value.

In our opinion the advantages to stockholders from the *appropriate* proportion of corporate debt will go beyond the indubitable tax saving and will fall close to those shown in Table 40-1. The appropriate amount of debt is that which the company can safely borrow, which in turn is no more and very little less than investors may safely lend to it. The upper limits of such borrowing have been spelled out in our specific standards for bond investment in Chapters 23 to 25. The debt issue of 35 percent of total capital, with interest coverage before taxes of over eight times, which we have selected for our Company B, would be approaching the upper limit of conservative borrowing for a typical industrial concern. For such a company the market's multiplier of its share earnings should be only slightly, if any, less than that of a similar company without bonds (Company A).

In Table 40-3 we seek to present the valuation picture more realistically, in terms of the market's probable reaction to the corporate struc-

Table 40-3. Effect of Differences of Capital Structure, Assuming Probable Market Prices for the Bonds and Stock Issues

	Company A	Company B	Company S
Assumed price of bonds.............	....	100	70
Resultant value of bond issue........	....	$ 3,500,000	$7,000,000
Assumed multiplier of earnings of common stock........................	12.5×	12.0×	6.0×
Resultant value of stock issue........	$9,000,000	7,630,000	2,590,000
Resultant enterprise value..........	$9,000,000	$11,130,000	$9,590,000

tures of Company *A* and Company *B* (together with a *possible* valuation of Company *S*). The previous assumptions accepted a valuation of Company *A* equal to the book value of the common stock. We now suggest that, since the concern earned only 7.2 percent thereon after taxes—a subnormal rate—the market might well apply a multiplier as low as $12\frac{1}{2}$, thus producing a value less than book value for the enterprise. Company *B*, on the other hand, will show earnings of about 10 percent on its common-stock component. Thus a multiplier of 12 for these earnings might be a reasonable expectation. (In fact, it might well be somewhat higher.) The two multipliers of $12\frac{1}{2}$ and 12, respectively, produce total values of $9,000,000 for Company *A* and $11,130,000 for Company *B*—an advantage of over 23 percent in favor of the one with a moderate debt proportion. To this final figure the tax saving and the "leverage" factor contribute about equally.

If these conclusions are correct, two important consequences ensue. The first is that where debt (and/or preferred stock) is conservative, the security analyst need not adjust his earnings and dividend multiplier downward for the debt factor. Thus he can virtually disregard the senior securities in selecting the capitalization rate. The second consequence relates to corporate financial policy. It suggests that frequently the stockholders will be better off if the company has a moderate amount of debt than if it has none.[3]

Company S: A Case of Excessive Debt. Let us now consider Company *S* (for "Speculative"), which was taken as an extreme case. Here the entire investment has been bonded, and the common holders are receiving the substantial residual earnings without having to put up any money. Will the enterprise value of Company *S*, in theory in the market, be higher than that of Company *B*? That is by no means sure; at most times it would be highly unlikely. Company *S* clearly has a speculative capital structure, with consequent instability and even possible insolvency. Since the bond interest is covered only $2\frac{1}{2}$ times before taxes the issue is obviously unsuitable for conservative investment. For this reason the bond issue would normally sell well below par, despite its 6 percent rate, and the common stock would sell at a relatively low multiplier of its average or current earnings. However, one of the effects of a highly leveraged capital structure is to make the market value of the enterprise largely unpredictable. In a favorable financial climate Company *S* might be valued at a good premium above the $10 million invested; but when sentiment is adverse, or even indifferent, it might just as easily sell at a discount from book value. At such times the hazards created by the excessive bond component may more than offset the impressive tax saving. Hence the assumption made in Table 40-2—that Company *S* will sell at

[3] In some growth-stock cases the cost of common-stock capital is less than net bond interest, when measured in terms of current income; but this is not true in terms of expected income.

the same multiplier of total earnings as the others—has no sound basis, and the calculations for Company S in both Tables 40-1 and 40-2 may well be disregarded.

Avoidance of Formal Valuations of Speculative Companies. The analyst would find great difficulty in selecting an appropriate multiplier to apply to Company S's projected earnings and dividends, for purposes of appraisal. The capital structure itself throws the company into a speculative category, just as uncertainties about the future of the business would, for other industrial concerns, invite the same designation. As we have stated before, the analyst should avoid making formal valuations of essentially speculative enterprises.

Capital Structures and Actual Earnings Multipliers. The conclusions we have drawn as to the desirability of Company B—or a conservatively leveraged type of capital structure—require further elucidation, and we shall supply it a little later in this chapter. At this point, however, it might be well to inquire what support or negation of our view may be found in the *actual* stock-market relationships between stock-bond ratios and earnings multipliers. By using the common-stock ratio as the criterion, we shall lump preferred stock together with bonds as "senior securities." While in theory a given component of preferred stock involves less potential risk to the common than an equal component of bonds, in practice the amount of preferred stock at issue is rarely large enough to warrant separate treatment.

The most satisfactory material for our purpose is found in the list of operating electric companies. Although one of these may vary considerably from another, they present enough homogeneity, when studied in quantity, to suggest that if actual capital structures have an appreciable effect on actual multipliers this fact should be demonstrated by the data. In Table 40-4 we summarize the figures on 98 such utility companies taken from a brokerage-firm review.[4]

Our table suggests a number of conclusions. The first is that the common-stock ratios of the 98 companies were strongly concentrated in the range of 30 to 45 percent. Within this large modal group there was no indication that the multiplier increased with the common-stock ratio. In the relatively few companies outside the modal range the results are the reverse of those called for by anyone's theory, since the stocks with the largest debt ahead of them tend to sell at higher multipliers than those with the smallest proportion of debt.

It is clear that within the limits of capital-structure variation actually shown by the electric utilities, this factor of debt had so minor an effect on the earnings multipliers as to be completely submerged by other

---

[4] *Annual Review of Electric Utility Companies,* published by Carl M. Loeb, Rhoades & Company, June 1960. The relationships studied are all as of a single date rather than an average for a period, but we consider them highly significant for our present purpose.

determinants. Table 40-5 gives some data bearing on this question, as related to the electric utilities showing the largest and the lowest earnings multipliers.

These figures would indicate that neither the capital structures nor the payout ratio played any part at all in setting the price-earnings ratios for the two subgroups. The very large difference between them arises almost entirely from the contrasting expectations as to the rate of future growth

Table 40-4. Capital Structures and Earnings Multipliers of 98 Electric Utility Companies in June 1960

Stock equity	Price-earnings ratio			Number of companies
	High	Low	Mean	
Under 30 percent........ (average 26.1 percent)	36.7×	15.4×	22.7×	9
30–34 percent..........	27.9×	12.7×	19.9×	34
35–39 percent..........	27.9×	11.6×	18.7×	32
40–44 percent..........	33.2×	13.5×	21.0×	20
Above 44 percent........ (average 47.3 percent)	23.6×	18.8×	20.5×	3
All companies..........	36.7×	11.6×	20.0×	98

Table 40-5

	Average P/E ratio	Average dividend yield	Average payout	Average common-stock ratio	1955–1959 Average growth per share
15 companies above 25 times...............	28.6×	2.59%	61%	34.5%	8.9%
12 companies under 15 times...............	13.9×	4.68	64	35.8	5.8

of earnings. These expectations, in turn, are based, in part at least, on the faster growth of the favored group in 1955–1959.

Table 40-6 sets forth the average percent which the common-stock equity and senior securities constituted of total capital over the 1955–1959 span, and the average price-earnings ratio for each of 30 major American industries. Two facts stand out. First, no close relationship exists between capital-structure proportions and the price-earnings ratios of the individual industries. (Moreover, a check of the leverage and price-earnings ratios of the individual companies comprising a number of the industries reveals no consistent pattern which would indicate that the amount of senior securities had a discernible influence on the valuation of the common stock.) Second, the use of senior securities is modest. In no instance was the senior-security proportion more than 35 percent of total capital, and in four industries it was 10 percent or less.

If we extend our study of actual capital structures to other groups we shall find that a double condition prevails: (1) There is a tendency for

Table 40-6. Comparison of Leverage and Price-Earnings Ratios of 30 Major Industries: 1955–1959 Averages

(Industries ranked by price-earnings ratios)

Industries	Common stock as % of total capital	Senior securities as % of total capital	Price-earnings ratio
Electrical supplies and equipment..........	76	24	23.7×
Chemicals............................	69	31	23.2×
Ethical Drugs........................	87	13	17.9×
Proprietary Drugs.....................	85	15	17.3×
Paper and allied products..............	77	23	17.3×
Toilet preparations and soap...........	81	19	16.0×
Meat packing.........................	69	31	16.0×
Apparel and accessories chain stores........	90	10	15.2×
Automobiles..........................	86	14	14.8×
Radio and television....................	72	28	14.8×
Glass and metal container...............	66	34	14.7×
Nonferrous Metals incl. copper...........	91	9	14.6×
Mail-order...........................	90	10	14.4×
Rubber..............................	69	31	14.2×
Corn products........................	84	16	13.9×
Building materials.....................	89	11	13.9×
Oil industry..........................	85	15	13.5×
General industrial machinery.............	83	17	13.3×
Dairy products........................	79	21	13.1×
Grain-mill products....................	70	30	12.8×
Limited-price variety stores.............	84	16	12.3×
Grocery chain stores...................	72	28	12.1×
Steel................................	80	20	11.7×
Distilling............................	72	28	11.7×
Department stores.....................	65	35	11.6×
Aircraft.............................	84	16	11.0×
Automobile parts and accessories..........	92	8	10.8×
Agricultural machinery.................	76	24	10.2×
Cigarette............................	65	35	10.2×
Textile fabrics.......................	67	33	8.9×

the senior-security ratio to be concentrated in a rather narrow modal range; and (2) the modal or average senior ratio is well below what we would consider a conservative limit. Viewing industrials as a whole, we set forth in Table 40-7 the distribution of debt ratios for several groups of important concerns.

If, instead of taking the ratio of debt to book value of total capital, we used the market value of the enterprise, the ratios for nearly all companies would be much lower. For example, on the basis of average market prices for 1955–1959 about three-fourths of the large companies would have a debt component under 20 percent of the enterprise value.

Our conclusions from these data, and from other experience, is that for the bulk of common-stock issues the actual common-stock ratios do not have a noticeable effect on the earnings multipliers. This is explained by the fact that within most industrial groups the large majority of companies have capital structures falling within a comparatively narrow band, which reflects current financial standards for that industry. The difference between the lower and upper limits of these ranges is not

Table 40-7. Percent of Selected Groups of Industrial Corporations with Senior Securities Constituting Stipulated Proportions of Book Value of Total Capital

Sample	Date	Senior securities as percent of total capital			Total
		0–30%	30–50%	Over 50%	
29 industrial shares—Dow-Jones Industrial Average	1959	83%	17%	0%	100%
First 200 industrial companies—Moody's *Handbook of Widely Held Stocks**	1959	76	18	6	100
Studley-Shupert *Analyses of Corporate Securities*—300 companies	1959	72	23	5	100

* First 1961 edition.

large enough to affect the multiplier to any degree, and its very minor influence is obliterated by the powerful factor of the expected growth rate. (For a moderately different view see Chapter 43.)

Thus we find nothing in our studies of actual experience which is seriously opposed to our thesis that companies with moderate debt are likely to have a larger enterprise value than the same type of company without debt. This would certainly be true if the common-stock multipliers for moderate debt companies are generally no lower than those of lower-debt or no-debt companies. Most of the available data indicate just such a condition. We thus appear to be confirmed in our recommendation to the analyst that, within the appropriate limit of *sound* indebtedness, he need make no adjustment of his multipliers for variations in the common-stock ratio.

The Question of Corporate Debt Examined Further. The foregoing discussion leads naturally from the field of arithmetical calculations and common-stock appraisals into that of corporate policy. Our conclusions that Company *B* will have a substantially larger enterprise value than Company *A*, *merely because its capital structure is more suitable*, suggests that the stockholders of Company *A* would be better off if that concern were capitalized with 35 percent in bonds instead of having only common stock outstanding. Many corporate managements and experienced investors may disagree with this conclusion. It is traditional to regard corporate debt as something inherently unfavorable and to view a "clean balance sheet"—i.e., an all-common-stock capitalization—as a praiseworthy achievement by management.

In Defense of Debt. That damage is done by *excessive* debt needs no argument, and the history of our railroads points up that moral only too well. But it would be naïve to assume, from such examples, that *all* corporate debt is bad and to be avoided. If that were so, the only companies that would deserve good credit would be those that never borrowed. Furthermore, how would it be possible to identify *conservative* investment with bond investment—as is done by life insurance companies, savings banks, trust funds, etc.—if the very contraction of a bonded debt meant that the company had taken a dangerous and unwise step? Obviously, the objection to debt capital per se is more of a cliché than a serious principle of corporate finance.

In our view the question whether corporate borrowing is desirable or undesirable is to be decided not as a matter of general principle, but by reference to the circumstances of the case. For some companies it is dangerous to owe more than a nominal amount; hence not enough money could be soundly borrowed to make the transaction worthwhile. For most public utility companies, on the other hand, a substantial debt is warranted by the inherent stability of their operations, and the gain to the stockholders from the use of low-cost money (after tax saving) is essential to make their own investment profitable. It has been customary to consider a representative utility structure as consisting of about 50 percent debt, 15 percent preferred stock, and 35 percent common stock and surplus. For reasons developed elsewhere, we question the inherent logic of preferred-stock financing. Thus we should recommend as a preferable capital structure for utilities the simpler combination of about three-fifths debt and two-fifths common-stock equity.

In the case of nonutility enterprises the soundness of the debt structure cannot be judged by reference to the book value of the stock equity, since there is no assurance that earnings will be commensurate with the book investment. (The railroads appear to offer the opposite and melancholy assurance that earnings will *not* support the asset values.) Thus the primary criterion of sound borrowing is not the balance sheet but the income account over a number of years past and a businesslike appraisal of the hazards of the future.

Principle of the Optimal Capital Structure. The criteria we developed in the preceding section for sound bond selection may be taken also as criteria of sound bond financing by corporations. In most enterprises a bond component no more than—and not too far below—the amount that careful financial institutions would be ready to lend, at the going rate for sound risks, would probably be in the interest of the owners and would make for what may be called an "optimal capital structure." The bond component will rarely be as high as 50 percent of the capital fund for industrial concerns; for the typical case, the figure might be set at about one-third of the total.

Factors Favoring a Bond Component. As we see it, there are two reasons why an industrial company of good size and reasonable stability of earnings should have a bond component of conservative but appreciable size. One of the reasons is positive and the other is negative. First, the favorable income tax status of the bond-interest charge effectively reduces the cost of bond money by 52 percent in most instances, and brings its net cost well below that of common-stock capital, except for a few highly favored growth companies. In our Company B example, we found that $175,000 of earnings before taxes was worth $3,500,000 on a bond basis, while the remaining $1,325,000 of net before taxes was worth only $8,840,000 (Table 40-1) on a stock basis—a differential of 3 to 1 in favor of bond money.

In contrast, it is to be noted that the Dow-Jones Industrial Average sold in 1961 at more than 20 times the after-tax earnings for the year— or on an earnings-yield basis of less than 5 percent. Even in terms of this market condition and prevailing taxes, common-stock capital costs are still over twice as much as that of high-grade bond capital.

What may be called the negative reason for adopting an optimal rather than an all-common structure is the fact that on common stock alone some companies cannot earn a return sufficiently high to carry or justify the investment in terms of average market valuation. If, for example, the standard earnings multiplier for a good company with average prospects is taken to be 15, this will require 6⅔ percent on market value after taxes *and about 13.9 percent before income tax* at 52 percent in order to support the stockholders' investment in terms of average market value. In other words, unless such a company can earn nearly 14 percent on book value before taxes, the market price will be less than book value and the company will not be worth what the stockholders have invested in it. For a variety of reasons there are a number of all-common-stock concerns which do not earn enough on their total capital to make it worth book value on the market.

By using lower-cost bond money in place of some of the higher-cost common-stock capital, subprofitable all-stock companies could be transformed into more profitable concerns, which might then earn and pay enough on the stockholders' equity to make it worth in the market what the books say it is worth. Stockholders may legitimately insist that the capital structure be set up with this objective in view.

In practice, the important areas for applying the principle of an optimal capital structure are likely to be found in companies with a good financial position, including little or no debt, and with insufficient earnings on their capital. These are likely to sell persistently at market prices below book value. For such companies acquisition of other enterprises with significant earning power, through issuance of senior securities, is very likely to prove of real benefit to the stockholders.

Leverage Effects of "Excessive" Senior Securities. In our schematic discussion of three imaginary companies early in this chapter, we pointed out that the highly speculative capital structure of Company S would produce highly speculative and therefore unpredictable, results for the company and its shareholders. This subject will be dealt with in detail in Chapter 48 on Leverage.

Capital-structure Policy, Dividend Policy, and Income Taxes. In our chapters on the dividend factor we stressed the gradually increasing impact of high personal income taxes on the investor's attitude toward cash dividends. In this chapter we have emphasized the substantial savings in income taxes to the corporation, and consequent increase in enterprise value, that may result from the bond component in the capital structure. In these concluding paragraphs we might make a broad comparison between these two impacts of the income tax on corporate financial policies.

It is appropriate that such policies seek to minimize, as far as is legally and prudently possible, the burden of income taxes on the company and its owners. To minimize personal income taxes we have suggested that companies with good opportunities for the reinvestment of profits should move in the direction of substituting periodic stock dividends for cash dividends—and particularly where all or part of the cash-dividend drain is now recouped by the sale of additional shares. The analogous policy to reduce corporate income taxes would lie in the substitution of *income bonds* for that part of the capital structure that would otherwise be in the form of preferred stock, and the use of income bonds also to increase the percentage of total capital that could safely be issued as senior securities.

It is questionable whether the full possibilities of the income-bond device have been explored. We consider it one of the important possibilities for the future development of corporate financial policy, paralleling in good part the regularization of the periodic stock-dividend device.

CHAPTER FORTY-ONE

THE ASSET-VALUE FACTOR IN COMMON-STOCK

VALUATION

GENERAL STATEMENT

In Chapter 16 we developed in some detail the technique of determining the net asset value of a given common stock as well as certain related calculations on a per-share basis. We must now consider the significance of such calculations in valuing and selecting common stocks.

The basic fact is that—except in certain limited parts of the common-stock universe—asset values are virtually ignored in the stock market. Not only that; there is a sense in which tangible asset values are a negative factor in the company's exhibit. For, given any amount of earnings, the larger the net worth, the lower the profitability or percent earned on capital; hence the less favorable the showing. There is a temptation to accept this verdict of the market place and to confine our treatment of the asset factor to the exceptional cases or the special areas in which the net worth can be clearly shown to exert an influence on average price.

We think that security analysts should endeavor to attain a wider perspective in their work than is reflected in the current attitude of the stock market. At the least they should understand all the implications of this widespread ignoring of the asset factor. Most of all they should reflect fully on the rather startling truth that as long as a business remains a *private* corporation or partnership the net asset value appearing on the balance sheet is likely to constitute the point of departure for determining what the enterprise is "worth." But once it makes its appearance as a "publicly held company"—even though the shares distributed to the public may constitute only a small part of the total—the net-worth figure seems to lose virtually all its significance. "Value" then becomes dependent almost exclusively on the expected future earnings. (The change seems to take place as if by the waving of a magic wand.) Since in recent years many hundreds of private businesses—generally of small size—have been turned into publicly held ones, at an accelerating pace, this metamorphosis of their main criterion of value should provoke some searching questions. One of these would be: "If net worth no longer counts for anything in valuation, why do all the financial services continue to calculate and publish it for every common stock?"

Viewing the picture broadly, we shall find that in the majority of companies taken at any one time the net-worth figure properly plays so small a part as to warrant our excluding it in the process of valuation. This predominant group may be said to fall in the wide band of issues valued at between, say, two-thirds and twice their asset value. But the analysts will find it worthwhile, for various reasons, to pay attention to the asset factor in the smaller but still considerable proportion of cases falling outside our roughly drawn limits. In addition, net worth has recognized importance in the major fields of public utility and financial companies. Furthermore, "asset values"—as distinguished from the balance-sheet equity—are often a major consideration in the appraisal of concerns owning substantial natural resources.

Illustrative Data. Some initial statistics will give the reader a general idea of the relationships subsisting between market price and net worth. At this writing we have available a compilation of asset values and market prices for a large number of manufacturing companies at the end of 1959.[1] The two figures were provided for 1,218 issues, which we have arranged in the following segments:

Table 41-1

Ratio of price to assets		*Number of companies*
Under 50 percent....................	59	
50 to 100 percent....................	284	
Total under 100 percent.................		343
100 to 200 percent.......................		535
200 to 500 percent....................	277	
500 to 1,000 percent..................	46	
Over 1,000 percent...................	17	
Total over 200 percent.................		340
Total.............................		1,218

This summary indicates that a large fraction of the companies had a December 1959 price between 100 and 200 percent of net worth. Almost exactly as many sold above twice asset value as sold below 100 percent thereof. An impressive number were quoted at levels five and even ten times their net worth. For more detail we supply in Table 41-2 a comparison of the price and net equity of the 30 DJIA issues at the end of 1947 and of 1960. This compilation indicates the wide range covered by these relationships within so homogeneous a group of major companies. In 1947 the ratio of price to net assets was $4\frac{1}{2}$ times as large for Union Carbide as for U.S. Steel. In 1961 it was $10\frac{1}{2}$ times as large for General Electric as for Chrysler.

[1] The data used were compiled by the magazine *News Front* in its 1961 "Directory of 7500 Leading Manufacturers." Its early schedules did not include net asset value; thus many important concerns are excluded from our count.

Table 41-2. Price-Asset Ratios for DJIA Issues, 1960–1961 and 1947*

Company	Book value, year end, 1960	Average price, 1961	1961 price/1960 book value ratio	1947 price/book value ratio
Allied Chemical.............	$ 23.20	58½	226%	45%
ALCOA....................	36.20	69	233	—
American Can..............	31.00	42	135	110
American Smelting & Refining.	—	—	—	117
American Tel and Tel........	59.30	121½	242	113
American Tobacco...........	37.40	88	233	188
Anaconda..................	87.70	54½	62	—
Bethlehem Steel.............	35.90	47	123	57
Chrysler...................	75.80	42½	55	170
Corn Products..............	—	—	—	178
du Pont....................	57.70	220	380	207
Eastman Kodak.............	19.20	108½	555	204
General Foods..............	17.30	70½	405	211
General Electric............	15.10	88	582	170
General Motors.............	19.60	47	238	210
Goodyear..................	18.50	40½	218	55
International Harvester......	67.40	49	72	87
International Nickel.........	20.50	71½	350	158
International Paper..........	20.20	34	166	133
Johns-Manville.............	32.50	65	200	66
Loew's, Inc................	—	—	—	81
National Distillers...........	—	—	—	113
National Steel..............	—	—	—	100
Owens-Illinois Glass.........	52.40	93	177	—
Procter & Gamble...........	16.30	84	515	210
Sears Roebuck..............	19.50	74	380	187
Standard Oil of Calif.........	37.50	52	140	110
Standard Oil of N.J..........	31.80	46	145	114
Swift......................	66.40	44½	66	—
Texaco....................	22.20	50½	250	93
Union Carbide..............	32.50	130	395	247
United Aircraft.............	39.50	47	120	65
U.S. Steel.................	56.60	83	147	52
Westinghouse..............	26.10	44	169	114
Woolworth.................	49.90†	80	160	166
Woolworth.................	107.00‡	80	75	—

* The list of companies reflects changes between 1947 and 1961. The 1947 figures used were year-end price and book values.

† Based on book value as stated on balance sheet.

‡ Based on book value adjusted for market value of Woolworth, Ltd., shares owned, less provision for capital-gain tax.

The Net-worth Factor in Private Business. We return to the striking fact pointed out at the beginning that net worth is a primary factor of value in most privately owned businesses, but seems to be not even of minor moment in most publicly owned concerns. An obvious explanation of this anomaly is that the private owner has no clear-cut measure of the value of his business other than that shown on his balance sheet. Hence he always starts with this figure and often ends with it; any adjustment he makes will be in the direction of adding a tentative increment for "goodwill," which is calculated along conservative lines. If a formal valuation becomes necessary—for example, when estate taxes are due—he is likely to apply a standard formula which may go back to the last century. Such a formula will value goodwill less liberally than the tangible assets.

A typical calculation of this kind, based on a U.S. Treasury formula, may be summarized as follows: Assume a business with $1 million of net assets and average net profits in the preceding five years of $140,000. The formula assumes that $80,000 of the earnings are needed for a fair return of 8 percent on the tangible capital; the remaining $60,000 is "excess," creating a "goodwill" component. The goodwill will be valued at a 15 percent rate, or at "$6\frac{2}{3}$ years' purchase"—i.e., at $6\frac{2}{3}$ times $60,000, or $400,000. The total valuation for estate-tax purposes will thus be $1,400,000. In this case it is equivalent to 10 times average earnings, but that figure is a composite of an 8 percent capitalization rate for the earnings "produced" by the tangible assets and a 15 percent rate for those ascribed to the intangibles.[2]

The Stock Market's Treatment of Net Assets. Nothing faintly resembling this procedure can be detected in the calculations and operations of investors, speculators, and financial analysts with respect to marketable common stocks. By studying the actual behavior of issues in the markets we can, however, infer some ruling relationships between the valuation of tangible assets and of goodwill, as we have defined the latter term above. The basic ratios seem to be the opposite of those obtaining in the field of privately owned business. This would necessarily be true if we made the plausible assumption that the market's multipliers for common stocks tend to vary more or less in proportion to the percent earned on capital. Companies earning a good return are recognized as prosperous in the past and promising for the future; hence their current or average earnings are valued liberally. Conversely, those with a low return on net worth are viewed as unsuccessful and unpromising; their earnings (unless extremely small) tend to be given low multipliers. The arithmetical consequences of this market attitude can be shown in Table 41-3, which is based on certain oversimplified assumptions.

Table 41-3 is not intended as a definitive picture of stock-market valuations—which vary from period to period and among types of companies—but it is fairly representative of familiar relations between profitability and multipliers. The most significant factor, perhaps, is the negative goodwill, or "bad will," created by the low profitability of Company C. (The term may seem less awkward if we think of good and bad will as applying to the attitude of potential investors rather than potential

[2] This subject is treated at length in J. C. Bonbright's authoritative work *The Valuation of Property*, McGraw-Hill Book Company, Inc., New York, 1937, pp. 720–735; also in memoranda of the Internal Revenue Service subsequently issued.

customers towards the enterprise.) This is just another way of saying that companies earning a low return on invested capital tend to sell at a discount from asset value. The remarkable fact about the figures themselves is that the multipliers for the excess earnings ascribed to goodwill (or the earnings deficiency creating bad will) work out at 20 (or 5 percent), while those for the earnings on tangible assets at only 12½ (or 8 percent).

The reader may object that the above calculation, which derives the multiplier exclusively from the rate earned on capital, is inconsistent with our reiterated statement that stock-market multipliers are governed mainly by the assumed rate of future growth. The contradiction is only

Table 41-3

	Company A	Company B	Company C
Equity per share......................	$100	$100	$100
Rate earned on equity................	8%	12%	6%
Assumed multiplier of earnings..........	12½×	15×	10×
Resultant market price................	100	180	60
Resultant goodwill component..........	0	+80	−40
Earnings attributable to:			
Tangible assets@ 8 percent...........	$ 8	$ 8	$ 8
Goodwill@ plus or minus 5 percent....	0	+4	−2
Total earnings....................	$ 8	$ 12	$ 6

apparent, however, because high profitability and good growth tend to go together.

Assets as a Negative Factor in Value. A more serious objection to our type of calculation is that it makes a large asset investment less valuable than a small asset investment—and thus, in a sense, turns assets into liabilities. For if Company C had an equity of $50 per share, instead of $100, it would be earning 12 percent on capital and be entitled to Company B's multiplier of 15, and thus sell at $90 per share instead of $60. Does this mean that the second $50 per share of Company C's assets actually functions as a negative factor, or virtual liability, of no less than $30? If so, could not Company C benefit its stockholders by marking down its assets to half, and by a stroke of the pen double its profitability and add 50 percent to its market price?

This is perhaps an intriguing idea, but fortunately it is not practical.[3] (Too many tricks are still played with corporate figures, as it is, without adding wholesale mark-downs of assets to our troubles.) Security

---

[3] The reader is reminded of moves of this kind actually made by some companies in the 1930's which marked down their plant values to $1. Their purpose, however, was chiefly to relieve the income account of depreciation charges. See references in Chapter 12, pp. 134–135.

analysts would not be led astray by such a blatant bit of financial juggling. Furthermore, as we have already explained, the test of profitability rests on the comparative margin of profit on sales as well as on the indicated rate of return on capital.

Effects of the Market's Disregard. In spite of theoretical objections to the market's ignoring of asset values, we believe that the analyst may accept this well-established attitude when it is applied over a fairly wide range of price-asset relationships. However, he should be cognizant of the possible dangerous consequences of this general philosophy, and also of the areas and situations in which asset values actually do or probably will play a role of some significance in determining market price. One set of harmful results, we are sure, is to be seen in the widespread flotation of new common stocks of relatively small companies which has become so prominent a feature of the early 1960's. It is here that the discrepancy between private-business valuations and stockmarket valuations produces its most spectacular and ominous results.

In past years the main dividing line between shares deemed eligible and ineligible for first-time distribution to the public was the size of the enterprise. Among the millions of small businesses in operation it was never difficult to find a considerable number which were earning a large return on invested capital and had also increased their profits at a high percentage rate over several years past. As is well known, high percentage figures of this sort are more readily attainable by a successful small business, with an investment perhaps under $100,000, than by our large and well-established enterprises with a formidable amount of capital to figure earnings against. But the flourishing small companies were recognized as subject to special hazards growing out of their limited size; and these weaknesses, in the judgment of responsible investment-banking houses, disqualified them from public distribution. This prudent barrier was overcome not long ago, and a flood of little companies began to inundate the market. For most of them the high returns on capital plus apparently impressive growth rates (generally for only a few recent years) permitted an offering price equal to several times the net equity and a subsequent market price well above that.

We think that the purchase of such issues at a price, say, five or more times their net worth must carry great risks to the buyers as a whole, and that these risks are related directly to the net-worth situation. In past periods of similar offerings—always in the higher ranges of bull markets —the invariable sequel was for most of these unseasoned issues to fall *below* their asset values. They were then, belatedly, recognized as unsuitable for public ownership because of their inadequate size, and their shares found buyers in the market only on a *bargain basis*. This meant that, instead of valuing them more generously than from a privately owned ("Main Street") viewpoint, Wall Street now considered them to be worth a good deal less to its buyers than their value to a private owner. If a similar sequel should follow the present spate of new common-stock offerings, the losses will be that much heavier because of the huge multipliers now being paid soon after issuance, and the carnage will indeed be terrible.

There is a perhaps not unimportant detail that bears on the foregoing discussion. A large number of the companies now making their public appearance are engaged in "space-age," "missile-age," and other defense activities. A preponderant part of their business may come from government orders. The Renegotiation Act makes their profits subject to review and possible refund if found unreasonably high. A very high return on invested capital, if derived from government contracts, may be prima facie evidence that the profits have been excessive. We cannot specify the degree of vulnerability that resides in this factor—which has a direct relation with asset value as against market price—but it is not one to be ignored. Nor should it be forgotten that an excess-profits tax—imposed in our last three wars—would be likely to fall most heavily on companies of this sort.[4]

Asset-value Factor in Larger Companies. High ratios of market price to net worth occur, of course, in major prosperous companies as well as in the small concerns we have just been discussing. (However, it is an unprecedented phenomenon of the early 1960's that speculation in "hot issues" of the latter type has undoubtedly produced a greater number of enormous premiums over book value in these than in our strongest stocks.) It would be difficult to develop from experience any proof that a high multiplier of net worth in the case of a leading company will per se make its purchase hazardous and unwise. The danger, if any, would seem to be associated more clearly with a very high multiplier of current or average *earnings*—i.e., with an overgenerous discounting of future prospects. By the nature of the market's valuation process the two ratios tend to go together.

Some plausible reasons may be advanced, at least from the theoretical standpoint, for giving separate weight to the asset factor in all analysts' valuations, and thus for penalizing any stock to some degree when the appraisal based on other factors reaches a high multiplier of net worth. One reason is that asset values are never ignored in legal valuations, which are made for a variety of purposes. (In a number of valuation cases with which we are familiar, the asset values have been given as much as 25 percent weight and the earnings-and-dividend factors 75 percent weight.) As we shall see, this point will almost always increase the trading value of companies which sell at a *discount* from net worth and which for that very reason are often candidates for merger or sale. The opposite effect may be visibly produced for "high-premium" companies under special conditions, such as renegotiation or excess-profits

[4] See Appendix Note 17, p. 750, for some relevant data on a group of "applied-science stocks," taken from a January 1962 study.

taxes previously alluded to. If the excess-profits impost allows an exemption equal to certain percentages on invested capital, it will fall most heavily on the high-premium companies. Economists would here stress the point that high returns on capital attract competition, which ultimately forces down the rate of profit. For long-run calculations this factor must be taken into account. Since high market multipliers of asset value and of earnings must necessarily look forward to many years of growth and superior profitability for their vindication, the "economic law" just alluded to may prove more significant than it currently appears.

Quantitative Adjustments for Small Asset Values. We have always hesitated to lay down any hard and fast rule for evaluating the asset factor in the case of premium companies. In the 1951 edition we suggested, quite tentatively, that the analyst might deduct one-quarter of the amount by which his earning-power valuation exceeded twice the asset value. This "formula" imposed no penalty on an asset deficiency up to 50 percent of the basic appraisal. In the atmosphere of the early 1960's such a rule would doubtless appear unrealistically deflationary, especially as applied to rapidly growing companies. To use an extreme illustration, consider a company assigned a 20 percent growth rate for the next four to seven years, and for which we have posited our maximum recommended multiplier of $41\frac{1}{2}$ times current profits. Such a concern might easily be earning 20 percent on its invested capital, and hence our indicated value would be 8.3 times its net worth. If the analyst then applies the asset-value "deflator" suggested in this paragraph, he would take off about one-fifth of his earning-power valuation, reducing the multiplier to around 33.

Very few, if any, practicing analysts would favor any such reduction—or any rebate at all—in the computed value of a growth stock because of the large premium over asset value which is virtually implicit in the whole growth-stock concept. The reader must decide for himself whether he will accept all, or part, or none of our 1951 suggestion. At bottom the issue is between conservatism (or perhaps "old-fogyism") and optimism.

Valuations Equal to Asset Value. In only a small minority of cases will the standard methods of appraisal, based mainly on expected earnings and dividends, produce a value approximating closely the stated net worth. The wider the analyst makes his range of valuation, the greater the chance, of course, that the asset value will fall within it. In such cases the appraiser may take the net worth itself as a convenient and somehow satisfying measure of "best" value. In so doing, he will find himself in harmony with the practice often followed in formal or legal valuations and will also associate himself with the time-honored private, or "Main Street," point of view.

At former, more tractable levels of the market it was possible for an investor to gear his common-stock investment policy to the net worth as a kind of norm. He could find a wide selection of issues which appeared to have an earning power sufficient to support their book value, but which could be bought at an attractive discount therefrom. This was by no means the only logical basis of investment, and not necessarily the best. (By its nature it excluded nearly all the companies of highest quality and with the most exciting prospects.) But it had special advantages for those who had rather homespun notions of conservative investment. In our present market this kind of common-stock policy is scarcely practicable; most Wall Street people are convinced that it will never again be practicable. But never is a long time.

"Sub-asset" Common Stocks. In schematic opposition to the many companies selling well above asset value we find the inglorious array of those that cannot earn enough to carry their net worth in the market. The reasons for these inadequate earnings are various. They may be inherent in the industry. As is well known, only a handful of our many railroads have been able to earn a fair return on capital under the unfavorable competitive and regulatory conditions afflicting them for many decades. Ironically enough, the airlines, which took away most of the profitable long-haul passenger business from the rail carriers, found themselves in so tight a competitive bind in 1961 that the industry in its entirety showed an operating deficit.

In the manufacturing field, the *News Front* compilation showed that every company detailed in some industry classifications—e.g., 37 concerns in "Communication Equipment"—were quoted above asset value in December 1959. But the majority of those in other industries—e.g., "Furniture and Fixtures" and some "Textile" subdivisions—were quoted below their net worth.

The rate of return on capital often varies widely among companies in the same industry, producing correspondingly diverse relationships between price and asset value. To illustrate this point we present in Table 41-4 a condensed analysis of the comparative exhibits in 1960 of 14 shoe-manufacturing companies, many of which have retail stores and at least one of which is engaged in other lines. (They constitute all those in the Standard & Poor's list which had 1960 sales above $10 million.) The companies are ranked in descending order of ratio of 1960 average price to book value. The earnings figures are those for 1960 only; an average of several years might give a slightly different comparative picture.

Comment: It will be noted that a good general correlation exists between profitability (rate of return on common-stock capital) and the ratio of price to asset value. The price-earnings ratio does not vary here with profitability, as we have suggested above would be a logical expectation. In some individual cases the price appears out of line with other ratios. It is the purpose of this type of analysis to disclose such first-glance discrepancies. They provide leads for the analyst to follow up in a more comprehensive study, which may or may not confirm the indications in the table. It is to be noted that there is no correlation to speak of between the size of these companies and their performance or popularity.

The concerns that do poorly against the industry average may be unfavorably situated in one or more external respects, or they may suffer from bad management. Our concern at this point is to inquire only whether the possession of net assets is a factor to be considered by analysts apart from the inadequate earnings on these assets.

Table 41-4. Comparative Ratios for Shoe-manufacturing Companies, 1960

| Company | Sales (in millions) | Per-share figures | | | Ratios | | |
		Earned	Book value	Price average	Price/ book value	Earnings/ book value	Price/ earnings
Melville..................	$161.6	$1.92	$ 8.10	28	345 %	23.6 %	14.6 ×
U.S. Shoe.................	51.4	2.72	13.90	40	288	19.6	14.7
Green Shoe...............	21.8	1.53	8.00	20*	250	19.1	13.0
Agnew Surpass...........	16.7	1.48	11.00	19	173	8.1	12.8
Brown Shoe..............	295.8	5.96	47.40	72	152	12.6	13.8
Genesco..................	321.1	2.05	23.20	33	142	8.8	16.1
International Shoe.........	296.5	2.61	32.20	35	108	8.1	13.4
Weyenberg Shoe...........	18.4	5.65	44.20	45½†	103	12.8	8.0
Shoe Corporation of America	126.7	2.00	21.80	20	92	9.2	10.0
Julian & Kokenge.........	13.7	4.62	36.60	32½	88	14.2	7.0
National Shoes............	28.1	.84	12.00	10	83	7.0	11.9
A. S. Beck...............	61.7	.61	20.80	11½	55	2.9	19.3
Nunn-Bush..............	16.5	1.53	32.40	15	46	4.7	10.2
Endicott Johnson..........	141.4	2.22(d)	70.10‡	31	43	§	§

* First offered at 20 in October 1960.
† Split 3 for 1 in 1961.
‡ Including inventory reserve, later added to surplus.
§ Deficit.

It is clear that in the extreme case the assets must be given some consideration. A company with no earnings, and even with no definite prospect of earnings, will not sell for zero in the market. For the same reason a truly marginal company, with very small earning power, will usually sell at a large multiplier of its microscopic earnings—apparently rivaling the market favorites in this purely arithmetical ratio. In such cases the investor is paying for the assets rather than for the earning power. The assets are expected in some way to produce a satisfactory result for the buyer who gets them at a low fraction of their book value—either by being made more productive, or by bulk sale to, or merger with, some other enterprise, or—very rarely indeed —by piecemeal liquidation.

The sale or merger of a "sub-asset" company is a far from negligible possibility. The number of such transactions has greatly increased in recent years. The acquiring enterprise is able to obtain tangible assets at well below their reproduction cost less depreciation, plus a certain added volume of sales, plus at least some worthwhile personnel. One might say that the longer and the farther a company sells below its net worth, the greater the pressure from various sources either to improve its operating results or to sell or merge. In a merger the net assets are bound to receive serious consideration in arriving at the terms of the deal.

Example: Diamond T Motor Co. For several years the shares of this concern were quoted below book value because of insufficient earnings. In 1955, for example, they showed earnings of only 66 cents on net assets of $30 per share, and sold as low as 13¾. In 1958 the company sold its inventories to White Motors at about cost, turned over its business to the purchaser, and later liquidated its remaining assets. The high price in 1959 was 39½—above the last stated book value.

It would be logical, therefore, to suggest to the analyst that he assign some plus value for an appreciable excess of net assets above the valuation he makes based on anticipated earnings and dividends. We have not done so in the past, in quantitative terms, except in the special cases of "sub-current-asset" stocks, to be discussed below. Our reason has been both general conservatism and the absence of clear-cut statistical indications that such an excess of ordinary asset value over price may be counted on to be made up in the market within a reasonable number of years. Developments since 1950—especially the rise in the general level of the market and the wide extension of the merger movement—make the case for a quantitative recognition of excess assets somewhat stronger than before. We might suggest, again tentatively, that the analyst give weight to ordinary net worth only when it exceeds 150 percent of his earning-power value. He might arbitrarily add one-third of the amount by which two-thirds of net worth exceeds his earning-power appraisal. For example, say a company has estimated earning power of $3 and book value of $100 per share and assume the earnings and dividends warrant a value of $30. If the analyst follows this formula he would add one-third of the difference between $67 and $30, making his final valuation about $42.[5]

NET-CURRENT-ASSET VALUE

We feel on more solid ground in discussing those cases in which the market price or the computed value based on earnings and dividends is less than the *net current assets* applicable to the common stock. (The reader will recall that in this computation we deduct all obligations and preferred stock from the working capital to determine the balance for the common.) From long experience with this type of situation we can say that it is always interesting, and that the purchase of a

---

[5] The student will note a parallelism between this "formula" and that suggested above for the opposite situation.

diversified group of companies on this "bargain basis" is almost certain to result profitably within a reasonable period of time. One reason for calling such purchases bargain issues is that usually net-current-asset value may be considered a conservative measure of liquidating value. Thus, as a practical matter most such companies could be disposed of for not less than their working capital, if that capital is conservatively stated. It is a general rule that at least enough can be realized for the plant account and the miscellaneous assets to offset any shrinkage sustained in the process of turning the current assets into cash. (This rule would nearly always apply to a negotiated sale of the business to some reasonably interested buyer.) The working-capital value behind a common stock can be readily computed. Consequently, by using this figure as the equivalent of "minimum liquidating value," we can discuss with some degree of confidence the actual relationship between the market price of a stock and the realizable value of the business.

The historical development of this relationship has been interesting. Before the 1920's, common stocks selling under current-asset value were practically unknown. During the "new-era" market, when prime emphasis was placed on prospects to the exclusion of other factors, a few issues in depressed industries sold below their working capital. In the Great Depression of the early 1930's this phenomenon became widespread. Our computations show that about 40 percent of all industrial companies on the New York Stock Exchange were quoted at some time in 1932 at less than their net current assets. Many issues actually sold for less than their net cash assets alone. Writing about this situation in 1932, we stated that the market prices as a whole seemed to indicate that American business was "worth more dead than alive."[6] It seemed evident that the market had carried its pessimism much too far—to compensate, no doubt, for its reckless optimism of the 1920's.

Ratio of Sub-current-asset Stocks a Key to Market Levels. At the top of the ensuing bull market, in 1937, this situation had all but disappeared; but in the following recession about 20 percent of all industrials sold on a "sub-current-asset" basis. For a number of years thereafter the variations in the number of such issues on the New York Stock Exchange could have been taken as a fairly dependable guide to the technical position of the stock market. When the number was large, the market had reached a buying range; when it was very small, the market was dangerously high. (In May 1946, for example, it was difficult to find any "sub-current-asset" issues.)

In 1947–1950, however, we witnessed a new and more extraordinary phase of this phenomenon. The prevailingly high earnings built up working capital for many companies at a rapid rate, but the prevailingly cautious attitude toward the future prevented stock prices from moving

[6] See three articles by Benjamin Graham on this subject, published in *Forbes Magazine* on June 1, 1932, June 13, 1932, and July 1, 1932.

up in the same proportion. The result was not only that many issues sold persistently between 1947 and 1950 at less than their working capital, but, more strangely, that this relationship was largely due to the very fact that the companies had been showing such large earnings. Thus the large earnings themselves might paradoxically be called at least half the cause of this disparity, because they had raised working capital to a figure that exceeded the lagging market prices. In former years a low price in relation to current assets almost always indicated unsatisfactory current earnings. But between 1946 and 1950, if it reflected anything else than the market's heedlessness, it must have indicated only a distrust of the future in the face of a highly satisfactory current performance.

Example: As an illustration of the extraordinary relationship to be found between price and all factors of value in 1949 we append data pertaining to Grinnell Corporation (sprinkler systems) in that year.

Table 41-5. Grinnell Corporation, 1949

Average price of common, 1949	$27\frac{1}{4}$
Number of shares	500,000
Average market value of common issue	$13,625,000
Average market value of capital funds	$13,625,000
Net assets for capital funds, December 1949	35,085,000
Per share of common stock:	
Net current assets (less senior issues)	$44.62*
Net tangible assets (book value)	70.17
Earned 1947	10.78
Earned 1948	14.50
Earned 1949	12.51
Total, 3 years, 1947–1949	$37.79
10-year average 1940–1949 (balance-sheet basis)	6.17
Compared with 1939, per share:	
Increase in market price of common (average for year)	$13\frac{1}{2}$
Increase in net current assets for common (year-end figure)	$30.80
Increase in asset value of common (year-end figure)	47.90

* Includes estimated working capital of Canadian subsidiary.

As the market advanced determinedly after 1950, the proportion of sub-current-asset issues declined. Somewhat surprisingly, however, as late as 1958 they were still in plentiful supply.[7] But the subsequent further rise in the market reduced this group to a mere handful, consisting chiefly of companies that had made an unusually dismal profit showing for years in succession. From the vantage (or disadvantage) point of our experience we are inclined to regard the drying up of these bargain opportunities as an additional indication that the general market has reached a hazardous level. Most Wall Street people will say, of course, that this detail is only another indication that past measures and guides are no longer useful, and that the forward-looking investor will not be misled by their indications.

[7] A compilation published in 1958 by Stock-Statistics, Inc., listed 169 issues selling at the beginning of the year at or below their working-capital value.

Cash Assets—Special Factor in Valuation. Some companies sell at too low a price because their cash assets are too large. This sounds like a paradox, but a moment's thought will show that the statement can be true. Market price depends chiefly on earnings; cash assets bring in no earnings or very little. A company with nothing but cash in bank could not possibly earn enough to support a market price equal to its cash-asset value.

It has been by no means unusual to find companies that are so rich in cash that they are necessarily poor in earning power as related to book value.

We shall reprint, with its sequel, material given at this point in our 1951 edition (page 490):

Example: As a detailed example we supply figures for F. H. Shattuck (operating the "Schrafft's" chain) comparing them with B/G Foods, which is in the same general field [Table 41-6]. B/G Foods sold in 1950 at 50% above book value, while Shattuck sold 50% below book value. This difference is explained by the much more effective use of capital made by the smaller chain. Its sales per dollar of common capital were nearly 3.8 times those of Shattuck. A good part of this divergence, in turn, may be traced to the huge amount of idle cash assets held by Shattuck. From the stockholder's viewpoint Shattuck's policy makes it impossible to earn a fair return on its capital or to support an average market price equal to book value. From the bargain hunter's viewpoint the situation may be attractive for the very reason the outside stockholder is suffering. For this $9 per share he would be getting $7.70 of free-cash assets and $10.80 of other assets. Hence, even though the earnings on total price are not particularly attractive, those on the noncash portion of the price work out at a very high percentage.[8]

Sequel: Shattuck had a singularly uneventful history for the next seven years, its price fluctuating each year quite narrowly about the 9 level. The earnings and dividends made no progress at all, and the cash assets were drawn down for various capital expenditures. Nonetheless, the stock "came to life" in 1958, and by 1961 it had advanced above 31. In this case the development of speculative interest and a major rise in price coincided with the disappearance of the redundant cash.

During the same period, B/G Foods made modest progress in its earnings and maintained a liberal dividend, but its price did not rise above 17.

Another Example: An illustration of a somewhat different sort, current as we write, is supplied by Burton-Dixie Corporation, maker of

---

[8] Quite a few companies sold at times in 1949 below their free-cash assets per share. These include Pullman, American Hawaiian Steamship, Saco-Lowell, Easy Washing Machine, Stewart-Warner, N.Y. Shipbuilding, Douglas Aircraft, Gisholt Machine, U.S. Freight. Some of these had large earnings on the full market price without deduction for the surplus cash.

cushions, pads, mattresses, etc. The calculation of the cash-asset value of its shares as of November 1961 appears on page 217 above. The earnings had fallen from $3 in 1959 to only 55 cents per share in 1961. In early 1962 the company passed completely its long-maintained dividend of at least $1.20 per annum, and the price declined below 20. This was just a little less than the "free-cash-asset value," and compares with a full asset value of more than 50.

Table 41-6. Two Restaurant Chains Compared

	F. H. Shattuck ("Schrafft's")	B/G Foods
Price of common, July 1950	9	10
Number of shares of common	1,120,000	126,000
Market value of common issue	$10,080,000	$1,260,000
December 31, 1949:		
Cash assets	$ 8,610,000	$ 565,000
Other current assets	5,236,000	176,000
Less current liabilities	2,628,000	614,000
Senior securities at par	....	372,000
Working capital for common, excluding cash items	2,608,000	810,000(d)
Other assets, net	9,501,000	1,112,000
Total assets for common	20,719,000	867,000
Sales	41,742,000	6,720,000
Net earnings for common stock	925,000	164,000
Per-share figures, 1949:		
Free cash assets	$ 7.70	$ 0
Net current assets	10.03	*
Net tangible assets	18.50	6.49
Market price less free cash assets	1.30	10.00
Earned for common stock	0.83	1.31
(Earned for common stock, average 1945–1949)	(1.20)	(1.59)
Percent earned on book value of common	4.5%	20.0%
Percent earned on market price of common	9.2%	13.1%
Percent earned on book value less free cash assets	7.7%	20.0%
Percent earned on market price less free cash assets	63.9%	13.1%

* Deficit.

It is not possible to predict the future results of an individual stock purchase of the type described in our two examples, especially since most of these will show subnormal profit margins and earning power. But unless they are in a kind of business that may produce large operating losses they can hardly fail to work out satisfactorily on a group basis.

A Tax Aspect of Sub-asset Situations. The student may reflect on the fact that the 52 percent partnership held by the U.S. Treasury in the profits of earning companies carries with it an equivalent 52 percent interest in most types of losses. Operating losses are carried backward against prior years' or forward against later years' profits. Under certain conditions, not too difficult to meet, they can be availed of by a profitable company which takes over another with tax losses to its "credit." In somewhat the same way a decline of *enterprise value* to a figure well below its net worth (presumably its tax base) may possibly be recouped to the extent of one-half. This would be done by the realization of the indicated loss under circumstances which permit it to be offset against equivalent operating profits of the same or another company. The purpose of this cryptic utterance is to indicate that somewhat the same kind of tax advantages, which have recently been stressed so much in the case of concerns "blessed" with carry-forward losses, may exist with respect to companies valued in the market at well below their asset values, even though operating losses are absent.

A Stockholder-Management Problem Sometimes Involved in These Issues. In quite a number of instances companies selling below working capital have had disappointing past records. Either they have lost money or they have earned less than enough to justify a price equal to the working-capital figure. Under such conditions the current assets alone could not establish investment value in excess of the market price. They are not necessarily "bargain issues."

But these issues supply an interesting problem of another sort. Why should the stockholders be satisfied to permit matters to continue on so unsatisfactory a basis? Should not they insist that management take some steps to improve this situation—so that the company will be worth as a going concern, and on an earning-power basis, at least as much as the stockholders could realize out of it by sale or liquidation? This is one of the issues that may arise between the owners of the business and those responsible for directing its affairs. We shall discuss it in Chapter 50, which is devoted to stockholder-management relations.

Adjustment for Net Current Assets. On page 558 we suggested an arbitrary reduction of the earning-power value when it exceeds twice the asset value. A similar adjustment in the opposite direction may properly be made when the net-current-asset value alone exceeds the earning-power value. Our suggestion is that one-half of such excess be added to the earning-power value to give the final appraisal figure.

INDUSTRIES WHERE ASSET VALUES ARE IMPORTANT

Our chapters on public utilities stress the central fact that as regulated enterprises their profits may be limited, in nearly all jurisdictions, by enforced rate reductions. The basic criterion of rate regulation is the actual percentage return shown on capital, as compared with an allowable figure. Thus invested capital, or net worth plus debt, plays a large part in determining the permissible earnings. This does not mean that all public utilities should be valued at net worth or at the same ratio to net worth. As the next two chapters will make clear, there are differences in both the regulatory philosophy of the various state commissions, and also in the past and expected growth rates in the territories served. These will justify a significant variation in the earnings per dollar of asset value and in the multipliers assigned to the earnings. It will be found, however, that in most years of stock-market history the ratios of utility market prices to asset values tended to cluster around a fairly modest premium above 100 percent, and that wide divergencies from the mean were quite exceptional.

In most groups of *financial* enterprises the asset-value factor has exerted a greater influence than in industrial companies. Since their assets are mainly cash, investments, and receivables, their stated net worth is taken to be fairly representative of their actual liquidating value—subject to certain adjustments, such as allowance for an equity in unearned premiums of insurance companies, etc. The closest relation to asset value is to be found, of course, in the open-end investment funds. This is the necessary consequence of their fixed policy of issuing and redeeming shares at about current liquidating value. The closed-end companies, which do not redeem shares on demand, are subject to significant variations between asset value and price. Yet the range tends to be much narrower than for industrial companies. A compilation at the end of 1959 shows that 22 such companies sold at between 1 and 29 percent discounts from net asset value; one, of the holding company type, was quoted at a 50 percent discount. (Some had shown premiums up to 20 percent in the previous ten years; but there were no premiums in December 1959.[9])

Until recent years, the price-asset ratios for banks and (non-life) insurance companies had a tendency to bunch within a fairly narrow area, which varied with the times. Somewhat surprisingly, the modal figure stayed below 100 percent for a long period—a fact which called into question the basic profitability of these important enterprises. It was quite rare to find issues selling at more than twice or less than half of asset values. A greater scattering of ratios was discernible among the various types of finance companies. Also, a goodly number of life insurance stocks—as distinct from the casualty companies—have sold at many times their stated asset values.

The valuation of life insurance companies is something of a specialized affair, chiefly because of actuarial complexities. It has become customary in this field to ascribe a definite value to the insurance in force—at so much per $1,000 of face value—the rate varying between the different forms of policy. These policy values are included with the tangible assets in figuring the "adjusted book value" of the shares; and the increase in

[9] Source: Arthur Wisenberger, *Investment Companies*, 1960 edition, p. 258.

the policy values for a given year is added to the reported earnings to give "adjusted earnings" for the year.

We consider the latter treatment fundamentally unsound, for reasons that are developed in Appendix Note 6, p. 730. (This note deals first with a companion thesis of "net worth accounting" advanced by Sheraton Corp. in its 1960 report.) There are many ways in which increases in capital values can be presented in the guise of capitalizable earnings. The investor must be on his guard against them, and the analyst must oppose them.

Natural Resources Companies. Primary producers of raw materials usually own substantial reserves which can be valued on the basis of their quantities and grades. This statement would apply in general to those producing metals, oil and gas, lumber, sulphur, and many other minerals. Analyses of such enterprises will often assign a monetary value to their developed reserves and use this value as at least one of the tests of the attractiveness of the shares at current market. We have seen this method applied most often among the oil and gas companies, and also fairly regularly for lumber companies with large timber reserves. For the latter a value of, say, $2–$4 per thousand board feet of standing timber owned or controlled may be used. For oil and gas companies customary rates in 1961 would be about $1.10 per barrel for domestic oil, $0.40 for South American oil, $0.30 for Near East reserves, and 6–7 cents per 1,000 cu ft for gas reserves—all as estimated by the companies to be contained in their developed acreage. (A supplemental calculation may be made for semideveloped reserves.) The value of reserves in undeveloped acreage is usually not computed separately from their book cost, but it can exert a determining influence on the market price ultimately reached by the shares.

Advantage of Small Companies. In the early 1960's a rather paradoxical situation developed in the oil and gas group. Many small companies sold out to larger ones. The price netted by the shareholders was usually quite high in relation to their earnings and sometimes several times the market price ruling before the negotiations. In effect, all these smaller companies proved to have a realizable value for their owners considerably higher than that paid in the market for either the comparable earnings or the comparable stated reserves of the larger and presumably stronger units.

A 1962 Example. An interesting example of the working out of this anomaly is found in the history of TXL Oil Corporation. This entity came into being in 1954 through a spin-off of oil interests by the old-established Texas Pacific Land Trust. The actual earnings of the new concern were not large—about 50 cents per share on 5.6 million shares—but its ownership of mineral rights on 1.7 million undeveloped acres in Texas gave the shares speculative appeal. Thus in 1954 they sold above 41, or about 80 times the earnings. When nothing spectacular hap-

pened in the company's affairs the stock declined to 12½ in 1957 and
again to 14⅞ in 1960. But in February 1962, Texaco, Inc., offered to take
the company over on a share-exchange basis equivalent to 35 for the
TXL stock. This price was equal to 75 times the 1961 earnings of 46
cents per share; while Texaco itself—one of the largest and most successful of the petroleum companies—was concurrently selling at 16 times
its 1961 earnings.[10]

For an analogy with this phenomenon one may have to go back to
the late 1930's when the giant distilling companies were building up their
whisky reserves by buying small concerns. The price paid by them per
barrel of whisky acquired would have given their own shares a value far
above their market price. Alas! There was no one available to buy out
the giants on such terms.

[10] Similar take-overs occurred in 1960–1961 in Monterey Oil, Anderson-Prichard,
Bishop Oil, Honolulu Oil, and others. Most of these were aided by a rather complicated tax-saving device, known as an "A-B-C transaction."

CHAPTER FORTY-TWO

THE VALUATION OF PUBLIC UTILITY COMMON

STOCKS

Public utility common stocks are susceptible, we believe, of valuation for investment purposes within considerably more precise limits than the common stocks of either railroads or industrial companies. This results from the high degree of stability of utility earnings, the reasonable predictability of growth trends, and the general improbability of any sudden or unexpected developments that might have a marked effect on operations. Moreover, the industry typically does not possess the speculative growth possibilities found in certain manufacturing and industrial enterprises, elements which magnify the problems of investment-valuation techniques.

By this we do not, of course, mean that the electric industry is lacking in growth characteristics. The very opposite is true; continued and substantial long-term growth can be looked forward to with a high degree of confidence. Generally speaking, however, the benefits of this growth in terms of increasing per-share earnings for the common stock will be moderate, ranging for most companies between about 4 and 8 percent per year, an important determinant being the factor of leverage resulting from variations in the capital or security structure. This results, of course, from the impact of the regulatory procedure, which closely relates earnings to the investment in productive facilities.

Despite this, however, the recurrent tendency of market prices to deviate, sometimes widely, from reasonable investment values presents with interesting frequency investment opportunities for both advantageous buying and profitable selling. The discovery and recognition of these opportunities test the skill and experience of the analyst.

In Chapters 20 and 21 we have discussed in general terms the analysis of utility balance sheets and income statements. We have pointed out that perhaps the unique factor affecting the earning power of public service enterprises is their subjection to governmental regulation. In effect, this sets a ceiling on earnings, a ceiling which varies largely in accordance with the policies of the regulatory body having jurisdiction.

570

Public utility analysis, therefore, when directed toward determining the sound investment value of a common stock, must first arrive at a reasonable estimate of what a company is likely to earn under the impact of the economic forces, and second, what it will be permitted to earn within the regulatory framework. Third, the analyst must exercise an informed judgment as to the present reasonable value of the earnings, by applying an appropriate capitalization rate thereto.

This represents a three-pronged attack on the problem of utility common-stock valuation. In the following pages the problem will be considered in the above sequence.

ESTIMATING FUTURE EARNINGS

The present investment value of a common stock essentially depends upon the future income to be expected from it, plus future capital appreciation. This requires that an estimate or projection of future earnings and dividends be made by the analyst. The technique of such a forecast must be based upon a step-by-step analysis and projection of the factors that determine earnings, i.e., number of customers, sales, revenue, and operating and capital costs. Each of these factors should be broken down into its component parts, so that the forecast may be made on the basis of the fullest understanding of the determinants involved.

For example, the projection of operating revenue should take into account the make-up of the company's total load in terms of the various customer classifications and should reflect a composite of projections of revenue to be obtained from each group. Only in this way can the varying impact of the different group characteristics be correctly weighted. Projections of operating expenses must similarly be based upon a breakdown more complete than that commonly given in the income statement, and we suggest that the analyst use the method of presentation discussed in Chapter 21.

It should be emphasized, perhaps, that projections of this sort are subject to a considerable factor of possible error and that the best the analyst can do is to try to make his assumptions as reasonable as possible in the light of all the facts at hand. The object is not to determine exactly what earnings figure may be realized as of some specified date in the future, but rather to arrive at a level of earnings, with a certain margin of give and take, that may reasonably be looked forward to as achievable within a future period of time. When and as new and unforeseen developments occur, it will, of course, be necessary to review and perhaps revise the forecast.

During the 1940's when public utility holding companies were being liquidated under the impact of the Holding Company Act of 1935, the SEC consistently made use of earnings projections for the purpose of determining security values. In a memorandum on "Charges in Lieu of

Taxes," dated Nov. 16, 1945,[1] the Commission pointed out that "notwithstanding the uncertainty inherent in estimates of future earnings, it is apparent that the formation of a considered investment judgment ordinarily involves a conclusion as to the future prospects of the company."

Emphasis has been carefully placed, however, on the lack of mathematical exactness of such projections. In its opinion approving the reorganization plan of Public Service Corporation of New Jersey, the Commission stated:

> We use such earnings estimates emphasizing that the estimation of prospective income is, under the best of circumstances, an "appraisal of many factors that cannot be reduced to fixed formula." A "prediction as to what will occur in the future, an estimate, as distinguished from mathematical certitude, is all that can be made." Our judgment in this regard does not imply that we believe that the books will show in any given year in the future net income in the same amount as that which we have estimated, but only that, in the foreseeable future, the earnings of the company will on the average so approximate such amount that it may appropriately be employed for the purpose of testing the fairness of the proposed treatment of security holders.[2]

Various techniques have been developed and are used by different analysts for the purpose of projecting earnings. Perhaps the simplest method is to make an estimate of future capital investment, assume a certain over-all rate of return, and compute the results in terms of per-share earnings on the common stock.

While this approach is useful and should be used as a supplementary test, it cannot be relied on alone. It assumes that under virtually all circumstances a company will in fact earn its full allowable return and that this is all that the investor need to take into consideration. Actually, we know that a utility's earnings are only partially determined by the rate levels which, in regulatory theory, are designed to produce a fair return. A utility company has to compete with many other demands made on the consumer's dollar, and this competition is increasing as expanding utility services partake more and more of a semiluxury nature. Competitive business methods are assuming an increasingly important role in maintaining the financial well-being of a utility company.

Thus the utility analyst realizes that while regulation is supposed to guarantee an *opportunity* to earn a fair return, it by no means guarantees that a fair return will be earned in fact. The analyst, therefore, must try to forecast future earnings, absent major rate changes, and then form some opinion as to whether the forecast indicates the likelihood of some rate adjustment, either upward or downward.

An illustration of methods that we have used in making earnings projections is shown in Tables 42-1 to 42-4. The projections and comments

[1] Holding Company Act Release No. 6,200.
[2] Holding Company Act Release No. 8,002, Feb. 27, 1948.

pertaining thereto were made in the late spring of 1955 for the purpose of estimating the reasonable investment value of the common stock of Puget Sound Power & Light Company. Comment will be made later on developments subsequent to the date of this analysis.

Puget Sound Power & Light Company. *Earnings Projection.* The study required a projection of revenues and operating expenses. For the purpose of estimating depreciation accruals, fixed charges, and per-share earnings, it was also necessary to make projections of plant growth and the components of capitalization.

Table 42-1. Utility Plant

(Dollar figures in thousands)

	Actual	Projected		
	1954	1955	1956	1957
Plant at beginning of year..........	$105,973	$111,448	$117,448	$132,448
Gross additions*...............	7,015	7,000	16,000	17,000
Total.......................	$112,988	$118,448	$133,448	$149,448
Retirements†..................	1,540	1,000	1,000	1,000
Plant at end of year..............	$111,448	$117,448	$132,448	$148,448
Depreciation reserve				
Reserve at beginning of year........	$16,663	$16,945	$17,445	$18,045
Accruals......................	1,441	1,500	1,600	1,700
Total.......................	$18,104	$18,445	$19,045	$19,745
Retirements...................	1,159	1,000	1,000	1,000
Reserve at end of year............	$16,945	$17,445	$18,045	$18,745
Percent plant.................	15.2%	14.9%	13.6%	12.6%

* Based on statement in 1954 annual report that new construction for period 1955–1959 would aggregate about $75,000,000. Annual amounts based on our then estimates of spreading.

† Based on assumption that retirements average about 8 percent of gross additions.

The plant-account projection was based on a statement in the company's 1954 annual report that expenditures for construction would aggregate about $7 million in 1955 and some $75 million for the period 1955–1959. In our projection we made an arbitrary allocation of this amount to the years 1956 and 1957.

1. *Projected Plant and Reserve Growth.* Table 42-1 shows total utility plant at the beginning and end of each year. Gross additions represent our own spreading of the construction program mentioned above. While the table above shows only the figures for a three-year period, actually our projection was extended for the full five years.

2. *Projected Capitalization Growth.* At December 31, 1954, the company's capital structure consisted of 26 percent mortgage bonds, 15.6 percent long-term notes, and 58.4 percent common stock and surplus. These capital ratios were unusually conservative and placed the company in a position where it could finance substantial growth through the issuance of bonds or other senior securities. Thus we contemplated no sale of additional common stock over the period of the projection. By the end of 1957 our projected capitalization still showed a common-stock equity ratio of 45.1 percent, a very conservative ratio for an electric utility.

Table 42-2. Capitalization Growth

(Dollar figures in thousands)

	Actual Dec. 31, 1954	Projected					
		Additions	Dec. 31, 1955	Additions	Dec. 31, 1956	Additions	Dec. 31, 1957
Mortgage bonds.........	$25,000	....	$ 25,000	$10,000	$ 35,000	$15,000	$ 50,000
Interest requirement...	875	....	875	350	1,225	525	1,750
Percent..............	3.5%	....	3.5%	3.5%	3.5%	3.5%	3.5%
Long-term note.........	15,000	....	15,000	....	15,000	....	15,000
Interest requirement...	450	....	450	....	450	....	450
Percent..............	3.0%	....	3.0%	....	3.0%	....	3.0%
Bank loans............	....	$3,000	3,000	4,000	7,000	....	7,000
Interest requirement...	....	90	90	120	210	....	210
Percent..............	....	3.0%	3.0%	3.0%	3.0%	....	3.0%
Common stock.........	21,779	....	21,779	....	21,779	....	21,779
Earned surplus.........	34,443	930	35,373	970	36,343	1,270	37,613
Total...............	$96,222	....	$100,152	....	$115,122	....	$131,392
Depreciation accruals.'...	....	$1,500	....	$ 1,600	....	$ 1,700	....
Cash at beginning of year	....	3,988	....	2,418	....	2,988	....
Total available cash...	....	$9,418	....	$18,988	....	$20,958	....
Less gross additions to property..............	....	7,000	....	16,000	....	17,000	....
Cash at end of year......	....	....	$ 2,418	....	$ 2,988	....	$ 3,988

3. *Projected Operating Revenue.* Because of substantial sales of properties in 1948, 1949, and 1951, the company's operating revenue record could not be used as a guide to projecting future growth. In this instance it was necessary to go to the company's management to obtain past figures adjusted for the effect of property sales. We were informed that over the prior eight years, kwh sales, as adjusted, had increased at an average annual rate of about 11 percent and that the company expected a continuation of this rate of growth for at least the next several years. As a matter of our own judgment we used a 9 percent annual rate of increase in projecting revenue.

4. *Operating Profit.* On account of the sale of properties mentioned above, the company's longer-term past record was of limited use as a guide to the future, and this limitation considerably increased the difficulties of making any projection of operating profit that could be used with confidence. During the period 1951–1954 operating profit rose sharply

from 40.8 percent to 49 percent, as shown in Table 42-3, primarily reflecting reduced operating taxes and miscellaneous expenses. As is shown below in our earnings projection, however, we did not think it prudent to assume that the 1954 level of operating profit would be maintained.

5. *Projected Earnings.* The data now developed permit a projection of earnings for the company, from operating revenue all the way down to balance for surplus (Table 42-4). Operating revenue is projected at an approximate 9 percent growth rate, and a moderate decline is assumed

Table 42-3. Operating Profit

(Dollar figures in thousands)

	1951	1952	1953	1954	Average 1951– 1954, %
Operating revenue............	$21,296	$19,749	$20,334	$20,980	
Operating expenses:					
Wages....................	6,169	5,946	6,306	6,065	
Percent revenue.........	29.0%	30.1%	31.1%	29.0%	29.8
Fuel cost.................	377	1,623	594	24	
Percent revenue.........	1.8%	8.2%	2.9%	0.1%	3.2
Purchased power...........	973	710	8	596	
Percent revenue.........	4.6%	3.6%	....	2.8%	2.8
Operating taxes............	2,605	2,219	2,291	2,284	
Percent revenue.........	12.2%	11.2%	11.3%	10.9%	11.4
Other expenses............	2,493	1,698	1,673	1,726	
Percent revenue.........	11.6%	8.6%	8.2%	8.2%	9.2
Total operating expenses.......	$12,617	$12,196	$10,872	$10,695	
Percent revenue...........	49.2%	61.7%	53.5%	51.0%	56.4
Operating profit.............	8,679	7,553	9,462	10,285	
Percent revenue...........	40.8%	38.3%	46.5%	49.0%	43.6

in operating profit. Depreciation provisions are taken from Table 42-1, and fixed charges are based on Table 42-2, with consideration given to the estimated effect of the credit for interest charged to construction. In view of the planned heavy construction program, this last item could be expected to be considerably larger than in the preceding several years.

The annual provision for depreciation shown in the table appears distinctly low. This is explained by two factors: The company is predominantly hydroelectric and depreciation is based on the sinking-fund or compound-interest method, which provides lower accruals in the early years of property life and higher accruals in the later years. In respect to Federal income taxes, we used a "judgment" rate of 50 percent in our projection. While the corporate rate at the time of our analysis was 52 percent, and still is, at that time there seemed to be grounds for expecting some reduction. The lower ratio of the income tax to the balance of earnings, shown in Table 42-4, reflects the impact of the significantly larger depreciation provisions taken for tax purposes.

As we mentioned earlier, a projection such as this is not intended to be an exact forecast of what the figures will be as of any specified date. It is rather an attempt to show a level of earnings which can reasonably be anticipated in the foreseeable future, and which can be used

Table 42-4. Earnings
(Dollar figures in thousands)

	Actual		Projected		
	1953	1954	1955	1956	1957
Operating revenue..........	$20,234	$20,980	$23,000	$25,000	$27,200
Operating profit............	9,462	10,285	11,000	11,700	12,600
Percent revenue..........	46.5%	49.0%	47.8%	46.8%	46.4%
Depreciation.............	1,381	1,441	1,500	1,600	1,700
Percent plant..........	1.3%	1.3%	1.3%	1.2%	1.2%
Charges.................	1,195	1,288	1,300	1,400	1,500
Percent debt...........	3.3%	3.2%	3.3%	2.8%	2.6%
Balance....................	$ 6,886	$ 7,556	$ 8,200	$ 8,700	$ 9,400
Federal income tax........	2,889	3,178	3,400	3,600	3,800
Percent balance...........	42.0%	42.0%	42.0%	41.0%	40.0%
Balance....................	$ 3,997	$ 4,378	$ 4,800	$ 5,100	$ 5,600
Other income.............	31	83	50	50	50
Net income................	$ 4,028	$ 4,461	$ 4,850	$ 5,150	$ 5,650
Gross income..............	$ 5,223	$ 5,749	$ 6,150	$ 6,550	$ 7,150
Percent capital and surplus.	5.7%	6.0%	6.2%	5.7%	5.4%
Net income................	4,028	4,461	4,850	5,150	5,650
Preferred dividends........	....	....	....	....	....
Balance for common........	$ 4,028	$ 4,461	$ 4,850	$ 5,150	$ 5,650
Common dividends........	2,777	3,496	3,920	4,180	4,380
Balance to surplus..........	$ 1,251	$ 965	$ 930	$ 970	$ 1,270
Earnings per share*.........	$1.23	$1.37	$1.48	$1.58	$1.73
Dividends per share*........	0.85	1.07	1.20	1.28	1.34
Common shares (000)*.......	3,267	3,267	3,267	3,267	3,267

* 1953–1954 figures adjusted for 3-for-2 stock split in 1955.

as a basis for a current investment appraisal of the company's common stock. Although the figures are broken down in detail, it is not the individual figures that are important, but rather the enveloping pattern that they reveal. While the figures are precise, they should be considered an indication of a general area or level rather than an exact forecast. The same attitude should be taken toward the end result, or earnings per share.

As we have mentioned previously, these projections were made in the late spring of 1955 and were based, of course, on the information available at that time. Actually the company made a somewhat better showing than our estimate and subsequently reported per-share earnings of $1.51 for 1955, $1.67 for 1956, and $1.82 for 1957.

The Factor of Growth in Utility Earnings. In the 1951 edition we made the statement that growth, in the sense of a *substantial* increase in per-share earnings, is not ordinarily a factor to be taken into consideration in the valuation of utility common stocks. Whether or not this statement is quite accurate is, perhaps, a matter for argument; certainly, it depends upon one's definition of the word "substantial." Our subsequent discussion of the growth factor in utility earnings, however, was inadequate and failed to give sufficient recognition to the very real importance of this factor in utility common-stock values.

Over the past 22 years (1937–1959) the electric industry's total kwh sales to ultimate customers have increased at an average compound rate of 8 percent per year. Operating revenue over this period has increased at an average annual rate of 7 percent and earnings for common stock at a rate of about 6.7 percent per year. During the postwar period (1946–1959) the average annual gain in kwh sales has been 8.2 percent, in revenue 8.3 percent, and in earnings for common, about 10 percent. Industry forecasts project a continuation of this general pattern of growth over the next 10 to 20 years.

The necessity of financing expansion in part by the sale of additional common stock has resulted in a lesser rate of increase in *per-share* earnings. While industry statistics are not available on this point, studies that we have made indicate that per-share earnings have typically increased at approximately 45 to 55 percent of the rate of increase in total earnings available for common. For the companies included in Moody's 24 Electric Utility Common Stock Average, total earnings available for common, for the 12-year period, 1946–1957, increased at an average rate of close to 10 percent per year, while per-share earnings increased at an average annual rate of about 5 percent. Other studies indicate that an average growth rate of about 5 percent per year in per-share earnings has been generally representative of the industry. Certain companies, of course, particularly those in the rapidly expanding areas of Florida and Texas, have shown considerably higher rates of gain in per-share earnings. (Florida Power & Light Company makes about the best showing, with a postwar rate of increase averaging about 13 percent annually. Very few companies, however, have been able to show per-share earnings growth rates approaching this magnitude.)

From the common stockholders' viewpoint, the benefits of expansion in a company's operations result from two factors: (1) the reinvestment of earnings that are not paid out in dividends and (2) the fact that new common shares are almost invariably sold at prices that are materially higher than the book value of the outstanding shares.

From the standpoint of sales, revenue, and investment, we believe that confidence in the substantial further growth of the electric industry is fully justified. Unless there is to be a constant and permanent decline in the allowable rate of return (which we do not anticipate), the increase in gross income should parallel the increase in investment.

If senior capital costs do not increase and common stock equity ratios continue at approximately present levels, the increase in the balance for common would parallel the increase in gross income. This is simply a matter of arithmetic. It should be pointed out, however, that the present cost of senior money, bonds and preferred stock, is in fact higher than the present average cost of senior capital now on the books of most companies. If interest rates continue at present levels, the aggregate cost of borrowed capital will rise slowly as new increments are added to the capital structure. This, however, should be given consideration by the regulatory agencies in the determination of a fair rate of return, which should also gradually work higher in at least sufficient degree to offset this higher cost of senior capital.

A portion of the increase in investment, of course, will have to be financed by the sale of additional shares of common stock. Typically this stock will be sold at prices substantially above book value. In view of the higher price, a lesser number of new shares will have to be sold in order to obtain a desired number of dollars than would be the case if the new shares were sold at book value. If the earned rate of return on the total enlarged equity remains the same (as it is reasonable to expect), it is obvious that *per-share* earnings will increase, since the increase in the number of shares will be less than the increase in the dollar amount of the equity.

How this works out is shown below in Table 42-5. In this hypothetical case we assume a 10 percent growth trend over a period of five years. The expansion in investment is financed so as to maintain capitalization ratios of 50 percent bonds, 15 percent preferred stock, and 35 percent common stock and surplus. We assume that the over-all earned return is stabilized at $6\frac{1}{2}$ percent and that the common-stock dividend payout is approximately 75 percent of available earnings.

As shown below, the 61 percent increase in investment is accompanied by a similar increase in gross income and total earnings for common stock. The increase in per-share earnings is at a typically lower rate, or 32 percent, because of the increased number of shares.

There is, however, an actual increase in the percentage return on the common stockholders' investment over the period, even though the company's over-all rate of return does not increase. For simplicity, let us assume that an investor buys the entire outstanding common stock in year *A* at its average market price of 68. His investment, therefore, is $680,000, and in year *A* his earned return (balance for common) is $37,000, or 5.5 percent. Over the five-year period he subscribes to all the additional shares issued; the subscription requires an additional investment of $156,500. In year *B*, therefore, his aggregate investment totals $836,500, on which a return of $60,700, or 7.3 percent is earned.

The increase in earned return, moreover, should normally be reflected in a higher market value for the stock. For example, in year *B*, the aggregate market worth of the stock, at 18 times earnings, would be $1,097,000, representing an appreciation of $260,000 (compared with the investment of $836,500) over the period. This gain in value should be considered as part of the return, in addition to dividends received. If this is done in

Table 42-5

	Year A		Year B		Percent increase	Average annual percent increase†
	Amount	Percent	Amount	Percent		
Bonds, 4 percent................	$ 500,000	50.0	$ 805,000	50.0		
Preferred stock, 5 percent..........	150,000	15.0	242,000	15.0		
Common and surplus.............	350,000	35.0	564,000*	35.0	....	
Totals......................	$1,000,000	100.0	$1,611,000	100.0	61.0	10.0
Gross income....................	$65,000	.....	$105,000	.....	61.0	10.0
Interest charges.................	20,000		32,200			
Net income......................	$45,000	.....	$ 72,800	.....	61.0	10.0
Preferred dividends..............	7,500	.....	12,100			
Balance for common.............	$37,500	.....	$ 60,700	.....	61.0	10.0
Common dividends..............	28,000	.....	45,300			
Percent payout..................	74.7%	.....	74.6%			
Number of common shares........	10,000	.....	12,185	.....	22.0	4.1
Book value per share............	$35.00	.....	$46.30	.....	32.0	5.7
Earnings per share..............	3.75	.....	4.99	.....	32.0	5.7
Dividends per share.............	2.80	.....	3.72	.....	32.0	5.7
Market price....................	68	.....	90	.....	32.0	5.7
Price-earnings ratio..............	18.1×	.....	18.0×			
Dividend yield..................	4.1%	.....	4.1%			
Initial investment at market.......	$680,000					
Additional investment at cost......	....	.....	$156,500*			
Total investment...............	....	.....	$836,500			
Balance for common.............	$ 37,500	.....	60,700			
Return on investment............	5.5%	.....	7.3%			

* 2,185 shares sold during the period at approximately 6 percent discount from prevailing market prices provide $156,500. Retained earnings provide $57,500.
† Compounded.

the illustration used, it works out to an average annual total return of approximately 10 percent.[3]

Any increase in leverage, of course, will magnify the results in terms of per-share earnings. In other words, if property expansion is financed by relatively low-cost senior capital and the existing over-all return is maintained on the enlarged investment, the increase in per-share earnings will be greater in relation to the increase in gross income than that shown in Table 42-5.

On the other hand, if at the inception of the expansion period the common-stock equity is too "thin" and has to be built up, the increase in

[3] For additional comments on earnings growth, see "The Growth Factor in Electric Utility Earnings," by Charles Tatham, *Analysts Journal*, Mar. 1, 1952.

gross income will be moderated, if not nullified, in terms of per-share earnings accruing to the common.

If for any reason the over-all return being earned is less than that which can be looked forward to with reasonable assurance, then gross income can be expected to show greater gains than those which would normally accompany plant growth. This will result from either improving operating ratios or from rate increases, or in part from both.

Using a hypothetical example again, the effect of this on per-share earnings is shown in Table 42-6. Here also we assume a 10 percent growth trend over a period of five years.

Table 42-6

	Year A		Year B		Percent increase
	Amount	Percent	Amount	Percent	
Bonds, 4 percent	$ 500,000	50.0	$ 805,000	50.0	
Preferred stock, 5 percent	150,000	15.0	242,000	15.0	
Common and surplus	350,000	35.0	564,000*	35.0	
Totals	$1,000,000	100.0	$1,611,000	100.0	61.0
Gross income	$45,000	.....	$105,000	.....	133.0
Interest charges	20,000	.....	32,200		
Net income	$25,000	.....	$ 78,200	.....	191.0
Preferred dividends	7,500	.....	12,100		
Balance for common	$17,500	.....	$ 60,700	.....	247.0
Common dividends	13,500	.....	46,000		
Percent payout	77.1%	.....	75.1%		
Number of common shares	10,000	.....	14,150	.....	42.0
Book value per share	$35.00	.....	$39.80	.....	14.0
Earnings per share	1.75	.....	4.29	.....	145.0
Dividends per share	1.35	.....	3.25	.....	141.0
Market price	32	.....	77	.....	140.0
Price-earnings ratio	18.3×	.....	18.0×		
Dividend yield	4.2%	.....	4.2%		
Initial investment at market	$ 320,000				
Additional investment at cost	....	.....	$173,700*		
Total investment	....	.....	$493,700		
Balance for common	$17,500	.....	60,700		
Return on investment	5.5%	.....	12.3%		

* 4,150 shares sold during the period at approximately 6 percent discount from prevailing market prices provide $173,700. Retained earnings provide $40,300.

In this instance, the company is initially earning a 4½ percent return on its investment, and over the expansion period it succeeds in raising the earned return to 6½ percent. The increase in investment is financed as in Table 42-5 so as to maintain the existing capitalization ratios. Gross income, it will be seen, increases by 133 percent (although the investment increases only 61 percent), and the balance for common shows a considerably greater gain.

While the increase in per-share earnings is typically at a lesser rate, nevertheless it is substantial and should justify a considerable increase in the price of the stock. It should also be noted that the return on investment rises from 5.5 to 12.3 percent, a highly satisfactory performance.

This suggests that a favorable time to buy electric utility common stocks is when the earned return is low in relation to the property-value base apt to be used by the regulatory commission in setting rates. This allows for an increasing return, provided the economic characteristics of the service permit it, with resultant higher earnings on the stock. As mentioned above, the improvement in earnings will come about either through lower expense ratios or through rate increases, or in part from both.

Opportunities of this sort occur with varying frequency and justify considerable searching by the analyst. Usually they require a "full-dress" analytical job in order to develop the necessary assurance that earnings will increase within a reasonable period of time.

THE IMPACT OF REGULATION

In projecting earnings the analyst must, of course, bear in mind the regulated nature of the company's business and remember that earnings which might from an economic standpoint be reasonably *achievable* may not be *retainable* under regulatory policy. Since the projections shown above for Puget Sound Power & Light Company indicated earnings well below a ceiling likely to be imposed by Commission action, this factor did not have to be taken into account.

In many cases, however, the impact of regulation is an element of primary importance. If a carefully made projection of earnings produces results that indicate a vulnerably high return on the earnings base, the analyst should either accept a reasonable return figure as the maximum capitalizable earnings, or else apply a very low multiplier (say two or three times) to the earnings in excess of the estimated reasonable return, on the theory that the excess earnings may in fact be realized for a limited period of time.

For the electric power industry the essential significance of regulation, from the investor's viewpoint, lies in the restrictions that it imposes on rate of earnings. The same thing may be said of the telephone industry and to a considerable extent of the natural gas business. Gas companies, however, are faced by the problem of increasing competition if rates get too high, particularly in areas where high-cost natural gas is purchased for distribution. Gas competes with other fuels, and potentially with electricity, for the space-heating load, and with electricity for residential and commercial cooking and refrigeration.

Electricity, on the other hand, has an economic worth well above its cost, certainly as far as the residential, rural, and commercial customers are concerned, and the history of the industry's earning power has showed that profits have been held down by regulation, via rate reductions, rather than by economic forces. At present we can see no essential change in the outlook in this respect.

We realize, of course, that during the postwar years, sharply rising costs curtailed profits of many companies to a point where rate increases have been required. These have been generally granted with a promptness that has been reassuring to investors. The regulatory commissions have recognized that adequate earnings are necessary in order to keep the industry financially strong and in a position to satisfy the country's growing demands for utility services. As one of the most rapidly expanding segments of our economy, the electric utility industry has been calling, and will continue to call, for very substantial amounts of new capital from investors. The economics of the electric power business do not permit the financing of growth and expansion with retained earnings. Generally speaking, only about 40 percent of funds for new construction come from retained earnings, including depreciation accruals, while 60 percent must be obtained from outside sources. For example, of the $36.3 billion spent by the investor-owned electric utilities from 1947 through 1960 for new construction, 62 percent, or $22.5 billion, was financed by the sale of securities for new capital.

Looking ahead, we see a continued inevitable demand for substantial amounts of new capital, which will be forthcoming only if investors are confident that regulation will permit an adequate return to be earned thereon. An "adequate" return, however, does not mean an excessive return or even necessarily a "generous" return. A level of earnings sufficient to attract new capital is widely considered by the regulatory agencies as the key to fair rate of return, but what this level is has not always received the enlightened understanding which it requires. This is a subject on which the analyst should attempt to develop an informed opinion, both as to what the earnings level *should* be and what a particular commission is apt to *think* it should be. Knowledge concerning the latter point will be gained by reading the rate orders handed down by the different commissions.

In studying a company's earnings, therefore, an important figure for the analyst to keep in mind is what we would describe as the *estimated earnings potential*. This expression is one we use to indicate the maximum per-share earnings reasonably expectable under the regulatory policies of the state in which the company operates. It represents the earnings resulting from a "full" over-all return, after deduction of the annual service requirements on all senior securities outstanding.

It is derived by applying an appropriate rate of return either to the known rate-base value or to an estimate of what the latter might be considered to be by the regulatory authorities. Where no rate base has been determined by the Public Service Commission, as is the case with regard to the great majority of companies, an intelligent assumption must be based upon the analyst's knowledge of the policy and practice usually followed.

Generally speaking, the estimated earnings potential should represent the highest figure for per-share earnings that can be counted on with any reasonable assurance under favorable economic and operating conditions and with either the presently existing or a certain assumed or projected investment in plant and facilities. Higher earnings may, of course, be actually realized, but they will be subject to the threat of extinction through regulatory action and consequently should add but little to a soundly appraised value for the common stock.

In the case of Puget Sound Power & Light (to continue to use this company as an example) our earnings projection as shown in Table 42-4 indicated a rate of return of 5.4 percent on the projected 1957 year-end capital investment, a distinctly low figure. Unless the company should succeed in showing a better earnings performance, it would seem logical to expect some eventual increase in rates. The extent to which this might be expected to improve per-share earnings is indicated in Table 42-7.

Table 42-7. Estimated Earnings Potential of Puget Sound Power & Light Company, December 31, 1957

Estimated-earnings base	$131,000,000
Estimated rate of return	6.5%
Estimated allowable earnings	$ 8,500,000
Interest requirements	2,200,000
Resultant net income	$ 6,300,000
Earnings per share	$1.93
Common shares outstanding	3,266,819

In this table it should be noted that interest requirements in the amount of $2.2 million are deducted from the estimated allowable earnings, whereas in Table 42-4 the amount deducted for interest charges for the year 1957 was $1.5 million. The reason for this is that when computing the "estimated earnings potential," it is assumed that a full return will be earned on the entire amount of capital used as the earnings base. Thus, it becomes necessary, in computing earnings for the common stock, to deduct a full year's interest requirements on senior capital, without any credit for interest charged to construction. The resultant per-share earnings figure of $1.93 provided a better figure for stock-valuation purposes than the $1.73 per-share earnings shown in Table 42-4, since it could be assumed to be more representative of the *earning power* to be associated with the projected capital investment.

Actually, as mentioned above, the company reported earnings of $1.82 for the year 1957. The over-all earned rate of return, however, was still decidedly low, and in 1959 the company applied for, and subsequently received, a significant rate increase.

The estimated earnings potential is not, of course, a static concept, except in relation to (1) the existing capital investment or (2) some specific projected capital investment. As the property grows, its earning power will expand and an increase in per-share earnings should normally result, subject to the additional influence of changes in the capitalization structure. Normally, however, the growth process is one of reasonable consistency, and it can usually be correctly evaluated in the determination of expectable earnings.

It should also be pointed out that the estimated earnings potential does not represent a forecast of what a company *will* earn, but represents rather the maximum reasonably expectable earnings, based upon an assumed full over-all return on the estimated earnings base after deduction of the annual requirements of senior securities. Whether, or when, earnings of this order will actually be attained is a matter for determination by the analyst in his projection and forecast.

CHAPTER FORTY-THREE

THE VALUATION OF PUBLIC UTILITY

COMMON STOCKS (*Continued*)

THE EARNINGS-CAPITALIZATION RATE

In the determination of common-stock investment values, the selection of an appropriate earnings-capitalization rate, or earnings multiplier, is just as important a factor as is a correct forecast of earnings. The two might be called the primary determinants of value. In recent years, as we have pointed out earlier, practicing security analysts have directed their efforts increasingly toward the development of a rational approach to the selection of an appropriate price-earnings ratio in relation to the rate of expected increase in per-share earnings.

Common-stock values are not static and can reasonably be expected to increase over a period of time if the business of the company expands and prospers. In fact, this expectation of *future enhanced worth* is an important factor in the *current value* of a stock. If the expectation did not exist, the stock's value in relation to current earnings would almost invariably be less. Expressed somewhat differently, it can be said that the investment value of a common stock is normally measured by the present worth of: (1) the future income payments to be received, plus (2) the stock's future expectable increase in capital value.

Since both future dividends and future capital appreciation will normally be a function of future earnings, it seems perfectly logical to place a higher present worth, in relation to current earnings, on a stock which has superior prospects for earnings growth as compared with a stock with less dynamic expectations. In other words, a more rapidly rising trend of future earnings has a higher present value than a future trend with a slower growth rate.

While we think that this concept is perfectly sound, nevertheless we should perhaps point out that we also think that it lends itself to possible dangerous abuse. As in past bull markets, this can come about through a failure to use reasonable standards in relating earnings growth to current value. Without standards no rational method of measurement is possible.

Capitalization rates for both earnings and dividends have fluctuated widely over past periods of time and will undoubtedly continue to do so in the future. In the case of electric utility stocks, however, there has been a sufficiently recurrent central tendency so that we believe that historical averages can be used as a basis from which to develop an appropriate guide to value.

A standard of measurement developed from past performance, of course, will be a valid guide to the future only if future financial relationships can be expected on average to adhere to experienced patterns. An average of historical price-earnings ratios, for example, would be of no help in measuring future values if there are basic and fundamental reasons why future corporate earnings are likely to command a higher price, that is, be given a higher capital value. Such a divergence from the past could readily occur for any particular company; the past might have represented a period of product development, inexperience in the field of activity, and a high degree of speculative risk, while the future might promise a strong and secure competitive position, a high level of management know-how, and a well-developed market for the company's product. Under these circumstances, a past *low* average of price-earnings ratios would obviously be no guide at all to the future rate at which the market might logically capitalize earnings. And the opposite set of circumstances might equally well exist, under which *high* past price-earnings ratios, if applied to current earnings, would overstate the value of the stock.

This inapplicability of a past standard to the future is less probable when it is developed from a group of representative and generally comparable companies which have had a long and consistent record of performance like that of the electric utilities. Changes in basic considerations, such as the broad element of risk, a sharp variation in expectable growth, or a real change in supply-demand factors, would appear to be necessary to invalidate the past as a guide to the future in regard to financial relationships.

Our approach, therefore, to the problem of selecting an appropriate rate for capitalizing either current or expectable future earnings is founded on a study of average earnings-capitalization rates and dividend yields going back over a period of many years. These data show what *in the past* have been the generally prevailing levels at which earnings and dividends have been valued. The decision must then be made as to whether these past ratios will be appropriate to use in the future. This subject will be discussed below.

Table 43-1 shows the average price-earnings ratio, earnings-price ratio (percentage earned on price), dividend yield, and proportion of earnings paid out in dividends, for a group of predominantly electric operating utilities for the 35-year period, 1926–1960.[1]

---

[1] The companies used in computing these averages are the same as those mentioned on p. 300.

Table 43-1. Price-Earnings Ratios and Dividend Yields

Year	Price-earnings ratio	Earnings-price ratio	Dividend yield	Percent payout
1926	12.1×	8.30%	5.24%	67.6
1927	13.4×	7.46	4.64	65.5
1928	16.8×	5.96	3.67	64.2
1929	19.9×	5.03	3.21	64.0
1930	19.5×	5.14	3.81	74.1
1931	14.4×	6.96	5.43	78.6
1932	11.5×	8.66	8.37	96.0
1933	13.1×	7.64	7.91	103.1
1934	11.9×	8.38	8.19	98.0
1935	11.3×	8.84	6.77	76.4
1936	15.9×	6.29	4.98	78.3
1937	13.1×	7.64	6.29	82.0
1938	12.5×	8.00	6.94	87.4
1939	13.7×	7.28	6.03	80.7
1940	13.0×	7.71	6.34	82.3
1941	9.9×	10.11	8.38	83.2
1942	10.1×	9.87	9.19	93.6
1943	12.8×	7.82	7.08	90.8
1944	15.3×	6.52	5.94	91.9
1945	18.4×	5.43	4.88	88.3
1946	15.7×	6.37	4.71	73.9
1947	14.8×	6.77	5.33	78.8
1948	13.4×	7.46	6.16	82.9
1949	12.4×	8.06	6.02	74.6
1950	12.5×	8.00	5.79	72.2
1951	13.9×	7.20	5.87	81.5
1952	13.8×	7.25	5.50	76.1
1953	14.1×	7.10	5.50	77.5
1954	15.5×	6.45	4:82	74.5
1955	16.1×	6.21	4.46	71.6
1956	15.2×	6.58	4.69	71.4
1957	14.7×	6.80	5.00	73.5
1958	16.3×	6.14	4.36	71.0
1959	17.2×	5.81	3.95	68.0
1960	17.0×	5.89	3.90	66.3
Average 1926–1960....	14.3×	7.00%	5.69%	81.3%
Average 1941–1960....	14.4×	6.95	5.58	80.4
Average 1951–1960....	15.4×	6.50	4.81	74.0

In the third edition of this book, published in 1951, the above table presented the same data for the period 1926–1949. At that time we stated that it was "significant to observe that there has been no discernible *trend* in either the price-earnings ratio or the dividend yields over the years." This same observation was noted by the Cowles Commission in its study of common-stock prices which covered the 68-year period from 1871 to 1938.[2] The Commission stated:

It will be noted that the long-range trend of yields is nearly horizontal. The average of 5.30 per cent for the 20 years from 1871 to 1890 was almost exactly repeated from 1911 to 1935 when an average yield of 5.31 per cent was recorded. The figures indicated no evidence that the return on common stock investments has shown a long-range declining trend. In analyzing the record of earnings-price ratios, a similar picture is presented. The average ratio of 7.58 per cent prevailing for the 20 years from 1871 to 1890 is slightly lower than that for 1911–1935, which is 8.03 per cent.

The Cowles Commission study covered all stocks listed on the New York Stock Exchange, and the above comments apply to this group. While not necessarily applicable to the historical record of utility stocks, because of the past extreme diversity of companies in this field, we think that the force of the observation applies to this group as to any other.

Since 1949, however, a somewhat different picture has presented itself. This is revealed in Table 43-1, which shows that since that year there has been a definite rising trend in the price-earnings ratio and a declining trend in the dividend yield. The puzzling question arises as to whether this is merely a concomitant of a long, persistent bull market or whether it portends a permanently higher capital value to be placed on corporate earnings. During 1961 utility common-stock prices continued to rise strongly, and by the year-end Moody's 24 Electric Utility Common Stock Average showed a price-earnings ratio of 23.2 times. In recent years, the price-earnings ratio for this Average has deviated very little from our own figures, as shown in Table 43-1.

At the time of this writing, in January 1962, a substantial body of opinion believes that electric utility common stocks will in the future command a significantly higher price in relation to earnings than they have in the past. The principal reasons advanced for this prediction include a growing public awareness of inflation, which will intensify a preference for equity securities over fixed-income issues; an increasing demand for stocks in relation to supply, coming from institutional funds; and a declining supply of available shares due to the tax barriers to their sale, even though prices look high. In addition to this, there has been an increasing realization on the part of investors of the strong, inherent growth aspect of the electric utility industry as well as of its resistance, from an earnings standpoint, to temporary or short-lived declines in general business activity.

The impact of these factors must be recognized, although we hesitate to believe that their weight will be irresistible, irrespective of stock-price levels. In a bull market plausible reasons are always advanced as to why

[2] *Common Stock Indexes,* by Alfred Cowles, 3d, and Associates, Principia Press, Inc., Bloomington, Ind., 1939, pp. 43–44.

stock prices should remain high and continue higher. The fallacy in the reasoning is seldom recognized until the reaction has developed.

Moreover, two distinctly disconcerting thoughts intrude themselves. The prediction that investors are going to place a higher capital value on corporate earnings really seems the same as a contention that, in the future, corporate capital will be satisfied with a lower rate of return. This may be true, but, if so, it would seem indicative of a more mature, less enterprising economy than that which most people, we suspect, anticipate. Morever, in publicly regulated businesses, i.e., public utilities, a trend toward lower permitted rates of earned return, which would almost certainly follow if corporations in general earned less, could sharply reduce price-earnings ratios for utility common stocks.

The whole subject has enigmatic aspects, and we doubt if it has been thoroughly thought through. At the time of this writing, however, we do not think that current high price-earnings ratios signify that investors are or will be satisfied with *less* in the way of earnings on their capital, but rather that they mean that they are presently willing to look further into the future, with confidence in a rising trend of earnings, for a satisfactory return.

The difference is, perhaps, a subtle one. We think its force lies in the possibility that the present level of price-earnings ratios could rapidly fall if investors, for any reason, lost confidence in a future rising stream of earnings, or in the rate at which it will rise.

In the appraisal of common-stock investment values, the analyst should never let the market-price level of equities be his determining guide. To do so would be to enter into the worst sort of circular reasoning. On the other hand, a certain amount of respectful attention must be paid to the market place, since a concept of investment value would be of little practical help if quoted prices varied from it significantly and for a long period of time.

The problem is not easy to solve. It calls for judgment that will be proved right or wrong only after, perhaps, a considerable passage of time. Our own conclusion is that, looking ahead, we may expect price-earnings ratios to be somewhat higher than the historical average, but not as high as those which generally prevailed during the second half of 1961.

In Chapter 42, we pointed out that since World War II (1946) an average growth rate of about 5 percent per year in per-share earnings has been generally typical of the electric industry. Close to this same rate of average annual per-share-earnings increase has been shown by Moody's Electric Utility Average over the 25-year period, 1935–1959. Thus the long-term past average price-earnings ratio of 14 to 15 times for electric utility common stocks has historically been associated with a per-share earnings-growth rate of about 5 percent annually.

Looking to the future, however, and giving weight to the reasons mentioned above, we think it reasonable to expect a somewhat higher value appraisal of strongly situated equities in relation to earnings. In the summer of 1961 we made a rather extensive survey of the thinking of well-informed security analysts on this point, and the consensus of their opinions supports our own conclusion that, looking ahead, a price-earnings ratio of 18 times appears to be a reasonable multiplier to use for a stock with an expectable average annual per-share earnings increase of 5 percent.[3] This produces what might be called a normal, central-value figure approximately 25 percent higher than the historical multiplier of 14 to 15 times.[4]

If these two figures are acceptable (an 18 times price-earnings ratio and a 5 percent growth rate in per-share earnings), it then becomes possible to develop mathematically a series of price-earnings ratios to be associated with differing growth rates over varying periods of time. These are shown in Table 43-2.

In correlating these price-earnings ratios with the various earnings growth rates, an important assumption is that at the end of the selected time period, five, seven, ten, etc., years, the then future growth rate will approximate that for the industry as a whole, which we assume will continue at about 5 percent annually. It is impossible, of course, to pinpoint with any pretense of accuracy a future date at which a company's earnings growth, which may currently be superior to that of the industry, will level off to the industry average. Actually, it would be extraordinary if any particular company performed in exactly this manner. On the other hand, it would be equally unrealistic to expect an exceptionally rapid rate of earnings increase to continue indefinitely. Some eventual leveling off must be anticipated, and individual judgment must determine the time period during which the estimated growth rate is expected to

---

[3] In Chap. 37, p. 511, we suggest that a standard earnings multiplier for a good industrial company with average prospects be taken at 15 times current earnings and 13 times expected average earnings for the next seven years. We think it is logical to use a somewhat higher multiplier for a sound electric utility, in view of its inherent earnings stability and growth characteristics.

[4] In this connection it is interesting to refer again to the Cowles Commission study mentioned above. In its discussion of points revealed by its study (as previously cited, p. 486) it stated, " . . . for the 68 years from 1871 to 1938, the average amount of earnings annually retained by corporations is 2.5 percent of the value of their common stocks. As previously noted, all stocks on the average advanced in price at the rate of 1.8 percent a year for the period under consideration. This means that every $2.50 of earnings retained by a corporation has, on the average, been associated with an increase of $1.80 in the value of its stock." The Commission considered that reported retained earnings of $2.50 might have overstated the true earnings, but concluded that "perhaps a more satisfactory explanation, however, is that during the last 68 years common stocks in the United States have in general sold at about 72 percent of their true value; that is, their true value has been about 39 percent higher than their market price." The average earning-price ratio for the All Stock Index over the entire period was 7.53 percent, equivalent to a price-earnings ratio of 13.3 times. If this were increased by 39 percent it would indicate an average price-earnings ratio for the period of 18.5 times.

persist. Similarly, if a company is showing a substandard rate of increase in earnings, a careful evaluation of all the factors must precede any conclusion that the earnings growth rate will improve in the future.

As a practical matter, in our own approach to valuing utility common stocks, our practice is to assume that the estimated growth trend will continue for seven years. We hesitate to look further ahead than this. However, for those who wish to take a longer look into the future, Table 43-2 correlates price-earnings ratios with varying earnings growth rates

Table 43-2. Price-Earnings Ratios and Growth Rates

Annual increase in per-share earnings, percent	Justified price-earnings ratios (number of years of earnings increase*)				
	5 years	7 years	10 years	15 years	20 years
2	15×	15×	13×	12×	10×
4	17×	17×	16×	16×	15×
5	18×	18×	18×	18×	18×
6	19×	19×	20×	21×	22×
8	21×	22×	24×	28×	30×
10	23×	25×	28×	35×	45×
12	25×	28×	33×	48×	—
14	27×	32×	40×	—	—

* Assumes earnings growth rate continues at 5 percent at the end of period.

for periods of time of from five to twenty years. In this approach to value measurement, the "Justified Price-Earnings Ratio," is applied to the current year's per-share earnings.

At this point, perhaps, we should issue a warning that the definiteness of the figures in Table 43-2 should not be construed as producing a precise measure of value. No such device has yet been invented, and what we have designated as Justified Price-Earnings Ratios are *indications* of an appropriate earnings multiplier rather than attempts at exact measurement.

Factors Affecting the Earnings-Capitalization Rate. The various factors influencing the earnings multiplier, or price-earnings ratio, may be broadly classified under two headings:

1. Those associated with prospective *growth* of the enterprise
2. Those reflecting the known or expected *stability* of the business

In the 1951 edition of this work we listed as a third independent factor the dividend payout, or percentage of available earnings distributed to stockholders. However, as we point out in Chapter 21, this now has limited significance. Various studies that we and others have made in recent years indicate little, if any, clearly discernible relationship between payout and price-earnings ratio in respect to electric utility common stocks, except possibly insofar as the payout reflects variations in the capital structure.

1. *Growth.* We have already indicated that the expected future rate of increase in earnings is a major factor in determining both the price and the investment value of a common stock. It is, of course, a speculative factor, in the noninvidious sense of the word, since the anticipated earnings increase must to some extent be conjectural and is less susceptible of accurate measurement than earnings based on demonstrated performance. The weight which has been given to it by the securities markets seems to have varied proportionally to the degree of general optimism in investors' thinking. In recent years it has been of dominant influence. We think that this emphasis is perfectly logical, provided that too high a price is not paid for the expectation.

2. *Stability.* Traditionally, however, earnings stability has been at least an equal, if not a major, factor causing a low earnings-capitalization rate, i.e., a high multiplier. If we look beyond the common-stock field, that is at bonds and preferred stocks, we see that the very high assurance of stable, periodic income payments supports price-interest and price-dividend ratios that are normally considerably higher than the price-residual earnings ratios for most common stocks.

In other words, the higher the degree of assurance that a given income will continue to be received, the higher the capitalized value of the income. As compared with both industrials and railroads, the electric utilities have a record of enviable stability.

In the analysis of individual companies, one of the factors generally considered to have a significant bearing on the price-earnings ratio is the balance of earnings available for the common stock expressed as a percentage of operating revenue. A relatively high percentage balance ordinarily justifies a higher price-earnings ratio. This, of course, is essentially a measure of stability, since the thicker the equity in earnings, the less marked is the impact of any variation in revenues or in operating expenses.

Value Based on Estimated Capitalizable Earnings. In appraising the current value of a stock, an expected future increase in earnings can be recognized either in the capitalization rate or in the selection of an anticipated earnings figure higher than that being currently shown. So far, we have discussed the first method of approach, that of using a variable earnings multiplier depending upon the rate of increase that is anticipated in per-share earnings.

In Chapter 21 we suggested that in order to correlate the common dividend payout ratio with the factor of capital leverage, the appropriate payout should equal the balance for common less 10 percent of gross income. We pointed out that this proportionate distribution of earnings closely corresponded to actual average practice of independent electric utilities over a period of years prior to 1946. While the practice has not been so generally followed since World War II, we still believe that the formula can be used as a basis for evaluating utility stocks.

As is also explained in Chapter 21, the formula compels the percentage payout to adjust for the impact of senior charges, or that portion of leverage which is caused by the capital structure. Since the degree of leverage has an important bearing on earnings stability, the use of an automatic adjustment of this sort eliminates the necessity for varying the earnings-capitalization rate to compensate for this factor. The second major factor influencing the price-earnings ratio—per-share earnings increase—is given effect by the selection of a future year's expected results. The use of the formula, therefore, permits the use of a uniform capitalization rate for all companies.

The indicated payout, as determined by the formula, we would term the *estimated capitalizable earnings,* i.e., the normally distributable earnings (rather than the reported earnings) which, in this approach, should be capitalized for the purpose of determining investment value. This is predicated on the assumption that the investor is primarily interested in the earnings that he might, under normal or average conditions, expect to receive in the form of dividends and that this actual or potential future income determines the capital value of his investment.

The foregoing assertion may seem inconsistent with the statement we made earlier that investment value represents the present worth of future dividends *plus* future capital appreciation. However, we think the conflict is more apparent than real. In respect to electric utility common stocks, capital appreciation (except that resulting from increasing price-earnings ratios) can only result from and be supported by earnings growth paralleling the continuing expansion in property investment. The possibility of speculative profits resulting from new developments or products does not exist in this industry as it does in many nonregulated manufacturing or industrial fields. From the stockholder's standpoint, the benefits of earnings growth are largely receivable via normal dividend increases, which, in turn, produce enhanced capital values. In view of the regulated nature of the industry, it seems probable that this pattern will continue.

The estimated capitalizable earnings represent what would ordinarily be the maximum expectable payout, or dividend, in relation to the earnings under consideration. In Table 43-1 it was shown that utility common-stock dividend yields, over the 35-year period, 1926–1960, averaged 5.69 percent, and over the past 20-year period, 5.58 percent. More recently, of course, dividend yields have been significantly lower; for the latest 5-year period, 1956–1960, the average yield has been 4.38 percent.

Looking to the future, however, we believe that a somewhat higher yield level will prevail on average, and as a matter of judgment we are using a figure of about 5¼ percent as a future "norm." This is equivalent to a dividend-price ratio of about 19 times, and the application of this multiplier to the "potential" dividend, or "estimated capitalizable earnings," produces, in our opinion, a figure of reasonable central value for a typical utility stock.

Actually, we are of the opinion that an estimated *range of value* is preferable to the use of a single figure. Value cannot realistically be pinned to a precise number and an attempt to do so will produce an illusion of accuracy that will be misleading.

We suggest, therefore, that the estimated capitalizable earnings, computed according to the formula described above, be valued at both 17 and 20 times, bracketing the 19-times multiplier referred to.[5] These correspond to capitalization rates of 5.9 percent and 5 percent and produce a range of value with approximately a 16 percent differential. We doubt that this range can be narrowed by the application of any analytical procedure. Within this area a mutually satisfactory price agreement at which a stock changes hands calls for a meeting of minds between buyer and seller, a compromise of many factors not determinable by security analysis.

Having selected 17 and 20 times as the appropriate multipliers to apply to the estimated capitalizable earnings, the determination of value is derived by the following formula:

$$RV = \begin{cases} \dfrac{20(BC - 0.10GI)}{\text{Number of shares}} \\ \dfrac{17(BC - 0.10GI)}{\text{Number of shares}} \end{cases}$$

where RV = range of value

BC = balance for common

GI = gross income

Example: If we apply this formula to the common stock of Puget Sound Power & Light Company, for which we developed earnings projections in Chapter 42, it produces a range of investment value as shown in Table 43-3. In this table we show the company's actual earnings for 1954 and as we projected them for the subsequent four years. As stated in Chapter 42, these projections were made in the late spring of 1955 for the purpose of estimating the reasonable investment value of the company's common stock.

Value Determined by Future Earnings. When using this technique for estimating the value of a common stock, the earnings figure to be used is that which a careful appraisal indicates should be reached within some reasonably foreseeable period in the future. We have already suggested

[5] In the 1951 edition, we recommended multipliers of 15 and 18 times when using this formula. For reasons discussed, we now think that higher multipliers should be used.

that the fourth year's projected earnings be used, as generally represent-ing the average earnings in a seven-year projection. In the case of Puget Sound, the fourth year's (1958) projected earnings were $2.06 per share, and estimated capitalizable earnings, as shown in Table 43-3, were $1.82. Using the multipliers suggested above, we found that this indicated a range of investment value of $31 to $36 for the stock. In 1955, when the study was made, the stock had a price range of 22½ to 27⅛. The con-clusion to be drawn at that time was that the stock was then under-valued in the market. Subsequent price action confirmed the validity of the value appraisal.

Table 43-3. Puget Sound Power & Light Company

(Dollar figures in thousands)

	Actual 1954	Projected	
		1955	1958
Gross income	$5,749	$6,150	$8,150
Balance for common	4,461	4,850	6,750
Less 10 percent of gross income	575	615	815
Estimated capitalizable earnings	$3,886	$4,235	$5,935
Per share	$1.19	$1.29	$1.82
Estimated range of value:			
At 20 times estimated 1958 capitalizable earnings		36	
At 17 times estimated 1958 capitalizable earnings		31	
Price range:			
High	22½*	27⅛	35¼
Low	16*	22½	26⅞
Number of common shares	3,267*	3,267	3,267

* Adjusted to reflect 3-for-2 stock split in 1955.

Value Based on Justified Price-Earnings Ratio. Our projection for Puget Sound for the period 1955–1958 indicated an average annual rate of increase in per-share earnings of about 11 percent. This was a higher growth rate than we were willing to assume would persist for a seven-year future period, but we felt that an 8 percent rate could be used with some justification. From Table 43-2 it will be seen that an 8 percent growth rate, expected to persist for seven years, should justify a current price-earnings ratio of 22 times. This ratio, applied to our estimate of 1955 per-share earnings, $1.48, indicated a value of just about $33, about the midpoint of the value range reached above.

Value Based on "Estimated Earnings Potential." We stated in Chapter 42 that the term *estimated earnings potential* might be used to describe the maximum per-share earnings reasonably expectable under the exist-ing regulatory jurisdiction and that ordinarily it should represent the highest figure used as a base for determining investment value. In the case of Puget Sound we indicated an estimated earnings potential of $1.93 per share in relation to the capital investment as projected to December 31, 1957. Applying the 10 percent formula described above and the earnings figures shown in Table 42-7, we find that the estimated capitalizable earnings would be $1.67 and the stock's estimated range of value, using multipliers of 17 and 20 times, $28 to $33. This value range supports those reached above.

Under certain circumstances, however, earnings computed on this basis might be significantly higher or lower than those being reported or than those which the analyst's projections indicate are expectable in the foreseeable future. In this case, he should review his figures carefully and attempt to develop an informed judgment as to whether action in respect to rates is apt to be taken by the regulatory commission.

Additional Components of Value. To any valuation reached by capitalizing earnings should be added the value of assets owned which are not contributing to the earnings that are being capitalized. These might include investments from which no income is currently being received and any working capital, including cash funds, in excess of that needed in operations.

However, when value is based on the estimated earnings potential and that potential is determined in relation either to total net plant plus net current assets, or to total capitalization including surplus, obviously no additional increment should be included for excess working capital.

In most cases, however, these additional components of worth are of a minor nature.

Significance of Book Value. In industrial common-stock analysis, book value is seldom regarded as an important determinant of investment value, largely for the reason that it usually bears little relationship to the earning power of the company. Goodwill, for example, or the value of a trade name, may be carried at a negligible figure in the balance sheet and yet may be a major factor in the competitive position and consequently in the earning ability of a manufacturing concern.

In the regulated utility industries, however, earnings are restricted by public policy to some appropriate return on the capital actually employed in the public's service. The corporate balance sheet shows this capital in terms of dollars paid in and dollars of retained earnings. Market-price quotations, particularly of the common-stock component of the capital, reflect investors' appraisals of expectable future earnings in relation to this investment.

In our view, there are a number of reasons why fairly substantial market-price premiums over book value are not only justified but are essential if utility common stocks are to continue an attractive medium for investment.

One of the basic objectives of the fair rate of return, which regulation must allow a utility company to earn, is to provide earnings sufficient to maintain the integrity of the company's capital. The word "integrity" means the state or quality of being unimpaired or complete, and when used in reference to capital or monetary investment, it means unimpaired capital, that is, capital which has not suffered a decline in exchange value. The economic value of money lies in its purchasing power, and financial integrity as applied to money means maintenance of purchasing power or exchange value. From the standpoint of the investor this is the only value that has any reality when applied to monetary savings or investment, and it is this value which must be preserved under our system of regulation.

It is common knowledge, of course, that inflation has substantially reduced the purchasing power of the dollar in recent years. Since 1940, the Consumer Price Index has approximately doubled. If the integrity of the capital invested in regulated utilities is to be maintained, it is obvious that the effect of price changes of this magnitude must be given consideration in one way or another. In theory, at least, changes in the value of the dollar can be given recognition either in the rate base or through the rate of return, and in "fair-value" jurisdictions the adjustment for inflation is usually made in the rate base.

From the investor's standpoint, we do not see that it makes much difference which method is used, so long as the adjustment carries through to the area of his own interest, which is the market value of the common stock. Equity capital committed to corporate enterprise is not ordinarily subject to possible withdrawal, and it is only through the medium of the securities markets that investors retain some measure of control over the funds which they have contributed to the business, i.e., by being able to sell their interest to others. It thus necessarily follows that market value constitutes the sole measure of "economic value" of corporate capital at the crucial time when such capital is to be rendered liquid.

Thus, if the "integrity" of the common stockholders' capital is to be maintained, the stock, in times of reasonably normal securities markets, must command an average market price sufficiently above book value *at least* to offset the decline in the value of the dollar. And since price is a function of earnings, regulation should allow sufficient earnings for this to happen.

Apart from this, the fact that utility common stocks sell at significant premiums above book value provides an important element of growth potential. This results from the fact that when new common stock is sold at a price above book value the *per-share* book value of the old stock is increased and thus permits higher *per-share* earnings, even though the over-all rate of return does not increase.

Example: A somewhat extreme example of how the book value of a utility stock can be increased when new shares are sold at a substantial market premium is afforded by Florida Power & Light Company. In May

1960 this company sold to the public 400,000 shares of common stock at a price of $59.125 per share, obtaining thereby $23,202,000 of new capital, which it needed for expansion. Prior to the sale, the book value of the 13,200,000 shares of common outstanding was $14.47 per share. As a result of the high price received for the new stock, the book value of the 13,600,000 shares then outstanding was $15.78 per share. As a result of the stock sale, the per-share book value was increased by $1.31, or 9 percent, although the increase in number of shares was only 3 percent. For the 12 months ended March 31, 1960, the company reported earnings for common equal to 13.9 percent on total common-stock capital per books. If the company continues to show this rate of earned return on its equity capital, the increase in *per-share* earnings would be 9 percent.

A third reason for a market-price premium lies in the fundamental investment principle that the risk of capital loss must be counterbalanced by the possibility of capital gain. The risk of loss is ever-present in a common-stock investment, and this must be offset by a reasonable possibility that per-share earnings can increase and thus support higher per-share values. As long as regulation restricts earnings to some determined rate of return on capital, the only way that per-share earnings can show real growth is by increasing the per-share book value of the common stock. In a period of expansion, the sale of new stock at a price premium is a very important factor in achieving this earnings growth.

If utility-company earnings were restricted to a level that supported common-stock prices at say, not more than 10 percent above book value so that new common shares could be sold only at book value, then utility equities would lose a major part of their investment appeal and could only be sold on the basis of considerably higher dividend yields and lower price-earning ratios than those discussed in this chapter. This is for the reason that under such circumstances a large part of their growth potential would be eliminated.

What the appropriate price premium should be will vary from company to company, depending upon a number of factors. For Moody's 24 Electric Utility Common Stock Average it averaged approximately 60 percent over the five-year period 1956–1960, and close to 78 percent for the year 1960. As a result of the sharp rise in electric utility common-stock prices in 1961, the year's average price for this index was approximately 115 percent above book value.

Generally speaking, the market-price premium will be determined by three fundamental factors:

1. The over-all rate of return which the company is earning
2. The leverage provided by senior capital, which will affect the earned return on the common equity
3. The optimism with which investors view the future

The analyst should study each of these factors with an eye to possible change before concluding whether or not a prevailing market-price premium is dangerously high.

Summary. In closing, it might be well to summarize briefly the salient points developed in this and the previous chapter concerning the valuation of utility common stocks and to add a few general comments. The electric power industry is one of the fastest-growing segments of our economy. It is constantly seeking new capital, and for a long time to come it will provide a large and expanding field for investment.

Equities of the electric light and power companies provide, in our opinion, one of the soundest and most attractive investment media as long as they are not bought at an excessive price. Essentially, the purchase price must be determined in accordance with the investor's conception of a satisfactory "total" return, that is, a combination of income plus long-term capital appreciation. The elements of stability characteristic of electric utility earnings, resulting from the coexistence of persistent growth combined with the restrictive forces of regulation, facilitate the problem of valuation for investment purposes.

In the past, market prices have periodically tended to exceed and fall below investment value based on the longer-term considerations, largely as a result of changes in investor psychology, or what Lord Keynes has termed the "state of confidence," or "spontaneous optimism" of the public. It appears safe to assume that in the future, also, price deviations from value will sooner or later be followed by corrective action that will in turn go beyond reasonable limits. So long, therefore, as investment value can be determined with some measure of assurance, these changes in market sentiment should offer attractive investment opportunities.

Essentially, the valuation of a utility common stock must proceed from (1) an analysis of the expectable earnings in the light of all the economic forces; (2) a consideration of the regulatory factor as it may require a reduction in rates, with an attendant retardation of earnings, or permit an increase in rates and consequently earnings; and (3) a selection of an appropriate capitalization rate for the expectable earnings and dividends.

In addition to the factor of regulation, the analyst should keep in mind the fact that a good many people in this country believe that government ownership and operation of the electric-power industry is desirable. The impact of political moves designed to further this objective should be watched carefully, since they could have a major bearing on investors' appraisals of utility common stocks.

PART FIVE

SENIOR SECURITIES WITH

SPECULATIVE FEATURES

CHAPTER FORTY-FOUR

PRIVILEGED ISSUES

In our present arrangement of the general subject we have dealt first with bonds and preferred stocks of the stable-value type and then with common stocks bought for investment—the two representing the major divisions of ordinary investment securities. There remains to be discussed the intermediate class of *senior issues with speculative features,* which partake in some degree of the characteristics of both the typical senior security and the typical common stock. In our introductory discussion (Chapter 8) we subdivided this group under two heads: issues which are speculative because of inadequate safety, and those which are speculative because they possess a conversion or similar privilege which makes possible substantial variations in market price.

A senior issue may have a speculative feature without being speculative in the sense that it involves an appreciable risk to the buyer. Convertible bonds may combine adequate safety with an attractive chance for profit. In a number of instances—though not as many as investors seem to think—the speculative opportunity (popularly referred to as "kick" or "sweetening") may be added to full investment quality. On rare occasions a nonprivileged, or "straight," senior issue may be found which sells at a large discount from par and offers an abnormally high yield even though it is a safe investment.[1] We shall refer briefly to this

---

[1] These were plentiful in the 1931–1933 period, when the prevailing pessimism depressed the price of many sound bonds and preferreds, and we had a section on these opportunities in the 1934 edition of this book. Since they later became very scarce, as was to be expected, such treatment has been curtailed in the revisions.

type of "bargain issue" in Chapter 52, page 693, when dealing with un-dervalued senior securities.

In addition to enjoying a prior claim for a fixed amount of principal and income, a bond or preferred stock may also be given the right to share in benefits accruing to the common stock. These privileges are of three kinds, designated as follows:

1. Convertible—conferring the right to exchange the senior issue for common stock on stipulated terms
2. Participating—under which additional income may be paid to the senior security holder, dependent usually upon the amount of common dividends declared
3. Subscription or warrant—by which holders of the bond or preferred stock may purchase common shares, at prices, in amounts, and during periods, stipulated[2]

The conversion privilege is now by far the most popular of the three. Prior to 1940 the sum of participating issues and those with warrants was about equal, together, to the number of convertibles. There was then a distinct decline in the use of warrants and participating features as against convertible issues. Since 1959 the issuance of securities with warrants attached has again become very frequent. Conversion privileges are still widely used in new financing, and because of their dominance we shall frequently use the term "convertible issues" to refer to privileged issues in general.

Such Issues Attractive in Form. By means of any one of these three provisions a senior security can be given virtually all the profit possibilities that attach to the common stock of the enterprise. Such issues must therefore be considered the most attractive of all in point of *form*, since they permit the combination of maximum safety with the chance of un-limited appreciation in value. A bond that meets all the requirements of a sound investment, including an adequate yield. and in addition possesses an interesting conversion privilege would undoubtedly constitute a highly desirable purchase.

Securities of this type are claimed to be especially advantageous to both the investor and the issuing corporation. The investor receives the superior protection of a bond or preferred stock, plus the opportunity to participate in any substantial rise in the value of the common stock. The issuer is able to raise capital at a moderate interest or preferred-dividend cost, and if the expected prosperity materializes the issuer will get rid of the senior obligation by having it exchanged into common stock. Thus both sides to the bargain will fare unusually well.

Obviously the foregoing paragraph must overstate the case somewhere, for you cannot by a mere ingenious device make a bargain much better

---

[2] A fourth type of profit-sharing arrangement—the "optional" bond or preferred stock—has not been seen since 1929. It is discussed on p. 522 of the 1951 edition.

for both sides. In exchange for the conversion privilege the investor usually gives up something important in quality or yield, or both. Conversely, if the company gets its money at lower cost because of the conversion feature, it is surrendering in return part of the common stockholder's claim to future enhancement of value. On this subject there are a number of tricky arguments to be advanced both pro and con. The safest conclusion that can be reached is that convertible issues are like any other form of security, in that their form itself guarantees neither attractiveness nor unattractiveness. The solution will depend on all the facts surrounding the individual issue.

Two Typical Convertible Issues. The general principle that the buyer of a privileged issue gives up something for the advantage gained may be illustrated by two representative convertible issues offered in 1961.

Example 1: FMC Corporation Convertible Subordinated Debenture $3\frac{1}{8}$s, due 1981, sold at 100; convertible into common at 100, against a current price of about 90. This is a bond of high quality, with a mathematically attractive conversion privilege. However, the buyer gave up about $1\frac{1}{2}$ percent per annum in yield, as measured by the concurrent price of the same issuer's nonconvertible bonds. The offering price of 100 for the $3\frac{1}{8}$s comprised about 20 points paid for the conversion right.

Example 2: Nuclear Corporation of America Convertible $5\frac{1}{2}$s, due 1976, offered to stockholders at 100; convertible into common at 4, against a current price of about $3\frac{1}{2}$. In this case the yield was satisfactory and the conversion rate apparently attractive. However, the company had reported deficits in each year since incorporation in 1958, and the bonds were obviously lacking in *investment* protection.

Varied Investment Record of Privileged Issues. The attitude of the typical security buyer toward such issues in 1961 was undoubtedly far different from his attitude in 1949. When our previous edition was in the writing, convertibles were highly unpopular. Many had been offered in the bull market of 1945–1946 and then had fared poorly in the subsequent decline. A similar outpouring of new convertible and warrant issues has taken place in recent years. With the continued strength of the stock market, a majority of these privileged securities have rewarded their purchasers quite handsomely, as the related common stocks have participated in the general advance. Many investors are now convinced that convertible issues afford an ideal combination of small risk and good chance for profit.

If privileged issues are viewed in longer perspective we must conclude that for the most part they are fair-weather investments. They are bound to do well in bull markets but typically not so well as common stocks as a whole. They are equally bound to do badly in bear markets—and it is even possible that they may do worse than a representative list of common stocks.

It may be well to bring home this point, in the midst of the current enthusiasm for privileged securities, by reproducing our material on the behavior of all convertible preferred stocks offered in 1946 as compared with the "straight" preferreds sold to the public in the same year. This is done in Table 44-1.

The greater weakness of the privileged issues in the 1946–1947 period was without question a reflection of their poorer investment quality. The extent of their decline in the space of about a year indicates that *on the whole* the privileged preferred stocks offered to the public are likely to prove unsatisfactory investments if bought at the issue price shortly before a fairly severe decline in stock prices. (It should be observed that the privileged issues in our table declined more than did the indexes of *common stocks* during the same period.)

Table 44-1. Price Record of New Preferred-stock Issues Offered in 1946

Price change from issue price to low up to July 1947	"Straight" issues	Convertible and participating issues
No decline...............	7 issues	0 issues
Declined:		
0–9.99 percent...........	16	2
10–19.99 percent..........	11	6
20–39.99 percent..........	3	22
40 percent or more........	0	12
Totals................	37	42
Average decline............	About 9%	About 30%

An Inherent Price Problem in Such Issues. A second reason for hesitancy about buying privileged issues is related to the conditions under which profit may accrue from the privilege. Although there is indeed no upper limit to the price that a convertible bond may reach, a very real limitation is set on the amount of profit that the holder may realize while still maintaining an *investment position.* After a privileged issue has advanced with the common stock, its price soon becomes dependent *in both directions* upon changes in the stock quotation, and to that extent the continued holding of the senior issue becomes a *speculative* operation. An example will make this clear.

Let us assume the purchase of a high-grade 4½ percent bond at par, convertible into two shares of common for each $100 bond (i.e., convertible into common stock at 50). The common stock is selling at 45 when the bond is bought.

First stage: (1) If the stock declines to 35, the bond may remain close to par. This illustrates the pronounced technical advantage of a convertible issue over the common stock. (2) If the stock advances to 55, the price of the bond will probably rise to 115 or more. (Its "immediate conversion value" would be 110, but a premium would be justified because of its advantage over the stock.) This illustrates the undoubted speculative possibilities of such a convertible issue.

Second stage: The stock advances further to 65. The conversion value of the bond is now 130, and it will sell at that figure, or slightly higher. At this point the original purchaser is faced with a problem. Within wide limits, the future price of his bond depends entirely upon the course of the common stock. In order to seek a larger profit he must risk the loss of the profit in hand, which in fact constitutes a substantial part of the present market value of his security. (A drop in the price of the common could readily induce a decline in the bond from 130 to 110.) If he elects to hold the issue, he places himself to a considerable degree in the position of the stockholders, and this similarity increases rapidly as the price advances further. If, for example, he is still holding the bond at a level, say, of 180 (90 for the stock), he has for all practical purposes assumed the status and risks of a stockholder.

Unlimited Profit in Such Issues Identified with Stockholder's Position. The unlimited profit possibilities of a privileged issue are thus in an important sense illusory. They must be identified not with the ownership of a bond or preferred stock but with the assumption of a common stockholder's position—which any holder of a nonconvertible may effect by exchanging his bond for a stock. Practically speaking, the range of profit possibilities for a convertible issue, *while still maintaining the advantage of an investment holding,* must usually be limited to somewhere between 25 and 35 percent of its face value. For this reason original purchasers of privileged issues do not ordinarily hold them for more than a small fraction of the maximum market gains scored by the most successful among them, and consequently they do not actually realize these very large possible profits. Thus the profits taken may not offset the losses occasioned by unsound commitments in this field.

Examples of Attractive Issues. The two objections just discussed must considerably temper our enthusiasm for privileged senior issues as a class, but they by no means destroy their inherent advantages or the possibilities of exploiting them with reasonable success. Although a significant proportion of convertible issues are inadequately secured or unattractive in yield, there are many exceptions to this rule. These exceptions should be of prime interest to the alert investor. Some opportunities are presented at the time of first issuance; others are created by a subsequent decline in the price of the convertible. We append an example of each.

Example 1: Avco Corporation Convertible Subordinated Debenture 5s, due 1979, offered to stockholders at 100 in February 1959 and traded first at about 107 to yield 4.40 percent. The debentures are convertible into common at 11½, which was the approximate price at the time of the offering. Earnings after taxes but before interest averaged about 5½ times 1959 interest charges. Net current assets were over twice the total debt. These debentures appeared reasonably well protected and carried a call on the stock at only slightly above the current market. (Their price advanced to 157 in the same year.)

Example 2: McCrory Stores 3½ percent cumulative convertible preferred ($100 par) sold as low as 60 in 1957, to yield 5.83 percent, although originally offered at 104 in 1946. It was convertible into 5 shares of common, and its conversion parity of 12 was only slightly above the current market and well below prices registered in most of the preceding 10 years. The company had a very small debt; the preferred dividend had been earned more than fourteen times for many years past; the working capital covered debt and preferred with a large margin. (In 1959 the common advanced to 19¾, making the preferred worth about 100 on a conversion basis. The company is now called McCrory Corp.)

Example of an Unattractive Issue. By way of contrast with these examples we shall supply an illustration of a superficially attractive but basically unsound convertible offering, such as characterized the 1945–1946 period.

Example: Samson United 55-cent convertible preferred stock, par $8. 125,000 shares of this issue were offered in May 1946 at $10 per share. Each share was convertible into 1½ shares of common stock, then selling at 6¾ to 7¾.

The company, makers of electric household appliances, had lost money each year from 1937 through 1942. It made fair profits on war business in the next three years. At the end of 1945, the balance sheet showed only $284,000 of working capital and a common-stock equity of $873,000 (for 324,000 shares). The price of the common had advanced from 7/16 in 1943 to 11¼ in 1945. The preferred appeared attractive because of its conversion privilege "right at the market," and 15,000 shares were converted during 1946.

Sequel: The company sustained large losses in 1946 and subsequently. At the end of 1949, the equity of the preferred stock had virtually disappeared, and the price had fallen to 1⅝.

Principle Derived. From these contrasting instances an investment principle may be developed that should afford a valuable guide to the selection of privileged senior issues. The principle is as follows: *A privileged senior issue, selling close to or above face value, should meet the requirements either of a straight fixed-value investment or of an attractive common-stock commitment, and it should be bought with one or the other qualification clearly in view.*

The alternative given supplies two different approaches to the purchase of a privileged security. It may be bought as a sound investment with an incidental chance of profit through an enhancement of principal, or it may be bought primarily as an attractive form of commitment in the common stock. Generally speaking, there should be no middle ground.[3] The *investor* interested in safety of principal should not abate his requirements in return for a conversion privilege; the *speculator* should not be attracted to an enterprise of mediocre promise because of the pseudo-security provided by the bond contract.

Our opposition to any compromise between the purely investment and the admittedly speculative attitude is based primarily on doubt as to whether the purchaser is psychologically prepared for the adventure. When he takes an intermediate stand, the result is usually confusion, clouded thinking, and self-deception. The investor who relaxes his safety requirements to obtain a profit-sharing privilege is frequently not prepared, financially or mentally, for the inevitable loss if fortune should frown on the venture. The speculator who wants to reduce his risk by operating in convertible issues is likely to find his primary interest divided between the enterprise itself and the terms of the privilege, and he will probably be uncertain in his own mind as to whether he is at bottom a stockholder or a bondholder. (Privileged issues *selling at substantial discounts from par* are not in general subject to this principle, since they belong to the second category of speculative senior securities to be considered later.)

Reverting to our examples, the student will see at once that McCrory Stores Preferred could properly have been purchased as an investment without any regard to the conversion feature. The strong possibility that this privilege would be of value made the shares almost uniquely attractive at their low price in 1957. Both this issue and the Avco convertible debentures should also have been attractive to a speculator who was persuaded that the related common stock was due for an advance in price.

On the other hand Samson United Preferred could not have passed stringent qualitative and quantitative tests of safety. Hence it should properly have been of interest only to a person who had full confidence in the future value of the common stock. It is hardly likely, however, that most of the buying of this issue was motivated by the primary desire to invest or speculate in Samson United common stock; it was based rather on the attractive terms of the conversion privilege and on the feeling that the issue was "fairly safe" as a senior security. It is precisely this compromise between true investment and true speculation that we disapprove, chiefly because the purchaser has no clear-cut idea of the purpose of his commitment or of the risk that he is incurring.

Rules Regarding Retention or Sale. Having stated a basic principle to guide the *selection* of privileged issues, we ask next what rules can be established regarding their subsequent retention or sale. Convertibles

[3] If the common stock is regarded as a sound and attractive commitment, then a convertible issue at close to parity must also be a sound investment. Hence the real alternative in this case is between buying the senior issue as an investment or as a superior way of making a commitment in the junior issue.

bought primarily as a form of commitment in the common stock may be held for a larger profit than those acquired from the investment standpoint. If a bond of the former class advances from 100 to 150, the large premium need not in itself be a controlling reason for selling out; the owner must be guided rather by his views as to whether or not the common stock has advanced enough to justify taking his profit. But when the purchase is made primarily as a safe bond investment, then the limitation on the amount of profit that can conservatively be waited for comes directly into play. For the reasons explained in detail above, the conservative buyer of privileged issues will not ordinarily hold them for more than a 25 to 35 percent advance. This means that a really successful investment operation in the convertible fields does not cover a long period of time. Hence such issues should be bought with the *possibility* of long-term holding in mind but with the *hope* that the potential profit will be realized fairly soon.

The foregoing discussion leads to the statement of another investment rule, viz.:

In the typical case, a convertible issue should not be converted by the investor. It should be either held or sold.

It is true that the object of the privilege is to bring about such conversion when it seems advantageous. If the price of the convertible issue advances substantially, its current yield will shrink to an unattractive figure, and there is ordinarily a substantial gain in income to be realized through the exchange into stock. Nevertheless, when the investor does exchange his senior issue for the stock, he abandons the prior claim to principal and interest upon which the purchase was originally premised. If after the conversion is made things should go badly, his shares may decline in value far below the original cost of his senior issue, and he will lose not only his profit but part of his principal as well.

Moreover, he is running the risk of transforming himself—generally, as well as in the specific instances—from an investor into a stock speculator. It must be recognized that there is something insidious about even a good convertible bond or preferred; it can easily prove a costly snare to the unwary. To avoid this danger the investor must cling determinedly to a conservative viewpoint. When the price of his bond has passed out of the investment range, he must sell it; most important of all, he must not consider his judgment impugned if the bond subsequently rises to a much higher level. The market behavior of the issue, once it has entered the speculative range, is no more the investor's affair than the price gyrations of any speculative stock about which he knows nothing.

Example: The following history of the Eversharp, Inc., convertible issues during the 1945–1948 period is interesting in itself; it also serves to point up our thesis that most convertibles present a peculiar combination of opportunity and risk which is likely to prove tantalizing and disappointing to the investor. During 1945 Eversharp sold at 103 two issues, each for $3 million, of income debenture 4½s, convertible into common stock at $40 per share. The stock advanced rapidly to 65½, and then (after a 3-for-2 split-up) to the equivalent of 88. The latter price made the convertible debenture worth no less than 220. During this period the two issues were called at a small premium; hence they were practically all converted into common stock, which was retained by many of the original buyers of the debentures. The price promptly began a severe decline, and in March 1948 the stock sold as low as 7⅜. This represented a value of only 27 for the debenture issues, or a loss of 73 percent of the original price instead of a profit of over 100 percent.

Effect of Recommended Policy. If the course of action here recommended is followed by investors generally, the conversion of senior issues would be brought about only through their purchase for this specific purpose by persons who have decided independently to acquire the shares for either speculation or supposed investment.[4] The arguments against the investor's converting convertible issues apply to some extent against his exercising stock-purchase warrants attached to bonds or preferreds bought for investment purposes.

A continued policy of investment in privileged issues would, under favorable conditions, require rather frequent taking of profits and replacement by new securities not selling at an excessive premium. More concretely, a bond bought at 100 would be sold at, say, 125 and be replaced by another good convertible issue purchasable at about par. It is not likely that satisfactory opportunities of this kind will be continuously available or that the investor will have the means of locating all those that are at hand. Yet the unusually large amount of financing by convertibles in recent years has undoubtedly included a fair number of truly attractive offerings. The field can be exploited to advantage by the careful investor as well as by the speculator, but a special degree of discrimination and skill may be needed to protect the former against an ultimately disappointing experience.

[4] In actual practice, conversions often result also from arbitrage operations involving the purchase of the bond and the simultaneous sale of the stock at a price slightly higher than the "conversion parity."

CHAPTER FORTY-FIVE

TECHNICAL CHARACTERISTICS OF PRIVILEGED

SENIOR SECURITIES

In the preceding chapter privileged senior issues were considered in their relationship to the broader principles of investment and speculation. To arrive at an adequate knowledge of this group of securities from their practical side, we need to undertake a more intensive discussion of their characteristics. Such a study may conveniently be carried on from three successive viewpoints: (1) considerations common to all three types of privilege—conversion, participation, and subscription (i.e., "warrant"); (2) the relative merits of each type, as compared with the others; (3) technical aspects of each type, considered by itself.[1]

CONSIDERATIONS GENERALLY APPLICABLE TO PRIVILEGED ISSUES

The attractiveness of a profit-sharing feature depends upon two major but entirely unrelated factors: (1) the *terms* of the arrangement and (2) the *prospects* of profits to share. To use a simple illustration:

Company A	Company B
5 percent bond selling at 100	5 percent bond selling at 100
Convertible into stock at 50 (i.e., two shares of stock for a $100 bond)	Convertible into stock at 33⅓ (i.e., three shares of stock for a $100 bond)
Stock selling at 30	Stock selling at 30

Terms of the Privilege vs. Prospects for the Enterprise. The *terms* of the conversion privilege are evidently more attractive in the case of Bond *B;* for the stock need advance only a little more than 3 points to assure a profit, whereas Stock *A* must advance over 20 points to make conversion profitable. Nevertheless, it is quite possible that Bond *A* may turn out to be the more advantageous purchase. For conceivably Stock *B* may fail to advance at all while Stock *A* may double or triple in price.

[1] This subject is treated at what may appear to be disproportionate length because of the numerical importance of privileged issues and the absence of thoroughgoing discussion thereof in the standard descriptive textbooks.

As between the two factors, it is undoubtedly true that it is more profitable to select the right *company* than to select the issue with the most desirable *terms*. There is certainly no mathematical basis on which the attractiveness of the enterprise may be offset against the terms of the privilege and a balance struck between these two entirely dissociated elements of value. But in analyzing privileged issues of the investment grade, the *terms* of the privilege must receive the greater attention, not because they are more important but because they can be more definitely dealt with. It may seem a comparatively easy matter to determine that one enterprise is more promising than another. But it is by no means so easy to establish that one common stock at a given price is clearly preferable to another stock at *its* current price.

Reverting to our example, if it were quite certain, or even reasonably probable, that Stock *A* is more likely to advance to 50 than Stock *B* to advance to 33, then both issues would not be quoted at 30. Stock *A*, of course, would be selling higher. The point we make is that the market price in general *reflects already* any superiority that one enterprise has demonstrated over another. The investor who prefers Bond *A* because he expects its related stock to rise a great deal faster than Stock *B* is exercising independent judgment in a field where certainty is lacking and where mistakes are necessarily frequent. For this reason we doubt that a successful policy of buying privileged issues *from the investment approach* can be based primarily upon the purchaser's view regarding the future expansion of the profits of the enterprise. (In stating this point we are merely repeating a principle previously laid down in the field of fixed-income investment.)

Where the speculative approach is followed, i.e., where the issue is bought primarily as a desirable method of acquiring an interest in the stock, it would be quite logical, of course, to assign dominant weight to the buyer's judgment as to the future of the company.

Example: The difference between the *terms* and the *quality* of a privileged issue may be illustrated by a comparison of two convertible preferred stocks in August 1950 (Table 45-1). Seaboard Finance Preferred was offered at slightly below its immediate conversion value of parity—an unusual occurrence. American Cyanamid Preferred was then selling 25 percent above parity. On its *terms*, including the dividend yield, the Seaboard issue was much more attractive than the other. The investor's choice, however, would be governed in addition by his views on the relative safety of the two issues—which appeared much greater in the case of American Cyanamid—and the relative prospects of market appreciation in the common stock.

Sequel: Both of the common stocks made large advances in subsequent years, and the preferred issues as a result were highly profitable. They were all converted into common—the final conversions being compelled, as is customary, by the nominal "calling" of the issue.

Three Important Elements. In examining the terms of a profit-sharing privilege, we are aware of three component elements. These are:

1. The *extent* of the profit-sharing or speculative interest per dollar of investment
2. The *closeness* of the privilege to a realizable profit at the time of purchase
3. The *duration* of the privilege

1. *Extent of the Privilege.* The amount or extent of speculative interest attaching to a convertible or warrant-bearing senior security is equal to

Table 45-1. Comparison of Two Convertible Issues

	Seaboard Finance Co. ($1.35 Conv. Pfd. Series B)	American Cyanamid Co. ($3.50 Conv. Pfd. Series B)
Price of preferred.........................	23¼*	106¼
Yield......................................	5.8%	3.3%
Conversion rate...........................	1.34 common for 1 preferred	1.4 common for 1 preferred
Price of common..........................	17¾	61
Conversion value or parity of preferred.....	23¾	85½
Debt......................................	$52,600,000	$ 57,600,000
Preferred stock at par.....................	8,300,000	55,400,000
Common stock at market..................	18,000,000	216,600,000
Common at market as percentage of total capital...................................	23%	66%
Earned after taxes, year ended June 30, 1950, before interest.........................	$3,702,000	$28,930,000
Interest charge...........................	1,283,000	1,488,000
Preferred requirements....................	448,000	1,809,000
Coverage, including preferred dividends, after tax................................	2.14×	8.60×

* Offering price Aug. 8, 1950.

the current market value of the number of shares of stock covered by the privilege. Other things being equal, the larger the amount of the speculative interest per dollar of investment, the more attractive the privilege.

Example 1: Each $1,000 of Mack Trucks 5⅛ percent debentures, issued in 1961, carried a warrant to buy 5 shares of common at 46, expiring in 1971. The "speculative interest" here was thus about $230 per $1,000 bond, or 23 percent.

Example 2: A very old example of a huge speculative interest attaching to a bond issue may be reoffered here as a curiosity. Intercontinental Rubber Products 7 percent notes, issued in 1922, were convertible into stock at 10, and each $1,000 note also carried the right to purchase 400 additional shares at 10. When the stock sold at 10 in 1925 the speculative interest per $1,000 note amounted to 500 × 10 or $5,000—i.e., 500 percent. (By contrast, Reliable Stores 6s, offered in 1927, carried warrants to buy 5 shares per $1,000, at 10. The speculative interest here was only about 5 percent.)

The practical importance of the amount of speculative interest can be illustrated by the comparison in Table 45-2, covering the two bond issues just referred to.

2 and 3. Closeness and Duration of the Privilege. The implications of the second and third factors in valuing a privilege are readily apparent. A privilege having a long period to run is in that respect more desirable than one expiring in a short time. The nearer the current price

Table 45-2

Item	Reliable Stores 6s	Intercontinental Rubber 7s
Number of shares covered by each $1,000 bond..	5	500
Base price..	$10.00	$ 10.00
Increase in value of bond when stock advances:		
25 percent above base price.................	12.50	1,250.00
50 percent above base price.................	25.00	2,500.00
100 percent above base price.................	50.00	5,000.00

of the stock to the level at which conversion or subscription becomes profitable, the more attractive does the privilege become. In the case of a participation feature, it is similarly desirable that the current dividends or earnings on the common stock should be close to the figure at which the extra distribution on the senior issue commences.

COMPARATIVE MERITS OF THE THREE TYPES OF PRIVILEGES

From the theoretical standpoint, a participating feature—unlimited in time and possible amount—is the most desirable type of profit-sharing privilege. This arrangement enables the investor to derive the specific benefit of participation in profits (viz., increased income) without modifying his original position as a senior-security holder. These benefits may be received over a long period of years. By contrast, a conversion privilege can result in higher income only through actual exchange into the stock and consequent surrender of the senior position. Its real advantage consists, therefore, only of the opportunity to make a profit through the sale of the convertible issue at the right time. Similarly the benefits from a subscription privilege may conservatively be realized only through sale of the warrants (or by the subscription to and prompt sale of the stock). If the common stock is purchased and held for permanent income, the operation involves the risking of additional money on a basis entirely different from the original purchase of the senior issue.

Example of Advantage of Unlimited Participation Privilege. An excellent practical example of the theoretical advantages attaching to a well-entrenched participating security was long afforded by Westinghouse Electric and Manufacturing Company Preferred. This issue was entitled to cumulative prior dividends of $3.50 per annum (7 percent on $50 par) and in addition participated equally per share with the common in any dividends paid on the latter in excess of $3.50. As far back as 1917, Westinghouse Preferred could have been bought at 52½, representing an attractive straight investment with additional possibilities through its participating feature. In the ensuing 15 years to 1932, a total of about $7 per share was disbursed in extra dividends above the basic 7 percent. In the meantime an opportunity arose to sell out at a large profit (the high price being 284 in 1929), which corresponded to the enhancement possibilities of a convertible or subscription-warrant issue. If the stock was not sold, the profit was naturally lost in the ensuing market decline. But the investor's original position remained unimpaired, for at the low point of 1932 the issue was still paying the 7 percent dividend and selling at 52½—although the common had passed its dividend and had fallen to 15⅝.

In this instance the investor was able to participate in the surplus profits of the common stock in good years while maintaining his preferred position, so that when the bad years came, he lost only his "paper" *profit.* Had the issue been convertible instead of participating, the investor could have received the higher dividends only through converting and would later have found the dividend omitted on his common shares and their value fallen far below his original investment.[2]

Participating Issues at a Disadvantage in the Market. Although, from the standpoint of long-pull investment holding, participating issues are theoretically the most desirable, they may behave somewhat less satisfactorily in a major market upswing than do convertible or subscription-warrant issues. During such a period a participating senior security may regularly sell below its proper comparative price. The price of Westinghouse Preferred, for example, during 1929 was usually from 5 to 10 points lower than that of the common, although its intrinsic value per share could not be less than that of the junior stock.

---

[2] Each share of Westinghouse Preferred was subsequently replaced in two steps by $100 par value of new nonparticipating preferred carrying a $3.50 dividend plus two shares of new common par $12.50. At the time of retirement, the old preferred was worth in the market the equivalent of 141, against the equivalent of 92½ for the old common.

The reason for this phenomenon is as follows: The price of the common stock is made largely by speculators interested chiefly in quick profits, to secure which they need an active market. The preferred stock, being closely held, is relatively inactive. Consequently the speculators are willing to pay several points more for the inferior common issue simply because it can be bought and sold more readily and because other speculators are likely to be willing to pay more for it also.[3]

Relative Price Behavior of Convertible and Warrant-bearing Issues. From the standpoint of price behavior under favorable market conditions, the best results are obtained from securities with detachable stock-purchase warrants equivalent in their amount to a conversion privilege. Such issues are now very rare, since it has become customary to have the warrants represent a purchase price of less than half the face amount of the issue to which they are attached. However, because of the speculative attractiveness attaching to warrants alone they usually command a greater premium in the market over their realizable value than would a comparable convertible issue. We shall deal with this aspect of warrants in a separate section (page 621).

Warrant-bearing issues have two other general advantages over convertibles. The warrant period usually may not be terminated at the option of the company through exercise of a call privilege, such as is found in most convertibles.[4] Furthermore, their holders have the option of selling their warrants (or exercising them) and retaining their original senior issue. Holders of a convertible can cash in on a price rise of the common only be selling out their investment—unless they pursue the generally unwise alternative of converting and holding the common stock.

Summary. To summarize this section, it may be said that, for *long-pull holding,* a sound participating issue represents the best form of profit-sharing privilege. From the standpoint of maximum *price advance* under favorable market conditions, a senior issue with detachable stock-purchase warrants is likely to show the best results. Furthermore, subscription-warrant issues as a class have definite advantages in that the privilege is ordinarily not subject to curtailment through early redemp-

---

[3] A striking anomaly of this kind formerly existed between the prices of voting and nonvoting common stocks of several listed companies, e.g., American Tobacco, Bethlehem Steel, Liggett & Myers Tobacco, Pan-American Petroleum. The nonvoting shares regularly sold several points *higher* than the shares with the presumably valuable voting privilege, merely because the former were the more active in the market. These nonvoting issues have all disappeared through stockholder action which turned them into voting shares. A group of nonvoting issues has appeared among the numerous common-stock offerings at the beginning of the 1960's. None of these sold above the voting issue.

[4] However, unless protected by an antidilution clause, the warrant privilege may be impaired by payment of a stock dividend or a similar reduction in the value of each share. (See next page.) In rare cases warrants may be callable by the issuer. Those attached to the Keyes Fibre subordinated convertible 5¼s, due 1985, may be called by the company after 1965 at $1 per share covered by the warrants.

tion of the security, and they permit the purchaser to realize a speculative profit while retaining the original investment position.

The effective terms of a conversion privilege are frequently subject to change during the life of the issue. These changes are of two kinds: (1) a decrease in the conversion price, to protect the holder against "dilution," and (2) an increase in the conversion price (in accordance usually with a "sliding-scale" arrangement) for the benefit of the company.

Dilution, and Antidilution Clauses. The value of a common stock is said to be diluted if there is an increase in the number of shares without a corresponding increase in assets and earning power. Dilution may arise through split-ups, stock dividends, offers of subscription rights at a low price, and issuance of stock for property or services at a low valuation per share.[5] The standard "antidilution" provisions of a convertible issue endeavor to reduce the conversion price proportionately to any decrease in the per-share value arising through any act of dilution.

The method may be expressed in a formula, as follows: Let C be the conversion price, O be the number of shares now outstanding, N be the number of new shares to be issued, and P be the price at which they are to be issued.

Then

$$C' \text{ (the new conversion price)} = \frac{CO + NP}{O + N}$$

A much less frequent provision merely reduces the conversion price to any lower figure at which new shares may be issued. This is, of course, more favorable to the holder of the convertible issue.[6]

Protection against Dilution Not Complete. Although practically all convertibles now have antidilution provisions, there have been exceptions.[7] As a matter of course, a prospective buyer should make certain that such protection exists for the issue he is considering.

It should be borne in mind that the effect of some of these provisions is to preserve only the principal or par value of the privileged issue

[5] Railway & Light Securities Company Preferred stock was protected against an unusual type of "dilution"—viz., the payment of dividends on the common out of security profits. By the operation of this provision the conversion rate changed from an initial two shares of common for one preferred to 2.378 shares in October 1950, when it was called for redemption. The company was renamed Colonial Fund, Inc., in December 1952.

[6] An old example was Consolidated Textile Corporation 7s, due 1923, described in the 1940 edition, p. 764.

[7] An old example was American Telephone and Telegraph Company 4½s, due 1933, described in the 1940 edition, p. 764.

against dilution. If a convertible is selling considerably above par, the *premium* will still be subject to impairment through additional stock issues or a special dividend. A simple illustration will make this clear.

A bond is convertible into stock, par for par. The usual antidilution clauses are present. Both bond and stock are selling at 200. Stockholders are given the right to buy new stock, share for share, at par ($100). These rights will be worth $50 per share, and the new stock (or the old stock "ex-rights") will be worth 150. No change will be made in the conversion basis, because the new stock is not issued below the old conversion price. However, the effect of offering these rights must be to compel immediate conversion of the bonds, since otherwise they would lose 25 percent of their value. As the stock will be worth only 150 "ex-rights," instead of 200, the value of the unconverted bonds would drop proportionately.

The foregoing discussion indicates that, when a large premium or market profit is created for a privileged issue, the situation is vulnerable to sudden change. Although prompt action will always prevent loss through such changes, their effect is to terminate the effective life of the privilege.[8] The same result will follow, of course, from the calling of a privileged issue for redemption at a price below its then conversion value.

Where the number of shares is *reduced* through recapitalization, it is customary to *increase* the conversion price proportionately. Such recapitalization measures include increases in par value, "reverse split-ups" (e.g., issuance of one share in place of, say, five old shares), and exchanges of the old stock for fewer new shares through consolidation with another company.[9]

Sliding Scales Designed to Accelerate Conversion. The provisions just discussed are intended to maintain equitably the original basis of conversion in the event of subsequent capitalization changes. On the other hand, a "sliding-scale" arrangement is intended definitely to reduce the value of the privilege as time goes on. The underlying purpose is to accelerate conversion, in other words, to curtail the effective duration and hence the real value of the option. Obviously, any diminution of the worth of the privilege to its recipients must correspondingly benefit the donors of the privilege, who are the company's common shareholders.

The usual terms of a sliding scale prescribe a series of increases in the conversion price in successive periods of time.

[8] To guard against this form of dilution, holders of convertible issues are sometimes given the right to subscribe to any new offerings of common stock on the same basis as if they owned the amount of common shares into which their holdings are convertible. Older examples were the New York, New Haven and Hartford Railroad Company Convertible Debenture 6s, due 1948, and Commercial Investment Trust Corporation Convertible Debenture 5½s, due 1949.

[9] An old example was Dodge Brothers, Inc., Convertible Debenture 6s, due 1940, when they became convertible into Chrysler shares after the merger in 1928 (described in the 1940 edition, p. 765).

Example: American Machine & Foundry subordinated debenture 4¼s, due 1981, are convertible into common stock at 60 to 1971 and then at 65 until maturity.

A variation makes the conversion price increase as soon as a certain portion of the issue has been exchanged.

Example 1: An $8,000,000 issue of Hiram Walker-Goderham and Worts 4¼s, due 1945, was convertible as follows: at $40 per share for the first $2,000,000 block of bonds; at $45 per share for the next $2,000,000 block of bonds; at $55 for the third block; and at $60 per share for the final block.

Example 2: In 1955 Sunray-Mid-Continental Oil issued 956,000 shares of 5½ percent Second Preferred, par $30, in exchange for shares of Mid-Continent Petroleum. This issue was made convertible into common at $28.75 until one-third of the shares had been converted; then at $31.15 until the next third had been turned in; and finally at $33.54. The company had created an issue with similar provisions in 1950, all of which was converted into common.

Changes in the conversion price based on the extent to which privilege is exercised give the first lot of bonds or preferred stocks converted an obvious advantage over the next; hence this method provides a *competitive* stimulus to early conversion. By so doing it creates a conflict in the mind of the holder between the desire to retain his senior position and the fear of losing the more favorable basis of conversion through prior action by other bondholders. This fear of being forestalled will ordinarily result in large-scale conversions as soon as the stock advances moderately above the initial conversion price, i.e., as soon as the bond is worth slightly more than the original cost. Accordingly, the price of the senior issue can oscillate over a relatively narrow range while the common stock is advancing and while successive blocks of bonds are being converted.

Example: The sequence of events normally to be expected is shown fairly well by the market action of Hiram Walker-Goderham and Worts Convertible 4¼s described above. The bonds, issued in 1936 at par, ranged in price between 100 and 111¼ during 1936–1939. In the same period the stock ranged between 26⅛ and 54. If the initial conversion price of 40 for the stock had prevailed throughout the period, the bonds should have sold for at least 135 when the stock sold at 54. But meanwhile, as the price of the stock rose, successive blocks of the bonds were converted (partly under the impetus supplied by successive calls for redemption of parts of the issue), thus tipping off higher conversion prices until the $55 bracket was reached in 1937. In consequence the bonds did not appreciate commensurately with the rise in the price of the stock.

When the last block under such a sliding scale is reached, the *competitive* element disappears, and the bond or preferred stock is then in the position of an ordinary convertible, free to advance indefinitely with the stock.[10]

Special Features of Some Convertibles. Many years ago it was customary to make short-term note issues convertible into long-term bonds deposited as collateral thereof. There were also quite a few bond issues convertible into preferred stock or a class A stock with preference rights. These arrangements seem to have gone out of style. A definitely objectionable device of the past was the issuance of bonds or "convertible obligations" convertible into some junior issue at the *option of the company*. This was one of the features of the fantastic financial structure of Associated Gas & Electric Company under the Hopson regime. Under all the circumstances the device was little short of a fraud perpetrated on untrained security buyers.

However, some of the financing of new pipelines in the past decade has included the sale of bonds convertible at the option of the company into preferred stock. The purpose of this arrangement, which was not deceptive, was to permit payment of interest to the investor during the initial years of no profits; had the security been sold in the first instance as a preferred stock, the payment of equivalent preferred dividends would have been illegal. The original buyer expected to own a preferred stock after the company had begun profitable operations.

Example: Transwestern Pipe Line Company sold $40 million of subordinated debenture 5s in May 1959 in units of $100 of debentures and 5 shares of common for $153.75. The 5s were made "payable at the company's option" after October 1961 in 5½ percent preferred.

Another peculiarity of 1928–1929, which has not yet been imitated in the 1960's, was the offering of convertible issues with an original market issue greatly in excess of par, by way of rights given to the stockholders. This created an immediate speculative risk for the "investors" therein. It was also the custom to delay the operation of the conversion privilege until a date several years after issuance. This practice introduced an added factor of uncertainty into the status of these issues and tended to make the privilege less valuable than it would have been otherwise.[11]

---

[10] In some cases (e.g., International Paper and Power Company old First Preferred) the conversion privilege ceases entirely after a certain fraction of the issue has been converted. This maintains the competitive factor throughout the life of the privilege and in theory should prevent it from ever having any substantial value.

[11] Examples of these earlier variations in the terms of convertibles are given in the 1940 edition, pp. 313–317. We should point out, for completeness, the unusual case of Reading Company (Railroad) $2 Second Preferred, which when issued in reorganization in 1896 was made convertible *at the option of the company* into one-half share of $2 First Preferred and one-half share of common. When the common stock sold at high prices, as in the 1920's, the second preferred regularly commanded a higher quotation than the first preferred, on some vague notion that the company would make the conversion and thus benefit the second preferred. Conversely, in certain years the second preferred has sold for more than it would be worth if the

The American Telephone and Telegraph Pattern. American Telephone and Telegraph Company has been the most consistent user of convertible-bond financing, and the amounts of such issues far exceed those of any other enterprise. At the beginning of 1950 it had $690 million of convertibles outstanding in three issues. At the end of 1960 virtually all the convertible bonds had disappeared through conversion, but there were outstanding $2,950 million in "straight" debentures, in 15 issues, all rated Aaa.

Special Factor in American Telephone and Telegraph Financing. The company has used the special device of issuing one share of stock upon tender of a $100 bond plus the cash required to bring the total up to the conversion price of the stock. That arrangement is a more liberal one to the bondholder than a straight conversion privilege, because it gives each $1,000 bond a call on 10 shares of stock. On a straight conversion at, say, 142 the call would cover only seven shares.[12]

Comment: We should like to comment as follows on the bearing of American Telephone and Telegraph convertible financing upon the general question of the attractiveness of convertible securities to both the issuer and the investor. For this huge corporation the use of the convertible medium was almost compulsory until fairly recently, because only in this way was it able to attract the equivalent of equity money from life insurance companies and other sources of funds that were not then permitted to buy common stocks. The interest return has been less than half the corresponding dividend yield on the stock, so that as long as the bonds remained outstanding they saved the company an important sum in capital costs. Because the dividend was maintained at its liberal $9 rate on the old shares for many years, the result was the eventual conversion of all the older convertible issues and the rapid conversion of the newer ones.

The buyers of the convertibles have thus fared quite well during the years, but not as well as they would have done if they had bought the stock in the first place and received the high dividend return from the beginning. In sum, American Telephone and Telegraph convertibles have proved good investments because the company has remained prosperous. To prove the convertible *form* sound in practice it would be necessary to have a number of instances in which the convertible issue worked out well even though the common stock proved definitely disappointing. Such instances are not easy to find.

---

company actually required conversion—presumably on the theory that the conversion right of the company is not to be taken seriously. This contrasting market behavior—in both instances resulting in a higher price for the second preferred than its contract rights would warrant—sheds a curious light on the reasoning of investors and speculators.

[12] The few 4¼s due 1973 remaining at the end of 1960 were convertible originally at the rate of 1 share for each $100 bond plus $42 in cash. This was changed to 3 shares after the stock split in 1959.

CHAPTER FORTY-SIX

PARTICIPATING AND WARRANT-BEARING ISSUES.

PRIVILEGED ISSUES VS. THE RELATED

COMMON STOCKS

Participating Issues. At the time of our 1951 edition this type of security had become quite rare. However, it has been revived in recent years, chiefly in the form of a class A stock with both a limited priority right over, and a participating right with, the common or class B issue.

The participating right to additional dividends is usually dependent upon the amounts paid to the common. The extra payments to the senior issue may be limited or unlimited.

Example 1: Each share of Arden Farms Company Cumulative Preferred Stock, no par, receives $3 annually plus one-fourth of the dividend paid on each common share, but not more than $1 additional in any calendar year. It has received an (extra) 25-cent participating dividend in each year since 1948.

Example 2: Molson's Brewery, Ltd., class A, is entitled to 40 cents noncumulative in each year and then shares equally, without limit, in dividends paid on the class B above 40 cents. It has received participating dividends of varying amounts in each year since issuance in 1950.

The participating right may be dependent on the amount of earnings only, without regard to common dividends.

Example: American Service Company Cumulative Participating Preferred received $3 annually; then $220,000 of earnings were reserved for the common (but not necessarily paid); and then the preferred received 25 percent of the balance. (This issue was exchanged for Income Debenture 4½s in 1959.)

Calculation of Earnings for Participating Issues. Two kinds of calculation are required for a participating senior issue. The first is the number of times the regular interest or dividend is earned; the second is the amount available for distribution under the participating provision.

Example: Foote Bros. Gear & Machine, 1960. Its class A stock receives 50 cents annually and shares equally in dividends with the common after 50 cents on the common. There are 461,000 shares of class A and 612,000 shares of common. The 1960 earnings of $866,000 equaled $1.88 per share, or 3.8 times the priority dividend on the class A. It also equaled 81 cents per share on the two classes combined.

It is customary to present this situation as follows: Earned for class A on priority basis $1.88 per share. Earned for class A on participating basis $0.81 per share.

Senior Securities with Warrants. This type of privileged issue has also been revived in recent years, and in 1961 such senior securities were becoming quite numerous. They may have the same technical features of convertibles in the matter of antidilution provisions[1] and sliding-scale changes of subscription price dependent either on a time schedule or on the number of warrants exercised. In a number of cases the warrant can be exercised either by paying cash for the common stock or by turning in the senior security at par. The latter arrangement is directly equivalent to a conversion privilege. The warrants are made either nondetachable, detachable, or detachable only after a certain period. Detachable warrants may be traded in separately. Since they are popular with speculators—who like the "call" on the common stock—they have sold in bull markets at far above their exercise value. Issues with nondetachable warrants are similar in their characteristics to convertible issues— except that the warrants generally call for a smaller dollar amount of common than the par value of the senior issue.

The various complexities of warrant-bearing issues, as well as their speculative possibilities, are illustrated by the following account of two issues of Coastal States Gas Producing Company: (1) $5 million of 5½ percent Debentures, due 1977, were sold at 100 in 1957. A sinking fund, commencing in 1959, must retire all but $50,000 of the issue before maturity. Each $1,000 bond carried a warrant to buy 60 shares of common at 7½, payable either in cash or in debentures at par. One half of the warrants (Series A) were immediately detachable, the other half (Series B) were nondetachable for two years. The indenture limited the company's total debt to four times the capital stock and surplus— an 80 percent debt component. (2) $20 million of Debenture 6s, due 1980, were sold in 1960 at 100. A sinking fund commences in 1968 and will retire about 58 percent of the issue before maturity. Each $1,000 bond carries a warrant (detachable after about six months) to buy 17 common shares at $32. Payment could be made one-half in debentures and one-half in cash, or all in cash.

Both series of warrants are protected against dilution.

---

[1] An interesting controversy over this point developed in 1950 in connection with Merritt-Chapman & Scott perpetual warrants entitling the holder to buy one share of common at an initial price of 30. Following payment of a 40 percent stock dividend, it was finally held by the courts that, even without a specific antidilution provision, the warrants should then call for 1.4 shares at about $20.70 per share.

The 5½ percent debentures with warrants sold down to 88 in 1957, but rose to 590 in 1961 when the common advanced to 92½. The warrants were then quoted at their exercisable value of $85 each, or $5,100 for those attached to a $1,000 bond. The apparent market value of the bonds ex-warrants was then only 80, but their real quotation was undoubtedly higher, indicating that an arbitrage profit was to be made by buying bonds with warrants and simultaneously selling the warrants (or the stock) and the bonds ex-warrants separately. (See below, footnote 3, page 623.)

The 6 percent debentures with warrants advanced from a low of 100 in 1960, to a high of 215 in 1961. The difference in market value between the two issues reflected, of course, the much more liberal warrant terms of the 1957 issue.

Warrants as Separate Securities. When subscription warrants were made detachable from the related senior issue, they were bound to assume an existence and characteristics of their own. From a mere appendage of bond financing they developed into an independent form of security and a major vehicle of speculation during the madness of 1928–1929. It is an amazing fact that the option warrants created by one company, American and Foreign Power, reached an indicated market value in 1929 of over a billion dollars, a figure that exceeded the market value of *all* the railroad common stocks of the United States listed on the New York Stock Exchange in July 1932, less than three years later.

It will be necessary, therefore, to consider in a later chapter the characteristics of stock-purchase warrants, viewed as an independent speculation medium. At that time we shall discuss the relationships between the prices of such warrants and the prices of the preferred and common shares of the same corporations.

Privileged Issues Compared with the Related Common Stocks. In our previous discussion of the merits of privileged issues as a class it was pointed out that they sometimes offer a very attractive combination of security and chance for profit. More frequently, a decision may be merely that the privileged senior security is preferable to the common stock of the enterprise. Since a conclusion of this kind is based on comparative elements only, it is likely to involve smaller risks of error than one that asserts the absolute attractiveness of an issue.

Example: The example of Graham-Paige Convertible 4s and stock (now somewhat old) is still impressive. In May 1946 the bonds were selling at 102, which was slightly less than the current value (at 13¼) of the 76.9 shares into which each $1,000 bond was convertible. The common stock was paying no dividends and had shown very small earnings. Obviously the bonds were a better purchase than the common stock: (1) they offered the same opportunities for profit, because of their conversion privilege; (2) they yielded an income return; and (3) they were much better protected against loss.

Sequel: Both the bonds and the stock declined sharply in price after May 1946, but the bondholder's shrinkage was much less than the stockholder's. He received full interest on his bonds until they were retired at 100 in 1955, during which year the stock sold as low as 1¾.

"Parity," "Premium," and "Discount." When the price of a convertible bond of preferred is exactly equivalent, on an exchange basis, to the current price of the common stock, the two issues are said to be selling at a parity.[2] When the price of the senior issue is above parity, it is said to be selling at a premium, and the difference between its price and conversion parity is called the amount of the premium, or the "spread." Conversely if the price of the convertible is below parity, the difference is sometimes called the "discount."[3]

A Fruitful Field for Dependable Analysis. The Graham-Paige example gives us that infrequent phenomenon—an absolutely dependable conclusion arrived at by security analysis. Holders of the common could not possibly lose by exchanging into the convertible issue, and they had excellent prospects, which in fact were realized, of deriving substantial benefits in the form of both increased income and greater market value. In this respect privileged issues offer a fruitful field for the more scientific application of the technique of analysis. The foregoing example is typical also of the price relationships created by an active and advancing market. When there is a senior issue convertible into common, the concentration of speculative interest in the latter often results in establishing a price level closely equivalent to (and sometimes even higher than) the price of the senior issue, to which the public pays little attention.

Conclusion from Foregoing. It is clear that a convertible issue selling on a parity with the common is preferable thereto, except when its price is so far above an investment level that it has become merely a form of commitment in the common stock.

[2] This term should not be confused with "par," which means simply the face value of the security in question, and sometimes $100 per share, without reference to the real par value of the share, which may be quite different.

[3] Discounts occur fairly often when the conversion privilege is not immediately operative. If the senior issue may be promptly exchanged for the common, a discount results in creating an arbitrage opportunity. This is a chance to make a profit (usually small) without risk of loss. The profit is made by (1) simultaneously buying the senior issue and selling the common stock; (2) immediately converting the senior issue into the common stock; and (3) delivering the common stock against the sale, thus completing the transaction. Arbitraging of this "open-and-shut" kind is done rather extensively in active, rising markets, but the opportunities are usually monopolized by brokers specializing in such operations. Other forms of inter-security arbitrage operations arise from reorganizations, mergers or purchase offers, stock split-ups, rights to buy additional shares, etc. For detailed discussion see Meyer H. Weinstein, *Arbitrage in Securities,* Harper & Brothers, New York, 1931. In the older sense, the term "arbitrage" applied to simultaneous purchases and sales of the same security in different markets (e.g., New York and London) and to similar operations involving foreign exchange. See also our discussion of the "discount price" of Studebaker-Packard Preferred in 1959, on p. 31 above.

Example: An extreme example of our exception would be the American Telephone and Telegraph convertible 4¼s, due 1973, previously mentioned. Because of their valuable conversion rights they sold above 350 in 1961. Obviously the bonds were not as attractive as the stock, since they carried the same risk of a market decline, and their current yield was only half as great.

It is generally worthwhile, however, to pay some moderate premium in order to obtain the superior safety of the senior issue. This is certainly true when the convertible yields a higher income return than the common, and it holds good to some extent even if the income yield is lower.

Switching. As a practical rule, therefore, holders of common stocks who wish to retain their interest in the company should always exchange into a convertible senior issue of the enterprise, whenever it sells both at an investment level on its own account and also close to parity on a conversion basis. Just how large a premium a common stockholder should be willing to pay in making such an exchange is a matter of individual judgment. Because of his confidence in the future of his company, he is usually unwilling to pay anything substantial for insurance against a decline in value. But experience shows that he would be wise to give up somewhat more than he thinks is necessary in order to secure the strategic advantages that even a fairly sound convertible issue possesses over a common stock.

Example: Western Maryland $1.60 Preferred (par $40) is convertible, share for share, into common. Both sold at about 31½ in 1961. The common was receiving 45 cents quarterly and the preferred 40 cents. In 1955, when nothing was paid on either issue, the preferred had sold at the equivalent of 25 against 12 for the common. Merely on general grounds of prudence, and without opinion as to future possibilities in either direction, a Western Maryland common stockholder should have switched into the preferred, even though he sacrificed about ¾ of 1 percent per annum in dividend return. (The common dividend was reduced to 25 cents quarterly, late in 1961, and in 1962 the preferred sold twice as high as the common.)

It may be prudent to switch from a speculative common stock into a convertible preferred paying a higher dividend return, even if the preferred sells several points above its conversion parity.

Example 1: Kaiser Aluminum & Chemical 4¾ percent Preferred is convertible into common at 47½, or at about 2.1 shares for 1. When the common sold at close to 55 in 1960 the preferred sold at 123 or 7 points above its parity. But its dividend return was about 4 percent against 1.7 percent from the common, and the earnings of only $1.17 on the common in 1959 suggested that its price was speculative.

Sequel: The next year the common sold down to 32, equivalent to only 67 for the preferred, while the latter did not sell below 101. The spread of 7 points had thus widened to 34 points, and the exchange would have proved a very wise one.

Example 2: Baldwin-Montrose Chemical Preferred is convertible into 1.3 shares of common until 1966. In 1961 it sold at 17¾ against a concurrent price of 13¼ for the common—equivalent to 17⅛ for the preferred. The preferred paid a $1 annual dividend; the common paid nothing. A switch at these prices was undoubtedly prudent and was likely to prove advantageous.

Sequel: This prediction was verified that very year.

Hedging. The advantages of a strong convertible issue over a common stock become manifest when the market declines. The price of the senior issue will ordinarily suffer less severely than the common, so that a good-sized spread may thereby be established, instead of the near-parity previously existing. This possibility suggests a special form of market operation known as "hedging," in which the operator buys the convertible and sells the common stock short against it, at an approximate parity.[4] In the event of a protracted *rise*, he can convert the senior issue and thus close out the transaction at only a slight loss, consisting of the original spread plus carrying expenses. But if the market declines substantially, he can "undo" the operation at a considerable profit, by selling out the senior issue and buying back the common.

With favorable surrounding conditions, operations of this kind offer a chance for large gains against a small maximum loss. They are particularly suitable as a form of protection against other financial commitments, for they yield their profit in a declining market when other holdings are likely to show losses.

Some Technical Aspects of Hedging. Hedging has numerous technical aspects, however, which make it less simple and foolproof than our brief description would indicate. An exhaustive discussion of hedging would fall outside the scope of this volume, and for this reason we shall merely list below certain elements that the experienced hedger will take into account in embarking upon such operations:

1. Ability to borrow stock sold and to maintain short position indefinitely[5]
2. Original cost of establishing position, including spread and commissions

---

[4] "Hedging" in commodities is a superficially similar but basically different type of operation. Generally speaking, its purpose is to protect a normal manufacturing or distributing profit against the chance of speculative loss through commodity price changes. A miller, having bought wheat that he will sell as flour some months later, will sell wheat futures as a "hedge" against the possibility of a decline in wheat destroying his profit margin. When the flour is disposed of, he covers (buys back) the wheat sold as protection. Most commodity hedging is thus designed as a safeguard, whereas security hedging is usually intended to yield direct profits.

[5] Regulations of the SEC and the stock exchanges have made short selling more difficult since 1934. For example, short sales could be made for a time only at a price higher than the last previous trade. The rule was later relaxed to permit short sales at a price no lower than the last trade. The obstacle imposed by these rules is mitigated in part by the fact that hedges of the kind under discussion are ordinarily set up only in a rising and fairly active market.

3. Cost of maintaining the position, including interest charges on long holdings, dividends on short stock, possible premiums payable for borrowing stock, and stamp taxes in connection with reborrowing of stock—less offsets in the forms of dividends or interest receivable on long securities and possible interest credit on short position

4. Amount of profit at which operation will probably be closed out if opportunity offers; relationship between this maximum profit and probable maximum loss, consisting of (2) plus (3) plus cost of undoing position

It should be borne in mind in these, as in all other operations in securities, that the potential profit to be taken into account is not the *maximum* figure that might conceivably be reached in the market but merely the highest figure for which the operator is likely to wait before he closes out his position. Once a given profit is taken, the additional profit that might have been realized subsequently becomes of merely academic or rueful interest.

An Intermediate Form of Hedging. An intermediate form of hedging consists of purchasing a convertible issue and selling only part of the related common shares, say one-half of the amount receivable upon conversion. On this basis a profit may be realized in the event of either a substantial advance or a substantial decline in the common stock. This is probably the most scientific method of hedging, since it requires no opinion as to the future course of prices. An ideal situation of this kind would meet the following two requirements:

1. A strongly entrenched senior issue that can be relied on to maintain a price close to par even if the common should drop precipitously. A good convertible bond, maturing in a short time, is an ideal type for this purpose.

2. A common stock in which the speculative interest is large and which is therefore subject to wide fluctuations in either direction.[6]

The advantages possessed by convertibles, along the lines described in this chapter, are shared to some degree by participating and purchase-warrant issues. The latter types of privileged securities may be used as media for hedging operations. Similarly, it may be found most desirable to switch from common stocks into such issues. But hedging operations between a nonconvertible participating preferred and the common would involve special hazards, since the hedger cannot limit his maximum market loss.

[6] An old example of such an intermediate hedge is Pierce Oil notes and stock. See page 767 of the 1940 edition.

CHAPTER FORTY-SEVEN

SENIOR SECURITIES OF QUESTIONABLE SAFETY

At the low point of the 1932 securities markets, the safety of at least 80 percent of all corporate bonds and preferred stocks was open to some appreciable degree of doubt. Even prior to the 1929 crash the number of speculative senior securities was very large; in spite of improvements in corporate financing and of the many railroad reorganizations, they were still numerous in 1950. Their number has been greatly diminished by the prosperity of the past decade. This change is shown strikingly by the following sampling of senior issues selling below 70 percent of face value at various times in the past.

Table 47-1. Proportion of Senior Issues Selling at Speculative Prices

At some time during year	Bonds		Preferred stocks	
	No. of issues examined	% below 70	No. of issues examined	% below 70
1932	4,500	70%*		
1939	1,100	57		
1949	100	57	100	57
1960	100	12	100	13†

* Fifty-two percent sold below 50.
† In addition, eight had arrears or yielded more than 6 percent.

A low-grade bond or preferred stock constitutes a relatively unpopular form of commitment. The conventional investor must not buy either of them, and the speculator generally prefers to devote his attention to common stocks. There seems to be much logic in the view that if one decides to speculate he should choose a thoroughly speculative medium and not subject himself to the upper limitations of market value and income return, or to the possibility of confusion between speculation and investment, both of which difficulties attach to the lower-priced bonds and preferred stocks.

Opportunities in This Field. But however impressive may be the objection to these nondescript securities, the fact remains that they have existed in large amounts, that they have been owned by innumerable security holders, and that hence they must be taken seriously into account in any survey of security analysis. We may add our belief that the large outpouring of inadequately protected senior issues—most of them with conversion or warrant features—that began several years ago is almost certain to produce a new crop of "below-70" issues some time in the future. It is reasonable to conclude that a large supply of such issues, coupled with the lack of a natural demand for them, will make for a level of prices below their intrinsic value. Even if an inherent unattractiveness in the form of such securities be admitted, this may be more than offset by the attractive price at which they may be purchased. Furthermore, the limitations of principal profit in the case of a low-priced bond, as compared with a common stock, may be of only minor practical importance, because the profit actually realized by the common-stock buyer is ordinarily no greater than that obtainable from a speculative senior security. If, for example, we are considering a 4 percent bond selling at 35—e.g., Graham-Paige 4s, due 1956, at the beginning of 1950[1]—its maximum possible price appreciation was about 70 points, or 200 percent. The average common-stock purchase at 35 cannot be held for a greater profit than this without a dangerous surrender to bull-market psychology.

Two Viewpoints with Respect to Speculative Bonds. A speculative bond may be viewed from two directly opposite angles. It may be considered in its relation to investment standards and yields, in which case the leading question is whether or not the low price and higher income return will compensate for the concession made in the matter of safety. Or it may be thought of in terms of a common-stock commitment, in which event the contrary question arises, viz., "Does the smaller risk of loss involved in this low-priced bond, as compared with a common stock, compensate for the smaller possibilities of profit?" The nearer a bond comes to meeting investment requirements—and the closer it sells to an investment price—the more likely are those interested to regard it from the investment viewpoint. The opposite approach is evidently suggested in the case of a bond in default or selling at an extremely low price. We are faced here with the familiar difficulty of classification arising from the absence of definite lines of demarcation. Some issues can always be found which reflect any conceivable status in the gamut between complete worthlessness and absolute safety.

Common-stock Approach Preferable. We believe, however, that the sounder and more fruitful approach to the field of speculative senior securities lies in the direction of common stocks. This will carry with it a more thorough appreciation of the risk involved and therefore a

---

[1] These bonds were paid off at par in 1955. (See p. 622.)

greater insistence upon either reasonable assurance of safety or especially attractive possibilities of profit, or both. It induces also—among intelligent security buyers at least—a more intensive examination of the corporate picture than would ordinarily be made in viewing a security from the investment angle.

Such an approach would be distinctly unfavorable to the purchase of slightly substandard bonds selling at moderate discounts from par. These, together with high-coupon bonds of second grade, belong in the category of "businessman's investments," which we considered and decided against in Chapter 22. It may be objected that a general adoption of this attitude would result in wide and sudden fluctuations in the price of many issues. Assuming that a 4 percent bond deserves to sell at par as long as it meets strict investment standards, then as soon as it falls slightly below these standards its price would suffer a precipitous decline to, say, 70; and, conversely, a slight improvement in its exhibit would warrant its jumping suddenly back to par. Apparently there would be no justification for intermediate quotations between 70 and 100.

The real situation is not so simple as this, however. Differences of opinion may properly exist in the minds of investors as to whether or not a given issue is adequately secured, particularly since the standards are qualitative and personal as well as arithmetical and objective. The range between 70 and 100 may therefore logically reflect a greater or lesser agreement concerning the safety of the issue. This would mean that an investor would be justified in buying such a bond at, say, 85, if his own considered judgment regarded it as sound, although he would recognize that doubt on this score in the minds of other investors would account for its appreciable discount from a prime investment price. According to this view, the levels between 70 and 100, approximately, may be designated as the range of "subjective variations" in the status of the issue.

Example: Northern Pacific Railway 4½s, due 2047, sold in 1949 at an average price of 80, to yield 5.65 percent, which represented a partially speculative appraisal of the issue at the time. Although bond yields rose and bond prices in general have declined greatly since then, the improvement of the credit of the Northern Pacific created an average price of 97 for this issue in 1961.

The field of speculative values proper would therefore commence somewhere near the 70 level (for bonds yielding over 5 percent) and would offer maximum possibilities of appreciation of at least 50 percent of the cost. (In the case of other senior issues, 70 percent of *normal value* might be taken as the dividing line.) In making such commitments, the investor is advised to take the same general attitude that he would adopt in the careful purchase of a common stock; in other words, to submit the income account and the balance sheet to the same intensive analysis and to make the same effort to evaluate future possibilities— favorable and unfavorable.

Important Distinctions between Common Stocks and Speculative Senior Issues. We shall not seek, therefore, to set up standards of selection for speculative senior issues in any sense corresponding to the quantitative tests applicable to fixed-income securities. On the other hand, although they should preferably be considered in their relationship to the common-stock approach and technique, it is necessary to appreciate certain rather important points of difference that exist between common stocks as a class and speculative senior issues.

Low-priced Bonds Result from Corporate Weakness. The limitation on the profit possibilities of senior securities has already been referred to. Its significance varies with the individual security, but in general we do not consider it a controlling disadvantage. A more emphatic objection is made against low-priced bonds and preferred stocks on the ground that they are associated with corporate weakness, retrogression, or depression. Obviously the enterprise behind such a security is not highly successful, and furthermore, it must have been following a downward course, since the issue originally sold at a much higher level.

The financial history of past decades has shown that a large proportion of companies of this type have recovered sufficient earning power to meet their fixed obligations and eventually to restore their bonds or preferred stocks to an investment status. This experience suggests that there may be as much reason to expect substantial recoveries in the quotations of depressed senior issues as to look for a rise in the price of common stocks generally when the market is at a low level. The favorable economic conditions since World War II have converted most of the low-priced bonds and preferred stocks of the early 1940's into investment-grade issues, or have permitted their retirement at about their par value and accumulated dividends, if any. Our discussion following will apply more to conditions existing prior to the market rise of the 1950's than to those of 1961. It may well be found relevant, however, to conditions of future years.

Many Senior Securities Are Undervalued in Relation to Their Status and Contractual Position. We have already mentioned that the unpopularity of speculative senior securities tends to make them sell at lower prices than common stocks, in relation to their intrinsic value. From the standpoint of the intelligent buyer this undervaluation must be considered a point in their favor. With respect to their intrinsic position, speculative bonds—and, to a lesser degree, preferred stocks—derive important advantages from their contractual rights. The fixed obligation to pay bond interest will usually result in the continuation of such payments as long as they are in any way possible. If we assume that a fairly large proportion of a group of carefully selected low-priced bonds will escape default, the income received on the group as a whole over a period of time will undoubtedly far exceed the dividend return on similarly priced common stocks.

Preferred shares occupy an immeasurably weaker position in this regard, but even here the provisions transferring voting control to the senior shares in the event of suspension of dividends will be found in some cases to impel their continuance. Where the cash resources are ample, the desire to maintain an unbroken record and to avoid accumulations will frequently result in paying preferred dividends even though poor earnings have depressed the market price.

Example: Publicker Industries failed to earn anything on its preferred stock in five of the six years 1954–1959, but it has maintained the $4.75 dividend uninterruptedly since issuance in 1945 (through 1961). The price of the stock has been as low as 63½.[2]

Contrasting Importance of Contractual Terms in Speculation and Investment. The reader should appreciate the distinction between the *investment* and the *speculative* qualities of preferred stocks in this matter of dividend continuance. From the investment standpoint, i.e., the *dependability* of the dividend, the absence of an enforceable claim is a disadvantage as compared with bonds. From the speculative standpoint, i.e., the possibility that dividends may be continued under unfavorable conditions, preferred stocks have certain semicontractual claims to consideration by the directors that undoubtedly give them an advantage over common stocks.

Bearing of Working-capital and Sinking-fund Factors on the Safety of Speculative Senior Issues. A large working capital, which has been characteristic of many nonprosperous industrials for some years past, is much more directly advantageous to the senior securities than to the common stock. Not only does it make possible the continuance of interest or preferred-dividend payments, but it has an important bearing also on the retirement of the principal—at maturity or by sinking-fund operations or by voluntary repurchase. Sinking-fund provisions, for bonds as well as preferred stocks, contribute to the improvement of both the market quotation and the intrinsic position of the issue. This advantage is not found among common stocks.

Examples: Frances H. Leggett Company, manufacturers and wholesalers of food products, issued $2,000,000 of 7 percent preferred stock carrying a sinking-fund provision which retired 3 percent of the issue annually. By June 30, 1932, the amount outstanding had been reduced to $608,500, and, because of the small balance remaining, the issue was called for redemption at 110, *in the depth of the Depression.* Similarly, Century Ribbon Mills Preferred was reduced from $2,000,000 to $544,000 between 1922 and 1938; and Lawrence Portland Cement Company Debenture 5½s were reduced from $2,000,000 to $650,000 on

---

[2] See the older examples of Century Ribbon Mills and Electric Bond and Share Preferred stocks on pp. 550–551 in the 1951 edition. Despite a poor earnings showing for a number of years and frequent low market prices, these issues received regular dividends until retirement.

December 31, 1938, the balance being called for redemption on April 1, 1939.

Importance of Large Net-current-asset Coverage. Where a low-priced bond is covered several times over by net current assets, it presents a special type of opportunity, because experience shows that the chances of repayment are good, even though the earnings may be poor or irregular.

While the investor should attach considerable weight to the net-current-asset position in selecting speculative bonds, he must not assume that whenever a bond is fully covered by working capital its safety is thereby assured. The current assets may be greatly reduced by subsequent operating losses, and to some extent the stated values are likely to prove undependable in the event of insolvency. But when the working capital covers the price paid many times over, the chance of payment in full, with consequent profit, is better than that of default. Even in the latter case the ultimate realization may exceed the price paid.

Example: This point may be illustrated by two periods in the history of McKesson & Robbins 5½s, due 1950. In 1932 the bonds sold as low as 25. Their face amount was covered twice by working capital; i.e., net current assets were *eight times* the low price. The past-earnings record had been good. By 1935 their price had recovered to above par. In 1938 the issue was affected by the disclosure of extraordinary defalcations by the president. Trustees in bankruptcy were appointed, and the price fell to 50. In 1939 interest was deferred. However, the issue was amply protected by assets and earning power. In 1940 the price again recovered to above par. The bonds were paid off in full in the subsequent reorganization.

Speculative Preferred Stocks. *Stages in Their Price History.* Speculative preferred stocks are more subject than speculative bonds to irrational activity, so that from time to time such preferred shares are overvalued in the market in the same way as common stocks. We thus have three possible stages in the price history of a preferred issue, in each of which the market quotation tends to be out of line with the value:

1. The first stage is that of original issuance, when investors are persuaded to buy the offering at a full investment price not justified by its intrinsic merit.

2. In the second stage the lack of investment merit has become manifest, and the price drops to a speculative level. During this period the decline is likely to be overdone, for reasons previously discussed.

3. A third stage sometimes appears in which the issue advances speculatively in the same fashion as common stocks. On such occasions certain factors of questionable importance—such as the amount of dividend accumulations—are overemphasized.

An example of this third or irrational stage will be given a little later.

The Rule of "Maximum Valuation for Senior Issues." Both as a safe-guard against being led astray by the propaganda that is characteristic of the third stage and also as a general guide in dealing with speculative senior issues, the following principle of security analysis is presented, which we shall call "the rule of maximum valuation for senior issues."

A senior issue cannot be worth, intrinsically, any more than a common stock would be worth if it occupied the position of that senior issue, with no junior securities outstanding.

This statement may be understood more readily by means of an example.

Company X and Company Y have the same value. Company X has 80,000 shares of preferred and 200,000 shares of common. Company Y has only 80,000 shares of common and no preferred. Then our principle asserts that a share of Company X preferred cannot be worth more than a share of Company Y common. This is true because Company Y common represents the same value that lies behind *both* the preferred and common of Company X.

Instead of comparing two equivalent companies such as X and Y, we may assume that Company X is recapitalized so that the old common is eliminated and the preferred becomes the sole stock issue, i.e., the new common stock. (To coin a term, we may call such an assumed change the "commonizing" of a preferred stock.) Then our principle merely states the obvious fact that the value of such a hypothetical common stock cannot be *less* than the value of the preferred stock it replaces, because it is equivalent to the preferred *plus* the old common. The same idea may be applied to a speculative bond, followed either by common stock only or by both preferred and common. If the bond is "commonized," i.e., if it is, presumably, turned into a common stock with the old stock issues eliminated, then the value of the new common stock thus created cannot be less than the present value of the bond.

This relationship must hold true regardless of how high the coupon or dividend rate, the par value or the redemption price of the senior issue may be and, particularly, regardless of what amount of unpaid interest or dividends may have accumulated. For if we had a pre-ferred stock with accumulations of $1,000 per share, the value of the issue could be no greater than if it were a common stock (without div-idend accumulations) representing complete ownership of the business. The unpaid dividends cannot create any additional value for the com-pany's securities in the aggregate; they merely affect the division of the total value between the preferred and the common.

Excessive Emphasis Placed on the Amount of Accrued Dividends. Al-though a very small amount of analysis will show the above statements to be almost self-evident truths, the public has often failed to observe the simplest rules of logic when once it is in a gambling mood. Hence pre-ferred shares with large dividend accruals have lent themselves readily to market enthusiasm (and even manipulation) in which the accumulations are made the basis for a large advance in the price of both the preferred and common. An excellent example of such a performance was provided by Crystal Oil Refining Preferred and common in 1952. The summary that follows may give the reader some insight into the extraordinary discrepancies that often exist between the behavior of speculative issues in the stock market and the financial facts behind the securities.

Crystal Oil Refining no longer owned a refinery but had some modest oil royalty and land interests. Outstanding were 25,000 shares of $6 cumulative preferred (with the deceptive par value of $10), on which a total of only $9½ per share had been received since their issuance in 1926. At the beginning of 1952 accumulations thus had reached $153 per share. In that year its receipts from all sources were less than $300,000, and its net income was $150,000, or just $6 per share.

Speculative activity advanced the price of the preferred on the American Stock Exchange from a low of 26 in 1948 to a high of 200 in 1952, with no visible change in the company's affairs. The 103,000 shares of common stock had a concurrent advance from 1⅜ to 29⅜. At the high prices the market valued the preferred at $5 million and the common at $3 million, for an old and unsuccessful company with maximum earnings of $150,000 and net assets of some $500,000. No doubt the speculators in the shares were told (1) that the company's oil lands would prove very valuable; (2) that there would be a plan for paying off the preferred arrears; and (3) that with the back dividends "out of the way" the common could have a large further advance.

Sequel: No significant change took place in the company's earnings. However, in 1955 it did put through a plan to dispose of the accumulated preferred dividends by exchanging each share for 4 shares of new $1.125 preferred (again with the misleading par of $2.50) plus a bonus of 10 shares of common. The old common was left unchanged. The company also entered a new asset on its books reading "mineral rights . . . $1,600,000," wrote up its land value as well, and thus created a "capital surplus" of $1,767,000. In 1960 the new preferred sold as low as 15 and the common at 4½, representing a loss of about one-half of the previous high quotation of the preferred and five-sixths that of the common.[3]

Variation in Capital Structure Affects Total Market Value of Securities. From the foregoing discussion it might be inferred that the value of a single capital-stock issue must always be equivalent to the combined values of any preferred- and common-stock issues into which it might be split. In a theoretical sense this is entirely true, but in practice it may not be true at all, because a division of capitalization into senior securities

[3] On pp. 553–555 of the 1951 edition we discuss in detail a closely parallel situation that developed in American Zinc Preferred and common shares in 1928.

and common stock may have a real advantage over a single common-stock issue.

The distinction between the idea just suggested and our "rule of maximum valuation" may be clarified as follows:

1. Assume Company X = Company Y.
2. Company X has preferred (P) and common (C); Company Y has common only (C').
3. Then it *would appear* that

$$\text{Value of } P + \text{value of } C = \text{value of } C'$$

since each side of the equation represents equal things, viz., the total value of each company.

But this apparent relationship may not hold good in practice because the preferred-and-common capitalization method may have real advantages over a single common-stock issue.

On the other hand, our "rule of maximum valuation" merely states that the value of P *alone* cannot exceed the value of C'. This should hold true in practice as well as in theory, except insofar as manipulative or heedlessly speculative activity brushes aside all rational considerations.

Our rule is stated in negative form and is therefore essentially negative in its application. It is most useful in detecting instances where preferred stocks or bonds are *not worth* their market price. To apply the rule positively, it would be necessary, first, to arrive at a value for the preferred on a "commonized" basis (i.e., representing complete ownership of the business) and then to determine what deduction from this value should be made to reflect the part of the ownership fairly ascribable to the existing common stock. At times this approach will be found useful in establishing the fact that a given senior issue is worth more than its market price.

CHAPTER FORTY-EIGHT

LEVERAGE

Our Chapter 40, "Capitalization Structure," discussed in somewhat general terms the effect of variations in the proportion of senior securities in the total capitalization. We summarized the academic controversy over the subject, and set forth our own views as to the advantages to be gained from an "optimal" capital structure, which for many companies would include a moderate debt component. We reserved for this later chapter an exposition of the consequences of what we termed a speculative structure—i.e., one which had a larger proportion of senior securities than the maximum allowable by conservative standards.

The effects of such a capitalization set-up on per-share earnings and market price are familiarly referred to under the term "leverage." (In England the word used is "gearing.") In a strict sense leverage applies to any appreciable percentage of senior issues; hence the advantages we have asserted for an optimal structure against an all-common structure are products of the leverage factor. However, the popularly conceived and interesting aspects of leverage appear in the more extreme cases of speculative capital structure, and we propose to discuss the term here as if it were limited to such situations.

In a 1961 article Professor Pearson Hunt pointed out that leverage effects are of two different sorts.[1] One he calls "balance-sheet leverage" —related to the old term "trading on the equity." This has to do with the effects on common-stock earnings of structures which include *various proportions* of senior securities as against a structure built only of common stock. It would be measured on the assumption of a given or fixed amount of earnings for the total common, with a series of assumed changes in the common-equity proportion. The second effect comes from what Hunt calls "income-statement leverage." In this aspect the capital structure (or debt percentage) is kept constant, and the measurement is made of the effect on the common stock of various assumed changes in

---

[1] In "A Proposal for Precise Definitions of 'Trading on the Equity' and 'Leverage,'" *Journal of Finance*, September 1961. Professor Hunt supplies equations for measuring each type of leverage.

earnings on total capital, as against the consequences of similar changes applied to an all-common structure. The reader should keep Hunt's distinction in mind in the following discussion.

The general effects of leverage can be quickly summarized. The presence of a substantial proportion of senior capital, carrying a limited charge for interest or preferred dividends, permits the relatively small common issue to benefit from the earnings of a much larger capital fund. Under normal or average conditions, the fund will earn more than the cost of the senior capital; hence, the return on the common will be considerably above the rate on the entire capital. (This will appear from our subsequent examples.) Furthermore, an increase in the rate earned on total capital will produce a magnified increase in the earnings for the common. The same is true with respect to asset values—a point which is of major importance in dealing with investment-fund common stocks. Those that are leveraged will show a more rapid increase in their asset value than in the total portfolio value—which means that it is more rapid than the increase in the general market level.

Leverage a Two-way Street. The principle of leverage works both ways, however. If earnings or asset value *decrease*, the effect on the common stock is proportionately more severe. Under unfavorable conditions the earning power of the common can disappear entirely, even though there are some profits for the capital fund as a whole. Similarly, the common stocks of highly leveraged investment funds can lose all their asset value—thus going "under water"—when the general market level is low. Practically all the common stocks of leveraged funds were under water for long periods after 1929. Even under the vastly improved market levels of 1950, some issues remained in this state.

Examples: Selected Industries common and North American Investment common were both in this category at the end of 1950.

Leverage a Favorable Speculative Factor. It is clear that leverage is an inherently speculative factor and one that intensifies the possibilities of both gain and loss. Abstractly considered, leverage would seem to be more favorable than unfavorable, on balance, to common stocks—first, because in the average case it tends to increase the percentage earned on the common; and second, because the amount of possible profit from future changes is likely to exceed the amount of loss. But large leverage is always a bad thing for the senior securities, since it means that the common holders are exploiting the senior capital without offering an adequate "cushion" or margin of safety.

Because of these facts the effect of leverage on market quotations tends to be eccentric and unpredictable. At times the senior issues sell at investment levels, although the absence of adequate protection would warrant a lower price. At other times the common stock fails to reflect the opportunities present in the leverage factor. These anomalies are typical products of the injection of speculative factors into a financial picture. The market's appraisal of such factors is likely to be governed by psychological and often irrational considerations.

A speculative structure usually produces a number of interesting and often spectacular phenomena over the years, affecting the position of the company itself and causing gyrations in the price of the common stock. As we stated above, in Chapter 40, "Capitalization Structure," it is difficult to predict under what circumstances a speculative structure will result in a premium value for the company as a whole and when it will produce a discount value. We do know, however, that the common stock will advance sharply under favorable conditions and decline under adverse conditions.

To show concretely the effects of leverage under relatively recent market conditions we shall first present two pairs of contrasting examples which were described as then current in our 1951 edition. The advantage of reusing these illustrations lies in the opportunity they give of following them through time. This should add to the reader's appreciation of the factor of change which underlies most corporate life-histories. We repeat these examples from our 1951 text (pages 471–474) and add brief sequels.

Example 1: Keyes Fibre and Hinde & Dauch [Table 48-1]. Our first pair of examples brings out what we may call the classic relationship between capital structure, earnings on common-stock equity, and market value of the enterprise. Hinde & Dauch earned substantially more on its capital funds in 1946–1949 than Keyes and slightly more in 1949 alone, but it sold in the market at 25 percent under book value, while the total enterprise value of Keyes is 20 percent more than book value. On the other hand, Keyes represents the extreme case of using senior capital to the extent of more than 100 percent of book value, when full provision is made for the effective liability—here taken as the same as call price—of the two preferred-stock issues. In other words, there was no *book equity* for Keyes common at the end of 1949, but it had an equity in more than half the total *earnings* after taxes.

The respective multipliers for the two common stocks—about 5 for Hinde & Dauch and 4.4 for Keyes—show very little recognition of the great difference in capital structures. This may be explained, of course, by a more favorable stock-market appraisal of the prospects of Keyes Fibre. But it is clear that the presence of senior securities in Keyes is largely responsible for the fact that the *enterprise as a whole* was valued in the market at about ten times its average 1946–1949 earnings, while in the case of Hinde & Dauch the multiplier was as low as 5.

Sequel: The most influential factor affecting Keyes Fibre after 1949 appears to have been the conversion privilege of its two senior stock issues. The 5.6 percent preferred was convertible into $1\frac{1}{2}$ shares of common for 1 preferred; the $3 class A was convertible into common at the rate of $1\frac{1}{2}$ common for 1 class A. Because of the disparities in market prices at the end of 1949 we did not deem it necessary to mention these conversion rights, since they could become operative only under conditions establishing a large profit for the common stock. As it happened, the large profit actually developed, after which the virtually complete conversion of the two senior issues operated to change the company from high to quite moderate leverage. The conversions more than doubled the

Table 48-1. Comparison of Two Pulp-products Companies

	Keyes Fibre	Hinde & Dauch Paper
Capital funds at book value, Dec. 31, 1949:		
3 percent bonds at 100..........	$2,440,000	
5.6 percent preferred stock at call price (110 percent of $25 par)..	2,750,000 = 5% rate	
$3 class A at call (55)...........	3,300,000 = 5.4% rate	
Common at book value........	*704,000(d)*	$20,670,000
Total capital fund...........	$7,786,000	$20,670,000
Capital fund at market value, Dec. 31, 1949:		
Bonds at 100.................	$2,440,000	
Preferred stock at 103..........	2,575,000	
Class A at 34.................	2,040,000	
Common.....................	(149,000 shares @ 15)	(935,000 shares @ 16)
	2,240,000	$14,960,000
Total capital fund...........	$9,295,000	$14,960,000
Average available earnings after taxes, 1946–1949..............	$ 902,000	$ 3,010,000
Bond interest (1950 basis)........	79,000	
Preferred dividends..............	140,000	
Class A dividends...............	180,000	
Balance for common.............	503,000	3,010,000
Ratios, 1946–1949:		
Percent earned on capital fund at book value.................	11.6%	14.8%
Percent earned on capital fund at market value...............	9.7	19.9
Percent earned on common stock at market value.............	22.5	19.9
Percent market value of capital fund to book value..........	120.0	74.0
1949 alone:		
Available earnings after taxes....	$ 883,000	$ 2,388,000
Percent earned on capital fund...	11.5%	11.6%

common issue (on its 1949 basis) and thus reduced its participation in later favorable developments. The over-all consequence was that the common had an excellent advance—from 15 in December 1949 to the equivalent of 52 at the end of 1959—but, secondly, this advance actually proved less than that for industrial commons generally. (In the same period the Standard & Poor's Index of 425 Industrials rose from 16.4 to 64.5.)

The Hinde & Dauch common issue had a different history. The company was acquired by West Virginia Pulp and Paper Company in 1953, on an exchange of 1⅓ shares for each share of Hinde & Dauch. West Virginia had a reasonable amount of senior securities. At the end of

Table 48-2. Comparison of Two Natural-gas Companies

(Dollar figures in thousands)

	Consolidated Natural Gas, December 1949	Transcontinental Gas Pipeline, December 1949
Capital fund:		
Bonds at par.................	$ 30,400	$143,000
Notes (to be exchanged for pre-ferred) at par...............	....	26,500
Common stock at book value....	190,000	31,400
Total at book value.........	$220,400	$200,900
Common stock at market, December 1949....................	$142,400	$ 67,100
	(3,274,000 sh. @ 43½)	(3,530,000 sh. @ 19)
Capital fund at market value......	172,800	236,600

	Actual 1949	Projection
Income account:		
Gross.......................	$106,800	$34,300
Balance for capital fund........	12,582	11,490
Interest and preferred dividends.	837	6,780
Balance for common stock.......	11,745	4,710
Earned on capital fund at book value....................	5.7%	6.0%*
Earned on capital fund at market value....................	7.3	4.9
Earned on common stock at book value....................	6.2	15.0
Earned on common stock at market value.................	8.2	7.0

* The prospectus dated Dec. 2, 1948, estimated first year's sales at $34.3 million and stated that the company expects "it will be able to earn a satisfactory return on its estimated rate base of $191.5 million within the 6% rate of return heretofore allowed by the [Federal Power] Commission."

1959 the exchanged Hinde & Dauch shares were worth about 75, showing a better-than-average advance, which must be ascribed to their metamorphosis.

Example 2: Consolidated Natural Gas and Transcontinental Gas Pipeline [Table 48-2]. The two companies are in the same general field. Consolidated Natural Gas (organized by Standard Oil Company of New Jersey, to take over its natural-gas interests) produces, purchases, and transports gas and sells it directly to nearly a million customers. Transcontinental Gas Pipeline was formed in 1946 to construct and operate large transmission lines for gas. It proposes to buy gas under contract from producers and to sell it at the other end of its lines to public utilities in the New York City area.

The difference in capital structure of the two companies is extraordinary. Consolidated has 14 percent of its total capital in bonds and 86 percent in common stock; Transcontinental has 85 percent in senior securities and only 15 percent in common stock. (In 1950 the common-stock proportion was further reduced to about 12½ percent by the issuance of additional $42 million of bonds and bank loans.)

The leveraged capital structure of Transcontinental Gas Pipeline produces estimated earnings of 15 percent on the book value of the common as against only 6 percent on its total capital fund. This expected rate of earnings in turn undoubtedly was responsible for a market price of the stock of more than twice its book value. Contrariwise, the extremely conservative capital structure of Consolidated held down the earnings on the common-stock equity to only 6.2 percent in 1949 and to similar amounts in previous years. Evidently this earnings rate was not considered attractive, since the stock sold considerably below book value in the years 1947–1950.

The student should be impressed by these illustrations that capital-structure variations in the same industry can be carried to extremes in either direction. The structure of Consolidated Natural Gas appears too conservative to give the stockholders a chance to earn an adequate return on their investment. That of Transcontinental appears so speculative—especially for a new venture with its line not even built—that the purchase of its senior securities with their limited return could scarcely appear prudent.

Sequel: In the next 12 years Consolidated Natural Gas raised its bond component from 14 to 42 percent of total capitalization. Its earnings per share increased about 60 percent, and the price of the stock advanced about 180 percent, to very moderately above its book value. This appears a good performance, but it did not quite keep pace with the 225 percent rise in the price of Standard & Poor's 50 Utility Stock Index.

Transcontinental Gas Pipeline expanded its business greatly, with a slight reduction in its leverage, senior issues falling from 84 percent to about 80 percent of total capital. Its earnings per share advanced from the $1.35 projected in 1949 to an actual (adjusted) $3.60 per share in 1961. The price rose just about as much as the public utility index.

General Comment: These "case histories" may be called typical of corporate experience since 1949. The expansion of the economy, accompanied by only minor setbacks, gave scope to the advantageous aspects of a speculative capital structure, and did not put its possible disadvantages to the test.

Another Set of Examples. We shall turn now to another group of illustrations of the effects of leverage. The three companies chosen cover a wide expanse of time, and the first will be carried through a period of both great improvement and great decline in business and financial conditions—viz., 1921 to 1941. The second, placed in 1945–1949, will be governed by its particular exhibit rather than by fluctuations in the general economy. Our third will reflect the vicissitudes of the railroad industry in quite recent years.

Example 1: American Water Works and Electric Company. The record of American Water Works and Electric Company common stock between 1921 and 1929 presents an almost fabulous picture of enhancement in value, a great part of which was due to the influence of a highly speculative capitalization structure multiplied by that of an unexampled stock-market boom. The exhibits for 1921 and 1929 are summarized in Table 48-3.

Table 48-3. Four Annual Exhibits of American Water Works and Electric Company

Item	1921	1929	1938	1941
Total operating revenues*.......	$20,574	$ 54,119	$ 50,004	$ 62,866
Net for charges*..............	6,692	22,776	17,593	18,689
Fixed charges and preferred dividends*.....................	6,353	16,514	15,498	16,081
Balance for common*..........	339	6,692	2,095	2,608
1921 basis:				
Number of shares of common†.	92,000	130,000	185,000	185,000
Earned per share............	$3.68	$51.00	$4.80	$14.00
High or low price of common..	6½ high	2,500 high	128 low	32 low
Earnings multiplier at price shown....................	1.8×	48.5×	26.0×	2.3×
As reported:				
Number of shares of common..	92,000	1,657,000	2,343,000	2,343,000
Earned per share............	$3.68	$4.00	$0.38	$1.11
High or low price of common..	6½ high	199 high	10 low	2½ low

* 000 omitted.
† Number of shares adjusted to eliminate effect of stock dividends.

The purchaser of one share of American Water Works common stock at the high price of 6½ in 1921, if he retained the distributions made in stock, would have owned about 12½ shares when the common sold at its high price of 199 in 1929. His $6.50 would have grown to about $2,500. While the market value of the common shares was thus increasing some 400-fold, the operating revenues had expanded to only 2.6 times the earlier figure. The tremendously disproportionate rise in the common-stock value was due to the following elements, in order of importance:

1. A much higher valuation placed upon the per-share earnings of this issue. In 1921 the company's capitalization was recognized as top-heavy; its bonds sold at a low price, and the earnings per share of common were not taken

seriously, especially since no dividends were being paid on the second preferred. In 1929 the general enthusiasm for public utility shares resulted in a price for the common issue of nearly 50 times its highest recorded earnings.

2. The speculative capitalization structure allowed the common stock to gain an enormous advantage from the expansion of the company's properties and earnings. Nearly all the additional funds needed were raised by the sale of senior securities. It will be observed that whereas the gross revenues increased about 160 percent from 1921 to 1929, the balance per share of old common stock grew to fourteenfold during the same period.

3. The margin of profit improved during these years, as was shown by the higher ratio of net to gross. The speculative capital structure greatly accentuated the benefit to the common stock from the additional net profits so derived.

The picture of a drastic rise based on pyramiding and market madness is succeeded by another of equally spectacular collapse, portrayed in the same table. The reader will note that the same stock that soared from 6½ to some 2,500 in eight years then fell in the next twelve to the equivalent of 32. Correspondingly, the multiplier that rose from 2 to nearly 50 now fell back to an abysmal 2.3 times. The latter development was the direct outcome of dissolution proceedings initiated for public utility–holding-company systems. The concept of unlimited value for these financial concoctions that held sway in 1929 was followed by unrelieved pessimism as to their future. This is an extraordinary story; it should convey to the reader some inkling of the great ups and downs in corporate affairs that have occurred during the lifetime of many of us.

Example 2: Another extreme example of the working of leverage—this time in only four years on the upside—was presented by the stock of San Francisco Bay Toll Bridge between 1945 and 1949. There were only 8,584 shares outstanding, junior to $4,303,000 in 3 percent income bonds. The results for 1945 and 1949 are shown in Table 48-4.

Table 48-4. San Francisco Bay Toll Bridge

	1945	1949
Revenue..................	$321,000	$780,000
Available for interest.......	51,000	252,000
Balance for stock..........	69,000(d)	159,000
Per share.................	$8.06(d)	$18.52
Price of stock.............	1½–2 (in 1946)	150 bid

Here we see the same interrelationships that were evident in the exhibits of American Water Works. Revenue rose 150 percent; net increased 400 percent; the balance for common changed from a large deficit per share to more than a doubly large rate of earnings per share. The price rose 75-fold.

Example 3: Our last example brings us up to date. It is provided by Missouri Pacific Railroad class B common stock. In the reorganization consummated in 1956 the holders of old common received one share of this new issue in exchange for each 20 shares formerly owned. Only 40,658 shares were thus created; they had no par, but were carried in the balance sheet at $100 per share, or $4,065,000 for the entire issue. They were preceded by debt and class A shares having an aggregate par amount of no less than $835 million. Thus the common-stock "equity" represented about one two-hundredth of the total capitalization. This tiny issue was given the right to all the surplus earnings above the fixed rates for the senior issues. The 1.8 million shares of class A stock were actually made a noncumulative preferred, limited to $5 per annum. If this amount were earned and not paid—as the directors had the right to decide—such a decision would in a single year transfer the equivalent of $225 per share of class B to that issue from the class A holders. Substantial annual earnings were required to be set aside for sinking and capital funds, but all of these sums at least added to the book equity and possible value of the class B common.

It is not surprising that the staid Moody's *Transportation Manual* (1961 edition, page 444) makes the breathless statement: "The leverage position of the class B stock is fantastic."

Table 48-5. Earnings and Price Fluctuations of Missouri Pacific Railroad, Class B Common, 1955–1961

Year	Operating revenues*	Available for charges*	Net income*	Earned per share of class B	Price of class B
1955	$260,700	$41,914	$14,595	$123.20	145 low†
1956	264,600	45,785	19,593	231.80	700 high
1957	260,300	44,039	18,446	223.50	170 low
1958	253,400	41,712	15,758	157.40	160 low
1959	262,200	41,180	15,559	152.50	550 high
1960	256,300	37,976	11,837	61.00	265 low
1961	248,100	35,920	9,883	13.00	500 high

* 000 omitted.
† Equivalent of low price of old stock (7¼) in 1954.

The earnings of Missouri Pacific available for fixed charges between 1955 and 1961 have been unusually stable for a railroad, as appears from our Table 48-5. But the leveraged capitalization has caused the earnings accruing to the class B stock to fluctuate from a high of $232 per share in 1956 to a mere $13 in 1961. The price of the shares (largely held by one owner) advanced from the equivalent of 142 in 1954—based on the price of the old stock—to a high of 700 in 1956, followed by a fall to 170 in the very next year. These price variations show no close connection with the operating results; the relationships between price and earnings in 1957 and 1961 seem quite bizarre. But this apparent absurdity follows from the doubly speculative quality of highly leveraged situations; they can respond violently to changes in the current earnings picture, or to more or less arbitrary variations in market psychology, or to the naked supply-and-demand situation.

Recent Tendencies toward Leveraged Capitalizations. In our Chapter 40, on capitalization structure, we stated that industrial companies as a whole have conservative debt components, and that some all-common companies might be well advised to contract a moderate amount of debt for the purpose of bringing up the earnings on the common equity to a satisfactory figure. But this general statement has always been subject to exceptions, and it would appear that the proportion of companies with nonconservative structures has tended to increase with the rise in the stock market.

In our previous edition we criticized the low common-stock proportions in the capitalization of various natural-gas pipeline companies then being financed. (Transcontinental Gas Pipeline Company discussed above is representative of the group.) In our view the purchasers of bond and straight-preferred issues were the reverse of shrewd in putting up nearly all the capital for a limited return, and in permitting a small common equity to garner all the surplus profits and appreciation in capital value. This financing scheme appeared to us to run counter both to ordinary prudence and to the pattern which the SEC had imposed on other regulated utilities when it had jurisdiction over their capital structures.[2]

Since all these enterprises have been successful, or were protected by adequate guarantees,[3] the bondholders have not suffered any damage or worry, and they doubtless feel that their judgment has been well vindicated. A cautionary remark may be in order, however. The soundness of straight bond investment can be demonstrated only by its performance under unfavorable business conditions; if the bondholders needed prosperity to keep them whole they would have been smarter to have bought the company's stock and made the profits that flow from prosperity.

A number of smaller enterprises, recently offered to the public, have larger than conservative bond components. There is also a tendency for more substantial enterprises to move in that direction, as is indicated by three quite varied examples given below.

---

[2] See Chapter 51 for comments on the *limited* control exercised by the SEC in this field.

[3] Trans-Canada Pipeline, Ltd., failed to earn interest charges between 1956 and 1960, but the deficits were made up by the purchase of junior bonds by controlling (gas-producing) stockholders.

Example 1: Ling-Temco Electronics. At the end of 1960 this company showed a tangible common equity of about $21 million, preceded by $20.3 million of long-term debt and preferred, *plus* $29.3 million of current notes payable to banks. (Since August 1961 Ling-Temco-Vought, Inc.)

Example 2: Apco Oil Corporation. This company was formed in 1961 to take over the gathering, refining, and marketing business of Anderson-Prichard Oil. (The producing properties were sold to other interests; see the reference above, page 569*n*.) Apco financed the purchase as follows: bank loans $10.5 million; long-term debt $10.1 million; and common-stock equity $5.8 million. Senior financing to this degree was formerly a rarity in the oil industry.[4]

Example 3: Punta-Alegre Sugar. This company seems to have carried the concept of profitable debt creation to an interesting extreme. As a case history, it illustrates among other things the interaction of tax considerations and corporate moves. When its Cuban sugar properties were expropriated in 1960 (with no good prospects of compensation), the company was left with $3.7 million of United States net assets, or $4.70 per share. The market price fell to 4¼. Nothing daunted, the management proceeded to buy a grain elevator in Kansas for $40,250,000. The financing terms were unusual. The company paid $3,250,000 in cash, all of which was borrowed from a bank. The remaining $37 million was to carry no interest, and to be repayable over an expected 15-year period out of the annual depreciation (running at about $3 million annually) plus part of the profits after depreciation. Income taxes on the profits would presumably be offset during the next five years by a carry-forward loss of some $13 million resulting from the seizure of the Cuban properties. Net profit before tax from the elevator was running at about $1.60 per share of Punta-Alegre.

The company's 1961 balance sheet showed as an asset only its down payment on the grain elevator subsidiary, as adjusted; the listing of the approximately $37 million still owing ahead of the $4.0 million stock equity might have made some stockholders nervous. At least one thing could have been said for this unorthodox deal; the terms of financing were easy.[5]

Speculative Attractiveness of Leveraged Common Stocks Considered.
Our discussion of fixed-income investment has emphasized as strongly as possible the disadvantage (amounting to unfairness) that attaches to the senior security holder's position where the junior capital is propor-

---

[4] The student might be interested in looking into some curious tax consequences of the Anderson-Prichard split-up. When the refining business was part of the integrated system, the old company paid no tax on its substantial profits; in the separate operation Apco paid a tax of $2.8 million on its 1961 profits of $5.5 million.

[5] In many respects this deal followed the pattern set by the purchase of Union Underwear by Philadelphia & Reading Coal & Iron in 1955. This was the first major step in that company's climb back from large losses to great prosperity.

tionately slight. Questions would logically arise as to whether there are not corresponding *advantages* to the common stock in such an arrangement, from which it gains a very high degree of speculative attractiveness. This inquiry would obviously take us entirely outside the field of common-stock *investment* and would represent an expedition into the realm of intelligent or scientific speculation.

We have already seen from our American Water Works example that in bad times a speculative capitalization structure may react adversely on the market price of both the senior securities and the common stock.[6] During such a period, then, the common stockholders do not derive a present benefit at the expense of the bondholder. This fact clearly detracts from the speculative advantage inherent in such common stocks. It is easy to suggest that these issues be purchased only when they are selling at abnormally low levels because of temporarily unfavorable conditions. But this is really begging the question, because it assumes that the intelligent speculator can consistently detect and wait for these abnormal and temporary conditions. If this were so, he could make a great deal of money regardless of what type of common stock he buys, and under such conditions he might be better advised to select high-grade common stocks at bargain prices rather than these more speculative issues.

Practical Aspects of the Foregoing. To view the matter in a practical light, the purchase of speculatively capitalized common stocks must be considered under general or market conditions that are supposedly normal, i.e., under those which are not obviously inflated or deflated. Assuming (1) diversification and (2) reasonably good judgment in selecting companies with satisfactory prospects, it would seem that the speculator should be able to profit rather substantially in the long run from commitments of this kind. In making such purchases, he should evidently show partiality to those companies in which most of the senior capital is in the form of preferred stock rather than bonds. Such an arrangement removes or minimizes the danger of extinction of the junior equity through default in bad times and thus permits the common stockholder to maintain his position on a shoestring until prosperity returns. (But just because the preferred-stock contract benefits the common shareholder in this way, it is clearly disadvantageous to the preferred stockholder himself.)

We must not forget, however, the peculiar practical difficulty in the way of realizing the full amount of prospective gain in any one of the purchases. As we pointed out in the analogous case of convertible bonds, as soon as a substantial profit appears, the holder is in a dilemma, because he can hold for a further gain only by risking that already accrued. Just as a convertible bond loses its distinctive advantages when the price

---

[6] In the 1951 edition we demonstrated this at length in our comparison between A. E. Staley and American Maize Products during 1924–1933 (pp. 558–560).

rises to a point that carries it clearly outside of the straight investment class, so a shoestring common-stock commitment is transformed into a more and more substantial commitment as the price continues to rise. In the American Water Works example the price had become too high by established investment standards as early as 1924; hence nearly all the subsequent twelvefold further rise represented the most dangerous sort of speculative heedlessness; in fact it epitomizes the wanton stock market of the late 1920's.

CHAPTER FORTY-NINE

LOW-PRICED COMMON STOCKS. OPTION

WARRANTS

LOW-PRICED STOCKS

The characteristics discussed in the preceding chapter are generally associated in the mind of the public with *low-priced stocks*. The majority of issues of the speculatively capitalized type do sell within the low-priced range a good part of the time. The definition of "low-priced" must, of course, be somewhat arbitrary. Prices below $10 per share belong in this category beyond question; those above $20 are ordinarily excluded; the dividing line would therefore be set somewhere between $10 and $20.

Arithmetical Advantage of Low-priced Issues. Low-priced common stocks appear to possess an inherent arithmetical advantage arising from the fact they can advance so much more than they can decline. It is a commonplace of the securities market that an issue will rise more readily from 10 to 40 than from 100 to 400. This fact is due in part to the preferences of the speculative public, which generally is much more partial to issues in the 10-to-40 range than to those selling above 100. But it is also true that in many cases low-price common stocks give the owner the advantage of an interest in, or "call" upon, a relatively large enterprise at relatively small expense.

Some older statistical studies covered the price behavior of low-priced stocks between 1897 and 1935.[1] Their conclusions showed a better overall performance for diversified lists of low-priced shares as compared with high-priced shares. The former advanced more in bull markets and lost only part of their superior gains in the recessions that followed.

---

[1] Louis H. Fritzemeier, "Relative Price Fluctuations of Industrial Stocks in Different Price Groups," *Journal of Business of the University of Chicago*, April 1936, pp. 133–154. See pp. 473–474 of the 1934 edition of this work for reference to an earlier study devoted to the relative behavior of low-priced and high-priced issues when purchased at or near the bottoms of depressions in 1897, 1907, 1914, and 1921. Within its more limited scope this study, published in 1931 by J. H. Holmes and Company, led to conclusions similar to those of Fritzemeier.

Two indexes of low-priced shares have been available for different periods. That of Standard & Poor's runs from 1926 (though started some years later) and continues to the present. It seeks to maintain its low-priced character by eliminating issues that advance beyond a certain level and substituting for them new lower-priced issues. Barron's, also, made up a list of issues selling below $5 in 1938, but discontinued that index in May 1946 after it had advanced (sixfold) to a level where "low price" was a misnomer for the group. A second index of stocks selling under $5 was set up in 1947.

In Table 49-1 we compare the price movements of the two low-priced indexes with that of the Standard & Poor's 425 Industrials between

Table 49-1. Relative Price Movements of Low-priced Stocks
and 425 Industrials, 1926–1961

	Standard & Poor's 425 Industrials	Standard & Poor's low-priced index	Barron's low-priced index	
			No. 1	No. 2
1926 low..............	8.6	21.6		
1929 high............	25.4	47.9		
1932 low.............	3.5	3.0		
1936–1937 high........	18.1	21.7		
1938 low.............	8.4	7.2	107	
1938–1939 high........	13.7	15.4	—	
1942 low.............	7.5	7.1	—	
1946 high............	18.5	45.3	620	173
1947–1949 low........	13.2	14.7	abt. 300	63
1956 high............	53.3	42.4		
1957 low.............	42.0	32.1		
1959 high............	65.3	78.6		
1961 close...........	75.7	72.0		

various significant dates. These figures show a rather remarkable change in relative behavior after 1949. During 1938–1946 both low-priced indexes had spectacular advances, far exceeding that of the general market, but then lost all this comparative advantage in the 1946–1949 bear market. But from 1946 through 1961 the low-priced issues advanced and declined in about the same degree as other stocks. In fact, at the end of 1961 they had scored a somewhat smaller advance from their 1949 low and from their base figure of 10 in 1941–1943. These data would seem to indicate that the once characteristic comparative behavior of low-priced issues can no longer be counted upon.

Some Reasons Why Buyers of Low-priced Issues Lose Money. Even during the long period when low-priced shares appeared to enjoy an inherent advantage over others, the general public—which had always been partial to "cheap stocks"—did not do very well with them. Undoubtedly more money was lost than made in this department. Why was this so? The underlying reason is that the public buys issues that are *sold* to it, and the sales effort is put forward to benefit the seller and not the buyer. In consequence the bulk of the low-priced purchases made by the public are of the wrong kind; i.e., they do not provide the real advantages of this security type. The reason may be either because the companies are in bad financial condition or because the common stock is low-priced in appearance only and actually represents a full or excessive commitment in relation to the value of the enterprise. The latter is preponderantly true of new security offerings in the low-priced range. In such cases, a pseudo-low price is accomplished by the simple artifice of creating so large a number of shares that even at a few dollars per share the total value of the common issue is excessive. This has been true of mining-stock flotations from of old and has been evident in other offerings of miscellaneous sorts that have been made to the public in recent years.

The True Meaning of "Low Price." A low-priced stock of the genuine variety will show an aggregate value for the issue which is small in relation to the company's assets, sales, and past and prospective profits under favorable business conditions. It will ordinarily have sold repeatedly in former years at many times the current low price. None of these points is likely to hold for the "intentionally low-priced" issue, with its millions of shares outstanding—except that it may have shown a larger percentage advance in bull markets than that of common stocks generally.

We shall illustrate this contrast by reproducing one pair of examples which has appeared in the first three editions of our book. The two companies were Barker Brothers (retailer of furniture) and Wright Hargreaves Mines (a gold producer). These concerns were initially compared as of July 1933 in our first edition. We present here in Table 49-2 the figures as of December 1939 and 1949 used in the next two editions. The 1939 exhibit of the two companies shows clearly the difference between genuine low price and "pseudo"–low price. The sequel in 1949 demonstrated the advantage of the genuine over the pseudo-article in somewhat too pat a manner. Such results are by no means guaranteed to the analyst. (Subsequently Barker Brothers was acquired by new interests and became part of a rather involved financial picture. Wright Hargreaves sold below $1 per share at the close of 1961.)

In Table 49-3 we add another pair of examples taken at dates between 1956 and 1961. The Atlas Sewing Center shares at the end of 1961 represented a low-priced issue of the genuine variety. When this occurs at the height of a bull market the company's performance and financial position must necessarily be unsatisfactory, and the issue must be considered highly speculative. (The delay in publishing the May 1961 re-

Table 49-2. Low-priced Stocks Contrasted: First Pair

Basic data	Barker Brothers		Wright Hargreaves Mines	
	1939*	1949	1939	1949
Average price of common........	4¾	18	7.80	1.81
Number of shares.............	356,000	356,000	5,500,000	5,500,000
Total market value of common..	$ 1,690,000	$ 6,408,000	$42,900,000	$9,955,000
Sales........................	12,135,000	28,212,000	7,828,000	3,022,000
Net for common...............	141,000	863,000	4,044,000	833,000
Earned per share..............	$0.40	$2.42	$0.74	$0.15
Dividend paid................	0.12½	2.00	0.70	0.15
Book value of common.........	11.08	22.06	1.25	1.18
Sales per dollar of common at market......................	7.20	4.40	0.18	0.30

* 1939 figures are adjusted for a later 2-for-1 split.

Table 49-3. Low-priced Stocks Contrasted: Second Pair

Basic data	Atlas Sewing Centers, 1961	Sapphire Petroleums, 1956
Price of common*.....................	1⅞	3.90
Number of shares.....................	798,000	9,143,000‡
Market value of common...............	$ 1,500,000	$ 35,700,000
	(May 1960 year)†	
Sales............................	18,700,000	709,000
Net income........................	91,000	*463,000*(d)
Earned per share....................	$ 0.11	§
Book value per share.................	5.81	$1.22‡
Sales per dollar of market value.........	12.46	0.02
1959 earnings per share...............	1.25	§
1959 high price......................	16	1.70

* Closing and low price for Atlas; high price for Sapphire.
† Latest available.
‡ Adjusted for conversion of bonds convertible at 2½.
§ Deficit.

port was a bad sign.) But its possibilities under favorable conditions are demonstrated by the reported earnings and the market price as recently as 1959.[2]

The Sapphire Petroleum shares, on the other hand, at their price of $3.90 in 1956 showed the amazing picture of a common-stock issue selling for over $35 million, while its gross receipts were only $700,000, and

[2] Not surprisingly the company went into bankruptcy in 1962; after the above was written. This is a useful example of the risks often implicit in a low-priced situation.

it had been reporting deficits for many years. In 1961 this enterprise underwent some metamorphoses rather characteristic of the times. It branched out into bowling centers, in addition to oil, gas, and uranium; it changed its name to Cabol Enterprises, Ltd., and it made a reverse (1-for-10) split of its stock, issuing 1,410,000 new shares for the 14,100,000 old. The price of 2⅜ for the new issue at the end of 1961 compares with a former high equivalent of over 50 for the same shares.

Observation of the stock market will show that the stocks of companies facing receivership are likely to be more active than those which are very low in price merely because of poor current earnings. This phenomenon is caused by the desire of insiders to dispose of their holdings before the receivership wipes them out, thus accounting for a large supply of these shares at a low level and also sometimes for unscrupulous efforts to persuade the unwary public to buy them. But where a low-priced stock fulfills our conditions of speculative attractiveness, there is apt to be no pressure to sell and no effort to create buying. Hence the issue is inactive and attracts little public attention. This analysis may explain why the public almost always buys the wrong low-priced issues and ignores the really promising opportunities in this field.

Speculative Capitalization. Speculatively capitalized enterprises, according to our definition, are marked by a relatively large amount of senior securities and a comparatively small issue of common stock. Although usually the common stock will sell at a low price per share, it need not necessarily do so if the number of shares is small. In the case of Missouri Pacific, for example (referred to on page 644), even at $700 per share for the class B common in 1955 the capitalization structure was still speculative, since the bonds and preferred at par represented over 90 percent of the total. It is also true that even where there are no senior securities the common stock may have possibilities equivalent to those in a speculatively capitalized enterprise. These possibilities will occur wherever the market value of the common issue represents a small amount of money in relation to the size of the business, regardless of how it is capitalized.

To illustrate this point we fall back on an old example and append in Table 49-4 a condensed analysis of Mandel Brothers, Inc., and Gimbel Brothers, Inc., two department-store enterprises, as of September 1939.

Gimbel Brothers presented a typical picture of a speculatively capitalized enterprise. On the other hand, Mandel Brothers had no senior securities ahead of the common, but despite this fact the relatively small market value of the entire issue imparted to the shares the same sort of speculative possibilities (though in somewhat lesser degree) as were found in the Gimbel Brothers setup. Note, however, that the rental payments of Mandel Brothers were proportionately much higher than those of Gimbel Brothers and that these rental charges were equivalent in good part to senior securities.

Large Volume and High Production Cost Equivalent to Speculative Capital Structure. This example should lead us to widen our conception of a speculatively situated common stock. The speculative or *marginal* position may arise from any cause that reduces the percentage of gross available for the common to a subnormal figure and that therefore serves to create a subnormal value for the common stock in relation to the volume of business. Unusually high operating or production costs have

Table 49-4. Two Department Stores Compared

Item	Gimbel Brothers	Mandel Brothers
September 1939:		
Bonds at par....................	$ 26,753,000	
Preferred stock.................	197,000 sh. @ 50	
	$ 9,850,000	
Common stock...................	977,000 sh. @ 8	297,000 sh. @ 5
	$ 7,816,000	$ 1,485,000
Total capitalization............	$ 44,419,000	$ 1,485,000
Results for 12 months to July 31, 1939:		
Sales.........................	$ 87,963,000	$17,883,000
Net before interest............	*1,073,000*	155,000
Balance for common.............	*1,105,000(d)*	155,000
Earned per share...............	*$1.13(d)*	$0.52
Period 1934–1938:*		
Maximum sales (1937)...........	$100,081,000	$19,378,000
Maximum net earnings (1937) for common	2,032,000	414,000
Maximum earnings per share of common, (1937).........................	$2.08	$1.33
High price of common...........	29¾ (1937)	18 (1936)
Average earnings per share of common....	$0.23	$0.46
Jan. 31, 1939:		
Net current assets..............	$ 22,916,000	$4,043,000
Net tangible assets.............	75,614,000	6,001,000
Rentals paid 1937..............	1,401,000	867,000

* Based on report for succeeding Jan. 31.

the identical effect as excessive senior charges in cutting down the percentage of gross available for common. The hypothetical examples of three copper producers, shown in Table 49-5, will make this point more intelligible and also lead to some conclusions on the subject of large output vs. low operating costs.

It is scarcely necessary to point out that the higher production cost of Company *C* will have exactly the same effect as the bond-interest requirement of Company *B* (assuming output and production costs to continue as stated).

General Principle Derived. The foregoing table is perhaps more useful in showing concretely the inverse relationship that usually exists between profit per unit and output per dollar of stock value.

The general principle may be stated that the lower the unit cost, the lower the production per dollar of market value of stock and vice versa. Since Company A has a 21-cent cost, its stock naturally sells at a higher price *per pound of output* than Company C's stock with its 28-cent cost. Conversely Company C produces more pounds per dollar of stock value than Company A. This fact is not without significance from the standpoint of speculative technique. When a rise in the price of the commodity

Table 49-5

Item	Company A	Company B	Company C
Capitalization:			
6 percent bonds.............	....	$75,000,000	
Common stock.............	3,000,000 sh.	3,000,000 sh.	3,000,000 sh.
Output.....................	100,000,000 lb	150,000,000 lb	150,000,000 lb
Cost of production (before interest).....................	21¢	21¢	28¢
Interest charge per pound.....	....	7¢	
Total cost per pound*.........	21¢	28¢	28¢
A			
Assumed price of copper.......	30¢	30¢	
Profit per pound.............	9¢	2¢	
Output per share.............	331 lb	50 lb	
Profit per share.............	$ 3	$1	
Value of stock at 10 times earnings.....................	$30	$10	
Output per $1 of market value of stock....................	1.11 lb	5 lb	
B			
Assumed price of copper.......	39¢	39¢	
Profit per pound.............	18¢	11¢	
Profit per share.............	$ 6	$5.50	
Value per share at 10 times earnings..................	$60	$55	
Output per $1 of market price of stock....................	0.56 lb	0.9 lb	

* For convenience income tax is ignored in this table.

occurs, there will ordinarily be a larger advance in terms of percentage, in the shares of high-cost producers than in the shares of low-cost producers. The foregoing table indicates that a rise in the price of copper from 30 to 39 cents would increase the value of Company A shares by 100 percent and the value of Company B and C shares by 450 percent. Contrary to the general impression in Wall Street, the stocks of high-cost producers are more logical commitments than those of the low-cost producers when the buyer is convinced that a rise in the price of the product is imminent and he wishes to exploit this conviction to the utmost.[3] Exactly the same advantage attaches to the purchase of speculatively capitalized common stocks when a pronounced improvement in sales and profits is confidently anticipated.

STOCK-OPTION WARRANTS

Option warrants were discussed briefly in Chapter 44, as a form of privilege attached to senior securities. They need to be considered also as independent entities. Until recently most warrants have attained the status of separate security by being detached from a senior issue of which they originally formed a part. In the past few years many have been created not only in the traditional way but also through other financing arrangements. These include:

1. Sale of common stock and warrants together as a "unit"
2. Issuance of warrants in whole or partial exchange for other securities
   a. In a reorganization
   b. In a voluntary exchange
3. Sale of warrants at a nominal price—often 1 cent each—to underwriters as part of their compensation and to others connected with the company's financing and management
4. Sold separately to the public (very rarely)

Examples: We illustrate the sale of warrants to the public along with common stock, and the "sale" of warrants at a nominal price to underwriters and other "insiders" in our discussion of the financing arrangements of two typical companies that "went public" in 1960—viz., Boonton Electronics and American Bowling Enterprises. These thumbnail "case histories" will be found in Appendix Note 19, page 751.

The issuance of warrants in a corporate reorganization is illustrated by the case of Erie Railroad, discussed later in this chapter. Warrants were issued in partial exchange for shares taken over by Lynch Corporation in 1962 and by McCrory Corp. in 1961. The examples of a separate sale of warrants to the general public by the issuing corporation go back to Fourth National Investors in 1929 and to Phillips Packing Company in 1936.

Varied History of Warrants. Warrants were known but little used before the bull market of the 1920's. (Perhaps the earliest instance of their appearance is as part of an issue of American Power & Light notes in 1911.) About 1925 their possibilities—mainly for evil, we are certain—began to be exploited. As a result, not only were warrants issued for the variety of purposes listed above, but also their market value in dollars

---

[3] The action of the market in advancing Company *B* shares from 10 to 55 because the price of copper rises from 30 to 39 cents is in itself extremely illogical, for there is ordinarily no warrant for supposing that the higher metal price will be *permanent*. However, since the market does in fact act in this irrational fashion, the speculator must recognize this behavior in his calculation.

became an important factor in the financial scene. The culmination of this movement was undoubtedly the creation of warrants for 7,100,000 shares of common stock of American & Foreign Power Company, which were originally attached to $270,000,000 of Second Preferred Stock. At their peak price of 175 in 1929 these warrants had an indicated market value of over a *billion dollars*. In the recapitalization of American & Foreign Power, consummated in 1952, the warrants were eliminated out completely as having no value despite the fact that the company remained solvent.

This extraordinary generation and disappearance of market value depicts, in exaggerated proportions, the rise and decline of stock-option warrants generally prior to recent years. One respect in which the stock market of the early 1960's is imitating its great and ill-starred predecessor of a generation ago is undoubtedly seen in the new vogue and multiplication of warrant issues.

Basis of Trading. Warrants are now generally dealt in on the basis of "one warrant" calling for one share of stock. If the terms of the warrant change, however, it may be dealt in on the modified basis.

Example: One Tri-Continental warrant now entitles the owner to buy 1.27 shares of common at $17.76 without time limit. (The odd figures result from operation of antidilution provisions.)

As in the case of conversion privileges, the terms of a warrant may change unfavorably with the passage of time.

Example: Textron, Inc., warrants entitle the holder to buy 1.078 shares (adjusted from 1 share) of common at $25 to 1964, then at $30 to 1969, and at prices increasing $5 at the end of each five-year period, ending with a price of $45 between 1979 and 1984.

A new wrinkle—not seen in the 1920's—is a provision giving the company the right to redeem the warrants for cash at a date prior to their expiration.

Example 1: Keyes Fibre warrants, which expire in 1970, may be "called" by the company at $1 each after 1965.

Example 2: Morris Shell Homes, Inc., in 1961 sold units of $20 8 percent Subordinated Debentures, together with one share of common stock, one "First Warrant," and one "Second Warrant"—all for $22 per package. The First Warrants gave the holder the right until 1971 to buy a simpler unit, consisting of $20 of the debentures plus one share of common, this time for $28. The Second Warrants called for $40 of debentures and one share of common, at an aggregate price of $55. By some careful calculation the company made the First Warrants callable at 50 cents each after July 1, 1963, and the Second Warrants callable at 50 cents after July 1, 1964.

To add to the fun, the company created 100,000 "Third Warrants," which gave the right to buy only common at $20 per share, running to 1971, and not callable. These were sold for 1 cent each to the president and chief stockholder, who turned over half of them at the same price to the underwriter of the debentures.

The Valuation of Warrants. The value of a warrant depends (1) on its terms, i.e., the option price and duration; (2) on the current price of the stock; (3) on the number of warrants outstanding relative to the common-stock issue; (4) on the presumed speculative possibilities of the related common. The implications of these criteria of value are obvious. If the stock is selling above the option price, the warrant has "an exercisable value" equal to the difference. However, warrants will have some potential value and related market value even though the stock may be selling well below the option price. This is true because the stock *may* rise above the option price at some time during the life of the warrant, and such a future possibility has present value.

In the past most warrants have behaved in the market like low-priced common stocks of the sort which lack immediate earning power and are essentially a "call" on the company's future. They offered opportunities for spectacular percentage gains when purchased at the low levels produced by a depressed stock market.

This point may be illustrated by reproducing relevant material from the 1940 and 1951 editions, as set forth in Table 49-6.

Table 49-6. Warrants vs. Common Stocks

Name of corporation issuing warrant	Purchase price of stock named in warrant	Dec. 31, 1939		Dec. 31, 1949	
		Market price of stock	Market price of warrant	Market price of stock	Market price of warrant
American & Foreign Power........	25*	1⅞	⅜	2⅜	⅜†
Atlas Corporation..............	25	8⅝	⅞	23⅜	5⅝
Electric Power & Light Corporation.......................	25*	6⅞	2⅝	31½‡	10½‡
Merritt-Chapman & Scott Corporation......................	30	4½	½	20½	4⅞
Tri-Continental Corporation......	22½	2¾	½	9⅛	3
United Corporation..............	27½	2⅜	¼	5	¼†

* In lieu of cash, the purchaser could tender $25 par value of preferred stock selling in 1939 at a large discount.

† Corporate simplification plans pending at the end of 1949 gave no recognition to these warrants. United Corporation warrant holders were resisting such treatment.

‡ These warrants were given a value equivalent to one-third of a common share in the corporate simplification of the system. The prices stated are the market value of the new securities allotted to the stock and the warrants.

It will be noted that what seemed at the end of 1939 an unprepossessing assortment of valueless pieces of paper actually had potentialities of large profits per dollar "invested." The moral would seem to be: "Never underestimate the power of a warrant"—especially if it is selling below a dollar.

In Appendix Note 18, page 751, we present a summary description of the 28 warrants which were separately dealt in and quoted in the Standard & Poor's "Stock Guide" at the end of 1961. The pattern of price relationships is by no means uniform or consistent. Where the stock was selling fairly close to the option price, the warrants were usually quoted between 40 and 60 percent of the price of the stock. Our data thus indicate that a fairly long-term "call" on a typical common stock at about its current price is likely to be valued in the market at about one-half such current price. This would mean that the shares would have to advance by about 50 percent before the warrant buyer reached the break-even point, in the meantime receiving no return on his investment. (See especially the price relationships of stock and warrants for McCrory Corp., Molybdenum, and Sperry-Rand in Appendix Note 18.)

Our table shows some contrasts in both directions. For example, Symington-Wayne warrants sold proportionately lower than those of Sperry-Rand, although the former had a large immediate value and the latter had none.

Table 49-7. Price of Stock and Warrants of Two
Companies on December 31, 1961

	Sperry-Rand	Symington-Wayne
Subscription price of warrants............	25 to Sept. 1963*	10 to May 1963†
Price of stock........................	23⅞	16¾
Price of warrants......................	13⅜	8¾
Parity price of stock....................	38⅜	18¾
Percent rise in stock needed to reach parity..	58%	12%

* Then at 28 to Sept. 1967. Each warrant calls for 1.04 shares of common.
† Then at 15 to May 1968.

The analyst may easily be misled in such comparisons by vagaries in the terms of the warrant and the basis of trading. We have made such an error ourselves at this point in discussing the apparently excessive price of McLean Industries warrants. (The Stock Guide failed to indicate that the warrants, as traded, called for three shares of stock instead of the usual one.) Some of the differences in relative prices are ascribable to the varying durations of the warrants, including changes in their terms, and some no doubt reflect appraisals of the chances of a wide price movement in the near future.

Warrants Represent a Subtraction from the Related Stock. This point may be illustrated concretely by reference to the effect of the issuance of warrants upon the value of the stock in the following classic case.

Example: The earnings reported for 1926 by Barnsdall Oil were $6,077,000, or $5.34 per share on 1,140,000 shares outstanding. However, there were also in existence warrants to buy 1,000,000 shares at $25, the proceeds to be applied to retire $25,000,000 of 6 percent bonds. The analyst should have *assumed* exercise of the warrants, thus reducing the 1926 earnings from $5.34 to $3.45 per share. In 1929, the warrants having actually been exercised, the earnings were $3.25 per share, as against $4.85 if there had been no warrants created. The average price of 35 for the stock was equivalent to a value of 10 for the warrants. This meant, substantially, that about $8 per share had been taken away from the value of the common stock (which otherwise would have been worth 43) by the creation of the warrants.

These illustrations show clearly that the effect of the creation of warrants is to diminish the benefits realized by the common from a large increase in the earnings or in the value of the business. Warrants to buy stock, even at a price above the market, detract from the present value of the common stock, because part of this present value is based upon the right to benefit from future improvement.

In Chapter 17 we suggested that in computing the true earnings available for the issue, the analyst should consider warrants the equivalent of a suitable amount of common stock. The simplest way to make the computation is to divide the total market value of the warrants by the current price of the stock. This will give the number of additional shares of common equivalent to the outstanding warrants. We performed this operation in the case of Del E. Webb stock and warrants on page 227 above.

The similar effect on net asset value by the creation of a large number of subscription warrants is best shown in the case of Tri-Continental Corporation, since asset values have primary importance in analyzing investment company shares. At the end of 1955 the company had outstanding 4,438,000 shares of common and perpetual warrants to buy an additional 3,891,000 shares at $17.76 per share. The asset value of the common was stated to be $49.44 per share, and at the year's closing price of 25¾, the discount was calculated in various manuals as high as 48 percent. But for such purpose the impact of the warrants should obviously be taken into account. If exercise of the warrants were assumed, the per-share net asset value would drop to $31, and the discount would fall to about 17 percent—quite a change.[4] (Were the market value of the warrants—equivalent to $8 per share called for—to be added to that of the common, the resultant sum would show a discount of about 25 percent from the net assets available for stock and warrants.)

A Dangerous Device for Diluting Stock Values. The option warrant is a fundamentally dangerous and objectionable device because it effects

---

[4] The company spelled out these consequences in footnotes to its annual statements.

an indirect and usually unrecognized dilution of common-stock values. The stockholders view the issuance of warrants with indifference, failing to realize that part of their equity in the future is being taken from them. The stock market, with its usual heedlessness, applies the same basis of valuation to common shares whether warrants are outstanding or not. Hence warrants may be availed of to pay unreasonable bonuses to promoters or other insiders without fear of comprehension and criticism by the rank and file of stockholders. Furthermore, the warrant device has facilitated the establishment of an artificially high aggregate market valuation for a company's securities, because (with a little manipulation) large values were established for a huge issue of warrants without reducing the quotation of the common shares.

We think the use of warrants is now being carried to absurd lengths in the numerous new offerings of "units" of common stocks combined with warrants to buy additional amounts of the same issue. (These are illustrated by our American Bowling and Boonton Electronics examples in Appendix Note 19.) The right to buy additional shares of common stock, when such financing is done by the company, is vested by law in the existing common stockholders, unless waived by charter provisions. It should be part of the basic "package" of values represented by the common stock and its market quotation. To issue to stockholders—in fact, to sell to them—a separate piece of paper representing a portion of the general subscription rights they possess without such paper, appears to us to border on financial chicanery. From the viewpoint of corporate financial policy it is equally absurd to place the decision to add to the company's capital in the hands of individual stockholders, to be exercised when market conditions make this apparently desirable, instead of having it based on the needs and opportunities of the business.

Warrants as Part of the Capitalization Structure. Stock-option warrants have proved a convenient and appealing instrument in corporation reorganizations, because they have enabled the reorganizers to give the old stockholders a sop of some kind while ostensibly turning the company over entirely to the creditors. The SEC, however, has taken a stand against this practice, contending that if the old stockholders really have no equity they are not even entitled to warrants. This view was followed by the ICC in its action on railroad reorganization plans and was sustained by the United States Supreme Court.[5]

Our viewpoint on this matter as expressed in 1940 was as follows: "In our opinion the broad objections to the warrant device in principle

[5] See the SEC's advisory opinion in the Childs Company case (in September 1946— Corporate Reorganization Release No. 67), which led to the dropping of a warrant provision for the old stockholders; also the opinion dated Mar. 15, 1943, of the United States Supreme Court in the Chicago, Milwaukee, St. Paul & Pacific Railway reorganization, in which warrants were referred to as "presently worthless pieces of paper."

may justify the rather Draconian stand of the SEC. But a warrant arrangement under which old stockholders can buy out old creditors at a price that will pay them off, e.g., the Erie plan, dated January 1939, has much to recommend it." Under the Erie plan the old stockholders of all classes received for each share held (1) ⅕ share of new common stock and (2) a warrant to buy 1¼ shares of common stock at $37.17 per share, expiring at the end of 1944. If the warrants were exercised the proceeds would, in effect, be paid over to the holders of the old Refunding and Improvement Mortgage bonds, in lieu of corresponding shares of new common stock otherwise reserved for them. This arrangement gave the old stockholders the right, for a limited period, to take over the controlling ownership of the new company by "making whole" the old junior bondholders. As it happened, the warrants failed to attain any realizable value during their life.

Warrants for Old Stockholders in Reorganizations. The history of the 1940's suggests that the warrant device of the Erie type should certainly be availed of whenever there appears any reasonable possibility that the common stock is being deprived of potential value by being denied participation in a reorganization. Some of the railroad common stocks were wiped out at a time of extraordinarily large earnings. Although in most cases the profits failed to continue at such high levels, there is the outstanding exception of St. Louis Southwestern (the "Cotton Belt") to be recorded here as a warning to all analysts and regulatory or judicial bodies that conditions do change; that the possibility of change must always be recognized; and, a fortiori, that a change that has actually taken place must never be ignored.[6]

We have here one of several areas of finance in which purely theoretical criteria might well give way to considerations of equity and practicality. Option warrants may be objectionable in principle, but it is better to create less than perfect securities than to commit a possible injustice to stockholders facing extinction.[7]

---

[6] The stocks of the "bankrupt" Cotton Belt escaped extinction by the narrowest of margins in 1947; soon thereafter the road was declared solvent, and the price of the common rose to 320 in 1951.

[7] The same type of reasoning would dictate the maintenance of a substantial amount of debt, in income-bond form, for a reorganized company, in order to conserve the important tax advantage of deductible interest charges. The difference in money value to the old security holders, through the company's continuing to have this deduction, could well be so large as to outweigh the desirability of a thoroughly sound capital structure. This was the situation in the reorganization of Associated Gas & Electric, now General Public Utilities Company, consummated in 1946. In our opinion, the decision to exchange the old debentures entirely for new common stock destroyed a substantial amount of previously existing value resident in a vested tax-deduction privilege.

PART SIX

OTHER ASPECTS OF SECURITY ANALYSIS

CHAPTER FIFTY

STOCKHOLDERS AND MANAGEMENT

GENERAL APPROACH

In recent years considerable attention has been given to the matter of relations between stockholders and managements. The movement has taken two directions. On the one hand, management has felt it desirable to cultivate the goodwill of stockholders. For this purpose many have engaged "public relations counsel," or similarly styled agencies, who issue press releases of various kinds and who advise on the preparation of financial reports and proxy material. On the other side, agencies have sprung up to represent stockholders. The most widely publicized have been identified with a few colorful figures who take a prominent part in numerous annual meetings.[1]

Some things of value have resulted from both types of activities. Through the public relations counsel an increasing amount of information has been made available to security analysts and to stockholders generally. Annual reports have steadily improved in appearance and convenience, as well as in the quantity and quality of the data supplied. The stockholders' representatives have waged a number of battles on matters

---

[1] The best known of these has been Lewis D. Gilbert. For an excellent statement of his views, see his article "Management and the Public Stockholder," in the July 1950 issue of the *Harvard Business Review*. The brothers Gilbert have long published annual reports of their activities. The 1961 report is amusingly reviewed by A. Wilfred May, in the *Commercial & Financial Chronicle*, Mar. 8, 1962, p. 4 (1156).

of protocol in the conduct of annual meetings. Now and then they have joined issue on some question of substantive importance—usually involving managerial compensation.

We are convinced, however, that neither form of activity has as yet come to grips with the real issues involved in the confrontation of stockholders and their managements. These issues fall into two main categories, viz.:

1. Is the management capable and worthy of confidence?
2. Is the management treating the stockholders fairly?

Closely allied to the second question is another:

3. Are the interests of the public or outside stockholder being subordinated to those of the management, including insiders or controlling stockholders?

We may restate these questions with somewhat greater precision, and with some preliminary comments, in the following order:

1. General Competence of Management. This is universally considered to be of prime importance in investment theory and practice. But the ratings of management are mainly matters of opinion or hearsay. It would seem logical that the accomplishments of good management should be clearly established and well rewarded. Conversely, a poor showing of earnings would seem to call for a careful and unbiased appraisal of the management's responsibility therefor. However, very little evaluation of this sort has as yet actually been made.

2. Compensation of Management. Up to now this has been the most frequent subject of formal objection by stockholders. Although there have been real abuses in the matter of compensation—especially through overgenerous stock options and profit-sharing rights—we consider it much less vital to the stockholders' pocketbook than other policies and actions of management.

3. Dividend Policy. This is the most important aspect of management's policy directly toward stockholders. A dividend inadequate under the circumstances can be as bad for the typical outside stockholder as inadequate earnings. Dividend policy lends itself to factual analysis and to definite conclusions more readily than does managerial ability.

4. Unprofitable or Otherwise Unsatisfactory Use of Stockholders' Capital. Within this broad subject we shall indicate several kinds of unwise use of capital, all of which may be of practical consequence. In a fair proportion of all companies which fail to show really satisfactory over-all results for their owners—measured by earnings, dividends, and the average market price of their shares—stockholders should consider carefully how their capital is used.

a. The stockholder suffers unnecessarily if more of his capital is employed in the business than is required for its efficient operation. This unnecessary use often takes the form of excessive working capital. Negatively, it may arise from failure to employ a reasonable amount of senior capital (debt) in place of equity money, when such an "optimal" capital structure is essential to produce an adequate return for the stockholders.

b. Expansion policies, including ventures in new lines of business, are often resorted to in order to make use of otherwise redundant capital belonging to stockholders. Managements seem to have a natural bias toward taking risks with capital rather than toward relinquishing control over it by returning it to its owners.

c. The holding-company device has been used to the advantage of controlling stockholders despite the fact that this arrangement has tended to penalize other stockholders severely by making their shares sell at a large and unnecessary discount.[2]

d. When a *private* enterprise turns definitely unprofitable or unprosperous and there is no clear indication of near-term improvement, the owner naturally thinks of getting out of the business and recovering as much of his capital as he can. This is not true of publicly owned corporations. No matter how poor the performance, their continuance in the field seems to be taken as a matter of course. The result is often an extraordinary depreciation of the market price of the common stock, forcing many of the owners to sacrifice their shares at ridiculously low levels compared with the realizable value of the business.

Thus if a company's showing is bad or unpromising, it is thought to be the logical and proper move for stockholders to sell their shares *individually*, but not a logical and proper move to consider selling or discontinuing the business as a whole. Why should this be so? Is it necessary and sound that public stockholders of unsuccessful companies should make sacrifices to a degree not expected of private business? This matter has not received thoroughgoing consideration by investors or their advisers.

Conflicts of Interests. The reader will have observed that in all the issues described above the interests of the operating management and outside stockholders are likely to be in conflict. The officers, even though they may be inefficient, want to keep their jobs. Their bias is in the direction of large working capital, low dividends, maximum expansion, an all-common-stock capital structure, and the continuance of the business at all costs—even though under many circumstances one or more of these policies may react to the disadvantage of the typical stockholder. (On some questions—particularly that of low vs. adequate dividends—the interests or desires of the controlling stockholders may be opposed to those of the rank and file.)

---

[2] A typical instance of this kind, Mission Corp., was discussed in Appendix Note 43, p. 723, of the 1951 edition. We believe that closed-end investment companies represent a disadvantageous corporate form, of similar type—though more virtuously motivated.

Majority of Managements Well Qualified. Fortunately, this conflict of interest—which may be said to be latent in the very nature of our corporate organization—is not so serious in practice as it may seem to be in theory. We believe most managements are sufficiently competent, and we are certain that the overwhelming majority of them are honest and conscientious. In matters involving their own advantage they will often lean backward to avoid the color of unfairness toward their stockholders. When the business is prosperous there is enough in it to take care of everybody on a satisfactory basis; and the outside stockholders will almost always have grounds for thankfulness to management rather than complaint.

The significant problems of stockholder-management relations occur therefore in only a minority of cases, but this minority is sufficiently large to warrant giving considerable attention to the subject. Strangely enough, if Wall Street opinion were consulted, it would be found to hold that a large proportion of companies are not as well managed as they should be.[3] If this view is correct it is high time that methods were devised for checking up on the competence of management, and high time that stockholders were educated to do something about making improvements when they are badly needed. Fully as great is the need for a new and searching approach to the question of proper dividend policy from the standpoint of the average stockholder. Here the problem has been complicated by a maze of conflicting developments and interests, with results unnecessarily harmful to the cause of successful investment in common stocks.

The third group of problems—related to the effective use of stockholders' capital—is perhaps as basic as the other two in investment theory, but hardly so in practice. There are, however, many individual cases of the third type in which a really intelligent analysis by stockholders would show the need for specific action to remedy an unsatisfactory condition, or at least to reduce the impact of inadequate earning power on capital.

Relationship of These Problems to Security Analysis. Investment policy as a whole should include the matter of intelligent attitudes and decisions by stockholders while they hold their securities. It may be just as important to do the wise thing during the period of owning a stock as it is to act wisely in *becoming* or *ceasing* to be a stockholder. Even in the narrower area of the analysis and evaluation of securities, the question of proper action by stockholders is by no means an extraneous consideration. If value is held down by inferior management, the analyst may properly consider what is the likelihood of a change taking place in this vital factor—either as a consequence of the supposedly "normal" super-

---

[3] See Appendix Note 51, p. 736, of the 1951 edition for the opinion of practicing security analysts on this point and others related thereto, as disclosed in answers to a questionnaire.

vision by the directors or through stockholder pressure. The same may be said if value is held down by a niggardly dividend policy or by other specific policies which prevent the stockholders from obtaining a satisfactory result from their investment.

Advising Present Stockholders on Managerial Quality. The determination whether the management is superior, passable, or inadequate is generally considered to be a most important function of the security analyst in his efforts to appraise the value or prospects of a given security. But for some peculiar reason the analyst is supposed to use this determination solely in advising on purchases or sales. It has not been recognized as part of his function to advise stockholders, in their capacity as continuing owners, on the apparent excellences or shortcomings of their management. This strikes us as scarcely logical. We think that security analysts and financial counselors could and should play a most helpful role in promoting effective action by stockholders as a group, not only in their own interest but in that of a healthy free-enterprise system.

The heedlessness and inertia of American stockholders as a class have long been notorious. This laxity has invited exploitation, and a certain amount of it has inevitably followed.[4] The consequences have been more serious than the loss of money by investors. We think the flow of equity capital has at times in the past been sensibly retarded by the fact that many possible venturers have a feeling that they are helpless to control their capital after it has been committed into common stocks, and that they cannot rely upon receiving a square deal from those who will control it. In our view the establishment of sound attitudes by stockholders who realize that they are owners of the business is the best way to remove this distrust and thereby to promote the flow of the public's money into free enterprise.[5]

STOCKHOLDERS AND MANAGERIAL EFFICIENCY

This is the logical place at which to attack the broad question of the attitude of stockholders toward management and its policies. If there

---

[4] This subject was treated in a well-known book, *The Modern Corporation and Private Property*, by A. A. Berle, Jr., and G. C. Means, New York, 1932. The authors drew the conclusion that the control of corporations had been abdicated by the stockholder-owners and had been transferred *de facto* to management. Under these conditions, they suggested that the control should more properly be exercised on behalf of the public as a whole. *The Managerial Revolution* by James Burnham (New York, 1942), starting with the same thesis that the managers had seized control of corporations through default by their owners, predicted that the same managing class would take over control of the state.

[5] This statement is not in conflict with the widely held view that adverse policies of government have discouraged the raising of equity capital. We are not concerned with the latter question here. Stockholders may well need to be alert to conditions both within and without their companies.

are inefficient managements, they themselves are not likely to correct their deficiencies. The remedial action must come from the owners of the business. Yet despite the vital importance of having good management, stockholders have as yet no recognized procedure by which they can assure themselves that their business is being well run; none by which they can ascertain where the responsibility rests for a relatively poor corporate record; and none by which they can move effectively to make corrections when these are needed.

The appraisal of management is considered an essential—perhaps the essential—factor in determining whether an investment should be made in a given business and often whether holdings in a business should be disposed of. Experienced investors and their advisors are greatly influenced in their buy-and-sell decisions by their individual conclusions or by the commonly accepted view as to the caliber of management. It is worth asking why such views rarely lead to action of any kind by the stockholders as a whole, the composite owners of the business. If investors are right in avoiding a company because its management is poor, must not the stockholders of that company be wrong in doing nothing to change the way things are run?

Our answers to these questions would fall into two related parts. First we should concede that while opinions about managerial competence may be strongly held, they are for the most part only opinions. They are not backed by a body of clearly recognized evidence or by the application to such evidence of well-established rules of appraisal. Consequently, while the individual investor may be guided by such views in making his personal commitments or sales, they are not well enough documented to serve as a basis for a public appeal to stockholders generally or for concerted action by them. Partly because of this difficulty and partly because American custom is strongly against independent action by stockholders in corporate affairs, the idea that the owners collectively should sit in judgment on their managements would seem to most investors quite impractical.

But the foregoing concession should not end the matter. Without underestimating the obstacles to progress in this area, we think the time is ripe for some new thinking and new action by and on behalf of stockholders generally. If we start from the indubitable fact that many companies show unsatisfactory results, it seems clear that the question whether the management is good enough can sometimes be raised without injustice. Nor is it at all impossible to arrive at a fair and intelligent answer to such a question. Progress has been made in the art of appraising managements. There are experts in the field, and a body of technical knowledge is gradually being accumulated.

Management Domination of the Board. After all, the board of directors does at times form an independent and carefully grounded conclusion regarding the merits of the executive officers. In theory the directors should do this regularly, and it is their duty to change the operating management when it fails to make the grade. The theory works badly in practice, because in the typical case the board of directors is not sufficiently independent of the executives. The nonexecutive directors—often themselves a minority of the board—are generally bound to the officers by close ties of friendship and of business dealings. The practical and basic point here is that the officers choose the directors more often than the directors choose the officers. If every board were thoroughly independent of management, the problem of obtaining and keeping good top executives would nearly always be solved, as it should be, by businesslike action at directors' meetings. But so often the boards and the executives form an indistinguishable whole—i.e., a single "management"—that the businesslike approach must be taken by the stockholders if it is to be taken at all.

The frequent lack of an effective distinction between the board of directors and the operating management makes necessary at least a minimum amount of vigilance and initiative on the part of the stockholders acting independently of their directors. Such vigilance is in fact required to assure the satisfactory working of our corporate economy and an adequate flow of new venture capital into publicly owned enterprises.

We do not propose in this chapter to develop the tests and standards by which a fair decision may be reached as to managerial efficiency. That is part of the science of business management. We shall simply repeat that the job can be done and properly done if the stockholders make up their minds that it is needed. Our concern in the subject of security analysis is to indicate the circumstances under which a demand for such an appraisal of management may properly emanate from stockholders.

Management's Performance as the Point of Departure. In our chapter on key ratios in statement analysis, we developed three basic figures which indicate how successful the company's operations have been. First and foremost is the rate of return on stock and bond capital, including both contributed capital and retained earnings. The second, which is generally the key to the first, is the margin of profit on sales. The third is the growth of sales and profits. These ratios measure the success of the company; they also measure the performance of management and, presumably or prima facie, its quality or competence. We thus have a comparatively simple starting point from which to determine whether the stockholders should be concerned at all about their management and whether further study of the question is called for.[6]

---

[6] A well-managed company, such as du Pont, applies tests of this sort to the performance of each operating department. The final figure to which all the others lead is Return on Investment. See the illuminating paper by T. C. Davis, treasurer of E. I. du Pont de Nemours & Company, entitled "How the Du Pont Organization Appraises Its Performance," presented at the Financial Management Conference of the American Management Association in December 1949.

Standards Are Both Absolute and Relative. Performance is judged both absolutely and relatively, and the management is entitled to credit for a good showing on either count. If the return on capital is satisfactory in itself, the fact that most other companies in the industry have done still better is hardly to be taken too seriously. Conversely, even if the return on capital is unsatisfactory, there is no prima-facie ground for criticism if the results have been no worse than those of the industry as a whole.

Thus the cases requiring stockholders' attention narrow down to those where performance has been bad both absolutely and relatively. Conversely and importantly, when performance has been good on both counts, management is entitled to have this fact realized and appreciated by the stockholders. Excellent performance should be well compensated —not only as a matter of fairness to the executives but also in the interest of the stockholders. The way to retain good management is to pay it well. It is an axiom of business that the net cost of good management, no matter how highly paid, is less than that of bad management.

This question of good or bad management would be advanced beyond its present hit-or-miss or hearsay stage in Wall Street if security analysts would work out simple performance figures for the various companies, both absolutely and in relation to the industry as a whole. They could readily be made part of the statistical analysis supplied by the various financial services under some such title as "Indicated Performance of Management." When these ratios are arranged in order in an industry survey, the companies at the top and the bottom of the list should properly stand out, not only in the calculations and preferences of stock buyers and sellers but also in the minds of their stockholders. Bouquets may well be called for in one group and brickbats in the other.

An Accounting of the Stewardship. Let us emphasize here a point we have tried to make all along, viz., that the performance figures are prima-facie but not conclusive indications of management's competence. Bad over-all results may be associated with good management and vice versa. But it would be silly to conclude that because the evidence they offer is insufficient, the performance figures are not worth careful study. If managements expect to receive credit for good results, as they do, it is only common sense to require them to defend their stewardship when the results are poor. Stockholders are fully entitled to inquire and to complain. More than that, they are entitled to a full, frank, and convincing report from their directors on the reasons for the bad showing. An independent study of the executives' competence and specific policies, made by outside consultants on management, would undoubtedly be a sound move in *nearly* all these cases.[7] In such a study the merely prima-

---

[7] Compare the report on its management obtained by Green Giant Packing Company as described in *Business Week* of July 15, 1950. This step was taken by an outstandingly successful management desirous of doing a still better job. For obvious

facie indications will be either confirmed or disproved by facts not apparent on the surface. Whatever the conclusions, they should be of great assistance to the directors in discharging their obligation to see that the company is properly and efficiently managed.

The Growth Factor in Relation to Management Performance. Our performance ratios include a measure of growth of sales and profits, a factor to which major attention is given by the stock market and by investors generally. An outstanding company increases its profit more rapidly than the rest of the industry. As far as stockholders are concerned, an expansion in sales alone not accompanied by an increase in net earnings is of no real benefit, and it may hurt them by tying up too much of their capital. Even when profits expand, the stockholders may not benefit therefrom if the growth has required so large an increase in capital as to reduce significantly the rate of return on their investment.

A good record of growth in addition to a satisfactory return on capital is of course an added reason for congratulating and rewarding management. Failure to expand as fast as the industry as a whole is generally considered an unsatisfactory element in the picture and a sign of weakness in the company's position or management. This is a matter that may properly concern the board of directors. However, we do not consider that it supplies an adequate reason for stockholder unrest and independent action, if the other basic factors in the performance—earnings and dividends in relation to capital—are reasonably satisfactory.

Other Methods of Appraising Management. We referred at the outset to the fact that beginnings have been made in the formal evaluation of management as part of publicly available material. *Forbes Magazine* publishes "yardstick of Corporate Performance," which now (1962) gives comparative figures for growth, profitability, and recent trend of earnings. Formerly it rated management performance on a percentage scale, covering various categories, including relations with the stockholders, labor, the community, and the public.[8] Undoubtedly the evaluation of management will make further progress in years to come. Whatever is accomplished in this direction will be only half effective if it is used solely as a guide to the buying and selling of securities. The

---

reasons managements with a poor record are likely to oppose such outside studies. They are usually more successful in maintaining the managerial status quo than they are in making money for their stockholders.

[8] In 1950, Jackson Martindell, president of the American Institute of Management, published his book *The Scientific Appraisal of Management,* which covers the theory of the subject in comprehensive detail. Martindell explains an elaborate point system of evaluating management, which he uses in his investment-counsel work. Much of the basic material is obtained through an extensive questionnaire sent out to the chief executives of numerous corporations. The book was revised in 1961.

more dependable such measures become, the more reason there will be to employ them as a means to recognize and reward good management and to recognize and change inferior management.

COMPENSATION OF MANAGEMENT

The ordinary compensation of the executives is determined by the board of directors, usually on an annual basis. It has now become common practice to add various types of special compensation to the basic salary. These take the major forms of profit sharing, stock options, and retirement pay. As a matter of law or universal policy such arrangements are submitted to the stockholders for their approval at an annual or special meeting. (Year-end bonuses, paid at the discretion of the board, remain a matter within its sole jurisdiction.) Thus, technically speaking, the compensation of management falls partly within and partly without the purview of stockholder decision. However, since all elements of compensation are required to be disclosed in proxy statements relating to the election of directors, it seems to be the intention of our present laws that stockholders should exercise at least secondary control over the entire field.

The more thought we give to the matter of executives' salaries, the less important it appears to us as compared with other questions which affect the stockholders' interests vitally but which quite escape their attention. Experience shows that really good management is practically never overpaid. Poor management is often paid more than it deserves; but here, if the stockholders bestir themselves at all, they should devote their efforts to changing personnel rather than pay. Thus the practical questions would seem to arise when the management is fairly good but its compensation appears unfairly high.

It is quite rare to find the ordinary salaries of such executives so far out of line as to make a substantial dollar-and-cents difference to the stockholders. The fact that all large salaries are now published, and that comparisons may readily be made within an industry, tends to keep all the figures within a normal range.[9] Naturally, the size of the company often has an important bearing on the salary schedule.

With the increasing use of special arrangements of the types mentioned above, the stockholders are sometimes called upon to allot to management far too large a portion of the future earnings. The SEC is careful to see that the full implications of any special plan are made

---

[9] The dollar range in salaries, however, is a wide one. The *Corporate Director* for June 1950, published by the American Institute of Management, contains a statistical study of the chief executives of 204 "leading and excellently managed companies." The highest salary (and bonus) was $598,000, and the lowest was only $24,000. The group average was $119,000, and the modal range was between $100,000 and $149,000.

clear in the proxy statement, but for most companies its jurisdiction extends solely to disclosure.

Rationalization for Management Compensation. It would be a salutary development if, when important amounts are involved, the directors were called upon to justify in a fairly explicit and elaborate way the generous treatment they are asking the stockholders to approve. The stockholders are entitled to be told (1) just what are the excellent results for which these arrangements constitute a reward; and (2) by what analogies or other reasoning the board determined that the amounts accorded are appropriate.

We are strongly in favor of paying liberal over-all compensation for outstanding managerial achievement. In many cases stockholders would gladly vote executives higher pay than they now receive if the quality of their performance could be brought home by concrete figures, absolute and comparative. Thus we consider that this matter of fair compensation is closely tied in with the more important objective of recognizing and retaining good management, and of replacing inadequate management. The key figures that can be used to measure the success of the enterprise may serve as a basis for determining appropriate compensation through some reasonable formula. But any profit-sharing plan should not permit distributions unless the stockholders are concurrently receiving an adequate dividend in relation either to the book value of their investment, or to some other rationally determined value—or unless they have voted explicitly in favor of a low dividend policy.

Management often does a remarkably good job under conditions so unfavorable that the dollar results are not a proper measure of their accomplishment. In some cases it may take genius just to break even. When a new management is brought into a run-down business, some years may have to pass before its hard work can be translated into satisfactory profits. It seems to us that during these periods of stress and change the pay must remain moderate even though the management's ability may be high. The executives must be reconciled to waiting for good times and good results before they can draw anything in the nature of bonus compensation. If good results are out of the question, something drastic should probably be done about the business itself. A new management, with a proved record in another company, may properly ask to be compensated in the form of stock options, at prices preferably somewhat above the current market, and certainly not below the net-current-asset value of the shares.

OTHER ASPECTS NOW SUMMARIZED

The 1951 edition of this book contained three additional chapters (48–50) in this section, dealing with dividend policy, stockholders' capital, and stockholder-management controversies. They discussed the areas in which conflicts in interest may arise between the management and nonmanagement stockholders, and also the important differences in strategic position between controlling and noncontrolling shareowners. The chapters had a threefold purpose. The first was to cover in some detail a region of investment policy to which insufficient attention had been given elsewhere. The second was to advance the thesis that security analysts themselves could be of great service to investor-stockholders by guiding them along the paths of intelligence and self-protection in their dealings with their managements. Finally, in quixotic fashion perhaps, we wanted to combat the traditional but harmful notion that if a stockholder doesn't like the way his company is run he should sell his shares, no matter how low their price may be.

We have decided to omit most of the material referred to, especially since it has been summarized at the beginning of this chapter.

One of our particular concerns was the failure of stockholders to use independent judgment in matters affecting their interests, and their habit of voting, sheeplike, in favor of anything the management proposes regardless of its merits or of arguments advanced against it. Not much improvement in that supine attitude has been shown in the past decade. Incompetent or unfair management is not being remedied, as it should be, through action by rank-and-file stockholders—action which follows expert and disinterested guidance or supports justified efforts by some of the larger holders to correct the situation. Where a change does take place, it is almost always the result of the acquisition of so large a holding of shares by new interests that they win by the votes they control rather than by convincing their fellow owners of the rightness of their cause.

Let us repeat the paragraph that closed this section of the previous edition:

Sound investment in common stocks requires sound attitudes and actions by stockholders. The intelligent choice of securities is, of course, the major factor in successful investment. But if the stockholder is to regard himself as a continuing part-owner of the business in which he has placed his money, he must be ready at times to act like a true owner and to make the decisions associated with ownership. If he wants his interests fully protected he must be willing to do something on his own to protect them. This requires a moderate amount of initiative and judgment. It is not beyond the competence of American investors, especially if they are counseled in these matters by agencies in which they can have confidence.

CHAPTER FIFTY-ONE

REGULATION BY THE SECURITIES AND EXCHANGE COMMISSION

THE SECURITIES AND EXCHANGE COMMISSION

A series of legislative acts, beginning in 1933, established the Securities and Exchange Commission—now invariably referred to as the S.E.C. or the SEC—and prescribed its duties and powers. The result has been a far-reaching and intricate scheme of regulation of the security business and of corporate affairs. Undoubtedly it has revolutionized Wall Street. The SEC has had a major impact upon the following six aspects of finance:

1. The issuance of new securities
2. Security trading both on the exchanges and over the counter
3. Financial statements of corporations, including accounting practices
4. Practically every important financial matter concerned with public utility holding-company systems, including their continued existence as such
5. Corporate reorganizations, except those of railroads
6. The conduct of investment funds (investment companies)

In addition, the SEC has much to say about proxy statements, about disclosure of stock holdings and security trading of "insiders," about the conduct of investment advisers, and about trust indentures and trustees thereunder.

The Legislative Background. The statutes under which the Commission operates are the following:[1]

1. The Securities Act of 1933, relating to new issues of securities
2. The Securities Exchange Act of 1934, relating to trading on organized exchanges; this was enlarged by
3. The "Maloney Act" of 1938, conferring jurisdiction over unlisted trading

[1] In the intervening years there have been legislative amendments. The *25th Annual Report of the Securities and Exchange Commission* (Fiscal 1959), in part II, reviews a number of recent proposals.

4. The Public Utility Holding Company Act of 1935, to eliminate abuses in that field

5. The Chandler Act of 1938, which added Chapter X to the Bankruptcy Act, setting up new procedures for corporate reorganizations

6. The Trust Indenture Act of 1939, which defines the responsibilities of corporate bond trustees

7. The Investment Company Act of 1940, regulating publicly held investment funds

8. The companion Investment Advisers Act of 1940

SEC Authority Limited. The regulatory powers given the SEC by these laws, while extensive, are far from complete. They vary greatly in their scope from one aspect of finance to another. It is important for the investor and the security analyst to recognize what these powers do and do not comprehend.

Under the 1933 Act, the Commission has jurisdiction over public offerings of new securities (not confined to a single state) in amounts of $300,000 or more in a twelve-month period. Its duties extend solely to the disclosures made in connection with these offerings, as set forth in the formal registration statement and the related prospectus. It may refuse registration if the statement is "deficient" from the standpoint of full and fair disclosure. But it has no power to prevent the sale of stock at unjustifiably high prices or in companies clearly unsuited for public participation.[2]

Prospectuses and Individuals. In our 1951 edition, we advanced the view that prospectuses were overly informative, and pointed to the fact that the prospectus for Clinton Industries[3]—a typical one—was 52 pages long. We also noted that many students of the subject believed that because of the very wealth of detail, the prospectuses were largely failing in their purpose. The ordinary investor simply will not wade through all the minutiae of information. In the intervening years the length of prospectuses has been reduced—quite probably by something like one-half. *Example:* A review of a recent cross-section sample disclosed that the 28-page prospectuses covering the January 22, 1962 offering of 1,500,000 common shares of Southern California Edison and the January 24, 1962 offering of $35,000,000 debenture 4¾s of 1987 of W. T. Grant Company were typical. This is a marked improvement, but

---

[2] Two statements taken from the Foreword of the *25th Annual Report of the Securities and Exchange Commission* bear on this: "The Federal securities laws were not designed to prevent investors from losing money in the stock market; indeed, it is extremely doubtful whether any laws could do this in a free economy" (p. xiii). "The Commission's examination relates only to the accuracy and adequacy of the disclosures. The Commission is not empowered to, and does not, appraise the merits of the securities or otherwise pass upon the soundness of the venture" (p. xxi).

[3] Subsequently changed to Clinton Foods, Inc., and in 1956 acquired by Standard Brands.

we still propose in a subsequent paragraph (as we did ten years ago) the use of a supplementary one-page summary. Perhaps it could be in the form of a cover sheet.

The Wall Street machinery for offering new securities is geared to quick results. It is customary to sell the entire offering of many issues on the first day of public announcement. Such announcement is made almost simultaneously with the appearance of the printed prospectus in final form. The law requires that the buyer be furnished with a prospectus "before" the sale is made. On such a time schedule it would be virtually a physical impossibility for public buyers to read a *final* prospectus before deciding whether and how much to buy.

Under a relaxation of the regulations, in part to meet the exigencies of this situation, the SEC has permitted the dissemination of the quaintly named "red herrings." These are nonfinal drafts of the prospectus containing a legend in red ink across each page that warns the reader that the text is subject to change. The more experienced investors, including mainly the institutional buyers, can undoubtedly make an adequate study of a particular issue by feasting on these "red herrings."

The Prospectus in Profile. But the 1933 Act was designed to protect mainly the general public—individuals. There is some question whether any amount of disclosure will deter a security-buying victim from being victimized, especially when his own cupidity plays a large role in the proceeding. This is particularly true in a bull market.[4] Certainly a prospectus—which inevitably embodies a good deal that is somewhat technical—will not deter him. We have a concrete suggestion on this point. It is that each prospectus be accompanied by a one-page summary of the more important facts about the issue, in a form approved by the SEC. The summary should contain at least a brief reference, citing page numbers, to every unfavorable factor described in the prospectus itself and deemed to be of more than incidental importance. Such a one-page summary could tell the investor pretty well what he is getting for his money. If he has any sense at all, he will read it. If he has no sense, nothing will save him.

We are concerned over the quality of new offerings of common stocks that appear in the latter stages of bull markets. Most of the companies are too small; their prosperity is of recent vintage; either their offering price is inordinately high or they are bid up sharply after they "go

---

[4] In its 1960 Annual Report, p. 2, the SEC states, "The fraudulent sale of securities remains a major problem for the Commission and has continued to occupy the time of a large portion of its staff. During the second half of the fiscal year, activity in the securities market generally receded somewhat from its mid-year peak. However, public interest in securities remained at a high level and furnished a fertile field for fraud and manipulation in the sale of securities. Recent publicity in regard to certain successful traders seems to have instilled in the minds of some persons a desire to duplicate their success in the market."

public"; and the subsequent price declines are dishearteningly great. These new issues are successful because the public is in a stock-buying —even gambling—mood and is willing to overpay for all types of speculative equities.[5] Under such circumstances it is hardly possible to interfere with the laws of supply and demand and to regulate the prices which either existing shares or new offerings should command in the open market. Congress has been wise to refrain from any attempt to interfere with the price levels of securities—except in a highly indirect manner by giving the Federal Reserve Board the power to vary the margin requirements on loans against listed stocks and bonds.[6]

Example: Consolidated Airborne Systems, Inc., (according to the prospectus—"specializes in the design, engineering, and manufacturing of servo-type electronic test equipment, temperature systems and instrumentation for uses related to military and commercial jet and propeller-driven aircraft") is an illustration of a new and small company. It was incorporated in New York in 1957 and for the year ending May 31, 1961, reported sales of $1,398,000 and earnings of $91,000 before a "non-recurring special charge"[7]—after such charges of $29,000, earnings of $62,000. Per-share earnings before special charges were 25 cents (based on year-end shares), and after charges about 19 cents (vs. a reported 7 cents in 1960 and 14 cents in 1959). In early 1961, 180,000 shares were offered to the public at $5. They were promptly bid up to 15½ and have since fallen back to a bid of 3½.

Flood of New Issues. Some pronounced changes have occurred in recent years in regard to registrations under the Securities Act of 1933. First, the dollar volume has increased greatly. In the 27 years from the beginning of the administration of the Act to June 1961, over $203 billion of securities have been registered. However, in the last five years in excess of $80 billion—40 percent of the 27-year aggregate—was registered. Second, there has been a marked increase in the number of small issues. Third, out of the total number of registration statements, those filed by companies which had not previously filed statements has risen rapidly—jumping from 28 percent of the total in 1958 to 52 percent in fiscal 1961—a record 958 out of a total of 1,830 statements filed. Fourth, there has also been a significant increase in the percentage which common stock represents of total dollar amount of registrations for cash

[5] That the SEC is also much concerned with what the public is willing to buy is shown by the foregoing footnote. In fact, the Commission made the following opening statement in the 1960 Annual Report: "Previous annual reports have reflected the need for, and the expenditure of, considerable time and money in meeting the challenge of the rising band of promoters and others who attempt to take unlawful advantage of the desire of the investing public to share in the increased prosperity and consequent rising security markets of our nation."

[6] And except for SEC regulation of stock-market manipulation referred to below.

[7] The special charge arose out of the settlement of a claim in connection with a default under a prior-year contract.

sales.[8] This is shown by the following data from the 1961 *Annual Report* of the SEC:

Fiscal year	Common stock as percent of total registrations
1935	24.5%
1940	14.7
1945	16.8
1950	40.8
1955	46.7
1960	59.0
1961	54.7

"The 1934 Act." *Regulation of Stock-market Trading.* In the 1951 edition we wrote as follows in regard to this Act:

The chief effect of SEC regulation in this area has been the virtual ending of stock-market manipulation. That is indeed a striking accomplishment. Every now and then some manipulative activities are engaged in by hardy souls, but they generally find their schemes exposed and themselves in serious trouble. In every major sense, the market has been free of manipulation since the middle 1930's.

In the intervening decade much has happened. The public participation in the securities markets has increased tremendously. For example, a study by the New York Stock Exchange states that during the period from 1952 to 1959 the number of shareholders doubled.[9] To serve them, there has been a great increase in the number of brokers, dealers, and customers' men. In this connection the SEC reports that there were 5,500 brokers and dealers registered with the Commission at the end of fiscal 1961 vs. 3,930 at the end of 1950.[10] Over the same period, the number of customers' men registered with the NYSE increased from less than 11,000 to nearly 28,000 and with the National Association of Securities Dealers (the NASD) from 29,000 to over 93,000. (In the aggregate the number of security salesmen has more than tripled.) At the same time, the branch offices of stock-exchange firms have also multiplied. It is not surprising, therefore, that the total reported annual dollar volumes of the New York and American Stock Exchanges have skyrocketed—from $525 billion in 1950 to almost $940 billion in 1961 and from $108 billion to nearly $450 billion, respectively.[11] The aggregate total number of shares traded on *all* stock exchanges in the United States has increased

[8] There has also been a pronounced increase in the proportion of registrations for cash sales registered by investment companies. For example, it increased from less than 22 percent in 1957 to over 40 percent in 1960. In 1961 it was about 32 percent.

[9] *Share Ownership in America: 1959,* New York Stock Exchange, June 1959, p. 3.

[10] The *27th Annual Report of the Securities and Exchange Commission,* 1961, p. 1.

[11] *Organization, Management, and Regulation of Conduct of Members of the American Stock Exchange,* Securities and Exchange Commission Staff Report, Jan. 3, 1962, p. 55.

from 468 million shares in 1939 and 516 million in 1949 to 1,700 million in 1959 and over 1,260 million in the *first half* of 1961.

This tremendous influx is changing the securities market into a mass market. The combination of a large body of new investors and salesmen —both of whom are inexperienced—and a surging bull market has not been without its problems. Irrational price movements in issues and feverish activity have caused the financial press to speak of "hectic trading." In fact, in April 1961, the President of the NYSE stated in regard to such trading that:[12]

Reports reaching us indicate that some would-be investors are attempting to purchase shares of companies whose names they cannot identify, whose products are unknown to them, and whose prospects are, at best, highly uncertain.

There is a disquieting evidence that some people have not yet discovered that it is impossible to get something for nothing, and they are attempting to make improper use of the facilities of the investment community.

Apparently, in a different sense, others were also improperly using the facilities of the investment community. For in early January 1962, the SEC published its study of the ASE. This staff report concluded:[13]

There can be little doubt that in the case of the American Stock Exchange the statutory scheme of self-regulation in the public interest has not worked out in the manner originally envisioned by Congress. The manifold and prolonged abuses by specialists and floor traders and other instances of misconduct described in this report make it clear that the problem goes beyond isolated violations and amounts to a general deficiency of standards and a fundamental failure of controls.

In an extended bull market the temptations become much greater than usual. Undoubtedly, the improved institutional framework has made it possible to withstand them far better than in the late 1920's. But there have been offenders. To its credit, the financial community itself is moving vigorously to correct what needs correction.

"Insiders' " Short-term Gains. Section 16a of the 1934 Act requires so-called "insiders" to report to the SEC changes in their holdings of equity securities, including convertible bonds, on a monthly basis. These figures are published regularly. For the purpose of preventing unfair use of information, the law declares (in Section 16b) that any profits realized by such an insider from trades concluded within a six-month period shall be forfeitable to the corporation itself.[14]

[12] *Wall Street Journal*, Apr. 5, 1961.

[13] Staff report of SEC, *op. cit.*, p. 53.

[14] Insiders are defined as officers, directors, and those owning directly or indirectly more than 10 percent of the voting securities of the company. Provisions similar to those of Sec. 16b are found in the 1935 Act (Sec. 17b) and in the 1940 Act (Sec. 20f).

Peculiarly enough, the SEC is not given power to enforce this provision. It is left to the corporation itself or some interested stockholder to bring suit to recover such "short-term profits."[15] This section of the law has been severely criticized on the ground that it interferes with the legitimate activities of directors, including their efforts to support the price for the shares when the market breaks. We think the statute should be changed, more for ethical than for practical reasons. Under present tax laws, wealthy men have little reason to take short-term stock-market profits. Hence, assuming there is some improper buying on inside information, the profits made therefrom are unlikely to come within the compass of the law.[16] But in our view it is unjust to declare an act improper and punishable because it *might* represent an abuse of trust. Perhaps the correct solution is to amend the law so as to make these profits prima-facie evidence of improper trading. The presumed "wrongdoer" would then have his day in court and an opportunity to show that his purchases and sales were made without benefit of special information.

The SEC compiles and publishes a considerable amount of data on the division of total trading between "professionals" (stock-exchange members), odd-lot traders, and full-lot traders. (As a separate service, the New York Stock Exchange publishes monthly the amount of the short interest in each security, where the figure is more than nominal.) Of special interest is the elaborate study made by the SEC of the trading on September 6, 1946, an historic 3-million-share day on which the market had a sudden collapse. This study covers the details of the market's action, minute by minute; more interestingly, it indicates the number and classes of buyers and sellers, and also the results of many sample interviews designed to elicit the reasons for the decisions to sell.[17]

It must always be borne in mind that the SEC is given no authority over, or responsibility for, the prices of individual stocks or of the market as a whole.

Regulation of Corporate Statements and Reports. These powers are conferred in Section 19 of the 1933 Act, Section 13 of the 1934 Act, Sections 14 and 20 of the 1935 Act, Sections 30–32 and 38 of the 1940 Act.

---

[15] For a summary reference to one of the rather infrequent proceedings brought by a stockholder under Sec. 16b, see an advertisement on the financial page of the *New York Times* of Aug. 2, 1950, announcing a court hearing on a proposed settlement of such an action, which involved trading in shares of L. A. Young Spring and Wire.

[16] These limitations on the actions of insiders have the effect of discouraging suitable persons from becoming directors. Real "insiders," if not overscrupulous, can place dummies on the board and trade on the basis of information supplied to them.

[17] In connection with the sharp decline in stock prices following the President's heart attack in 1955, the NYSE made a rather detailed study of that day's market. See G. K. Funston, *The Stock Market: September 26*, published by the New York Stock Exchange. (Reprint of an article in the *Exchange*—monthly publication of the NYSE—November 1955.)

In 1960 Congress passed Public Law 86–750 which amends the Investment Advisers Act of 1940, and among other things, authorizes the Commission to require the keeping of books and records and filing of reports and permits the periodic examination of a registrant's books. Section 19(*a*) of the 1933 Act gives the Commission

. . . authority from time to time to make, amend, and rescind such rules and regulations as may be necessary to carry out the provisions of this title, including rules and regulations governing registration statements and prospectuses for various classes of securities and issuers, and defining *accounting*, technical, and trade terms used in this title. Among other things, the Commission shall have authority, for the purposes of this title, to prescribe the form or forms in which required information shall be set forth, the items or details to be shown in the balance sheet and earning statement, and the methods to be followed in the preparation of accounts, in the appraisal or valuation of assets and liabilities, in the determination of depreciation and depletion, in the differentiation of recurring and nonrecurring income, in the differentiation of investment and operating income, and in the preparation, where the Commission deems it necessary or desirable, of consolidated balance sheets or income accounts of any person directly or indirectly controlling or controlled by the issuer, or any person under direct or indirect common control with the issuer. (Italics supplied.)

Pursuant to this statutory authority, the SEC has set up an elaborate system of corporate reports, for a variety of purposes. Registration statements for new securities supply full financial information for the last three years plus a fraction of the current year, to the extent that such material is available. (The body of the prospectus generally supplies more summary data for a longer period of years.) Similar data are required for the registration of securities for dealings on a stock exchange. Supplements to the latter statement—in most cases on forms known as "10-K"—provide the figures for each succeeding year. This material is required also from registrants under the Securities Act if the offering aggregates $2 million or more. For the great majority of companies the Commission requires submission of *quarterly sales* figures. (On the other hand, the interim figures for *net earnings* are made public—generally quarterly—pursuant to agreements with the stock exchanges, or on the initiative of the companies themselves.)

The SEC has taken an active part in improving the standards of corporate accounting and reporting. On the whole it has worked closely with the leaders of the accounting profession and has generally supported the far-reaching recommendations of the American Institute of Certified Public Accountants.[18]

---

[18] See "The Independent Accountant and the SEC," by Andrew Barr (Chief Accountant for the SEC) in the *Journal of Accountancy*, October 1959. From a somewhat different standpoint, see the action of the SEC in connection with the Londontown Manufacturing Company case, reported in *Business Week*, May 19, 1962, p. 128.

"The 1935 Act." Regulation of Public Utility Companies. These powers stem from the Public Utility Holding Company Act of 1935. They extend to holding companies and their operating-company subsidiaries. The functions assigned the SEC have been by far the most comprehensive in this area. They were required to terminate the grave abuses associated with the holding companies—by breaking up systems considered by the standards of the law to be harmful and unnecessary, by recapitalizing companies which had excessive amounts of senior securities, and by changing the voting powers where these were inequitably distributed. Supplementing the jurisdiction of local commissions over intrastate operations, the Commission was given wide powers over the financing of the operating subsidiaries within the systems.

The SEC has done a monumental job in discharging its duties under the 1935 Act. By the beginning of 1962 its labors toward geographical integration and corporate simplification were practically at an end. At one time or another between 1938 and 1961 a total of 2,413 companies had been subject to the Act as registered holding companies or subsidiaries thereof. By June 1961, 2,226 of these companies had been released from the regulatory jurisdiction of the Act or had ceased to exist as separate corporate entities. There remain 187 companies, of which 163 are members of 18 active, registered holding-company systems, and 24 are members of 5 small additional systems. The aggregate valuation for the 18 systems was $12 billion at the end of 1960.[19] These systems will remain subject to the 1935 Act and the Commission's jurisdiction.

Security Valuations by the SEC. The process of simplification of holding-company systems has required the elimination of many security issues by repayment in cash or more often by exchange for new securities of the issuing company or its subsidiaries. In many of these cases the SEC has been required to find the value of such securities for the purpose of their proper treatment in a simplification plan, and we thus have numerous opinions of the Commission in which formal principles of valuation are developed and applied to specific utility securities. This work of the SEC constitutes a major contribution to valuation technique. As the reader knows, it is a central thesis of this book that the appraisal technique may be carried over with sound results into the general field of common stocks considered as investments.

To a considerable extent the policy of the SEC in passing upon the fairness of proposed security exchanges has been to match the reasonably expectable earnings of the securities in question. If income to be received was judged compensatory for income to be given up, the standards of fairness were generally considered to be met. This made un-

---

[19] See the 27th Annual Report of the SEC, p. 102.

necessary a formal finding of *value* of the securities involved.[20] There is
a very interesting discussion of this approach in the 25th anniversary
Annual Report of the SEC, pp. xxvi and xxvii. It states in part:

The Commission developed the so-called "investment value" doctrine under
which the claims of security holders are evaluated for purposes of reorganization on a going-concern basis rather than on the liquidation basis followed in
reorganizations in equity receivership and bankruptcy proceedings where the
claims are treated as matured. Under the investment value doctrine, which was
duly sustained by the courts, plans of reorganization were approved which
accorded participation to senior claimants upon the basis of the present worth
of their securities on a going-concern basis, and similarly to junior security
holders on the basis of their secondary claim to future earnings, even though
they would not have had a right to participate if the senior claims were
evaluated upon the basis of their liquidation preferences.

Advisory Opinions under the Bankruptcy Act. Since 1938 the SEC has
played a prominent part in corporate (nonrailroad) reorganizations. These
and related procedures are discussed in suitably condensed form in Appendix Note 9, p. 737. Under the statute, the SEC is called upon to provide
advisory opinions to assist the Federal courts in passing upon the fairness and feasibility of reorganization plans filed in certain Chapter X
proceedings. (Such advisory opinions are mandatory when the liabilities
exceed $3 million, and may be requested by the judge in other cases.)
The role of the Commission in Chapter X proceedings is unique, in that
it involves an obligation without any related powers. However, in the
majority of cases the courts have followed the SEC's recommendations—
both positive and negative—in passing upon the plans. Consequently the
staff has been able to exercise great influence over the actual formulation of reorganization plans; in most instances the trustees "clear" their
plans with the Commission in advance of submission to the court.

Regulation of Investment Companies. The Investment Company Act
of 1940 was devised by extensive conferences between representatives of
the investment-fund industry, the legislators, and the Commission. As a
result, the law gives comparatively little discretionary power to the
Commission, but rather directs it to enforce a number of specific standards and prohibitions spelled out in the various sections.

The scope of the Act is summarized by the SEC as follows:[21]

---

[20] There were, however, some cases where an actual estimation of value was
made and others where valuation techniques were discussed at some length. These
include United Light and Power Company, Holding Company Act Release No. 4215,
Apr. 6, 1943; Portland Electric Power Company, Holding Company Act Release No.
5132, July 5, 1944, also Release No. 6365, Jan. 15, 1946; North American Company
and Its Subsidiary Companies, Holding Company Act Release No. 7514, June 26,
1947; American & Foreign Power Company, Inc., Holding Company Act Release No.
7815, Nov. 5, 1947.

[21] From 15th Annual Report, p. 151.

The Investment Company Act of 1940 requires registration of and regulates investment companies—companies engaged primarily in the business of investing, reinvesting, and trading in securities. Among other things, the act requires disclosure of the finances and investment policies of these companies in order to afford investors full and complete information with respect to their activities; prohibits such companies from changing the nature of their business or their investment policies without the approval of the stockholders; bars persons guilty of security frauds from serving as officers and directors of such companies; regulates the means of custody of the assets of investment companies and requires the bonding of officers and directors having access to such assets; prevents underwriters, investment bankers, and brokers from constituting more than a minority of the directors of such companies; requires management contracts in the first instance to be submitted to security holders for their approval; prohibits transactions between such companies and their officers and directors except on the approval of the Commission; forbids the issuance of senior securities of such companies except in specified instances; and prohibits pyramiding of such companies and cross-ownership of their securities. The Commission is authorized to prepare advisory reports upon plans of reorganizations of registered companies upon request of such companies or twenty-five per cent of their stockholders and to institute proceedings to enjoin such plans if they are grossly unfair. The act also requires face-amount-certificate companies to maintain reserves adequate to meet maturity payments upon their certificates.

In the twenty-odd years since the passage of the 1940 Act the growth of investment funds has been phenomenal. In 1941, 436 companies with total assets of $2.5 billion were registered. By 1961 there were 663 companies—including 44 small business investment companies (SBIC's) —with estimated total assets at market of $29 billion, or more than 11 times their 1941 aggregate.[22] (Under a 1959 Supreme Court ruling, variable annuities are now held to be "investment contracts" subject to the jurisdiction of the SEC under the Securities Act and the Investment Company Act.)[23]

The striking growth in the mutual fund business (investment funds) and in the number of people involved in the administration and sale of these rapidly growing funds has—as in the case of the securities market itself—created problems. There has been some litigation under the Act, and the press has noted particularly the 1959–1960 episode at Managed Funds, Inc., ("the first scandal of any size to hit the mutual funds since the 1930s . . . ").[24] This case, undoubtedly, was one of the factors in SEC's "study" of practices in the mutual fund industry (not completed at

[22] 27th Annual Report, p. 142.

[23] SEC v. Variable Annuity Life Insurance Company of America, et al., 359 U.S. 65 (1959).

[24] See "How Good Are Mutual Funds?" by G. B. Bookman in *Fortune*, June 1960, p. 188. Also "Shaken Trust," a series of two articles in *Barron's*, Apr. 4 and 11, 1960. A principal allegation of misbehavior here consisted of the misuse of brokerage commissions and excessive trading ("churning") to maintain capital distributions.

this writing). The fact remains that mutual funds provide the small investor especially with investment opportunities which otherwise would not be available; moreover the over-all integrity of their management is unquestioned.

Regulation of the Over-the-counter Markets.[25] Under the Maloney Act of 1938 (which added Section 15a to the 1934 Act), the SEC is given police powers and duties with respect to the over-the-counter or unlisted securities markets. It discharges these functions in cooperation with the National Association of Security Dealers (NASD), a body organized by the industry itself for the purpose of prescribing standards of conduct, making trading rules, deciding disputes, and correcting abuses in the over-the-counter markets.[26] A fair amount of day-to-day policing is done by the NASD and the SEC. Unlisted trading is a field which could lend itself readily to the entry of unscrupulous persons and the victimizing of the public were it not for the vigilance shown by these regulatory bodies.[27]

Investment Advisers Act of 1940. The scope of this Act is described by the SEC as follows:

The Investment Advisers Act of 1940 requires the registration of investment advisers, persons engaged for compensation in the business of advising others with respect to securities. The Commission is empowered to deny registration to or revoke registration of such advisers if they have been convicted or enjoined because of misconduct in connection with security transactions or have made false statements in their applications for registration. The act also makes it unlawful for investment advisers to engage in practices which constitute fraud or deceit; requires investment advisers to disclose the nature of their interest in transactions executed for their clients; prohibits profit-sharing arrangements; and in effect, prevents assignment of investment advisory contracts without the client's consent.

A person is not an adviser within the meaning of the Act if, among other things, he has fewer than 15 clients and does not present himself gen-

---

[25] For an outstanding analysis of the over-the-counter market, see Friend, Hoffman, and Winn, *The Over-the-counter Securities Markets*, McGraw-Hill Book Company, Inc., 1958.

[26] In an address before the Practising Law Institute (New York, Jan. 13, 1962) entitled, "Improving Corporate Standards," Joseph L. Weiner, in making "some suggestions for improving investor protection under existing machinery and without additional legislation," proposed that the NASD "should have listing requirements appropriate for its activities just as the exchanges have theirs. They need not be identical but should be designed to achieve an adequate measure of investor protection."

[27] For a favorable appraisal of the operation of the Maloney Act, see the article by H. V. Cherrington, entitled "The National Association of Security Dealers," in the *Harvard Business Review* of November 1949. On the other hand, the *Commercial and Financial Chronicle* has been severely critical of the entire scheme of regulation of the over-the-counter markets.

erally to the public as an investment adviser. In the 1951 edition, on page 630, we added the following comment: "Severe penalties are provided for the violation of the law. However, the powers of the Commission are quite limited in this area, and it may prove advisable to extend them."

Under amendments to the Act effective September 13, 1960, the powers of the SEC have been broadened. Earlier in this chapter we cited the fact that the Commission can now require registered investment advisers to keep prescribed books and records and that it is empowered to inspect them. Among other things, the amendments have provided additional grounds for denying, suspending, or revoking the registration of an adviser.

Trust Indenture Act of 1939. The purpose of this Act was to remedy shortcomings and abuses that had been revealed in the 1930's, growing out of inaction or questionable actions by indenture trustees. The scope of the act is described by the SEC as follows:

The act operates by requiring the inclusion in indentures to be qualified of specified provisions which provide means by which the rights of holders of securities issued under such indentures may be protected and enforced. These provisions relate primarily to the corporate trustee, who must not possess conflicting interest; must not after default, or within 4 months prior thereto, improve his position as a creditor to the detriment of the indenture securities; must make annual and periodic reports to bondholders; must maintain bondholders lists to provide a method of communication between bondholders as to their rights under the indenture and the bonds; and must be authorized to file suits and proofs of claims on behalf of the bondholders. The act outlaws exculpatory clauses used in the past to eliminate the liability of the indenture trustee to his indenture security holders and imposes on the trustee, after default, the duty to exercise the rights and powers vested in it, and to use the same degree of care and skill in their exercise as a prudent man would use in the conduct of his own affairs.

The passage of the Act has been followed by a definite improvement in the performance of the banks and trust companies acting as indenture trustees. Bondholders may now rely upon them for positive action when necessary—which was not true before 1940.

Miscellaneous Activities of the Commission. The SEC engages in a considerable number of activities not described above. The most important of these, in our opinion, relate to the compilation and distribution of various kinds of economic data.

The breadth and variety of the Commission's activities will be evident from a reading of its annual reports. The "anniversary" 25th Annual Report, for fiscal 1959, contains 288 pages, including a large number of statistical tables.

From time to time the Commission's actions have been subject to criticism, but in the aggregate such criticism has been surprisingly limited in view of the wide impact of the Commission's activities on all members of the financial community, who must now operate "as ever in their great Taskmaster's eye." There can be little doubt that the work of the SEC has been well done and has been a benefit to the investing public. If the scope of the investigations now in progress is any indication, it is quite probable that the powers of the Commission will be expanded in certain respects. Some enlargement may be in order. But our legislators must face here, as elsewhere, the basic problems not only of reconciling the principle of liberty with the protection of the public interest but also of weighing the advantages of the objectives sought against the difficulties and costs of attaining them.

CHAPTER FIFTY-TWO

SECURITY ANALYSIS IN ACTION

In this chapter we shall try to illustrate various types of positive conclusions which may be reached by practicing security analysts. We shall draw mainly upon the discussion and examples presented early in this book, our purpose now being to give the reader an orderly and fairly complete view of the end products of security analysis. We shall add a rather long new section on "The Analyst and Selectivity."

Conventional Recommendations. The analyst should be able to make up lists of bonds and preferred stocks meeting the rigorous requirements of stable-income investment. He should reject many issues which sell at full prices but which do not pass his test of safety. These issues are frequently bought, nonetheless, by investors who have confidence in the enterprise and are attracted by their higher-than-standard yields. We think the trained analyst can help the investor by pointing out the logical objections to such securities.

In the field of standard or primary common stocks, the analyst will be called upon to select those which are most attractive at their current prices, and he will usually be asked to recommend "those which are likely to perform best in the future." By intensive study of the various industries and their prospects, and by close familiarity with individual companies and their managements, the expert analyst can undoubtedly reach conclusions of value. To a great extent these are the result of the application not of formal standards to a set of facts and figures, but rather of business judgment and foresight to an intimate knowledge of conditions in the industry and its companies.

Our textbook, long as it is, does not offer much positive assistance to security analysts in this interesting and important part of their work. One cannot be taught how to weigh the future. Our emphasis has, in fact, been in the opposite direction. We have warned the analyst not to trust his projections of the future too far, and especially not to lose sight of the price of the security he is analyzing. No matter how rosy the prospects, the price may still be too high. Conversely, the shares of companies with unpromising outlooks may sell so low that they offer excellent opportunities to the shrewd buyer. Also, the wheel of time brings many changes and reversals. Let us repeat here, from our epigraph, the lines which Horace applied to the works of poets and which our experience tells us are equally applicable to the more prosaic life histories of our business enterprises:

> *Multa renascentur quae iam cecidere, cadentque*
> *Quae nunc sunt in honore.*
> Many shall be restored that now are fallen, and many
> Shall fall that now are in honor.

The Analyst and the Defensive Investor. In the field of standard stocks the analyst can do a simple but highly worthwhile job if he selects for his client a group of issues that are fairly priced and thoroughly representative of our leading American businesses. The great majority of investors, whom we have placed in the "defensive" class, should find a list of that sort well suited to their financial and temperamental requirements. For this major investing group the analyst will perform his best service by keeping them from buying inferior stocks during periods of enthusiasm and high prices. His next service is to induce them to buy their standard issues when the market level is below, rather than above, its indicated long-term normal figure. His third service is to guard the investor from paying extremely high prices for good stocks. The work he is likely to apply himself to with greatest interest is the selection of the most promising issues at the particular time. We shall have a good deal to say about this function of the analyst at the end of the chapter.

Nonconventional Recommendations by the Analyst. When the analyst leaves the safe haven of standard issues and devotes his attention to secondary companies, he usually finds he has two powerful enemies to contend with and one strong ally to help him. His enemies are (1) market psychology and (2) the uncertainties of the future. His essential ally is a low price. We can state it as a positive rule that the analyst should not recommend a secondary stock for investment if it sells at a full price —i.e., unless it is selling at substantially less than indicated by his calculation of the value of the enterprise. This means that when a secondary stock is popular—because of some substantial improvement in its position and prospects—it is practically never a sound purchase for investment. On the contrary, the investor who bought it when it was unpopular and the price was low should now be strongly moved to sell it despite the promising development. This is his chance to cash in on his earlier shrewdness. It should not be missed.

A number of individual instances will occur in which this important principle will seem to work out poorly, because the company will continue to forge ahead and the average price of the future will be much higher than the level at which the analyst counseled the sale. Experience indicates that such occurrences, while very possible, are exceptional and delusive. If they did not happen the market would never go to its extremes. They resemble the cases of large winnings at roulette, without which encouragement there would be no customers for the wheel. Let us repeat here the example we gave in the 1951 edition, page 638, with sequel added.

It would be too easy to supply examples from the past of secondary stocks that rose too far on favorable developments and then found a much lower average level. Let us rather take a current instance, related to one of our former examples, and run the chance of its proving the exception to the rule.

Example: In our 1940 edition (pages 516 to 518), we discussed the then-current exhibit of Intertype Corporation as a typical example of an undervalued security. In March–June 1939 its average price was $8, its net current assets about $20 per share, and its average earnings for 1934–1938 were $0.87 per share. In 1950, Intertype sold at an average price of 36½ and reached a high price of 45. Business had greatly improved, of course, over the indicated levels of the 1930's. The earnings of 1945–1949 had averaged $4 per share and had advanced to $7.81 in 1949. The net current assets were about $30 per share, and the book value was $38. It is clear from the sequel after 1939 that at $8 per share Intertype was undoubtedly a bargain issue. Reasoning of the correlative kind applied to the quite different state of facts in 1950 would mark it as a comparatively risky buy at 40 or more.

Sequel: The stock declined to 25½ in 1952, but following a merger with Harris-Seybold-Potter in 1957, it enjoyed a great advance. (See page 477 above.)

When a security is popular the relationship of its price to indicated value is an entirely different matter than when the same or a similar security is unpopular. This fact may be shown quite vividly by the comparison of Company A and Company B in Table 52-1.

Table 52-1. Comparison of a Popular and an Unpopular Common Stock

	Company *A*	Company *B*
Price of common.........................	35	21½
Number of shares.........................	722,000	1,082,000
Market value of common equity...............	$25,270,000	$23,263,000
Net current assets for common equity..........	4,006,000	37,811,000
Book value of common equity.................	7,095,000	43,555,000
Earned for common stock, current year.........	*555,000(d)*	1,716,000
Earned for common stock, following year........	*3,284,000(d)*	4,411,000

Company *A* is the Boeing Airplane Company, selling at 35 on December 31, 1938. The market was so enthusiastic about its prospects, based on preparations for a European war, that it paid 3½ times the book value in spite of the current year's loss. The next year's loss proved tremendous and cut the equity almost in two. In 1940 the stock sold at 12¾. After the United States entered World War II, the company did a tremendous war job and earned a good deal of money; but despite these developments—certainly not to be anticipated at the end of 1938—the stock never sold higher than 35 in 1941–1949 and averaged far below that figure.

Company *B* is also Boeing Airplane Company, taken exactly ten years later, at the end of 1948. The profits made in 1941–1945, plus about $5 million received from the sale of stock, had increased the equity very greatly. Excellent earnings were to be realized in the next year. Yet the market valued Boeing at about one-half of its asset value and only 60 percent of its working capital. The contrast with the figure of ten years earlier is extraordinary. It illustrates how far the stock market departs from a rational valuation of the securities it deals in, and how prone it is to go to extremes in the direction of optimism and pessimism on the flimsiest of foundations. In a later section of this chapter, on the origin of discrepancies between price and value, we shall give some broader examples which apply to whole fields of securities as they were valued by the market in times of popularity and unpopularity. (The stock of Boeing Company—name changed in 1961—advanced to 56 in 1951, and after several splits, to the equivalent of nearly 400 in 1956.)

Frequency of Opportunities in Secondary Companies. In the longer past the number of such opportunities has constituted a trustworthy guide to the general situation of the stock market. They could be found in relative abundance under most conditions, and were really scarce only in the upper ranges of bull markets, like those which culminated in 1937 and 1946. This very scarcity was a timely indication that the price level of stocks generally had reached dangerous heights. The undervaluations could have been determined either by the use of formal appraisal methods—such as we have developed in previous chapters—or by a simpler comparison between the price on the one hand and the earnings, dividend, and assets on the other. In 1948–1950 investors were offered an unprecedented combination of large earnings plus a large excess of assets over price, often including an excess of working capital over price. Our data in Table 41-5 on Grinnell Corporation in December 1949 (taken from our 1951 edition) described one of many such situations. In the markets of 1960–1961 really "cheap" issues were very few in number and were not without their weaknesses. Instead of the typical secondary issue selling at less than its value to a private owner, we have seen an unprecedented outpouring of new offerings of this kind at prices relatively much higher than those commanded by many first-rate enterprises—e.g., the large integrated oil companies.

Undervalued Senior Securities. Our discussion of senior securities of questionable safety (Chapter 47) pointed out that once a preferred stock or bond is recognized as inadequately protected its price tends to fall to an unduly low level. The reasons are that (1) *investors* consider such issues unsuitable for their needs, and (2) most *speculators,* who are very common-stock-minded, are not interested in this type of commitment. When preferred dividends are unpaid and accumulate over the years, the price tends to decline while the amount of the claim increases. The price often remains low, even though the earning situation has improved, as long as dividends are not resumed. At some stage these issues become definitely undervalued and are appropriate for study and recommendation by the security analyst.

Example: What might be called a classic example of this phenomenon was presented by Cities Service Company First Preferred stock in 1943 and subsequently. The company had passed its preferred dividend in September 1932 and paid nothing until May 1947 except $3 in 1941. Thus by 1947 accumulations amounted to over $84 per share. However, net earnings from 1933 to 1946 inclusive aggregated about $215 million or over $400 per share of first preferred. In 1943 the first preferred stock earned $31 per share, but it sold as low as $37, although its claim was for at least $160 per share including the back dividend. In 1947 the preferred stock was exchanged for $196 per share in 3 percent debentures, due 1977, which originally sold at about 90 percent but in 1950 sold above par.

The example of McCrory Stores $3½ Preferred, which sold below 60 in 1957 and was given on page 605 to illustrate opportunities in convertible issues, exemplifies also the undervaluations of certain well-protected issues which have existed from time to time in most types of markets. Even without its conversion privilege so close to the market, this issue was apparently selling somewhat below its proper investment level in 1957.

Senior securities are sometimes undervalued because their formal contractual arrangements involve complications that alienate the typical investment buyer. This matter is treated below in our discussion of the origin of discrepancies between price and value.

Special Situations. These are the happy hunting grounds for the simon-pure analyst who prefers to deal with the future in terms of specific, measurable developments rather than general anticipations. As the name implies it is a specialized subject which we do not have space to treat adequately in the present revision. The interested reader will find in Appendix Note 48, p. 729, of the 1951 edition the text of an article by Benjamin Graham, entitled "Special Situations," reprinted from the (financial) *Analysts Journal,* fourth quarter, 1946—with sequels added.

DISCREPANCIES BETWEEN PRICE AND VALUE

We have divided the practical work of the analyst into the conventional and the nonconventional. The conventional work relates to the selection of sound senior securities and the choice of primary or representative common stocks. His nonconventional work is in all the other fields. As we see it, he is justified in recommending a nonconventional security only when his conclusion is that it is selling for less than its intrinsic or calculated value. His activities may include the recommendation of the sale of any kind of security selling well above its intrinsic value, *provided* he is asked to give his advice on the basis of investment values rather than expected market action.

It may be well to summarize here the various ways in which discrepancies between price and value originate.

1. Price above Value. *a. General Speculative Enthusiasm—the Typical Bull Market.* The majority of common stocks are overvalued at the height of a typical bull market. The degree of overvaluation varies greatly, however, depending on the degree of speculative emphasis and on accidental factors. Stocks of lowest value are often overvalued proportionately more than others. Their subsequent price decline is that much greater. This fact is illustrated by the figures showing the comparative advance and decline of *Barron's* weekly indexes of low-price stocks during 1938–1946 and 1946–1950, which appear on page 650, Chapter 49. These indexes may be viewed as roughly representing the behavior of stocks of poorer quality, while the Dow-Jones Industrial index would reflect the behavior of stocks of high quality.

b. Specific Enthusiasm or Overbullishness. Many securities sell too high in normal markets. The most important group, we believe, is that of the "blue chips"—the prosperous leaders of industry—whose popularity for many years has given their price level a strong upward bias. Certain industries will attract a tenacious bullishness that gives strange results from the analyst's viewpoint. Let us again reproduce our 1951 text at this point.

Examples: The leading examples are the air-line issues during the past decade. Their prices have been consistently above their net worth, but the earnings record has so far been most disappointing. (In 1947, a very prosperous year for general business, the air-line companies reported large aggregate losses, despite their subsidized mail operations.)

The reader may find it interesting to compare the statistical showing (Table 52-2) of two companies that follow each other on the stock list, as at the end of 1947, viz., Trans World Airlines and Transamerica Corporation (mainly a bank-holding company).

Sequel (added in 1962): TWA had difficulty in avoiding repeated deficits, and the stock closed 1961 at 12. Transamerica Corporation did well, made some large distributions to its stockholders, and closed at 48½ in 1961.

c. Overvaluations within a Company. When a company has senior issues and common stock, and all its securities are of speculative caliber, the common usually sells too high because of the speculator's frequent

Table 52-2. Two Companies Compared in 1947

	Transamerica Corporation	Trans World Airlines
Per share figures:		
Market price, December 1947...	$13	$17
Net-asset value..............	18.59	*2.85(d)*
Earned 1947.................	1.39	*8.19(d)*
Earned 1946.................	1.57	*14.55(d)*
Earned 1945.................	1.86	1.84
Earned 1944.................	1.63	2.82
Earned 1943.................	1.55	2.12
Total figures:		
Net assets for debt and stock....	$230,600,000	$50,000,000
Funded debt.................	46,000,000	52,800,000
Balance for capital stock.......	184,600,000	*2,800,000(d)*
Number of shares outstanding...	9,934,000	986,000

exclusive interest in common stocks and his preference for low-priced issues.

Examples: The prices of the three stock issues of J. I. Case Company at the end of 1961 affords us a current example of this type. The picture appears in Table 52-3.

Table 52-3. J. I. Case Preferred vs. Common in December 1961

Total debt, including current bank loans, Oct. 31, 1961...........	$126,300,000
7 percent Cumulative First Preferred (par $100)*	
93,000 shares at 60..	5,580,000
6½ percent Cumulative Second Preferred (par $7)*	
1,199,000 shares at 3⅛.....................................	3,700,000
Common stock, 2,863,000 shares at 8⅛........................	23,200,000
Net tangible equity for common stock ($2.79 per share)..........	8,000,000
Earned for stock issues, October 1960 and 1961 years combined...	*72,200,000(d)*

* No dividend since October 1960.

Clearly the common is overvalued here in relation both to the price of the two preferreds and the company's financial position. The working out of a similar situation in American & Foreign Power is shown later in this chapter.

These overvaluations within a company are not so much in a class by themselves as they are vivid illustrations of the general tendency for speculators to buy regardless of price. When a senior issue is available for comparison, the fact of overvaluation may often be established almost mathematically.

2. Value above Price. These situations are pretty much the reverse of those cited above. Thus we have

a. General Pessimism. The typical bear market or sometimes a temporary "scare market."

b. Specific Pessimism or Disfavor. It is our thesis that the stocks of companies with disappointing showings usually sell lower than they should, for the same basic reason that stocks as a whole sell too low during periods of depression. The significance of the unfavorable conditions is exaggerated. If this view is correct, the "poorer issues" will normally be undervalued in the market in relation to the better issues, with the possible exception of low-priced stocks as a whole, which attract a special sort of speculative interest. Broadly speaking, this generalization is valid.

Our view is based on the principle that in the majority of cases companies showing an unfavorable trend of earnings will reach a bottom at some time and that thereafter their earnings will fluctuate irregularly around some indicated average or normal base. The market price will usually have fallen well below the value indicated by the latter as well as by the asset-value factors. Consequently there is an undervaluation and a practical opportunity for profitable purchase.

A 1949 Example: At this point in the 1951 edition we gave as a current or recent example the stock of Bond Stores, which had declined from a high of 48 in 1946 to a low of 13 in 1949, accompanied by a shrinkage of earnings from $5.93 to $1.78 per share. Book value was $23.81 at the end of 1949. We added the lines:

Thus the price swung from a large premium above, to a large discount below, net assets. If Bond Stores develops in the future in a typical fashion for a large company of its class, we should see an earning power established sufficient to support the book value. Thus the price levels of 1949 should prove to have offered an investment opportunity.

Sequel: The price did reach 24⅝ in 1959, and so in a technical sense the above recommendation was vindicated. Actually, the subsequent history of Bond Stores was far from impressive when set against the market as a whole. (Current examples are like an investment list; not every issue can be expected to work out brilliantly.)

The reader should be warned that our view of business vicissitudes does not seem to be generally held in Wall Street. There is, indeed, a sector of investment theory which holds quite the contrary. It asserts that once a company or even an industry has started definitely on the downward path, it is likely to lose its earning power completely. The conclusion must be, therefore, that the securities of such a company or industry should be sold regardless of price.

The less extreme version of this theory is that all industries follow a cycle or pattern like that of living things and go through well-defined periods of growth and decay. The shrewd investor recognizes the beginning of the growth period and buys; he later recognizes the onset of the decay period and sells. We think this view has only partial validity, because it fails to recognize the basic factors of *permanence* and *fluctuation,* which characterize nearly all our large industries.[1] It is these fluctuations in operating results and in the market's appraisal of prospects that produce the recurrent overvaluations and undervaluations of practically every class of common stock. As a consequence they generate recurrent opportunities throughout the list to purchase at low levels and to sell at full levels or better.

Clear-cut undervaluations of *leading* common stocks tend to occur only during bear markets. Since 1922 the intervals between successive market bottoms have been much longer than in earlier years, so that this type of opportunity must now be considered infrequent. In the *secondary* field, by contrast, undervaluations may be found at all times except when a bull market is well advanced. Thus the investor or analyst who is strongly interested in the undervaluation approach will find what he is looking for, more continuously or consistently, among the secondary issues.

c. The Factor of Unfamiliarity or Neglect. Undervaluation may often be explained in part by the public's unfamiliarity with the issue. It is assumed that if the stock were better known it would sell higher. We are inclined to believe that neglect of an issue almost always implies some lack of confidence about its future. For a company of any size at all, there are enough people interested in its affairs to create a buying interest in the shares *if they have the requisite confidence in its future.* It is because this confidence is lacking that the stock remains definitely undervalued.

Our viewpoint is supported by the price behavior of these secondary issues both during bull markets and when some unusually favorable development is taking place in the company's position. At such times sufficient interest develops in this type of concern to create a fair degree of market activity at rising prices. In a typical case the stimulus comes from the groups familiar with the company's operations, and it may be communicated rapidly to the public by brokerage houses and financial services which are attracted to the issue for a transitory period. In this way the undervaluation is ended and in fact may give way to overvaluation. In many cases, perhaps most, the enthusiasm passes with the condition that engendered it; the stock relapses to its normal state of relative disfavor and neglect; and the cycle has begun again. Thus the factor of "unfamiliarity" as a cause of unduly low prices is likely to be a mask for the lack of popular appeal which characterizes the average secondary company during large portions of the market's ups and downs. The reader should note that the vast majority of secondary common stocks sold at

---

[1] The actual abandonment and disappearance of a large enterprise is comparatively rare. True, the names of many companies have disappeared from the Stock Exchange list; but over 90 percent of these either have changed their title or have been taken over in a purchase or merger deal by some other concern.

full or excessive prices in 1946, especially in relation to their past achievements. The same was broadly true of new offerings in 1960–1962.

d. The Factor of "Complications." When a security is subject to a serious corporate or legal complication, it is likely to sell for less than its value. This statement embraces the broad field of special situations referred to earlier in this chapter. Both the investing public and the speculative public shy away from all types of long-drawn-out litigation or corporate readjustments. This is true to such an extent that a suit intended to get *better* treatment for a security in a readjustment plan will usually put its price *down,* merely because it adds the factor of uncertainty and long delay.

A 1949 Example: South Western Railroad Common. A plan proposed by Central of Georgia Railway would have given this stock new securities which, with an expected cash distribution, would have created a value of about $65 per share at the end of 1949. A substantial group of minority stockholders opposed the plan vigorously, on the basic ground that the stock should receive considerably more. Because of this opposition and the resultant uncertainty, the current price of the stock at the end of 1949 was about $40.

Sequel: In 1953 most stockholders sold their shares at $75 to Central of Georgia Railway.

The presence of a large accumulated dividend on a preferred issue is a complication which generally depresses the market value of the enterprise as a whole. However, in somewhat exceptional cases it operates as a bullish factor and therefore may even create overvaluation. This happens when speculative interest is aroused by indications that a plan will soon be forthcoming to clear up the arrearages. The market price of the common may then advance disproportionately to its true value, merely because some "favorable development" is deemed imminent.

In Chapter 47 we gave as an example of this situation the behavior of Crystal Oil Refining Preferred and common in 1951 and mentioned that American Zinc Preferred in 1928 presented a similar situation.

These cases may serve to illustrate further our thesis that it is possible to generate speculative interest in almost any type of security if some plausible basis can be found for it, and particularly if some initial effort is made by interested parties. Under favoring conditions the speculative fervor will feed on itself, so as ultimately to transform an unpopular and undervalued issue to one that is temporarily quite active and definitely overvalued.

A Companion Error Made by the Investment Fraternity. The pendulum swings of speculative feelings are motivated as much by eagerness for quick profits as they are by ignorance and by a lack of interest in the fundamentals of security values. Investors are not as greedy as speculators, but they often display a similar lack of poise and penetration. We can illustrate what may unfortunately be called the standard psychology of investors as a class by two broad examples taken from the field of real estate mortgage bonds and railroad bonds.

In the 1920's real estate mortgage bonds were considered a prime form of investment; they were recommended by investment advisers and bought by trustees of estates. Billions of dollars worth were placed at their issue price of about par. Little attention was paid to the fact that nearly all these bonds were woefully deficient in the margin of safety required to justify an investment with a limited return.

In the early 1930's the debacle came, and a large portion of these bonds defaulted. The price fell to as low as 20 cents on the dollar or even less. At that time they were considered risky speculations and were avoided by investors and their advisers. However, the security behind these bonds was now more than adequate to cover them *at their low price*, just as it had been deficient in relation to the high issue price. Shrewd buyers, who were guided by values rather than popularity factors, were thus able to acquire these issues at quotations that were sure to return them a handsome profit as the situations worked themselves out.

A similar history has been recorded by the bonds of the weaker railroads. During relatively good years they sold at full prices—i.e., at about par—and they were bought and held by the large financial institutions. When adverse conditions brought on financial troubles, their prices fell to extremely low levels. At that time most of the financial institutions, under pressure from banking and insurance authorities, sold their holdings for whatever they would bring. They were bought by really intelligent investors, who realized that the market decline had been largely overdone and whose judgment was handsomely vindicated by later events.[2]

"Unsuitability" as a Type of Complication. A basic cause of persistent undervaluation is a corporate form or security form not suited to the needs or preferences of some major class of security buyers. Unsuitable corporate setups, under present conditions, include the following:

1. Holding companies in the stock-market sense of owning large interests in one or more separate enterprises
2. Companies with a large part of their resources in cash or low-yielding investments
3. Companies combining disparate forms of activities
4. Closed-end investment funds
5. Companies of the all-common-stock type, in an enterprise where a substantial amount of senior capital is needed to create an adequate earning power for the common

In previous chapters we have pointed out the disadvantages to the stockholders of most of the above. In some of them the cause of their un-

---

[2] We have been told of an insurance company financial executive who remarked when he reluctantly placed an order to sell some railroad bonds at 30 that his company would doubtlessly buy them back when the price returned to par.

suitability may be viewed in the nature of a "complication" which militates against their acceptance by the typical investor.

Complicated security forms usually operate in the same way as corporate complications, i.e., to prevent the establishment of fair value in the market under ordinary conditions. An example of such a complication is the combination of a fixed-interest and a contingent-interest provision in the same bond issue. There is no clear-cut class of buyer for such a mixture. The adverse effect of such an arrangement—which has become by no means uncommon—is shown by the following calculation applied to Chicago, Terre Haute & South Eastern Income $2\frac{3}{4}$–$4\frac{1}{4}$s, due 1994, which sold at 66 in October 1949 and at 54 in December 1961.

These bonds are obligations of the "Milwaukee Railroad," i.e., the Chicago, Milwaukee, St. Paul and Pacific. They came through the trusteeship and reorganization with relatively favorable treatment, and evidently cover mileage of strategic value. They receive fixed interest of $2\frac{3}{4}$ percent, ranking equally in this regard with the Milwaukee First 4s, due 1994. They are further entitled to contingent interest of $1\frac{1}{2}$ percent, ranking equally with the Milwaukee General income $4\frac{1}{2}$s, Series A. It may be assumed that intrinsically the Terre Haute issue is worth as much, per dollar of interest income, as the two Milwaukee issues with which it ranks on a parity. Thus the Terre Haute issue has a value equal to $2\frac{75}{400}$ or $1\frac{1}{16}$ the price of the Milwaukee First 4s plus $\frac{1}{3}$ the price of the Milwaukee Income $4\frac{1}{2}$s. The relationship between such value and the price in 1949 and 1961 is worked out in Table 52-4.

Table 52-4. Value vs. Price of Chicago, Terre Haute & South Eastern Income $2\frac{3}{4}$–$4\frac{1}{2}$s in 1949 and 1961

	October 1949		December 1961	
	Price of Milwaukee issue	Equivalent for Terre Haute issue	Price of Milwaukee issue	Equivalent for Terre Haute issue
Fixed-interest component: Chicago, Milwaukee, St. Paul & Pacific first 4s............	98	67.5	76	$52\frac{1}{4}$
Contingent-interest component: Chicago, Milwaukee, St. Paul & Pacific Income $4\frac{1}{2}$s.....	56	18.7	60	20
Equivalent value of Terre Haute issue......................	...	86.2	...	$72\frac{1}{4}$
Current price of Terre Haute issue......................	...	66	...	$54\frac{1}{2}$

A striking point in this calculation is that the Terre Haute issue was selling in 1949 for slightly less than the value of its fixed-interest component alone, and that thus the substantial contingent-interest right was ostensibly given no value. (In 1961 and most of the years between, the case was not very different.) In our view the discrepancy is caused by the unsuitable security form involved in combining fixed and contingent components of interest. For the security analyst, however, the substantial undervaluation of the issue affords a sound basis for recommending it to alert bond investors. Most such discrepancies are corrected with the passage of time. It is extraordinary, we think, that this one has persisted for so many years. That fact underlines the undesirable quality of a mixed security.

Recurrent Value-Price Discrepancies. The example presented here in 1951 is worth retaining. In Table 52-5 we give the prices of the various

Table 52-5. American & Foreign Power Company, Inc.

(Dollar and share figures in thousands)

Item	5% Debentures	$7 1st Preferred	$6 1st Preferred	$7 2d Preferred	Common	Warrants
Outstanding*	$50,000	480	387	2,655	1,850	6,874
High price 1930	90½	111½	101	100¾	101¾	76⅛
Market value	$45,200	$53,500	$39,100	$267,500	$188,200	$523,200
Low price 1932	15¼	5	3¾	2¾	2	1⅛
Market value	$ 7,600	$ 2,400	$ 1,500	$ 7,300	$ 3,700	$ 7,700
High price 1937	87¼	68⅞	58⅞	38½	13¾	4½
Market value	$43,600	$33,100	$22,800	$102,200	$ 25,400	$ 30,900
Dec. 31, 1949 price	92	65	55⅞	16¼	2⅝	⅜
Market value	$46,000	$31,200	$21,600	$ 43,100	$ 4,800	$ 2,600

* Outstanding amounts show par value of bonds and number of shares or warrants. Compiled from 1949 figures, but roughly constant throughout the period.

securities of American & Foreign Power Company for certain dates between 1930 and 1949, together with the aggregate market values represented by such prices. The picture is extraordinary from two points of view. The first is that of the vicissitudes of the general market, reflected by the wide swings in price for each of the six security issues quoted. The second is the recurrence of illogical relationships among the various issues. The first point needs no elaboration; we shall discuss the second in summary fashion.

At the low point in 1932 the *warrants* could hardly be assigned any intrinsic value in view of the fact that the first and second preferred shares were selling for 5 cents on the dollar and less. Nevertheless, the warrants had an ostensible aggregate *market* value of $7.7 million, which exceeded that of either the first or second preferred issues. In the recovery of 1937 the junior issues were still clearly overvalued in relation to the seniors.

In 1947 the SEC approved a reorganization plan which provided for repayment of the 5 percent debentures at 102½; for exchanging the first preferred issues for new debentures and most of the new common stock; for giving the second preferred under $6 per share in new common (valued at $15); for giving the common 30 cents per share on the same basis; and for wiping out the warrants. The plan was approved by the United States District Court; but financing difficulties, tied in with frozen foreign exchange, compelled the company to withdraw the plan.

It might have been expected that this untoward development would have reduced the value of the junior issues in relation to the first preferred shares, since in theory the brunt of adversity should fall on the juniors. Instead, it permitted speculators to put up the price of the second preferred and even the common—apparently on the theory that some favorable "break" was possible in working out a new recapitalization plan. Conversely, the price of the first preferred issues fell far below the values assigned to them in the SEC-approved plan, because the people interested in that type of security were worried about the delays and difficulties involved in formulating a new proposal.

The result was that at the end of 1949 the first preferred issues were selling at only 45 percent of the values assigned them in the reorganization plan, while the second preferred was selling at nearly three times such value. We consider this a prime demonstration that Wall Street thinking can just as easily be completely irrational as not.[3]

A minor but astonishing detail in the American & Foreign Power situation is the fact that over 25 percent of the publicly owned second preferred stock was converted into common, by exercising the warrant privilege, between 1932 and 1949. During all this time dividends were accumulating on the preferred shares, so that their exchange for common was about as ridiculous as giving a dollar bill for four pennies. However, the *market-price* relationships of the second preferred, the common, and the warrants were such as to make this Alice-in-Wonderland exchange a profitable arbitrage.[4]

[3] One of the financial services recommended the second preferred stock at 17½ in January 1950, on the ground that it "appeared to offer good possibilities for trading profits, based on the generally improved position of the company." This was said although the service expected any new plan to be about the same as the old plan, and the preceding analysis showed that the second preferred was selling much too high in relation to the first preferred issues in terms of what they were to get under the 1947 plan.

The second preferred did advance to 25¼ not long after this recommendation, but it relapsed to 15 shortly before publication of the revised plan at the beginning of 1951. Evidently stock trading and stock investing are two very different activities.

[4] Each share of second preferred accompanied by four warrants could be exchanged for four shares of common stock.

Sequel: The plan was consummated on about the above-stated terms in 1952, and the absurd price discrepancies perforce disappeared.

Let us return here to a subject broached in the early pages of this chapter. Few analysts are satisfied with the limited and unimaginative role of making up a representative portfolio of standard-type common stocks. Nearly all feel that their training, skill, and labor should be devoted to the selection of the most promising issues, whether of primary or secondary classification. In administering the capital of an investment fund, the standard approach consists of allocating the equity money to a number of industries, excluding those deemed basically unattractive, and dividing the holdings among the chosen industries in some proportion to their relative quality and prospects. It is customary to follow a fairly rigid policy which limits the percentage placed in one industry or a single issue and requires a certain minimum number of industries to be represented in the portfolio. To a large degree the stockholdings of a substantial individual investor (including trust accounts) are selected by or for him in accordance with this general policy, though the number of issues held is likely to be much lower than for a typical mutual fund.

The analyst therefore endeavors to rank industries in proportion to their attractiveness vis-à-vis the others, and individual companies in similar proportion to their attractiveness within their industry group. The choices made by these procedures reflect the concept of *selectivity*, which has become the watchword and battle cry of Wall Street. As we have remarked before, some senior analysts now seem to believe that they can do such a good job of selecting the best industries and issues that they can ensure successful investment regardless of the fluctuations of the general market.

Selectivity Procedures. A good part of comparative analysis must necessarily rest on past and current performance. Most of the detailed treatments in this book have been devoted to methods of analyzing past results, including modification of nonrepresentative figures, and the application of various ratios and other tests to aid in their evaluation. We have repeatedly warned the student, however, that this paper-and-pencil work, however essential to a complete analysis, is far from sufficient to establish dependable conclusions as to value in the future. For this, extra ingredients are needed. They almost always include a knowledge in depth of the factors affecting the company's volume, price received, and costs; usually, also, a full acquaintanceship with the technological opportunities (and hazards) residing in the company's sphere of operations; often knowledge of nonpublished but available information as to the company's plans for the future; finally, the judgment to decide well whether the management has the capability to carry out such plans, and whether the surrounding conditions will be propitious or unfavorable. These are comprehensive and difficult requirements for the senior analyst. He will not master them by reading our book; much of the most valuable skills he must acquire for himself, through a combination of ability and experience.

A CASE STUDY OF THE PAST-PERFORMANCE FACTOR

In Chapter 19 we gave an outline of a comprehensive study of the chemical industry, and added a comparative analysis of seven individual company results. At the end of that chapter we raised some questions, which we left to be answered at this distant point.

First Question: What definite conclusions as to investment choices can properly be drawn from this study?

With regard to the chemical industry as a whole, we found a mixture of favorable and unfavorable factors. The industry was not especially profitable in terms of rate of return, nor did it enjoy better than average stability; but it had shown the ability to grow more rapidly than the economy as a whole and to maintain a good (though recently declining) return on its enlarged capital. This study did not show convincing reasons why a dollar of earnings of the chemical industry should be valued at the high ruling premium over earnings dollars as a whole. If the analyst had been guided in his decisions by this study, he would probably have recommended some reduction in the relative percentage (of a good-sized portfolio) invested in chemical stocks.

A Rating System for Comparative Analysis. To evaluate the relative performance of the individual companies in the samples shown in our Tables 19-5 to 19-9, the analyst would need to follow some rating scheme or system. A simple one would be to rank the companies from 1 to 7 in each of the comparative tests, and then to determine their overall rank by addition. Some details of this operation appear now in Table 52-6. It will be noted that du Pont ranked far above its nearest rivals, which were Hercules, followed closely by American Cyanamid and Union Carbide. Monsanto and Allied ranked sixth and seventh. In terms of price-earnings ratios—ranked in reverse to show "cheapness"—Cyanamid came first, du Pont (including its General Motors component) fifth, and Dow Chemical last.

Had the analyst sought to make a provisional choice from these comparisons, he would have been compelled to decide what weight to give past performance on the one hand[5] and cost of the stock (price-earnings ratio) on the other. If equal weight were given to both factors—a simple and plausible concept—then the composite rating would place

---

[5] Many analysts consider the relative *price* advance over a given period as a positive factor in the "past performance." We are unable to convince ourselves that this test has value for security analysis.

American Cyanamid in first position, closely followed by Hercules, and then du Pont. Lowest rating would go to Dow, next lowest to Allied.

If the analyst were to base his recommendations solely on this study, as evaluated above—a course we are far from suggesting—he would probably have advised buying American Cyanamid and Hercules and selling Allied and Dow.

Second Question: How would the recommendations have fared in regard to earnings and price to the end of 1961?

As to the chemical sample as a whole, its per-share earnings rose 11.2 percent (taking one share of each company) from 1957 to 1961, while those of Standard & Poor's 425 Industrials declined about 3 percent. However, the price picture was somewhat different. The Standard & Poor gain was 57 percent; the average gain of the seven chemicals was 46 percent. More important, excluding the phenomenal advance of 167 percent of Hercules, the average gain was only 26 percent, and none of the others equaled the Standard & Poor figure. (The gain of the Standard & Poor's Chemical Stock Index, comprising 12 issues, was 24 percent.)

It would seem that the study's intimation that the chemical stocks looked too high as against the general market was supported by the ensuing market action. That this happened despite a better earnings gain for the chemicals should not be too surprising, since the higher-than-average price-earnings ratio presupposed a superior earnings performance in the following years.

The choice of two individual issues—on the basis of statistical showing combined with "cheapness"—would have produced anomalous results. The second choice had the best gain in earnings and an extraordinary price advance; the first had a slight loss in both earnings and price. The average of the two would have outperformed the market; but such an "average" has little evidential value. The two stocks "sold" did somewhat worse than the sample average in earnings gain and in market gain.

Had the two "best" stocks been selected solely on the basis of corporate record, without regard to price, they would have been du Pont and Hercules, and their average price gain would have been 100 percent. Had the choice been made solely on the basis of market multipliers, without regard to indicated quality, first place would have gone to American Cyanamid, and second would have been divided between Hercules and Monsanto. The average price gain for this 50-25-25 percent package would have been 50 percent.

Third Question: What inferences may be drawn from the above as to the practical utility of security analysis?

In respect to the conclusions re the chemical industry as a whole and the sequel, we should claim—modestly enough—that they had sufficient value to justify their cost in time or money. As for the in-

Table 52-6. Seven Chemical Stocks Ranked by Various Criteria

	Allied	American Cyanamid	Dow	duPont	Hercules	Monsanto	Union Carbide
1. Post-war sales growth (Table 19-5)	7	4	1	5	6	2	3
2. Return on capital, 1957 (Table 19-6)	6½	3½	5	1	2	6½	3½
3. Return on capital, 1953–1957 (Table 19-6)	6½	4	5	1	2	6½	3
4. Return on capital, 1953–1957, before depreciation (Table 19-7)	7	5	3	1	2	6	4
5. Earnings margin, 1957 (Table 19-8)	6½	3	4	1	5	6½	2
6. Earnings margin, 1953–1957 (Table 19-8)	5	4	3	1	7	6	2
7. Capital turnover, 1957 (Table 19-8)	5½	3	7	2	1	5½	4
8. Capital turnover, 1953–1957 (Table 19-8)	6	3	7	2	1	4	5
9. Increase in earnings per share, 1953–1957 vs. 1947–1951 (Table 19-9)	7	3	2	1	4	6	5
10. Increase in earnings, 1957 vs. 1947–1951 (Table 19-9)	7	2	4	1	3	6	5
11. Total of 10 rankings	64	34½	41	16	33	55	36½
12. Rank on basis of total	7	3	5	1	2	6	4
13. Comparative P/E ratio	4	1	7	5*	2½	2½	6
14. Rank on performance and P/E ratio combined	6	1	7	3	2	4	5
15. Gain in earnings, 1961 vs. 1957	5	7	2	6*	1	3	4
16. Gain in price, Dec. 1961 vs. 1957 average	3½	7	5	3½	1	2	6

* Including General Motors component.

dividual choices, we have already short-circuited the reply to the question by insisting that *in general,* recommendations to buy or sell must not be based solely on past-performance analysis. (We go further in suggesting that advice to exchange from one common stock into another must not only be based on a full analysis, comprising both quantitative and qualitative factors, but must also show a substantial margin in value —say one-third—in favor of the issue recommended.) Only in the exceptional case of bargain issues may one be justified in buying merely on a combined assets-and-earnings basis, as is shown by the analyzed figures; but even here diversification is essential to assure a good over-all result. (Perhaps this basis of purchase constitutes the best *definition* of a bargain issue.)

The remarkably good performance of one of the issues favored by the chemical comparison and the unsatisfactory results from the other point up in salutary fashion the ordinarily preponderant influence of future developments not foreshadowed in the past figures. The reader will note a fairly good correlation between the relative rank in earnings gain from 1957 to 1961 and that in price advance. To the extent that conclusions may be drawn from this limited study it would indicate that the largest single factor governing subsequent price behavior within an industry will be the subsequent earnings performance. This is no new discovery.

Selectivity Based on Intensive Study. What can the average analyst achieve by extending his work from the mere figures to a searching study of the company's management, program, and prospects? We have thought long and hard on this problem, and our answer may be something of a shocker. We think that at bottom the analyst's comparative results—i.e., how his recommendations fare as against the market averages—will depend largely on his competition. The more skillful analysts there are, the harder it will be for the average practitioner to "beat the averages." The superior man will do it; otherwise he would not be called superior.

The real accomplishment of the many thousand analysts now studying not so many thousand companies is the establishment of proper relative prices in today's market for most of the leading issues and a great many secondary ones.[6] (New offerings of the "hot-issue" type are excluded here, as well as others in which greed and undisciplined speculation are the dominant price-making influences.)

This is worthwhile work from the standpoint of the public interest, and it justifies our profession's existence. But insofar as stock prices are relatively "right" on the basis of known and foreseeable facts, the oppor-

---

[6] To the extent that "fantasy" has become a pervasive and controlling element in determining the price level of whole groups of stocks—mainly the "technological" issues—as has been claimed by prominent analyst Walter Gutman, our thesis will not hold.

tunities for consistently above-average results must necessarily diminish. It is largely the combined work of all analysts which creates the general market performance that each analyst aims to beat.

The analogy that comes to mind here is that of a tennis or a duplicate-bridge tournament. Let us take the second. If the players consisted mainly of average enthusiasts, plus a relatively few bridge experts, the latter would be sure to run off quite consistently with the top scores. But if all players had already won "master points," then only the very best would end up on top, and even some highly skilled practitioners would rank near the very bottom. (Were they playing for money, the latter experts would be heavy losers.) In some cases the relative standing would depend on some lucky guesses as to how the cards were divided. We think a like situation has been developing in Wall Street. The bulk of investment-type purchases—e.g., those of the mutual funds—are made on the basis of careful studies by trained analysts. Although all are seeking much the same objectives and nearly all follow the same general methods, there is considerable variation in the issues selected. These differences show that for analysts a basic difficulty is that relative market prices already reflect pretty well those facts and expectations on which nearly all analysts would agree. Each actual choice will therefore be dictated by considerations which are not so valid for analysts as a group. They may reflect a special interest or familiarity, but for the most part they are the outcome of different judgment weights given by different analysts to factors bearing on future earnings. If one chooses Company A rather than Company B, and the other does the reverse, the relative results achieved by these individual choices is likely to depend more on the "breaks" of the future than on true insight.

The superior analyst will have a combination made up from the following advantages: (1) high innate ability (perhaps aided by the best training); (2) a predilection for hard work; and (3) an independent mind. His ability will show itself mainly in his good judgment and in a certain flair for quickly identifying the key points in a corporate or security situation. (The French call the latter the *coup d'oeil.*) The superior man or woman is likely to select certain approaches to analysis or certain areas in the common-stock field which are best suited to his special temperament or skills. The majority will probably emphasize the twin elements of managerial capacity and company prospects. In those areas they will be competing with most of their fellow analysts, but they will show the best over-all results. Some will devote themselves chiefly to science and technology—today a controlling element in the fortunes of numerous enterprises. Others—definitely a minority— will interest themselves mainly in undervalued securities of the statistical type. Their work will depend on a thorough search of the list, on reasonable assurance against corporate disaster in each security selected, and on wide diversification. Finally, many will subordinate their security analysis to market analysis, and rely chiefly on their interpretation of past price movements by one or another system. It would be unfair to read the latter group out of our party, but we suspect that the really good market analysts would not have to bother with security analysis.

Effect of the 1949–1961 Market on Security Analysis.[7] The previous part of this discussion compares the results that security analysts may achieve by means of selectivity with those registered by the market averages.[8] In our former editions we stated the view that competent security analysis could identify levels of the general market that were dangerously high as well as those that were appealingly low. A general investment policy based on buying in the low markets and selling out—at least partially—in the high ones would thus prove both feasible and profitable. The persistent market strength since 1949, punctuated only by three setbacks of less than 20 percent each, has called this viewpoint into serious question. Even if analysts had been able to come fairly close to locating the turning points in the last three minor cycles, it is doubtful if much of value could have been realized by sales at some distance below the highs and purchases safely above the lows, with payment of capital-gains tax based on the original low cost. There was a near-fatal risk of miscalculating the extent of the decline and thus missing the chance to buy back.

In consequence, the great majority of analysts have admittedly or unconsciously renounced all pretension to identifying a selling level for stocks generally. Most say there is no need to do this, since (good) selectivity will protect adequately against future market declines. Some investment funds have adopted the policy of virtual 100 percent investment in common stocks at all times, leaving to their stockholders the decision to withdraw from equities by turning in their shares.

This "full-investment" policy has been eminently successful for thirteen years—a span long enough to make it appear the correct one not only for the past but for the indefinite future. But there is at least the possibility that the opposite may be true, and that the very length of our only briefly interrupted market rise will make it ultimately more vulnerable to a serious decline. Is it not true that the longer the inevitable is postponed the more inevitable it becomes—and the less expected? If there is any validity in the conclusions reached by our painful en-

---

[7] This section was written before the market break of May 1962 and has been left unchanged.

[8] We assume that a comparatively simple process of diversification can bring results similar to those of a 30-stock or 500-stock average. Wall Street men often claim that the uncounseled investor-speculator cannot "buy the averages," and usually fares far worse than they do. Hence it is both an achievement and a service to the public, for, say, a mutual fund to net results for its rank-and-file shareholders about equal to that of Standard & Poor's 500 Composite. We agree that this is a real service to the public, but we find it difficult to regard it as an achievement by security analysis.

deavors to evaluate the market averages at the beginning of 1962 (in Chapter 31), then there is equal validity in the fear that market excesses on the upside will some day be succeeded by corresponding excesses on the downside.[9] We belong to the perhaps ridiculously old-fashioned and stubborn minority which holds that this fear has at least an even chance of being justified.

Hence we feel that ordinary prudence and common sense should prompt the countless people who have already done quite well from the market's advance to place themselves in an invulnerable position by dividing their funds in some appropriate way between equities and tax-free bonds.

By the nature of their business and professional activities it is scarcely practicable for the majority of security analysts to take an alarmist position on a market that has confounded the alarmists for so many years. After the ultraconservative has finally given up crying "Wolf! Wolf!", the cry is not likely to be taken up by those who for over a decade have found the key to success in a "constructive and selective" attitude. This whole discussion may be summed up in the simple statement that if there is to be a real bear market some day, it will come—as all have come in the past—without being forecast by the financial community.

---

[9] This is not really a "law of the stock market" though it used to be propounded as such. The amount of the "excesses" on either side is largely determined ex post facto by taking the midpoint of the swing as "normal."

CHAPTER FIFTY-THREE

MARKET ANALYSIS AND SECURITY ANALYSIS

Forecasting security prices is not properly a part of security analysis. However, the two activities are generally thought to be closely allied, and they are frequently carried on by the same individuals and organizations. Endeavors to predict the course of prices have a variety of objectives and a still greater variety of techniques. Many analysts lay considerable emphasis upon the science, or art, or pastime, of prophesying the *immediate* action of the "general market," which is fairly represented by the various averages used in the financial press. Some of the services or experts desire to ignore day-to-day fluctuations and confine their aim to predicting the broader "swings" covering a period of, say, several months. A great deal of attention is given also to prophesying the market action of individual issues, as distinct from the market as a whole.

Market Analysis as a Substitute for or Adjunct to Security Analysis. Assuming that these activities are carried on with sufficient seriousness to represent more than mere guesses, we may refer to all or any attempts to predict security prices by the designation of "market analysis."

In this chapter we wish to examine the extent to which market analysis may seriously be considered a substitute for or a supplement to security analysis. The question is important. If, as many believe, we can dependably foretell the movements of stock prices without any reference to the underlying values, then it would be sensible to confine security analysis to the selection of fixed-income investments only. For when we are dealing with the common-stock type of issue, we should manifestly find it more profitable to master the technique of determining when to buy or sell, or of selecting the issues that are going to have the greatest or quickest advance, than to devote painstaking efforts to forming conclusions about intrinsic value. Many other people believe that the best results can be obtained by an analysis of the market position of a stock in conjunction with an analysis of its intrinsic value. If this is so, the security analyst who ventures outside the fixed-income field must qualify as a market analyst as well and be prepared to view each situation from both standpoints at the same time.

Our Adverse Position. In taking the stand that security analysts should not concern themselves with forecasting market movements, we enter upon highly controversial ground. To defend our viewpoint completely, it would be necessary to consider in comprehensive fashion the theories and techniques underlying all the major methods of stock-market analysis. For various reasons, including considerations of space, we shall confine ourselves to considering the broader lines of reasoning that are involved in the major premises of price forecasting. Even with this limited treatment it should be possible to reach some useful conclusions on the perplexing question of the relationship between market analysis and security analysis.

This relationship has some similarity to that between medicine and psychology. In recent years the psychosomatic element in illness has been emphasized to such an extent that most doctors apparently have to be psychologists. In the security field a like situation has obtained almost from the beginning. Security analysts have felt the need to gauge the psychology or "technical position" of the stock market and to base their buying and selling recommendations on a combined consideration of underlying value *and* prospective market movement.

We should like to see security analysis take a course opposite to the recent tendency in medicine and move toward divorcing itself from its ingrained preoccupation with the *short-term* behavior of the stock market. Long-term market considerations interest the investor, of course, because they are fundamentally identical with long-term value considerations.

Two Kinds of Market Analysis. A distinction may be made between two kinds of market analysis. The first finds the material for its predictions exclusively in the past action of the stock market. The second considers all sorts of economic factors, e.g., business conditions, general and specific; money rates; the political outlook. (The market's behavior is itself only one of these numerous elements of study.) The underlying theory of the first approach may be summed up in the declaration that "the market is its own best forecaster." The behavior of the market is generally studied by means of charts on which are plotted the movements of individual stocks or of "averages."

Those who devote themselves primarily to a study of these price movements are known as "chartists," and their procedure is often called "chart reading." (*Fortune* magazine has published two broad review articles on technical analysis which will be most helpful reading for the student.)[1]

But it must be pointed out that much present-day market analysis represents a combination of the two kinds described, in the sense that while the market's action alone is of predominant importance, it does not constitute the exclusive field of study. General economic indications play

[1] D. Seligman, "Playing the Market with Charts," *Fortune*, February 1962, and "The Mystique of Point-and-Figure," in the March issue.

a subordinate but still significant role.[2] Considerable latitude is therefore left for individual judgment, not only in interpreting the technical indications of the market's action but also in reconciling such indications with outside factors. The "Dow theory," however, which is the best-known method of market analysis, limits itself essentially to a study of the market's behavior. Hence we feel justified in dealing separately with chart reading as applied exclusively to stock prices. Moreover, there are purists who are not only uninterested in reports of sales, earnings, and dividends, but who feel that such information would interfere with the interpretation of their charts. Apparently some go to considerable length to avoid these external disturbances.[3]

Implication of the First Type of Market Analysis. It must be recognized that the vogue of such "technical study" has increased immensely during the past few decades. The growth has been particularly marked in recent years. In fact, one writer has gone so far as to say, "All over the U.S. tens of thousands of chartists are peering at their charts. . . . "[4] Many skeptics, it is true, are inclined to dismiss the whole procedure as akin to astrology or necromancy; but the sheer weight of its importance in Wall Street requires that its pretensions be examined with some degree of care. In order to confine our discussion within the framework of logical reasoning, we shall purposely omit a comprehensive summary of the main tenets of chart reading.[5] We wish to consider only the implications of the general idea that a study confined to past price movements can be availed of profitably to foretell the movements of the future.

Such consideration, we believe, should lead to the following conclusions:

1. Chart reading cannot possibly be a science.
2. It has not proved itself in the past to be a dependable method of making profits in the stock market, at least not one available to the general public.
3. Its theoretical basis rests upon faulty logic or else upon mere assertion.
4. Its vogue is due to certain advantages it possesses over haphazard speculation, but these advantages tend to diminish as the number of chart students increases.

[2] Seligman (p. 180 of the March 1962 *Fortune*) holds that many chartists "are students of the fundamentals too, and it is often hard to say on which grounds they are basing their recommendations."

[3] The *New Yorker*, in one of its profiles entitled "Onward and Upward with the Arts: Charting of Stocks," June 23, 1956, stated that one well-known chartist boarded up the window in his office to assist in eliminating outside influences.

[4] See Seligman's comment on p. 118 of the February 1962 issue of *Fortune*.

[5] For detailed statements concerning the theory and practice of chart reading the student is referred to Edwards and Magee, *Technical Analysis of Stock Trends*, 4th ed., published by John Magee, Springfield, Mass., and J. E. Granville, *A Strategy of Daily Stock Market Timing for Maximum Profit*, Prentice-Hall, Inc., Englewood Cliffs, N.J., 1960. See Appendix Note 13, p. 743, for a brief statement of the main tenets of the Dow theory.

1. *Chart Reading Not a Science.* That chart reading cannot be a science is clearly demonstrable.[6] If it were a science, its conclusions would be as a rule dependable; everybody could anticipate tomorrow's or next week's price changes; and hence everyone could make money continuously by buying and selling at the right time. This is patently impossible. A moment's thought will show that there can be no such thing as a scientific prediction of economic events under human control. The very "dependability" of such a prediction will cause human actions that will invalidate it. Hence thoughtful chartists admit that continued success is dependent upon keeping the successful method known to only a few people. But there is some doubt as to the success of at least some of the charting systems as they stand. In this connection, a special study by the staff of *Fortune* magazine of one point-and-figure system which could be specifically tested leads to the conclusion that "the results of one test inspire no special confidence in p. and f."[7]

2. *Its Practice Cannot Be Continuously Successful.* It follows that there is no generally known method of chart reading that has been continuously successful for a long period of time.[8] If it were known, it would be speedily adopted by numberless traders. This very following would bring its usefulness to an end.

3. *Theoretical Basis Open to Question.* The theoretical basis of chart reading runs somewhat as follows:

a. The action of the market (or of a particular stock) reflects the activities and the attitude of those interested in it.

b. Therefore, by studying the record of market action, we can tell what is going to happen next in the market.

The premise may well be true, but the conclusion does not necessarily follow. You may learn a great deal about the technical position of individual stocks by studying charts of their past market performances, but the question is whether you learn enough to predict the future with sufficient accuracy to operate profitably over time in the stock market. In other words, does the information which you derive from the past

---

[6] Although J. Magee, a leading chartist, refers to the "science of technical analysis," at the same time, in his already cited book, p. 277, he states that "judgment is required, and perspective, and a constant reversion to first principles." For a criticism of market analysis, see A. W. May, "On Market Forecasting and Timing," *Commercial & Financial Chronicle*, Nov. 14, 1957, p. 5.

[7] *Fortune*, March 1962, p. 180. A. W. May, *op. cit.*, also questioned seriously the accomplishments of market analysis.

[8] Adherents of the Dow theory have claimed extraordinary results for it. Some of the past record is open to doubt, turning, in part, on certain disputed interpretations of what the theory indicated on various key occasions. See a study of the indicated results of the Dow theory from 1897 through 1958 on p. 30 of *The Intelligent Investor* by Benjamin Graham, Harper & Brothers, New York, 1959. The results from 1897 through 1933 appear remarkably favorable; those since 1933 appear basically unprofitable.

market action of individual issues prove valuable *often enough* for you to invest profitably in common stocks?

At the same time, it is to be noted that a not entirely dissimilar question arises in security analysis itself. The past earnings of a company supply a useful indication of its future earnings—useful, but not *infallible*. Security analysis and market analysis are alike, therefore, in the fact that each deals with past data that are not conclusive as to the future. However, we are inclined to the view that for the typical analyst the so-called "fundamental" information for investment-quality shares—sales, earnings, asset and capital data, etc.—lends itself to more meaningful interpretation than does market information. Moreover, as we shall point out, there is the added difference that the security analyst can protect himself by a *margin of safety* that is denied to the market analyst.

Undoubtedly, there are occasions when the behavior of either the market as a whole or individual issues, as revealed on the charts, carries a definite and trustworthy meaning of particular value to those who are skilled in its interpretation. If reliance on chart indications were confined to those really convincing cases, a more positive argument could be made in favor of the "technical study." But such precise signals apparently occur at wide intervals, and all too often the chart configurations are such that chart readers "find themselves adrift on a sea of ambiguities."

4. *Other Theoretical and Practical Weaknesses.* The appeal of chart reading to the stock-market trader is something like that of a patent medicine to an incurable invalid. The stock speculator does suffer, in fact, from a well-nigh incurable ailment. The cure he seeks, however, is not abstinence from speculation but profits. Despite all experience, he persuades himself that profits can be made and retained; he grasps greedily and uncritically at every plausible means to this end.

The plausibility of chart reading, in our opinion, derives largely from its insistence on the sound gambling maxim that losses should be cut short and profits allowed to run. This principle usually prevents sudden large losses, and at times it permits the taking of a large profit. The results are likely to be better, therefore, than those produced by the haphazard following of "market tips." Traders, impressed by this advantage, are certain that by developing the technique of chart reading farther they will so increase its reliability as to assure themselves continued profits.

But in this conclusion lurks a double fallacy. Many players at roulette follow a similar system, which limits their losses at any one session and permits them at times to realize a substantial gain. But in the end they always find that the aggregate of small losses exceeds the few large profits. (This must be so, since the mathematical odds against them are inexorable over a period of time.) The same is true of the stock trader, who will find that the expense of trading weights the dice heavily against him. A second difficulty is that, as the methods of chart reading gain in popularity, the amount of the loss taken in unprofitable trades tends to increase, and the profits also tend to diminish. For as more and more people, following the same system, receive the signal to buy at about the same time, the result of this competitive buying must be that a higher average price is paid by the group. Conversely, when this larger group decides to sell out at the same time, either to cut short a loss or to protect a profit, the effect must again be that a lower average price is received. (The growth in the use of "stop-loss orders," formerly a helpful technical device of the trader, had this very effect of detracting greatly from their value as a protective measure.)

The more intelligent chart students recognize these theoretical weaknesses, we believe, and take the view that market forecasting is an *art* that requires talent, judgment, intuition, and other personal qualities. They admit that no rules of procedure can be laid down, the automatic following of which will ensure success. Hence the widespread tendency in Wall Street circles toward a composite or eclectic approach, in which a very thorough study of the market's performance is projected against the general economic background, and the whole is subjected to the appraisal of experienced judgment.

The Second Type of Market Analysis. Before considering the significance of this injection of judgment, let us pass on to the type of market forecasting which is based upon influences outside of the market itself. As far as the general market is concerned, the usual procedure is to construct indexes representing various economic factors, e.g., money rates, new orders, steel production, average hours worked, and carloadings, and to deduce impending changes in the market from an observation of a recent change in these indexes.[9] (In essence this method of market forecasting is mechanical.)

One of the earliest methods of the kind, and a very simple one, was based upon the percentage of blast furnaces in operation. This theory, developed by Col. Leonard P. Ayres of the Cleveland Trust Company, ran to the effect that security prices usually reached a bottom when blast furnaces in operation declined through 60 percent of the total and that conversely they usually reached a top when blast furnaces in operation passed through the 60 percent mark on the upswing in use thereof.[10] A

[9] These indexes may also be plotted on charts, in which case the forecasting takes on the aspect of chart reading. *Examples:* The A, B, and C lines of the Harvard Economic Service, which were published in weekly letters from Jan. 3, 1922 to Dec. 26, 1931; also the single composite Index Line in the "Investment Timing Service" offered by Independence Fund of North America, Inc., in 1939. While Value Line does not relate economic series directly to the movement of stock prices, it does publish a "business forecaster"—representing the combination in a single index of seven economic series—as part of its *Investment Survey*.

[10] See *Bulletin of the Cleveland Trust Company,* July 15, 1924, cited by David F. Jordan in *Practical Business Forecasting*, p. 203n., New York, 1927.

companion theory of Colonel Ayres was that the high point in bond prices is reached about 14 months subsequent to the low point in pig-iron production and that the peak in stock prices is reached about two years following the low point for pig-iron production.[11]

This simple method is representative of all mechanical forecasting systems, in that (1) it sounds vaguely *plausible* on the basis of a priori reasoning, and (2) it relies for its *convincingness* on the fact that it has "worked" for a number of years past. The necessary weakness of all these systems lies in the time element. It is easy and safe to prophesy, for example, that a period of high interest rates will lead to a sharp decline in the market. The question is, "How soon?" There is no scientific way of answering this question. Many of the forecasting services are therefore driven to a sort of pseudo-science, in which they take it for granted that certain time lags or certain coincidences that happened to occur several times in the past (or have been worked out laboriously by a process of trial and error) can be counted upon to occur in much the same way in the future.

Broadly speaking, therefore, the endeavor to forecast security price changes by reference to mechanical indexes is open to the same objections that were made to the methods of the chart readers. They are not truly scientific, because in highly dynamic economies there is no convincing reason for anticipating the maintenance in the future of some fixed (or given) relationship between stock prices and either an individual economic series or a composite index representing a number of series—irrespective of the duration of the historic support.

Disadvantages of Market Analysis as Compared with Security Analysis. We return in consequence to our earlier conclusion that market analysis is an art for which one must have special talent if he is to pursue it successfully. Security analysis is also an art; and it, too, will not yield satisfactory results unless the analyst has ability as well as knowledge. We think, however, that security analysis has several advantages over market analysis, which are likely to make the former a more successful field of activity for those with training and intelligence. In security analysis the prime stress is laid upon protection against untoward events. We obtain this protection by seeking a margin of safety. This margin should be represented by (a) an excess of calculated intrinsic value over the price paid, or (b) the excess of expected dividends for a period of years above a normal interest return, or (c) a corresponding calculation related to expected earnings. The underlying idea is that even if the security turns out to be less attractive than it appeared, the commitment might still prove satisfactory. In market analysis there are no margins of

[11] The conclusions of Colonel Ayres are summarized on p. 31 of a pamphlet entitled *Business Recovery Following Depression*, published by the Cleveland Trust Company in 1922.

safety; you are either right or wrong, and if you are wrong, you lose money.[12]

The cardinal rule of the market analyst that losses should be cut short and profits safeguarded (by selling when a decline commences) leads in the direction of active trading. This means in turn that the cost of buying and selling becomes a heavily adverse factor in aggregate results. Operations based on security analysis are ordinarily of the investment type and do not involve active trading.

At this point in our original (1934) edition the following paragraphs occur:

A third disadvantage of market analysis is that it involves essentially a battle of wits. Profits made by trading in the market are for the most part realized at the expense of others who are trying to do the same thing. The trader necessarily favors the more active issues, and the price changes in these are the resultant of the activities of numerous operators of his own type. The market analyst can be hopeful of success only upon the assumption that he will be more clever or perhaps luckier than his competitors.

The work of the security analyst, on the other hand, is in no similar sense competitive with that of his fellow analysts. In the typical case the issue that he elects to buy is not sold by someone who has made an equally painstaking analysis of its value. We must emphasize the point that the security analyst examines a far larger list of securities than does the market analyst. Out of this large list, he selects the exceptional cases in which the market price falls far short of reflecting intrinsic value, either through neglect or because of undue emphasis laid upon unfavorable factors that are probably temporary.

These paragraphs were retained in 1940 and in 1951. But in this revision we must express doubt as to their continued applicability. Our doubts were foreshadowed in the new material at the end of the preceding chapter (page 707), in which we pointed out that most of the present-day analysts seem to be engaged in a struggle with their numerous competitors to select the issues "most likely to succeed" in, say, the next year or two. In this occupation there is little room under current stock-market conditions for the application of a true margin-of-safety principle. To the extent that security analysis has also become a battle of wits—more by necessity, perhaps, than by choice—it has lost an important advantage over market analysis.

Market analysis seems easier than traditional security analysis, and its rewards may be realized much more quickly. For these very reasons, it is likely to prove more disappointing in the long run. There are no

[12] Viewing the two activities as possible professions, we are inclined to draw an analogous comparison between the law and the concert stage. A talented lawyer should be able to make a respectable living; a talented, i.e., a "merely talented," musician faces heartbreaking obstacles to a successful concert career. Thus, as we see it, a thoroughly competent security analyst should be able to obtain satisfactory results from his work, whereas permanent success as a market analyst requires unusual qualities—or unusual luck.

dependable ways of making money easily and quickly, either in Wall Street or anywhere else.

Prophecies Based on Near-term Prospects. Although to a less extent than when we wrote in 1950, a good part of the analysis and advice supplied in the financial district still rests upon the near-term business prospects of the company considered. It is assumed that if the outlook favors increased earnings, the issue should be bought in the expectation of a higher price when the larger profits are actually reported. In this reasoning, security analysis and market analysis are made to coincide. The market prospect is thought to be identical with the business prospect.

But to our mind the theory of buying stocks chiefly upon the basis of their short-run outlook makes the selection of speculative securities entirely too simple a matter. Its weakness lies in the fact that the current market price already takes into account the *consensus* as to future prospects. And in many cases the prospects will have been given *more* than their just meed of recognition. When a stock is recommended because next year's earnings are expected to show improvement, a twofold hazard is involved. First, the forecast of next year's results may prove incorrect; second, even if correct, it may have been discounted or even overdiscounted in the current price.

If markets generally reflected only this year's earnings, then a good estimate of next year's results would be of inestimable value. But the premise is not correct. The National Bureau of Economic Research, in its exhaustive studies of business-cycle indicators, has concluded that stock prices "are consistent leaders" of business conditions.[13] The same conclusion has been reached by others.[14] In our preceding editions of *Security Analysis*, we set forth data in support of the fact that no definite correlation exists between the *current* movement of stock prices and *current* earnings.[15] We have further compared over the 25-year span, 1935–1959, the quarterly earnings (on an annualized basis and seasonally adjusted) of Standard & Poor's 500 Composite stock group with the quarterly average stock-price index. It is impressive that in 46 out of the 100 quarters stock prices moved counter to the change in earnings; i.e., earnings rose, but prices declined, or vice versa.[16] Accordingly, if in each instance the analyst had correctly forecast the directional change in earnings for the next quarter, he would have had only about a 50/50 chance that this accuracy would be of assistance in forecasting whether stock prices would be higher or lower in that quarter.

[13] G. H. Moore, *Business Cycle Indicators*, Vol. I, National Bureau of Economic Research, Princeton University Press, Princeton, N.J., 1961, p. 619.

[14] For example, see E. A. Mennis, "Security Prices and Business Cycles," *Analysts Journal*, February 1955.

[15] See pp. 657–658 of the 1951 edition.

[16] It follows that the correlation between changes in stock prices and earnings is negligible in the short run.

Emphasis on Near-term Developments Fallacious. Market predictions based on economic analysis will almost always assume that if business improves then prices will advance, and that if business declines then prices will fall. This is the standard viewpoint, and it is applied both to the general market level and to trading or "investing" in individual stock issues. In the latter field it leads to so-called "analyses" of common-stock issues which are so concerned with near-term prospects that they lose sight entirely of the basic factors that determine value.[17]

We are skeptical of the ability of the analyst to forecast with a fair degree of success the market behavior of individual issues over the *near-term* future—whether he bases his predictions upon the technical position of the market or upon the general outlook for business or upon the specific outlook for the individual companies. More satisfactory results are to be obtained, in our opinion, by confining the positive conclusions of the analyst to the following fields of endeavor:

1. The selection of standard senior issues that meet exacting tests of safety; also the selection of standard or primary common stocks which are not selling above the range of reasonable value

2. The discovery of senior issues that merit an investment rating but that also have opportunities for an appreciable enhancement in value

3. The discovery of common stocks, or speculative senior issues, that in terms of their market prices and intrinsic values offer a margin of safety

4. The determination of definite price discrepancies existing between related securities, which situations may justify making exchanges or initiating hedging or arbitrage operations

A SUMMARY OF OUR VIEWS ON INVESTMENT POLICIES

If we transfer our attention, finally, from the analyst to the owner of securities, we may briefly express our views on what he may soundly do and not do under existing conditions.

1. The Individual Investor. *a. Investment for Fixed Income.* The most sensible investment for safety and current or accumulated income, under present conditions, is found in United States government bonds or tax-free civil obligations. Other good investments yield little more, and they

---

[17] To illustrate this fallacy, we reproduced in the 1934 and 1940 editions significant parts of the analysis and recommendations concerning two common stocks, made by an important statistical and advisory service in the latter part of 1933. The recommendations were based largely upon the apparent outlook for 1934. There was no indication of any endeavor to ascertain the fair value of the business and to compare this value with the current price. A thoroughgoing statistical analysis would have pointed to the conclusion that the issue of which the sale was advised was selling below its intrinsic value, just because of the unfavorable immediate prospects, and that the opposite was true of the common stock recommended as worth holding because of its satisfactory outlook. See pp. 822–828 of the 1940 edition.

have not equal protection against both ultimate and intermediate loss. Straight bonds and preferred stocks that offer a significantly higher return are almost certain to involve an appreciable factor of risk. (But the yield differentials may change sufficiently to make high-grade corporate bonds attractive to the individual investor. For tax reasons this is unlikely to happen in the case of prime-quality preferred stocks.)

b. Investment for Income, Moderate Long-term Appreciation, and Protection against Inflation. The investor has his choice here of purchasing shares of the established investment funds, or of making his commitment directly in a diversified list of primary common stocks. In either case he should make sure that he buys at a *not unreasonable* price level.

c. Investment Chiefly for Profit. Four approaches are open to both the small and the large investor:

(1) Purchase of representative common stocks when the market level is clearly low as judged by objective, long-term standards. This policy requires patience—particularly in terms of the markets of the last several years—and courage, and is by no means free from the possibility of grave miscalculation.

(2) Purchase of individual issues with special growth possibilities, when these can be obtained at reasonable prices in relation to actual accomplishment. Such a happy combination of circumstances is never easy to find, and it has become increasingly difficult in recent years. Where growth is *generally* expected, the price is rarely reasonable. If the basis of purchase is a confidence in future growth not held by the public, the operation may prove sound and profitable; it may also prove ill founded and costly.

(3) Purchase of well-secured privileged senior issues. A combination of really adequate security with a promising conversion or similar right is a rare but by no means unknown phenomenon. A policy of careful selection in this field should bring good results, provided the investor has the patience and persistence needed to find his opportunities.

(4) Purchase of securities selling well below intrinsic value. In 1950 this represented a practical suggestion. However, the investor will have to search diligently in the market of early 1962 for any issues which meet this requirement. Quite probably he will find his margin of safety more in terms of, say, a modest 5-year-yield differential of the type referred to on page 717 than in terms of a marked difference between market price and intrinsic value.

While care and discrimination are particularly important at prevailing stock-price levels, the search for and the recognition of security values of the types just discussed are not beyond the competence of the small investor who wishes to practice security analysis in a nonprofessional capacity. For this, however, he will undoubtedly need better than average intelligence and training. But we think it should be a necessary rule that the nonprofessional investor should submit his ideas to the criticism of a professional analyst, say one employed by a New York Stock Exchange firm. Surely modesty is not incompatible with self-confidence; and there is logic in the thought that unless a man is qualified to advise others professionally, he should not, unaided, prescribe for himself.

d. Speculation. The investor is privileged, of course, to step out of his role and become a speculator. (He is also privileged to regret his action afterwards.) There are various types of speculation, and they offer varying chances of success:

(1) Buying stock in new or virtually new ventures. This we can condemn unhesitatingly and with emphasis. The odds are so strongly against the man who buys into these new flotations that he might as well throw three-quarters of the money out the window and keep the rest in the bank.

(2) Trading in the market. It is fortunate for Wall Street as a business institution that a small minority of people can trade successfully and that many others think they can. The accepted view holds that stock trading is like anything else; i.e., with intelligence and application, or with good professional guidance, profits can be realized. Our own opinion is skeptical, perhaps jaundiced. We think that, regardless of preparation and method, success in trading is either accidental and impermanent or else due to a highly uncommon talent. Hence the vast majority of stock traders are inevitably doomed to failure. We do not expect this conclusion to have much effect on the public. (Note our basic distinction between purchasing stocks at objectively low levels and selling them at high levels—which we term shrewd investment—and the popular practice of buying only when the market is "expected" to advance and selling when it is "due" to decline—which we call speculation.)

(3) Purchase of "growth stocks" at generous prices. In calling this "speculation," we contravene most authoritative views. For reasons previously expressed, we consider this popular approach to be inherently dangerous and increasingly so as a result of its great popularity in recent years. But the chances of individual success are much brighter here than in the other forms of speculation, and there is a better field for the exercise of foresight, judgment, and moderation.

2. Investment of Surplus Funds by Nonfinancial Businesses. The ordinary manufacturing or distributing business does not or should not have funds for *permanent* investment in securities. For "temporary investment"—which may cover quite a number of years—the most suitable media are United States government securities or tax-free issues. It seems fairly evident, on the whole, that other types of investment by business enterprises—whether in bonds or in stocks—can offer an appreciably higher return only at the risk of loss and of criticism. A possible exception may be made in favor of well-protected preferred stocks or guaranteed common stocks, because of their attractive tax status when owned by a corporation.

3. Institutional Investment. Writing in 1950, we stressed the need of anticipating possible inflation in planning the investment program of educational and similar institutions. Our concluding statement was: " . . . we are convinced that it requires a more respectful attitude toward common stocks than that which prevailed ten years ago."[18] The increase in the equity proportion of institutional portfolios in recent years has been impressive. It has risen from about one-third to something like two-thirds in the course of the fifties.[19] Today different problems face the investment manager. Not only are interest rates substantially higher than in 1950 and stock yields substantially lower but, in addition, the inflationary pressure is somewhat mitigated. While this situation does not necessarily imply a basic change in investment policy, it certainly creates an environment in which the course of action for the 1960's is much less clear than it was in the beginning of the 1950's.

[18] 1951 edition, p. 662.

[19] See section headed *Subgroup 3. Investment Policies Not Controlled by Law,* Chap. 5, p. 64.

APPENDIX

NOTE A (PAGE 71 OF TEXT)

The following data on the amplitude and duration of the 11 stock-price cycles from 1885 to 1921 have been taken from Cottle and Whitman, *Investment Timing: The Formula Plan Approach,* McGraw-Hill Book Company, Inc., New York, 1953.

The method of measuring the amplitude of the cycles is explained therein as follows:[1]

Amplitude . . . may be measured in several different ways. For present purposes, the well-tested method used by Burns and Mitchell for measuring the cyclical movement of economic series is employed. It consists in expressing the peak and troughs of each cycle as percentages of the average value of the series during the cycle. For example, if the average value was 195 and the value at the initial trough was 156, at the peak 254 and at the terminal trough 146, these peak and trough values are converted into percentages of the average. Thus the initial trough is 80 percent of the average value, the peak is 130 percent, and the terminal trough 75 percent.

Duration and Amplitude of Common-stock Price Cycles, 1885–1921

Dates of cycles	Duration, months	Index of cycle limits			Amplitude		
		Initial trough	Peak	Terminal trough	Rise	Decline	Total cycle
Jan., 1885–May, 1887–June, 1888...	41	83.3	116.7	98.6	29.0	13.7	42.7
June, 1888–May, 1890–Dec., 1890...	30	96.4	104.5	88.9	8.1	15.6	23.7
Dec., 1890–Aug., 1892–Aug., 1893...	32	90.6	106.9	80.8	16.3	26.1	42.4
Aug., 1893–Sept., 1895–Aug., 1896..	36	95.1	104.9	89.4	13.0	18.7	31.7
Aug., 1896–Apr., 1899–Sept., 1900...	49	76.4	122.9	114.3	46.5	8.6	55.1
Sept., 1900–Sept., 1902–Oct., 1903..	37	76.0	112.3	81.4	36.3	30.9	67.2
Oct., 1903–Sept., 1906–Nov., 1907...	49	75.9	118.8	77.8	42.9	41.0	83.9
Nov., 1906–Dec., 1909–July, 1910...	32	73.5	115.7	100.5	42.2	15.2	57.4
July, 1910–Sept., 1912–Dec., 1914...	53	100.1	110.2	83.5	10.1	26.7	36.8
Dec., 1914–Nov., 1916–Dec., 1917...	36	84.1	114.5	80.3	30.4	34.2	64.6
Dec., 1917–July, 1919–Aug., 1921...	44	89.1	116.9	83.0	27.8	33.9	61.7

SOURCE: Based on Standard & Poor's Composite Long-term Stock Price Index.

NOTE 1 (PAGE 99 OF TEXT)

BOND CLAIM VERSUS TOTAL OWNERSHIP

Three widely separated examples[2] taken from the real estate field will illustrate our thesis that a bond claim is no safer, and less attractive, than a stock interest

[1] From pp. 3 and 4.

[2] Examples 1 and 2 are described in more detail on pp. 731–732 of the 1940 edition of this work.

of the same dollar size representing full ownership of the property with no debt ahead of it. Nevertheless, an all-stock company of this kind is likely to sell in the market for much less than the amount of mortgage debt which could be placed on the property; even though such a stock issue would include both a mortgage debt and the equity component of the total capital. It follows that a stock issue in such a position is likely to prove a profitable investment when and if the property is later sold or mortgaged.

Example 1: The U.S. Express Company Building. In 1918 full ownership of this building (and minor additional assets) were represented by 100,000 shares of stock selling at 15, or a total value of $1,500,000. In 1919 the building was sold for $3,725,000, the buyer placing a mortgage of $3,000,000 on the building. The U.S. Express Company stockholders received liquidating dividends aggregating $39.25 per share.

Example 2: Court-Livingston Building. In a reorganization the original first-mortgage bond issue on this building was exchanged for 3,880 shares of stock, which in 1939 was quoted at 30, indicating a total value of $116,000 for all the assets. In that year, the building was sold for $250,000, the purchase being financed by a mortgage loan of $285,000 (which covered some additional land). The Court-Livingston stockholders received about $110 per share in liquidation.

Example 3: City and Suburban Homes Company. At the beginning of 1950, this concern owned various real estate holdings free and clear of debt. In 1949 the average price of the stock was 12½ for 375,000 shares, indicating a total value of $4,700,000 for the assets, which included about $800,000 of working capital. At the end of 1950 the company placed mortgages of $5,000,000 on its property and distributed $14 per share as a return of capital. Shortly after this distribution, the stock sold above $10 per share.

In all these cases the common stock, on a free and clear basis, was both safer and more attractive than the mortgage (or mortgage bonds) later placed on the same property. It is equally true that in each case the all-stock capital structure had unduly depressed the market value of the enterprise.

NOTE 2 (PAGE 109 OF TEXT)

ACCOUNTING RESEARCH BULLETINS

The Committee on Accounting Procedure of the American Institute of Certified Public Accountants (AICPA) has issued many Accounting Research Bulletins. Practically all these bulletins are significant for the student of security analysis. Unfortunately, space does not permit us to reproduce or even to summarize them here. The serious student of security analysis is advised to consult the original documents, which are obtainable at nominal cost from the Institute. In our view the most important, from the standpoint of security analysis, are as follows:

Issuance dates	*Title*
Number 4, December 1939	*Foreign Operations and Foreign Exchange*
Number 11, September 1941	*Corporate Accounting for Ordinary Stock Dividends*
Number 20, November 1943	*Report of Committee on Terminology; Depreciation*
Number 22, May 1944	*Report of Committee on Terminology; Depreciation*
Number 23, December 1944	*Accounting for Income Taxes*
Number 29, July 1947	*Inventory Pricing*
Number 31, October 1947	*Inventory Reserves*
Number 32, December 1947	*Income and Earned Surplus*

NOTE 3 (PAGE 141 OF TEXT)

TWO ILLUSTRATIONS OF THE QUIRKS OF INVENTORY AND DEPRECIATION ACCOUNTING

Example 1: U.S. Steel. The report of United States Steel Corporation for the last quarter of 1949 presented some interesting features. Despite a protracted strike which reduced the operating rate to only 46 percent, as against 94.6 percent in the preceding three quarters, the company reported net earnings of $32.7 million in the three months—which were down only 25 percent from the average of the previous nine months. The chairman stated, however, that the earnings would have been only $6.7 million but for certain adjustments in the accounts which had to be made because of the steel strike.

The company had been charging accelerated depreciation (not tax-deductible) at the annual rate of $44 million, based on the 95 percent operating rate. The strike reduced the actual rate to 82.5 percent for the full year, which required the accelerated depreciation to be cut to $22 million. This meant that the charge made for the first nine months was $16 million more than necessary, and this amount was credited to the last quarter's results.

Inventories have been carried on a LIFO basis, for the most part at 1940 cost levels. Some of the low-cost inventory was drawn down, because shipments in the quarter exceeded production. This produced a special profit of $17 million, reduced by tax to $10 million. This item and the preceding one account for $26 million of the $32.7 million reported as net income.

It is obvious that the profits reported for the last quarter of 1949 did not "fairly reflect the results of the operations during the period"—to use auditors' language. The various devices for equalizing fluctuations and for stating results on a conservative basis operated in this case—and could do so in many others—to create a distorted picture of what had happened to earnings under strike conditions. This example confirms our belief that corporations could best serve their stockholders by reporting earnings: (1) on a FIFO inventory basis, (2) on the basis of depreciation charges allowed for tax purposes, and (3) with no charges or credits from the use of contingency reserves. Management should be entirely free to add its own interpretation of the "true results" for the period, by suggesting deductions from or additions to the reported profits; but such exegesis belongs in a comment outside of the statement itself.

Example 2: American Smelting & Refining Company. For the first half of 1949 and 1948 this company reported earnings as shown in the accompanying table. The tax deduction was considerably higher in 1949 than in 1948, although the net before taxes was 10 percent lower.

Item	First half of 1949	First half of 1948
Net before income tax......	$21,206,000	$23,561,000
Income tax...............	10,831,000	8,183,000
Net income...............	10,375,000	15,378,000

The company explained that about $6,300,000 had been charged to income to mark down the value of metals accumulated after January 1, 1949, to their lower value on June 30, 1949. This inventory write-down was not tax-deductible, because the company was carrying the balance of its inventory on a low LIFO basis, and it could not mark down the recent purchases to market without marking up similarly the old purchases to market. This would have meant the abandonment of the LIFO method.

The effect of this situation was that (1) the company received no benefit from its low-cost inventories in the first half of 1949 except that it was not required to mark them down; (2) it charged income with a considerable market loss on the additional metal acquired during the period; and (3) it was unable to take the usual income tax credit on this loss.

NOTE 4 (PAGE 154 OF TEXT)

DEPRECIATION AND AMORTIZATION POLICIES OF U.S. STEEL CORP. 1901–1961

During these sixty years U.S. Steel has employed a great variety of approaches to the treatment of depreciation and amortization. Most of these are summarized in the following account.

A. Amortization of Intangible Assets or Goodwill

On incorporation in 1901 the fixed-asset account contained no less than $769 million of written-up assets, popularly known then as "water." These intangibles represented the entire par value of the common, the initial surplus, and a good portion of the preferred stock as well. The company wrote off all the intangibles in its balance sheet by the following procedures: (1) Between 1901 and 1929 it made annual sinking-fund appropriations to retire parent-company bonds, charging these amounts to earnings as additional "depreciation"; (2) in the same period it made special write-offs, charged both to income and surplus; (3) in 1938 it made a final charge-off of $260 million, chiefly through decrease in the stated value of the common stock from $100 to $75 per share.

B. Amortization of Tangible Assets

1. Write-off of inflated costs in World War I.

Between 1917 and 1920 U.S. Steel charged earnings with $136 million and surplus with an added $12 million to write off "a proportion of the cost of war facilities installed," on the theory that such costs were excessive.

2. Regular depreciation policy.

U.S. Steel followed customary straight-line depreciation practice from 1902 to 1935. In that year it adopted the policy of varying the rate of depreciation with the operating rate of the plant, within certain limits, as described on p. 727 above.

3. A special arrangement which reduced depreciation charged to income.

In 1935 the company transferred $181 million from appropriated surplus to a reserve for future depreciation, plus another $89 million added to the past depreciation reserve. In the next nine years it reported that it had been using the future-depreciation reserve, instead of charging income, for annual amounts of depreciation varying between $5.2 and $9 million. (Today a device of that kind would be criticized since it operated to relieve the income account of part of the normal depreciation charge for the year. Carried to extremes, the consequence could be highly distorting.)

The 1935 transaction was reversed in its entirety in 1948 by transferring back $270 million from depreciation reserves to surplus. The company explained this reversal by stating that the large increase in the price level had made the earlier reduction in the net plant account unnecessary.

In our view this reversal and its explanation are basically inconsistent with U.S. Steel's strongly urged claim that much larger depreciation charges are required than those permitted as tax deductions, in order to provide for the replacement cost of the assets. (See below.) Proper replacement-cost accounting would require that (*a*) the gross plant be marked up on the books to replacement cost new; (*b*) the accrued depreciation be correspondingly increased to give the net depreciated value on the replacement basis; and (*c*) annual depreciation be taken on the same basis.

4. Accelerated amortization.

    (*a*) In 1941–1945 the company wrote off against earnings the entire expenditure of $184 million on war plants, as permitted by law. Similarly, in the Korean War, 1950–1953, the company obtained Certificates of Necessity for $816 million of war-connected plant expenditures, entitling it to write them off against income in 60 equal monthly installments.

    (*b*) Between 1947 and 1953 the company followed the policy of charging more depreciation on its non-war plants than permitted by the tax law. It wrote off up to 10 percent of the cost of new plant in the year of expenditure and also in the following year; but the write-off depended on the excess of the operating rate above a 70 percent base. Normal depreciation was taken in addition. The total amount of this accelerated depreciation, not tax-deductible, was $201 million.

    (*c*) The tax law was amended in 1954 to permit faster depreciation than the straight-line method. U.S. Steel adopted the "declining-balance" option, which permits double the straight-line rates as applied to the depreciated balance at the beginning of each year. The general effect was the continuance of the company's more liberal policies of former years, but with full tax deduction.

C. Calculation of Depreciation at Replacement Rates

Except for a single charge of $26 million in 1947, the company did not actually provide such replacement depreciation in its accounts, but it has presented calculations of the deficiency between its charges based on original cost and those required to take care of higher replacement cost. For the 17 years 1940–1956 its total amortization taken, including accelerated amounts, was $2.8 billion, while the requirement to meet replacement costs would have been $3.7 billion, or 32 percent greater. For 1956 alone the company calculated that its charge of $278 million would need to be increased by $67 million, or 24 percent, to recover the "buying power" of the dollar for replacement purposes. Again in 1960 the company reported that for the fifteen years 1946–1960 the total depreciation needed on a replacement basis was $4,276 million, while that recorded was $2,802 million. By subtraction from the previous report we may calculate that the increased deficiency in 1957–1960 amounted to $570 million against depreciation taken of $879 million.

These figures suggest a widening of the spread in 1957–1960, due chiefly to the smaller over-all depreciation taken in the last three years.

NOTE 5 (PAGE 169 OF TEXT)

EFFECT OF RETROACTIVE ADJUSTMENTS OF EARNINGS

The analyst should be aware of some rather subtle elements sometimes found in the presentation of reported earnings from year to year. In this note we shall discuss one such practice that may make a misleading impression on the superficial observer of successive statements. It has to do with changes in accounting practices, accompanied by revised reports for the previous year. The exhibit of Seaboard Finance Corporation (discussed on p. 169) is a case in point.

The sequential effects of a practice of this sort are as follows: In a given year, say 1960, the company excludes from income certain indicated deductions, which it may either ignore, or charge to surplus, or treat as a capitalizable expense. The consequence is that the 1960 report makes a better showing than it should relative to that of 1959. In the following year the accounting method is changed or a retroactive charge-off is made; the 1960 report is revised; and the 1961 results are published along with the revised 1960 figures (which show lower earnings than originally published). In this way the 1961 profits again make a better showing as against those of the year before. In sum, the accounts are so treated as to give more favorable comparable figures in successive years than the actual results will warrant. Since the chief emphasis of the daily stock market—mistakenly, but unmistakably—is on a comparison of the currently published earnings figures with those of the preceding period, these revisions are likely to produce at least obliquely misleading effects.

The relevant per-share figures of the company mentioned are as follows:

As published in 1962		As published in 1961	
1961	1960 (revised)	1960	1959
$1.02	68¢	$1.40	$1.42

NOTE 6 (PAGE 178 OF TEXT)

"NET-WORTH ACCOUNTING"

This term is employed by Sheraton Corporation of America to designate a novel approach to the presentation of the company's financial position at the end of its fiscal year and of its "economic performance" during the period. The results on this basis are provided in addition to those shown by "ordinary accounting." The company has made several other calculations of the results for its stockholders, as shown in the following summary of per-share figures:

Year ended April	Reported earnings		Adjusted earnings*		Cash flow	"Economic perform- ance" or "net worth profit"	Esti- mated net worth	Year-end market price
	Includ- ing capital gains	Exclud- ing capital gains	Without deferred- tax de- duction	After deferred- tax de- duction				
1961	$0.61	$0.39	$1.65	$1.00	$3.84	$1.60	$32.70	$17.75
1960	0.60	0.55	1.65	1.08	3.80	3.44	31.70	18.14
1959	1.10	0.69	1.70	1.18	3.60	3.66	28.85	17.78
1958	0.99	0.76	1.83	1.28	3.66	1.44	25.76	10.72
1957	1.10	0.97	1.72	1.33	3.40	3.52	24.84	11.66

* See later explanation.

In this note we shall deal chiefly with the "net-worth accounting" concept, but shall add some observations re the other per-share calculations provided by Sheraton. At the end of each fiscal year the company calculates the "fair value" of each property owned, thus arriving at a total estimated value for its fixed assets. The estimated values of the properties are determined by company officers by capitalizing the "basic earnings" at rates generally between 10 and 12 percent. The basic earnings are those shown before depreciation, interest paid, and income taxes. The capitalization rates used are intended to reflect conservatively the actual sales value of each property at the time of valuation.

The excess of such estimated value over book value is added to the stockholders' book equity to produce an "indicated net-asset value" per share. The increase in such asset value or net worth, plus dividends paid, is termed "economic or profit performance" for the year. Such economic performance is sometimes referred to as "earnings" (e.g., on page 17 of the April 1961 report). For the 10 years to April 1961 the "net worth profit" is shown to aggregate $143 million for the stock, versus an over-all $50 million by "ordinary accounting." These figures average $2.62 vs. $1.02 per share.

Comment: The fair market value of assets is an important factor in the valuation of the stock of many companies, including enterprises such as Sheraton. With respect to Sheraton's procedure, the analyst would raise two sorts of questions. The first is whether the valuations are reasonably conservative, as claimed by the company. It should be noted that the company's tabulation for 1947–1961 shows that during the 15 years the year-end market price remained constantly well below its estimated net asset value. (In 1947 the ratio of price to such value was 50 percent, in 1961 it was 54 percent, and it averaged 47 percent.) Such a persistent undervaluation in the long bull market would be exceptional.

The more important question for valuation theory, however, is whether the change in estimated net-asset value in any year, and the derived figure of "economic performance per share," may properly be regarded as "earnings," "income," or "profits." As such, may it properly be capitalized to calculate the value of the stock in the same way as reported earnings are generally capitalized? We hold strongly to the view that such a procedure is logically wrong. If followed in this and a variety of similar cases, it may produce grossly misleading results.

We present our argument in the following example: Assume that a company in 1962 has per-share earnings of $1, a payout of 60 percent, indicated growth of 8 percent, a consequent multiplier of 20, and a value of 20. The next year it earns $1.08, pays 65 cents, and its value increases to $21.60. This would represent a standard valuation procedure of security analysis.

Now assume that the company follows a Sheraton program of "net worth accounting," using the same valuations of its net assets as does the security analyst. Its "economic performance" for 1962 will consist of a gain of $1.60 in net asset value plus dividends of 65 cents, a total of $2.25 for the year. How are these $2.25 of "earnings" or "net worth profit" to be valued? If the multiplier of 20 is applied to them the stock becomes worth $45 per share, instead of the very $21.60 per share which was accepted as fair value to determine the economic performance. If the 20 multiplier is not to be used, what *would* be an appropriate multiplier for the $2.25 of "gainings" (another Sheraton word) for the year?

It should be obvious from this discussion that "economic performance" should in no sense be regarded as a measure of *earnings* for the year and in no sense capitalized as such. What it represents is not earnings or profits but the capitalized *results* of the actual earnings. Its sole utility is that of a measure of fair value and of changes in fair value over time. But the increase in the fair value of the stock does not itself constitute capitalizable earnings.

This point may be made clearer by passing from the hotel business to the field of investment companies. It has been the constant solicitude of the SEC to prevent the gains in asset values of such companies from being presented to the public as "earnings" or "profits," and thus having the price-level effects of the bull market of the 1950's and early 1960's compounded in the price of investment company shares—as it was, disastrously, in the 1920's.

An Analogy with Life Insurance Company Shares. It has become the practice among insurance stock analysts to increase the reported earnings of life insurance companies by giving them credit for the value of new insurance placed on the books. It may be typical to add in this way $15 for each $1,000 of net increase in ordinary life insurance in force. We believe our reasoning in the Sheraton situation applies to the life insurance companies as well. The $15 per thousand may properly be added to the capital value of the company's shares, but it should not be added to their year's earnings or earning power. What is involved here is the difference between treating $15 as $15, or as, say, 20 times $15 in valuing the shares. The reader may carry the analogy farther by assuming that an ordinary manufacturing or distributing company decides that each new customer has a capitalizable value and adds such capital value to its ordinary earnings for the year. Alternatively, it could consider each year's increase in sales and net earnings as adding proportionately to the "net asset value" of the business, and then report such increase in capital value as the chief part of the year's earnings or profits. The calculated increase in the value of the business may be justified, but the treatment of such increase as capitalizable earnings would be dangerously incorrect.

Note re Sheraton's "adjusted earnings." In a separate memorandum, entitled "Sheraton's True Earnings" and issued in 1962, the company presented a revised statement of its earnings for 1957–1962, adjusted to show depreciation at the rate of 6 percent of hotel sales—stated to be the average for the industry—instead of the substantially larger figure reported by Sheraton on both its tax returns and its reports to stockholders. This adjustment raised the average earnings from operations from 67 cents per share as reported, to $1.71 (capital gains were excluded in this calculation).

A company's depreciation charges may properly be revised by the analyst to make them fairly comparable with those of its industry generally. However, if charges are reduced for this purpose, it is essential that a counterallowance be made for income tax liability deferred as a result of the change. (Our views on this point, which are similar to those of the AICPA, are discussed in Chapter 15.) Sheraton failed to make such a provision in its own adjustment for lower depreciation, and we have added a column in the table in this note to allow for the deferred-income tax factor.

It will be noted that this counteradjustment reduces the average earnings for 1957–1961 from a revised $1.71 to a re-revised $1.18. We stress these figures to bring home the fact that both depreciation charges and tax allowances often exert a major effect on computed earnings and potentially on both appraised value and market price.

NOTE 7 (PAGE 182 OF TEXT)

INCREASED PLANT VALUATION WITH CONSEQUENT INCREASED DEPRECIATION

In 1960 a new enterprise, Needham Packing Company, bought the assets and business of Sioux City Packing Company for the equivalent of $3.8 million, against a stated equity of $2 million. Needham marked up the net property account from $1,472,000 to its appraised value of $3,125,000. (The balance of the excess of price paid over former book value was represented by a goodwill asset of $182,000.)

Prior to the transfer, Sioux City's depreciation—on a straight-line basis—was running at the annual rate of $121,000. On its higher plant value Needham charged depreciation of $252,000 in the following year.

The Sioux City-Needham transaction throws an interesting sidelight on the difference between private and public business valuations in 1960. The private stockholders of Sioux City sold $2,000,000 of net assets and recent net income of $881,000 for $3,834,000. Within two months the company sold about 30 percent of the (ultimate) stock equity on the basis of a corresponding value of $7,100,000 for the old equity.

The sale to the public involved a price of $9.50 per share for 200,000 shares. The prospectus, dated August 29, 1960 carried the following sentence in its first paragraph: "On June 1, 1960, the Company sold 240,500 shares of Common Stock to eleven persons at $1 per share and there have been no occurrences subsequent to that time which warrant an increase in the price of the shares."

This disarmingly frank statement—probably required by the SEC—did not seem to interfere with the sale of the shares to the public at 9½ times the earlier price.

NOTE 8 (PAGE 223 OF TEXT)

TWO LONG-TERM ANALYSES

I. UNITED STATES STEEL CORPORATION

A. Operating Results, Annual Averages

(Dollar figures in millions)

	1902–1910	1911–1920	1921–1930	1931–1940	1941–1950	1951–1960
Steel products shipped (net tons in thousands)	9,609	13,886	14,030	9,370	19,757	21,771
Gross sales.............	$423.1	$840.7	$945.9	$652.7	$2,064.6	$3,763.0
Net earnings for interest.	104.8	159.7	130.7	23.3	113.7	282.4
Bond interest...........	28.8	31.6	23.8	6.7	4.1	8.1
Preferred dividends......	26.9	25.2	25.2	25.2	25.2	25.2
Balance for common.....	49.1	102.9	81.7	8.6(d)	84.4	249.1
Common dividends......	12.1	35.6	61.4*	8.1	45.6	123.4
Balance to surplus.......	37.0	67.3	20.3	16.7(d)	38.8	125.7

* Including $203,000,000 paid in stock in 1927.

B. Balance-sheet Developments

(000,000 omitted)

	Dec. 31, 1902	Dec. 31, 1910	Dec. 31, 1920	Dec. 31, 1930	Dec. 31, 1940	Dec. 31, 1950	Dec. 31, 1960
Net assets:							
Fixed (less deprec.) and net misc.*....	$560	$885	$1,221	$1,556	$1,433†	$1,459	$2,817
Net current assets..	168	180	504	357	395	621	908¶
Totals..........	$728	$1,065	$1,725	$1,913	$1,828	$2,080	$3,725
Debt and stockholders' ownership (capital):							
Bonds.............	$400	$599	$586	$123	$203	$66	$423
Preferred stock.....	510	360	360	360	360	360	360
Common stock and surplus........	182(d)	106	237	1,430§	1,265†	1,654	2,942
Totals..........	$728	$1,065	$1,725	$1,913	$1,828	$2,080	$3,725

* Eliminating intangibles of $768,000,000 later written off.

† After restoring additional depreciation of $270,000,000 deducted from surplus in 1935 but cancelled in 1948.

§ Includes premium on capital stock of $80,000,000.

¶ Includes $300,000,000 "securities reserved for plant investment."

C. Relation of Earnings to Average Capital

(Dollar figures in millions)

	First period, 1902–1910	Second decade, 1911–1920	Third decade, 1921–1930	Fourth decade, 1931–1940	Fifth decade, 1941–1950	Sixth decade, 1951–1960
Capital at beginning............	$ 728	$1,065	$1,725	$1,913	$1,828	$2,080
Capital at end................	1,065	1,725	1,913	1,828	2,080	3,725
Average capital about..........	900	1,400	1,820	1,870	1,950	2,900
Percent earned on average capital per year....................	11.6%	11.4%	7.2%	1.2%	5.8%	9.7%
Percent paid per year in interest and dividends on average capital........................	7.5%	6.6%	4.9%*	2.1%	3.8%	5.4%
Average common-stock equity...	(None)	$ 443	$1,104	$1,347	$1,460	$2,350
Percent earned on common-stock equity about................	......	14.4%	7.4%	†	5.8%	10.6%
Percent paid on common-stock equity.....................	......	8.0%	3.7%*	0.6%	3.1%	5.3%
Depreciation and amortization per year.....................	$ 25	$ 49	$ 52	$ 54	$ 122	$ 228
Average fixed-property account net......................	720	1,050	1,390	1,500	1,450	2,125
Ratio of depreciation and amortization to fixed property, net...	3.5%	4.6%	3.7%	3.6%	8.4%	10.7%
Ratio of sales to average capital (turnover)...................	0.47×	0.60×	0.52×	0.35×	1.06×	1.30×
Ratio of net for interest to sales (after taxes) ("profit margin").	23.0%	19.0%	14.6%	3.5%	4.0%	7.5%

* Excluding stock dividend.

† Deficit.

Comment: The use of ten-year averages in the above tables might be expected to smooth out the well-known year-to-year fluctuations of the steel industry, and to supply a more informing picture of the company's secular progress. However, the results by successive decades also show a marked irregularity, which must be taken to be an inherent characteristic of this giant enterprise.

Our balance-sheet figures in the earlier years differ markedly from those published by the corporation, because we have eliminated retroactively the huge amount of intangibles originally included with the fixed assets and later written off in full by successive charges to income and surplus. The effect of this adjustment is to increase substantially the rate of earnings on capital in the first two decades and to intensify the contrast with the later periods. If we compare the 1941–1950 (wartime) averages with those for 1902–1910 (peacetime), we note that production approximately doubled, sales in dollars increased fivefold, average capital invested rose 200 percent, but net earnings available for the capital fund increased a bare 10 percent. It was only through the substantial reduction of funded debt and the related interest charges that U.S. Steel was able to show any substantial gain in earnings available for the common-stock equity.

The development of the earnings rate in successive decades may be summarized as follows:

1. The maximum rate of return on tangible capital was realized in the first peacetime period, 1902–1910.

2. Much larger dollar earnings were realized in the decade of World War I, but there was no increase in the rate of return on capital.

3. A substantial decline in the rate of return took place in the peace decade, 1921–1930, but the average results continued satisfactory.

4. In the depression decade, 1931–1940, the earning power virtually disappeared.

5. Earning power recovered in the war decade, 1941–1950, but government controls and taxes held the rate of profit to only half that of the previous war decade.

6. In the prosperity of the 1950's the return on capital reached a satisfactory average figure, exceeding that of the prosperous 1920's. The basic profit elements differed greatly between these two periods. In the 1950's the net profit margin was much lower—due in part to more liberal depreciation and heavier income taxes. This was more than offset, however, by the great increase in sales per dollar of capital. There was a minor increase in tons shipped per unit of capital, and a major rise from $69.50 to $172 in gross receipts per ton.

In our 1951 presentation of this material we concluded as follows: "The fifty-year record of U.S. Steel would raise doubts in the mind of the analyst as to the ability of this giant company, and possibly of the industry as a whole, to earn an adequate return on its greatly enlarged capacity under conditions of peace, unless the general economy develops quite differently in the future from its general development between 1920 and 1950." The economy did make a significant change for the better during the sixth decade, and the steel industry derived its full share of the improvement, though with some falling off toward the period's close. The variations in the performance of U.S. Steel, as in its industry, are more marked than those in the economy as a whole. Thus the chances for future *stability* may play as great a part in evaluating U.S. Steel stock for investment as would the expected rate of growth.

II. CONTINENTAL STEEL CORPORATION

This second method supplies both the income account and the balance sheet at ten-year intervals, with a summary of each decade's results. Per-share figures are adjusted to *initial* capitalization.

A. Income account (in thousands)	Years ended December			
	1930	1940	1950	1960
Sales..........................	$11,900	$18,400	$36,400	$46,400
Depreciation..................	488	484	602	1,475
Interest paid.................	133	59	......	66
Income tax....................	....	414	3,220	4,975
Net income...................	37(d)	978†	2,660	4,328
Shares of common:				
Actual.....................	180	201	501	1,038
Adjusted to 1930...........	180	201	201	207
Earned per adjusted share......	$1.38(d)	$4.23	$13.24	$20.91
Per-share earnings for decade:*				
High......................	4.80	6.78	$8.10	$27.38
Low.......................	1.38(d)	3.45	2.54	7.35
Average...................	2.48	1.22	4.28	12.14

B. Balance sheet (in millions)	Years ended December			
	1930	1940	1950	1960
Net current assets.............	$ 3.8	$ 6.3	$ 9.9‡	$18.0
Property, etc.:				
(Gross)....................	(14.0)	(15.9)	(15.5)	(34.6)
Net........................	9.1	8.4	6.8	15.7
Total..................	$12.9	$14.7	$16.7	$33.7
Debt........................	$ 1.9	$ 1.6	.....	$ 1.4
Reserves.....................	0.1	0.4	0.7	1.4
Preferred stock..............	3.0	1.9	.....	.....
Common-stock equity.........	7.9	10.8	16.0	30.9

* The 1930 period includes only 1928–1930.
† Before contingency-reserve deduction.
‡ Includes $4.5 million special fund for plant expansion.

Comment: The thirty-three-year history of this small steel company illustrates a basic factor in American business life not sufficiently appreciated by most investors and many analysts. It is that the typical enterprise is subject to wide vicissitudes over time; hence the performance in one period—even a fairly long one—is far from conclusive evidence as to what may be expected in the next.

The variations shown in the net income of Continental Steel are paralleled by price fluctuations of the shares, which (except for the deficit years 1931–1933) are considerably wider. The quotation fell from a 1929 high of 52 to a 1932 low of 1½; then recovered to 47 in 1937 and declined to 10 in 1938; rose to 33 in 1940 and fell to 15½ in 1941; advanced to 62 in 1945 and declined to 28 in 1949; and after again doubling and halving its price in 1951–1953, made a spectacular advance to the equivalent of 310 in 1961.

In the 1940's, Continental Steel was one of the very few steel companies that sold in the market for less than the working capital alone applicable to the common stock. This producer had made very small plant expenditures from its inception in 1927 to 1950. In consequence its balance sheet had been turned around. On the asset side, working capital had greatly expanded while net plant actually declined by 25 percent. On the liability side, the significant debt and preferred-stock components had disappeared, while the common-stock equity had doubled.

The tremendous rise in both per-share earnings and market price from 1941 to 1962 was hardly to be anticipated in the light of the company's small size, its exposure to competition, and particularly its clinging to what would appear to have been an old and obsolete plant. What clues did the analyst have to the company's brilliant future? What could he have discovered by intensive study of the company's position? What prior indications would have led him to make such a study of this company rather than of countless others which appeared more promising on the surface? These are intriguing questions, but we doubt if they have satisfactory answers except by hindsight.

NOTE 9 (PAGES 311 AND 684 OF TEXT)

REORGANIZATIONS AND RECAPITALIZATIONS

Corporate reorganization is an extremely complicated subject, and it is dealt with mainly in legal works. Moreover, the postwar prosperity has reduced the number of corporate bankruptcies significantly below the level of the 1930's. But, as the extent of the SEC's participation in reorganizations under Chapter X[1] indicates, the bankrupt we have always with us. Furthermore, the impact of corporate reorganizations upon the securities affected thereby is a matter to which the security analyst needs to give attention. Hence it is a part of his equipment to understand the process of trusteeship and reorganization, at least in its broader aspects.

The procedure for corporate reorganizations has changed greatly since the 1920's. The older plans were generally developed out of what was called an "equity receivership." This type of reorganization, while still legally permissible, is out of date. Instead, when a company is in need of reorganization, use is now made of one of four separate chapters or sections of the amended Bankruptcy Act, each designed to take care of a particular form of reorganization.

These are as follows:

1. Chapter X. Provides for appointment of trustees in bankruptcy and for subsequent reorganization. It is applicable to all corporations except railroads.

2. Section 77. A similar procedure applicable to railroads.

3. Chapter XI ("Arrangements"). Provides for a readjustment of the debt of the company without a prior trusteeship. The stock issues are not directly affected by an arrangement under this chapter.

4. Section 20b of the Interstate Commerce Act (the Mahaffie Act). Similar to Chapter XI, but applicable to railroads. The stock issues may be affected.

Chapter X Reorganizations. The steps in a Chapter X trusteeship and reorganization may be summarized as follows:

1. The company ("debtor") or a creditor applies to a United States district court for appointment of a trustee, admitting or alleging insolvency. After a hearing, the court appoints one or more trustees. At least one must be "disinterested"—i.e., not previously connected with the company in an important way. The trustees operate the company under court direction. They submit a "Section 167 report," describing the affairs of the company generally and suggesting that it be either reorganized or liquidated.

2. If reorganization is indicated, the trustees invite suggestions for a plan of reorganization from interested parties. In due course the trustees file a plan with the

[1] From September 1938 to June 1959, the SEC participated in reorganizations involving 457 debtor companies with stated total assets in excess of $3.5 billion. (*25th Annual Report*, p. xxxvi.)

court. Amendments to the trustees' plan or different plans may be filed by interested parties. Hearings are held on the plans.

If the debtor has liabilities of more than $3 million, the judge must determine what plans, if any, are "worthy of consideration" and refer them to the SEC for an advisory opinion thereon. The SEC submits such an opinion, analyzing the plans and stating its recommendations. The court may then approve a plan; generally, but not always, it accepts both the trustees' and the SEC's recommendations, but it often requires certain minor modifications in the plan submitted by the trustee.

3. The reorganization plan must be found by the court to be "fair and feasible," and also to conform with specific provisions of Chapter X. To be fair, the plan must provide adequate treatment for each class of debt, with proper recognition of its priorities, and similar treatment for such stock issues as are found to have an equity in the debtor. To be feasible, it must provide a sound capital structure and sufficient working capital for the reorganized company. The specific requirements include proper provision for selection of management, for the fair and equitable distribution of voting power among the stockholders, and for periodic reports to security holders. In addition, it must provide proper treatment for any class of creditors which does not accept the plan.

4. The court's action approving the plan may be appealed to the United States circuit court of appeals, and from there (if "certiorari" is granted) to the United States Supreme Court. As the next stage toward completion, a vote is taken of the various classes of creditors and of those classes of stockholders found to have an equity in the company. Approval by two-thirds of a class of creditors and 50 percent of a class of stockholders is sufficient. If a class fails to approve, the court may nonetheless confirm the plan if it makes equitable provision for the nonassenting classes. All parties, either assenting or not, are then bound by the terms of the plan. (If the plan fails of the required approvals, or if no plan is submitted, the court may "dismiss the proceedings." This would normally mean that the company reverts to the ordinary state of bankruptcy, subject to a sale of its assets to the highest bidder.)

5. The court appoints the first board of directors for the reorganized company, generally from names submitted to it by interested parties. On a consummation date, fixed by the court, the new regime takes over. The reorganized company may be the old company with a new capitalization, or a successor corporation which is usually—but not always—formed for the purpose. The trustees are discharged, unless retained for a limited purpose, such as carrying on unfinished litigation.

Example: The Chapter X reorganization proceedings of Central States Electric Corporation illustrate the time-consuming complexities of a situation of this sort involving a major company. (Central States was originally an "investment trust," formed mainly for the purpose of controlling North American Company, a large public utility–holding company system.) The bankruptcy petition was filed in February 1942, and after a long series of reports, plan filings, hearings, appeals, etc., the company emerged from bankruptcy under the name of Blue Ridge Mutual Fund, Inc., in June 1951.[2]

Section 77 Reorganizations. Section 77, originally passed in 1933, provides for railroads a scheme of trusteeship and reorganization which is essentially similar to that of Chapter X for nonrailroad companies. The important differences are that here the Interstate Commerce Commission takes the place of the Securities and Exchange Commission and that it is given considerable more authority than its companion

---

[2] A summary and "timetable" of the Central States Electric proceedings appear in Appendix Note 46, p. 727, of our 1951 edition. Examples current as we write include Davega Stores and Yuba Consolidated Industries. Both petitioned for bankruptcy under Chapter XI in 1961–1962, but were later required to enter the more formal Chapter X proceedings, with court-appointed trustees.

body. The ICC and the Federal courts have a sort of coordinate jurisdiction over reorganization plans. A plan must first be approved by the ICC before it can be approved by the judge. As a result, plans may be shuttled back and forth several times between the two agencies before final disposition is agreed upon. A plan approved by the ICC may be one previously submitted to it by the debtor or some other interested party, but in most cases the plan is drawn up by the Commission itself.

Example: One of the longest bankruptcy proceedings was that of Missouri Pacific Railroad Company. Trustees were appointed in March 1933, and the reorganization was not consummated until 1956—twenty-three years later.[3]

Section 20b (Mahaffie Act Reorganizations). This section of the Interstate Commerce Act was preceded by the so-called "Voluntary Railroad Readjustment Act of 1939" (the "Chandler Act") and then by the McLoughlin Act of 1942. Both were known as "Chapter XV" of the Bankruptcy Act, and both were operative for a limited period of time. They permitted "voluntary reorganization" of railroads without intervention of a trusteeship. Baltimore & Ohio, Lehigh Valley, and several other roads consummated voluntary reorganization under the provision of Chapter XV. In 1948 the Mahaffie Act was passed, which now permits a permanent scheme of voluntary reorganization under the supervision of the ICC and the courts. These plans may modify the debt structure of the railroad in one or more of the following ways:

1. By extending maturities
2. By reducing (or possibly increasing) coupon rates
3. By replacing fixed interest by contingent interest
4. By paying off back interest in the form of new securities

Mahaffie Act plans may affect the stockholders, or the bondholders, or both.

Example: The Bangor and Aroostook Railroad plan, submitted in May 1950, proposed to change only the terms of some of the bond issues and left the stock issues entirely unaffected. The Boston and Maine Railroad plan, filed in January 1949, affected only the numerous classes of preferred stock and the common stock. It left the debt structure unchanged. (However, in 1940, Boston and Maine had availed itself of Chapter XV, under which it extended some of its short-term maturities and also converted some of its fixed-interest debt into income bonds.) The Bangor & Aroostook plan was declared operative in July 1950; that of Boston & Maine was not consummated until May 1953.

Chapter XI Arrangements. The procedural setup here is similar to that provided in the Mahaffie Act, but applies to nonrailroad companies.[4] It is not availed of frequently, because most nonrailroad concerns do not have complicated debt structures; hence either they are insolvent and must go through a Chapter X reorganization, or else they are generally able to take care of their debt problems without a reorganization.

Examples: These proceedings were resorted to by Haytian Corporation in 1938 and by U.S. Realty & Improvement Company in 1939. However, U.S. Realty & Improvement later went into trusteeship under Chapter X and was reorganized by merger with Sheraton Corporation. See also the current (1962) cases of Davega Stores and Yuba Consolidated Industries cited in footnote 2.

[3] A summary of the numerous developments in this bankruptcy case to the middle of 1951 appears in Appendix Note 47, p. 728, of our 1951 edition.

[4] There is corresponding legislation providing a procedure for debt adjustment for defaulting municipalities and local government units. The first Municipal Bankruptcy Act was passed in 1934 but was declared unconstitutional; the successor act, passed in 1937, was upheld by the United States Supreme Court. See "The Federal Municipal Bankruptcy Act" by Harry W. Lehmann, in the *Journal of Finance*, September 1950.

NOTE 10 (PAGE 425 OF TEXT)

PERFORMANCE OF INVESTMENT COMPANIES

Result in 1927–1935. *The Statistical Survey of Investment Trusts and Investment Companies,* based on a compilation by the SEC staff, gave detailed figures of performance during the period. The results are summarized in the following sentence: "It can, then, be concluded with considerable assurance that the entire group of management investment companies proper (as opposed to the sample here studied) failed to perform better than an index of leading common stocks and probably performed somewhat worse than the index over the 1927–1935 period. . . . "

Results for 1934–1939. These are shown by the performance of the six largest companies, as presented in the accompanying table. On the whole, their results seem to be somewhat less favorable than those shown by the comprehensive market index.

Company	Asset value per share, Dec. 31			Dividend paid		Over-all gain in value, %	
	1933	1935	1939	1934–1939	1936–1939	1934–1939	1936–1939
Atlas Corporation.......	$11.03	$15.25	$12.80	$ 2.90	$ 2.60	42.4	1.0
Dividend Shares........	1.21	1.56	1.28	0.54	0.39	50.4	7.1
Incorporated Investors..	17.99	20.86	16.34	9.93	6.66	46.0	10.3
Lehman Corporation....	26.84	37.10	32.72	9.72	8.00	54.4	9.8
Mass. Investment Trust.	17.70	24.03	20.98	6.39	4.91	54.5	7.9
State Street Investment.	65.34	92.30*	71.81	39.30	36.00	70.6	16.8
Standard & Poor's 420 Stocks†	71.0	96.8	94.3	24.0	18.3	66.6	16.3

* Adjusted to cancel reserve.
† Market prices used instead of asset values. Dividends paid are estimated.

Results for 1940–1949. These are shown in the second table, by the performance of the same companies as in the preceding table. The results are on the whole appreciably better than those shown by the comprehensive market index.

Company	Asset value per share, year ending in		Dividends paid per share, 1940–1949 (including capital-gain distributions)	Over-all gain 1940–1949	
	1939	1949		Per share	%
Atlas Corporation.............	$12.80	$ 30.12	$ 8.80	$26.12	204
Dividend Shares..............	1.28	1.55	0.82	1.09	85
Incorporated Investors........	16.34	22.44	14.47	20.57	125
Lehman Corporation..........	32.72	52.82	27.95	48.05	146
Mass. Investment Trust.......	20.98	27.67	12.05	18.74	89
State Street Investment.......	71.81	94.28*	66.60*	89.07*	124
Standard & Poor's 420 Stocks†.	94.30	135.00	51.00	91.70	97
Standard & Poor's 90 Stocks†..	99.20	133.10	58.59	92.49	93

* 2-for-1 split in 1944 taken into account and the figures doubled.
† Market prices used instead of asset values. Dividends paid are estimated.

Results for 1951–1960. For this period we shall use a different approach than for 1934–1949. Moody's *Bank & Finance Manual* publishes a compilation of the management performance of the more important investment companies. The overall gain (or loss) is shown for each year, and a cumulative figure for the ten-year period is given, which is equivalent to assuming that all distributions are reinvested in the companies' shares at the end of the year in which made. The results for 58 companies for the decade 1951–1960 appear on page 43A of the 1961 *Bank & Finance Manual,* and are summarized herewith. For a general comparison we have made a similar assumption with respect to the Standard & Poor's Composite Index of 500 common stocks.

Company	Number of companies	Range of 10-year gain, %		
		Highest	Lowest	Mean
Closed-end leveraged..............	6	498	157	269
Closed-end nonleveraged...........	14	383	138	241
Open-end (nonleveraged)...........	38	361	95	207
All companies.....................	58	...	...	221
Standard & Poor's Composite........	...	...	...	322

The Standard & Poor's Composite performance was exceeded by only one (nonleveraged) open-end company, by one leveraged closed-end company, and by one closed-end company which was leveraged during the first half of the period. See also our summary of the performance of "Growth-appreciation Funds" for 1951–1960, on p. 536 above.

These results do not appear to us to be as satisfactory as they should be. They suggest that the investment companies as a whole—and practicing security analysts as a whole—might well reexamine their basic approaches to both the selection of common stocks for purchase and the decision to sell "less satisfactory" holdings.

NOTE 11 (PAGE 493 OF TEXT)

EARNING-POWER THEORY VS. FUTURE-DIVIDEND THEORY

It is possible to reconcile the "earning power" theory of value, as applied to low-dividend-paying growth stocks, with the discounted-value-of-future-dividends theory of value, by assuming that many years hence the growth companies will pay a stream of very large cash dividends, generated by their reinvestment policy. But such a reconciliation has an air of considerable unreality, for two important reasons. The first is that dividends deferred long into the future have only a small present value. Hence it will be necessary to assume extraordinarily large "normal" dividends, to begin, say, twenty years hence and to continue for a long time, to produce mathematically the high prices ruling for growth stocks generally. We think the elements of uncertainty and hence of risk must necessarily assume a more dominant position as the expectations counted upon both grow in magnitude and become longer deferred. Secondly, we do not think that either sophisticated or unsophisticated investors in popular growth stocks make such "future-dividend" calculations explicitly or think even vaguely in such terms.

For a possible bridging of the gulf between the two ideas, we may suggest an extension of the "dividend-stream theory" to read: "A common stock is worth the discounted value of future expectable dividends over any assumed period of time, plus the discounted value of its expected market price at the end of the period." If such market price in turn reflects only the discounted value of dividends expected later on, the original J. B. Williams thesis applies unchanged. But it is possible that the future market value may reflect other considerations not clearly related to the expectable dividends—e.g., value in merger, sale, liquidation, or even expropriation. This would allow also for the generalized case of the "Canadian Investment Companies," in which dividends are formally excluded from the investor's consideration and are replaced completely by expected increases in capital value. In the Canadian cases realization of such value is assured by the privilege of redeeming shares at net-asset values. But one may imagine an investment climate in which a growing company will pay no cash dividends over a period of years but the "earning-power value" will be adequately reflected in the market price—i.e., the market price will replace the redemption privilege of the Canadian shares. For investors in such companies, calculation of the present value of dividends to *commence* many years hence, possibly after the sale of their shares, would seem to be totally unrealistic.

In actual practice these investors are more nearly placing themselves in the position of owners of a private business, for which the dividend payments are largely a matter of personal requirements and legal penalty-tax pressure, but never a fundamental measure of the value of the enterprise.

Our suggested approach applies equally well to the more typical cases where the dividend payout is quite low and is expected to continue so almost indefinitely. It corresponds, also, to the theoretical valuation of any typical bond, which is the sum of the present value of all its interest payments plus the discounted value of the ultimate payment of its principal.

NOTE 12 (PAGE 501 OF TEXT)

TAX STATUS OF "INCOME" REALIZED BY ANNUAL SALES OF STOCK

Some analysts appear to assume, mistakenly, that if profits are reinvested by the corporation and concurrently realized by a stockholder through the sale of an equivalent amount of stock, then he will pay tax on such profit at the capital-gain rate rather than at the ordinary rate. In fact, his tax advantage is much greater than the foregoing, as is illustrated by the following example:

An investor buys 100 shares of a Canadian investment fund at $10; we assume no sales load. It earns 5.25 percent per annum on book value, and pays no dividend. The investor cashes in his first year's profit by redeeming 5 shares at 10.52, for about $52.50. His tax is based only on the difference between his cost of $50 for the 5 shares and his proceeds of $52.50. Thus he pays capital-gain tax on only $2.50, or a maximum of 62 cents, instead of full tax on $52.50 in cash dividends, or the erroneously suggested capital-gain tax on $52.50. The next year he would "theoretically sell" slightly under 5 shares at about 11.05, and pay capital gain tax on a difference of about $5. His capital gain will never reach the amount of earnings cashed in.

The operation could be simplified for the investor if the company paid annual stock dividends with book value equivalent to the year's earnings. Assume annual earnings of 5 percent and a stock dividend of like amount. The investor would merely turn back each year 5 shares at the constant book value of $50. His first year's capital gain would be calculated against a reduced cost of about 9.5; his second year's tax against a further reduced cost of about 9.02, etc. The taxes paid would correspond to those shown in the previous paragraph.

The same principle applies to the broader case of companies paying periodic stock dividends which the investor realizes upon by their sale in the market.

NOTE 13 (PAGE 508 OF TEXT)

THE PRINCIPAL TENETS OF THE DOW THEORY

1. There are three types of fluctuations manifested by the averages:

   a. Primary movements, which are broad, basic trends of bull or bear variety, extending over periods of less than a year to several years. Correct determination of such movements is the major objective of Dow theorists.

   b. Secondary movements, lasting from three weeks to several months but running counter to the primary trend.

   c. Day-to-day fluctuations in either direction, of minor character and of slight significance except in determining whether or not "lines" are being formed. They must be charted and studied, however, since they make up the longer term movements.

2. The industrial and railroad averages must corroborate each other if reliable inferences are to be drawn concerning the nature of the movement under way. Although, generally speaking, a bull market is one in which succeeding highs in each average exceed the preceding highs, and successive lows are higher than the preceding lows (and conversely for bear markets), each type of major movement is subject to interruption by countermovements of a secondary character. These secondary movements are supposed generally to retrace from a third to two-thirds of the primary price change in the averages since the preceding secondary movement terminated. It is apparent that the problem of determining from day to day or week to week whether a movement apparently under way is a secondary one or a reversal of a major trend presents a difficult task.

3. When movements of several weeks or longer are confined in both averages to a range of about 5 percent, a "line" is said to have been formed suggesting either accumulation or distribution. If both averages break out above the line simultaneously, accumulation is deduced therefrom, and higher prices predicted. If the averages break out below the line simultaneously, the reverse conclusions are deduced. If one average breaks through a line without being confirmed by similar action by the other the indication is inconclusive in character.

4. An overbought market—i.e., one which will decline fairly soon—becomes dull on rallies and active on declines; and oversold markets are dull on declines and active on rallies. Large volume characterizes termination of a bull market, and bull markets begin with light trading.

5. Active stocks tend to move in consonance with the averages, but individual issues may reflect conditions peculiar to them which will cause deviations from the pattern of the averages.

The foregoing statement of the main tenets of the Dow theory necessarily does not indicate many important details or the practical manner of operating under the theory. For more complete statements of the theory and its applications, see W. P. Hamilton, *The Stock Market Barometer,* New York, 1922; Robert Rhea, *The Dow Theory,* New York, 1932; Charles A. Dice, *The Stock Market,* pp. 485–506, New York, 1926; Floyd F. Burtchett, *Investments and Investment Policy,* pp. 672–688, New York, 1938; G. W. Bishop, Jr., *Charles H. Dow and the Dow Theory,* New York, 1960.

NOTE 14 (PAGE 510 OF TEXT)

THE CENTRAL-VALUE FORMULA

Calculation by Formula of Central Value of Dow-Jones Industrial Average, 1924–1951

Year	Average earnings of 10 previous years	Yield of Moody's all corporation Aaa bonds, April of same year	Central value: average earnings divided by twice interest rates	80% of central value	120% of central value	Range of Dow-Jones Ind. average, same year		Indicated policy
						High	Low	
1924	11.99	5.08	118.0	94.4	141.6	120.5	88.3	Buy
1925	12.62	4.87	129.6	103.7	155.5	159.4	115.0	Sell
1926	12.86	4.74	135.7	108.5	162.8	167.0	136.0	Sell
1927	12.36	4.58	133.8	107.1	160.6	201.5	152.0	Sell
1928	11.28	4.46	126.5	101.2	151.8	300.0	193.0	Sell
1929	11.21	4.69	119.5	95.6	143.4	381.2	199.0	Sell
1930	11.75	4.60	127.7	102.2	153.3	294.1	160.0	Sell
1931	11.98	4.40	136.1	108.9	163.4	193.0	74.6	Buy
1932	12.28	5.17	118.8	95.0	142.5	88.2	41.2	Buy
1933	11.41	4.78	119.4	95.5	143.2	108.5	50.2	Buy
1934	10.59	4.07	130.1	104.1	156.1	111.0	85.6	Buy
1935	9.86	3.66	134.7	107.8	161.6	149.9	96.7	Buy
1936	9.09	3.29	138.2	110.5	165.8	185.0	143.0	Sell
1937	8.60	3.42	125.7	100.6	150.9	194.4	113.0	Sell
1938	8.51	3.30	128.9	103.2	154.7	158.4	99.0	Buy–Sell
1939	7.45	3.02	123.3	98.7	148.0	155.9	121.5	Sell
1940	6.36	2.82	112.8	90.2	135.2	152.8	111.8	Sell
1941	6.35	2.82	112.6	90.1	135.1	133.6	106.3	
1942	7.11	2.83	125.6	100.5	150.7	119.7	92.9	Buy
1943	8.08	2.76	146.4	117.1	175.7	145.8	119.3	
1944	8.85	2.74	161.5	129.2	193.8	152.5	134.2	
1945	9.46	2.61	181.2	145.0	217.5	195.8	151.4	
1946	9.88	2.46	200.8	160.7	241.0	212.5	163.1	
1947	10.24	2.53	202.4	161.9	242.8	186.9	163.2	
1948	10.97	2.78	197.3	157.8	236.8	193.2	165.4	
1949	12.58	2.70	233.0	186.4	279.6	200.5	161.6	Buy
1950	14.02	2.60	270.0	216.0	324.0	235.0	196.8	Buy
1951	15.97	2.87	278.0	222.0	334.0	276.4	239.0	

Comment: (From 1951 Edition.) These valuations are based on a mechanical formula which would have yielded good practical results during the period 1924–1945. It should not be assumed that the method employed is either theoretically sound or practically dependable under all circumstances. The proper *theoretical basis* for valuing the Dow-Jones Unit or an individual common stock is to estimate average *future* earnings and to capitalize that figure at an appropriate rate. However, a formula valuation, such as shown above, should have collateral utility as a check upon valuations based on projected earnings.

Revision of the Central-value Formula.

1. Because of sudden and wide fluctuations in interest rates since the 1950's it appears preferable to use a moving three-year average of Aaa bond yields in place of the current yield.

2. The more liberal approach to common-stock valuation adopted in this edition requires a corresponding increase in the multiplier applied to the past ten-year-average earnings. At the beginning of 1961 the Central Value by the old formula was only 355, whereas our valuation based on estimated future earnings—developed in Note 15 below—gave a single figure of 572 or a more conservative range of 525–575. To make the two methods yield about equivalent results it would be necessary to increase the Central-value multiplier by 50 percent. This is done for the years 1952–1962 in the next table by using a capitalization rate of 1½ times instead of twice the Aaa bond rate.

Year	Average earnings of 10 previous years	Aaa bond yield*	Central value	80% of central value	120% of central value	Range of Dow-Jones Industrial Average same year		Indicated buy-or-sell policy
						High	Low	
1952	$17.58	2.71	480	392	588	292	256	Buy
1953	19.14	2.81	520	400	600	294	256	Buy
1954	20.80	3.01	520	416	624	427	280	Buy
1955	22.61	3.02	560	448	672	488	388	Buy
1956	25.13	3.05	620	496	744	521	463	Buy
1957	27.10	3.11	650	520	780	521	420	Buy
1958	28.82	3.44	630	504	752	584	437	Buy
1959	29.32	3.68	600	480	720	679	584	
1960	30.52	4.02	560	448	672	685	566	Sell
1961	30.68	4.19	530	424	636	735	610	Sell
1962	31.18	4.38	534	427	641	730		Sell

* Average of 3 preceding years.

Comment: The liberalization of the Central-value formula would have made stocks appear extraordinarily cheap in 1952–1954 and a purchase at all times through 1957. The indicated selling point would not have been reached until the 672 level was passed in 1960. (It should be borne in mind that a considerable element of hindsight enters into the application of the revised formula to earlier years.) At the beginning of 1962 the market level was about 40 percent the above Central Value—and more than double the old Central Value.

NOTE 15 (PAGE 511 OF TEXT)

CAPITALIZATION RATE FOR EARNINGS AND DIVIDENDS

Beginning with the price-earnings-ratio approach, we are inclined to the view that 13½ is reasonably indicative of the historic norm of the earnings multiplier for both series. We also believe that—as set forth in Chapter 31—a more liberal valuation of common stocks than formerly is now appropriate. This more liberal viewpoint rests principally on the prospect of greater stability for corporate earnings because of the government's commitment to stave off or to terminate quickly business depressions. Primarily for this reason, we feel it is reasonable to advance the basic multiplier for current normal earnings to, say, 15 times, which is about 11 percent above the historic average of 13½.

Since we have assumed a growth rate in earnings of 3½ percent per annum, the *basic multiplier* for the 7-year average *future* level of earnings would be 15 divided by 115 percent or 13 times. Thus, through this method, we arrive at the basic multiplier of 13 for *future* earnings of both Standard & Poor's Composite and the Dow-Jones Industrial Average.

Our second approach, the Central-value method, was summarized on page 422. The multiplier derived therefrom varies with the 3-year average interest rate. Our discussion in this note will be confined to the first method, which is applicable also to individual common stocks. The calculation of the value of the two indexes by this approach, at the beginning of 1962, is shown herewith.

	Standard & Poor's Composite	Dow-Jones Industrials
Estimated earnings 1962–1968.......	$4.25	$44.00*
Earnings multiplier.................	13×	13×
Resultant valuation.................	55½	572
High price in 1961.................	72	735

* Based on 1950–59 average earnings of $30.51 and a 3.5% growth rate.

Relationship of Earnings Multiplier to Expected Dividend Yield. To throw some additional light on the earnings multiplier which we have chosen for the two indexes, let us consider briefly the dividend return implicit in the valuations just arrived at. (These valuations were indeed disturbingly below the market prices prevailing at the time they were made.) The dividend yield should be derived by comparing the average expected dividends during the projected 7-year period with the *anticipated* average value[1] during the same period. This calculation works out as shown in the following tabulation:

	Standard & Poor's Composite	Dow-Jones Industrials
Current (1962) valuation...........	55½	572
Average expected value 1962–1968 (115 percent of 1962 value).......	64	658
Estimated average earnings.........	$4.25	$44.00
Average dividends:		
60 percent payout..............	2.55	26.40
66⅔ percent payout.............	2.83	29.33
Average dividend yield:		
60 percent payout..............	4.00%	4.00%
66⅔ percent payout.............	4.45%	4.45%

[1] The average value for the 1962–1968 period with an anticipated earnings growth rate of 3.5 percent would be 115 percent of current estimated value.

Market Valuation Data. Cowles Commission Index; Standard &
Poor's Composite Index, 1871–1960; Dow-Jones Industrial Average,
1926–1960

Cowles Commission Index

Period	Dividend yield	High-grade bond yield*	Earnings yield (E/P ratio)	Earnings multiplier (P/E ratio)	Payout (dividends ÷ earnings)
1871–1880	5.95%		8.92%	11.2×	67%
1881–1890	4.65		6.24	16.0×	75
1891–1900	3.95		6.21	16.1×	65
1901–1910	4.24	4.04%	7.51	13.2×	56
1911–1920	5.76	4.75	10.33	9.7×	56
1921–1930	5.11	4.92	8.12	12.3×	63

Standard & Poor's Composite Index

1926–1930	4.45%	4.63%	6.80%	14.7×	67%
1931–1935	5.38	4.34	5.42	18.7×	99
1936–1940	5.05	3.30	7.05	13.9×	71
1941–1945	5.62	2.74	8.72	11.4×	63
1946–1950	6.20	2.44	12.50	8.0×	50
1951–1955	5.22	3.00	9.35	10.7×	55
1956–1960	3.92	3.70	6.50	15.5×	61

Dow-Jones Industrial Average

1926–1930	4.47%	4.62%	6.80%	14.7×	66%
1931–1935	4.88	4.34	3.15	31.7×	155
1936–1940	4.60	3.30	6.45	15.5×	71
1941–1945	4.95	2.74	7.58	13.2×	65
1946–1950	6.05	2.44	11.62	8.6×	52
1951–1955	5.51	3.00	9.01	11.1×	61
1956–1960	3.93	3.70	6.06	16.5×	65

* 1901–1920 Standard & Poor's High-grade Railroad Bonds, 1920–1960; Moody's Aaa Bonds.

Either of these expected yields would be less than that for any of the 5-year spans from 1931 through 1955. We point out also that the 4 percent stock yield is below the 1957–1961 average yield on Moody's Aaa bonds, and the 4.45 percent stock yield would be only 106 percent of that bond average.

In terms of the historic record these anticipated relationships would hardly imply an unduly conservative valuation for common stocks. A number of compilations, one dating back to 1871, indicate that the modal ratio of stock yield to high-grade bond yields has been on the order of 120 to 130 percent. (This excludes the ratio of about 2 to 1 that obtained in the 20 years 1938–1957 and which we consider largely attributable to the artificially low interest rate maintained in that period.)

The historic relationships would indeed suggest our expected stock yields of 4 to 4.45 percent are too low, and that consequently our 1962 valuations of 572 for the DJIA and 55½ for the Standard & Poor's Composite are too high. However, we have assumed that somewhat less emphasis will be laid on dividends in the future than heretofore, and that a relatively low payout for stocks as a whole—say 60 percent—will be accepted without penalizing the multiplier of earnings. But it would indeed appear difficult to justify a valuation *higher* than those we have arrived at, when their yield implications are taken into account.

Relation of Present Valuation to Former Valuation. In the 1951 edition of this work we suggested the same current multiplier of 15 for the Dow-Jones Industrial Average that we suggest now. During 1945–1949 the actual multiplier had been only 10.1, so that this recommendation expressed our strong belief that common stocks had been much undervalued at the time we were making that revision. When this was first written (in late 1961) the suggested multiplier of 15 was well below that ruling in the market; thus we were expressing an equally strong conviction that recent market levels were too high by conservative valuation standards.

The explanation of this apparent paradox is found in the 50 percent advance in bond yields—from 2.90 percent to 4.35 percent—which has occurred between 1951 and 1962. By retaining the multiplier of 15 for *current* earnings (13 for *future* earnings) in the face of that change in bond yields we have in effect increased our *relative* valuation formula by a full 50 percent.

The jump from an old-basis appraisal of about 360 to a newly proposed basis giving a value of 534 (Central-value method) to 572 (P/E ratio approach) is the quantitative expression of our belief that common stocks should be valued more liberally than before *in relation to bond yields.* The improvement factor of more than 50 percent is in good part an arbitrary or judgment figure, but not entirely so. We have felt it necessary to use a valuation base which would produce current common-stock yields that might equal or approximate the recent average returns on high-grade bonds. For once this lower limit of yields is passed, we think that no restraint can be imposed on one's enthusiasm for common stocks; the analyst must perforce then take his valuation basis from the market itself—which is almost the same thing as saying that there is no such thing as value as distinguished from market price.

A second element of our reasoning was as follows: Our figure of 534–572 happens to lie reasonably close to the midpoint between the "old-style" value of 360 and the 1961 high of 735. We are persuaded that the huge market advance since 1949 must have included a considerable component of speculative ardor in addition to whatever upward shift in basic values may have been justified by the new economic climate, plus the new indispensability of common stocks for every investor. When we first wrote this section we added that our valuation figures, which approximately equated stock yields with bond yields, should not be considered unrealistically *low,* even though bull-market behavior had characteristically carried quotations to a much higher level. Our final revision in June 1962 overlaps a 200-point decline in the stock market and requires us to defend our valuations as not unrealistically *high.* Such are the pendulum swings of stock-market speculation!

NOTE 16 (PAGE 523 OF TEXT)

A. WILFRED MAY'S METHOD OF VALUING COMMON STOCKS

For a number of years Mr. May, an editor of the *Commercial and Financial Chronicle,* has expounded a method of determining "advantageous buying points" for common stocks, based on the concept of "recoupment of principal." It may be outlined as follows:

1. He estimates the average earnings for, say, the next 20 or 25 years, and the average future dividends therefrom.

2. He assumes that the price paid should return (*a*) an annual "rental" equal to the estimated average return on United States Treasury bonds or savings deposits,

plus (*b*) an annual "amortization reserve," not compounded, sufficient to return the purchase price in 20 or 25 years.

3. The choice of the valuation period would depend on the stock being valued. The stronger the company, the longer the period. In a 1957 lecture he suggested a 25-year period for American Tel and Tel and a 20-year period for U.S. Steel.[1] In similar calculations supplied to us in 1960 he used 25 years for General Motors and 20 years for Deere & Company.

Mr. May's calculation for General Motors in August 1960 follows:

Average annual per-share earnings in past ten years	$2.79
Average annual per-share earnings in past five years	3.19
Single-year 1959 earnings	3.06
Average payout—ten years	65%
Average payout—five years	70%
1. Estimated annual earnings—next 25 years	$4.50
2. Estimated annual dividends—next 25 years	3.25
3. Annual rental value of capital invested	3.5%
4. Annual amortization reserve—25-year life	4%
5. Annual requirement for (3) plus (4)	7.5%
6. Capitalization of $3.25 dividend at rate of 7.5% gives advantageous buying price of	44

Comment: The special feature of the May approach is the requirement that the cost of a common-stock investment be completely amortized out of dividends in the investor's calculation over a period of years. This relates common-stock investment closely to the older approach to real estate investment, as well as to the standard business calculations made to justify purchase of a machine tool, etc. The amortization approach, in his words, is a "way of getting your money back with income" over a period of time. Assuming the dividends work out as anticipated, the investor may view his stock purchase as returning him a bond result over a 20- or 25-year period, plus a residual value—the eventual market price of the shares—which is his extra reward for both his intelligence and his risk taking. (An additional "plus" of great importance resides in the absence of interest compounding in the calculations. This is an offset against the income tax on the annual dividends.)

While the theory behind the May valuations differs greatly from our own approach, its results in the typical case are likely to be quite similar. The reason is that the May calculations may readily be converted into a simple multiplier of the future average earnings, which then becomes identical in principle with our method. This relationship may be demonstrated by the following analysis of his valuation of General Motors:

May's appraisal of 44 equals 13.3 times the average expected dividends, or 9.8 times the expected earnings, for 25 years. (The assumed payout is 72 percent.) This, in turn, equals 14.4 times current "normal" earnings, which we take as $3.12. His assumed growth rate thus works out at just 3 percent. Under our method we would apply a multiplier of about 12½ (less than the 13 times for a 3½ growth rate) to the average of the next seven-years' earnings ($3.50), producing a present value of the same 44. Nor would the Molodovsky approach—which discounts both future dividends and the tenth-year market price to present value—produce a greatly different figure.[2]

[1] Published in the *Commercial and Financial Chronicle*, Oct. 15, 1957, p. (1905) 5.
[2] An elaborate valuation of General Motors by the older method was made by Molodovsky and published in the *Analysts Journal* of May 1959. This found a theoretical value of 45 in 1958 by simply applying a multiplier of about 13½ to the "level-of-earnings trend" for that year, taken at $3.30 per share.

May's "rental value" of capital invested is geared to current anticipations of the future rate of interest. As interest rates rise, the expected rate will usually rise also; hence the value of future dividends under his method would diminish. In this respect his method resembles our Central-value approach, except that in his case a change in interest rates affects only about half the capitalization rate.

May makes a separate allowance for the excess of current-asset value of a stock over his dividend-base valuation. For example, in 1957 he found Montgomery-Ward to have a value of 33 based on expected dividends; but the working capital alone applicable to the common was 47. He added $10 of this "excess equity" to the 33 value and reached a final "advantageous buying price" of 43. This technique corresponds to our own suggestion that the analyst add in one-half of the excess of working-capital value over his earnings-dividends valuation.

Limitations of the May Method. The May approach is necessarily based on the assumption that future dividends will bear a "normal" relationship to future earnings. Only dividends are taken into account in its arithmetic. Hence the method will not apply to the typical growth-stock situation in which dividends are definitely subordinated to reinvestment of profits. To the extent that cash dividends generally will play a smaller role than heretofore in corporate policy and investors' attitudes, the amortization approach will have diminishing applicability.

NOTE 17 (PAGE 557 OF TEXT)

"APPLIED-SCIENCE STOCKS" AND GOVERNMENT BUSINESS

In January 1962 a brokerage firm[1] published an interesting statistical and descriptive analysis of a group of 10 "applied-science stocks." The data showed that six of these had 60 percent or more of their sales in "military business"; two had small military sales; and for two the figures were not available. We give certain figures for the six companies dependent largely on government contracts.

Company	% Military business	Net assets for common per share	High price 1961–1962	Earned per share, 1961	Ratio of high price to 1961 earnings
Microwave Associates.......	70	$5.90	60	76¢	79×
Continental Connector......	70	3.20	27	53¢	51×
Elco Corporation...........	75	3.00	18	37¢	48×
Babcock Electronics........	100	3.60	36	78¢	46×
Dynamics Corporation of America................	80	4.15	20	45¢	44×
Geophysics Corporation of America................	60	2.30	60	15¢	40×

Comment: These shares sold, at their highs, at between 5 and 26 times their book value. To justify such prices they would have to attain earnings of 25 percent or more on their invested capital. But earnings from military business are subject to renegotiation, and earnings beyond a certain return on capital may be held to be

[1] Carl M. Loeb, Rhoades & Company.

excessive. (The return allowed depends on such factors as volume of sales, comparative costs, contribution made to the defense effort, etc.)

NOTE 18 (PAGE 557 OF TEXT)

DATA ON STOCK-PURCHASE WARRANTS QUOTED IN STANDARD & POOR'S STOCK GUIDE DECEMBER 1961

Company	Purchase price of common*	Expir. date of warrants	Out-standing warrants	Out-standing shares of common	Dec. 31, 1961 price		Range of warrants since issuance	
					War-rants	Stock	High	Low
Alleghany	3¾	Perpetual	1,099	9,848	7⅞	11	12	1 7/16
Armour	20	Dec. '64	246	5,350	32	52	36	3½
Atlas Corp	6¼	Perpetual	5,023	10,446	1⅛	2⅝	6⅛	⅛
BSF Co	1.67 @ 22	May '64	170	769	5⅜	14½	9¾	3½
Chadbourne-Gotham	8.86	Mar. '64	556	2,157	2¾	7½	2⅞	⅜
Coastal State Gas	3 @ 2½	June '67	291	6,062	83½	31½	85	2
Gen. Acceptance	20	Nov. '69	250	1,755	10½	26¾	10⅞	3¼
Gen. Tire & Rubber	25	Oct. '67	240	5,404	63¼	86½	67	5½
Guerdon Ind	½ @ 14¼	Jan. '63	130	1,040	15/16	5¾	2½	¾
Hilton Hotels	42 to 50	Oct. '63 Oct. '71	450	3,811	10⅛	32⅛	17⅜	5⅛
Keyes Fibre	18 to 21	Nov. '63 Nov. '70†	500	1,357	6⅛	18½	6¾	4
Mack Truck	1.40 @ 45 to 50	Sept. '63 Sept. '66	265	2,759	26	43¾	36⅜	7
Martin-Marietta	2.73 @ 40 to 45	Nov. '63 Nov. '68	420	21,357	38½	26⅞	46¼	10¼
McCrory	20	Mar. '76	1,092	5,695	10½	21⅞	11¾	6⅝
McLean Industries	3 @ 6	Feb. '67	180	8,100	3⅝	4¼	9¼	1
Miami Window	3½	Mar. '69	700	1,270	½	⅞	2¼	⅛
Molybdenum of America	1.04 @ 30	Oct. '63	176	1,701	16¼	27⅞	41¼	3½
Rio Algom	13/100 @ 3	Dec. '66	205	10,002	½	9¼	15/16	¼
Sperry-Rand	1.04 @ 25 to 28	Sept. '63 Sept. '67	2,288	29,498	13⅜	23⅞	20⅞	35
Symington-Wayne	10 to 15	May '63 May '68	264	1,611	8¾	16¾	11⅝	2⅝
Teleregister	15 to 17	May '63 May '65	120	2,776	8⅛	13	17	3½
Textron	25 to 50	May '64 May '84	600	4,918	11⅝	26⅞	14⅞	7½
TWA	20 to 23	June '65 June '73	2,700	6,674	5	12	5⅜	4⅛
Tri-Continental	127 @ 17.76	Perpetual	787	7,329	44	55	44⅝	1/32
United Air Lines	38.83	May '66	201	4,997	14¾	40	26½	10¼
United Ind	½ @ 17	Nov. '69	504	2,124	⅝	3	3⅝	⅛
Van Norman Ind	16	Mar. '65	125	624	3¾	11¼	7¼	1¼
Uris Buildings	1.03 @ 12½	May '75	824	3,296	13	21¾	12¾	3⅜
Webb, D. E	6¼	Dec. '75	800	5,675	10	14⅞	10	2

* A warrant can buy 1 share, unless otherwise stated.
† Redeemable at $1 each after 1965.

NOTE 19 (PAGE 656 OF TEXT)

TWO EXAMPLES OF COMMON-STOCK FINANCING IN 1960–1961, INVOLVING ISSUANCE OF WARRANTS

A. American Bowling Enterprises

1. Financing

This enterprise was formed at the end of 1959, and acquired certain bowling subsidiaries for $235,000. Private interests put up this sum in exchange for 80,000 shares of common stock together with Class A warrants to buy 80,000 additional shares. The original price paid for the units was thus about $3 each. In May 1960, for purposes of expansion, the company sold through underwriters 150,000 similar units at $7.50 each. The underwriters received a commission of $1.12 per share and also the right to buy 8,000 units for $2.94 each and 16,000 Class B warrants for 1 cent each.

Each of the 238,000 Class A warrants entitled the holder to buy a share of common at $7.50 to May 1961, $8 to May 1962, and $9 to November 1962. The company also created 50,000 Class B warrants, which entitled the holder to buy a share of common at $7.50 to May 1961, the price increasing by 37½ cents a year until expiration (at $9) in 1965. These were all sold at 1 cent each—i.e., virtually given—as follows: 16,000 to the underwriters, 9,000 to an officer and to a director, and 25,000 to an individual who loaned the company $200,000 four months after the public offering.

2. Balance sheet in June 1960

The public financing raised the stockholders' equity from $3 to $5 per share. However, one-third of this amount ($394,000) was represented by a variety of deferred charges relating to installation and financing of alleys and pinspotters. The current liabilities and notes payable exceeded the current assets.

3. Earnings

The company reported a small loss in its initial operating period ending in June 1960, but expected "a sizable profit" in fiscal 1961. (It actually reported a loss of $78,000 or 31 cents a share, in the June 1961 year.)

4. Market price of stock and warrants

The units advanced in price in 1960 to about $11, of which the Class A warrants represented about $3½ and the stock (ex-warrants) about $7½. The Class B warrants, having better terms, were worth more than the Class A warrants. At the prices stated the market valued the common at $1,750,000, the Class A warrants at $830,000 and the Class B warrants at, say, $200,000—a total of $2,780,000 for the equity. This was 2½ times the stated book value.

In June 1961 most of the Class B warrants were registered for possible sale to the public. The holder of 25,000 of these had contracted to sell them to an investment fund at 4½.

Comment: It will be noted that this enterprise issued more warrants to buy shares than shares themselves. Their market value shortly after creation was about two-thirds that of the shares. As stated in our text (p. 661), we consider that the combined stock-and-warrant form of financing serves no sound corporate purpose, and that its chief effect is to create market values for "equities" not represented in the balance sheet nor in the calculation of per share earnings.

Unless restraint is imposed from some source, the present vogue of common-stock financing may carry it to the height of absurdity represented by the American & Foreign Power financial structure in 1929. (See p. 657.)

B. Boonton Electronics Corporation

1. Financing

In March 1961 this was a small maker of electrical equipment. It had net worth of some $200,000 represented by 300,000 shares. The earnings had advanced during a three-year period to a high of $87,000 in the September 1960 year. It then raised about $300,000, net, of additional capital by selling 60,000 units to the public at $5.50, each consisting of one share of common plus half a warrant to buy an additional share at $5.50 to March 1962 and $6.50 to March 1963. The underwriters received a commission of 50 cents per unit, plus the right to buy 17,500 shares and 17,500 full warrants for $18,250.

2. Calculation of the public's "deal" and the underwriter's compensation

The $5.50 price paid by the public may be allocated $5 to the stock and 50 cents to the half-warrant. The $5 price compares with a preceding equity of 67 cents. (The public's purchase raised the book value of all the shares to about $1.30.) The public supplied funds equal to about 60 percent of the net assets after the transaction and received 17 percent of the equity, plus warrants to buy about 8 percent more. The aggregate value of the stock and warrants, represented by their public offering price, was some 22 times the recent (and record) profits.

On the basis of the price paid by the public the stock and warrants bought by the underwriters were worth about $87,000 above cost. Their total compensation may thus be set at $87,000 for raising $330,000 gross.

3. Subsequent earnings

In the year ended September 1961 sales increased from $741,000 to $952,000, but the net profits fell to $58,000, or 15 cents per share. This was a decline of about a third from those of the 1960 year.

Comment: Our two examples illustrate the following characteristic features of the common-stock financing of the early 1960's: (1) flotation of shares of much smaller enterprises than were formerly deemed suitable for public participation; (2) emphasis on a record of rising profits for a few years as promising long-term future growth; (3) a selling price several times the preceding equity per share, and more than 20 times the best year's profits; (4) the creation of stock-purchase warrants as a confusing part of the capital structure; (5) payment of various types of compensation to underwriters, aggregating a large percentage of the sum raised from the public; (6) the absence of convincing indications that these companies have inherent stability and dependable prospects of future growth needed to justify their sale to the public at a price above their book value.

NOTE 20 (PAGE 336 OF TEXT)

THE CALL PROVISION OF BONDS

Nearly all corporate bonds issued for some decades past have a call provision which enables the company to pay them off before maturity at a stipulated price, which often declines as maturity approaches. (Most preferred stocks carry a comparable provision, but the call price rarely if ever changes with time.) Comparatively little attention was paid to the significance of these call features until the sharp drop in interest rates after 1933—and the low rates continuing for more than 20 years thereafter—brought on an almost universal retirement of callable bond issues and their replacement by new ones carrying lower coupons. The effect of this provision was then seen to be the depriving of bondholders of most of the price benefit that should accompany a drop in interest rates, although they had no comparable option to safeguard them against a fall in the price of their bonds when interest rates advance. Otherwise stated, the call provision compels bondholders to accept a cut in their interest return when the general interest rate drops appreciably, but does not give them any increased income when the rate advances.

We have illustrated this point elsewhere[1] by the following typical example: In 1928, American Gas & Electric Co. sold an issue of 100-year 5 percent debentures to the public at 101, yielding 4.95 percent. Four years later, in the depths of the depression, the debentures sold as low as 60, with a yield of 8.25 percent. This reflected the impact of unusually unfavorable economic and market conditions on a good-quality investment bond. Conversely, and under favorable circumstances, the interest rate applicable to bonds of this quality fell under 3 percent. This *should* have meant an advance in the price of this 5 percent issue to 160 or better. But at this point, in March, 1946, the call feature was availed of and the company redeemed the issue at only 106.

[1] In B. Graham, *The Intelligent Investor*, 1959 Edition, pp. 77–79.

Since 1954 bondholders have experienced a third unfavorable experience of this sort—this time occasioned by a sharp rise in the basic interest rate. The low-coupon bonds issued in the long period of low-interest rates sustained a severe decline. In the case of American Gas & Electric, its 3⅜ percent debentures issued above par in 1952 sold as low as 80 in 1961. The purchasers of Consolidated Edison of New York 2¾'s at 102⅞ in 1947 had the more disconcerting experience of seeing their price drop below 70 in 1959.

In our view the call feature in the typical bond contract is a thinly disguised instance of "heads I win, tails you lose." Its results may be summarized as follows: When interest rates go down the call feature forces the investor to lose the income he counted upon; when the interest rate goes up the investor loses in the principal value of his bond.

The SEC has taken the stand that a call provision is a necessary feature in public utility bond issues (under their jurisdiction) to safeguard the company against paying higher interest on its old bonds than the going rate in future years. This view is logical as far as it goes, but it completely ignores the contrary and equally legitimate interests of the bond investor. Perhaps the correct solution of this problem would be to make the interest payments on long-term bonds vary with changes in the basic rate; if the company wishes to retain a right to call the bonds —presumably for reasons of convenience—then a corresponding right should be given the holders to tender their bonds to the company at discount equal to the premium that the company would have to pay on call.[2] A provision to vary the coupon with interest-rate conditions would bear some resemblance to that found in a number of foreign bonds which protect the holder against a fall in the gold or commodity value of the currency. However, our tentative suggestion would operate in both directions, to safeguard both parties to the bargain.

The triple "whipsawing" that institutional bondholders have submitted to since 1929 has led them to demand more protection as far as call features are concerned. Many, perhaps most, tax-free and industrial issues in recent years have been made noncallable for a substantial period after issuance.

Example: In 1961 the State of California issued $100 million of bonds with various coupon rates and maturing serially from 1963 through 1987. This issue was made callable only between 1983 and 1987.

A more sophisticated arrangement permits an early call provided that interest rates have not fallen appreciably—which means that the bondholder would be able to replace his called bonds at an equivalent coupon rate.

Example: In 1962 Ohio Oil Co. sold at 100 a large issue of 4⅜ percent debentures, due 1987. For the first five years they were made nonredeemable "through a re-funding operation at an interest cost to the company of less than 4.36 percent." They could be redeemed in whole or in part out of "spare cash" at prices ranging from 104.6 in 1962 to 103.9 in 1966. Beginning in 1967 the company will be free to redeem bonds with any funds at prices gradually declining toward par in 1986.

The analyst should be cognizant of the implications of the various types of call provisions, and pay due heed to them in making his bond selections.

---

[2] Note that an important feature of the United States Savings Bonds has been the right given the holders from their inception in 1934 to tender them for payment at short notice at appropriate prices. This provision had a substantial monetary value when interest rates rose; it compelled the United States Treasury to increase the rate of payment on outstanding bonds as well as on new ones. (Small investors did not have similar protection when interest rates rose steeply after World War I and the United.States Liberty Bonds dropped into the 70's.)

INDEX

NOTES

NOTES

NOTES

NOTES

NOTES

NOTES